DISCOURSE FEATURES OF NEW TESTAMENT GREEK

A Coursebook on the Information Structure of New Testament Greek

Second Edition

Stephen H. Levinsohn

International

© 2000 by SIL International
First edition 1992
Second edition 2000

Library of Congress Catalog No. 00-101266
ISBN: 1-55671-093-3

Printed in the United States of America

05 04 03 02 01   11 10 9 8 7 6 5 4 3

Copies of this and other publications of SIL International may be obtained from

International Academic Bookstore
7500 W. Camp Wisdom Road
Dallas, TX 75236

Voice: 972-708-7404
Fax: 972-708-7363
E-mail: academic_b00ks@sil.org
Internet: http://www.sil.org

CONTENTS

PREFACE

The second edition of this book is again aimed at instructional use, in connection with lectures, discussion groups, or a self-instruction environment. It has attempted to take account of the many comments and suggestions made during the seminars, teach-ins, and summer courses on Greek discourse structure that have been held since the first edition appeared.

My grateful thanks go to all who have shared their research with me, as well as to Dr. Katy Barnwell, who insisted that I take the time to develop a volume on this topic. I am particularly grateful to Tony Pope, who prepared a detailed critique of both editions and who shared many valuable insights about the Greek text and variants, and to Dr. Buist Fanning, who suggested various ways in which the material could be presented better and who spotted some unfortunate errors.

My thanks also to those SIL members whose work on Greek discourse is cited here. Many of their articles have appeared in SIL's *Selected Technical Articles Related to Translation* (START) or its successors *Occasional Papers in Translation and Textlinguistics* (OPTAT) and *Journal of Translation and Textlinguistics* (JOTT). Where relevant, I have taken over or adapted their conclusions as the basis for different chapters of this book. My apologies if at any point I have misrepresented their positions.

Much of the material in this volume draws upon the work of others. I have not provided a comprehensive bibliography of articles for each aspect of Greek grammar touched on in these chapters, but such bibliographies may be found in the articles mentioned in connection with each topic.

This book will have served its purpose only if the reader, consultant or translator benefits from it. So, first of all, my thanks to all who work through the book. Secondly, if you read through even a few of the chapters and notice errors, think of better ways to present the material and perhaps come up with improved analyses. Please, instead of keeping your observations to yourself, write and share them with me (e.g., to my E-Mail address Stephen_Levinsohn@sil.org), so that any future editions of this work can be that much more useful.

May the Lord cause his Word to be ever more living and active, as we increase our understanding of his written message to us and to all the people groups of this world.

INTRODUCTION

This book in no sense claims to offer a comprehensive coverage of the multitude of discourse features found in the Greek New Testament. Rather, it is an attempt to describe a limited number of features that I or other researchers have studied in depth.

If you have never taken any courses on discourse analysis, you will follow the argument of this book much more easily if you first read chapters 1-7 of *Analyzing Discourse: Basic Concepts* by Robert A. Dooley and myself (hereafter *SIL-UND*).[1]

With the above proviso, anyone with some knowledge of Koiné Greek grammar who wishes to learn what insights can be gained from a discourse approach to the original text of the New Testament will benefit from this book. The sort of knowledge you need is the ability to identify the case of a noun and the tense-aspect of a verb, to distinguish participial, relative and main clauses, etc. In other words, you need a basic knowledge of introductory Greek.

What you do *not* need to understand this book is a lot of Greek vocabulary. All examples are provided with a word-by-word translation, adapted from Brown, Comfort & Douglas' (1990) *The New Greek-English Interlinear New Testament*. Where it is not relevant to the point being taught, I have not even quoted the Greek text, but rather have provided the translation of the New Revised Standard Version (NRSV), adapted, where necessary, to reflect the Greek more closely. Incidentally, I have indicated textual variants only where the alternate reading(s) might affect the point under discussion.[2]

The book consists of seventeen chapters, each containing a presentation of one or more discourse features of Koiné Greek, illustrated from passages of the New Testament. Most sections end with review questions. The student should cover up the suggested answers and always attempt to answer them *before* looking at the answers. If the questions seem too hard to answer, then read the section over again.

Illustrative passages are provided in order that the principles taught in the chapter can be applied to them. Again, answer the questions about the illustrative passages *before* looking at the answers. (Model answers to some illustrative passages are given in the Appendix instead of in the chapter itself, precisely to make them less immediately accessible.)

The Theoretical Approach of This Book

It will quickly become obvious that this volume does not tackle Greek in the traditional way, but rather from the position of descriptive linguistics. Indeed, I have approached the Greek text just as I would approach texts in any other language of the world, using the same principles of discourse analysis. Furthermore, the conclusions I reach conform to the same overall principles that apply to other languages.

My approach to discourse analysis is *eclectic*, making use of the insights of different linguists and different linguistic theories to the extent that I feel they are helpful. Furthermore, I do not hesitate to take a seed idea that some linguist has come up with and develop it in a different direction. This is especially true of Givón; I find a number of his ideas to be very valuable, but at times the conclusions that I draw from them are the exact opposite of his (see Levinsohn 1990)!

My approach is also *functional*. Dooley (1989:1) defines the functional approach as "an attempt to discover and describe what linguistic structures are used for: the functions they serve, the factors that condition their use."

This functional approach contrasts with the *structural* one, which is "an attempt to describe linguistic structure ... essentially for its own sake" (ibid.). At its worst, the structural approach might tell you, for example, that Greek clauses manifest all six possible orders of subject (S), object (O) and verb (V)—

---

[1] *Analyzing discourse* may be obtained from the bookstore of the Summer Institute of Linguistics, 7500 West Camp Wisdom Road, Dallas TX 75236-5699.

[2] With a few exceptions, textual variants are considered only if they are noted in the apparatus of *Nestle-Aland*.

SVO, SOV, OSV, OVS, VSO, VOS)—without ever addressing the question of when to use which. A functional approach, on the other hand, starts from the existence of the six orders (i.e., it presupposes a structural analysis) and concentrates on identifying the factors that determine the selection of one order over against another.

One basic principle of a functional approach is that *choice implies meaning.*[3] (Too often, the terms "optional" and "stylistic variation" are synonyms of "don't know"!) So, when an author has the option of expressing himself or herself in more than one way, the ways differ in significance; there are reasons for the variations. For example, the subject of a Greek clause sometimes precedes and sometimes follows the verb. This is not just a question of style; there is a linguistic reason for the change of order (see chaps. 1 to 4). Similarly, successive sentences with the same subject refer to the subject at times only in the verb, at times with a pronoun such as αὐτός 'he' and at times with a noun phrase such as ὁ Ἰησοῦς '(the) Jesus.' Again, this is not just a question of style; there is a linguistic reason (see chap. 8). Likewise, references by name to a person sometimes include the article (ὁ Ἰησοῦς) and sometimes do not (Ἰησοῦς). This is not a just question of style, either; there is a linguistic reason (see chap. 9).

The converse of this principle is that, if there is no choice, there is nothing more to be said. For example, if certain names never take the article, there is nothing to investigate in that area. However, if a name sometimes takes the article and sometimes does not and there is no grammatical reason for the variation, it is the job of discourse analysis to discover the significance of the presence or absence of the article.

Using "stylistic variation" as an excuse for not investigating significance is not the only dangerous assumption analysts sometimes make. Equally wrong is to assume that all the New Testament writers use discourse features in the same way. I suspect that the failure of Greek grammarians to pin down the function of some of the features covered in this book is due to their expectation that one explanation would cover every author.[4]

My own approach is to assume that:

- an individual author uses the discourse features being studied in a consistent way
- there is potential for variation between authors and that it is therefore essential that the validity of conclusions reached about, say, Matthew's uses of the historical present (see secs. 12.2.1 and 14.3) be checked for Luke-Acts and Mark.

This highlights a weakness of this book and a huge (though, hopefully, diminishing) area where further research is needed. I have not undertaken an in-depth study of how every author uses the different devices. For example, when I describe the ways that Matthew uses the historical present, that is all I am describing (see secs. 12.2.3 and 15.1 for the somewhat different ways in which John uses the historical present). Unless I indicate to the contrary, I am not implying that Mark and Luke-Acts will use the historical present in exactly the same way. It is my hope that, among those who use this book, there will be some who will want to investigate how the features described are used by the authors not covered. The result, in the not too distant future, I trust, will be a more comprehensive volume.

The Value of Discourse Analysis

Discourse analysis is an analysis of language features that draws its explanations, not from within the sentence or word (i.e., the factors involved are not syntactic or morphological), but *extrasententially* (from the linguistic and wider context). In the case of written material, explanations are drawn mainly, though by no means exclusively, from the previous sentences of the text.

---

[3] *Meaning* is here used loosely to denote any semantic or pragmatic distinction; it is not used in contraposition to 'pragmatic effects' (see below). Furthermore, I accept that the domains of lexical items and functors (e.g., prepositions) may *overlap*, though their core meanings will be different. Similarly, where diachronic changes were in process at the time of the writing of a New Testament book (e.g., the use of the relative pronoun ὅστις instead of ὅς when its referent is not general and indeterminate), it *may* be the case that the author concerned uses both indiscriminately. However, this should always be checked. See *SIL-UND* chapter 3 on the use by the same author of different *registers* in different social contexts.

[4] J. Heimerdinger (p.c.) points out that different editors and copyists also have their own style, as is particularly evident in Codex Bezae. This means that the analyst of a modern edition of the Greek text such as that produced by the Bible Societies may still be faced with a conflation of styles, even when he or she concentrates on the works of a single New Testament author.

Discourse analysis is a vast topic. My primary interest is in those factors that have a direct payoff for exegesis and for translation into other languages, particularly those features that a translator might have some expectation of rendering in a receptor language. This gives rise to my constant concern with the *function* of the different features considered in the volume.

Porter (1995:108) has complained that, in looking at such features, I am essentially confining myself "to the level of the clause or sentence." It is true that, in some chapters, the primary unit of study is the clause or sentence (e.g., when examining constituent order in chapters 2-4). Nevertheless, some of the factors that determine the order of constituents are at least extrasentential. Lambrecht (1994:9) calls this area of linguistics *"information structure,"* the study of which "focuses on the interaction of sentences and their contexts." Nevertheless, other chapters do look at areas that Porter considers to be the proper domain of discourse analysis: "discourse boundaries, prominence, and coherence and cohesion" (loc. cit.).

Markedness

When the analyst seeks to explain some feature, it is important to find an explanation that works both when it is present and when it is absent. For example, if it is an explanation of when the historical present is used, the proposal should predict not only when the historical present occurs, but also when it does not.

Balancing this requirement is the concept of markedness. According to this concept, when a certain marker is present, the feature implied by the marker is present. However, when the marker is absent, nothing is said about the presence or absence of the feature—the sentence is unmarked for that feature. In other words, it is not necessarily true that the function of the unmarked form is the opposite of that of the marked form.

The concept of markedness is of particular importance in the case of the article, with proper names, for instance. One of the reasons for using the article is to indicate that the substantive refers to a particular item (Porter 1992:104). Consequently, it is appropriate that the article be used with Ἰησοῦς, since the referent is a particular known individual. However, the opposite is not true: Ἰησοῦς without the article also refers frequently to a particular known individual. The name is simply not marked for that feature when the article is absent (see further in chap. 9).

Semantic Meaning and Pragmatic Effects

There is a crucial distinction in my approach between the inherent or *semantic meaning* of a construction and the *pragmatic effects* of using that construction in a particular context. The progressive construction in English illustrates the usefulness of this distinction. The progressive construction has a semantic meaning of incompleteness, as in 'It's raining.' However, in certain contexts it carries an overtone of insincerity, as in 'John is being polite,' in contrast to 'John is polite' (see Zegarac 1989). Insincerity is not part of the semantic meaning of the progressive; it is a pragmatic effect that is achieved by the use of the progressive in certain specific contexts.

A Word to Consultants and Translators

Translation consultants and language workers who are working towards the translation of the New Testament should recognize that this book has consequences for the discourse analysis not only of Greek, but also of receptor languages. Those who take the trouble to understand Greek syntax from a discourse perspective need to undertake a similar analysis of texts in the receptor language in order to know how to render the force of the Greek text.

Of course, understanding the subtleties of the Greek text has value for its own sake; it helps us to better understand the flow of the writer's argument, to choose between possible interpretations, etc. However, much of the value of an in-depth understanding of the discourse features of the Greek text is lost if the translator has no understanding of how the same effects are achieved in the receptor language.

Overview of the Volume

Before summarizing the book chapter by chapter, let me say that I usually start discussion of a topic with what happens in narrative, then move to the Epistles and the teaching sections of the Gospels and Acts. I have two main reasons for this:

1. Discourse analysis of narrative is a lot easier than discourse analysis of the reasoned argument that characterizes the Epistles. Also, a lot more research has been done on narrative than on other discourse genres.
2. The factors that are identified for narrative tend to apply also to a reasoned argument without too much modification. In other words, once one understands how a feature works in narrative, it is not too difficult to understand its function in the Epistles. (This can be seen particularly in chap. 7.)

Part I of the book is devoted to the *order of constituents* in the clause and sentence. After an introductory chapter on the concepts of coherence and discontinuities, chapter 2 focuses on the significance of how the sentence begins, whether with a verb or with a nominal or adverbial constituent. Chapters 3 and 4 tackle the order of constituents in the rest of the sentence, as well as within the noun phrase. My aim is that the reader, having finished these chapters, will know when an author highlighted a constituent and when he did not, instead of wondering which commentator to believe.

Part II looks at the most common connectors or non-subordinating *conjunctions* that are found in the Greek New Testament. The choice of a particular conjunction communicates how an author intended the message to flow and develop (features which commentators and modern translators into English at times ignore). The combination of a conjunction and the sentence-initial constituent has a lot to tell us; if we understand their message aright, our exegesis will be much more accurate.

Part III considers *patterns of reference*, including why, once a participant has been introduced or activated, he or she is referred to at times only in the verb and, at other times, by means of a pronoun or a noun phrase as well. This topic contributes to understanding when an author intended a break in the story and when he was highlighting information. The presence versus absence of the article when referring to activated participants is then addressed, its absence often signaling the importance or local salience of the participant.

Part IV describes a number of features that have the effect of *backgrounding or highlighting* information. They include the encoding of information in a relative or participial clause, rather than an independent one, as well as one of the uses of ἐγένετο 'it happened' and of the historical present.

Part V addresses the reasons why *reported conversation* is introduced in different ways in narrative. These reasons include the status of the conversation in the overall story, the status of the concluding speech in the conversation, the signaling of efforts to take control of the conversation, and the desire to point forward to a subsequent speech or act. Part V also discusses the motivations for reporting conversation directly versus indirectly, and the significance of introducing direct speech with ὅτι '*recitativum*'.

Finally, in part VI, I review criteria that may be used to support or reject the segmenting of passages into sub-units. As Beekman and Callow (1974) point out, it is by no means impossible to decide with certainty on the presence or absence of a boundary, given the increased confidence with which we can say that a given feature provides supporting evidence.

ABBREVIATIONS

ADD	additive (τέ solitarium—sec. 6.3)
art	articular pronoun
BDF	Blass, Debrunner & Funk (1961)
DE	development marker (δέ—sec. 5.1)
fn.	footnote
GA	genitive absolute (anarthrous participial clause in the genitive case—sec. 11.1)
HP	historical present
intro	introduction
κ.τ.λ.	καὶ τὸ λοιπόν (Greek equivalent of *etc.*)
MGM	Moulton, Geden & Moulton (1978)
n.d.	no date
NEB	New English Bible
NIV	New International Version
NP	noun phrase
NPC	nominative participial clause (anarthrous participial clause in the nominative—sec. 11.1)
NRSV	New Revised Standard Version
OED	*The Oxford English Reference Dictionary* (Oxford University Press, 2nd. edition, 1996)
p.c.	personal communication
pn	pronoun
SIL-UND	*Analyzing Discourse: Basic Concepts* (1999—see p. vii)
TEV	Today's English Version
UBS	United Bible Societies *Greek New Testament* (3rd. corrected edition)
VIP	very important participant (sec. 8.3)
3P	verb inflected for third person plural
3S	verb inflected for third person singular
Ø	asyndeton, no overt reference
+	additive (adverbial καί—sec. 6.2)

PART I: CONSTITUENT ORDER[1]

Porter begins his discussion of patterns of constituent order and clause structure in New Testament Greek with the following assertion (1992:289):

> The flexibility of Greek syntax because of its inflected endings and its various ways of forming clauses does not mean that the order of various elements makes no difference.

Part I of the present volume describes some differences that are conveyed by changes in the order of constituents in clauses and sentences (chaps. 2–4) and in the noun phrase (sec. 4.5). These differences principally involve ways in which sentences relate to their context (chap. 2) and where the focus of a sentence falls (secs. 3.4–5).

The factors involved in determining the order of constituents at the beginning of sentences are presented in chapter 2 and sections 3.6–3.7. Factors involved in determining constituent order in the rest of positive sentences are described in the remainder of chapter 3. Constituent order in negated sentences and in information questions is considered in sections 4.1 and 4.2. Examples of *temporary* focus are given in section 4.3. Motivations for coordinative and other phrases being *discontinuous* are outlined in section 4.4, while factors determining whether a *genitive* precedes or follows its head noun are presented in section 4.5.

First, however, I devote a preliminary chapter to the concept of *coherence*, and to how thematic groupings of sentences or groups of sentences are characterized by the presence of various *discontinuities*.

---

[1] I use the term *constituent* order rather than *word* order, because the elements that are ordered in different ways in clauses and sentences are often phrases and clauses, not single words. See Cervin (1993:57) on this point.

1
COHERENCE AND DISCONTINUITIES

This chapter starts from the assumption that each book of the Greek New Testament is basically *coherent*.[1] This means that a reader who is reasonably conversant with the world-view of the author will be able to relate the information communicated in each new sentence of the book to the "mental model" (Johnson-Laird 1983:370) that he or she has formed from reading what has already been presented.

For example, consider the opening sentences of the book of **Colossians** (given below). The reader of vv. 1–2 will construct a mental model in which they form the beginning of a letter whose authors are two people identified as 'Paul an apostle of Christ Jesus' and 'Timothy the brother' (v. 1). The addressees, in turn, are a group of people identified as 'the saints and faithful brothers and sisters in Christ in Colossae' (v. 2). As each successive sentence of the text is processed, the reader adds to or modifies this mental model. Thus, the second half of v. 2 is added to the mental model as the opening greeting of the letter.

(1) Παῦλος ἀπόστολος Χριστοῦ Ἰησοῦ διὰ θελήματος θεοῦ
Paul apostle of.Christ Jesus through will of.God

καὶ Τιμόθεος ὁ ἀδελφὸς
and Timothy the brother

(2) τοῖς ἐν Κολοσσαῖς ἁγίοις καὶ πιστοῖς ἀδελφοῖς
to.the in Colossae saints and faithful brothers

ἐν Χριστῷ, χάρις ὑμῖν καὶ εἰρήνη ἀπὸ θεοῦ πατρὸς ἡμῶν.
in Christ grace to.you and peace from God father our

(3) Εὐχαριστοῦμεν τῷ θεῷ πατρὶ τοῦ κυρίου ἡμῶν Ἰησοῦ
we.give.thanks to.the God father of.the lord our Jesus

Χριστοῦ πάντοτε περὶ ὑμῶν προσευχόμενοι,
Christ always concerning you praying

The reader is aided in the build-up of his or her mental model by the linguistic signals of *cohesion*[2] which have been used. In the above passage from Colossians 1, for example, first person plural pronouns and verb inflection in vv. 2 and 3 indicate identity of reference with the authors of the letter, while second person plural pronouns indicate identity with its addressees. Similarly, an articular noun[3] typically implies that its referent is already to be found in the mental model that the reader has constructed from the previous verses. Thus, the articular reference to God in v. 3 constrains the reader to identify 'God the Father of our Lord Jesus Christ' with the God who was introduced in v. 2 as 'God our Father', notwithstanding the different form of reference.

When we examine the internal structure of a coherent text, we soon conclude that the sentences do not form a simple string. Modern editions of the Greek New Testament use one or more devices (e.g., paragraph indentation and blank lines) to signal *thematic groupings*. These are groupings of sentences

---

[1] See *SIL-UND* chap. 5 for an introduction to the concept of coherence. Many scholars question whether there is coherence between parts of certain books (e.g., 2 Corinthians), though most would accept that there is coherence *within* each part. For the majority of books, however, I take Turner's observation about the homogeneity of Acts to be applicable: "whatever his sources may have been, and however extensive,... the final editor has been able to impose his own style upon all his material" (1976:45) and thus ensure that the book is basically coherent.

[2] See *SIL-UND* chap. 6 for discussion and illustration of common types of cohesion.

[3] An *articular* noun is one that is preceded by an article (e.g., τῷ θεῷ 'to.the God'). Nouns without the article are described as *anarthrous* (e.g., ἀπὸ θεοῦ 'from God'). See further in chap. 9.

that seem to belong together over against other groupings of sentences, and groupings of groupings of sentences that seem to belong together over against other groupings of groupings of sentences.[4]

While editors often do not agree where one group of sentences ends and another begins, consciously or unconsciously they use as a basis for their segmentation changes "in scene, time, character configuration, event structure, and the like" (Chafe 1987:43). Givón (1984:245) formalizes these changes for narrative as *discontinuities* of time, place, action, and participants. Table 1 (taken from *SIL-UND* sec. 7.3) indicates how continuity and discontinuity manifests itself along each of these dimensions.

Table 1: Dimensions of continuity and discontinuity in narrative (based on Givón loc. cit.)

Dimension	Continuity	Discontinuity
time	events separated by at most only small forward gaps	large forward gaps or events out of order
place	same place or (for motion) continuous change	discrete changes of place
action	all material of the same type: event, non-event, reported conversation, etc.	change from one type of material to another
participants	same cast and usually same general roles vis-à-vis one another	discrete changes of cast or change in relative roles

In narrative, then, the speaker typically begins a new thematic grouping when there is a significant discontinuity in at least one of these four dimensions. Within a thematic grouping, there is usually continuity along all four dimensions. One can think of a new thematic grouping resulting when the speaker leaves one section of the mental representation and moves on to, or perhaps creates, another. (*SIL-UND* loc. cit.)

In the above table, *discrete* is descriptive of linguistic elements that have "definable boundaries, with no gradation or continuity between them" (Crystal 1991:107). A discrete change of *place*, for instance, may be discerned when one group of sentences describes events in one place while the next group switches to events in another place. For instance, the last part of **Acts 9** is set in Joppa, whereas the beginning of chapter 10 is set in Caesarea, so there is a discontinuity of place at the beginning of chapter 10 (DE = the development marker δέ—see sec. 5.1).

(9:43) And it happened that he [Peter] stayed in Joppa for some time with a certain Simon, a tanner.

(10:1) Ἀνὴρ   δέ   τις   ἐν Καισαρείᾳ ὀνόματι Κορνήλιος
       man   DE   certain   in Caesarea   named   Cornelius...

In contrast, when the description of a *journey* occurs between the presentation of events in the place where the journey begins and its destination, the change of place that is discerned is not a discrete one. For example, in the parable of the Prodigal Son (**Luke 15**), vv. 11–12 are set at the father's house whereas vv. 13b-19 are set in a distant country. Nevertheless, because v. 13a describes the younger son's journey from his father's house to the distant country, there is no discontinuity of place at the beginning of v. 13 (3S = a verb inflected for third person singular).

(11) A certain man had two sons. (12) And the younger of them said to his father, "Father, give me the share of the property that will belong to me." So he divided his property between them.

(13a) καὶ   μετ'   οὐ   πολλὰς   ἡμέρας   συναγαγὼν   πάντα
       and   after   not   many   days   gathering   all

---

[4] I refer to such groupings of sentences as *paragraphs*, and to groupings of groupings of sentences as *sections*. Where I need to refer to a subdivision of a section, I use the term *subsection*, which may or may not be larger than a paragraph. For narrative, I call the events that constitute a thematic grouping that is described in one or more paragraphs an *episode*.

ὁ   νεώτερος υἱὸς ἀπεδήμησεν   εἰς χώραν μακράν
the   younger   son   3S.departed   to   country far

(13b)   καὶ ἐκεῖ διεσκόρπισεν τὴν οὐσίαν αὐτοῦ ζῶν ἀσώτως.
        and there 3S.squandered the property his living loosely

Discontinuities of *time* occur when there are "large forward gaps." For example, there is a discontinuity of time at Luke 15:13a, since the events described in that sentence occur 'a few days later' than those of v. 12.

Discontinuities of time also occur when events are "out of order." A *flashback* by definition presents such a discontinuity, since it is "set in a time earlier than the main action" (OED). **Mark 6:17** is an instance of a flashback, because Herod's arrest of John occurs prior to his hearing of Jesus performing miracles.

(16)   But when Herod heard of it [Jesus performing miracles], he said, "John, whom I beheaded, has been raised."

(17)   Αὐτὸς γὰρ ὁ Ἡρῴδης ἀποστείλας ἐκράτησεν τὸν Ἰωάννην κ.τ.λ.
        himself for the Herod   having.sent   3S.arrested the   John

Discontinuities of *action* include changes in the type of action described. For example, a shift from the description of events to *non-events* constitutes an action discontinuity. This is illustrated in **Acts 19:14**. The act described in v. 15 resumes the sequence of events interrupted by the non-event material of v. 14 which identifies the 'some' of v. 13 (3P = a verb inflected for third person plural).

(13)   Then some of the itinerant Jewish exorcists undertook to pronounce the name of the Lord Jesus over those who had evil spirits...

(14)   ἦσαν δέ τινος Σκευᾶ Ἰουδαίου ἀρχιερέως ἑπτὰ υἱοὶ τοῦτο ποιοῦντες.
        3P.were DE of.one Sceva of.Jewish high.priest seven sons this   doing

(15)   But in answer, the evil spirit said to them...

Another noteworthy change in the type of action is *from the reporting of a conversation or long speech* to actions resulting from that conversation or speech. **Matthew 7:28**, which follows the Sermon on the Mount (5:3–7:27), illustrates such an action discontinuity.[5]

(28)   Καὶ ἐγένετο   ὅτε ἐτέλεσεν ὁ Ἰησοῦς τοὺς λόγους τούτους,
        and   3S.happened when 3S.finished the Jesus   the   words   these

        ἐξεπλήσσοντο   οἱ ὄχλοι ἐπὶ τῇ διδαχῇ αὐτοῦ·
        3P.were.amazed the crowds at   the teaching his

Another type of action discontinuity may be identified from Givón's definition of what constitutes continuity of action. He writes (1983:8):

[A]ction continuity pertains primarily to temporal sequentiality within [a] thematic paragraph... [A]ctions are given primarily in the natural sequential order in which they actually occurred and most commonly there is small if any temporal gap... between one action and the next.

It follows from the above definition that action discontinuities are to be discerned when a sentence describes an event that fails to move the narrative forward to the next action in sequence. This happens when simultaneous events or restatements are involved.[6]

---

[5] Οὖν is often used in John's Gospel at such points of action discontinuity—see sec. 5.3.3.

[6] Sentences describing simultaneous events or restating a proposition usually belong to the *same* thematic grouping. In other words, such action discontinuities tend not to form the basis for a new thematic grouping.

In an action discontinuity involving *simultaneous events*, the second event takes place at the same time as the first. It is not the next in sequence.[7] In **Acts 12:5**, for example, the prayers of the church for Peter (v. 5b) are simultaneous with Peter being kept in jail (v. 5a).

(5a) ὁ μὲν οὖν Πέτρος ἐτηρεῖτο ἐν τῇ φυλακῇ·
   the then Peter 3S.was.being.kept in the jail

(5b) προσευχὴ δὲ ἦν ἐκτενῶς γινομένη ὑπὸ τῆς ἐκκλησίας
   prayer DE 3S.was earnestly being.made by the church

   πρὸς τὸν θεὸν περὶ αὐτοῦ.
   to the God for him

Matthew 25:15 is an example of an action discontinuity involving a generic-specific *restatement*. The event of v. 15 is not the next in sequence after that of v. 14b; rather, it is a specific instance of that event.

(14a) For it is as if a man, going on a journey, summoned his slaves

(14b) and entrusted his property to them;

(15) καὶ ᾧ μὲν ἔδωκεν πέντε τάλαντα, κ.τ.λ.
   and to.whom 3S.gave five talents

Finally, discontinuities of *participants* typically involve discrete changes of cast. For instance, in Acts 10:1 (cited above), the previous scene has involved the apostle Peter and the disciples of Joppa (9:36–43). Chapter 10 begins with an interaction between the centurion Cornelius, an angel, and members of Cornelius' household. The cast of participants in the two scenes is completely different, so participant discontinuity occurs.

Givón's thematic dimensions in narrative may be generalized for other discourse genres[8] as three parameters:
- *situation*: continuity or discontinuities of time, place, conditions, circumstances, and assumptions (typically associated with adverbials—see sec. 2.2)
- *reference*: continuity or discontinuities of participants and topics (most often associated with nominals—sec. 2.2)
- *action*: as defined above.

As we shall see in the next chapter, situational information is typically encoded by adverbials, whereas referential information is most often encoded by nominals.

Review Questions[9]

(a) What does it mean for a text to be *coherent*?

(b) What are the four *dimensions* of continuity and discontinuity in narrative, according to Givón? How may they be generalized to other discourse genres?

(c) What type of discontinuity does a *flashback* display?

(d) Why does the description of *simultaneous events* and *restatements* involve discontinuities of action?

Suggested Answers

(a) A text is coherent if a reader who is reasonably conversant with the world-view of the author is able to relate the information communicated in each sentence to the "mental model" that he or she has formed from reading what has already been presented in the text.

---

[7] Simultaneous events typically are presented in the imperfect tense-aspect.

[8] See *SIL-UND* chap. 2 for a division of discourse genres into broad categories.

[9] The questions are followed by suggested answers. The reader should cover these answers and attempt to answer the questions without this help. Failure to answer correctly calls for reviewing the section.

(b) The four dimensions of continuity and discontinuity in narrative, according to Givón, are *time*, *place*, *action*, and *participants*. They may be generalized to other discourse genres as the dimensions of *situation*, *reference*, and *action*.

(c) A flashback displays discontinuity of *time*, since the events concerned are out of sequential order.

(d) The description of simultaneous events and restatements involves discontinuities of action because the events concerned fail to move the narrative forward to the next action in temporal sequence.

2
POINTS OF DEPARTURE

We now look at a device that signals discontinuities of situation, of reference, and sometimes of action, viz., the placement at the beginning of a clause or sentence of an adverbial or nominal constituent. In linguistic circles, this device is often called *topicalization*. However, because of the potential for confusion between this term and *topic*, I will use the term *point of departure*.

First, however, I distinguish three different ways in which information is arranged functionally within sentences (sec. 2.1). I then examine the significance of sentence-initial constituents that provide a *point of departure* for the communication (sec. 2.2). Most points of departure imply a *switch* to the initial constituent from a corresponding constituent in a previous clause or sentence. However, certain of points of departure *renew* an earlier point of departure or propositional topic (sec. 2.3). The implications of *not* starting a sentence with a potential point of departure are then examined (sec. 2.4). Section 2.5 contains a warning that constituents are placed at the beginning of a clause or sentence not only to establish points of departure, but also for "focus" or "emphasis" (see below). Section 2.6 briefly addresses the question of which order of constituents is basic in New Testament Greek sentences. The chapter closes with illustrative narrative passages (sec. 2.7) and non-narrative passages (sec. 2.8).

A comment is in order about my usage of the terms *focus* and *emphasis*. Greek grammarians tend to employ the term "emphasis" to denote any kind of *prominence*. K. Callow (1974:50) uses the term prominence to refer "to any device whatever which gives certain events, participants, or objects more significance than others in the same context." I follow Callow (op. cit. 52) in distinguishing three types of prominence: "thematic" ("what I'm talking about"), "focus" ("what is relatively the most important... information in the given setting"—Dik 1978:19), and "emphasis" proper (to express strong feelings about an item or indicate that an event is unexpected). See section 3.4 for more on focus (see also *SIL-UND* sec. 11.1).

2.1 Articulations of the Sentence

In order to discuss the concept points of departure, we need to recognize different functional or "pragmatic" sentence structures (Comrie 1989:64). Andrews (1985:77–80) distinguishes three principal "articulations" of the sentence: topic-comment, focus-presupposition, and presentational.

The following is an example of propositional *topic-comment* articulation. The sentence has a topic (which is usually the subject of the sentence) and a comment giving information about the topic.[1]

His older son / was in the field. (Luke 15:25)

The following is an example of *focus-presupposition* articulation. The sentence has a presupposition that is known to the hearer ('you received the Spirit'). The focus ("the most important... information in the given setting"—see above) is on how this happened.

[Was it] by works of law / you received the Spirit? (Gal. 3:2b)

The following is an example of *presentational* articulation. The sentence presents a participant to the story.

There was a certain disciple in Damascus named Ananias. (Acts 9:10)

Acts 9:10 involves an existential sentence (one which posits the existence of a participant). However, other types of sentence may also present a participant to the story. For example:

An angel of the Lord appeared to him. (Luke 1:11)

---

[1] Care must be taken not to confuse the term "(propositional) topic" with the topic of a paragraph or longer stretch of speech or writing. "A referent is interpreted as the topic of a proposition if in a given situation the proposition is construed as being about this referent, i.e., as expressing information that is relevant to and that increases the addressee's knowledge of this referent" (Lambrecht 1994:131).

The discussion of points of departure in the next section only concerns sentences with topic-comment or presentational articulation. Sentences with focus-presupposition articulation are considered in sections 4.1–2.

2.2   Propositional Topic, Comment, and Point of Departure

In chapter 1 we saw that coherent texts contain thematic subgroupings characterized by discontinuities of situation, reference, and action. One device that is used at points of discontinuity is the placement of an appropriate constituent at the beginning of the clause or sentence. This device, as will be seen below, indicates both the nature of the discontinuity and the relationship of what follows to the context.

In a single sentence with topic-comment articulation, as we noted in section 2.1, the speaker wishes to talk about something, viz., the propositional topic, and to make a comment about that topic, as in:

> *Topic*   *Comment*
> The younger son /   set off for a distant country.

A problem arises, however, if an analyst tries to divide all sentences with topic-comment articulation into just a topic and a comment. If 'the younger son set off for a distant country' were to be preceded by the temporal phrase 'not long after', I would still consider 'the younger son' to be the propositional topic. Consequently, following the Prague School linguist Beneš, I would divide the sentence into three functional parts:

> *Pt of Departure*   *Topic*   *Comment*
> Not long after /   the younger son /   set off for a distant country.

Many of those who have described the function of the point of departure concentrate on what follows it in the discourse. Thus, Chafe (1976:50) says that such a constituent "sets a spatial, temporal or individual domain within which the main predication holds."

Other linguists, however, recognize that points of departure are as much backward-looking as forward-looking (see, for example, Givón 1987:182). In other words, such constituents have a *bi-directional* function. This insight should probably be credited to Beneš. Back in 1962, he called such a constituent the "basis" which, "serving as a point of departure for the communication, is directly linked to the context" (as translated by Garvin 1963:508).

For example, in the sentence considered above, the initial temporal phrase 'not long after' has a bi-directional function. It looks forward, providing the temporal point of departure or setting for what follows. It also looks backward, indicating that what follows is to be related to the context primarily on the basis of time, involving a "switch" (Andrews 1985:78) from a previous temporal setting (whether explicit or implicit) to a new one.

Definition:

The term POINT OF DEPARTURE designates an element that is placed at the beginning of a clause or sentence with a dual function:

1. It provides a starting point for the communication; and
2. It "cohesively anchors the subsequent clause(s) to something which is already in the context (i.e., to something accessible in the hearer's mental representation)." *SIL-UND* sec 11.3.1

Note that conjunctions like καί, δέ and οὖν are ignored when identifying the initial element.

In narrative, points of departure relate events to their context on the basis of time, of place, or of reference. In argument, adverbial constituents expressing condition, reason, purpose, and other situational relations may also be placed initially in the sentence to act as points of departure.

We now look at a variety of adverbial phrases and clauses that begin sentences. In each case, they set a *situational* point of departure (underlined in the Greek text) for the following material. (Remember: to be a point of departure, the constituent must be *initial* in its clause or sentence.)

As we have already seen, a *temporal* point of departure is used in **Luke 15:13a**, viz., the adverbial phrase μετ' οὐ πολλὰς ἡμέρας 'after not many days'. This constituent sets the domain in time for what follows. It also indicates that the primary basis for relating what follows to the context is by a switch from the time of the father's dividing of the inheritance to a few days later.

(12b)   So he divided his property between them.

(13a)   καὶ <u>μετ' οὐ πολλὰς ἡμέρας</u> συναγαγὼν πάντα
           and after not many days gathering all

           ὁ νεώτερος υἱὸς ἀπεδήμησεν εἰς χώραν μακράν
           the younger son 3S.departed to country far

Matthew 6:2 contains a temporal point of departure which is an adverbial *clause*. In this case, the switch is from the habitual practice of τὴν δικαιοσύνην ὑμῶν 'your piety' (v. 1) to a specific instance of it (see also in vv. 5 and 16).

(1)   Beware of practicing your piety before others in order to be seen by them, for then you have no reward from your Father in heaven.

(2)   <u>Ὅταν</u> οὖν <u>ποιῇς ἐλεημοσύνην</u>, μὴ σαλπίσῃς ἔμποσθέν σου, κ.τ.λ.
           whenever then you.do alms not sound.trumpet before you

A *spatial* point of departure (i.e., one involving a discontinuity of place) occurs in **Acts 9:36a**. Here, the initial adverbial phrase Ἐν Ἰόππῃ establishes the spatial setting. It also indicates that the primary basis for relating what follows to the context is by a switch from Lydda and Sharon to Joppa.

(35)   And all the residents of Lydda and Sharon saw Aeneas and they turned to the Lord.

(36a)   <u>Ἐν Ἰόππῃ</u> δέ τις ἦν μαθήτρια ὀνόματι Ταβιθά
            at Joppa DE certain 3S.was disciple named Tabitha

(For a series of six spatial points of departure within *descriptive* material, see Rev. 4:4–6.)

Acts 14:26 exemplifies a spatial point of departure in the context of a *travelogue*. Here, the initial adverbial phrase κἀκεῖθεν 'from there', which refers back to the goal of the previous journey, establishes the point of departure for the next stage of the journey. It also indicates that the primary basis for relating what follows to the context is by a switch from the point of departure for the previous journey (Perga).

(25)   and, having spoken the word in Perga, they went down to Attalia.

(26)   <u>κἀκεῖθεν</u> ἀπέπλευσαν εἰς Ἀντιόχειαν, κ.τ.λ.
           and.from.there 3P.sailed.away to Antioch

Matthew 6:14, 15 begin with adverbial clauses of *condition*.[2] Verse 14 is related to the context by a switch from the set of petitions that make up the Lord's Prayer to the specific petition that appears in v. 12. This petition becomes the point of departure for the assertion that will be true if the condition is fulfilled. The opposite condition is the point of departure for v. 15. In this particular passage, the switch between these two points of departure has the effect of *contrasting* the consequences of fulfilling the two conditions; contrast is a special case of switch (+ = the additive non-conjunctive καί—see sec. 6.2).

(12)   And forgive us our debts, as we also have forgiven our debtors...

(14)   <u>Ἐὰν</u> γὰρ <u>ἀφῆτε τοῖς ἀνθρώποις τὰ παραπτώματα αὐτῶν</u>,
           if for you.forgive to.the men the trespasses their

---

[2]Ramsey observes that initial "if" clauses in English "are thematically associated to the preceding discourse" (1987:385).

ἀφήσει	καὶ	ὑμῖν	ὁ	πατὴρ	ὑμῶν	ὁ	οὐράνοις·
3S.will.forgive	+	to.you	the	father	your	the	heavenly

(15)

ἐὰν	δὲ	μὴ	ἀφῆτε	τοῖς	ἀνθρώποις,
if	DE	not	you.forgive	to.the	men

οὐδὲ	ὁ	πατὴρ	ὑμῶν[3]	ἀφήσει	τὰ	παραπτώματα	ὑμῶν.
neither	the	father	your	3S.will.forgive	the	trespasses	your

The reported speech of **1 Cor. 12:15b** begins with an adverbial clause of *reason* to establish a point of departure for the main assertion which follows. In this example, the point of departure begins the discourse, and the context that prompted the speech can only be surmised.

(15b)

Ὅτι	οὐκ	εἰμὶ	χείρ,	οὐκ	εἰμὶ	ἐκ	τοῦ	σώματος
because	not	I.am	hand	not	I.am	of	the	body

Finally, **Eph. 6:21** begins with an adverbial clause of *purpose* to establish a point of departure for what follows. It relates to the context by a switch from the purpose clause that immediately precedes it in v. 20.[4]

(19)   (Pray) also for me, so that (ἵνα) when I speak, a message may be given to me to make known with boldness the mystery of the gospel, (20) for which I am an ambassador in chains, so that (ἵνα) I may declare it boldly, as I must speak.

(21)

Ἵνα	δὲ	εἰδῆτε	καὶ	ὑμεῖς	τὰ	κατ᾽	ἐμέ,	τί
so.that	DE	you.may.know	+	you	the	about	me	what

πράσσω,	πάντα[5]	γνωρίσει	ὑμῖν	Τυχικὸς	κ.τ.λ.
I.do	all	3S.will.make.known	to.you	Tychicus	

So much for adverbial constituents which begin sentences to set situational points of departure! We look now at *referential* points of departure.

Some referential points of departure begin with the preposition περί 'concerning', and are used to set the *topic* for a paragraph or longer section. Typically, when a sentence begins with such a prepositional phrase, a switch from a previous paragraph topic is also indicated.

An example of this is found in **1 Cor. 8:1.** Here, the initial prepositional phrase Περὶ τῶν εἰδωλοθύτων 'concerning food sacrificed to idols' sets the topic for the chapter. It also indicates a switch from the topic of the previous section (Περὶ τῶν παρθένων 'concerning virgins'—7:25).[6]

(1)

Περὶ	δὲ	τῶν	εἰδωλοθύτων,	οἴδαμεν	ὅτι	πάντες	γνῶσιν	ἔχομεν.
concerning	DE	the	idolatrous.sacrifices	we.know	that	all	knowledge	we.have

Referential points of departure may also involve *nominal* constituents. In such instances, the point of departure may also be the propositional topic of a topic-comment sentence, especially if the point of departure is the subject of the sentence.

In **Acts 20:6a**, for example, the initial subject ἡμεῖς 'we' is both the point of departure and the propositional topic of the sentence. Its initial position in the sentence indicates that the basis for relating

---

[3] See sec. 4.1 for discussion of constituents that occur between the negative and the verb.

[4] On initial purpose clauses in English, see Thompson 1985.

[5] Πάντα precedes the verb for emphasis. See secs. 2.5 and 3.6. Variant orders of constituents in this sentence do not affect the point being made here.

[6] Initial constituents such as Περὶ τῶν εἰδωλοθύτων are said to be 'left-dislocated' because they are separated syntactically from the rest of the sentence (see *SIL-UND* sec. 11.3). Topics that are introduced in a left-dislocated constituent are "usually cognitively ACCESSIBLE" (Lambrecht 1994:183). In the case of 1 Cor. 7:25 and 8:1, the topics are cognitively accessible because the Corinthians had apparently asked about them in their letter (see Kistemaker 1993:237).

what follows to the context is by a switch from the activities of οὗτοι 'these men' to ἡμεῖς.[7] The switch has the effect of contrasting the activities of the two groups (compare Matt. 6:15 above).

(5)   These men, going before us, awaited us in Troas.

(6a)   *Pt of Departure/Topic*   *Comment*

ἡμεῖς   δὲ   ἐξεπλεύσαμεν   μετὰ   τὰς   ἡμέρας   τῶν
we   DE   we.sailed.away   after   the   days   of.the

                                               ἀζύμων   ἀπὸ   Φιλίππων
                                               unleavened.bread   from   Philippi

Similarly, in **Rev. 4:7a**, the initial position in the sentence of the subject τὸ ζῷον τὸ πρῶτον 'the first living creature' indicates that the basis for relating what follows to the context is by a switch from the four living creatures in general to one of them in particular. In other words, a *generic-specific* switch is involved.

(6b)   Around the throne, and on each side of the throne, are four living creatures, full of eyes in front and behind.

(7a)   *Pt of Departure/Topic*   *Comment*

καὶ   τὸ   ζῷον   τὸ   πρῶτον   ὅμοιον   λέοντι
and   the   living.being   the   first   like   lion

Occasionally, *two* points of departure begin a sentence, one situational and one referential. The first one will indicate the primary basis for relating the sentence to its context.

In **Rom. 11:30**, for instance, the referential point of departure ὑμεῖς 'you' marks a switch from 'all Israel' (v. 26), while the situational point of departure ποτε 'then' marks a secondary switch from the 'now' of v. 28.[8]

(26)   And so all Israel will be saved... (28) As regards the gospel they are enemies of God for your sake; but as regards election, they are beloved, for the sake of their ancestors; (29) for the gifts and the calling of God are irrevocable.

(30)   ὥσπερ   γὰρ   ὑμεῖς   ποτε   ἠπειθήσατε   τῷ   θεῷ,   κ.τ.λ.
just.as   for   you   then   you.disobeyed   the   God

See also 2 Cor. 5:16 (the referential point of departure ἡμεῖς 'we' indicates the primary basis for relating the sentence to its context, with the situational point of departure ἀπὸ τοῦ νῦν 'from now on' providing a secondary basis).

Review Questions

(a) What are the three principal articulations of the sentence, according to Andrews? Label the type of articulation of the following sentences:

At Joppa there was a certain disciple named Tabitha. (Acts 9:36)
From Miletus he summoned the elders of the church. (Acts 20:17)
Who has bewitched you? (Gal. 3:1)

(b) Divide the second of these sentences (Acts 20:17) into point of departure, (propositional) topic and comment.

(c) What is the primary basis for relating **Luke 1:57a** (below) to its context?

---

[7] In subject-initial languages such as English, strong claims about points of departure and discontinuities in relation to the subject are not possible. Nevertheless, a "spacer" (Dooley 1990:477) like *however* may be used in English to set off the subject (e.g., 'We, for our part...') and thus establish it as a point of departure.

[8] Codex Alexandrinus (A) reverses the order of ὑμεῖς and πότε.

(56)   And Mary remained with her (Elizabeth) about three months and then returned to her home.

(57a)   Τῇ   δὲ   Ἐλισάβετ   ἐπλήσθη   ὁ   χρόνος   τοῦ   τεκεῖν   αὐτήν
        to.the DE Elisabeth   3S.was.fulfilled the time   of.the to.bear   her

(d) In **Acts 27:41b, c**, which constituents are the point of departure, the (propositional) topic, and the comment? (Ignore the conjunctions καί, δέ and μέν, which will be discussed in part II.)

(41a)   But having fallen into a place of two seas, they ran the ship aground.

(41b)   καὶ   ἡ   μὲν   πρῷρα   ἐρείσασα   ἔμεινεν   ἀσάλευτος,
        and   the   prow   having.stuck   3S.remained   immovable

(41c)   ἡ   δὲ   πρύμνα   ἐλύετο   ὑπὸ   τῆς   βίας   [τῶν   κυμάτων].
        the   DE   stern   3S.was.being.destroyed by   the   force of.the   waves

Suggested Answers

(a) The first sentence has *presentational* articulation. (Tabitha is being presented to the scene.)
The second sentence has *topic-comment* articulation. (The comment is about the propositional topic 'he' [Paul].)
The third sentence has *focus-presupposition* articulation. (The presupposition is that 'someone bewitched you'. The focus is on 'who'.)

(b)   *Pt. of departure*   *Topic*   *Comment*
        From Miletus /   he /   summoned the elders of the church.

(c) The basis for relating Luke 1:57 to its context is a switch of attention from Mary (in v. 56) to Elisabeth. This could be reflected in English by opening the sentence with a phrase like "As for Elisabeth."

(d) In Acts 27:41b, ἡ πρῷρα 'the prow' is both the point of departure and the propositional topic about which the comment ἐρείσασα ἔμεινεν ἀσάλευτος 'having stuck, remained immovable' is made. Similarly, in v. 41c, ἡ πρύμνα 'the stern' is both the point of departure and the propositional topic about which the comment ἐλύετο ὑπὸ τῆς βίας [τῶν κυμάτων] 'was being destroyed by the force of the waves' is made.

2.3   Points of Departure involving Renewal

So far, I have illustrated only those points of departure that relate to the context by a switch from a corresponding constituent. However, points of departure may also relate to the context by *renewal*.[9]

Points of departure involving renewal have a number of possible referents.

- The point of departure may refer to the *point of departure* for the previous context.
- The point of departure may refer to the *propositional topic* of the previous sentence.
- The point of departure may refer to the participant who has just been *introduced* in a sentence with presentational articulation.

Because the referents of such points of departure have been featured in the immediate context, the point of departure often employs a "reduced" form (Werth 1984:9), i.e., a pronoun or pronominal adverb (see further in sec. 8.2).

Luke 2:36–37 illustrate points of departure that involve renewal. In v. 36b, the initial constituent αὕτη refers to Anna, who was introduced in v. 36a in a sentence with presentational articulation. Then, in v. 37a, the initial constituent αὕτη refers to the point of departure for v. 36b. (Both these constituents function not only as points of departure, but also as the propositional topic of their respective sentences.)

---

[9] Andrews (1985:78) refers to such points of departure as "expected topics."

(36a)   Καὶ   ἦν   Ἅννα προφῆτις, θυγάτηρ Φανουήλ, κ.τ.λ.
and   3S.was Anna prophetess daughter Phanuel

(36b)   αὕτη   προβεβηκυῖα   ἐν ἡμέραις πολλαῖς,
this   having.become.advanced in days   many

ζήσασα   μετὰ ἀνδρὸς ἔτη ἑπτὰ ἀπὸ τῆς παρθενίας αὐτῆς
having.lived with husband years seven from the virginity her

(37)   καὶ αὐτὴ χήρα ἕως ἐτῶν ὀγδοήκοντα τεσσάρων,
and she widow until years eighty   four

ἣ   οὐκ ἀφίστατο   τοῦ ἱεροῦ κ.τ.λ.
who not 3S.was.departing.from the temple

The initial constituent of **Mark 6:17** (cited above as an example of a flashback) refers to the propositional topic of the previous sentence, viz., Herod. (Note that Herod is the topic of the previous *narrative clauses*, not the topic of the reported speech, even though this intervenes. Reported speeches may be viewed as the complements of speech verbs, as they are embedded in the overall structure of the narrative, rather than being part of the narrative structure itself.)

(16)   But when Herod heard of it [Jesus performing miracles], he said, "John, whom I beheaded, has been raised."

(17)   Αὐτὸς γὰρ ὁ Ἡρῴδης ἀποστείλας ἐκράτησεν τὸν Ἰωάννην κ.τ.λ.
himself for the Herod   having.sent 3S.arrested the John

Although points of departure involving renewal are very common in non-narrative material (see sec. 2.8), in narrative, an initial *nominal* constituent that repeats a previous constituent is rare. There is one place in narrative where a nominal point of departure involving renewal is regularly used, however, viz., to introduce non-events or other '*background*' material (see part IV), as in Mark 6:17 above. Furthermore, if successive sentences begin with the same point of departure, then each presents a different background comment, as in Luke 2:36b and 37 (above). See also Rev. 11:4 and 6.

Occasionally in narrative, a nominal point of departure involving renewal introduces a foreground event. Such is the case in **Luke 22:41**; following Jesus' instruction to the disciples to pray (v. 40), the use of αὐτός ensures that attention remains on Jesus, rather than on the disciples' response to his instruction. This effect is captured in English by a translation like "He himself withdrew..." (NEB, rather than "Then he"—NRSV).

(40)   Having come to the place, he said to them, "Pray that you may not come into the time of trial."

(41a)   καὶ αὐτὸς ἀπεσπάσθη   ἀπ' αὐτῶν ὡσεὶ λίθου βολὴν
and he   3S.was.withdrawn from them about of.stone throw

Finally, **Mark 12:38** (UBS text) provides an example of an initial *adverbial* constituent that repeats the setting for the previous paragraph.[10] Typically, such points of departure introduce *different episodes* that occur in the same general setting (compare the renewal of nominal points of departure to present different comments about the same referent).

(35)   Jesus was saying, while teaching in the temple, "How can the scribes say that the Christ is the son of David?... (37) David himself calls him Lord; so how can he be his son?" And the large crowd was listening to him with delight.

(38)   Καὶ ἐν τῇ διδαχῇ αὐτοῦ ἔλεγεν,
and in the teaching his   3S.was.saying

---

[10] The setting for Mark 12:35 is not expressed in a temporal point of departure (contrast NRSV) but in a postnuclear participial clause (διδάσκων ἐν τῷ ἱερῷ). The pragmatic effect is to convey continuity with the context—see sec. 2.4.

Βλέπετε   ἀπὸ   τῶν   γραμματέων   κ.τ.λ.
beware   of   the   scribes

2.4   Potential Points of Departure that Do Not Begin a Clause or Sentence

In all languages in which adverbial constituents (and nominal constituents, where applicable) have the option of beginning a sentence or of occurring later in the sentence, a corollary follows from the principle that points of departure indicate the primary basis for relating the sentence to its context. This is that, if a potential point of departure is *not* the primary basis for relating the sentence to its context, it will *not* be placed initial in the sentence.

This is illustrated in **Acts 20:6a** (repeated below), which contains the temporal phrase μετὰ τὰς ἡμέρας τῶν ἀζύμων 'after the days of unleavened bread'.[11] The fact that the subject, rather than the temporal expression, is initial in Acts 20:6a indicates that the sentence is to be related to its context primarily on the basis, not of a switch of time, but of a switch of attention from one participant to another.

(5)   These men, going before us, awaited us in Troas.

(6a)   ἡμεῖς   δὲ   ἐξεπλεύσαμεν   μετὰ   τὰς   ἡμέρας   τῶν
        we   DE   we.sailed.away   after   the   days   of.the

        ἀζύμων   ἀπὸ   Φιλίππων   κ.τ.λ.
        unleavened.bread   from   Philippi

1 Cor. 11:25 (below) is similar. The second part of Paul's account of the Lord's supper is to be related to the first primarily on the basis of a switch from 'the bread' to 'the cup'. Contrast the NIV translation "In the same way, after supper he took the cup," which relates the two parts primarily on the basis of a switch of time from 'when he had given thanks' (v. 24) to 'after supper'.[12]

(23)   … the Lord Jesus on the night when he was betrayed took a loaf of bread, (24) and when he had given thanks, he broke it and said, "This is my body that is for you. Do this in remembrance of me."

(25)   ὡσαύτως   καὶ   τὸ   ποτήριον   μετὰ   τὸ   δειπνῆσαι   κ.τ.λ.
        similarly   +   the   cup   after   the   to.sup

Other passages in which one or more English translations change the primary basis for relating the material concerned to the context, include:

- Luke 16:20: the switch is from the rich man of v. 19 to πτωχὸς τις ὀνόματι Λάζαρος 'a poor man named Lazarus', not from the rich man's house to "at his gate" (NIV, NRSV).
- Acts 1:5b: the switch is from John (v. 5a) to ὑμεῖς 'you' (Newman and Nida 1972:15), not from the time that John was baptizing to "in a few days" (NIV).
- Col. 1:21: the switch is from the 'all things' that God was pleased to reconcile to himself (v. 20) to ὑμᾶς 'you' (who have now been reconciled), not from the time God was pleased to reconcile all things to himself back to "once" (NIV).[13]
- 1 Pet. 5:10: the switch is from 'your adversary the devil' (v. 8) to ὁ θεὸς πάσης χάριτος 'the God of all grace', not from the time of resisting the devil to "after you have suffered for a little while" (NIV, NRSV).

If *no* potential point of departure begins a sentence, then the pragmatic effect is often to convey *continuity* with the context. Since points of departure signal discontinuities of situation, reference and,

---

[11] As in many other languages, it is unusual in the Greek New Testament for references to a point in time *not* to be initial in the sentence. In Acts, for instance, only 13 out of 81 such expressions do not begin sentences.

[12] I am interpreting ὡσαύτως as a conjunction (see p. 94, fn. 1). See Rom. 11:30 (discussed in sec. 2.2) for the possibility of two points of departure occurring in the same sentence.

[13] Πότε 'once' precedes the verb in anticipation of a switch to the point of departure νυνί 'now' (v. 22); see sec. 4.3.

sometimes, action, the absence of a point of departure means that no such discontinuity has been indicated *by this means*. (This does not stop a discontinuity being signaled by some other means—see below.)

Acts 5:21 (below) is an instance in which no adverbial or nominal constituent begins the sentence.[14] If the sentence had started with the temporal phrase ὑπὸ τὸν ὄρθρον 'about the dawn', then the primary basis for relating the sentence to its context would have been through a switch to a new temporal setting. This might have raised the question as to why the apostles waited till morning to obey the angel's command. The fact that neither this nor any other potential point of departure is initial has the pragmatic effect of conveying continuity with the context, in this case with the command of v. 20. This relationship of command and appropriate response takes precedence over the change of temporal setting.[15]

(19)   An angel of the Lord... said, (20) "Go, stand and speak in the temple..."

(21)   ἀκούσαντες δὲ   εἰσῆλθον   ὑπὸ   τὸν   ὄρθρον   εἰς
        hearing   DE   3P.entered about the   dawn   into

        τὸ   ἱερὸν   καὶ   ἐδίδασκον.
        the temple   and   3P.were.teaching

In many narrative passages in which successive sentences begin with an event-type verb or participle, each sentence describes the next event in sequence and, in Givón's terms, there is action continuity between them. See, for example, Luke 1:59–65a.

Nevertheless, it is incorrect to suggest that, whenever a sentence begins with a verb or participle, rather than with a nonverbal constituent, *complete* continuity with the last events described is indicated. Such a claim is easily disproved. For instance, verb-initial sentences with presentational articulation often introduce participants to an ongoing story (see sec. 8.1), but not necessarily to the specific location of the last events.

Acts 9:10, a verb-initial presentational sentence, is an example of this. It introduces Ananias to the story in which Saul has met with the Lord Jesus on the road to Damascus (vv. 1–9). Although both Saul and Ananias are now in Damascus, it is clear from subsequent verses that they are not in the same specific location.[16]

(9)   and he (Saul) was without sight for three days, and neither ate nor drank.

(10a)   Ἦν   δὲ   τις   μαθητὴς   ἐν   Δαμασκῷ   ὀνόματι   Ἀνανίας,
        3S.was DE   certain disciple   in   Damascus   named   Ananias

A similar problem arises with certain classes of orienters or "complement-taking predicates" (Noonan 1985:110) that introduce new points in a discourse or epistle (Reed 1997:118 fn. 187). The combination of such an orienter and asyndeton (the absence of a conjunction) signals a discontinuity even though the sentence begins with a verb (see sec. 17.2.1). Examples include Ἠκούσατε ὅτι 'You have heard that' (Matt. 5:21, 27, 33, 38, 43), Μὴ νομίσητε ὅτι 'Do not think that' (Matt. 5:17), and Ἐλπίζω ... ἵνα 'I hope... that' (Phil. 2:19).

I conclude that all that can be said with certainty about verb-initial sentences in Greek is that they *mark* no discontinuity with the context. At the same time, if no potential point of departure begins a sentence with an event-type verb even though one or more is present in the sentence, the intended pragmatic effect is typically to convey continuity with the context.

---

[14] I will argue in sec. 11.1 that prenuclear participial clauses are not to be interpreted as points of departure.

[15] The TEV captures this relationship very nicely by beginning v. 21, "The apostles obeyed". NIV, in contrast, begins the verse, "At dawn."

[16] Furthermore, the verb ἦν 'was' signals an action discontinuity, as the story changes from events to a non-event. For a presentational sentence that begins with a point of departure, see Luke 4:33a (passage 2 of sec. 2.7).

Review Questions

(a) If a potential point of departure is not placed initial in the sentence, what does this indicate?

(b) In **Luke 20:19a**, why does the temporal phrase ἐν αὐτῇ τῇ ὥρα 'in the same hour' not begin the sentence? (Verse 18 is the end of a parable told by Jesus.)

(19a)	καὶ	ἐζήτησαν		οἱ	γραμματεῖς	...	ἐπιβαλεῖν
	and	3P.were.seeking		the	scribes		to.lay.on

	ἐπ′	αὐτὸν	τὰς	χεῖρας	ἐν	αὐτῇ	τῇ	ὥρα,
	on	him	the	hands	in	same	the	hour

(19b)   and they were afraid of the people,

(19c)   because they realized that he had told this parable against them.

Suggested Answers

(a) If a potential point of departure is not placed initial in the sentence, this indicates that it is not the primary basis for relating the sentence to its context.

(b) The temporal phrase ἐν αὐτῇ τῇ ὥρα does not begin the sentence in Luke 20:19a because the effort of the scribes (and chief priests) to lay hands on Jesus is in response to the parable he had told (see v. 19c). If the temporal phrase had begun the sentence, this would have indicated that the primary basis for relating their effort to the context was temporal. Any cause-and-effect relationship between the two events would then have been obscured. Furthermore, since the point of departure would have involved renewal (sec. 2.3), this would have implied that a different episode occurring in the same setting was beginning.

2.5   A Warning about Initial Constituents

All the adverbial and nominal constituents that have begun clauses and sentences to this point have been interpreted as points of departure. Unfortunately, constituents may be placed at the beginning of a sentence for other reasons, too. In particular, they may be placed there to *focus* on them or to *emphasize* them (to use the terms found in K. Callow 1974:52—see the introduction to this chapter).

In **Acts 14:3**, for example, ἱκανὸν χρόνον 'a long time' is placed first in its sentence for emphasis; "the duration of Paul and Barnabas' ministry is emphasized, because it was noteworthy and even surprising, in view of the prevailing circumstances (v. 2)" (Levinsohn 1987:52).[17]

(2)   But the unbelieving Jews stirred up the Gentiles and poisoned their minds against the brothers.

(3)	**ἱκανὸν**	μὲν	οὖν	**χρόνον**	διέτριψαν	παρρησιαζόμενοι	κ.τ.λ.
	long	then		time	3P.spent	speaking boldly	

See section 3.8.1 for a discussion of how to distinguish points of departure from constituents that have been placed initial for focus or emphasis. I simply note here that, like propositional topics, a point of departure "must either be already established in the discourse or is easily relatable to one that is already established" (Lambrecht 1994:164). Information that is focused, in contrast, either has *not* been established in the discourse (it is "new") or needs to be *re*established.

2.6   Implications for the Basic Constituent Order of New Testament Greek

Longacre (1995) addresses the identification of the basic order of subject, verb and object in languages in which the subject is commonly found both preceding and following its verb. On page 333 he makes the following claim, "If storyline clauses in a narrative discourse in a given language are VSO [verb - subject - object], then that language should be classified as a VSO language." I know of no way to prove the validity of this claim, but the following observations are in order.

---

[17] Constituents that are initial for focus or emphasis are given in bold in the Greek.

First of all, Porter points out (1992:293) that "the majority of Greek clauses do not express all of the elements," verb, subject, and object. Furthermore, "to base one's formulation of standard order on instances where all three elements are present misrepresents the evidence and its results" (ibid.). It is far more common for the verb to occur by itself or to be followed only by a direct or indirect object. The next most common patterns are object-verb and subject-verb structures.[18]

Secondly, note the following statistics for the narrative of Acts (Levinsohn 1987:3).

> Statistically, more clauses and sentences of the narrative in Acts begin with the verb than with the subject. Out of 720 clauses whose subject or theme is different from that of the clause or sentence to which they relate:
> in a maximum of 264, the subject precedes the verb;
> the subject follows the verb in 310;
> no separate subject is present in 146.

I have not compiled statistics for the narrative sections of the Gospels, but note that Terry, who argues (1995:154) for subject-initial as the basic constituent order in some Koiné Greek clause types, nevertheless concedes that VSO may be the norm for storyline clauses in narrative material. BDF make a similar observation concerning tendencies in the narrative of the New Testament, "The verb or nominal predicate with its copula stands immediately after the conjunction" (§472(1)).

Thirdly, I feel that, *pragmatically*, it is easiest to explain variations in constituent order by taking verb-initial as the default order.[19] The presence of adverbial or nominal constituents before the verb in individual sentences is then viewed as a marked order, motivated by the desire either to establish the constituent concerned as a point of departure or in order to focus on or emphasize that constituent. Furthermore, I argue in section 2.8 that, in non-narrative material, the same motivations determine whether or not an adverbial or nominal constituent is placed before the verb, even though this results in a majority of sentences beginning with the subject rather than the verb.[20]

Throughout this book, therefore, I treat verb-initial as the default pragmatic order in New Testament Greek, regardless of the discourse genre of the passage.

It follows that, when a phrase occurs between two verbs and could be construed with either, it is considered to be in its default position after the first verb, rather than to be preposed with respect to the second. For example, in Acts 3:12 (ἰδὼν δὲ ὁ Πέτρος ἀπεκρίνατο πρὸς τὸν λαόν 'and when Peter saw it, he responded to the people'), ὁ Πέτρος is *not* preposed with respect to ἀπεκρίνατο.

2.7   Illustrative Narrative Passages

In each of the following narratives from Luke's Gospel,[21] identify the type of discontinuity present when an adverbial or nominal constituent begins the sentence to provide the point of departure. Note, also, how the absence of a point of departure tends to correspond with continuity with the context. After studying each passage, try to answer the questions that follow it.

Initial constituents that are <u>underlined</u> are considered to be points of departure. Initial constituents in **bold** are considered to be preposed for focus or emphasis.

---

[18] Porter's conclusions are based upon analysis of Philippians, 1 and 2 Timothy, Matt. 5-7, Acts 21-23, Rom. 5-6, 1 Cor. 12-14, and 2 Cor. 10-13 (1992:293, fn. 2).

[19] Contrast Porter, for whom normal or default orders are those that "occur with high frequencies" (1992:295; see also Dryer 1997:74). Porter considers it "not incumbent upon the exegete to explain the normal patterns of usage," even though they include both the object-verb and verb-object orders.

[20] See also Porter's observation (ibid.), "The expressed subject is often used as a form of topic marker or shifter... and is appropriately placed first to signal this semantic function."

[21] The passages have been selected because καί is virtually the only conjunction used in them. I seek thereby to avoid addressing issues raised by the selection of one conjunction over against another until part II of this book.

Passage 1: Luke 5:27–32

(27a) Καὶ μετὰ ταῦτα ἐξῆλθεν
      and after these.things 3S.went.out

(27b) καὶ ἐθεάσατο τελώνην ὀνόματι Λευὶν καθήμενον ἐπὶ τὸ τελώνιον,
      and 3S.saw tax.collector named Levi sitting on the custom.house

(27c) καὶ εἶπεν αὐτῷ, Ἀκολούθει μοι.
      and 3S.said to.him follow me

(28) καὶ καταλιπὼν πάντα ἀναστὰς ἠκολούθει αὐτῷ.
      and abandoning all rising.up 3S.followed him

(29a) καὶ ἐποίησεν δοχὴν μεγάλην Λευὶς αὐτῷ ἐν τῇ οἰκίᾳ αὐτοῦ,
      and 3S.made feast great Levi for.him in the house his

(29b) καὶ ἦν ὄχλος πολὺς τελωνῶν καὶ ἄλλων οἳ
      and 3S.was crowd much of.tax.collectors and of.others who

      ἦσαν μετ᾽ αὐτῶν κατακείμενοι.
      3P.were with him reclining

(30) καὶ ἐγόγγυζον οἱ Φαρισαῖοι καὶ οἱ γραμματεῖς αὐτῶν
      and 3P.grumbled the Pharisees and the scribes their

      πρὸς τοὺς μαθητὰς αὐτοῦ κ.τ.λ.
      to the disciples his

(31–32) καὶ ἀποκριθεὶς ὁ Ἰησοῦς εἶπεν πρὸς αὐτούς, κ.τ.λ.
      and answering the Jesus 3S.said to them

Questions

Since the above narrative contains only one point of departure, the adverbial phrase of time in v. 27a:

(a) On what basis is the episode of vv. 27–32 to be related to its context?

(b) How does Luke relate the call of Levi in vv. 27–28 to the feast he gave (vv. 29ff.), as far as continuity or discontinuity is concerned?

Suggested Answers

(a) The episode is to be related to its context primarily on the basis of a switch to a later time.

(b) Luke signals no discontinuity between the call of Levi and the feast he gives. In fact, since the potential point of departure ἐν τῇ οἰκίᾳ αὐτοῦ 'in his house' does not begin the sentence, the initial verb in v. 29a tends to convey *continuity*.[22] The feast that Levi made for Jesus may be interpreted as a "concrete expression of Levi's 'following'" (Fitzmyer 1981:591). The logical relationship between Levi's decision to follow Jesus and his offering the feast in Jesus' honor then takes precedence over the change of spatial setting between vv. 27–28 and vv. 29ff.

Passage 2: Luke 4:31–37

(31a) καὶ κατῆλθεν εἰς Καφαρναοὺμ πόλιν τῆς Γαλιλαίας
      and 3S.went.down to Capernaum city of.the Galilee

---

[22] Luke 5:29b has presentational articulation, so an action discontinuity with v. 29a may be discerned, as essential non-event information is inserted. See after passage 2 for a further comment on this sentence.

(31b) καὶ   ἦν   διδάσκων   αὐτοὺς ἐν   τοῖς σάββασιν
and   3S.was   teaching   them   on   the   sabbath(s)[23]

(32a) καὶ   ἐξεπλήσσοντο   ἐπὶ τῇ   διδαχῇ   αὐτοῦ,
and   3P.were.astounded at   the teaching   his

(32b) ὅτι   **ἐν ἐξουσίᾳ**   ἦν   ὁ   λόγος   αὐτοῦ.
because with authority 3S.was the   word   his

(33a) καὶ   ἐν   τῇ   συναγωγῇ   ἦν   ἄνθρωπος ἔχων   πνεῦμα
and   in   the synagogue   3S.was man   having spirit

δαιμονίου   ἀκαθάρτου
of.demon   unclean

(33b) καὶ   ἀνέκραξεν φωνῇ   μεγάλῃ,   Ἔα, τί   ἡμῖν καὶ   σοί   κ.τ.λ.
and   3S.shouted with.voice great   ah   what to.us and   to.you

(35a) καὶ   ἐπετίμησεν αὐτῷ ὁ   Ἰησοῦς λέγων,   Φιμώθητι...
and   3S.rebuked   him   the Jesus   saying   be.muzzled

(35b) καὶ   ῥίψαν   αὐτὸν τὸ   δαιμόνιον εἰς τὸ   μέσον
and   having.thrown him   the demon   in   the midst

ἐξῆλθεν   ἀπ' αὐτοῦ κ.τ.λ.
3S.came.out from him

(36a) καὶ   ἐγένετο   θάμβος   ἐπὶ πάντας
and   3S.became   astonishment on   all

(36b) καὶ   συνελάλουν   πρὸς ἀλλήλους   λέγοντες,
and   3S.spoke.with to   one.another saying

Τίς ὁ   λόγος οὗτος ὅτι   **ἐν ἐξουσίᾳ** καὶ
what   the   word   this   since with authority and

δυνάμει ἐπιτάσσει   τοῖς ἀκαθάρτοις πνεύμασιν κ.τ.λ.
power   3S.commands the   unclean   spirits

(37) καὶ   ἐξεπορεύετο   ἦχος περὶ   αὐτοῦ εἰς πάντα τόπον κ.τ.λ.
and   3S.went.forth rumor about him   to   every place

Questions

(a) Does the point of departure in v. 33a (the sentence initial reference to the synagogue), involve switch or renewal?

(b) Since both 4:33a (in passage 2) and 5:29b (in passage 1) are presentational sentences that introduce new participants to the story, why does 4:33a include a point of departure, but 5:29b does not?

Suggested Answers

(a) The point of departure in v. 33a probably involves *renewal*. Even though the spatial setting of vv. 31b-32 was never actually stated, it is likely that Jesus' Sabbath teaching was in the synagogue.

(b) The presence of a point of departure in 4:33a indicates that a discontinuity in the storyline is to be perceived. Adverbial points of departure involving renewal are often used in narrative when *different episodes* occur in the same setting (sec. 2.3). Verses 31f. concern Jesus' *teaching*, emphasizing that his word was 'with authority' (v. 32b). While vv. 33ff. finish with a similar emphasis (v. 36b), the response this time is to his *command to a demon*.

---

[23] Marshall (1978:191) considers σάββασιν to be singular in reference. Fitzmyer (1981:542), in contrast, suggests that vv. 31-32 "contain a generic statement about Jesus' Sabbath teaching and of the reaction of the people of Capernaum to it."

In contrast, the presentational sentence of 5:29b provides detail about the *same* episode as that which has begun to be described in v. 29a.

Passage 3: Luke 14:16b-24

(16b)   "Ἄνθρωπός τις   ἐποίει   δεῖπνον μέγα,
      man   certain 3S.was.making supper   great

(16c)   καὶ ἐκάλεσεν πολλοὺς
      and 3S.invited   many

(17)   καὶ ἀπέστειλεν τὸν δοῦλον αὐτοῦ τῇ ὥρα τοῦ
    and 3S.sent   the   slave   his   at.the hour of.the

    δείπνου[24] εἰπεῖν τοῖς κεκλημένοις, Ἔρχεσθε   κ.τ.λ.
    supper   to.say to.the invited.ones   come

(18a)   καὶ ἤρξαντο ἀπὸ μιᾶς πάντες παραιτεῖσθαι.
     and 3P.began from one   all   to.beg.off

(18b)   ὁ   πρῶτος εἶπεν αὐτῷ, Ἀγρὸν ἠγόρασα κ.τ.λ.
     the   first   3S.said to.him farm   I.bought

(19)   καὶ ἕτερος εἶπεν, **Ζεύγη βοῶν** ἠγόρασα πέντε κ.τ.λ.
    and other   3S.said yoke of.oxen I.bought five

(20)   καὶ ἕτερος εἶπεν, **Γυναῖκα** ἔγημα κ.τ.λ.
    and other   3S.said wife   I.married

(21a)   καὶ παραγενόμενος ὁ δοῦλος ἀπήγγειλεν τῷ κυρίῳ αὐτοῦ ταῦτα.
     and coming.up   the slave   3S.reported to.the lord   his   these.things

(21b)   τότε ὀργισθεὶς ὁ οἰκοδεσπότης εἶπεν τῷ δούλῳ
     then being.angry the house.master   3S.said to.the slave

    αὐτοῦ,
    his   "Go out quickly... and bring in the poor and lame."

(22)   καὶ εἶπεν ὁ δοῦλος, Κύριε, γέγονεν   κ.τ.λ.
    and 3S.said the slave   Lord   3S.has.happened

(23)   καὶ εἶπεν ὁ κύριος πρὸς τὸν δοῦλον, Ἔξελθε κ.τ.λ.
    and 3S.said the lord   to   the slave   go.out

Note. "Ἄνθρωπός τις 'a certain man' begins v. 16b to set a point of departure for the story, because there is a discontinuity of reference with the speech which promoted the story ('Blessed is anyone who will eat bread in the kingdom of God!'). Sentences at the beginning of discourses commonly open with a non-verbal constituent for this reason.

Questions

(a) Why does 18b begin with the subject?
(b) Why do vv. 19 and 20 begin with the subject?
(c) How is the event of v. 17 related to the events of v. 16?

Suggested Answers

(a) Verse 18b begins with the subject because there is an action discontinuity with v. 18a involving a generic-specific restatement. Verses 18b-20 describe specific instances of people begging off, rather

---

[24] "The invitation is followed by an actual summons to the meal when it is ready" (Marshall 1978:587).

than events which occurred after they begged off. The event of v. 18b is therefore not presented as being in temporal sequence with that of v. 18a.

(b) Verses 19 and 20 begin with the subject because these sentences relate to the context on the basis of a switch from one subject to another.

(c) No discontinuity is signaled between the events of v. 16 and v. 17. In fact, since the potential point of departure τῇ ὥρᾳ τοῦ δείπνου 'at the hour of the supper' does not begin the sentence, the initial verb in v. 17 tends to convey *continuity*. The logical relationship in the culture of the time between inviting people to attend a supper at a future date and telling them that the date has arrived takes precedence over the change of temporal setting.

Passage 4: Luke 2:22–28

(22) καὶ ὅτε ἐπλήσθησαν αἱ ἡμέραι τοῦ καθαρισμοῦ...
    and when 3P.were.completed the days of.the cleansing

    ἀνήγαγον αὐτὸν εἰς Ἱεροσόλυμα παραστῆσαι τῷ κυρίῳ,
    3P.took.up him to Jerusalem to.present to.the Lord

(23a) καθὼς γέγραπται ἐν νόμῳ κυρίου
    as 3S.has.been.written in law of.Lord

(23b) ὅτι πᾶν ἄρσεν διανοῖγον μήτραν ἅγιον τῷ κυρίῳ κληθήσεται,
    that every male opening womb holy to.the Lord 3S.shall.be.called

(24) καὶ τοῦ δοῦναι θυσίαν κ.τ.λ.
    and of.the to.give sacrifice

(25a) καὶ ἰδοὺ ἄνθρωπος ἦν ἐν Ἱερουσαλήμ
    and behold man 3S.was in Jerusalem

(25b) ᾧ ὄνομα Συμεών
    to.whom name Simeon

(25c) καὶ ὁ ἄνθρωπος οὗτος δίκαιος καὶ εὐλαβὴς κ.τ.λ.
    and the man this just and devout

(25d) καὶ πνεῦμα ἦν ἅγιον ἐπ᾽ αὐτόν·
    and Spirit 3S.was Holy on him

(26) καὶ ἦν αὐτῷ κεχρηματισμένον ὑπὸ τοῦ πνεύματος τοῦ ἁγίου
    and 3S.was to.him communicated by the Spirit the Holy

    μὴ ἰδεῖν θάνατον πρὶν [ἢ] ἂν ἴδῃ τὸν Χριστὸν κυρίου.
    not to.see death before 3S.see the Christ of.Lord

(27a) καὶ ἦλθεν ἐν τῷ πνεύματι εἰς τὸ ἱερόν·
    and 3S.came by the Spirit to the temple

(27b) καὶ ἐν τῷ εἰσαγαγεῖν τοὺς γονεῖς τὸ παιδίον Ἰησοῦν κ.τ.λ.
    and in the to.bring.in the parents the child Jesus

(28a) καὶ αὐτὸς ἐδέξατο αὐτὸ εἰς τὰς ἀγκάλας
    and he 3S.received him in the arms

(28b) καὶ εὐλόγησεν τὸν θεόν
    and 3S.blessed the God

(28c) καὶ εἶπεν κ.τ.λ.
    and 3S.said

Notes.

- In v. 25a, ἰδού followed immediately by a reference to a new participant is used "to focus special attention on a major... participant as he/she/it is introduced onto the event line of an episode" (Van Otterloo 1988:34). This is discussed in section 8.1.
- Discontinuous constituents like πνεῦμα ... ἅγιον (v. 25c) are discussed in section 4.4.2.

Questions

(a) Why does v. 23b begin with the subject?
(b) Why does v. 25c begin with the subject?
(c) What is implied by beginning v. 28a with αὐτός?

Suggested Answers: see Appendix under 2(4), i.e., chapter 2, passage 4.

2.8   Points of Departure in Non-Narrative Passages

Although we have looked at examples of points of departure in sentences taken from non-narrative material, we have not yet examined their presence in more extensive passages. This is the task of the present section.

The most noteworthy feature of points of departure in non-narrative passages such as reasoned arguments is the increased frequency of *nominal* points of departure.[25] In narrative, nominal points of departure are used almost exclusively in connection with action discontinuities (e.g., to switch attention to a different participant or to introduce non-events). In the four passages of section 2.7, for instance, there is a total of only eight nominal points of departure in 38 sentences. In James 1:2–11 (parts of which are cited below), in contrast, seven nominal points of departure occur within 14 or 15 sentences.

My contention is that the greater frequency of points of departure in non-narrative text is due not to a change in their function but to the way reasoned argument is structured. In narrative, the same *spatio-temporal situation* is often shared by a series of sentences, so that any overt temporal or spatial point of departure applies to the whole series. *Referential* continuity is the norm, too, in that it is more common to introduce participants to an existing scene than to switch from one cast of participants to a different cast. In addition, narrative events tend to be arranged sequentially, preserving *action* continuity.

In reasoned arguments, however, neither action continuity nor continuity of time and place feature prominently. Rather, arguments progress as, every sentence or two, new propositional topics are established (often, by repeating a constituent of the comment of the previous sentence) or new conditions for the following assertions are proposed. Such changes are often achieved through points of departure.

In **James 1:3–4a**, for instance, the concept of endurance (ὑπομονή) is introduced in the comment of v. 3b. It is then taken up in a referential point of departure, as the topic switches from 'the testing of your faith' (v. 3b) to endurance itself (v. 4a).

(2)   Consider it nothing but joy, my brothers, whenever you face trails of any kind, (3a) because you know

(3b)   ὅτι   τὸ   δοκίμιον   ὑμῶν   τῆς   πίστεως   κατεργάζεται   ὑπομονήν.
       that   the   testing   of.your   the   faith   3S.works   endurance

(4a)   ἡ   δὲ   ὑπομονὴ   ἔργον   τέλειον   ἐχέτω,
       the   DE   endurance   work   perfect   3S.let.have

Similarly, in **James 1:4b-5**, the concept of 'lacking' (λειπόμενοι) is introduced in the comment of v. 4c. It is then taken up in a conditional point of departure (v. 5), as James switches from 'lacking nothing' to those who lack wisdom.

---

[25] My claim that nominal points of departure are more frequent in reasoned arguments than in narrative is impressionistic. I have undertaken a statistical check of the validity of the claim only for Matt. 5-7, Galatians, and James. See also Terry's (1995) statistics for the position of the subject in 1 Corinthians.

(4b)   so that you may be mature and complete,

(4c)   **ἐν   μηδενὶ**   λειπόμενοι.
        in   nothing   lacking

(5)   <u>Εἰ</u> δέ <u>τις</u> <u>ὑμῶν</u> <u>λείπεται</u> <u>σοφίας</u>, αἰτείτω παρὰ
       if   DE any of.you 3S.lacks wisdom, 3S.let.ask from

       τοῦ διδόντος θεοῦ πᾶσιν ἁπλῶς   καὶ μὴ
       the giving   God   to.all unreservedly and not

       ὀνειδίζοντος καὶ δοθήσεται αὐτῷ.
       reproaching   and 3S.will.be.given to.him

The same principle (introducing a concept in the comment of one sentence, then taking it up as the point of departure of the next) is often exploited when an author introduces supportive material with γάρ. In **James 1:6**, for instance, the concept of 'doubting' (διακρινόμενος) is introduced in the comment of v. 6a. It is then taken up in a referential point of departure in the supportive material of v. 6b, as James switches from 'doubting nothing' to 'the doubter'.

(6a)   αἰτείτω δὲ ἐν πίστει μηδὲν   διακρινόμενος·
       3S.let.ask DE in faith   nothing doubting

(6b)   <u>ὁ</u>   γὰρ <u>διακρινόμενος</u> ἔοικεν κλύδωνι θαλάσσης κ.τ.λ.
       the for doubting.one   3S.is.like wave   of.sea

The *absence* of a point of departure in reasoned argument is often related to *topic (referential) continuity* at some level.[26] For example, **James 1:7** continues with the topic of 'the doubter' (v. 6b above—ὁ ἄνθρωπος ἐκεῖνος has the same referent as ὁ διακρινόμενος). Consequently, the subject follows the verb.

(7)   μὴ γὰρ οἰέσθω   ὁ   ἄνθρωπος ἐκεῖνος
       not for 3S.let.suppose the man   that

       ὅτι λήμψεταί   τι   παρὰ τοῦ κυρίου,
       that 3S.will.receive anything from the Lord

Exhortations like the book of James deal "with how people... should behave" (Longacre 1996:9), so have "+ agent orientation" (see also *SIL-UND* sec. 2.2) around the addressees of the book. Points of departure are typically used in this passage as attention switches from 'you' to other referents.[27] Points of departure are *not* used when attention reverts to 'you', unless a switch of attention from another participant is intended (as happens in James 2:6).

This is illustrated in **James 1:9**. The exact relationship of v. 9 to the context is unclear, but the consensus among commentators seems to be that it builds in some way on the assertion of v. 2 about the trials which the 'brothers' are experiencing. It therefore appears that the subject of v. 9 (ὁ ἀδελφὸς ὁ ταπεινός) is not placed initial in the sentence because James has reverted to his original addressees (the rich are never referred to as brothers!).

(9)   Καυχάσθω δὲ ὁ   ἀδελφὸς ὁ   ταπεινὸς ἐν τῷ ὕψει αὐτοῦ,
       3S.let.boast DE the brother   the humble in the height his

---

[26] Although I consider verb-initial to be the default order (sec. 2.6), it is insightful to consider why, for example, subjects that follow the verb did not begin the sentence as points of departure.

[27] In 1 Cor. 5:7-13, virtually every clause containing an imperative or its equivalent begins with a verb, which leads Kathleen Callow to comment, "one function of the initial position seems to be the carrying of material most closely related to the theme of the unit" (1992:198). Since imperatives have the addressees as their subject, I would not expect many of them to begin with a point of departure.

A common pattern of argumentation in the Epistles is to begin with a point of minor significance that forms the ground or *counterpoint*[28] for the main assertion. This is seen in **James 1:9–10**. Verse 9 provides the counterpoint for the main assertion of v. 10. (Attention switches from the 'brother who is lowly' to the rich, so ὁ πλούσιος is placed first in v. 10.)

(9) Let the brother who is lowly boast in being raised up,

(10a) <u>ὁ</u> δὲ <u>πλούσιος</u> ἐν τῇ ταπεινώσει αὐτοῦ,
       the DE rich   in   the humiliation   his

(10b) ὅτι **ὡς ἄνθος χόρτου** παρελεύσεται.
       that as flower of.grass 3S.will.pass.away

The same pattern of argumentation is seen in **James 1:11**. As the presence of γάρ shows, this verse supports the assertion of v. 10 that 'the rich will disappear like a flower in the field'. However, the first two assertions (vv. 11a-b) only provide the ground for the assertions of vv. 11c-d, which are the ones that directly support v. 10b.[29]

(11a) ἀνέτειλεν γὰρ ὁ ἥλιος σὺν τῷ καύσωνι
       3S.rose   for the sun   with the hot.wind

(11b) καὶ ἐξήρανεν τὸν χόρτον
       and 3S.dried   the grass

(11c) καὶ <u>τὸ</u> <u>ἄνθος</u> <u>αὐτοῦ</u> ἐξέπεσεν
       and the flower its 3S.fell.out

(11d) καὶ <u>ἡ</u> <u>εὐπρέπεια</u> <u>τοῦ</u> <u>προσώπου</u> <u>αὐτοῦ</u> ἀπώλετο·
       and the comeliness of.the appearance its 3S.perished

In the above verse, the fact that ὁ ἥλιος does *not* begin v. 11 indicates that the material that is introduced with γάρ does not involve a switch to the topic of 'the sun' (contrast v. 6b). Within this supportive material, however, switches occur from τὸν χόρτον in v. 11b to τὸ ἄνθος αὐτοῦ in v. 11c and to ἡ εὐπρέπεια τοῦ προσώπου αὐτοῦ in v. 11d (vv. 11b-c is a quotation from the Septuagint).

Points of departure therefore occur in James 1:2–11 whenever there is a switch to other than the previous point of departure or to other than the addressees around whom the passage is oriented.

To further illustrate the above points, I now turn to Titus 1:10–16.

Passage 5: Titus 1:10–16

(10) Εἰσὶν γὰρ πολλοὶ [καὶ] ἀνυπότακτοι, ματαιολόγοι κ.τ.λ.
      3P.are for many   [+]   rebellious   idle.talkers

(11a) οὓς δεῖ   ἐπιστομίζειν,
       whom 3S.ought to.stop.mouth

(11b) οἵτινες **ὅλους οἴκους** ἀνατρέπουσιν διδάσκοντες ἃ   μὴ
       who   entire households 3P.overturn   teaching   what not

       δεῖ   αἰσχροῦ κέρδους χάριν.
       3S.ought dishonest gain   for.sake.of

(12a) εἶπέν τις   ἐξ αὐτῶν ἴδιος αὐτῶν προφήτης,
       3S.said certain of them own   their prophet

(12b) <u>Κρῆτες</u> ἀεὶ ψεῦσται, κακὰ θηρία, γαστέρες ἀργαί.
       Cretans   always liars   wicked beasts gluttons lazy

---

[28] counterpoint—"contrasting... idea, used to set off the main element" (OED)

[29] For further examples of this pattern of argumentation, see sec. 7.1.

(13a)   ἡ   μαρτυρία αὕτη ἐστὶν ἀληθής.
        the   witness   this   3S.is   true

(13b)   δἰ ἣν   αἰτίαν ἔλεγχε αὐτοὺς ἀποτόμως,
        for which cause reprove them   severely

(13c)   ἵνα   ὑγιαίνωσιν   ἐν τῇ πίστει,
        so.that 3P.may.be.healthy in the faith

(14)   μὴ   προσέχοντες   Ἰουδαϊκοῖς μύθοις κ.τ.λ.
        not   paying.attention   to.Jewish myths

(15a)   **πάντα** καθαρὰ   τοῖς   καθαροῖς·
        all.things pure   to.the   pure

(15b)   <u>τοῖς</u> δὲ <u>μεμιαμμένοις</u> <u>καὶ</u> <u>ἀπίστοις</u> οὐδὲν καθαρόν,
        to.the DE defiled   and unbelieving nothing pure

(15c)   ἀλλὰ μεμίανται   αὐτῶν καὶ ὁ νοῦς καὶ ἡ συνείδησις.
        but   3S.has.been.defiled their both the mind and the conscience

(16a)   **θεὸν** ὁμολογοῦσιν εἰδέναι,
        God   3P.profess   to.know

(16b)   <u>τοῖς</u> δὲ <u>ἔργοις</u> ἀρνοῦνται,
        by.the DE works   3P.deny

(16c)   **βδελυκτοὶ** ὄντες καὶ ἀπειθεῖς κ.τ.λ.
        detestable being and disobedient

The initial topic of this passage (πολλοὶ [καὶ] ἀνυπότακτοι, ματαιολόγοι καὶ φρεναπάται, μάλιστα οἱ ἐκ τῆς περιτομῆς) is not established by switching from a different topic by means of a point of departure. Rather, it is introduced to an ongoing argument in a presentational sentence (v. 10—see sec. 7.1; the last clause of v. 9 concerned the need for a bishop to be able to refute those that contradict sound doctrine).[30] The relative pronouns in v. 11 ensure that these same people remain the topic.

In v. 12a, the position of the subject after the verb indicates that attention remains on these people, rather than switching to a prophet of theirs. This might imply, in turn, that the quotation is made to confirm what v. 10 has said about the nature of Cretans. "The apostle supports his argument by appealing to a venerated Cretan critic of the Cretan character," according to Guthrie (1957:187). See section 7.1 for further discussion of this verse.

In v. 12b, the placement sentence-initial of the propositional topic Κρῆτες sets the point of departure for the quotation.[31]

In v. 13a, there is a switch of topic (reference) from the Cretans to ἡ μαρτυρία αὕτη (the quotation of v. 12b), after which attention reverts to 'them' for vv. 13c-14.[32] (See sec. 11.2 for the significance of the "continuative" relative clause in v. 13b.)

Verses 15–16 are not concerned primarily with 'the pure' but with 'the defiled and unfaithful', so τοῖς καθαροῖς does not begin the sentence. In v. 15b, however, the argument develops through a contrastive switch from 'the pure' to the other group, so τοῖς μεμιαμμένοις καὶ ἀπίστοις begins the sentence. Attention remains on this group in v. 15c, so the subject follows the verb (see sec. 4.5 on the position of αὐτῶν).

In v. 16b, however, the initial reference to τοῖς ἔργοις indicates that the argument now develops by a contrastive switch from what 'they profess' in v. 16a.

---

[30] It is the norm for the subject of a presentational sentence to follow the verb, see sec. 3.5.

[31] The context of this quotation would be needed to know why Epimenides needed to set a point of departure.

[32] See Greenlee 1989:41 for a summary of possible referents for αὐτούς.

Once again, then, the presence of a point of departure indicates a switch of attention to its referent. Failure to begin the sentence with the subject (in the absence of any other point of departure) implies either that the topic under consideration remains unchanged or that the topic has reverted to the original people of vv. 10–11.

The following passage should be studied for similar features.

Passage 6: Galatians 3:1–14

(1a) Ὦ   ἀνόητοι   Γαλάται,   τίς   ὑμᾶς   ἐβάσκανεν,
     oh   senseless   Galatians   who   you   3S.bewitched

(1b) οἷς   κατ'   ὀφθαλμοὺς   Ἰησοῦς Χριστὸς   προεγράφη   ἐσταυρωμένος;
     to.whom before   eyes   Jesus   Christ   3S.was.portrayed   having.been.crucified

(2a) τοῦτο   μόνον   θέλω   μαθεῖν   ἀφ'   ὑμῶν·
     this   only   I.wish   to.learn   from   you

(2b) ἐξ   ἔργων   νόμου   τὸ   πνεῦμα   ἐλάβετε   ἢ   ἐξ   ἀκοῆς   πίστεως;
     by   works   of.law   the   Spirit   you.received   or   by   hearing   of.faith

(3a) οὕτως   ἀνόητοί   ἐστε,
     so   senseless   you.are

(3b) ἐναρξάμενοι   πνεύματι   νῦν   σαρκὶ   ἐπιτελεῖσθε;
     having.begun   in.Spirit   now   in.flesh   you.are.perfected

(4)   τοσαῦτα   ἐπάθετε   εἰκῇ;   εἴ   γε   καὶ   εἰκῇ.
     so.much   you.suffered   in.vain   if   really   +   in.vain

(5)   ὁ   οὖν   ἐπιχορηγῶν   ὑμῖν   τὸ   πνεῦμα   καὶ   ἐνεργῶν   δυνάμεις
     the   then   supplying   to.you   the   Spirit   and   working   powerful.deeds

     ἐν   ὑμῖν,   ἐξ   ἔργων   νόμου   ἢ   ἐξ   ἀκοῆς   πίστεως;
     among   you   by   works   of.law   or   by   hearing   of.faith?

(6a) καθὼς   Ἀβραὰμ   ἐπίστευσεν   τῷ   θεῷ,
     as   Abraham   3S.believed   in.the   God

(6b) καὶ   ἐλογίσθη   αὐτῷ   εἰς   δικαιοσύνην.
     and   3S.was.reckoned   to.him   for   righteousness

(7a) Γινώσκετε   ἄρα
     (you).know   then

(7b)[33] ὅτι   οἱ   ἐκ   πίστεως,   οὗτοι   υἱοί   εἰσιν   Ἀβραάμ.
         that   the   of   faith   these   sons   3P.are   of.Abraham

(8a) προϊδοῦσα   δὲ   ἡ   γραφὴ
     having.foreseen   DE   the   Scripture

(8b) ὅτι   ἐκ   πίστεως   δικαιοῖ   τὰ   ἔθνη   ὁ   θεός,
     that   by   faith   3S.would.justify   the   nations   the   God

(8c) προευηγγελίσατο   τῷ   Ἀβραὰμ
     3S.before.preached   to.the   Abraham

---

[33] Οἱ ἐκ πίστεως is a left-dislocated constituent, used to introduce a cognitively accessible topic (see fn. 6). When a nominal constituent is left-dislocated, "its CANONICAL position is filled by a PRONOUN [in this case, οὗτοι] or a full LEXICAL NOUN PHRASE with the same REFERENCE" (Crystal 1991:197). Research is needed to determine the effect of using left-dislocation rather than simple preposing to establish a point of departure.

(8d)   ὅτι   Ἐνευλογηθήσονται   ἐν   σοὶ   πάντα   τὰ   ἔθνη·
      that   3P.will.be.blessed   in   you   all   the   nations

(9)   ὥστε   **οἱ ἐκ πίστεως**   εὐλογοῦνται   σὺν   τῷ   πιστῷ   Ἀβραάμ.
    so   the of faith   3P.are.blessed   with   the   faithful   Abraham

(10a)   ὅσοι   γὰρ   ἐξ   ἔργων   νόμου   εἰσὶν,   **ὑπὸ κατάραν**   εἰσίν·
     as.many.as   for   of   works   of.law   3P.are   under curse   3P.are

(10b)   γέγραπται   γὰρ
     3S.has.been.written   for

(10c)   ὅτι   **Ἐπικατάρατος**   πᾶς   ὃς   οὐκ   ἐμμένει   πᾶσιν
     that   cursed   everyone   who   not   3S.continues   in.all

     τοῖς   γεγραμμένοις   ἐν   τῷ   βιβλίῳ   τοῦ   νόμου   τοῦ   ποιῆσαι   αὐτά.
     the   having.been.written   in   the   book   of.the   law   of.the   to.do   them

(11a)*   ὅτι   δὲ   ἐν νόμῳ   **οὐδεὶς**   δικαιοῦται   παρὰ   τῷ   θεῷ   δῆλον,
     that   DE   by law   none   3S.is.justified   before   the   God   clear

(11b)   ὅτι   Ὁ   δίκαιος   **ἐκ πίστεως**   ζήσεται·
     since   the   just   of faith   3S.will.live

(12a)   ὁ   δὲ   νόμος   οὐκ   ἔστιν   ἐκ   πίστεως,
     the   DE   law   not   3S.is   of   faith

(12b)   ἀλλ'   Ὁ   ποιήσας   αὐτὰ   ζήσεται   ἐν   αὐτοῖς.
     but   the   doing   them   3S.will.live   by   them

(13a)   Χριστὸς   **ἡμᾶς**   ἐξηγόρασεν   ἐκ   τῆς   κατάρας   τοῦ   νόμου
     Christ   us   3S.redeemed   from   the   curse   of.the   law

     γενόμενος   ὑπὲρ   ἡμῶν   κατάρα,
     having.become   on.behalf.of   us   curse

(13b)   ὅτι   γέγραπται,
     since   3S.has.been.written

(13c)   **Ἐπικατάρατος**   πᾶς   ὁ   κρεμάμενος   ἐπὶ   ξύλου,
     cursed   everyone   the   hanging   on   tree

(14a)   ἵνα   εἰς τὰ ἔθνη   ἡ   εὐλογία   τοῦ   Ἀβραὰμ
     so.that   to the nations   the   blessing   of.the   Abraham

     γένηται   ἐν   Χριστῷ   Ἰησοῦ,
     3S.might.become   in   Christ   Jesus

(14b)   ἵνα   τὴν   ἐπαγγελίαν   τοῦ   πνεύματος   λάβωμεν
     so.that   the   promise   of.the   Spirit   we.might.receive

     διὰ   τῆς   πίστεως.
     through   the   faith

---

*I take the clause ὅτι ἐν νόμῳ **οὐδεὶς** δικαιοῦται παρὰ τῷ θεῷ 'that by law no-one is justified before God' in v. 11a to be a referential point of departure and propositional topic about which the comment δῆλον '(is) clear' is made. Within this clause, ἐν νόμῳ is also preposed as a point of departure.

Questions

(a) In v. 5, why does ὁ ἐπιχορηγῶν ὑμῖν τὸ πνεῦμα καὶ ἐνεργῶν δυνάμεις ἐν ὑμῖν begin the sentence?

(b) In v. 6a, why does Ἀβραὰμ begin the sentence?

(c) In v. 8a, why does ἡ γραφὴ NOT begin the sentence?

(d) In v. 14a, why is εἰς τὰ ἔθνη initial in the adverbial clause of purpose?

Suggested Answers: see Appendix under 2(6).

(Further questions on this topic occur at the end of chap. 3.)

3
CONSTITUENT ORDER IN THE COMMENT

The last chapter was concerned with the presence or absence of points of departure, i.e., of clause-initial constituents that set a domain for the material that follows and indicate the basis for relating what follows to its context. We now turn to the rest of the sentence, in particular, the arrangement of the constituents of the *comment* on the propositional topic.[1]

In languages like Greek with so-called 'free' order, a number of factors interact to influence the order of constituents. I first discuss four *default* ordering principles:

- the placement of *pronominal* constituents immediately following the verb (sec. 3.1),
- the placement of *core* constituents before *peripheral* ones (sec. 3.2),
- the placement of an overtly expressed propositional topic before the comment about that topic (sec. 3.3), and
- the placement towards the end of a clause or sentence of the most important or focal constituent of the comment (sec. 3.4).

I then turn to *marked* orders: the placement at the end of the clause or sentence (sec. 3.5) or prior to the verb (sec. 3.6) of a constituent that would have occurred elsewhere had the default rules of sections 3.1–4 been followed. In section 3.7 I consider when one position of focus is used rather than the other. Section 3.8 concerns *ambiguous* orderings, i.e., those that could be the product of more than one ordering principle, and suggests ways in which the ambiguity may sometimes be resolved. Finally, section 3.9 reviews some key questions to be asked about the constituent order of individual sentences.

I need to stress that what are presented in this chapter are ordering *principles*, not rules. The degree to which they are followed, particularly in the latter part of lengthy sentences, probably depends on the extent to which the original author had composed the sentence in his mind before he began to write or dictate it. Nevertheless, the vast majority of clauses and sentences do seem to follow these principles.

This chapter does not consider the ordering of words *within* noun phrases (or verb phrases); see section 4.5.

3.1 Pronominal Constituents

The default position for "unemphatic" pronominal constituents is immediately following the verb, preceding nominal constituents (BDF §472, Turner 1963:347).[2]

> Default Ordering Principle 1:
> **Verb - Pronominal Constituents - Nominal Constituents**

This ordering is found in many clauses that introduce reported speeches. In **John 2:7**, for example, the pronominal reference to the addressees precedes the nominal reference to the speaker. In **John 2:5**, in contrast, the reference to the addressees follows the reference to the speaker when both are nominal (see also sec. 3.3).

(7) λέγει / αὐτοῖς / ὁ Ἰησοῦς, κ.τ.λ.
    3S.says   to.them   the   Jesus

(5) λέγει / ἡ μήτηρ αὐτοῦ / τοῖς διακόνοις, κ.τ.λ.
    3S.says   the   mother   his   to.the   servants

---

[1] See sec. 4.1 for the order of constituents in negative sentences, and sec. 4.2 for the order of constituents in sentences such as information interrogatives.

[2] This observation conforms to the "Principle of Natural Information Flow" (Comrie 1989:127-28), which predicts that constituents will tend to be arranged from left to right according to the following hierarchy:

1st/2nd person pronoun > 3rd person pronoun > proper > human > animate (non-human) > inanimate.

For comparable examples in the other Gospels and Acts in which the pronominal reference to the addressees precedes the nominal reference to the speakers, see Matt. 4:7, Mark 1:17 (versus 6:22 when both references are nominal), Luke 20:34 (versus 15:12), and Acts 9:34 (versus 8:29; see sec. 3.2 for discussion of Acts 12:8).[3]

In **Gal. 1:24**, the pronominal constituent which precedes a nominal one is a *prepositional phrase* (see also Luke 19:9 and Acts 5:8).

(24) καὶ   ἐδόξαζον /   ἐν   ἐμοὶ /   τὸν   θεόν.
      and   3P.were.glorifying   in   me   the   God

Galatians 5:10 is similar, except that the sentence begins with a point of departure, which happens also to be a pronoun. ἐγώ is therefore in a marked position in the clause, while εἰς ὑμᾶς is in the default position for pronominal constituents.

(10) ἐγώ   πέποιθα /   εἰς   ὑμᾶς /   ἐν   κυρίῳ   κ.τ.λ.
      I   I.have.confidence   in   you   in   Lord

In **1 Cor. 5:2c**, the pronominal constituent is complex, yet still precedes the subject.

(2c) ἵνα   ἀρθῇ /   ἐκ   μέσου   ὑμῶν /   ὁ   τὸ   ἔργον
      so.that   3S.may.be.taken   from   midst   of.you   the.one   the   deed

      τοῦτο   πράξας;
      this   having.done

Finally, in **James 1:18c**, the pronominal constituent is the *subject* of the subordinate clause (see also sec. 3.3).

(18c) εἰς   τὸ   εἶναι /   ἡμᾶς /   ἀπαρχήν   τινα   τῶν   αὐτοῦ   κτισμάτων.
       to   the   to.be   we   firstfruit   certain   of.the   his   creatures

In section 3.4, see also Gal. 2:13a. See section 3.7 for instances in which the pronominal constituent immediately *precedes* the verb, when preceded by a focal constituent.

3.2   Core-Periphery

It is normal for core constituents to precede peripheral ones in natural languages. In the case of Koiné Greek, we may loosely classify the core 'arguments'[4] as the subject, object, and other nominal constituents not preceded by a preposition, together with the adjectival complement. Peripheral constituents consist largely of prepositional phrases plus adverbial phrases of time and location (see Andrews 1985:89).

```
Default Ordering Principle 2:
     Core Constituents - Peripheral Constituents
```

Colossians 1:6c is a typical example of a core constituent preceding a peripheral one.

(6c) καὶ   ἐπέγνωτε   τὴν   χάριν   τοῦ   θεοῦ /   ἐν   ἀληθείᾳ·
      and   you.knew   the   grace   of.the   God   in   reality

1 Cor. 1:11 illustrates the operation of this principle when two pronominal constituents occur in the same sentence. The core constituent μοι precedes the peripheral constituent περὶ ὑμῖν (with which the

---

[3] The UBS text of John 11:12 has the nominal reference to the speakers before the pronominal reference to the addressees (εἶπαν οὖν οἱ μαθηταὶ αὐτῷ), though variant readings reverse the order or change αὐτῷ to αὐτοῦ. See also Matt. 14:4 (although the UBS text has the nominal reference to the speaker before the pronominal reference to the addressees, other MSS reverse the order).

[4] The term 'argument' is "used to refer to any NOUN PHRASE position within a sentence" (Crystal 1991:24).

vocative ἀδελγοί μου is in apposition). The pronominal constituents are then followed by a nominal peripheral constituent—see default ordering principle 1.

(11) ἐδηλώθη   γάρ μοι / περὶ ὑμῶν, ἀδελφοί μου, /
      3S.was.made.clear for to.me about you   brothers my

      ὑπὸ τῶν Χλόης κ.τ.λ.
      by   of.the Chloe

James 2:18d is another example in which default ordering principles 1 and 2 both operate, since the pronominal constituent precedes both the core nominal and the peripheral constituents.

(18d) δεῖξόν μοι / τὴν πίστιν σου / χωρὶς τῶν ἔργων,
       show   to.me the faith   your without the works

In **Col. 1:22c**, the core constituent that follows the pronominal constituent and precedes the peripheral constituent is a complex adjectival complement.

(22c) παραστῆσαι ὑμᾶς / ἁγίους καὶ ἀμώμους καὶ
       to.present you   holy   and blameless and

       ἀνεγκλήτους / κατενώπιον αὐτοῦ,
       without.reproach before   him

It appears, however, that either ordering principle can take priority for some authors. This might explain why, in **Acts 12:8**, a peripheral *pronominal* constituent follows the core nominal one. In this example, ordering principle 2 appears to have taken precedence over ordering principle 1.[5]

(8) εἶπεν δὲ ὁ ἄγγελος / πρὸς αὐτόν, κ.τ.λ.
     3S.said DE the angel   to   him

3.3   Propositional Topic - Comment

In the vast majority of natural languages, the default order in sentences with topic-comment articulation is for the propositional topic to precede the comment about that topic. Tomlin (1986:37) considers such sentences to obey the "theme-first principle." In the case of New Testament Greek, this principle means that, if the propositional topic (Tomlin's "theme") is stated in the sentence, the default order is for it to precede the *nonverbal* constituents of the comment.[6]

> Default Ordering Principle 3:
> **Propositional Topic - Nonverbal Constituents of the Comment**

Statistics indicate that this order is the most common in New Testament Greek. In prototypical sentences (i.e., those in which the subject is the propositional topic), three of the six ways in which the subject (S), object (O) and verb (V) can be arranged conform to the Theme-First Principle. These three orders are all more common than the orders that do not conform to it. Thus, when S precedes V, SOV and SVO both obey the principle, and both are common. When S follows V, VSO obeys the principle and also is common. Orders in which O precedes S are rare.

In the book of James, for instance, out of the 80 sentences that contain both a subject and some sort of object, the frequency of the different orders is as follows:

SOV (34); SVO (24); VSO (12); thus, S precedes O 70 times.

---

[5] See also Acts 13:15 (UBS text; a group of late Byzantian MSS reverses the order of the constituents, "evidently to standardize it"—Pope p.c.). Further research is needed to identify the principle that determines which ordering principle takes precedence. It may be that a nominal subject precedes a peripheral pronominal constituent when there is a need to establish which is the propositional topic about which the comment is to be made (sec. 3.3).

[6] Tomlin's principle ignores the position of the verb, although it is normally considered to be part of the comment about the topic.

OSV (2); OVS (6); VOS (2); thus, O precedes S 10 times.

(Since O may be the propositional topic and S part of the comment, these figures are only illustrative.)

In **Luke 5:37b**, a nominal subject precedes a nominal direct object.

(37b) εἰ   δὲ   μή γε, ῥήξει   ὁ   οἶνος ὁ   νέος / τοὺς ἀσκοὺς
       if   DE   not   3S.will.burst the wine   the new   the   skins

John 2:5 (repeated below from sec. 3.1) is typical of clauses that introduce reported speeches and identify both the speaker and the addressee with a nominal constituent. The reference to the speaker (subject) precedes the reference to the addressee (as well as the speech itself, which can also be viewed as part of the comment about the propositional topic).

(5)   λέγει / ἡ   μήτηρ αὐτοῦ / τοῖς διακόνοις, κ.τ.λ.
       3S.says the mother his   to.the servants

James 1:19b provides an example in which the subject of a third person imperative precedes the nonverbal constituents of the comment.

(19b) ἔστω   δὲ   πᾶς   ἄνθρωπος / ταχὺς εἰς τὸ   ἀκοῦσαι,
       3S.let.be DE   every man   quick   to   the to.hear

See sections 2.2 and 2.3 for instances in which the subject as propositional topic precedes the comment when it is the point of departure for the sentence. See section 3.1 for an example (Jas. 1:18c) in which a pronominal subject/propositional topic precedes the comment.

3.4   Focal Constituent to the End

Prague School linguist Jan Firbas has noted that the constituents of the comment are not all of equal importance. He finds that, in some languages, the default position for the most *important* constituent of the comment is as far towards the end of the sentence as the grammar of the language permits.[7] This constituent he calls the "rheme" (Firbas 1964:115), but I shall follow Dik (1978:19) in referring to it as the *focus*, i.e., "what is relatively the most important... information in the given setting."[8]

This principle appears to be followed at times in New Testament Greek to determine the relative order of constituents when they are not determined by principles 1–3 (see Denniston 1952:45–46). This occurs, for example, when two peripheral or two core constituents occur in the same sentence.

> Default Ordering Principle 4:
>   **If ordering principles 1–3 do not determine the relative order of constituents, place the more focal constituent after the less focal one.**

When two *peripheral* constituents occur in the same sentence, ordering principles 1–3 do not determine their relative order. Principle 4 states that the more focal constituent will follow the less focal one. This is illustrated in **James 5:17c**, the focal constituent follows the supportive one.[9]

(17c) καὶ   οὐκ ἔβρεξεν   ἐπὶ τῆς γῆς / ἐνιαυτοὺς τρεῖς
       and   not 3S.rained on   the earth years   three

---

[7] For a discussion of Firbas' work, plus examples from English and Inga (Quechuan) which are considered to justify his approach, see Levinsohn 1975 and 1989.

[8] A more technical definition of focus, which reflects Lambrecht's (1994) work on mental representations, is the following (*SIL-UND* sec. 11.1): "The focus of an utterance is that part which is intended to make the most important... change in the hearer's mental representation."

[9] As Firbas notes (1959:43), the absence versus presence of the article often helps to identify which constituent is in focus and which is supportive or "thematic". See also secs. 3.7.2 and 9.3.

Another example in which this principle determines the relative order of two peripheral constituents is found in **Gal. 3:19d**. As the next verse confirms ("Now a mediator is one..."), the focus of the clause is the mediator, not the angels.

(19d) διαταγεὶς   δι'   ἀγγέλων /   ἐν   χειρὶ   μεσίτου.
       being.ordained through angels   by   hand   of.mediator

Galatians 1:14a illustrates the need to carefully identify the constituents of the sentence. The verb is followed by only *two* peripheral constituents, since ἐν τῷ γένει μου modifies συνηλικιώτας, not προέκοπτον. Once this is recognized, the sentence is seen to obey principle 4, with the supportive constituent ἐν τῷ Ἰουδαϊσμῷ preceding the focal constituent ὑπὲρ πολλοὺς συνηλικιώτας ἐν τῷ γένει μου.

(14a) καὶ   προέκοπτον   ἐν   τῷ   Ἰουδαϊσμῷ /   ὑπὲρ
       and   I.was.advancing in   the Judaism   beyond

       πολλοὺς   συνηλικιώτας   ἐν   τῷ   γένει   μου,
       many   contemporaries   in   the nation my

1 Cor. 5:5a illustrates the operation of the same principle, when two *core* constituents occur in the same clause. The more focal constituent (τῷ Σατανᾷ) is placed after the more supportive one (τὸν τοιοῦτον). In this particular clause, a peripheral constituent follows both core constituents.

(5a) παραδοῦναι   τὸν   τοιοῦτον /   τῷ   Σατανᾷ / εἰς   ὄλεθρον   τῆς   σαρκός,
      to.hand.over the   such.as.this to.the Satan   to   destruction of.the flesh

See also Rev. 15:7, in which the more focal constituent (ἑπτὰ φιάλας χρυσᾶς κ.τ.λ. 'seven golden bowls...') is placed after the less focal one (τοῖς ἑπτὰ ἀγγέλοις 'to the seven angels').

As I suggested in the introduction to this chapter, the degree to which the ordering principles I have just presented are followed in lengthy sentences probably depends on the extent to which the original writer composed the sentence in his mind. In particular, we cannot exclude the possibility that, rather than following principle 4 and placing the focal constituent after a supportive one, the writer thinks of supportive information after he has already written or dictated the focal constituent of the sentence.

Matthew 3:6 may provide an example of this, in that a pronominal constituent follows a nominal one (both are peripheral). However, it is possible that the reference to the Jordan in v. 5 makes the further mention of the Jordan river in v. 6 supportive rather than in focus (in Mark 1:5 (UBS text), the Jordan is only mentioned once and the order of constituents is reversed). In any case, the focal constituent of the sentence as a whole is the participial clause ἐξομολογούμενοι τὰς ἁμαρτίας αὐτῶν, which is at the end of the sentence, in conformity with principle 4.

(5)   Then the people of Jerusalem and all Judea were going out to him, and all the region along
      the Jordan,

(6)   καὶ   ἐβαπτίζοντο   ἐν   τῷ   Ἰορδάνῃ   ποταμῷ /
      and   3P.were.baptized in   the Jordan   river

      ὑπ'   αὐτοῦ /   ἐξομολογούμενοι   τὰς   ἁμαρτίας   αὐτῶν.
      by   him   confessing   the   sins   their

Review Question

What are the four default orderings of constituents in clauses or sentences in New Testament Greek?

Suggested Answer

The four default orderings of constituents are:

1. Verb - Pronominal Constituents - Nominal Constituents
2. Core Constituents - Peripheral Constituents

3. Propositional Topic - Nonverbal Constituents of the Comment
4. Supportive Constituent - Focal Constituent (for those constituents whose relative order was not determined by ordering principles 1–3).

Illustrative Clauses from 2 Timothy

Which default ordering principles determine the order of the postverbal constituents in the following clauses?

(1:8b)	ἀλλὰ	συγκακοπάθησον	τῷ	εὐαγγελίῳ /	κατὰ	δύναμιν	θεοῦ,
	but	suffer.together.with	for.the	gospel	according.to	power	of.God

(1:3b)	ᾧ	λατρεύω	ἀπὸ	προγόνων /	ἐν	καθαρᾷ	συνειδήσει,
	whom	I.serve	from	forefathers	in	clean	conscience

(2:7b)	δώσει	γάρ	σοι /	ὁ	κύριος /	σύνεσιν /	ἐν	πᾶσιν.
	3S.will.give	for	to.you	the	Lord	understanding	in	all

Suggested Answers

The default ordering principles that determine the order of constituents in these clauses from 2 Timothy are:

(1:8b) 2. The core constituent τῷ εὐαγγελίῳ precedes the peripheral constituent κατὰ δύναμιν θεοῦ.

(1:3b) 4. The focal constituent ἐν καθαρᾷ συνειδήσει follows the supportive constituent ἀπὸ προγόνων.

(2:7b) 1, 2, and 3. The pronominal constituent σοι occurs immediately after the verb. The propositional topic ὁ κύριος precedes the remaining nonverbal constituents of the comment. The core constituent σύνεσιν precedes the peripheral constituent ἐν πᾶσιν.

3.5   Marked Instances of End of Sentence Focus

This section concerns constituents whose default position is *not* at the end of a clause or sentence. Such constituents may be placed at the end in order to mark them as focused. They include pronominal constituents, subjects, core constituents of the comment that are placed after peripheral constituents, and verbs.

> Marked Ordering Principle 5:
>   **To mark as focused a constituent whose default position is not the end of a clause or sentence, place it at the end of the clause or sentence.**

Pronominal constituents will not normally be the focus of the comment, because their referent is already known, and the focus of the comment is usually new information (Firbas 1964:114). One way of making a pronominal constituent focal is by placing it at the end of the clause concerned, thus violating default ordering principle 1 (sec. 3.1).

This is illustrated in **1 Pet. 1:4**. The pronominal constituent is placed at the end of the verse to make it focal (the following verse concerns 'you', rather than heaven).

(4)	εἰς	κληρονομίαν	ἄφθαρτον	καὶ	ἀμίαντον	καὶ
	to	inheritance	imperishable	and	undefiled	and

	ἀμάραντον,	τετηρημένην	ἐν	οὐρανοῖς /	εἰς	ὑμᾶς
	unfading	having.been.kept	in	heavens	for	you

(5)   who are being protected by the power of God through faith for a salvation ready to be revealed in the last time.

At first sight, the presence at the end of **2 Cor. 13:4** of εἰς ὑμᾶς might be considered to be a supportive afterthought. However, Barnett (1997:603 fn. 60) points out, "Gk. εἰς ὑμᾶς is emphatic, coming at the end of the clause and sounding a note of warning to the Corinthians." In other words, this pronominal constituent has been placed at the end of v. 4d to make it focal (contrast the NRSV translation "but <u>in dealing with you</u> we will live with him by the power of God," which treats εἰς ὑμᾶς as a point of departure).[10]

(4a-c)   For he was crucified in weakness, but lives by the power of God. For we also are weak in him,

(4d)   ἀλλὰ   ζήσομεν   σὺν   αὐτῷ /   ἐκ   δυνάμεως   θεοῦ /   εἰς   ὑμᾶς.
         but   we.live   with him   by   power   of.God   to   you

The *subject* of a sentence with topic-comment articulation is normally the propositional topic about which the comment is made, so by definition it is not the focal constituent of the comment in prototypical sentences. One way to make the subject focal is to place it at the end of the sentence.

This is illustrated in **Gal. 2:20a, b**, in which the focus is on the contrastive constituents ἐγώ and Χριστός. Placing these constituents at the end of their respective clauses results, in the case of v. 20b, in the violation of default ordering principle 2, since the subject (a core constituent) follows a peripheral one.

(20a)   ζῶ   δὲ   οὐκέτι   ἐγώ,
         I.live DE   no.longer I

(20b)   ζῇ   δὲ   ἐν   ἐμοί /   Χριστός·
         3S.lives DE   in   me   Christ

In **Gal. 2:13a**, the subject follows a pronominal constituent, in conformity with default ordering principle 1. Its position at the end of the clause is consistent also with its being the focal constituent.[11]

(13a)   καὶ   συνυπεκρίθησαν   αὐτῷ /   [καὶ]   οἱ   λοιποὶ   Ἰουδαῖοι,
         and   3P.dissembled.along.with with.him +   the remaining   Jews

Sentences with *presentational* articulation have no propositional topic and the subject that is being presented is the focal constituent (Firbas 1971:97). This is the case in **Jas. 2:2**, which violates default ordering principle 2.

(2)   ἐὰν   γὰρ   εἰσέλθῃ   εἰς   συναγωγὴν   ὑμῶν /   ἀνὴρ   χρυσοδακτύλιος   κ.τ.λ.
        if   for   3S.enters into synagogue   your   man   gold.fingered

A *core* constituent of the comment may be placed after a peripheral constituent, in violation of default ordering principle 2, in order to bring it into focus. This is exemplified in **James 2:18e**, which the NRSV appropriately translates, "And I by my works will show you my faith." The core constituent τὴν πίστιν is placed after the peripheral constituent to bring it into focus. (See sec. 3.6 on the placement of σοι before the verb.)

(18d)   δεῖξόν   μοι /   τὴν   πίστιν   σου /   χωρὶς   τῶν   ἔργων,
         show   to.me   the   faith   your   without the   works

(18e)   κἀγώ   σοι   δείξω   ἐκ   τῶν   ἔργων   μου /   τὴν   πίστιν.
         and.I   to.you I.will.show   by   the   works   my   the   faith

See also the speech of Matt. 14:8 (Δός μοι... ὧδε ἐπὶ πίνακι / τὴν κεφαλὴν Ἰωάννου τοῦ βαπτιστοῦ 'Give me here on a platter the head of John the Baptist'), in which the core constituent τὴν κεφαλὴν Ἰωάννου τοῦ βαπτιστοῦ is placed after the peripheral constituent to bring it into focus.

---

[10] The New Living Translation renders v. 4d, 'but we live in him and have God's power—the power we use in dealing with you.'

[11] When the subject of a clause that introduces a reported speech follows a pronominal reference to the addressee (sec. 3.1), it is the speech which is sentence-final and in focus, not the subject.

Finally, the *verb* may be placed last in a clause or sentence to bring it especially into focus. As I have already suggested, the default position of the verb is clause-initial (sec. 2.6), and the default position for both pronominal and nominal constituents of the comment is following the verb (secs. 3.1–3.2). Now, the verb may end a clause or sentence because the only other constituent has been preposed, as in Luke 5:27a (Καὶ μετὰ ταῦτα ἐξῆλθεν 'and after these things he went out'—see also sec. 3.7). If that is not the case, however, the verb may have been placed at the end in order to bring it into special focus.[12]

In **James 1:11e**, for example, the verb follows a peripheral constituent. The articular nature of this constituent tends to confirm that the verb is the focal constituent (see fn. 9).

(11e)	οὕτως	καὶ	ὁ	πλούσιος /	ἐν	ταῖς	πορείαις	αὐτοῦ	μαρανθήσεται.
	thus	+	the	rich	in	the	goings	his	3S.will.fade.away

In **Gal. 2:19a**, the verb not only follows its propositional topic (the point of departure); it also follows a peripheral and a core constituent of the comment.[13] The verb appears, therefore, to be the focal constituent (see also the position of primary stress when this sentence is read aloud).

(19a)	ἐγὼ	γὰρ	διὰ	νόμου /	νόμῳ /	ἀπέθανον,
	I	for	through	law	to.law	I.died

'For I through the law died to the law'

See section 4.1 for sentences like John 1:5b (καὶ ἡ σκοτία αὐτὸ οὐ κατέλαβεν 'and the darkness did not overcome it'), in which the *negated* verb is placed last for focus.

Review Question

When may a constituent that ends a clause or sentence be judged to be there to bring it into focus?

Suggested Answer

A constituent that ends a clause or sentence may be judged to be there to bring it into focus if its position violates one of the default ordering principles.

Illustrative Clauses from 1 Corinthians

In the following clauses, what suggests that the final constituent has been brought into focus?

(10:8a) We must not indulge in sexual immorality as some of them did,

(8b)	καὶ	ἔπεσαν	μιᾷ	ἡμέρᾳ /	εἴκοσι	τρεῖς	χιλιάδες.
	and	3P.fell	in.one	day	twenty	three	thousand

(7:37a)	ὃς	δὲ	ἕστηκεν	ἐν	τῇ	καρδίᾳ	αὐτοῦ /	ἑδραῖος
	he.who	DE	3S.has.stood	in	the	heart	his	firm

(9:19a) For though I am free with respect to all,

(19b)	πᾶσιν	ἐμαυτὸν	ἐδούλωσα,
	to.all	myself	I.enslaved

Suggested Answers

In both 1 Cor. 10:8b and 7:37a, the core constituent follows a peripheral constituent, in violation of ordering principle 2 (μιᾷ ἡμέρᾳ is an adverbial phrase of time). This suggests that εἴκοσι τρεῖς χιλιάδες and ἑδραῖος are at the end of their respective clauses to bring them into focus.

---

[12] See sec. 3.7.1 for a proviso to this statement.

[13] The fact that the peripheral constituent precedes the core constituent in violation of default ordering principle 2 may indicate that there are two focal constituents or "information foci" (Halliday 1967:202) in this sentence, ἀπέθανον and διὰ νόμου (see sec. 3.6). See also fn. 14.

In 1 Cor. 9:19b, the verb is not in its default position. The other constituents appear to supply supportive information, so I judge ἐδούλωσα to have been placed last in the clause to bring it especially into focus.

3.6 Preverbal Focus

In many languages, constituents may be brought into focus by *preposing*, i.e., by placing them earlier in the sentence than their default position. New Testament Greek is no exception, as grammarians have long recognized (see, for example, BDF §472(2)), though they usually use the term "emphasis"— see the introduction to chapter 2).

In **James 1:2a**, for instance, πᾶσαν χαρὰν precedes the verb and is the focal constituent of the clause. (As in chap. 2, preverbal constituents that I judge to be in focus are given in **bold**. See sec. 4.4 for discussion of discontinuous constituents such as πειρασμοῖς ποικίλοις in v. 2b.)

(2a)　**Πᾶσαν　χαρὰν**　ἡγήσασθε,　ἀδελφοί　μου,
　　　　all　　　joy　　　consider　　brothers　my

(2b)　ὅταν　**πειρασμοῖς**　περιπέσητε　ποικίλοις,
　　　　whenever　into.trials　you.fall　　into.various

Similarly, in **Gal. 4:14b**, ὡς ἄγγελον θεοῦ precedes the verb and is the focal constituent of the clause.[14]

(14a)　and my condition which put you to the test you did not scorn or despise,

(14b)　ἀλλὰ　**ὡς ἄγγελον θεοῦ**　ἐδέξασθέ　με,　ὡς　Χριστὸν Ἰησοῦν.
　　　　but　　as　angel　of.God　you.received　me　as　Christ　Jesus.

In **Gal. 4:17b**, the pronoun αὐτοὺς 'them' precedes the verb, in violation of default ordering principle 1. This is because it is in focus; it corresponds to and contrasts with the implied 'us' of v. 17a.

(17a)　They are zealous for you, but for no good purpose; they want to alienate you [from us]

(17b)　ἵνα　**αὐτοὺς**　ζηλοῦτε·
　　　　that　them　　you.may.be.zealous.for

Any point of departure that is present will *precede* any preverbal focal constituent. This is illustrated in **James 2:18**. Both v. 18b and v. 18c begin with their propositional topics,[15] while the contrastive focal elements of the comments about them precede their respective verbs.[16] As for v. 18e, it contains *two* focal constituents: τὴν πίστιν (see sec. 3.5) and the pronominal constituent σοι, which is in contrast with μοι.

(18a)　But someone will say,

(18b)　<u>Σὺ</u>　**πίστιν**　ἔχεις,
　　　　you　faith　　you.have

(18c)　<u>κἀγὼ</u>　**ἔργα**　ἔχω·
　　　　and.I　　works　I.have

(18d)　δεῖξόν　μοι /　τὴν　πίστιν　σου /　χωρὶς　τῶν　ἔργων,
　　　　show　to.me　the　faith　your　without　the　works

(18e)　<u>κἀγὼ</u>　**σοι**　δείξω　ἐκ　τῶν　ἔργων　μου /　τὴν　πίστιν.
　　　　and.I　to.you　I.will.show　by　the　works　my　the　faith

---

[14] This clause has two focal constituents in apposition to each other, one preceding the verb, the other (ὡς Χριστόν Ἰησοῦν) at the end of the sentence.

[15] Alternative punctuations of v. 18c have been proposed; see Fung's (1992:149-50) discussion.

[16] Dik et al (1981:66) do not distinguish between contrastive points of departure and contrastive focus. They consider that "Contrast will necessarily imply Focus" (op. cit. 58).

We thus have a second ordering pattern involving focal constituents:[17]

Marked Ordering Pattern 6:		
(Point of Departure)	**Focal Constituent**	**Verb**

This means that there are two positions in the clause or sentence to which constituents may be moved from their default position in order to focus on them:
1. to the end of the clause or sentence (sec. 3.5)
2. prior to the verb (following the point of departure, if present).

3.7   Preverbal Focus versus End of Sentence Focus

I now address the question of when one position of focus is used rather than the other. I have already observed (sec. 3.5) that the default position of the *verb* is at the beginning of the sentence, and that *subjects* preceding the verb prototypically will be interpreted as propositional topics functioning as points of departure. For both of these constituents, therefore, the clause-final position is the only one available for focus (unless some other feature is present; see sec. 4.1 on subjects preceded by a negative particle, and sec. 6.2 on non-conjunctive καί with initial verbs).

Where a constituent may be placed for focus either prior to the verb or at the end of the sentence, however, grammarians have always taken the position that the preverbal position gives "emphasis" to the constituent. In other words, the preverbal position gives *more prominence* to the constituent than it would receive at the end of the clause or sentence. I see no reason to dispute this.

In the case of *copular* clauses whose complement is in focus, J. Callow observes that it is the *norm* for a focal complement to precede the copula, as in 1 Cor. 3:16b ((Do you not know) ὅτι **ναὸς θεοῦ** ἐστε 'that temple of.God you.are...?').[18]

Such complements follow the verb only when, in some sense, "they are off the theme-line" (1992:74). For example, in relative clauses in which the subject is a relative pronoun, the complement invariably follows the copula, as in 1 Cor. 3:11 (ὅς ἐστιν Ἰησοῦς Χριστός 'who is Jesus Christ').

Thus, even though it is the norm for focal complements to precede the copula, such complements still receive more prominence than those that follow the copula.

Another circumstance under which focal complements tend to follow the copula is when they are *long coordinative phrases*. For example, the list of the fruit of the Spirit in **Gal. 5:22–23** follows the copula.

(22) Ὁ   δὲ καρπὸς τοῦ πνεύματός ἐστιν ἀγάπη χαρὰ εἰρήνη,
      the DE fruit   of.the spirit   3S.is   love   joy   peace...

Similarly, in 1 Corinthians, focal complements whose structure is a coordinative phrase of the type οὐ/μή X ἀλλά Y always follow the verb when the subject precedes it (J. Callow 1992:77). This is the case in **1 Cor. 2:5**, for instance.

(5) ἵνα   ἡ   πίστις ὑμῶν μὴ   ᾖ   ἐν σοφίᾳ
     so.that the faith   your   not 3S.may.be in wisdom

     ἀνθρώπων ἀλλ' ἐν δυνάμει θεοῦ.
     of.men   but   in power   of.God

---

[17] Compare de Groot's analysis of Hungarian as a language in which, according to Dik (1989:363), "constituent ordering can be described according to the template **P1 P2 V X**, which is used in the following ways:

P1 can harbour one of more Topic constituents [i.e., points of departure]

P2 can harbour just one Focus constituent

constituents with neither Topic nor Focus function go to X."

[18] Complement is to be understood here in a broad sense, as "a word or phrase added to a verb to complete the predicate of a sentence" (OED). Complements of the copula include noun phrases (as in 1 Cor. 3:16b), adjectives (e.g., ἅγιός 'holy' in 1 Cor. 3:17), possessives (e.g., ὑμῶν 'yours' in 1 Cor. 3:21), and various prepositional phrases (as in 1 Cor. 2:5, cited in this section).

Nevertheless, an alternative order when coordinative phrases are involved is to place the first part of the coordination before the copula and the rest at the end of the sentence (e.g., in Gal. 4:2 [passage 1 of sec. 3.9] and Jas. 1:23—see sec. 4.4.1). Consequently, the length of the focal constituent does not guarantee that it will be placed at the end of the sentence.

Focal complements also follow the verb when the sentence begins with a pronoun whose function is *deictic*; i.e., to point out the topic about which a comment is to be made. This is exemplified in **Matt. 3:17**, where οὗτός identifies Jesus as the person about which the voice from heaven is making a comment.[19]

(17)　　And a voice from heaven said,

Οὗτός	ἐστιν	ὁ	υἱός	μου	ὁ	ἀγαπητός,	ἐν	ᾧ	εὐδόκησα.
this	3S.is	the	son	my	the	beoved	in	whom	I.am.well.pleased

The same order is found when the sentence begins with a personal pronoun such as ἐγώ and no switch from a corresponding constituent is intended (contrast James 2:18, discussed in sec. 3.6). An example is John 8:12: Ἐγώ εἰμι τὸ φῶς τοῦ κόσμου 'I am the light of the world.'

The existence in the clause of two focal positions means that a *chiastic* structure is available for parallel statements. Typically, the focal constituent of the first clause follows its verb, whereas the focal constituent of the second precedes it.

Mark 1:34 illustrates this (see sec. 3.8.1 below for why I consider the objects to be in focus, rather than the verbs).

(34a)	καὶ	ἐθεράπευσεν /	πολλοὺς	κακῶς	ἔχοντας	ποικίλαις	νόσοις
	and	3S.healed	many	ill	having	with.various	diseases

(34b)	καὶ	**δαιμόνια πολλὰ** /	ἐξέβαλεν
	and	demons many	3S.expelled

A change in the position of *pronominal constituents* often occurs when a focal constituent precedes the verb. If the pronominal constituent would otherwise end the sentence, it is nearly always found *before* the verb, in violation of default ordering principle 1 (sec. 3.1). In other words, such clauses typically have the structure: *Focal Constituent - Pronominal Constituent - Verb*.[20] **1 Cor. 2:14b** illustrates this order.

(14a)　　The natural man does not receive the things of God's Spirit,

(14b)	**μωρία**	γὰρ	αὐτῷ	ἐστιν·
	foolishness	for	to.him	3S.is

See also 1 Cor. 1:11b (ὅτι **ἔριδες** ἐν ὑμῖν εἰσιν 'that there are strifes among you'), which has presentational articulation. **1 Cor. 7:35** provides an example in which the verb is not a copula.

(35a)　　I say this for your own benefit,

(35b)	οὐχ	ἵνα	**βρόχον**	ὑμῖν	ἐπιβάλω
	not	so.that	noose	to.you	I.may.put.on

---

[19] A possible explanation for this order is that the use of a deictic or personal pronoun gives a certain amount of prominence to the topic. The juxtaposition of the focal constituent might detract from its prominence, so it is placed in the sentence final position for such constituents.

[20] For clauses in which the focal constituent precedes the verb but a supportive pronominal constituent follows it, see Gal. 4:14b (cited in sec. 3.6) and 1 Cor. 3:16c (cited in sec. 3.7.2).

Other languages also manifest changes in the order of *non*-focused constituents when a constituent is brought into focus. For example, Hannes Wiesemann (p.c.) reports that, in the Toussian language of Burkina Faso, the normal order of constituents is Subject-Object-Verb. When a focus marker is attached to the subject, however, the order becomes Subject+Focus-Verb-Object. In the Mambila language of Cameroon, when a constituent after the verb is in focus, non-focused constituents are "left-shifted" to before the verb (Perrin 1994:233).

This positioning of pronominal constituents is frequently found when the preposed constituent in focus follows a negative particle (see sec. 4.1).

Review Questions

(a) Into which two positions in a clause or sentence may constituents be moved from their default position in order to bring them into focus?

(b) Which of these positions has traditionally been judged to be more "emphatic"?

Suggested Answers

(a) The two positions in a clause or sentence into which constituents may be moved from their default position are:

- to the end of the clause or sentence
- prior to the verb (following the point of departure, if present).

(b) Traditionally, the preverbal position has been judged to be more "emphatic".

Illustrative Sentences

(a) In **1 Cor. 2:10**, why does ἡμῖν precede the verb?

<blockquote>

(9)   But, as it is written, "What no eye has seen, nor ear heard, nor the human heart conceived, what God has prepared for those who love him"—

(10)   ἡμῖν   δὲ   ἀπεκάλυψεν ὁ   θεὸς   διὰ   τοῦ   πνεύματος·
           to.us   DE   3S.revealed the God through the Spirit

</blockquote>

(b) In **Acts 13:44**, why do both τῷ ἐρχομένῳ σαββάτῳ and σχεδὸν πᾶσα ἡ πόλις precede the verb?

<blockquote>

(44)   Τῷ   δὲ   ἐρχομένῳ σαββάτῳ / σχεδὸν πᾶσα ἡ   πόλις
      on.the DE coming   sabbath   nearly all   the city

      συνήχθη   ἀκοῦσαι τὸν λόγον τοῦ κυρίου.
      3S.was.assembled to.hear the   word of.the Lord

</blockquote>

Suggested Answers

(a) In 1 Cor. 2:10, ἡμῖν precedes the verb to bring it into focus; it is in contrast with the 'no-one' who has previously been aware of what God has prepared for those who love him (v. 9).

(b) In Acts 13:44, τῷ ἐρχομένῳ σαββάτῳ and σχεδὸν πᾶσα ἡ πόλις precede the verb because they are respectively the point of departure and the focal constituent of the sentence. σχεδὸν πᾶσα ἡ πόλις is focused to emphasize the size of the crowd that assembled.

3.8 Ambiguous Constituent Orders

Let us now examine a couple of instances in which the operation of different principles produces the same order of constituents: one that sometimes occurs when a clause or sentence ends with a verb, and one that occurs when a single constituent precedes the verb.

3.8.1   Ambiguities when a Verb Ends a Sentence

A clause or sentence can *end with a verb* and the verb be preceded by another constituent of the complement as the result of two different ordering principles:

- the verb has been placed at the end of the sentence to bring it into focus (sec. 3.5)
- the other constituent has been placed before the verb to bring it into focus (sec. 3.6).

For instance, in **Mark 1:34b** (repeated below from sec. 3.7), the same order of constituents is obtained whether the focal constituent is judged to be δαιμόνια πολλὰ or ἐξέβαλεν.

(34a)   And he cured many that were sick with various diseases,

(34b)   καὶ   **δαιμόνια   πολλὰ** /   ἐξέβαλεν
        and   demons   many   3S.expelled

Firbas has argued (1959:48) that, in such instances, it is the norm for the object to be more in focus than its verb, unless it is information that is already known from the context.[21] Firbas would therefore consider δαιμόνια πολλὰ to be in focus in Mark 1:34b.

However, **James 4:11c** is not covered by Firbas' principle, since both 'law' and 'judging' have featured in the immediate context. In this case, the order of constituents does not indicate whether it is νόμον or κρίνεις that is in focus.

(11b)   ὁ   καταλαλῶν   ἀδελφοῦ   ἢ   κρίνων   τὸν   ἀδελφὸν   αὐτοῦ
        the speaking.against brother or judging the brother his

        καταλαλεῖ   νόμου   καὶ   κρίνει   νόμον·
        3S.speaks.against law and 3S.judges law

(11c)   εἰ   δὲ   νόμον   κρίνεις,
        if   DE   law   you.judge

(11d)   οὐκ   εἶ   ποιητὴς   νόμου   ἀλλὰ   κριτής.
        not   you.are doer of.law but   judge

The same ambiguity involving the verb results from the observed tendency for it to be placed final if it would otherwise have been the penultimate constituent in a clause or sentence of at least *four* constituents. I observed for Philippians that, if a clause or sentence begins with a point of departure followed by a focused constituent, then "a further non-verbal element may precede the verb, provided its referent is 'given' information and is of a supportive nature" (Levinsohn 1995:67).[22] In such instances, the focal constituent could theoretically have been either the constituent that follows the point of departure or the verb.

This ambiguity is illustrated in **Phil. 1:15b**. The verb is preceded by three constituents, the first of which (τινὲς) is readily interpreted as a point of departure, marking a switch from a different group identified by another τινὲς (v. 15a). The third constituent, an articular reference to Christ, appears to be merely of a supportive nature (see also v. 17). This leaves either καὶ δι' εὐδοκίαν or κηρύσσουσιν as the focal constituent. In reality, there seems to be no reason to suppose that the verb is in focus (v. 14 has already spoken about "speaking the word"). Furthermore, καὶ δι' εὐδοκίαν contrasts with καὶ διὰ φθόνον καὶ ἔριν (and includes a non-conjunctive καί—see sec. 6.2). I therefore deduce that καὶ δι' εὐδοκίαν is the focal constituent.

(15a)   Τινὲς   μὲν   καὶ   διὰ   φθόνον   καὶ   ἔριν,
        some   +   because.of envy and strife

(15b)   τινὲς /   δὲ   καὶ   δι'   εὐδοκίαν /   τὸν   Χριστὸν   κηρύσσουσιν·
        some   DE   +   because.of good.intention the Christ 3P.proclaim

James 1:25 illustrates the same potential ambiguity, but this time the main verb is a copula, which is most unlikely to be the focal constituent, anyway.

(25)   But the one who looks into the perfect law, the law of liberty, and perseveres, being not a hearer who forgets but a doer who acts—

---

[21] See Levinsohn 1967:15ff. for evidence from the Inga (Quechuan) language that validates Firbas' claim.

[22] Payne (1995:480) observes that, in verb initial languages, "there is evidence that thematic NPs may come right after the verb." Contrast Col. 3:4, in which the supportive constituent σὺν αὐτῷ 'with him' precedes the verb, but the anarthrous constituent ἐν δόξῃ 'in glory' does not.

οὗτος /	μακάριος /	ἐν	τῇ	ποιήσει	αὐτοῦ	ἔσται.
this	blessed	in	the	doing	his	3S.will.be

In **Gal. 2:11**, either κατὰ πρόσωπον or ἀντέστην could potentially be the focal constituent. In practice, however, as the NRSV translation "I opposed him to his face" suggests, κατὰ πρόσωπον is probably more in focus, whether or not the expression implies hostility (Burton 1921:103).

(11)	Ὅτε	δὲ	ἦλθεν	Κηφᾶς	εἰς	Ἀντιόχειαν, /	κατὰ
	when	DE	3S.came	Cephas	to	Antioch	to

	πρόσωπον /	αὐτῷ	ἀντέστην,
	face	to.him	I.stood.against

Galatians 5:5 provides a further example in which the verb is final and potentially in focus. However, it appears that *two* constituents have been placed before the verb because they are in focus. πνεύματι is contrasted with the flesh (v. 3—see Burton 1921:278), while ἐκ πίστεως is contrasted with law. The supportive constituent ἐλπίδα δικαιοσύνης '(the) hope of righteousness' (see v. 4) also precedes the verb.

(3)   Once again I testify to every man who lets himself be circumcised that he is obliged to obey the entire law. (4) You who want to be made righteous by the law have cut yourselves off from Christ; you have fallen away from grace.

(5)	ἡμεῖς	γὰρ	πνεύματι /	ἐκ	πίστεως /	ἐλπίδα	δικαιοσύνης	ἀπεκδεχόμεθα.
	we	for	by.spirit	by	faith	hope	of.righteousness	we.eagerly.await

3.8.2 Ambiguities when a Single Constituent Precedes the Verb

A single constituent may precede the verb and begin its clause or sentence for three very different reasons:[23]

1. to establish a point of departure for the communication (sec. 2.2)
2. to bring the constituent into focus (sec. 3.6)
3. to bring the verb into special focus (sec. 3.5).

Ambiguities resulting from the third reason have been considered in section 3.8.1, so I concentrate on the other two.

Although grammarians often refer to both operations 1 and 2 as "emphasis," they are quite distinct and, in many languages, are marked in different ways. In many Chadic languages, for example, points of departure are preceded by a "topic" marker, whereas focused constituents are not (see Levinsohn 1994:6). In many Bantu languages, focused constituents are followed by a special marker, whereas points of departure are not. In Inga (Quechuan), the suffix *-ca* is attached to points of departure, whereas an evidential clitic is attached to focused constituents (Levinsohn 1975:15, 25ff.).

As its name implies, a *point of departure* provides a starting place for a communication; it "cohesively anchors the subsequent clause to something which is already in the context" (*SIL-UND* sec. 11.3.1). Consequently, points of departure either refer to information that is accessible in the context or switch from information that is accessible in the context. As a result, points of departure are often *articular*.

Focal constituents, in contrast, typically are the most important piece of *new* information in the comment about the propositional topic. As a result, focal constituents are often *anarthrous*.

This means that, if the preverbal constituent is articular, it is more likely to be a point of departure, especially if some other constituent is anarthrous. If the preverbal constituent is anarthrous, it is more likely to be in focus.

---

[23] As I noted in sec. 3.6, when *two* constituents precede the verb, the point of departure typically precedes the focal constituent.

This is illustrated in **James 1:3–4**. In v. 3b, the preverbal constituent is articular, as it relates back to the reference to trials in v. 2, so is more likely to be a point of departure. This analysis is confirmed by the presence of an anarthrous constituent at the end of the sentence, which is more likely to be in focus. In v. 4a, this same constituent is articular, and is followed by another anarthrous constituent, so we conclude that the first constituent in v. 4a is the point of departure, whereas the second is in focus.

(3a) γινώσκοντες
knowing

(3b) ὅτι τὸ δοκίμιον ὑμῶν τῆς πίστεως κατεργάζεται ὑπομονήν.
that the testing of.your the faith 3S.works endurance

(4a) ἡ δὲ ὑπομονὴ **ἔργον τέλειον** ἐχέτω,
the DE endurance work perfect 3S.let.have

(4b) ἵνα ἦτε τέλειοι καὶ ὁλόκληροι
so.that you.may.be perfect and entire

(4c) **ἐν μηδενὶ** λειπόμενοι.
in nothing lacking

For passages in which the reason for a nonverbal constituent beginning a clause or sentence is not immediately apparent, there are three questions that can help to distinguish a point of departure from a focal constituent:

1. Does the initial constituent seem to be part of the *comment* about a given propositional topic? If so, it is unlikely to be a point of departure for what follows.
2. Does the initial constituent seem to *anchor* what follows to the context? If so, it is the point of departure—unless the answer to the previous question was yes.
   Now for a really subjective test:
3. When an English translation of the sentence is read aloud, does the *primary stress*, phonologically, fall on the initial constituent? If so, it is probably part of the comment.

Randall Buth (p.c.) suggests a further principle for interpreting the function of initial nonverbal constituents. He argues that the establishment of a point of departure is the unmarked purpose for preposing a constituent and that we should not consider that such a constituent is in focus unless it cannot be interpreted as the point of departure.

The following passages illustrate how the above principles may be applied to identify the function of an initial constituent.

In **Acts 8:3a** (see below), the initial constituent, Σαῦλος, is readily interpreted as a point of departure, anchoring the sentence to its context by a switch back to Saul from Stephen and the event of v. 2. It is also the most natural propositional topic and, subjectively, the primary stress would seem to fall later in the sentence (e.g., on 'ravaging').

In v. 3b, the initial constituent, κατὰ τοὺς οἴκους, occurs in a nominative participial clause, which typically has the same propositional topic as the clause to which it is subordinate (in this case, Saul). It appears to be part of the comment about Saul. In addition, it does not seem to anchor the clause to the context; it describes, not a spatial setting, but the extent of the persecution of v. 3a. Thus, this constituent is initial in order to *focus* on the thoroughness of the persecution.

(1) And Saul approved of their killing him (Stephen). That day a severe persecution began against the church in Jerusalem, and all except the apostles were scattered throughout the countryside of Judea and Samaria. (2) Devout men buried Stephen and made loud lamentation over him.

(3a) Σαῦλος δὲ ἐλυμαίνετο τὴν ἐκκλησίαν
Saul DE 3S.was.ravaging the church

(3b)   **κατὰ τοὺς οἴκους** εἰσπορευόμενος,
           house.by.house   entering

Although the initial constituent in **1 Cor. 10:9c** (ὑπὸ τῶν ὄφεων) is articular, it seems to be part of the comment about τινες αὐτῶν (v. 9b). It does not seem to anchor the clause to the context and, when read aloud, primary stress would fall on the constituent. It has therefore been placed before the verb to bring it into focus.

(9a)   μηδὲ   ἐκπειράζωμεν   τὸν   Χριστόν,
           neither   let.us.tempt   the   Christ

(9b)   καθώς   <u>τινες</u>   <u>αὐτῶν</u>   ἐπείρασαν
           as   some   of.them   3P.tempted

(9c)   καὶ   **ὑπὸ**   **τῶν**   **ὄφεων**   ἀπώλλυντο.
           and   by   the   serpents   3P.were.being.destroyed

An English translation of **1 Cor. 3:16c** can be read so that primary stress falls on either the initial constituent (God's **Spirit** dwells in you) or the final constituent (<u>God's Spirit</u> dwells **in you**). The fact that τὸ πνεῦμα τοῦ θεοῦ is articular and can be related to the context by a switch from ναὸς θεοῦ in v. 16b suggests that it should be interpreted as a point of departure, rather than having been placed before the verb to bring it into focus.

(16a)   οὐκ   οἴδατε
           not   you.know

(16b)   ὅτι   **ναὸς**   **θεοῦ**   ἐστε
           that   temple   of.God   you.are

(16c)   καὶ   τὸ   πνεῦμα   τοῦ   θεοῦ   οἰκεῖ   ἐν   ὑμῖν;
           and   the   spirit   of.the   God   3S.dwells   in   you

Review Questions

(a) When a clause or sentence ends with a verb that is preceded by another constituent of the complement, which two ordering principles could have produced this order?

(b) When a single constituent precedes the verb, what three reasons potentially explain the order of constituents?

Suggested Answers

(a) When a clause or sentence ends with a verb that is preceded by another constituent of the complement, either of the following ordering principles could have produced this order:
  • the placement of the verb at the end of the sentence to bring it into focus,
  • the placement of the other constituent before the verb to bring it into focus.

(b) When a single constituent precedes the verb, any one of the following three reasons potentially explains the order of constituents:
  1. the initial constituent is there to establish a point of departure for the communication,
  2. the initial constituent is there to bring the constituent into focus,
  3. the verb is final to bring it into special focus.

Illustrative Passages

(a) In **Gal. 6:14**, why is ἐμοὶ initial in the sentence?

(13)   For even the circumcised do not themselves obey the law. Rather, they want you to be circumcised so they may boast about your flesh.

(14a)   ἐμοὶ   δὲ   μὴ   γένοιτο   καυχᾶσθαι   εἰ   μὴ   ἐν
           to.me   DE   not   3S.may.be   to.boast   if   not   in

τῷ   σταυρῷ   τοῦ   κυρίου   ἡμῶν   Ἰησοῦ   Χριστοῦ,
the   cross   of.the lord   our   Jesus   Christ

(b) In **Gal. 4:1**, why is κύριος πάντων initial in the clause?

> (1)   My point is this: the heir, as long as he is a minor, is no better than a slave,
>
> κύριος   πάντων   ὤν,
> lord   of.all   being

(c) In **Rom. 8:24a**, why is τῇ ἐλπίδι initial in the sentence?

> (23)   and not only the creation, but we ourselves, who have the first fruits of the Spirit, groan inwardly while we wait for adoption, the redemption of our bodies.
>
> (24a)   τῇ   γὰρ   ἐλπίδι ἐσώθημεν·
>   with/by.the for   hope   we.were.saved
>
> (24b)   ἐλπὶς   δὲ   βλεπομένη   οὐκ   ἔστιν   ἐλπίς·
>   hope   DE   being.seen   not   3S.is   hope

Suggested Answers

(a) In Gal. 6:14, ἐμοὶ is initial in the sentence to establish a new point of departure, by a switch of attention from 'the circumcised' (v. 13) to 'me'. This constituent is readily interpreted as the propositional topic about which the rest of the sentence is a comment. Subjectively, primary stress falls later in the sentence.

(b) In Gal. 4:1, κύριος πάντων is initial in the (copular) clause to bring it into focus. It is readily interpreted as part of the comment about the propositional topic of the sentence, 'the heir'. Subjectively, primary stress falls on this constituent.

(c) In Rom. 8:24a, τῇ ἐλπίδι could be initial in the sentence because it provides the point of departure for the clause. This would explain the presence of the article. However, 'we' was the propositional topic of the previous sentence and can readily be taken as the topic of this clause, too. Godet (1883[1977]:319) claims that τῇ ἐλπίδι, "from its position at the beginning of the sentence, evidently has the emphasis." In other words, it is initial for focus. However, the constituent is articular (the concept of 'hope' was introduced in v. 20 and is implicit in 'waiting'—v. 23). It therefore seems more likely that ἐσώθημεν is in focus, with τῇ ἐλπίδι supportive ('It is <u>in hope</u> that we were **saved**').

3.9   Concluding Comments

By now, the reader may feel that there are just too many factors to consider and that it is not realistically possible to draw any conclusions from the constituent order of individual sentences in the Greek text. In fact, however, the situation is not that bad! The factors discussed in sections 3.1–3.4 explain what *usually* happens. They provide explanations for *default* orders of constituents. Thus, pronominal constituents usually occur immediately following the verb (sec. 3.1). Core constituents usually precede peripheral ones (sec. 3.2). The propositional topic usually precedes the comment (sec. 3.3). Two peripheral constituents (or core constituents or pronominal constituents) usually are ordered so that the more focal one follows the less focal one (sec. 3.4).

For expository purposes, all we need to be able to do is recognize when the order is significant, i.e., *marked*. For many clauses, it is sufficient to concentrate on any constituents (up to two) that precede a verb and, if more than one constituent follows the verb, be sure that the default order has been followed. It will be helpful to ask oneself the following three questions:

1. How does the sentence *begin*? Typically, if it begins with a verb, no discontinuity has been indicated (see sec. 2.4 for some exceptions). If it begins with a nonverbal constituent, determine whether this constituent is a point of departure or is in focus.

2. If a point of departure precedes the verb, does a *second* constituent also precede the verb? If so, it is usually in focus (in sec. 2.2, see Rom. 11:30 for an exception).

3. Does more than one constituent of the comment *follow* the verb? If so, have the default orderings been followed? If not, the final constituent is in focus.

Passage 1: Galatians 4:1–7

After studying the order of the constituents in each clause of the following passage, answer the questions that follow. They are based on both chapters 2 and 3, so review chapter 2 as well as chapter 3! (See sec. 4.4.1 on discontinuous coordinative constituents like ὑπὸ ἐπιτρόπους καὶ οἰκονόμους in v. 2.)

(1a)   Λέγω δέ,
             I.say DE

(1b)   ἐφ᾽ ὅσον χρόνον ὁ κληρονόμος νήπιός ἐστιν,
             for so.long time the heir infant 3S.is

(1c)   οὐδὲν διαφέρει δούλου
             nothing 3S.differs of.slave

(1d)   κύριος πάντων ὤν,
             lord of.all being

(2)   ἀλλὰ ὑπὸ ἐπιτρόπους ἐστὶν καὶ οἰκονόμους
             but under guardians 3S.is and stewards

             ἄχρι τῆς προθεσμίας τοῦ πατρός.
             until the previously.appointed.time of.the father

(3a)   οὕτως καὶ ἡμεῖς, ὅτε ἦμεν νήπιοι,
             so + we when we.were infants

(3b)   ὑπὸ τὰ στοιχεῖα τοῦ κόσμου ἤμεθα δεδουλωμένοι·
             under the elements of.the world we.were enslaved

(4a)   ὅτε δὲ ἦλθεν τὸ πλήρωμα τοῦ χρόνου,
             when DE 3S.came the fullness of.the time

(4b)   ἐξαπέστειλεν ὁ θεὸς τὸν υἱὸν αὐτοῦ,
             3S.sent.forth the God the son his

(4c)   γενόμενον ἐκ γυναικός,
             becoming from woman

(4d)   γενόμενον ὑπὸ νόμον,
             becoming under law

(5a)   ἵνα τοὺς ὑπὸ νόμον ἐξαγοράσῃ,
             so.that the.ones under law 3S.might.redeem

(5b)   ἵνα τὴν υἱοθεσίαν ἀπολάβωμεν.
             so.that the adoption.of.sons we.might.receive

Questions

(a) In Gal. 4:1b, assuming that ἐφ᾽ ὅσον χρόνον is a subordinating conjunctive phrase, why does ὁ κληρονόμος precede the verb? Why does νήπιός also precede the verb?

(b) What is the primary basis for relating v. 3a to the context?

(c) In v. 3a, why does νήπιοι follow the verb?

(d) In v. 3b, why does ὑπὸ τὰ στοιχεῖα τοῦ κόσμου precede the verb?

(e) Verse 4 is a single sentence. Which constituent is initial in v. 4 and why?

(f) In v. 4a, why is τὸ πλήρωμα τοῦ χρόνου final?

(g) In v. 4b, why is ὁ θεὸς not initial?

(h) In v. 5a, why does τοὺς ὑπὸ νόμον precede the verb?

(i) In v. 5b, why does τὴν υἱοθεσίαν precede the verb?

Suggested Answers: see Appendix under 3(1).

4
MORE ON CONSTITUENT ORDER

In this chapter, five more aspects of constituent order are discussed: the order of constituents in negated sentences (sec. 4.1) and information questions (sec. 4.2); temporary focus on a preposed constituent in anticipation of a switch of attention to a corresponding constituent that is the real focus of the sentence (sec. 4.3); discontinuous constituents (sec. 4.4); and the preposing of modifiers in the noun phrase (sec. 4.5).

4.1 Constituent Order in Negated Sentences

The order of constituents in negated sentences follows the same principles as those that were described in chapter 3 for positive sentences with topic-comment articulation. One advantage enjoyed by negated sentences is that the position of the negative particle μή or οὐ assists in the identification of points of departure and of constituents that have been preposed for focus.

If a negative *immediately precedes the verb*, then some or all of the comment about the propositional topic is negated. In **Gal. 4:30c**, for example, the propositional topic is 'the son of the maidservant', and it is the comment 'shall inherit with the son of the free woman' that is negated.

(30c) οὐ   γὰρ   μὴ   κληρονομήσει   ὁ   υἱὸς   τῆς   παιδίσκης
        not   for   not   3S.shall.inherit   the   son   of.the   maidservant

        μετὰ   τοῦ   υἱοῦ   τῆς   ἐλευθέρας.
        with   the   son   of.the   free.woman

John 1:5b illustrates the same point when the propositional topic precedes the verb as the *point of departure*. What is negated is the comment 'grasped it' about 'the darkness'. (The pronominal constituent αὐτὸ precedes the verb, in violation of default ordering principle 1 of sec. 3.1, because the verb is in focus.)

(5a)   And the light shines in the darkness,

(5b)   καὶ   ἡ   σκοτία   αὐτὸ   οὐ   κατέλαβεν.
        and   the   darkness   it   not   3S.grasped

See also Gal. 3:20a (ὁ δὲ μεσίτης ἑνὸς οὐκ ἔστιν 'now a mediator is not of one').[1] As I note in section 3.7, it appears to be the norm for a focal complement to precede the copula.

When a clause negated by οὐ or μή is followed by the conjunction ἀλλά, then what is negated is often just the constituent that corresponds to the one introduced by ἀλλά. See, for example, Matt. 5:17b (οὐκ ἦλθον καταλῦσαι ἀλλὰ πληρῶσαι), which the NRSV appropriately translates, "I have come not to abolish but to fulfill." In other words, what is negated is "to abolish," not "come to abolish."

In section 3.8.1 I noted the potential ambiguity that arises when the verb is the final constituent of the sentence. This order can result both from placing the verb at the end of the sentence to bring it into focus and from placing a nonverbal constituent before the verb to bring that constituent into focus. The same ambiguity theoretically arises in negated sentences that end in a verb.

In **Gal. 5:21c**, for instance, κληρονομήσουσιν could be at the end of the sentence either to focus on the verb or because βασιλείαν θεοῦ has been preposed to bring it into focus.

(21c)   ὅτι   οἱ   τὰ   τοιαῦτα   πράσσοντες   βασιλείαν θεοῦ   οὐ   κληρονομήσουσιν.
        that   the   the   such.things   practicing   kingdom   of.God   not   3P.will.inherit

---

[1] This is a counterexample to John Callow's suggestion (1992:86) that, in copular clauses, only those constituents that follow the verb are negated.

One way of specifically bringing a nonverbal constituent into focus while negating it is to place it immediately after the negative particle and before the verb (followed by a supportive pronominal constituent, when appropriate—see sec. 3.7). In other words, the order of constituents is:

Negative Particle   Focused Constituent   (Pronominal Constituent)   Verb.[2]

In **Gal. 2:5a**, for instance, πρὸς ὥραν is placed immediately after the negative particle to negate it and bring it into focus; see the NRSV translation, "we did not submit to them even for a moment," in which the intensified *even* is used to bring out the focus.

(5a)   οἷς   οὐδὲ[3]   **πρὸς ὥραν** εἴξαμεν   τῇ   ὑποταγῇ,
         to.whom   not   for   hour we.yielded by.the   subjection

In **Matt. 4:4b**, ἐπ' ἄρτῳ μόνῳ is placed immediately after the negative particle to negate it and bring it into focus. (See sec. 4.3 for discussion of such instances of "temporary focus" in anticipation of a switch of focus to another constituent.)

(4b)   Οὐκ   **ἐπ' ἄρτῳ μόνῳ** ζήσεται   ὁ   ἄνθρωπος,
         not   by   bread   alone   3S.will.live the   man

         ἀλλ' ἐπὶ   παντὶ   ῥήματι   ἐκπορευομένῳ   διὰ   στόματος θεοῦ.
         but   by   every   word   proceeding.from through mouth   of.God

In **Matt. 6:15b**, the *subject* ὁ πατὴρ ὑμῶν is brought into focus by placing it immediately after the negative (rather than at the end of the sentence—see sec. 3.5).

(15a)   ἐὰν   δὲ   μὴ   ἀφῆτε   τοῖς   ἀνθρώποις,
         if   DE   not you.forgive to.the men

(15b)   οὐδὲ   **ὁ πατὴρ ὑμῶν** ἀφήσει   τὰ   παραπτώματα ὑμῶν.
         neither the   father your   3S.will.forgive the   trespasses   your

Similarly, in **Gal. 5:6**, περιτομή is placed immediately after the negative particle to negate it and bring it into focus. The pronominal constituent τι also precedes the verb. (See sec. 4.4.1 on the placement of οὔτε ἀκροβυστία after the verb.)

(6)   ἐν   γὰρ   Χριστῷ   Ἰησοῦ οὔτε   **περιτομή**   τι
         in   for   Christ   Jesus   neither circumcision   anything

         ἰσχύει   οὔτε   ἀκροβυστία   κ.τ.λ.
         3S.avails nor   uncircumcision

If a constituent is preposed for focus but *not* negated, it precedes the negative particle. This is seen in **1 Cor. 16:12b**. Πάντως is placed before the verb to bring it into focus but, because it is not itself negated, it precedes οὐκ.

(12a)   Now concerning our brother Apollos, I strongly urged him to visit you with the other brothers,

(12b)   καὶ   **πάντως**   οὐκ   ἦν   θέλημα   ἵνα   **νῦν**   ἔλθῃ·
         and   altogether not   3S.was desire   that   now   3S.may.come

If the negative is a *content* word (e.g., οὐδείς 'no one', οὐδέν 'nothing') and immediately precedes the verb, the negative word itself is brought into focus. Pope (p.c.) points out that, since such words consist of the negative particle οὐδέ plus a form of εἷς 'one', they can be viewed as further instances in which the constituent that immediately follows the negative is brought into focus.

---

[2] This claim is stronger than Radney's assertion (1988:41), "If the main purpose of the negative is to deny that certain constituents participated in the action represented by the main verb of the clause at hand, *these constituents will occur before the verb immediately after the negative word.*"

[3] A few MSS omit οὐδέ.

In **James 3:8**, for example, οὐδείς is the focused constituent, following the point of departure τὴν γλῶσσαν.

(8)   τὴν   δὲ   γλῶσσαν / **οὐδεὶς** δαμάσαι   δύναται   ἀνθρώπων,   κ.τ.λ.
       the   DE   tongue   no.one   to.tame   3S.is.able of.men

In **Gal. 2:6b**, οὐδέν is the focused constituent. Once again, a supportive pronominal constituent also precedes the verb.[4]

(6b)   ὁποῖοί   ποτε   ἦσαν / **οὐδέν**   μοι   διαφέρει·
       of.what.kind then   3P.were nothing   to.me 3S.matters

In **Gal. 5:2b**, *two* constituents appear to have been preposed to bring them into focus: Χριστὸς (following the point of departure ἐὰν περιτέμνησθε) and οὐδέν.

(2b)   ἐὰν   περιτέμνησθε,   **Χριστὸς**   ὑμᾶς   **οὐδὲν**   ὠφελήσει.
       if   you.are.circumcised Christ   you   nothing   3S.will.profit

In **Phil. 4:15b**, οὐδεμία is the focused constituent, following a complex point of departure, and the clause terminates with an *exception* to οὐδεμία, introduced with εἰ μή.[5]

(15a)   You Philippians indeed know

(15b)   ὅτι   ἐν   ἀρχῇ   τοῦ   εὐαγγελίου,   ὅτε   ἐξῆλθον
        that in   beginning of.the gospel   when I.went.out

        ἀπὸ   Μακεδονίας,   **οὐδεμία**   μοι   ἐκκλησία   ἐκοινώνησεν
        from Macedonia   not.one   with.me church   3S.shared

        εἰς   λόγον   δόσεως   καὶ   λήμψεως   εἰ μὴ   ὑμεῖς   μόνοι,
        in   word   of.expenditures and   receipts   except you   only

John Callow (p.c.) points out that the *normal* position of a negative content word is preceding the verb (about 85% of the time in the New Testament). He feels that the combination of a negative particle prior to the verb plus the negative content word after the verb ought to be a more emphatic way of focusing on such a word. **Mark 14:61a** (UBS text) exemplifies this.

(61a)   ὁ   δὲ   ἐσιώπα   καὶ   οὐκ   ἀπεκρίνατο   οὐδέν.
        he DE   3S.was.silent and   not   3S.answered   nothing

However, it is not clear that, in fact, this is so. For example, **Mark 5:37** provides an example of the combination of a negative particle before the verb and a negative content word after it when an exception to the negative content word follows. Impressionistically, I would say that the negative content word is emphasized more when it precedes the verb in Phil. 4:15b (cited above), than when it follows it in Mark 5:37.[6]

(37)   καὶ   οὐκ   ἀφῆκεν   οὐδένα   μετ'   αὐτοῦ   συνακολουθῆσαι
       and   not   3S.permitted   no-one   with   him   to.follow

       εἰ μὴ   τὸν   Πέτρον   καὶ   Ἰάκωβον   καὶ   Ἰωάννην   κ.τ.λ.
       except the   Peter   and   James   and   John

---

[4] In the 1992 edition of this book, I stated (p. 87) that μοι was also highlighted. I now see no reason to claim this, or to assert (p. 88) that με is highlighted in Gal. 4:12b, particularly as non-emphatic forms of the pronoun are used in both passages.

[5] The rhetorical effect of placing μοι between οὐδεμία and ἐκκλησία may be to give extra prominence to the negative (Pope p.c.—see sec. 4.4.2).

[6] The same is true of Spanish, in my opinion. For example, I feel that 'nada' in 'nada respondía' is more emphatic than in '¿No respondes nada?' (Mark 14:61, 60).

Compare also Phil. 1:20b with 1:28a, both of which are cited below. In other words, I feel that the claim that the preverbal position gives more prominence to a constituent than the sentence final position (sec. 3.7) applies to both positive and negative sentences.[7]

When a *rhetorical question* begins with a negative, placing a constituent immediately after the negative and before the verb again gives it prominence. The constituent concerned may either be in focus, as in James 2:21 (below), or else be the propositional topic about which the rest of the sentence makes a comment, as in James 2:5-7.[8]

In the case of **James 2:21**, in which the focal constituent ἐξ ἔργων immediately follows the negative and precedes the verb, the negative is preceded by the point of departure Ἀβραὰμ ὁ πατὴρ ἡμῶν, as attention switches to him from 'you'. A translation that reflects all the details of the constituent order of this sentence might be, "Take our ancestor Abraham (as an example)! Was it not by works that he was justified when he offered his son Isaac on the altar?"

(20)　Do you want to be shown, you senseless person, that faith apart from works is barren?

(21)　Ἀβραὰμ　ὁ　πατὴρ　ἡμῶν　οὐκ　**ἐξ　ἔργων**　ἐδικαιώθη
　　　Abraham　the　father　our　not　by　works　3S.was.justified

　　　ἀνενέγκας　Ἰσαὰκ　τὸν　υἱὸν　αὐτοῦ　ἐπὶ　τὸ　θυσιαστήριον;
　　　offering.up　Isaac　the　son　his　upon　the　altar

In each of the rhetorical questions that occur in **James 2:5-7**, the propositional topic immediately follows the negative and a comment about that topic then follows. The prominence given to the topic is readily reflected in English by the use of a cleft construction, e.g., "Is it not the rich who oppress you?" (v. 6b NRSV).[9]

(5b)　οὐχ　ὁ　θεὸς　ἐξελέξατο　τοὺς　πτωχοὺς　τῷ　κόσμῳ
　　　not　the　God　3S.chose　the　poor　in.the　world

　　　πλουσίους　ἐν　πίστει　καὶ　κληρονόμους　τῆς　βασιλείας κ.τ.λ.
　　　rich　in　faith　and　heirs　of.the　kingdom

(6a)　ὑμεῖς　δὲ　ἠτιμάσατε　τὸν　πτωχόν.
　　　you　DE　you.dishonored　the　poor

(6b)　οὐχ　οἱ　πλούσιοι　καταδυναστεύουσιν　ὑμῶν
　　　not　the　rich　3P.oppress　you

(6c)　καὶ　αὐτοὶ　ἕλκουσιν　ὑμᾶς　εἰς　κριτήρια;
　　　and　they　3P.drag　you　to　tribunals

(7)　οὐκ　αὐτοὶ　βλασφημοῦσιν　τὸ　καλὸν　ὄνομα　τὸ　ἐπικληθὲν　ἐφ'　ὑμᾶς;
　　　not　they　3P.blaspheme　the　good　name　the　called.on　on　you

Review Questions

(a) When a negative immediately precedes the verb, what does this signify?

(b) When the negative is separated from the verb by some constituent(s), which constituent is focused? What does it signify if the negative that precedes the verb is a content word such as οὐδείς?

---

[7] Another possibility is that the difference between the two forms of negation is comparable to the difference in English between negating a *clause* (e.g., He didn't answer anything) and negating a *constituent* of a clause (He answered nothing). Although a negative content word can follow the verb in New Testament Greek without a negative particle preceding it (see, for example, James 1:13), the norm is for the particle to be present when a negative content word follows the verb (as in Spanish).

[8] For a rhetorical question that begins with a negative in which no constituent has been preposed, see James 2:4.

[9] These sentences are not to be interpreted as having focus-presupposition articulation (with the presupposition in v. 6b being 'someone oppresses you' and the focus being on 'who', viz., 'the rich'). If that were the case, the pronominal constituents (e.g. ὑμῶν) would have preceded the verb, rather than being in their default position immediately after the verb. Furthermore, the preposed constituents are articular—see sec. 9.4.

(c) When one or more nonverbal constituents *precede* a negative particle, what functions may these constituents have in the sentence?

Suggested Answers

(a) When a negative immediately precedes the verb, then part or all of the *comment* about the propositional topic is negated.

(b) When the negative is separated from the verb by some constituent(s), then the constituent that occurs immediately after the negative is both negated and focused. When the negative is a content word, then it is the negative that is focused.

(c) When one or more nonverbal constituents *precede* a negative particle, they may function as a *point of departure* or as a *focused* constituent that is not negated.

Illustrative Sentences from Philippians

(a) In **Phil. 1:22b**, why does τί αἰρήσομαι precede the negative particle?

> (21)   For to me, to live is Christ and to die is gain. (22a) If (I am) to live in the flesh, that (means) fruitful labor for me;

> (22b)   καὶ   τί   αἰρήσομαι   οὐ   γνωρίζω.
>   and   what   I.will.choose   not   I.know

(b) In **Phil. 2:6b**, why does ἁρπαγμὸν follow the negative particle?

> (6a)   ὃς   ἐν   μορφῇ   θεοῦ   ὑπάρχων
>   who   in   form   of.God   existing

> (6b)   οὐχ   ἁρπαγμὸν   ἡγήσατο   τὸ   εἶναι   ἴσα   θεῷ,
>   not   thing.to.be.grasped   3S.regarded   the   to.be   equal   to.God

(c) In **Phil. 3:9b**, which constituent(s) are negated?

> (8)   ... in order that I may gain Christ (9a) and be found in him,

> (9b)   μὴ   ἔχων   ἐμὴν   δικαιοσύνην   τὴν   ἐκ   νόμου
>   not   having   my.own   righteousness   the   of   law

>   ἀλλὰ   τὴν   διὰ   πίστεως   Χριστοῦ,   κ.τ.λ.
>   but   the   through   faith   of.Christ

(d) In **Phil. 1:20b**, why does the negative content phrase ἐν οὐδενὶ precede the verb?

> (20a)   according to my eager expectation and hope

> (20b)   ὅτι   ἐν   οὐδενὶ   αἰσχυνθήσομαι
>   that   in   nothing   I.will.be.put.to.shame

(e) In **Phil. 1:28a**, a negative particle and negative content phrase co-occur. Which ordering principle determines the order of the postverbal constituents and which constituent appears to be in focus?

> (27)   Only, live your life in a manner worthy of the gospel of Christ, so that... I will know that you are striving side by side with one mind for the faith of the gospel,

> (28a)   καὶ   μὴ   πτυρόμενοι   ἐν   μηδενὶ   ὑπὸ   τῶν   ἀντικειμένων,
>   and   not   being.frightened   in   nothing   by   the   opposing.ones

> (28b)   which is to them evidence of their destruction...

Suggested Answers

(a) In Phil. 1:22b, τί αἱρήσομαι precedes the negative particle because it provides a point of departure for the sentence, as the argument switches from one of the two possibilities that are being contemplated ('to live' over against 'to die') to joint consideration of them both.

(b) In Phil. 2:6b, ἁρπαγμὸν follows the negative particle to bring it into focus.

(c) In Phil. 3:9b, the negated constituent is ἐμὴν δικαιοσύνην τὴν ἐκ νόμου, since this is the constituent which corresponds to the one introduced by ἀλλά.

(d) In Phil. 1:20b, ἐν οὐδενὶ, which is a negative content word, precedes the verb to bring it into focus.

(e) In Phil. 1:28a, default ordering principle 1 determines the order of the peripheral postverbal constituents (the pronominal constituent ἐν μηδενὶ precedes the nominal constituent ὑπὸ τῶν ἀντικειμένων). I consider ἐν μηδενὶ to be strengthening μὴ πτυρόμενοι, but to be less focal than the second peripheral constituent.

Sentences 1: James 1:20 and 2:1.

(1:20) ὀργὴ γὰρ ἀνδρὸς δικαιοσύνην θεοῦ οὐκ ἐργάζεται.
wrath for of.man righteousness of.God not 3S.works

(2:1) Ἀδελφοί μου, μὴ ἐν προσωπολημψίαις ἔχετε τὴν πίστιν
brothers my not in respect.of.persons have the faith

τοῦ κυρίου ἡμῶν Ἰησοῦ Χριστοῦ τῆς δόξης.
of.the Lord our Jesus Christ of.the glory

Questions

(a) What does the position of the negative particle signify in James 1:20?

(b) What does the position of the negative particle signify in 2:1?

Suggested Answers: see Appendix under 4(1).

4.2   Constituent Order in Information Interrogatives

Most information interrogatives have *focus-presupposition* articulation (sec. 2.1), in which all but the question word is the presupposition, and the question word itself is the focus. It is not surprising, therefore, that the question word precedes the verb in the focal position.

In **Gal. 3:1**, for instance, the presupposition is that 'someone bewitched you'; the focus is on 'who'. As is normal when the focused constituent is preposed, the pronominal constituent ὑμᾶς also precedes the verb.

(1) Ὦ ἀνόητοι Γαλάται, **τίς** ὑμᾶς ἐβάσκανεν, κ.τ.λ.;
O senseless Galatians who you 3S.bewitched

The focused constituent may be a *phrase*, rather than just a question word. In **Matt. 21:23c**, for instance, the focused constituent is Ἐν ποίᾳ ἐξουσίᾳ.

(23c) **Ἐν ποίᾳ ἐξουσίᾳ** ταῦτα ποιεῖς;
by what authority these you.do

See also Matt. 19:16 (the focused constituent is τί ἀγαθὸν 'what good').

A *point of departure* may precede the question word. In **Matt. 12:27b**, for example, οἱ υἱοὶ ὑμῶν is the point of departure as attention switches from 'I'.

(27a)   And if I cast out demons by Beelzebul,

(27b) οἱ υἱοὶ ὑμῶν ἐν τίνι ἐκβάλλουσιν;
the sons your by whom 3P.cast.out

When the focused constituent asks *'why'*, e.g., with διὰ τί, the *rest* of the sentence has *topic-comment* articulation. A cleft sentence nicely captures the structure of such questions: "**Why** is it that 'topic-comment articulation proposition'?"

The topic-comment part of 'why' questions follows the normal principles of constituent order. In **Matt. 21:25b**, for example, a *pronominal* constituent follows the verb, in conformity with default ordering principle 1.

    (25b)   And they argued with one another, "If we say, 'From heaven,' he will say to us,

Διὰ τί	οὖν	οὐκ	ἐπιστεύσατε	αὐτῷ;
why	then	not	you.believed	him

Where appropriate, a *point of departure* may begin the rest of a 'why' question.[10] In such instances, there is *no* switch from some previous point of departure (contrast Matt. 12:27b, cited above). In **Matt. 15:2a**, for instance, the propositional topic about which the questioners wish to make a comment is stated immediately after the question word. A cleft sentence that captures the significance of the different parts of the sentence might read, "**Why** is it that <u>your disciples</u> break the tradition of the elders?"[11]

    (1)   Then Pharisees and scribes came to Jesus from Jerusalem and said,

    (2a)

Διὰ τί	οἱ	μαθηταί	σου	παραβαίνουσιν	τὴν	παράδοσιν	τῶν	πρεσβυτέρων;
why	the	disciples	your	3P.transgress	the	tradition	of.the	elders

The rest of a 'why' question may begin with a constituent preposed for *focus*. In **Matt. 13:10**, for instance, ἐν παραβολαῖς is preposed for focus.

    (10)   Then the disciples, approaching, asked him,

Διὰ τί /	ἐν	παραβολαῖς	λαλεῖς	αὐτοῖς;
why	in	parables	you.speak	to.them

Review Questions

(a) What type of sentence articulation do most information questions have?

(b) What principles determine the order of constituents in a 'why' question?

Suggested Answers

(a) Most information questions have *focus-presupposition* articulation, in which the question word is the focus and the rest of the sentence, the presupposition.

(b) In a 'why' question, the question word begins the sentence, but the remaining constituents are ordered according to the principles applicable to sentences with topic-comment articulation.

Illustrative Sentences

(a) In **Matt. 21:23d**, why does σοι precede the verb?

    (23c)   By what authority are you doing these things?

    (23d)

καὶ	τίς	σοι	ἔδωκεν	τὴν	ἐξουσίαν	ταύτην;
and	who	to.you	3S.gave	the	authority	this

(b) In **Matt. 22:28a**, which is the focused constituent? Why does ἐν τῇ ἀναστάσει begin the sentence?

    (28a)

ἐν	τῇ	ἀναστάσει	οὖν	τίνος	τῶν	ἑπτὰ	ἔσται	γυνή;
in	the	resurrection	then	which	of.the	seven	3S.will.be	wife

---

[10] I find no examples in which a point of departure *precedes* διὰ τί, though I see no inherent reason why one could not occur.

[11] Contrast Mark 7:5 (UBS text) (Διὰ τί οὐ περιπατοῦσιν οἱ μαθηταί σου κατὰ τὴν παράδοσιν τῶν πρεσβυτέρων κ.τ.λ.;). Verse 2 has already recorded that the Pharisees and scribes noticed that some of Jesus' disciples were eating 'with defiled hands', so a point of departure for the speech does not need to be established. The postverbal constituents of this verse are ordered according to default principle 2.

(c) In **Matt. 9:11b**, why does μετὰ τῶν τελωνῶν καὶ ἁμαρτωλῶν precede the verb, and ὁ διδάσκαλος ὑμῶν follow it?

    (10)   And as he (Jesus) sat at dinner in the house, many tax collectors and sinners came and were sitting with him and his disciples. (11a) When the Pharisees saw this, they said to his disciples,

    (11b)   Διὰ τί μετὰ τῶν τελωνῶν καὶ ἁμαρτωλῶν ἐσθίει ὁ διδάσκαλος ὑμῶν;
                why with the tax.collectors and sinners 3S.eats the teacher your

Suggested Answers

(a) In Matt. 21:23d, σοι precedes the verb because the question word τίς is in focus. It is normal for a pronominal constituent to precede the verb when a focal constituent has been preposed.

(b) In Matt. 22:28a, the focused constituent is τίνος τῶν ἑπτά. Ἐν τῇ ἀναστάσει begins the sentence to provide a point of departure, as attention switches from life in this world to life at the resurrection.

(c) Matt. 9:11b is a 'why' question in which the rest of the sentence follows the principles for ordering constituents in a sentence with topic-comment articulation. Μετὰ τῶν τελωνῶν καὶ ἁμαρτωλῶν precedes the verb to bring it into focus. Ὁ διδάσκαλος ὑμῶν presumably follows the verb because the questioners were responding to what they and their addressees could see (v. 11a). It would therefore be unnecessary to establish a point of departure.

Sentence 2: Galatians 5:7

    (7a)   You were running well;

    (7b)   τίς ὑμᾶς ἐνέκοψεν
              who you 3S.hindered

    (7c)   [τῇ] ἀληθείᾳ μὴ πείθεσθαι;
              by.the truth not to.be.persuaded

Questions

(a) In v. 7b, what is the presupposition and what the focus?
(b) In v. 7c, why does [τῇ] ἀληθείᾳ precede the verb?

Suggested Answer: see Appendix under 4(2).

4.3   Temporary Focus

    This section involves instances in which a constituent is brought into focus by placing it before the verb, when the real focus is presented later in the sentence. We may think of such instances as bringing the initial constituent *temporarily* into focus, in anticipation of a switch of attention to the corresponding constituent that is presented later.

    For example, when a sentence begins with a *demonstrative pronoun* like οὗτος 'this' and the sentence then specifies what 'this' refers to, οὗτος has been brought temporarily into focus, with the purpose of directing the reader's attention to its referent. In **Gal. 3:2a**, for instance, τοῦτο directs the reader's attention to the following clause (v. 2b).

    (2a)   **τοῦτο** μόνον θέλω μαθεῖν ἀφ' ὑμῶν·
              this only I.want to.know from you

    (2b)   **ἐξ ἔργων νόμου** τὸ πνεῦμα ἐλάβετε ἢ ἐξ ἀκοῆς πίστεως;
              by works of.law the Spirit you.received or by hearing of.faith

See also Philemon 15 (διὰ τοῦτο), 1 John 2:25 (αὕτη), and Rev. 9:17 (οὕτως).

Alternatives may be presented in such a way that the first alternative is brought temporarily into focus by occurring before the verb, in anticipation of a switch of attention to the more important alternative that is presented later in the sentence.

In Gal. 3:2b (above), for instance, focus rests temporarily on ἐξ ἔργων νόμου, before switching to the real center of attention, ἐξ ἀκοῆς πίστεως. This particular sentence has focus-presupposition articulation; it is presupposed that 'you received the Spirit' by some means and the focus is on the two possible means.

In **Gal. 3:16a**, τῷ Ἀβραὰμ is brought temporarily into focus, in anticipation of a switch of attention to the 'seed' to whom the promises were *also* made. Τῷ σπέρματι αὐτοῦ, rather than Abraham, is the concern of the rest of the verse. (See also sec. 4.4.1.)

(16a)	τῷ	δὲ	Ἀβραὰμ	ἐρρέθησαν	αἱ	ἐπαγγελίαι
	to.the	DE	Abraham	3P.were.spoken	the	promises

	καὶ	τῷ	σπέρματι	αὐτοῦ.
	and	to.the	seed	his

(16b)   it does not say, "And to seeds," as of many; but it says, "And to your seed,"...

James 2:14b is a little different, in that πίστιν is brought temporarily into focus in one clause, in anticipation of a switch of attention to ἔργα, which is brought into focus in the next clause.

(14a)   What good is it, my brothers,

(14b)	ἐὰν	πίστιν	λέγῃ	τις	ἔχειν
	if	faith	3S.may.say	anyone	to.have

(14c)	ἔργα	δὲ	μὴ	ἔχῃ;
	works	DE	not	3S.may.have

Review Question

What are the characteristics of *temporary* focus?

Suggested Answer

Temporary focus involves bringing a constituent into focus by placing it before the verb in anticipation of a switch of attention to a corresponding constituent, later in the sentence, which is the *real* focus of the sentence.

Illustrative Sentences

(a) In **James 3:15**, why does ἄνωθεν precede its verb (κατερχομένη)?[12]

(15)	οὐκ	ἔστιν	αὕτη	ἡ	σοφία	ἄνωθεν	κατερχομένη
	not	3S.is	this	the	wisdom	from.above	coming.down

	ἀλλὰ	ἐπίγειος,	ψυχική,	δαιμονιώδης.
	but	earthly	natural	demonic

(b) In **John 13:35**, why does ἐν τούτῳ begin the sentence? And why does ἀγάπην precede its verb?

(34)   I give you a new commandment, that you love one another—just as I have loved you, that you also should love one another.

(35)	ἐν	τούτῳ	γνώσονται	πάντες	ὅτι	ἐμοὶ	μαθηταί	ἐστε,
	by	this	3P.will.know	all.people	that	my	disciples	you.are

---

[12] The combination of ἔστιν and the participle is not periphrastic, as the grammatical subject occurs between them (see Porter 1992:45-46).

ἐὰν   ἀγάπην   ἔχητε   ἐν   ἀλλήλοις.
if   love   you.have   among   one.another

Suggested Answers

(a) In James 3:15, ἄνωθεν precedes its verb to bring it temporarily into focus, in anticipation of a switch of attention to the 'correct' alternative, ἐπίγειος, ψυχική, δαιμονιώδης.

(b) In John 13:35, ἐν τούτῳ begins the sentence to bring it temporarily into focus, with the purpose of directing the reader's attention to its referent, viz., the conditional clause that ends the sentence. Ἀγάπην precedes its verb to give particular prominence to it as the focal constituent of the clause.

Passage 3: John 18:7–8

(7)   So he again asked them, "For whom are you looking?" And they said, "Jesus of Nazareth."

(8a)   ἀπεκρίθη   Ἰησοῦς,   Εἶπον   ὑμῖν   ὅτι   ἐγώ   εἰμι·
        3S.answered Jesus   I.said to.you that   I   I.am

(8b)   εἰ   οὖν   ἐμὲ   ζητεῖτε,   ἄφετε   τούτους   ὑπάγειν·
        if   then me   you.seek   let   these   go.away

(a) In v. 8a, why does ἐγώ precede εἰμι?
(b) In v. 8b, why does ἐμὲ precede ζητεῖτε?

Suggested Answer: see Appendix under 4(3).

4.4   Discontinuous Constituents

A phrase is considered to be discontinuous (or 'split'—Healey 1984) when it consists of more than one word but the words are *not contiguous* because another constituent occurs between them. In **Rom. 12:4b**, for instance, the object, τὴν αὐτὴν πρᾶξιν, occurs on both sides of the verb ἔχει, so is discontinuous.

(4a)   For as in one body we have many members,

(4b)   <u>τὰ</u>   δὲ   <u>μέλη</u>   <u>πάντα</u>   οὐ   **τὴν αὐτὴν**   ἔχει   πρᾶξιν,
        the   DE   members   all   not   the same   3S.has   function

Note: I will not be discussing the splitting of phrases like τὰ μέλη by "postpositive" particles such as δέ.

There appear to be two basic reasons why some constituents are discontinuous, a processing one and a pragmatic one. The *processing* reason is usually related to the preposing of focused constituents; if the constituent to be preposed is complex, then it is normal for only the first part to precede the verb (sec. 4.4.1).[13] The *pragmatic* reason applies when two parts of a constituent are of unequal importance, as when only part of a constituent relates to what follows or is to be focused (sec. 4.4.2).

4.4.1   Discontinuity of a Focused Constituent Due to Its Complexity

Winer (1882:685) observes, "if the subject is complex, [the NT writers] place the principal subject only before the verb, leaving the rest to follow... that the reader's attention may not be kept on the stretch too long." Thus, if a complex constituent is in focus, it is normal for only part of it to precede the verb, with the rest of it occurring after the verb in accordance with the ordering principles of sections 3.1–3.5.

Coordinative constituents are frequently discontinuous when they are in focus, with the first part before the verb and the second part after it. Such is the case in **Rev. 17:14c**, for instance.

---

[13] In most of the examples of this section, the discontinuous constituent is separated by the verb, though the reasons for other constituents being discontinuous appear to be similar to those described here.

(14b)   and the Lamb will conquer them

(14c)   ὅτι   **κύριος κυρίων** ἐστὶν καὶ βασιλεὺς βασιλέων
        since   lord of.lords 3S.is and king   of.kings

In **James 3:14a**, the focused constituent ζῆλον πικρὸν καὶ ἐριθείαν contrasts with ἐν πραΰτητι 'in meekness' in v. 13 (Bratcher 1984:39). The first part of the coordinative phrase precedes the verb, while the second part follows it in the default position for core constituents, viz., prior to the peripheral constituent ἐν τῇ καρδίᾳ ὑμῶν (sec. 3.2).

(13)   Who is wise and understanding among you? By his good life let him show his works in the meekness of wisdom.

(14a)   εἰ   δὲ **ζῆλον πικρὸν** ἔχετε   καὶ ἐριθείαν ἐν τῇ   καρδίᾳ ὑμῶν,
        if   DE jealousy bitter   you.have and rivalry   in the heart   your

(14b)   do not be boastful and false to the truth.

In **1 Cor. 3:7**, the negated subject οὔτε ὁ φυτεύων οὔτε ὁ ποτίζων is brought into temporary focus (sec. 4.3) in anticipation of a switch of attention to the positive counterpart, ὁ αὐξάνων θεός. The first part of the coordinative phrase precedes the verb, while the second part follows it in the usual place for focused subjects, viz., following the object (sec. 3.5).

(7)   ὥστε οὔτε   **ὁ   φυτεύων**   ἐστίν τι   οὔτε ὁ   ποτίζων
        so.that neither the planting.one 3S.is anything nor the watering.one

        ἀλλ᾽ ὁ   αὐξάνων   θεός.
        but the giving.growth.one God

See also Gal. 5:6 (cited in sec. 4.1) and Gal. 6:16b, which is verbless (εἰρήνη ἐπ᾽ αὐτοὺς καὶ ἔλεος 'peace on them and mercy'); the second part of the coordinative phrase follows the pronominal constituent (see sec. 3.1).

Contrast James 1:4b, in which both parts of the coordinative complement τέλειοι καὶ ὁλόκληροι 'mature and complete' follow the copula. As the next few verses do not take up either of these concepts, it is appropriate for the complement, though in focus, to follow the copula—see the discussion of copular clauses in sec. 3.7.

4.4.2   Discontinuity of a Constituent Due to Its Parts Being Unequally Relevant

Constituents often are discontinuous for a pragmatic reason. In this section I consider two such reasons in turn:
- the constituent is discontinuous because only the first part is in focus
- the constituent is discontinuous because only the second part relates to what follows.

First of all, constituents may be discontinuous because only the *first* or preposed part is in focus, whereas the remainder is supportive.

In **Gal. 6:11**, for example, it is the *size* of the letters that is in focus, rather than the phrase πηλίκοις γράμμασιν as a whole. (In this sentence, a pronominal constituent, rather than the verb, comes between the two parts of the phrase.)

(11)   Ἴδετε **πηλίκοις** ὑμῖν γράμμασιν ἔγραψα τῇ   ἐμῇ χειρί.
        you.see how.large to.you letters   I.wrote with.the my hand

In **Rom. 11:24a**, the focus is on the particular *type* of olive tree, as the rest of the verse shows, rather than on the whole of the phrase ἐκ τῆς κατὰ φύσιν ἀγριελαίου.

(24a)   εἰ γὰρ σὺ **ἐκ** τῆς **κατὰ** **φύσιν** ἐξεκόπης   ἀγριελαίου
        if for you from the according.to nature you.were.cut wild.olive.tree

(24b) καὶ **παρὰ φύσιν** ἐνεκεντρίσθης εἰς καλλιέλαιον,
and against nature you.were.engrafted into cultivated.olive.tree

(24c) πόσῳ μᾶλλον <u>οὗτοι</u> <u>οἱ</u> <u>κατὰ</u> <u>φύσιν</u>
by.how.much more these the according.to nature

ἐγκεντρισθήσονται τῇ ἰδίᾳ ἐλαίᾳ.
3P.will.be.grafted.into the own olive.tree

In **James 1:13c**, it is ἀπείραστός that relates to and contrasts with πειράζομαι in v. 13b, whereas κακῶν is only supportive.

(13a-b) <u>μηδεὶς</u> <u>πειραζόμενος</u> λεγέτω ὅτι **Ἀπὸ θεοῦ** πειράζομαι·
no.one being.tempted 3S.let.say that from God I.am.tempted

(13c) <u>ὁ</u> γὰρ <u>θεὸς</u> **ἀπείραστός** ἐστιν κακῶν,
the for God untempted 3S.is of.evil

(13d) and he himself tempts no-one.

See also Rev. 16:3c (καὶ **πᾶσα ψυχὴ ζωῆς** ἀπέθανεν τὰ ἐν τῇ θαλάσσῃ 'and every living soul in the sea died'), in which the second part of the phrase is supportive (v. 3a records that the second angel poured his bowl into the sea).

In the case of **James 4:4b**, both parts of the discontinuous phrase (φίλος τοῦ κόσμου) occur also in v. 4a. However, James' point is that his readers are like adulteresses (v. 4a), so it is appropriate that he focus on the relation of friendship with other than God, rather than on the whole phrase.

(4a) μοιχαλίδες, οὐκ οἴδατε ὅτι <u>ἡ</u> <u>φιλία</u> <u>τοῦ</u> <u>κόσμου</u>
adulteresses not you.know that the friendship of.the world

ἔχθρα **τοῦ** **θεοῦ** ἐστιν;
enmity of.the God 3S.is

(4b) ὃς ἐὰν οὖν βουληθῇ **φίλος** εἶναι τοῦ κόσμου,
whoever then 3S.resolves friend to.be of.the world

ἐχθρὸς **τοῦ** **θεοῦ** καθίσταται.
enemy of.the God 3S.is.constituted

Secondly, constituents may be discontinuous because, even though the whole phrase is focused, only the *second* part relates to what follows.[14] Typically, the following clause(s) build only on the part of the constituent that is closest to what is to follow.

An example of this is in **Gal. 2:20d**. The nominalized clauses that follow relate to 'the Son of God' (τῇ τοῦ υἱοῦ τοῦ θεοῦ), not to 'by faith' (ἐν πίστει).

(20d) **ἐν πίστει** ζῶ τῇ τοῦ υἱοῦ τοῦ θεοῦ
by faith I.live by.the of.the son of.the God

(20e) τοῦ ἀγαπήσαντός με καὶ παραδόντος ἑαυτὸν ὑπὲρ ἐμοῦ.
of.the loving me and giving.up himself for me

In **Gal. 2:9**, the discontinuous constituent is δεξιὰς κοινωνίας. Lenski (1937:88) observes, "κοινωνίας is placed last in order that ἵνα may define it."

(9) καὶ γνόντες τὴν χάριν τὴν δοθεῖσάν μοι,
and realizing the grace the having.been.given to.me

Ἰάκωβος καὶ Κηφᾶς καὶ Ἰωάννης, οἱ δοκοῦντες
James and Cephas and John the seeming

---

[14] See BDF's comment (§473), "The connection with the following clause may also be decisive for a final position."

στῦλοι	εἶναι,	δεξιὰς	ἔδωκαν	ἐμοὶ	καὶ	Βαρναβᾷ
pillars	to.be	right.hands	3P.gave	to.me	and	to.Barnabas

κοινωνίας,	ἵνα	ἡμεῖς	εἰς	τὰ	ἔθνη,	αὐτοὶ	δὲ	εἰς	τὴν	περιτομήν·
of.fellowship	that	we	to	the	Gentiles	they	DE	to	the	circumcision

See also Gal. 3:16a (discussed in sec. 4.3).

4.4.3   Conclusion

The factors identified in this section will not provide an explanation for every instance of a discontinuous constituent found in the New Testament. (For example, why is πνεῦμα ἅγιον 'spirit holy' discontinuous in the UBS text of Luke 2:25c and Acts 1:5?) However, it does appear that Healey's (1984) concern with the *syntactic* function of constituents that split other constituents or which themselves are discontinuous seems largely misdirected. It would appear to be more productive to look for *processing* or *pragmatic* reasons for discontinuous constituents.

Review Questions

(a) What is a common processing reason for making a constituent discontinuous?
(b) What are two pragmatic reasons for making a constituent discontinuous?

Suggested Answers

(a) A common processing reason for making a constituent discontinuous is its complexity. The discontinuity occurs when the whole constituent would otherwise be placed before the verb because it is in focus.
(b) Two pragmatic reasons for making a constituent discontinuous are that:
- only the first part of the constituent is in focus
- only the second part of the constituent relates to what follows.

Illustrative Sentences

(a) In **Gal. 4:2**, why is ὑπὸ ἐπιτρόπους καὶ οἰκονόμους discontinuous?

(1)   My point is this: the heir, as long as he is a minor, is no better than a slave, though he is the owner of all the property;

(2)

ἀλλὰ	ὑπὸ	ἐπιτρόπους	ἐστὶν	καὶ	οἰκονόμους	ἄχρι	τῆς
but	under	guardians	3S.is	and	stewards	until	the

προθεσμίας	τοῦ	πατρός.
time.previously.appointed	of.the	father

(b) In **Rom. 12:4b**, why is τὴν αὐτὴν πρᾶξιν discontinuous?

(4a)

καθάπερ	γὰρ	ἐν	ἑνὶ	σώματι	πολλὰ	μέλη	ἔχομεν,
as	for	in	one	body	many	members	we.have

(4b)

τὰ	δὲ	μέλη	πάντα	οὐ	τὴν	αὐτὴν	ἔχει	πρᾶξιν,
the	DE	members	all	not	the	same	3S.has	function

(5)   so we, who are many, are one body in Christ, and individually we are members of one another.

(c) In **Heb. 2:3b**, why is τηλικαύτης σωτηρίας discontinuous?

(2)   For if the message declared through angels was valid, and every transgression or disobedience received a just penalty,

(3a)

πῶς	ἡμεῖς	ἐκφευξόμεθα
how	we	we.will.escape

(3b) τηλικαύτης   ἀμελήσαντες   σωτηρίας,
      so.important having.neglected salvation

(3c) which (ἥτις) at first having been declared through the Lord, was confirmed by those who heard him?

(d) In **Gal. 2:6c**, why do the constituents πρόσωπον ἀνθρώπου and [ὁ] θεὸς precede the negated verb (see sec. 4.1)? Why is πρόσωπον ἀνθρώπου discontinuous?

(6a–b) And from those who seemed to be something—what they actually were matters nothing to me;

(6c) πρόσωπον [ὁ] θεὸς ἀνθρώπου οὐ   λαμβάνει—
      face   the God   of.man   not 3S.accepts

Suggested Answers

(a) In Gal. 4:2, ὑπὸ ἐπιτρόπους καὶ οἰκονόμους is discontinuous because it is a focused complex constituent. The first part of the coordinative phrase precedes the verb, while the second part follows it in the default position for core constituents.

(b) In Rom. 12:4b, τὴν αὐτὴν πρᾶξιν is discontinuous because only the first part is in focus, contrasting with the focal constituent of v. 4a, πολλὰ μέλη.

(c) In Heb. 2:3b, τηλικαύτης σωτηρίας is discontinuous because, whereas it is appropriate to prepose it for focus (to emphasize τηλικαύτης), the author then takes up the topic of this salvation, so it is appropriate to end the clause with σωτηρίας.

(d) If anarthrous θεός is read in Gal. 2:6c, then πρόσωπον ἀνθρώπου precedes the negated verb because it is the point of departure (marking a shift from 'what they actually were' in v. 6b). In turn, θεός precedes the verb because it is a focused constituent ("the emphatic θεός"—Eadie 1869:120) that is not negated (it occurs before the negative particle). If the articular reading is followed, it is more likely that πρόσωπον ἀνθρώπου is preposed for focus. Ὁ θεός is then a supportive constituent (sec. 3.8.1). Πρόσωπον ἀνθρώπου is discontinuous because it is the 'face' of a person that relates back to 'what they actually were' in v. 6b (Arichea & Nida 1975:35) rather than the phrase πρόσωπον ἀνθρώπου as a whole.

Passages 4

Why are the constituents in James 1:2b, 2:15 and 4:6a (below) discontinuous?

Passage 4a: James 1:2–3

(2a) Πᾶσαν χαρὰν ἡγήσασθε, ἀδελφοί μου,
      all   joy   deem   brothers my

(2b) ὅταν πειρασμοῖς περιπέσητε ποικίλοις,
      when into.trials you.fall   various

(3)   knowing that the testing of your faith produces endurance.

Passage 4b: James 2:15–16

(15) ἐὰν ἀδελφὸς ἢ   ἀδελφὴ γυμνοὶ ὑπάρχωσιν
      if   brother   or sister   naked   3P.are

      καὶ λειπόμενοι τῆς   ἐφημέρου τροφῆς
      and lacking   of.the daily   food

(16) and one of you says to them, "Go in peace; keep warm and eat your fill," and yet you do not supply their bodily needs, what is the good of that?

Passage 4c: James 4:5–6

(5)   Or do you suppose that it is for nothing that the scripture says, "He yearns jealously for the spirit that he has made to dwell in us"?

(6a)   μείζονα   δὲ   δίδωσιν   χάριν;
        greater   DE   3S.gives   grace

(6b)   therefore it says, "God opposes the proud, but gives grace to the humble."

Suggested Answers: see Appendix under 4(4).

4.5   Preposing in the Noun Phrase: The Genitive

I turn now to the relative order of the head noun and its modifiers within the noun phrase, with particular attention to the position of the genitive.

Smith claims (1985:22) that, in noun phrases, the constituent orders genitive-noun, adjective-noun, and dative-noun are marked orders, used to give prominence to the constituent that precedes the head noun. He, therefore, considers Noun-Modifier to be the default order.

Statistics confirm that it is the norm for the *genitival* modifier to follow its noun (Porter 1992:291). In the case of the *adjectival* modifier, however, whereas it "follows its noun approximately 75% of the time in Luke and Mark," it "precedes its noun approximately 65% of the time in Paul" (op. cit. p. 290, following Davison 1989). Furthermore, when the article also precedes the noun in Pauline writings, the adjective almost invariably precedes the noun.[15] Further research is therefore needed to determine whether Robertson's (n.d.:776) claim that the adjective "receives greater emphasis than the substantive" when it follows the article but precedes the noun is applicable to all NT authors.

Pronominal genitives frequently precede their head noun even when they are not "emphatic" (Turner 1963:189–90), so I first consider genitival constituents that are *nominal*.

A genitival constituent that is nominal is preposed within the noun phrase for two purposes:
- to bring it into focus
- within a point of departure, to indicate that it is the genitive in particular which relates to a corresponding constituent of the context.

First of all, the genitive may be preposed for the purpose of bringing it into *focus*. In **Gal. 4:31**, for instance, παιδίσκης 'of a bondwoman' is preposed, because it is brought into temporary focus (sec. 4.3) in anticipation of a switch of attention to τῆς ἐλευθέρας.

(31)   διό,   ἀδελφοί,   οὐκ   ἐσμὲν   **παιδίσκης**   τέκνα
        therefore brothers   not   we.are   of.bondwoman   children

        ἀλλὰ   τῆς   ἐλευθέρας.
        but   of.the   free.woman

In **Gal. 1:10d**, Χριστοῦ is preposed for focus because it (rather than 'slave of Christ') is the specific point of contrast with ἀνθρώποις (v. 10c).

(10c)   εἰ   ἔτι   **ἀνθρώποις**   ἤρεσκον,
        if   still   to.men   I.were.pleasing

(10d)   **Χριστοῦ**   δοῦλος   οὐκ   ἂν ἤμην.
        of.Christ   slave   not   I.would.be

Other examples in Galatians in which a genitive is preposed to bring it into focus include 2:15 (ἐξ ἐθνῶν ἁμαρτωλοί 'sinners from the Gentiles', which is the specific point of contrast with Ἰουδαῖοι 'Jews' earlier in the same clause); 3:29b (τοῦ Ἀβραὰμ σπέρμα 'seed of Abraham'); 4:28 (ἐπαγγελίας

---

[15] I am grateful to Buist Fanning (p.c.) for pointing this out to me.

τέκνα 'children of promise'); and 6:2 (ἀλλήλων τὰ βάρη 'one another's burdens'). See also Rev. 7:17 (ζωῆς πηγὰς ὑδάτων 'of.life fountains of.waters').[16]

Secondly, the genitival constituent may be preposed within a *point of departure*. Usually, this is done to indicate that the *switch* of attention is specifically to the genitive from a corresponding constituent, rather than to the whole of the noun phrase.

In **James 3:3**, for example, τῶν ἵππων is preposed within the point of departure to indicate that the primary basis for relating what follows to the context is by a switch of attention from people (v. 2) to horses (rather than to 'horses' bridles'). Τοὺς χαλινοὺς then provides the specific point of departure and propositional topic for the sentence.

(2)   For all of us make many mistakes. If anyone makes no mistakes in speaking, such a one is
        perfect, able to bridle also the whole body.

(3)   εἰ   δὲ   <u>τῶν</u>   <u>ἵππων</u>   <u>τοὺς</u>   <u>χαλινοὺς</u>   **εἰς**   **τὰ**   **στόματα**   βάλλομεν   κ.τ.λ.
        if   DE   of.the   horses   the   bridles   into   the   mouths   we.put

In **Matt. 1:18**, the genitival constituent τοῦ Ἰησοῦ Χριστοῦ (or any of its textual variants) is preposed within the point of departure to indicate a switch of attention from αἱ γενεαὶ 'the generations' (v. 17) to Jesus Christ (rather than to 'the birth of Jesus Christ'). In turn, ἡ γένεσις provides the specific point of departure for the events that are described in the immediately following verses.

(17)   … and from the deportation to the Christ, fourteen generations.

(18)   <u>Τοῦ</u>   δὲ   <u>Ἰησοῦ</u>   <u>Χριστοῦ</u>   ἡ   γένεσις   **οὕτως**   ἦν.
        of.the   DE   Jesus   Christ   the   birth   thus   3S.was

In **Gal. 3:15b**, however, the genitival constituent ἀνθρώπου, which is part of the point of departure, is preposed to bring it into temporary focus in anticipation of the switch in v. 17b to διαθήκην προκεκυρωμένην ὑπὸ τοῦ θεοῦ 'a covenant previously ratified by God'.

(15b)   ὅμως   <u>ἀνθρώπου</u>   <u>κεκυρωμένην</u>   <u>διαθήκην</u>   οὐδεὶς
        also   of.man   having.been.ratified   covenant   no-one

        ἀθετεῖ   ἢ   ἐπιδιατάσσεται.
        3S.sets.aside   or   3S.adds.to

I now look at sentences in which an *unemphatic pronominal* genitive precedes a noun. As (Turner loc. cit.) notes, such genitives are *not* necessarily in focus.[17] I am particularly concerned with Turner's set (b); viz., those that occur before the article, as in αὐτοῦ τὸν ἀστέρα 'his the star' (Matt. 2:2). Three of the principles discussed in chapter 3 may contribute, at least by analogy, to the pronominal genitive being preposed without being brought into focus:

1. default ordering principle 1, that pronominal constituents precede nominal constituents (sec. 3.1)
2. the principle of sec. 3.5 that a focal constituent whose default position is not the end of a clause or sentence is placed at the end to give it extra prominence
3. default ordering principle 3, that propositional topics precede comments about their topics (sec. 3.3).

First of all, in 51 of the sample of 55 "unemphatic" examples which Turner cites, the phrase as a whole is a core constituent which immediately follows the verb, so that the order is:

        verb - pronominal genitive - rest of the noun phrase.

In these examples, the genitives occur in the default position for pronominal constituents of the comment (sec. 3.1), so it is possible that they have been preposed by analogy with this ordering

---

[16] Turner (1963:218) says that, when two genitives modify the same noun, one will be placed on either side of the noun. However, Turnbull (1997) points out that, in Rev. 7:17, ζωῆς precedes the head noun to bring it into focus.

[17] See also Pierpont's distinction between preposed pronominal genitives that occur for "emphasis" and those that occur for "contrast/comparison" (1986:11).

principle.[18] However, pronominal genitives sometimes follow the rest of a core noun phrase (as in Matt. 9:29a below), so further reasons for such an ordering are needed.

Secondly, the pronoun may be preposed when the rest of the noun phrase is in focus. This allows the focal part of the phrase to occur at the end of the clause and thus receive extra prominence (compare the ordering principle of sec. 3.5). For example, in Mark 9:24 (except D—βοήθει μου τῇ ἀπιστίᾳ 'help my the unbelief'), μου may have been preposed to give extra prominence to τῇ ἀπιστίᾳ by placing it at the end of the clause. See also:

Matt. 17:15 (Κύριε, ἐλέησόν μου τὸν υἱόν 'Lord, pity my the son')
Luke 6:47 (καὶ ἀκούων μου τῶν λόγων 'and hearing my the words')
John 1:27 (ἵνα λύσω αὐτοῦ τὸν ἱμάντα τοῦ ὑποδήματος 'that I.untie his the thong of.the sandal')
Acts 21:11 (UBS text—δήσας ἑαυτοῦ τοὺς πόδας καὶ τὰς χεῖρας 'having.bound of.self the feet and the hands')
1 Cor. 8:12 (καὶ τύπτοντες αὐτῶν τὴν συνείδησιν ἀσθενοῦσαν 'and wounding their the conscience being.weak')
Phil. 4:14 (συγκοινωνήσαντές μου τῇ θλίψει 'having.become.partners.with my the affliction')
Col. 2:5 (βλέπων ὑμῶν τὴν τάξιν 'seeing your the order')
2 Tim. 1:4 (μεμνημένος σου τῶν δακρύων 'having.rememberance your of.the tears')
Rev. 14:18 (πέμψον σου τὸ δρέπανον τὸ ὀξὺ 'send your the sickle the sharp').

Thirdly, pronominal genitives may sometimes be preposed when the referent of the pronoun is *thematically salient* (i.e., the center of attention). While the referent of the pronoun may or may not also be the propositional topic, there is a sense in which the rest of the sentence is organized around that referent and is a comment about it. In such instances, the placement of the reference to the 'topic' before its noun head is analogous to ordering principle 3 (sec. 3.3), which states that it is normal for a propositional topic to precede the comment about the topic.

This is illustrated in **Matt. 2:2**. The question of v. 2a establishes 'king of the Jews' as the center of attention. The rest of the sentence concerns this king of the Jews and, in v. 2b, αὐτοῦ precedes τὸν ἀστέρα as a comment is made about him.[19]

(2a)   λέγοντες, Ποῦ   ἐστιν ὁ   τεχθεὶς βασιλεὺς τῶν   Ἰουδαίων;
        saying   where 3S.is the born   king   of.the Jews

(2b)   εἴδομεν γὰρ αὐτοῦ τὸν ἀστέρα ἐν   τῇ   ἀνατολῇ
        we.saw   for his   the star   in   the east

(2c)   καὶ   ἤλθομεν προσκυνῆσαι αὐτῷ.
        and   we.came to.worship   him

See also:[20]
Matt. 8:3 (καὶ εὐθέως ἐκαθαρίσθη αὐτοῦ ἡ λέπρα 'and immediately was.cleansed his the leprosy')
Matt. 9:2 and 5 (UBS text—ἀφίενταί σου αἱ ἁμαρτίαι 'are.forgiven your the sins')
Matt. 24:48 (UBS text—Χρονίζει μου ὁ κύριος 'is.lingering my the master')
Matt. 26:43 (ἦσαν γὰρ αὐτῶν οἱ ὀφθαλμοὶ βεβαρημένοι 'were for their the eyes weighed.down')
John 1:27 (cited above) and 3:33 (ὁ λαβὼν αὐτοῦ τὴν μαρτυρίαν 'the.one having.received his the testimony')
Rom. 14:16 (μὴ βλασφημείσθω οὖν ὑμῶν τὸ ἀγαθόν 'not let.be.spoken.against your the good')

---

[18] Concerning the other four examples in Turner's list (b), the pronominal genitive immediately follows the verb in John 3:19 (UBS text), too, but is separated from the rest of the noun phrase by πονηρὰ 'evil'. In Mark 5:30 (except D), the pronominal genitive occurs between the question word τίς and the verb; compare Gal. 3:1, discussed in sec. 4.2. In Matt. 8:8 and 1 Tim. 4:15, the pronominal genitive begins a preposed constituent; see discussion below.

[19] In these next examples, the rest of the phrase either does not occur at the end of the clause or appears not be in focus.

[20] I have not investigated whether Mark and Luke prepose the pronominal genitive because its referent is the center of attention.

Gal. 2:13b (ὥστε καὶ Βαρναβᾶς συναπήχθη αὐτῶν τῇ ὑποκρίσει 'so.that also Barnabas was.carried. away.with their the hypocrisy')

Tit. 1:15c (μεμίανται αὐτῶν καὶ ὁ νοῦς καὶ ἡ συνείδησις 'has.been.defiled their both the mind and the conscience'—see discussion of passage 5 in sec. 2.8).

If the referent of the pronominal genitive is *not* the center of attention, then the pronoun is not preposed. This is illustrated in **Matt. 9:29a**. The question of v. 28b concerns whether Jesus is 'able to do this', so his action of v. 29a is a comment about him. Since αὐτῶν does not refer to Jesus, it follows its head noun. In contrast, the speech of v. 29b shifts the attention to 'you'. Since αὐτῶν in v. 30a refers to these same participants, it precedes its head noun.

(28a) When he entered the house, the blind men came to him;

(28b) and Jesus said to them, "Do you believe that I am able to do this?"

(28c) They said to him, "Yes, Lord."

(29a) τότε   ἥψατο   τῶν   ὀφθαλμῶν   αὐτῶν
      then   3S.touched of.the eyes   their

(29b) saying, "According to your faith let it be done to you."

(30a) καὶ   ἠνεῴχθησαν   αὐτῶν   οἱ   ὀφθαλμοί.
      and   3P.were.opened their   the eyes

Compare also Matt. 9:25 (αὐτῆς follows its head noun because it does not refer to Jesus, who is the center of attention) with Matt. 28:9 (αὐτοῦ precedes its head noun because it refers to Jesus, who is the center of attention; in addition, τοὺς πόδας 'the feet' is in focus).

In summary, when an unemphatic pronominal genitive immediately follows the verb and precedes the rest of the phrase, it has probably not been preposed for focus. Rather, its position may enable extra prominence to fall on the rest of the phrase and/or its referent is thematically salient.[21]

When a pronominal genitive begins a *preposed* constituent, however, it has been preposed for the same reasons as a nominal genitival constituent; viz., to bring it into focus or to indicate that it is specifically the genitive that relates to a corresponding constituent of the context.

Ephesians 2:10 may provide an instance in which a pronominal genitive has been preposed for focus (Turner classifies it as "emphatic"). Αὐτοῦ is brought into focus to contrast what God has done with what 'we' have not done. (The constituent is also discontinuous—see sec. 4.4.2.)

(8) For by grace you have been saved through faith, and this is not your own doing; it is the gift of God—(9) not the result of works, so that no one may boast.

(10) **αὐτοῦ**   γάρ   ἐσμεν   ποίημα,   κτισθέντες   κ.τ.λ.
     his   for   we.are work   having.been.created

See also Matt. 8:8 (Κύριε, οὐκ εἰμὶ ἱκανὸς ἵνα **μου ὑπὸ τὴν στέγην** εἰσέλθῃς 'Lord not I.am worthy that my under the roof you.may.come); μου would appear to be preposed for focus within the focused constituent, even though Turner (loc. cit.) classifies it as "unemphatic".

Alternatively, a pronominal genitive is preposed within a preposed constituent to indicate that it is specifically the genitive that relates to a corresponding constituent of the context. In **Phil. 3:20**, for instance, ἡμῶν is preposed because there is a switch, in the first instance, from those who live as enemies of the cross (v. 18) to 'us'.

---

[21] Turner (p. 190) classifies as "emphatic" only one example in which the pronominal genitive occurs between the verb and the rest of noun phrase. This is Luke 22:53 (most MSS—αὕτη ἐστιν ὑμῶν ἡ ὥρα κ.τ.λ. 'this is your the hour'). For ὑμῶν to be unambiguously 'emphatic,' I would have expected it to precede the verb (as is the case in a few MSS).

Turner (p. 189) also states, "where the noun has an attribute the gen. pers. pronoun follows the attribute." In such instances, the attributive adjective, rather than the pronoun, is in focus. Turner cites the following examples: Matt. 27:60; 2 Cor. 4:16, 5:1; 1 Peter 1:3, 2:9, 5:10.

(18)   For many live as enemies of the cross of Christ; I have often told you of them, and now I
        tell you even with tears. (19) Their end is destruction; their god is the belly; and their
        glory is in their shame; their minds are set on earthly things.

(20a)   ἡμῶν   γὰρ   τὸ   πολίτευμα   **ἐν οὐρανοῖς**   ὑπάρχει,
        our   for   the   citizenship   in heavens   3S.exists

Other "emphatic" examples of preposed pronominal genitives cited by Turner (loc. cit.) which fit
into this category are Luke 12:30 (ὑμῶν δὲ ὁ πατὴρ οἶδεν κ.τ.λ. 'your DE the father has.known') and 1
Tim. 4:15 (ἵνα σου ἡ προκοπὴ **φανερὰ** ᾖ πᾶσιν 'so.that your the progress manifest may.be to.all').

In **1 Cor. 9:11b**, ἡμεῖς is a point of departure by renewal and the constituent which begins with
ὑμῶν is preposed for focus. This would lead us to expect that ὑμῶν has also been preposed for focus.
However, since ὑμῶν relates back to ὑμῖν in v. 11a and the focal constituent in v. 11a appears to be τὰ
πνευματικὰ, I think it more likely that ὑμῶν has been preposed to provide a second point of departure
for v. 11b.

(11a)   εἰ   ἡμεῖς   ὑμῖν   τὰ   **πνευματικὰ**   ἐσπείραμεν,
        if   we   to.you   the   spiritual.things   we.sowed

(11b)   μέγα   εἰ   ἡμεῖς   ὑμῶν   τὰ   **σαρκικὰ**   θερίσομεν;
        great   if   we   your   the   material.things   we.will.reap

I conclude, therefore, that when a pronominal genitive begins a preposed constituent, it has been
preposed for focus or to provide the specific point of departure for what follows.

Review Questions

(a) For what purposes are *nominal* genitives placed before their head noun in a noun phrase?
(b) When a core constituent that begins with an unemphatic *pronominal* genitive immediately follows a
    verb, what are three reasons for suspecting that the genitive is not in focus?

Suggested Answers

(a) Nominal genitives are placed before their head noun in a noun phrase for two purposes:
    • to bring the genitive into focus
    • within a point of departure, to indicate that it is the genitive in particular which relates to a
      corresponding constituent of the context.

(b) When a core constituent that begins with an unemphatic pronominal genitive immediately follows a
    verb, the following are three reasons for suspecting that the genitive is not in focus:

    1. The pronominal genitive may precede the rest of the noun phrase by analogy with default
       ordering principle 1 (that pronominal constituents precede nominal constituents).
    2. The pronominal genitive may have been preposed to place the rest of the noun phrase at the end
       of the clause or sentence to give it extra prominence.
    3. The pronominal genitive may have been preposed because its referent is thematically prominent,
       to allow a comment about its referent to follow.

Illustrative Sentences

(a) In **Gal. 2:17c**, why does ἁμαρτίας precede διάκονος?

(17a)   εἰ   δὲ   ζητοῦντες   δικαιωθῆναι   ἐν   Χριστῷ
        if   DE   seeking   to.be.justified   in   Christ

(17b)   εὑρέθημεν   καὶ   αὐτοὶ   ἁμαρτωλοί,
        we.were.found   +   selves   sinners

(17c)   ἆρα   Χριστὸς   ἁμαρτίας   διάκονος;
        then   Christ   of.sin   minister

(b) In **John 19:32b**, why does τοῦ πρώτου precede the verb, whereas τὰ σκέλη follows it?

> (31b) So they asked Pilate to have the legs of the crucified men broken and the bodies removed. (32a) Then the soldiers came

> (32b) καὶ   τοῦ   μὲν   πρώτου   κατέαξαν   τὰ   σκέλη
> and   of.the   first   3P.broke   the   legs

> καὶ   τοῦ   ἄλλου   τοῦ   συσταυρωθέντος   αὐτῷ·
> and   of.the   other   the   having.been.crucified.with   him

> (33a) ἐπὶ   δὲ   τὸν   Ἰησοῦν   ἐλθόντες   κ.τ.λ.
> upon   DE   the   Jesus   having.come

(c) In **1 Thess. 3:10**, why does ὑμῶν precede τὸ πρόσωπον?

> (9) How can we thank God enough for you in return for all the joy that we feel before our God because of you,

> (10) νυκτὸς   καὶ   ἡμέρας   ὑπερεκπερισσοῦ   δεόμενοι
> night   and   day   exceedingly   asking

> εἰς   τὸ   ἰδεῖν   ὑμῶν   τὸ   πρόσωπον   καὶ   καταρτίσαι
> into   the   to.see   your   the   face   and   to.supply

> τὰ   ὑστερήματα   τῆς   πίστεως   ὑμῶν;
> the   shortcomings   of.the   faith   your

Suggested Answers

(a) In Gal. 2:17c, ἁμαρτίας precedes διάκονος to bring it into focus.

(b) In John 19:32b, τοῦ πρώτου precedes the verb whereas τὰ σκέλη follows it because only the first part is in focus. Τοῦ πρώτου is brought into temporary focus in anticipation of the switch of attention to Jesus (see also μέν). Incidentally, τοῦ πρώτου καὶ τοῦ ἄλλου τοῦ συσταυρωθέντος αὐτῷ may be interpreted as a discontinuous coordinative phrase (sec. 4.4.1).

(c) In 1 Thess. 3:10, ὑμῶν precedes τὸ πρόσωπον to place τὸ πρόσωπον at the end of the clause and give it extra prominence.

Passage 5a: Matthew 5:20b (UBS text)

Why does ὑμῶν precede ἡ δικαιοσύνη?

> ἐὰν μὴ   περισσεύσῃ   ὑμῶν   ἡ   δικαιοσύνη   πλεῖον   τῶν   γραμματέων   καὶ
> unless   3S.exceeds   your   the   righteousness   beyond   the   scribes   and

> Φαρισαίων,   οὐ μὴ   εἰσέλθητε   εἰς   τὴν   βασιλείαν   τῶν   οὐρανῶν.
> Pharisees   not   you.may.enter   into   the   kingdom   of.the   heavens

Passage 5b: John 18:10

In v. 10b, why does τοῦ ἀρχιερέως precede δοῦλον? In v. 10c, why does αὐτοῦ precede τὸ ὠτάριον τὸ δεξιόν?

> (10a) Then Simon Peter, having a sword, drew it

> (10b) καὶ   ἔπαισεν   τὸν   τοῦ   ἀρχιερέως   δοῦλον
> and   3S.struck   the   of.the   high.priest   slave

> (10c) καὶ   ἀπέκοψεν   αὐτοῦ   τὸ   ὠτάριον   τὸ   δεξιόν·
> and   3S.cut.off   his   the   ear   the   right

Suggested Answers: see Appendix under 4(5).

PART II: SENTENCE CONJUNCTIONS

Part II concerns the most common "non-subordinating conjunctions" (Buth 1992:144) that are found in the New Testament, viz., ἀλλά, γάρ, δέ, καί, οὖν, τέ and, following BDF (§459), τότε, together with the absence of any conjunction ("asyndeton"). A conjunction is "a word used to connect clauses or sentences or words in the same clause" (OED), and the following chapters focus on the functions of these conjunctions when connecting sentences and groupings of sentences (paragraphs, sections, etc.).

I find two basic approaches to the way in which the functions of conjunctions in New Testament Greek are described.

One approach is to describe each conjunction in terms of the different *"senses"* in which it is employed. For example, Porter (1992:207) identifies two senses for γάρ: "The inferential sense is widespread... The explanatory sense is also found."

A second approach, which is reflected in Blakemore's 1987 book *Semantic Constraints on Relevance*, is to describe each conjunction in terms of the single *constraint* that it places on the way the sentence concerned is to be processed with reference to its context.[1] When a reader encounters a conjunction in a text, the conjunction always constrains him or her to relate what follows to the context in the *same* way. The different senses that grammarians identify are produced by the same constraint being applied in different contexts.

For example, γάρ constrains the reader to interpret the material it introduces as *strengthening* an assertion or assumption that has been presented in or implied by the immediate context. (Relevance Theory uses the term *"confirmation"*—Sperber & Wilson 1986:76, see Denniston 1954:58.) The *nature* of that strengthening, viz., explanation versus inference or cause, is deduced from the content of the material, not from the presence of γάρ.

Thus, Heckert (1996:32–36) finds γάρ used in 1 Timothy to introduce something akin to the *cause* of the previous assertion,[2] as in 4:5, and the *reason* for previous material, as in 4:8. It also introduces material that "can be said to confirm and strengthen" when "even 'reason' seems too strong a word to describe the function of the proposition introduced by γάρ, as in 1 Tim. 4:10" (p. 36). These different senses are not produced by γάρ, but by the different perceived relations between the material introduced by γάρ and the material that is to be strengthened.[3]

It might appear from the above example that the constraint one identifies for each conjunction will be nothing more than the "lowest common denominator" of the senses which grammarians have proposed. This is not so. Rather, once the constraint on processing that each conjunction imposes has been identified, it is possible to reject senses and glosses that cannot be reconciled with this constraint. Examples of unacceptable senses which are addressed in chapters 5–7 include the "adversative" sense of καί (sec. 7.3) and of οὖν (sec. 7.4), δέ translated as "for" (sec. 7.1), and τέ translated as "but" (sec. 6.3). Furthermore, whereas two conjunctions may have the same list of senses (e.g., δέ and καί—see sec. 5.1), if one expresses the function of each conjunction in terms of the constraint on processing that it imposes, this enables the difference between them immediately to be discerned.

Now for a very obvious comment! A different constraint is associated with each conjunction. This means that, where variant readings exist for conjunctions in the text of a passage, the different readings will constrain the material to be related to its context in different ways.

---

[1] See fn. 3 (p. viii) for a proviso to this assertion. Wallace (1996:510, 512) warns against the danger of "seeing an 'invariant' meaning for a feature" and failing to allow for the fact that "all languages change over time."

[2] The American Heritage Dictionary defines a *cause* as that which "must exist for an effect logically to occur" and a *reason* as that which "explains the occurrence or nature of an effect."

[3] For further discussion of γάρ, see sec. 5.4.2. See sec. 7.1 for a detailed discussion of how the adversative and connective senses associated with δέ are determined by the contexts in which δέ occurs.

69

In **Mark 13:22**, for example, both γάρ and δέ are attested. If γάρ is read, the reader is constrained to interpret v. 22 as strengthening v. 21. If δέ is read, the reader is constrained to interpret v. 22 as moving on from v. 21 to a new point (see sec. 7.1).

(21)   And then if anyone says to you, "Look! Here is the Messiah!" or "Look! There he is!"—
        do not believe it.

(22)   ἐγερθήσονται   γάρ*   ψευδόχριστοι   καὶ   ψευδοπροφῆται   κ.τ.λ.
        3P.will.be.raised.up   for   false.Christs   and   false.prophets   (*variant: δὲ)

We begin consideration of the different conjunctions by distinguishing the functions of καί and δέ in narrative material (chapter 5). This chapter also covers the functions of οὖν and asyndeton in John's Gospel, and the significance of introducing background material with γάρ, δέ, καί or asyndeton. Chapter 6 looks at two other conjunctions that are found almost exclusively in narrative material, τότε and τέ, and compares the function of the latter to that of non-conjunctive καί. Finally, chapter 7 moves on to asyndeton, καί, δέ, and οὖν in non-narrative material, and compares the function of δέ to that of ἀλλά.

In part I of this book, we were able to look at the general principles involved in determining the order of constituents in clauses and sentences, without needing to restrict the application of the principles to specific authors. That is not the case with the function of the sentence conjunctions, as the following table indicates.

The table compares the function of the most common forms of linkage found in the narrative sections of the Gospels and Acts. The symbol Ø represents asyndeton. See chapter 5 for discussion of the term "development."

	Matthew	Mark	Luke	John	Acts
default[4]	καί	καί	καί	Ø (intersententially)	καί
development	δέ	(δέ)	δέ	δέ, οὖν	δέ
other	Ø, τότε	-	-	καί	τέ, τότε

---

[4] Καί is also the default form of linkage in Revelation.

5
Καί AND Δέ IN NARRATIVE

The main purpose of this chapter is to distinguish the functions of the conjunctions that are used most frequently in the Gospels and Acts, viz., καί and δέ. I begin by defining their function in general terms for the Synoptic Gospels and Acts (sec. 5.1), then comment on differences of detail between these books, particularly Mark's Gospel (sec. 5.2). I then (sec. 5.3) turn to John's Gospel, where I look also at the functions of asyndeton and οὖν. Finally, I consider the implications of beginning background material with δέ versus γάρ, καί, and a point of departure but no conjunction (sec. 5.4).

5.1   Καί and Δέ in the Synoptic Gospels and Acts

It is possible to relate a whole episode of a narrative in New Testament Greek using a single sentence conjunction, viz., καί. Such passages are comparable to narratives in Hebrew in which the single conjunction *waw* is used. You can think of such passages as "straight narrative."

Thus, every sentence of the narrative of Luke 5:27–32 (i.e., ignoring the reported speeches that are embedded in the narrative) begins with καί (see also Mark 2:13–17).

Passage 1: Luke 5:27–32

(27a)	Καὶ	μετὰ	ταῦτα	ἐξῆλθεν	
	and	after	these.things	3S.went.out	

(27b)   καὶ   ἐθεάσατο   τελώνην   ὀνόματι Λευὶν   καθήμενον ἐπὶ   τὸ   τελώνιον,
        and   3S.saw   tax.collector   named Levi   sitting   on   the   custom.house

(27c)   καὶ   εἶπεν   αὐτῷ,   Ἀκολούθει   μοι.
        and   3S.said   to.him   follow   me

(28)   καὶ   καταλιπὼν   πάντα   ἀναστὰς   ἠκολούθει   αὐτῷ.
     and   abandoning   all   rising.up   3S.followed   him

(29a)   καὶ   ἐποίησεν   δοχὴν   μεγάλην Λευὶς   αὐτῷ   ἐν   τῇ   οἰκίᾳ αὐτοῦ,
     and   3S.made   feast   great Levi   for.him   in   the   house his

(29b)   καὶ   ἦν   ὄχλος   πολὺς   τελωνῶν   καὶ   ἄλλων
     and   3S.was   crowd   much   of.tax.collectors   and   of.others

         οἳ   ἦσαν   μετ'   αὐτῶν   κατακείμενοι.
         who   3P.were   with   him   reclining

(30)   καὶ   ἐγόγγυζον   οἱ   Φαρισαῖοι καὶ   οἱ   γραμματεῖς αὐτῶν
     and   3P.were.grumbling   the   Pharisees and   the   scribes   their

         πρὸς   τοὺς   μαθητὰς αὐτοῦ κ.τ.λ.
         to   the   disciples   his

(31-32) καὶ   ἀποκριθεὶς   ὁ   Ἰησοῦς   εἶπεν   πρὸς   αὐτούς, κ.τ.λ.
        and   answering   the Jesus   3S.said   to   them

Though Luke and Mark in particular present some passages as straight narrative, using only the default conjunction καί, all the authors have the option of linking sentences in other, more marked ways. The conjunction they most frequently use instead of καί is δέ.

Some New Testament grammarians take the position that δέ is "usually... indistinguishable from καί" (Turner 1963:331, see also Thrall 1962:51). The problem is captured nicely by a comparison of Porter's list of "senses" for the two conjunctions:

"δέ   (... Adversative or Connective or Emphatic...)"   (1992:208)
"καί   (... Connective or Adversative or Emphatic)"   (p. 211)

Thus, although conjunctive καί can generally be translated "and" (i.e., it is "connective"), there are times when it seems that "but" would be more appropriate (i.e., it would appear to be "adversative"). See, for example, the NRSV translation of Rom. 1:13, in which "but" is the rendering for καί: "... I have often intended to come to you (but thus far have been prevented)."

Conversely, although δέ can generally be translated "but" or "now," there are times when it seems that "and" would be more appropriate. See, for example, **Acts 5:10.**

(9)   Then Peter said to her (Sapphira), "How is it that you have agreed together to put the Spirit of the Lord to the test? Look, the feet of those who have buried your husband are at the door, and they will carry you out."

(10a)   ἔπεσεν   δὲ   παραχρῆμα πρὸς τοὺς πόδας αὐτοῦ
        3S.fell   DE   immediately at   the   feet his

(10b)   καὶ   ἐξέψυξεν·
        and   3S.died

Some grammarians have defined the conditions under which δέ may be used without explaining why it often does *not* occur even though the conditions are met. For instance, Winer correctly observes (1882:552), "Δέ is often used when the writer subjoins something new, different and distinct from what precedes." However, "at least a hundred times in Acts, καί introduces a sentence containing something distinctive" (Levinsohn 1987:86).

My research into the distribution of καί and δέ in Acts determined that, for δέ to be used, a factor of distinctiveness (a change of spatio-temporal setting or circumstances, a change in the underlying subject, or a change to or from background material) had to be present (op. cit. 96). However, the presence of such a factor did not guarantee that δέ would be used. In Luke 5:27-32 (passage 1 above), for instance, changes of subject occur in vv. 28, 29b, 30, and 31, while v. 29b is also background material, yet δέ is not used at all. (See further below.)

The factor that is missing in Winer's description of the function of δέ is the author's purpose in presenting his material. If δέ is to be used, not only must the sentence contain something distinctive, as defined above; it must also represent *a new step or development in the author's story or argument.* The following passages illustrate this.

First, a passage in which δέ is used whenever a sentence contains something distinctive (as defined above). Δέ occurs in Matt. 1:18-25 whenever there is a change of subject between the independent clauses of successive sentences (vv. 18, 19, 20, 22, 24a). In some of these instances, other changes can also be discerned that would warrant the use of δέ. For example, v. 18 opens the passage with a change of circumstances from the genealogy of vv. 1-17 to the events leading up to the birth of Jesus Christ, while v. 22 presents a change from an event to background material. In contrast, καί is used in vv. 24-25 when the subject (Joseph) remains the same in successive clauses.

Note: This and other passages are given in English, with only the conjunction in Greek, so that the overall development of the passage may be more readily discerned by those who do not read Greek fluently. As in part I of the book, underlining identifies points of departure, while constituents preposed for focus are in **bold.**

Passage 2: Matthew 1:18-25

(18)   <u>Of.the</u> δέ <u>Jesus Christ the birth</u> **thus** 3S.was: being.engaged the mother his Mary to.the Joseph, <u>before to.come.together they</u> 3S.was.found **in womb** having by Spirit Holy.

(19)   <u>Joseph</u> δέ <u>the husband her</u>, **righteous** being and not wishing her to.disgrace, 3S.decided **secretly** to.divorce her.

(20)   These.things δέ he having.thought, **behold angel of.Lord** in dream appeared to.him saying, "Joseph, son of.David, not be.afraid to.take Mary the wife your,..."

(22)   This δέ all 3S.happened so.that 3S.might.be.fulfilled the spoken by Lord through the prophet saying, (23) "**Behold the virgin** in womb 3S.will.have..."

(24a)   Rising.up δέ the Joseph from the sleep, 3S.did as 3S.commanded him the angel of.Lord

(24b)   καί 3S.took the wife his,

(25a)   καί not 3S.knew her until 3S.bore son;

(25b)   καί 3S.called the name his Jesus.

We now look at passages in which an analysis of δέ as a marker of distinctiveness is inadequate.

First of all, it is very common for the *initial* events of an episode to be linked with καί, even when the sentences contain distinctive information. This is because the scene needs to be set for the first step or development of the story to occur (see Levinsohn 1987:97–106 for detailed discussion of passages in Acts that illustrate this).

In Matthew's account of the temptation of Jesus, for instance, vv. 1–3 each contain distinctive information (v. 2 presents a change of circumstances and v. 3, a change of subject), yet they are linked by καί. This is because the first development of the story requires Jesus to be in the wilderness (v.1), to have become hungry (v. 2), and the devil to have become involved (v. 3).[1]

Passage 3: Matthew 4:1–4

(1)   Τότε the Jesus 3S.was.led.up into the wilderness by the Spirit to.be.tempted by the devil.

(2)   καί having.fasted days forty and nights forty, afterwards 3S.hungered.

(3)   καί having.approached the tempter 3S.said to.him, "If **son** you.are of.the God, speak so.that the stones these **bread** 3S.may.become."

(4)   He δέ answering 3S.said, "3S.has.been.written,..."

It is common also for the *final* events of an episode to be linked by καί, even when they contain distinctive information. This typically happens when the subsequent story will develop through participants or actions other than those involved in the current episode (see Levinsohn 1987:107–17 for detailed discussion of passages in Acts that illustrate this).

The closing sentence of the story of the Magi (Matt. 2:1–12) illustrates this. In vv. 1–11, δέ or τότε is used whenever the sentence concerned presents distinctive information, whereas καί links sentences with the same subject (vv. 3–4, 7–8, 10–11). In v. 12, καί is again used, even though a change of circumstances is presented in the initial participial clause. This is because the subsequent story develops, not through the Magi, but through events directly affecting Joseph, Mary and Jesus.

Passage 4: Matthew 2:10–13

(10)   Seeing δέ the star, 3P.rejoiced joy great exceeding.

(11a)   καί coming into the house, 3P.saw the child with Mary the mother his,

(11b)   καί falling.down 3P.worshiped him

(11b)   καί having.opened the treasure.bags their 3P.offered to.him gifts...

(12)   καί having.been.warned in dream not to.return to Herod, **by another way** 3P.departed to the country their.

(13)   Having.departed δέ they, **behold angel of.Lord** 3S.appears in dream to.the Joseph saying, "Rising.up take the child and the mother his and flee to Egypt..."

Then there are whole *paragraphs* in which the sentences may be linked by καί even though they contain distinctive information. This happens when the paragraph itself does not represent a new development in the story, but rather provides the setting for the next development.

---

[1] Matthew often uses τότε where Luke has δέ. Τότε may be viewed as a "marked form of δέ" (Levinsohn 1987:151). See sec. 6.1 for discussion of τότε.

Matthew 4:23–25 exemplifies this. The paragraph occurs between the calling of the first four disciples (vv. 18–22) and the "Sermon on the Mount" (5:1ff.), both of which feature δέ. The events of 4:23–25 appear to provide the setting for the sermon by explaining the presence of such large crowds, rather than themselves developing the story (see sec. 8.3 for further evidence for this analysis).

Passage 5: Matthew 4:21–5:1

(21a)   Καί having.gone.on from.there 3S.saw other two brothers, James the of.the Zebedee and John the brother his, in the boat with Zebedee the father their, repairing the nets their

(21b)   καί 3S.called them.

(22)   They δέ **immediately** leaving the boat and the father their, 3P.followed him.

(23)   Καί 3S.went.about in all the Galilee teaching in the synagogues their and preaching the good.news of.the kingdom and healing every disease and every illness among the people.

(24a)   καί 3S.went.out the report of.him into all the Syria;

(24b)   καί 3P.brought to.him all the **ill** having, **from.various diseases and from.torments** suffering [and] demon.possessed and epileptics and paralytics,

(24c)   καί 3S.healed them.

(25)   καί 3P.followed him crowds many from the Galilee and Decapolis and Jerusalem and Judea and beyond the Jordan.

(5:1)   Having.seen δέ the crowds, 3S.went.up to the mountain…

See also Luke 5:27–32 (passage 1 above), which leads to the exchange of vv. 33–39, both speeches of which are introduced with δέ. Acts 13:16–41 (Paul's sermon in Antioch) is similar, in that δέ does not occur until v. 25 (see Levinsohn 1987:103).

Matthew's Gospel has a number of passages in which only the *conclusion* is introduced with δέ. This suggests that the author's primary intent in relating the episode is to lead up to that conclusion.

In Matt. 9:1–8, for instance, δέ is used only to introduce the response of the crowds to the manifestation of Jesus' authority (preceded by a concluding speech introduced by τότε, see sec. 6.1.1). This suggests that the author has a larger purpose than the simple narration of the episode; his primary interest is rather in the response of those with whom Jesus is interacting (see also 8:27).

Passage 6: Matthew 9:1–8

(1a)   καί having.embarked into boat, 3S.crossed.over

(1b)   καί 3S.came into the own city.

(2a)   καί behold 3P.brought to.him paralytic on stretcher lying

(2b)   καί having.seen the Jesus the faith their, 3S.said to.the paralytic, "Cheer.up, child, 3P.are.forgiven your the sins."

(3)   καί **behold some of.the scribes** 3P.said among themselves, "This 3S.blasphemes."

(4)   καί having.seen the Jesus the thoughts their, 3S.said, "Why you.are.thinking evil in the hearts your?…"

(6b)   τότε 3S.says to.the paralytic, "Rising.up, take your the stretcher and go to the house your."

(7)   καί rising.up 3S.went.away to the house his.

(8a)   having.seen δέ the crowds 3P.were.afraid

(8b)   καί 3P.glorified the God the having.given authority such to.the men.

See also Matt. 9:9–13 (δέ is used only to introduce Jesus' teaching point of vv. 12–13). Luke 2:21–40 may be similar (δέ is used only in v. 40 to introduce the concluding comment about Jesus).

It is often useful to think of δέ as introducing an *event cluster* (a group of events that are linked by καί).[2] This is particularly the case when the significant event that develops the story is not the first one

---

[2] Unger (1996:408) refers to conjunctions like 'so' that connect "a cluster of utterances."

in the cluster. In **Acts 5:7**, for instance, the significant event is not that three hours passed (v. 7a), but that Ananias' wife entered in ignorance of what had happened to her husband (v. 7b).

(7a)   Ἐγένετο   δὲ   ὡς   ὡρῶν   τριῶν   διάστημα
       3S.became DE about of.hours three   interval

(7b)   καὶ ἡ   γυνὴ αὐτοῦ μὴ εἰδυῖα   τὸ   γεγονὸς   εἰσῆλθεν.
       and the wife his   not having.known the.thing having.happened 3S.entered

Now look at the use of καί and δέ in passage 7, which is followed by comments about their distribution.

Passage 7: Luke 2:1–20

(1)   3S.happened δέ <u>in the days</u> those 3S.went.out decree from Caesar Augustus to.register all the world.

(2)   Ø <u>this registration</u> first 3S.happened, governing the Syria Cyrenius.

(3)   καί 3P.were.going all to.register, each to the own city.

(4)   3S.went.up δέ also Joseph from the Galilee... (5) to.register with Mary...

(6)   3S.happened δέ <u>in the to.be</u> them <u>there</u>, 3P.were.fulfilled the days of.the to.bear her,

(7a)   καί 3S.bore the son her the firstborn,

(7b)   καί 3S.swathed him

(7c)   καί 3S.laid him in manger, because not 3S.was for.them place in the inn.

(8)   καί **shepherds** 3P.were in the region the same living.outside...

(9a)   καί **angel of.Lord** 3S.appeared to.them

(9b)   καί **glory of.Lord** 3S.shone.around them,

(9c)   καί 3P.feared fear great.

(10)   καί 3S.said to.them the angel, 'Not be.afraid... '

(13)   καί **suddenly** 3S.happened with the angel multitude of.army heavenly...

(15)   καί 3S.happened, <u>when 3P.went.away from them to the heaven the angels</u>, the shepherds 3P.were.saying to one.another...

(16a)   καί 3P.came having.hastened

(16b)   καί 3P.found the both Mary and the Joseph and the infant lying in the manger.

(17)   seeing δέ 3P.made.known about the word the spoken to.them about the child this.

(18)   καί <u>all the hearers</u> 3P.marvelled about the spoken by the shepherds to them;

(19)   <u>the</u> δέ **Mary** all 3S.was.keeping the words these pondering in the heart her.

(20)   καί 3P.returned the shepherds glorifying and praising the God...

In the above passage, the following sentences contain something distinctive, as defined earlier (changes of subject, circumstances, etc.): vv. 1, 2, 3, 4, 6, 8, 9a, 9c, 10, 13, 15, 18, 19, and 20. However, δέ is employed only five times—in vv. 1, 4, 6, 17, 19—in one of which (v. 17) no change of subject is involved. Nevertheless, when the presence of δέ is related to new developments as they affect Jesus and his parents (the principal characters of the episode), a pattern emerges.

The presence of δέ in v. 1 may be thought of as a high-level usage, indicating that the episode as a whole represents a new development in the story. See further below.

Verses 1–3 together set the scene in general for the episode, recording the decree that led to Mary and Joseph going to Bethlehem (v. 1), further identifying the registration that had been decreed (v. 2), and describing its consequences for the general population (v. 3). These sentences are linked by καί or by a form of the demonstrative οὖτος (see sec. 5.4.3). The presence of δέ in v. 4 corresponds to the shift from the scene-setting events to the first event specifically involving Joseph and Mary, i.e., to the first significant development in the episode.

The presence of δέ in v. 6 corresponds to the next distinctive event: the birth of Jesus and what Mary did with him (v. 7).

The absence of δέ throughout vv. 8–16 is noteworthy, as several sentences contain something distinctive, yet all are introduced with καί. In fact, the events concerned occur away from the scene of Jesus' birth. The implication is that, together, they set the scene for the next development of the story, which only occurs when the shepherds interact with the principal characters. This occurs in v. 17 (δέ), when they "made known what had been told them about this child."

The sentence-initial reference to Mary in v. 19 indicates a switch of attention to her from the general group of people who heard the shepherds' report (and whose reaction is introduced in v. 18 with καί). The presence of δέ indicates that Luke views Mary's act as a new development, as far as his purpose is concerned, perhaps because of the authenticity this gives to his report. In contrast, the departure of the shepherds from the scene (v. 20) is not marked as a new development, as it has no recorded impact on the principal characters.

In summary, δέ is used in Luke 2:1–20 when a distinctive event involves the principal characters in the story. Otherwise, καί is used, even if the sentence contains something distinctive.

As I noted above, the presence of δέ in Luke 2:1 may be thought of as a *high-level* usage. This observation is in line with K. Callow's observations about δέ in 1 Corinthians (1992:184), "Even a superficial reading... reveals that δέ occurs at a variety of different discourse levels. It may occur with *high-level significance*, initiating a new topic that will form a major discourse-block... It may occur with *low-level significance*, being relevant only to the clause or sentence in which it is located..."[3]

In the case of a narrative like a gospel, "high-level significance" means that, when δέ introduces an episode like Luke 2:1–20, the episode as a whole represents a new development in the larger story. In fact, every new episode of Luke 1:5–2:7 is introduced with δέ (1:8, 24, 26, 39, 56, 57, 80, 2:1, 6). In other words, each episode represents a new development of the overall storyline.

Incidentally, the series of episodes would appear to culminate with the one that describes the birth of Jesus, since no further episodes in Luke 2 are introduced with δέ. The next series of episodes that are introduced with δέ begins in 3:1 (3:1, 15, 21, 4:1), after which further episodes are introduced with καί (4:14, 16, 31). Research on the high-level distribution of δέ in the Synoptic Gospels is needed.

The claim that the information introduced by δέ represents a new step or development in the story or argument as far as the purpose of the author is concerned[4] implies that this information *builds* on what has preceded it. The significance of this implication may be seen by comparing Luke 4:1, which employs δέ, with Luke 1:67, which uses καί. In both examples, the subject is initial as a point of departure/propositional topic.

In **Luke 4:1**, the initial reference to Jesus reestablishes him as the center of attention, as the narrative resumes following the genealogy of 3:23–38. Δέ indicates that the new episode builds on and develops from the events of 3:21–22 (Jesus' baptism in the river Jordan, the coming of the Holy Spirit upon him and the voice from heaven).

(1) Ἰησοῦς δὲ πλήρης πνεύματος ἁγίου ὑπέστρεψεν ἀπὸ τοῦ Ἰορδάνου
     Jesus   DE   full   of.Spirit   holy   3S.returned from the Jordan

     καὶ ἤγετο   ἐν τῷ πνεύματι ἐν τῇ ἐρήμῳ
     and 3S.was.being.led in the Spirit   in the desert

The initial reference to Zacharias in **Luke 1:67** indicates a switch of attention to him from those who heard that he had regained his speech (vv. 65–66). The fact that δέ is not used here indicates that,

---

[3] The use of δέ with an articular pronoun in reported conversations should possibly be viewed as having significance at a third level. See below and sec. 13.1.

[4] Δέ cannot be described as an exclusively developmental conjunction, since it also introduces background material, which can be viewed as a new *step* in a narrative, but scarcely as a new development. In Levinsohn 1976, I classified the comparable Inga (Quechuan) suffix *ca* as a marker of "progression-digression." Buth's term "significant change" (1992:145) covers both new developments and background material, but does not capture the idea of an advancement in the author's purpose.

notwithstanding this switch of attention, Zacharias' prophecy does *not* develop from what has preceded. It is not in response to the events of vv. 65–66; they may even have occurred after his speech.

(65)   And fear came over all their neighbors. And, throughout the entire hill country of Judea, all these things were talked about; (66) and all who heard them laid them up in their hearts, saying, "What then will this child be?" For, indeed, the hand of the Lord was with him.

(67)   καὶ   Ζαχαρίας   ὁ   πατὴρ   αὐτοῦ   ἐπλήσθη   πνεύματος   ἁγίου
     and   Zacharias   the   father   his   3S.was.filled   of.Spirit   holy

     καὶ   ἐπροφήτευσεν   λέγων,
     and   3S.prophesied   saying

I now want to emphasize that development and points of departure are *different* parameters.

Points of departure relate to *coherence*. They enable discontinuities of situation, topic, participants and action to be presented in such a way that the overall coherence of the book is preserved. Points of departure also specify how different parts of the whole cohere at the points of discontinuity at which they occur.

Development, on the other hand, relates to the *purpose* of the story or argument. Δέ indicates when a particular event or episode represents a new development in the story or argument, in the sense that it advances the author's purpose.

In the opening sentences of the parable of the "Prodigal Son" (below), for instance, Luke 15:13 begins with a point of departure, indicating a discontinuity of time (see sec. 2.2). However, the conjunction used is καί, as vv. 11–13 *together* set the scene for the development of v. 14. There is thus a mismatch between the parameter of continuity and that of development, which is suggested by the horizontal lines in the following diagram.

Passage 8: Parameters of Coherence and Development in Luke 15:11–14

	Coherence	Development
11b	Man certain had two sons.	Man certain had two sons.
12a	and 3S.said the younger of.them to.the father, "Father, give me my share!"	καί 3S.said the younger of.them to.the father, "Father, give me my share!"
12b	and he 3S.distributed to.them the property.	καί/ὁ δὲ[5] 3S.distributed to.them the property.
13a	and after not many days having gathered everything the younger son 3S.journeyed to country far	καί after not many days having gathered everything the younger son 3S.journeyed to country far
13b	and there 3S.squandered the property his living loosely	καί there 3S.squandered the property his living loosely
14a	having.spent and he everything 3S.happened famine severe...	having.spent δέ he everything 3S.happened famine severe...

A similar mismatch is found at the beginning of the book of Acts. Δέ is usually found in Acts whenever a sentence contains distinctive information. This does not happen in 1:9–2:4, however, even though several sentences begin with temporal expressions (1:10, 13, 15, and 2:1). Although discontinuities of time are discernible at these points, the story of the "acts of the apostles" only starts to develop after Jesus has ascended to heaven and the Holy Spirit has come upon them. The presence or absence of δέ does not affect the coherence of the book of Acts, but it does add the dimension of the author's purpose.

---

[5] As I noted earlier (fn. 3), the use of δέ with an articular pronoun may be a third level at which δέ functions. If the textual variant ὁ δὲ is read in v. 12b, I would interpret δέ as a marker of development *within* the exchange of v. 12.

Review Questions

(a) What is inadequate about Winer's observation that "Δέ is often used when the writer subjoins something... distinct from what precedes"?

(b) When καί links sentences that contain something distinctive at the *beginning* of an episode, what does this indicate?

(c) When the only sentence of an episode that is introduced with δέ is the *conclusion*, what does this suggest?

(d) In narrative, what is the difference between δέ having *high-level* versus *low-level* significance?

(e) When δέ is used, what two conditions are true about the information associated with it?

(f) If a sentence begins with δέ plus a temporal expression such as τῇ ἐπαύριον 'the next day' (Matt. 27:62), what two things does this indicate?

(g) What is an event cluster, and when is the concept particularly useful?

Suggested Answers

(a) What is inadequate about Winer's observation that δέ is often used when a writer subjoins something distinctive is that it does not explain why a sentence may contain something distinctive yet be introduced with καί.

(b) When καί links sentences that contain something distinctive at the beginning of an episode, this indicates that *together* they set the scene for the first step or development of the story.

(c) When the only sentence of an episode that is introduced with δέ is the conclusion, this suggests that the author's primary intent in relating the episode is to lead up to the conclusion.

(d) When δέ occurs with *high-level* significance in narrative, it indicates that the episode concerned builds on and develops from a previous episode. When it occurs with *low-level* significance, it relates primarily to the clause or sentence in which it is located.

(e) When δέ is used, the information concerned (1) *builds* on the preceding context and (2) represents a new step or *development* of the storyline or argument, as far as the author's purpose is concerned.

(f) Preposing a temporal expression such as τῇ ἐπαύριον indicates a switch to a new temporal setting. Δέ indicates that the event(s) that take place at the new time represent a further development of the storyline.

(g) An *event cluster* is a group of events that are linked by καί and which are introduced by a development marker such as δέ. The concept is particularly useful when the significant event that furthers the author's purpose is not the first one in the cluster.

Illustrative Passage 9: Matthew 8:14–22

Note the distribution of δέ and καί in the following passage. Then answer the questions that follow it.

(14) Καί coming the Jesus into the house of.Peter, 3S.saw the mother-in-law his bedridden and fever.stricken;

(15a) καί 3S.touched the hand her,

(15b) καί 3S.left her the fever,

(15c) καί 3S.arose

(15d) καί 3S.was.serving him.

(16a) Evening δέ having.become, 3P.brought to.him demon.possessed many;

(16b) καί 3S.cast.out the spirits with.word

(16c) καί **all the illness having** 3S.healed.

(17) Ø ὅπως (thus) 3S.was.fulfilled the spoken through Isaiah the prophet saying, "He **the weaknesses our** 3S.took and **the diseases** 3S.removed."

(18) Seeing δέ the Jesus crowd around him, 3S.commanded to.go to the other.side.

(19) καί having.approached one scribe 3S.said to.him, "Teacher, I.will.follow you wherever you.may.go."

(20) καί 3S.says to.him the Jesus, "The <u>foxes</u> **holes** 3P.have and the birds of.the heaven nests, the but <u>Son</u> of.the <u>Man</u> not 3S.has where the head 3S.may.lay."

(21)   <u>Another</u> δέ <u>of.the</u> <u>disciples</u> [his] 3S.said to.him, "Lord, allow me first to.go and to.bury the father my."

(22)   <u>The</u> δέ <u>Jesus</u> says to.him, "Follow me and permit the dead to.bury the of.themselves dead."

Questions

(a) The previous episode (Matt. 8:5–13) concerns the healing of the centurion's servant. What is the significance of beginning the episode of vv. 14ff. with καί?

(b) In v. 15b-c, why is καί used, rather than δέ? And why is δέ appropriate in v. 16a?

(c) What is the significance of beginning the episode of vv. 18ff. with δέ?

(d) In vv. 19 and 20, why is καί used, rather than δέ?

Suggested Answers

(a) By beginning the episode of Matt. 8:14ff. with the default conjunction καί, Matthew avoids suggesting that the episode builds on and develops from the previous one. (Mark 1:21–28 and Luke 4:31–37 both record the healing of a demoniac in the synagogue immediately before Jesus enters Peter's house.)

(b) In v. 15b-c, καί is probably used, rather than δέ, because the purpose of relating vv. 14–16 is to show how a prophecy of Isaiah was fulfilled by Jesus' actions. The episode of vv. 14–15 then serves as the setting (and stimulus) for the evening gathering of v. 16 which is seen as specifically fulfilling the prophecy. Verse 16 thus represents a significant development, as far as the author's purpose is concerned.

(c) By beginning the episode of vv. 18ff. with δέ, it "is obviously the intention of St. Matthew to bind on the following episodes to the occurrence which he had just related" (Alford 1863.I:81). Hendriksen observes (1973:401), "the theme of suffering and self-denial clearly implied in verse 17… is underscored here in verses 18–22."

(d) In vv. 19 and 20, καί is apparently used, rather than δέ, to treat the episode of vv. 18–20 as a single event cluster on which the next exchange (vv. 21–22) builds. (I suggest in sec. 14.3 that the historical present is used in v. 20 to point forward to the exchange that follows.)

Passage 10: Luke 24:13–31 (UBS text)

Note the distribution of δέ and καί in the following passage. Then answer the questions that follow it.

(13)   καί **behold two of them** on same the day 3P.were journeying to village… to.which name Emmaus,

(14)   καί <u>they</u> 3P.were.talking to each.other about all the having.occurred these.

(15)   καί 3S.happened in the to.talk they and to.discuss,
        καί <u>self</u> Jesus drawing.near 3S.was.journeying.with them,

(16)   the δέ <u>eyes</u> their 3P.were.being.held of.the not to.recognize him.

(17a)   3S.said δέ to them, "What (are) the words these… ?"

(17b)   καί 3P.stood sad.faced.

(18)   answering δέ one named Cleopas 3S.said to him, "(Are) you only visiting Jerusalem and not you.know the having.happened in it in the days these?"

(19a)   καί 3S.said to.them, "What.things?"

(19b)   <u>they</u> δέ 3P.said to.him, "The about Jesus of.the Nazarene,…"

(25)   καί <u>he</u> 3S.said to them, "O foolish.ones… (26) Was it not necessary that the Christ should suffer…?"

(27)   καί having.begun from Moses… 3S.explained to.them in all the Scriptures the about himself.

(28a)   καί 3P.drew.near to the village to.which 3P.were.journeying,

(28b)   καί <u>he</u> 3S.pretended farther to.journey.

(29a)   καί 3P.urged him saying, "Stay with us,…"

(29b)   καί 3S.went.in of.the to.stay with them.
(30a)   καί 3S.happened in the to.recline he with them having.taken the bread 3S.blessed
(30b)   καί having.broken 3S.was.handing to.them;
(31a)   their δέ 3P.were.opened.up the eyes
(31b)   καί 3P.recognized him;
(31c)   καί he **invisible** 3S.became from them.

Questions

(a) The first *event* of the episode that is introduced with δέ is the one described in v. 17a (the significance of δέ in v. 16 is discussed in sec. 5.4.1). Why is δέ used in v. 17a and not before?

(b) Both vv. 17b and 19a involve changes of subject, which is a distinctive feature often associated with δέ. Why did Luke not use δέ in these instances?

(c) The events of vv. 25–30 are not introduced by δέ, but the events in v. 31 are. What does this tell us about the author's purpose in telling the story? (The next occurrence of δέ is in v. 36, after the two disciples have returned to Jerusalem and have learned that Jesus has appeared to Simon; v. 36 begins, "While they were speaking these things, Jesus himself stood among them.")

Suggested Answers: see Appendix under 5(10).

5.2   Notes on Δέ in Mark's Gospel

In sec. 5.1 I implied that δέ is used in Matthew, Luke and Acts in basically the same way. Matthew does use τότε in a number of places where Luke would use δέ, and δέ is used with much greater frequency in Acts than in any of the Synoptic Gospels. To some extent this may reflect the Semitic sources of the Gospels and the absence, presumably, of a developmental conjunction in these sources. However, I believe that further research will reveal a satisfactory developmental explanation for the presence and absence of δέ throughout Matthew and Luke, and that the relative absence of δέ in certain passages will be explained in terms of the high-level purposes of the respective authors.

It remains to be seen whether δέ in Mark's Gospel can be explained in developmental terms (see Levinsohn 1977b for discussion of δέ in 14:1–16:8 from a developmental perspective).

Buth (p.c.) has suggested that the *threshold* at which Mark perceives distinctiveness is much higher than in the other Synoptics and Acts. This generally means, in practice, that *adversative* overtones must be present in Mark before δέ occurs, whether this is manifested as contrast or as a switch from something different (e.g., in connection with a point of departure or from narrative events to background material).

Examples of δέ with a *point of departure* in the narrative of Mark include:[6]
- a temporal setting with contrastive overtones, as in 4:29
- other points of departure involving contrast, as in 4:34
- a reference to the new individual through whom the story will develop, as in 5:33, 36, and 15:16.

Examples of δέ with *background material*, particularly that which is significant for the further development of the story, include 1:30a and 2:6 (see also sec. 5.4.1).

Examples of sentences containing δέ that begin with a verb when there are adversative overtones include 2:20 and 6:16. Only occasionally does δέ occur in sentences with an initial verb when there are *no* adversative overtones. Examples include 7:20 and 9:25.

Mark practically never uses δέ to introduce a new *episode* (1:32 and 10:32 are rare exceptions in which καί is not a textual variant).[7] In other words, Mark seldom uses δέ to indicate that one episode develops from the previous one.

---

[6] See sec. 13.1 on responses by the addressee of the previous speech which are introduced with an articular pronoun plus δέ.

The following table shows that Mark uses καί when Luke (19:32, 33, 36, 37) and Matthew employ δέ but there are no adversative overtones. A line across the column indicates the presence of δέ to signal a new development. A broken line is used when δέ follows an articular pronoun.

Passage 11: Luke 19:28–37, (Matthew 21:1–9,) and Mark 11:1–9

	Luke 19 (and Matthew 21)		Mark 11
28	Καί having.said these, 3S.was.traveling ahead going.up to Jerusalem.		
29	Καί it.happened, as 3S.came.near to B & B to the mount the called of.Olives, 3S.sent two of.the disciples	1	Καί when they.draw.near to Jm to B & B to the mount of.the Olives, 3S.sends two of.the disciples his
30f	saying, "Go...!"	2f.	καί 3S.says to.them, "Go...!"
	(Matt 21:4 This δέ took.place that 3S.may.be.fulfilled the spoken through the prophet...)		
32	Having.departed δέ the sent.ones 3P.found as 3S.said to.them.	4a / 4b	καί 3P.left / καί 3P.found colt...
33	Untying δέ they the colt, 3P.said the masters its to them, "Why you.are.untying the colt?" *(not in Matthew)*	4c / 5	καί 3P.untie it. / καί some of.the there standing 3P.were.saying to.them, "What are.you.doing untying the colt?"
34	They δέ 3P.said that "The lord its need has" *(not in Matthew)*	6a	They δέ 3P.said to.them as told the Jesus,
		6b	καί 3P.permitted them.
35a	καί 3P.led it to the Jesus	7a	καί 3P.bring the colt to the Jesus
35b	καί having.thrown their the garments on the colt 3P.put.on the Jesus.	7b / 7c	καί 3P.lay.on it the garments their, / καί 3S.sat on it.
36	Going δέ he 3P.were.spreading.out the garments their on the road.	8a	καί many **the garments their** 3P.spread on the road,
		8b	others δέ **leafy.branches** having.cut from the fields.
37	Nearing δέ he already to the descent of.the mount of.the Olives 3P.began all the multitude of.the disciples rejoicing to.praise the God...	9	καί the leading & the following 3P.were.crying out,...

5.3   Δέ, Καί, Οὖν, and Asyndeton in John's Gospel

The ways in which καί and δέ are used in John's Gospel do not correspond exactly with how they are employed in the Synoptic Gospels and Acts. This is because two other forms of linkage are employed in John's Gospel in contexts in which καί and δέ would have occurred had the material been written in the style of the Synoptics.[8] One of them is *asyndeton* (the absence of a conjunction), which is John's default means of conjoining sentences (Poythress 1984:331), instead of καί. John's other common marker of

---

[7] Pope (p.c.) notes the following as possible instances of high-level δέ in Mark, in each of which καί is either the preferred reading or a textual variant: 1:16, 15:33 and, with a temporal or spatial point of departure, 1:14, 4:10, 7:24.

[8] Some writers have suggested that the genre of John is different from that of the Synoptics (see, for example, Robinson 1985:225, fn. 30). However, I do not think the differences in conjunction use can be explained solely in terms of genre change, notwithstanding the similarity between the function of οὖν in John's Gospel and the epistles (see sec. 5.3.3).

linkage is οὖν; he uses it as a low-level development marker in certain contexts in which the Synoptics and Acts use δέ.[9]

Buth (1992:157) captures the differences between asyndeton, δέ, καί and οὖν in John's Gospel in the following table. The minus sign means that the form is *not* marked for the feature concerned. (Buth uses the term "significant change," instead of development.)

	– close connection	+ close connection
– development	Ø	καί
+ development	δέ	οὖν

Asyndeton in John's Gospel is discussed in sec. 5.3.1 and καί in sec. 5.3.2. The functions of δέ and οὖν are compared in sec. 5.3.3.

5.3.1 Asyndeton in John's Gospel

Asyndeton, rather than καί, is the default means of conjoining sentences in John's Gospel. It is found both at points of discontinuity (with a point of departure—see Poythress 1984:334)[10] and when no discontinuity is indicated (with the verb initial).[11]

Throughout this section, illustrations are taken wherever possible from John 1:19–2:12 (below). For convenience, I have divided the passage into sections according to the occurrence of temporal points of departure.

Passage 12: John 1:19–2:12

1:19–28

(19)   καί this 3S.is the witness of.the John, when 3P.sent [to him] the Jews from Jerusalem priests and Levites that 3P.might.ask him, "You, who are.you?"

(20)   καί 3S.confessed... that "I not I.am the Christ."

(21a)   καί 3P.asked him, "What then? You Elijah are.you?"

(21b)   καί 3S.says, "Not I.am."

(21c)   Ø, "**The prophet** are you?"

(21d)   καί 3S.answered, "No!"

(22)   3P.said οὖν to.him, "Who are.you?... What do.you.say about yourself?"

(23)   Ø 3S.affirmed, "I (am) voice crying in the desert..."

(24)   καί having.been.sent.ones 3P.were of the Pharisees.

(25)   καί 3P.asked him and 3P.said to.him, "Why then do.you.baptize... ?"

(26–27) Ø 3S.answered to.them the John saying, "I baptize in water..."

(28)   Ø these **in Bethany** 3S.happened beyond the Jordan...

1:29–34

(29a)   Ø on.the next day 3S.sees the Jesus coming to him

(29b)   καί 3S.says, "Behold the Lamb of.the God..."

(32)   καί 3S.testified John saying that "I.have.seen the Spirit..."

1:35–42

(35)   Ø on.the next day again 3S.was.standing the John and of the disciples his two

(36)   καί having.looked.at the Jesus walking 3S.says, "Behold the Lamb of.the God..."

(37a)   καί 3P.heard the two disciples his speaking

---

[9] Particularly in Luke-Acts, δέ and οὖν are textual variants in a number of narrative passages. For example, see Luke 10:37b, 22:36, and Acts 15:2, 16:10, 16:11, 20:4, 25:1. See sec. 10.1 on μέν οὖν.

[10] Although Poythress views asyndeton as a default conjunction in narrative, he then details six specific circumstances in which it occurs between sentences in narrative (op. cit. 332-33).

[11] "John abounds in instances of asyndeton of the most varied and unexpected kind... especially with an initial verb" (Abbott 1906:70).

(37b)   καί 3P.followed the Jesus.
(38a)   having.turned δέ the Jesus... 3S.says to.them, "What do.you.seek?"
(38b)   they δέ 3P.said to.him, "Rabbi... where are.you.staying?"
(39a)   Ø 3S.says to.them, "Come and see!"
(39b)   οὖν* 3P.went (*variant: Ø)
(39c)   καί 3P.saw where 3S.stays
(39d)   καί with him 3P.were.remaining the day that;
(39e)   Ø hour 3S.was about tenth.
(40)   Ø 3S.was Andrew... one of the two... having.followed him;
(41a)   Ø 3S.finds this first the brother the own Simon
(41b)   καί 3S.says to.him, "We.have.found the Messiah" (which is translated Christ).
(42a)   Ø* 3S.led him to.the Jesus. (*variant: καί)
(42b)   Ø* having.looked at.him the Jesus 3S.said, "You you.are Simon..." (*variant: δέ)

1:43-51

(43a)   Ø on.the next day 3S.wanted to.go.out into the Galilee
(43b)   καί 3S.finds Philip.
(43c)   καί 3S.says to.him the Jesus, "Follow me!"
(44)   3S.was δέ the Philip from Bethsaida, of the city of.Andrew and Peter.
(45a)   Ø 3S.finds Philip the Nathanael
(45b)   καί 3S.says to.him, "Whom 3S.wrote Moses in the law... we.have.found,..."
(46a)   καί 3S.said to.him Nathanael, "Out.of Nazareth can anything good be?"
(46b)   Ø 3S.says to.him [the] Philip, "Come and see!"
(47a)   Ø 3S.saw the Jesus the Nathanael coming toward him
(47b)   καί 3S.says about him, "Behold genuine Israelite in whom **guile** not 3S.is."
(48a)   Ø 3S.says to.him Nathanael, "How me you.know?"
(48b)   Ø 3S.answered Jesus and 3S.said to.him, "Before the you Philip called, being under the fig.tree, I.saw you."
(49)   Ø 3S.answered to.him Nathanael, "Rabbi, you are the son of.the God..."
(50)   Ø 3S.answered Jesus and 3S.said to.him, "**Because I.said to.you that I.saw you under the fig.tree** do.you.believe? **Greater things** you.will.see."
(51)   καί 3S.says to.him, "Truly, truly I.say to.you, you.will.see the heaven opened..."

2:1-11

(2:1a) καί on.the day the third **wedding** 3S.happened in Cana of Galilee
(1b)   καί 3S.was the mother of.the Jesus there;
(2)   3S.was.invited δέ also the Jesus and the disciples his to the wedding.
(3)   καί lacking wine, 3S.says the mother of.the Jesus to him, "Wine not they.have."
(4)   [καί] 3S.says to.her the Jesus, "What to.me and to.you, woman?..."
(5)   Ø 3S.says the mother his to.the servants, "**Whatever he.says to.you** do!"
(6)   3S.was δέ there stone water.jars six...
(7a)   Ø 3S.says to.them the Jesus, "Fill the water.jars with.water!"
(7b)   καί 3P.filled them up.to top.
(8a)   καί 3S.says to.them, "Draw now and take to.the feast.master!"
(8b)   they δέ* 3P.carried (*variant for οἱ δέ: καί)
(9a)   When δέ 3S.tasted the feast.master the water wine having.become and not 3S.knew whence 3S.is—
(9b)   the δέ servants 3P.knew the having.drawn the water—
        3S.calls the bridegroom the feast.master
(10)   καί 3S.says to.him, "Every man first **the good wine** 3S.sets.out..."
(11a)   Ø this 3S.did beginning of.the signs the Jesus in Cana of.the Galilee
(11b)   καί 3S.manifested the glory his,
(11c)   καί 3P.believed in him the disciples his.

2:12

> (12)   Ø after <u>this</u> 3S.went.down to Capernaum he and the mother his...

In the above passage, asyndeton is found at a number of points of discontinuity. It introduces separate sections in which a different topic is developed, at 1:29a, 35, 43a and 2:12 (all involving a temporal point of departure). It also introduces the author's concluding comment about the preceding events, at 1:28 and 2:11a. (These last involve an initial demonstrative pronoun—sec. 5.4.3. See sec. 5.3.2 on καί with a temporal point of departure at 2:1a.)

When asyndeton is used in connection with a clause that begins with a verb, it is the equivalent of a default coordinative conjunction in straight narrative. Examples include conversational exchanges such as 1:47b-50, background material such as v. 39e (sec. 5.4.3), and events such as vv. 41a and 45a that follow background material. See also the events of v. 42 (if the UBS text is followed).

Note. Asyndeton is occasionally found in the narrative sections of the Synoptic Gospels and Acts. See sec. 5.4.3 for background material that begins with a demonstrative pronoun and no conjunction, and sec. 14.2 for asyndeton in connection with the reporting of conversation in Matthew's Gospel.

Asyndeton is sometimes found also when a narrative unit opens with a genitive absolute participial clause (GA) beginning with the adverb ἔτι 'yet' (see p. 94, fn. 1). An example is in Mark 5:35: Ἔτι αὐτοῦ λαλοῦντος ἔρχονται ἀπὸ τοῦ ἀρχισυναγώγου 'While he was still speaking, some people come from the leader's house'. The GA indicates that the next event takes place while the previous event was still in process; the event described following the GA introduces participants who change the direction of the story (see sec. 11.1.1).[12]

Other examples in which a narrative unit begins with a GA and ἔτι but no conjunction are found in Matt. 12:46 (variant δέ) and 17:5, Luke 8:49 and 22:47 (variant δέ), and Acts 10:44. In some of these, asyndeton may have resulted from the verse being the start of a reading in an early church lectionary. In Acts 18:1, some manuscripts begin the unit with μετὰ ταῦτα 'after these things' but no conjunction, while others insert δέ. In John's Gospel and Revelation, in contrast, it is common for narrative units to begin with μετὰ τοῦτο/ταῦτα and asyndeton. See, for example, John 2:12 (passage 12 above) and Rev. 4:1.

5.3.2   The Conjunction καί in John's Gospel

Conjunctive καί has two uses in John's Gospel:
1. to associate information together in certain specific contexts.[13]
2. to add one or more events (compare the additive function of non-conjunctive καί—sec. 6.2).

Examples of the first of these uses are found in John 1:29b and 1:41b, where καί associates information into what may be thought of as a coordinative sentence. In both examples, the event and the following speech are linked to form a single *event cluster* (sec. 5.1—see Poythress 1984:330-31).

Intersententially, as in the Synoptics and Acts (sec. 5.1), καί associates *initial* events or speeches that together set the scene for the foreground events or speeches. For instance, the individual speeches of the exchange of 1:19-21 between John and the Pharisees are associated, as together they set the scene for the key exchange of vv. 22-23 in which John states who he is, rather than who he is not. Similarly, the events of 1:35-37 are associated because together they set the scene for the more important interaction between Jesus and those who had been with John.

The other function of καί is to *add* one or more events to the preceding material.

---

[12] A conjunction may be used at the beginning of a narrative unit that begins with a GA and ἔτι. See, for example, Matt. 26:47 (with καί) and Luke 9:42, 15:20 and 24:41 (with δέ). Pope notes (p.c.), "The examples with δέ seem to operate at a lower level in the narrative."

[13] Titrud (1991:23) says, "καί informs that the following is to be closely united with the preceding." He also points out that, unlike English *and*, the items linked by καί are not necessarily distinct.

In 1:32 and 1:51, for instance, a further *speech* by the same speaker is added to a previous speech. When a speech has been reported, it is the norm for the addressee to respond, so the presence of καί may counteract this expectation.

In the case of 9:39, the episode revolving around a blind man that Jesus had healed culminates in the man's profession of faith (v. 38). Καί indicates that the *exchange* of vv. 39-41 between Jesus and the Pharisees has been added to this episode.

Passage 13: John 9:38–41

(38a)   He δέ 3S.affirmed, "I.believe, Lord."

(38b)   καί 3S.worshiped him.

(39)   καί 3S.said the Jesus, "**For judgment** I into the world this I.came, so that the not seeing 3P.may.see, and the seeing **blind** 3P.may.become."

(40a)   Ø*   3P.heard   some   of   the   Pharisees   these.things   the   with   him   being (**variants*: δέ, καί, οὖν)

(40b)   καί 3P.said to.him, "Not **also we** blind we.are?"

(41)   Ø 3S.said to.them the Jesus, "If blind you.were, not you.would.have sin. Now but you.say that we.see, the sin your 3S.remains."

In 2:1a (passage 12), καί adds a whole *episode* to the preceding material ("To the attestation through the word is now added that of the deed"—Lenski 1943:183).

5.3.3   The Conjunctions Δέ and Οὖν in John's Gospel[14]

Both δέ and οὖν are development markers, in that both are used to introduce information that represents a significant development, as far as the author's purpose is concerned. The contexts in which δέ is used in the Synoptic Gospels and Acts have been divided between the two conjunctions in John's Gospel.

Οὖν may be thought of as a marked developmental conjunction,[15] employed in specific contexts in which δέ would have been used in the Synoptics. It is used in John's Gospel in two specific contexts (see also sec. 7.4):

1. in connection with a return to the storyline[16] (i.e., as a *resumptive*), provided the event concerned represents a new development, as far as the author's purpose is concerned
2. when an *inferential* (logical) relation with the preceding event is to the fore.

Passage 14 (below) provides three examples of the *resumptive* usage of οὖν. Verse 1 returns to the storyline as it concerns Jesus (the temporal point of departure relates back to the events of 3:22) and further develops it, following a passage which mainly concerns John and in which Jesus is not an active participant (3:25–36). Following the author's comment of 4:4, verse 5 resumes and further develops this storyline, as Jesus arrives at the general location for the following events. Finally, following the background material of v. 6a, verse 6b again returns to the storyline with a further development, as Jesus seats himself at the specific location where the interaction with the woman from Samaria will take place.

---

[14] The following analysis is the result of interaction with Dr. Randall Buth during a Greek discourse teach-in held in Cameroon in November 1989.

[15] Poythress, however, considers οὖν, rather than δέ, to be "the unmarked way of continuing the narrative whenever there is a shift to a new agent" (1984: 328). The developmental nature of οὖν may be seen in his statement that its presence "assures [the reader] that [what follows] is directly related to something preceding" (p. 330); see also Reimer 1985:35.

[16] See Abbott 1906:472-74, Waltz 1976:3-4, Poythress 1984:327. See sec. 7.4 for discussion of the extent to which οὖν conveys some inferential force when used as a resumptive. In the same section I argue that οὖν marks a return to the same topic as before, whereas δέ permits a change of topic.

Passage 14: John 4:1–7

(1)   When οὖν 3S.knew Jesus/the Lord that 3P.heard the Pharisees that Jesus **more disciples** 3S.makes and 3S.baptizes than John…, (3a) 3S.left the Judaea

(3b)   καί 3S.went.away again into the Galilee.

(4)   3S.was.necessary δέ him to.pass through the Samaria.

(5)   3S.comes οὖν to city of.the Samaria called Sychar near the parcel which 3S.gave Jacob to.[the] Joseph the son his;

(6a)   3S.was δέ there well of.the Jacob.

(6b)   the οὖν Jesus having.become.weary from the journey 3S.was.sitting thus at the well;

(6c)   Ø hour 3S.was about sixth.

(7)   Ø 3S.comes woman of the Samaria to.draw water.

Notice that, although v. 6c is background material, οὖν is *not* used in v. 7. Asyndeton is preferred, as no further development in the story is perceived until after Jesus has started interacting with the woman. In other words, the next development in the story only occurs after Jesus is sitting at the well *and* the woman arrives at the same place.

The inferential use of οὖν, to introduce an event in *logical* sequence with the preceding event, is illustrated in 4:53a (below). The servants tell the father what time his son became better οὖν he realized that this was the hour when Jesus had said to him that his son would live.

Passage 15: John 4:51–53

(51)   Already δέ he going.down, the slaves his 3P.met him saying that the child his 3S.lives.

(52a)   3S.inquired οὖν the time from them in which **better** 3S.became;

(52b)   3P.said οὖν* to.him that "**Yesterday hour seventh** 3S.left him the fever." (**variant:* καί)

(53a)   3S.knew οὖν the father that [in] same the hour in which 3S.said to.him the Jesus, "The son your 3S.lives."

See also 1:39b (passage 12 of sec. 5.3.1, if the UBS text is followed): Jesus invites the disciples to come (v. 39a) οὖν they go with Jesus.[17]

The inferential use of οὖν is particularly common in the reporting of conversations (see 4:52 above). The reply to a preceding speech typically enjoys a logical relation with that speech and, when it represents a new development in the exchange, οὖν is employed in the speech margin. This is seen also in John 1:22 (passage 12): at the point that the exchange between John and the Pharisees moves from what John is not (vv. 19–21) to what he is, οὖν is employed.[18]

Δέ is used as a development marker in John's Gospel in the remaining contexts in which it is employed in the Synoptics. The following are typical contexts in which it is employed.

Δέ is used in connection with *changes of initiative*, when the story is to develop through the actions of a different participant. In 1:38a (passage 12), for instance, the storyline shifts from John's initiatives (in v. 36) to Jesus' initiative; 2:9a is similar, in that the storyline shifts from actions performed by the servants in response to Jesus' orders (vv. 7–8) to those performed by the master of the feast.

Δέ plus an articular pronoun whose referent is the addressee of the previous speech is used to introduce what, in sec. 13.1, I shall call an "*intermediate step.*" In passage 12, see 1:38b and 2:8b (UBS text) for examples.

---

[17] Many instances of inferential οὖν occur at points of action discontinuity (chap. 1), where there is a shift from the reporting of conversation to events resulting from that conversation.

[18] Reimer (1985:34) suggests that the *absence* of οὖν in connection with the miracle at Cana (2:1-11) and certain conversations (e.g., Jesus' discussion with Nicodemus in John 3:1ff.) reflects an absence of conflict or tension. However, the presence of οὖν in 4:52 (passage 15) appears to be a counterexample. It seems more likely that οὖν is absent when the conversation is not an end in itself (see chap. 15), but rather leads to non-speech events.

Δέ is often used to introduce *background material*. In passage 12, see 1:44 and 2:6, 9b for examples. See also 3:1, which is a sentence with presentational articulation used to introduce a participant to an ongoing story (secs. 2.4 and 8.1). (For further discussion of the conjunctions used to introduce background material, see sec. 5.4.)

Δέ is used also in connection with temporal *points of departure*, to mark a further development in the storyline when a logical relation with the immediate context is not to the fore. See, for example, 4:43, 7:37, and 20:1.

The concept of an *event cluster* (a group of events that is linked by καί) was introduced in sec. 5.1— a concept that is particularly useful when the significant event that furthers the author's purpose is not the first one in the cluster. In John's Gospel, both δέ and οὖν may introduce such clusters.

This is illustrated in 2:9–10 (When δέ the master tasted the water now become wine... he called the bridegroom καί said to him, "Every man serves the good wine first... but you have kept the good wine until now"). The key event in connection with the change of initiative is not the master calling the bridegroom, but his pronouncement about the wine.

John 4:28 (below) provides a similar example involving οὖν. This verse resumes the storyline as it concerns the woman from Samaria, following the reintroduction of the disciples (v. 27). The key event as far as the development of the story is concerned is not her leaving her water pot (v. 28a) but what she says to the men when she arrives in the city (v. 28c).

Passage 16: John 4:28–34

(28a)   3S.left οὖν the water pot her the woman

(28b)   καί 3S.went.away into the city

(28c)   καί 3S.says to.the men, "Come see man who 3S.said to.me all whatsoever I.did, not **this** 3S.is the Messiah?"

(30a)   Ø* 3P.came from the city (*variants:* καί, οὖν)

(30b)   καί 3P.were.coming to him.

(31)   Ø* <u>in the meantime</u> 3P.were.asking him the disciples saying, "Rabbi, eat." (*variant:* δέ)

(32)   he δέ 3S.said to.them, "<u>I</u> **food** I.have to.eat which <u>you</u> not you.know."

(33)   3P.were.saying οὖν the disciples to one.another, "not **someone** 3S.brought to.him to.eat?"

(34)   Ø 3S.says to.them the Jesus, "<u>My food</u> 3S.is that I.may.do the will of.the having.sent me and I.may.complete his the work..."

See also John 11:54, which puzzled Buth (1992:149); οὖν introduces not just the collateral event of v. 54a (what Jesus did not do), but also the actual event of v. 54b (what he did do), which is introduced with ἀλλά.

In the same way, οὖν is often used in connection with the introduction of *speech clusters*, when each individual speech is linked by asyndeton. This is illustrated in 4:33–34 (above). The new development, in logical sequence with previous events, would appear to be Jesus' response in vv. 34ff., not the disciples' speculation in v. 33. Thus, οὖν is used here to introduce the speech cluster of vv. 33ff., rather than a single speech.

Another example of a speech cluster is in 1:22 (passage 12), in which οὖν may be viewed as introducing the exchange of vv. 22–23, rather than just the speech of v. 22.

The functions of δέ, καί, οὖν and asyndeton in John' Gospel may therefore be summarized in the following expansion of the table that introduced this section.

	– close connection	+ close connection
– development	Ø (default)	καί: associative, additive
+ development	δέ	οὖν: resumptive, inferential

Review Questions

(a) What is the default means of conjoining sentences in the Synoptic Gospels? What is the default means of conjoining sentences in John's Gospel?

(b) What are the two specific functions of καί in John's Gospel?

(c) What are the two specific circumstances in which οὖν is used as a development marker in John, rather than δέ?

Suggested Answers

(a) In the Synoptic Gospels, καί is the default means of conjoining sentences. In John, asyndeton is the default means of conjoining sentences.

(b) The functions of καί are to associate information together (e.g., into event clusters) and to add one or more events to the preceding material.

(c) Οὖν is used as a development marker in connection with a return to the storyline (its resumptive usage) and when a logical relation with the previous event is to the fore (its inferential usage).

Illustrative Passage 17: John 6:1–11

Read this passage carefully to see how each sentence is linked to the context by δέ, καί, οὖν, or asyndeton. Some questions follow the passage. (See sec. 5.4.2 on γάρ.)

(1)   Ø after these.things 3S.went.away the Jesus across the sea of.the Galilee of.the Tiberias.

(2)   3S.was.following δέ* him crowd much, because 3P.were.seeing the signs which 3S.was.doing on the ailing. (*variant: καί)

(3a)   3S.went.up δέ* to the mountain Jesus (*variant: οὖν)

(3b)   καί there 3S.was.sitting with the disciples his.

(4)   3S.was δέ near the Passover, the feast of.the Jews.

(5)   having.lifted.up οὖν the eyes the Jesus and having.seen that **much crowd** 3S.is.coming to him, 3S.says to Philip, "From.where may.we.buy bread, so.that 3P.may.eat these?"

(6a)   this δέ 3S.was.saying testing him;

(6b)   he γάρ 3S.knew what 3S.was.about to.do.

(7)   Ø 3S.answered to.him [the] Philip, "**of.200 denarii** loaves not 3P.be.enough for.them that each.one **little [something]** 3S.may.take."

(8)   Ø 3S.says to.him one of the disciples his, Andrew..., (9) "3S.is lad here who 3S.has five loaves barley and two fish; but these **what** 3P.are to so.many?"

(10a)   Ø* 3S.said the Jesus, "Make the men to.recline!" (*variants: δέ, οὖν)

(10b)   3S.was δέ grass much in the place.

(10c)   3P.reclined οὖν the men the number about 5000.

(11a)   3S.took οὖν* the loaves the Jesus (*variants: δέ, καί)

(11b)   καί having.given.thanks 3S.distributed to.the reclining...

Questions

(a) What is the function of asyndeton in v. 1?

(b) What is the function of asyndeton in vv. 7 and 8?

(c) Why is οὖν used in vv. 5 and 10c? Why is it not used in v. 7?

(d) What is the function of οὖν in v. 11a, if the UBS text is followed?

(e) What is the function of δέ in v. 2, if the UBS text is followed? What relation with v. 1 is suggested if καί is read?

(f) What is the function of asyndeton in v. 10a, if the UBS text is followed? What relation with vv. 8–9 is implied if οὖν is read? And if δέ is read?

Suggested Answers

(a) Asyndeton is used in v. 1, in connection with a switch to a new temporal setting, to introduce a new episode in which a different topic is developed. There is no developmental or associative relation between the episodes of chapters 5 and 6.

(b) Asyndeton is used in vv. 7 and 8 to introduce the second and subsequent speeches of the conversation of vv. 5ff.

(c) Οὖν is used as a resumptive in vv. 5 and 10c, following the background material of vv. 4 and 10b, to introduce the next development in the story. It is not used in v. 7, following the background material of v. 6, because the story returns to the conversation that began in v. 5, rather than presenting an event or speech that John considers to be a new development in the story.

(d) Οὖν is used inferentially in v. 11a; the logical relation with v. 10b is to the fore, as the next development of the story is presented.

(e) If δέ is read in v. 2, the sentence is probably to be interpreted as background material (sec. 5.4.1). If καί is read, it would associate the material in vv. 1–2 as initial events that together set the scene for the foreground events that follow.

(f) If asyndeton is read in v. 10a, then it is used to introduce a further speech of the conversation that began in v. 5 (see answer (c)). If οὖν is read, then the speech of v. 10a represents the next development in the story and the logical relation with the speech of vv. 8–9 is to the fore, i.e., Andrew tells Jesus about the lad with the food *so* he tells the people to sit down. If δέ is read, then the speech of v. 10a again represents the next development in the story, but no logical relation with the speech of vv. 8–9 is marked.

Passage 18 continues the episode that began in passage 17.

Passage 18: John 6:12–21

Read this passage carefully to see how each sentence is linked to the context by δέ, καί, οὖν, or asyndeton. Concerning τέ in v. 18, see sec. 6.3. Concerning the articular pronoun plus δέ in v. 20, see sec. 13.1.

(12)   when δέ 3P.were.filled, 3S.says to.the disciples his, "Gather the left.over fragments, that not **anything** 3S.may.be.lost!"

(13a)   3P.gathered οὖν

(13b)   καί 3P.filled 12 baskets of.fragments from the five loaves...

(14)   the οὖν men seeing what 3S.did sign 3P.were.saying that "**This** 3S.is truly the prophet the coming into the world."

(15)   Jesus οὖν knowing that 3P.are.about to.come and to.seize him that 3P.might.make king, 3S.departed again to the mountain self alone.

(16)   when δέ **evening** 3S.became, 3P.went.down the disciples his to the sea

(17a)   καί having.embarked in boat 3P.were.going across the sea to Capernaum.

(17b)   καί **darkness** now 3S.had.become

(17c)   καί not.yet 3S.had.come to them the Jesus,

(18)   the τέ sea, of.wind great blowing, 3S.was.being.roused.

(19a)   having.rowed οὖν about furlongs 25 or 30 3P.see the Jesus walking on the sea and **near the boat** becoming,

(19b)   καί 3P.feared.

(20)   he δέ 3S.says to them, "**I am**; not be.afraid!"

(21a)   3P.were.wishing οὖν to.take him into the boat,

(21b)   καί **immediately** 3S.became the boat at the land to which 3P.were.going.

Questions

(a) Why is καί used in v. 21b?

(b) Why is καί used in v. 17a? Why is it used in vv. 17b and 17c?

(c) Why is οὖν used in v. 13a? Why is it used in vv. 14 and 15? And in v. 19a?

(d) Why is δέ used with a temporal point of departure in vv. 12 and 16, rather than asyndeton or οὖν?

Suggested Answers: see Appendix under 5(18).

5.4   Background Material

Background material in narrative typically employs a nonevent verb such as the copula; it may even have no verb. It is called background material not to imply that the information it conveys is unimportant, but because the information is off the event line, which is considered to be foreground information in narrative (Grimes 1975:55–56).

Background material is usually introduced with δέ or γάρ (with or without a point of departure), or with a point of departure but no conjunction, though καί is sometimes used. The reader is constrained to relate it to its context in a way that is consistent with the basic function of the conjunction used. Thus, δέ introduces background material that moves the story to something *distinctive* (sec. 5.4.1), whereas γάρ introduces background material that *strengthens* some aspect of what has just been presented (sec. 5.4.2). A point of departure but no conjunction typically provides further information about some *item* that has just been mentioned, and καί may be used to *add* further background material about that item (sec. 5.4.3).

5.4.1   Background Material with Δέ

When δέ introduces background material, the sentence moves the narrative to something *distinctive*, as defined in sec. 5.1. Furthermore, this distinctive information is often significant for the further development of the storyline that was being followed before the background material.

Two types of background material are commonly introduced with δέ:
- material with presentational articulation, to introduce an item to the ongoing story
- material with topic-comment articulation that begins with a point of departure, to relate the background material to the context by a switch from some other constituent.

Background material with *presentational* articulation is commonly used to introduce participants or props that will feature in the ongoing story. See, for example, Mark 2:6 (ἦσαν δέ τινες τῶν γραμματέων ἐκεῖ καθήμενοι καὶ διαλογιζόμενοι ἐν ταῖς καρδίαις αὐτῶν 'Now there were some scribes sitting there, questioning in their hearts'). Other examples include the presentation of Nicodemus (John 3:1), of the stone jars that will hold the water to be turned into wine (John 2:6—passage 12 of sec. 5.3.1), and of the well by which Jesus will sit (John 4:6a—passage 14).

(Note that background material with presentational articulation does not have to begin with δέ. For instance, no conjunction is used in Matt. 21:33b (Ἄνθρωπος ἦν οἰκοδεσπότης 'there was a landowner') because it is the opening sentence of a parable and there is no previous material from which to develop. See Luke 5:29b (passage 1 of sec. 2.7) and Luke 4:33a for instances in which background material with presentational articulation is introduced with καί; as noted in sec. 5.1, Mark and Luke tell some stories as 'straight narrative.'[19])

Although the information contained in background material introduced by δέ is usually of significance for the further development of the story, it does not have to be. Sometimes, the material appears only to supply "information such as the number of people present" (Levinsohn 1987:91). An example of this is found in Acts 19:7 (ἦσαν δέ οἱ πάντες ἄνδρες ὡσεὶ δώδεκα 'There were about twelve of them in all').

When background material with *topic-comment* articulation begins with a point of departure plus δέ, it typically relates to the context by a switch from a corresponding constituent. See, for example, Luke 24:16 (passage 10 of sec. 5.1). In **Mark 1:30a**, attention switches to a new participant with whom Jesus will interact.

---

[19] See sec. 2.7 for why Luke 4:33a begins with a spatial point of departure.

(29)   καί immediately out of.the synagogue going.forth 3P.came into the house of Simon and of.Andrew with James and John.

(30a)   the δέ mother.in.law of.Simon 3S.was.lying.down fever.stricken,

(30b)   καί immediately 3P.say to.him about her.

(31a)   καί having.approached 3S.raised her holding the hand;

Occasionally, background material begins with a form of the demonstrative pronoun *οὗτος* 'this' and the conjunction δέ. Although the referent of the demonstrative is found in the immediate context, the background material presents distinctive information that advances the author's purpose.

For example, in Matthew's Gospel, several events are followed immediately by a sentence like Τοῦτο δὲ ὅλον γέγονεν ἵνα πληρωθῇ τὸ ῥηθὲν ὑπὸ κυρίου διὰ τοῦ προφήτου ('All this took place to fulfill what had been spoken by the Lord through the prophet' Matt. 1:22—passage 2 of sec. 5.1; see also 21:4 and 26:56). The presence of δέ in these passages indicates that these fulfillments of Old Testament prophecies further develop the author's purpose in narrating the events.

Among background material with topic-comment articulation that is introduced with δέ but does not begin with a point of departure, see John 1:44 (passage 12 of sec. 5.3.1), 2:9b (οἱ διάκονοι is preposed for focus), and 4:4 (passage 14 of sec. 5.3.3).

5.4.2 Background Material with Γάρ

Background material introduced by γάρ provides explanations or expositions of the previous assertion (see Winer 1882:566–67, Robertson n.d.:1190, Harbeck 1970:12). The presence of γάρ constrains the material that it introduces to be interpreted as *strengthening* some aspect of the previous assertion, rather than as distinctive information.

In **Matt. 4:18**, for instance, the material introduced with γάρ explains why Simon and Andrew were casting a net into the sea. It strengthens the implication that they might be fishermen because they were doing so.

(18a)   As he walked by the Sea of Galilee, he saw two brothers, Simon, who is called Peter, and Andrew his brother, casting a net into the sea;

(18b)   ἦσαν   γὰρ   ἁλιεῖς.
        3P.were   for   fishermen

See also Mark 2:15b (καὶ **πολλοὶ τελῶναι καὶ ἁμαρτωλοὶ** συνανέκειντο τῷ Ἰησοῦ καὶ τοῖς μαθηταῖς αὐτοῦ· ἦσαν γὰρ πολλοὶ καὶ ἠκολούθουν αὐτῷ 'and many tax collectors and sinners 3P.were reclining with Jesus and his disciples—for there were many who were following him').

Background material introduced by γάρ is relatively uncommon in the narrative sections of the Gospels and Acts. In non-narrative, however, γάρ is used very frequently to strengthen some aspect of a previous assertion. Modern versions in English often leave γάρ untranslated and, while asyndeton may be appropriate in some contexts, in others the constraint that is placed on the interpretation of the passage by the presence of γάρ is lost.

At **Rom. 8:22**, for instance, the NIV begins a new paragraph. As a result, the English reader is likely to assume that v. 22 begins a new point when, in fact, the presence of γάρ constrains it to be interpreted as strengthening vv. 20–21. One way to avoid this problem is to use an expression like "After all" or "In this regard," which also indicates that what follows is to be interpreted as strengthening some aspect of the context.

(20)   for the creation was subjected to futility, not of its own will but by the will of the one who subjected it, in hope (21) that the creation itself will be set free from its bondage to decay and will obtain the freedom of the glory of the children of God.

(22)   οἴδαμεν   γὰρ   ὅτι   πᾶσα   ἡ   κτίσις   συστενάζει   καί
        we.know   for   that   all   the   creation   3S.groans.together and

συνωδίνει	ἄχρι	τοῦ	νῦν·
3S.travails.together	until	the	now

5.4.3 Background Material with a Point of Departure and No Conjunction

When no conjunction introduces background material, the sentence always concerns the point of departure/propositional topic with which it begins, to provide a comment about its referent. As with γάρ, such information relates back to the context though, unlike γάρ, its function is not to explain, expound or otherwise strengthen some aspect of the previous assertion.

When an author wishes to make a comment about an item that has just been mentioned, he commonly begins the comment with a form of the *demonstrative pronoun οὗτος* 'this' (see sec. 2.3 on points of departure involving renewal).

For an example, see Acts 8:26 (αὕτη ἐστὶν ἔρημος 'This is deserted'), which is preceded by the account of an angel telling Philip to go south 'on the road that goes down from Jerusalem to Gaza'. The point of departure/propositional topic αὕτη refers to the road, and the comment gives further information about it. Other examples are in Matt. 27:46 (τοῦτ' ἔστιν 'this means'), Luke 2:2 (passage 7 of sec. 5.1), Luke 2:36b (sec. 2.3), John 21:24, and Rev. 20:5b (v. 5a is also background material with a point of departure and no conjunction, though no demonstrative pronoun is used).

Καί plus a pronoun as point of departure/propositional topic may supply an *additional* comment about the same referent, as in Luke 2:37 (sec. 2.3).

In a couple of sentences in John's Gospel, ὥρα 'hour' is the point of departure/ propositional topic for background material that lacks a conjunction. See 1:39e (passage 12 of section 5.3.1) and John 4:6c (passage 14 of section 5.3.3). I suspect that this is another instance in which John prefers asyndeton when the other writers would have used a conjunction; see Mark 15:25 and Luke 23:44, which respectively use δέ and καί (with δέ as a variant).

Review Questions

(a) What difference does it make when background material begins with γάρ rather than δέ?
(b) What information is supplied by background material that begins with a point of departure but no conjunction?

Suggested Answers

(a) Background material introduced with γάρ strengthens some aspect of the previous assertion, whereas background material introduced with δέ moves the narrative to something distinctive, which is often significant for the future development of the storyline.
(b) Background material that begins with a point of departure but no conjunction supplies further information about the point of departure/propositional topic. Typically, the referent of the point of departure has been mentioned in the immediate context.

Illustrative Passages

(a) In **Acts 13:8b**, why is the background material introduced with γάρ?

(8a)	ἀνθίστατο	δὲ	αὐτοῖς	Ἐλύμας	ὁ	μάγος,
	3S.was.opposing	DE	them	Elymas	the	magician

(8b)	**οὕτως**	γὰρ	μεθερμηνεύται	τὸ	ὄνομα	αὐτοῦ,	κ.τ.λ.
	thus	for	3S.is.translated	the	name	his	

(b) In **Acts 9:10a**, why is the presentational material introduced with δέ?

(8)　　… so they led him (Saul) by the hand and brought him into Damascus. (9) For three days he was without sight, and neither ate nor drank.

(10a) Ἦν   δέ   τις   μαθητὴς ἐν Δαμασκῷ ὀνόματι Ἀνανίας,
      3S.was DE certain disciple in Damascus named Ananias

(10b) and the Lord said to him in a vision, "Ananias."

(c) **John 19:29** contains background material that begins with a point of departure but no conjunction. However, variant readings insert δέ or οὖν. Which reading(s) would the analysis of sec. 5.4 lead you to expect?

    (28)   After this, when Jesus knew that all was now finished, he said (in order to fulfill the scripture), "I am thirsty."

    (29a)   Ø* σκεῦος ἔκειτο   ὄξους   μεστόν· (*variants: δέ, οὖν)
             vessel 3S.was.set of.vinegar full

    (29b)   They put οὖν* a sponge full of the vinegar on a branch of hyssop and held it to his mouth. (*variants: δὲ, οἱ δὲ)

Suggested Answers

(a) In Acts 13:8b, the background material is introduced with γάρ because it relates back to v. 7 and justifies referring to Elymas as a magician.

(b) In Acts 9:10a, the presentational material is introduced with δέ because it introduces a new participant who will be involved in the ongoing story.

(c) Concerning John 19:29a, it is not unusual for background material in John's Gospel that begins with a point of departure to have no conjunction. However, the information about the vinegar appears to relate to what follows rather than to what precedes. Indeed, it is pertinent to the further development of the storyline. I would, therefore, have expected δέ to be present, even though the variant is weakly attested. If οὖν were read, then its domain would have to be the event cluster (sec. 5.3.3) of the whole of v. 29.[20]

Now we return to John 6 (passage 17) to look at three instances of background material that are found in vv. 1–6.

Passage 19: John 6:1–6

    (1)   Ø after these.things 3S.went.away the Jesus across the sea of.the Galilee of.the Tiberias.

    (2)   3S.was.following δέ* him crowd much, because 3P.were.seeing the signs which 3S.was.doing on the ailing. (*variant: καί)

    (3a)   3S.went.up δέ to the mountain Jesus

    (3b)   καί there 3S.was.sitting with the disciples his.

    (4)   3S.was δέ near the Passover, the feast of.the Jews.

    (5)   having.lifted.up οὖν the eyes the Jesus and having.seen that **much crowd** 3S.is.coming to him, 3S.says to Philip, "From.where may.we.buy bread, so that 3P.may.eat these?"

    (6a)   this δέ 3S.was.saying testing him;

    (6b)   he γάρ 3S.knew what 3S.was.about to.do.

Question

Why is the background material of vv. 4, 6a and 6b encoded differently?

Suggested Answer: see Appendix under 5(19).

---

[20] I am grateful to Pope (p.c.) for this observation. Σκεῦος ὄξους μεστόν is discontinuous because what is important is the vinegar, not the vessel; see sec. 4.4.2.

6
Τότε, NON-CONJUNCTIVE Καί, AND Τέ SOLITARIUM

In this chapter, I treat two conjunctions that are found predominantly in narrative material: the adverb τότε (sec. 6.1) and τέ solitarium (sec. 6.3). However, because τέ is an "additive," I devote sec. 6.2 to consideration of another additive, non-conjunctive καί (also known as adverbial καί).

6.1   Τότε

Τότε is one of a number of adverbs that, in the absence of a conjunction such as δέ or καί, may begin a sentence and themselves function as a conjunction.[1] It is often used, especially in Matthew and Acts, as "a connective particle" (BDF §459(2)), perhaps because of Semitic influence (Turner 1963:341).

First, though, some examples of τότε when it is accompanied by a conjunction: Matt. 24:21 (ἔσται γὰρ τότε θλῖψις μεγάλη 'for there will be great tribulation at that time') and Matt. 26:16 (καὶ ἀπὸ τότε ἐζήτει εὐκαιρίαν ἵνα αὐτὸν παραδῷ 'and from that time he sought an opportunity to betray him').

Often, the presence of τότε appears to highlight the fact that the event is to occur *then* and not at some previous time. See, for example, Matt. 5:24 (ἄφες ἐκεῖ τὸ δῶρόν σου ἔμπροσθεν τοῦ θυσιαστηρίου καὶ ὕπαγε πρῶτον διαλλάγηθι τῷ ἀδελφῷ σου, καὶ **τότε** ἐλθὼν πρόσφερε τὸ δῶρόν σου 'leave your gift there before the altar and go; first be reconciled to your brother, and *then* come and offer your gift'); the gift was not to be offered while 'your brother has something against you' (v. 23), but only when reconciliation has taken place.

Τότε may be used in a similar way between clauses, especially after an adverbial clause of time subordinated by ὅτε or ὅταν. **Luke 21:20** illustrates this: in reply to the disciples' question as to when the destruction of Jerusalem would take place (v. 7), Jesus first mentions events that would precede that occasion (v. 9) and then states when the destruction would actually take place.

(20)	Ὅταν	δὲ	ἴδητε	κυκλουμένην	ὑπὸ	στρατοπέδων	Ἰερουσαλήμ,
	when	DE	you.see	surrounded	by	camps	Jerusalem

	τότε	γνῶτε	ὅτι	ἤγγικεν	ἡ	ἐρήμωσις	αὐτῆς.
	then	know	that	3S.has.drawn.near	the	desolation	its

Another example of this is in Acts 28:1 (Καὶ διασωθέντες τότε ἐπέγνωμεν ὅτι **Μελίτη** ἡ νῆσος καλεῖται. 'Having escaped, *then* we found out that the island was called Melita'); earlier, they did not know the name of the island (see 27:39).

Alternatively, τότε may follow an adverbial clause to highlight the events that immediately follow (see sec. 12.1 for other instances of "redundancy" (pleonasm) to slow down the storyline immediately before a particularly significant development). For example, **Matthew 21:1** introduces an episode that France (1985:295) describes as a "climactic visit" for which "from 16:21 on Matthew has been preparing" his readers.

(1)	Καὶ	ὅτε	ἤγγισαν	εἰς	Ἰεροσόλυμα	καὶ	ἦλθον
	and	when	3P.drew.near	to	Jerusalem	and	3P.came

	εἰς	Βηθφαγὴ	εἰς	τὸ	Ὄρος	τῶν	Ἐλαιῶν,
	to	Bethphage	to	the	mount	of.the	Olives

	τότε	Ἰησοῦς	ἀπέστειλεν	δύο	μαθητὰς
	then	Jesus	3S.sent	two	disciples

---

[1] Other adverbs that may take on a conjunctive role at the beginning of a sentence include ἔτι 'yet' (see sec. 5.3.1), ὅπως 'thus' (Matt. 8:17—see passage 9 of sec. 5.1), and ὡσαύτως 'similarly' (1 Cor. 11:25—sec. 2.4).

When *no* conjunction occurs with τότε in a narrative passage, it seems most appropriate to interpret τότε itself as the conjunction, since asyndeton is so rarely found in the Synoptic Gospels and Acts (see sec. 5.3.3). However, this does not mean that τότε has lost its adverbial characteristics. For instance, in some passages it still implies "then and not at some previous time" (see the examples at the end of sec. 6.1.1).

Τότε as an adverbial conjunction may be compared to 'then' or "thereupon" (BDF loc. cit.) in English (and the equivalent of 'then' in a good many other languages), in that it occurs in narrative at "low level divisions within an episode" (Schooling 1985:18). It both signals the division and functions as a "cohesive device" (Akin 1987:83), indicating continuity of time *and of other factors* between the subsections.

What these factors are will depend on the context, as Matt. 2:16–17 (passage 1 below) illustrates. Verse 16a begins with a preposed reference to Herod that reintroduces him to the story and establishes him as the new point of departure/propositional topic. The discontinuity in the cast of participants between the events of v. 16 and those of vv. 14–15 is evident. Notwithstanding this discontinuity, τότε indicates continuity of time and of other factors between the two units. In particular, it implies that the units belong to the *same episode* and that Herod's initiative represents the next significant development of the episode.

As for the author comment of v. 17, by its very nature there is a discontinuity of action between it and the narrative events that have just been described. Notwithstanding this discontinuity, the presence of τότε indicates continuity of time and of other factors with the previous unit. In particular, it signals that the Scripture concerned was fulfilled at that time and by the events just described.[2]

Passage 1: Matthew 2:14–18

(14a) He δέ having.risen 3S.took the child and the mother his by.night

(14b) καί 3S.departed to Egypt

(15) καί 3S.was there until the death of Herod, that 3S.might.be.fulfilled the spoken by the Lord through the prophet saying, "Out of Egypt I have called my son."

(16a) τότε Herod seeing that 3S.was.mocked by the magi 3S.was.angered greatly

(16b) καί having.sent 3S.killed all the male.children the in Bethlehem...

(17) τότε 3S.was.fulfilled the thing.spoken through Jeremiah the prophet saying, (18) "A voice was heard in Ramah... Rachel weeping.for her children... because they are no more."

The cohesive function of τότε may be seen also by contrasting its usage with that of ἐν ἐκείνῳ τῷ καιρῷ 'at that time' (found in Matt. 11:25, 12:1, 14:1). As a point of departure involving renewal (sec. 2.3), this phrase typically opens an episode that, while occurring in the same general time frame as the previous episode, is not otherwise associated together. Material linked by τότε, in contrast, is closely associated together.

In both Matthew and Acts, τότε as an adverbial conjunction is used both at subsections of an ongoing story and "at a peak in a paragraph or as a concluding event" (Buth 1990:46—see the end of sec. 6.1.1). In Luke's Gospel, however, only the former usage is found, and that infrequently. Mark and John never use τότε as a sentential conjunction. The following table summarizes how each Gospel author employs τότε intersententially when no other conjunction occurs.[3]

τότε as a sentential conjunction	Matthew	Luke	Acts	Mark/John
at subsections of an ongoing story	yes	(few)	(few)	no
highlights the conclusion	yes	no	yes	no

---

[2] Greek grammarians seem to have overlooked this usage of τότε when they describe it as "consecutive" (Porter 1992:217) or introducing "a subsequent event" (BDF loc. cit.).

[3] Τότε is not used as a conjunction in the Epistles, except in the quotation from Ps. 40 cited in Heb. 10:7,9, where it translates ʾaz.

The most frequent use of τότε as an adverbial conjunction is in Matthew, so I concentrate on that Gospel in sec. 6.1.1.[4] Section 6.1.2 looks at how τότε is used in the other Gospels and Acts.

6.1.1 Τότε as an Adverbial Conjunction in Matthew's Gospel

Both of the conjunctive functions of τότε indicated in the previous table are found in Matthew's Gospel. Most commonly, τότε occurs at subsections of an ongoing story. However, it is used also to introduce conclusions that achieve the goal of one of the participants involved in the episode.

As I note above, the presence of τότε both signals divisions of an episode into subsections and provides cohesion between them by indicating continuity of time and of other factors. The event introduced by τότε is also presented as the next significant development of the episode.

In the following five paragraphs I group instances in Matthew's Gospel in which τότε provides cohesion and signals development between units. I am not suggesting that these groupings represent a significant classification. Rather, they serve as illustrations of how τότε is used to indicate that there is continuity of time and of other factors between subsections of an episode.

Most commonly, τότε provides cohesion and signals development between units that deal with the *same topic* but involve a *modified cast*—usually, participants who featured earlier in the episode. Thus, in both Matt. 2:16 (passage 1) and 13:43, participants who featured earlier in the episode are reintroduced in a point of departure as another part of the same episode is recounted.

In Matt. 13:36 (Τότε ἀφεὶς τοὺς ὄχλους ἦλθεν εἰς τὴν οἰκίαν 'Then, leaving the crowds, he went into the house'), τότε links Jesus' telling of a series of parables with the disciples' request that he interpret one of the parables. No point of departure occurs, so τότε signals the commencement of a new subsection of the overall episode. Nevertheless, there is continuity of time and of other factors between the subsections. Similarly, in Matt. 16:20, τότε links the unit in which Jesus responds to Peter's declaration that he is the Christ with his warning to all the disciples not to tell people that he is the Christ. In each case, τότε signals a division in the episode, indicates that the material so linked shares continuity of time and of other factors, and introduces the event that represents the next significant development of the episode.

Τότε also provides cohesion and signals development between sets of events that involve the *same cast* of participants. In Matt. 4:5, for instance, τότε links two exchanges between the devil and Jesus. In 26:31, τότε links successive interactions involving Jesus and the apostles. In both cases, τότε signals a division of the material into subsections. At the same time, it indicates that the units enjoy continuity of time and of other factors, and it introduces the next significant development of the episode.

In other passages, τότε provides cohesion and signals development between units in which the *same major participant* successively interacts with different participants. In Matt. 2:7, after Herod has interacted with his counselors, τότε introduces his subsequent interaction with the magi. In 11:20, after Jesus has reproached 'this generation', τότε introduces his reproach of three unbelieving cities. Similarly, in 23:1, after Jesus has interacted with the Pharisees, τότε introduces his subsequent interaction with the crowds, in which he criticizes the Pharisees. In each passage, τότε signals a division of the material into subsections, indicates that the units share a continuity of time and of other factors, and introduces the next significant development in the storyline.

Similar to these passages are those in which τότε opens a narrative unit in which a *presentational* verb introduces new participants to an existing scene. In Matt. 3:13 (Τότε παραγίνεται ὁ Ἰησοῦς 'then Jesus arrives'), Jesus is introduced to the place where John was baptizing (3:5–12). Similarly, in 19:13 (Τότε προσηνέχθησαν αὐτῷ 'then children were brought to him'), little children are introduced to the place where Jesus was teaching (19:3–12). In both instances, τότε signals a division of the material into subsections, indicates that the units share continuity of time and of other factors, and introduces the next significant development in the storyline.

---

[4] Τότε is often followed, in Matthew, by a verb in the historical present; see sec. 12.2.1.

Finally, in Matt. 2:17 and 27:9, τότε introduces a reference to a Scripture. Its presence indicates that the Scripture concerned was *fulfilled* at the time of and by the events that had just been described.

In each of the examples of τότε that have been cited so far, its presence signaled a division of an episode into subsections. However, τότε is used also to introduce the *concluding* event or speech to which an episode has been building up, even though the conclusion does not constitute a separate subsection. This may be thought of as a *marked* (rhetorical) usage of τότε, treating the conclusion as though it were a separate subsection in order to highlight it.

Typically, conclusions introduced with τότε attain the goal sought or predicted in earlier events. In Matt. 26:74, for instance, τότε opens the concluding "event complex" (sec. 5.3.3), viz., Peter's final denial and the crowing of the cock. It was these events that Jesus had earlier predicted, as v. 75 reminds the reader.

Sometimes, realization of the goal that was sought or predicted is delayed by intervening speeches or events (compare the interclausal usage of τότε that was described earlier). This is illustrated in Matt. 15:28 (passage 2); the goal that the woman had sought was first expressed in v. 22.

Passage 2: Matthew 15:21–28

    (21)   καί having.gone.out from.there the Jesus 3S.withdrew into the districts of.Tyre and of.Sidon.

    (22)   καί behold woman Canaanite from the borders those having.come.out 3S.was.crying. out saying, "Have mercy on me, Lord, son of.David; my daughter is severely demon-possessed."

    (23a)   he δέ not 3S.answered to.her word.

    (23b)   καί having.approached the disciples his 3P.were.asking him saying, "Send her away, for she keeps shouting after us."

    (24)   he δέ answering 3S.said, "I was sent only to the lost sheep of the house of Israel."

    (25)   she δέ having.come 3S.was.worshiping him saying, "Lord, help me."

    (26)   he δέ answering 3S.said, "It is not fair to take the children's food and throw it to the dogs."

    (27)   she δέ 3S.said, "Yes, Lord, yet even the dogs eat the crumbs that fall from their masters' table."

    (28a)   τότε answering the Jesus 3S.said to her, "Woman, great is your faith! Let it be done for you as you wish."

    (28b)   καί 3S.was.healed the daughter her from the hour that.

Matthew 8:26b, 9:6b, 9:29, 12:13 and 16:12 provide other examples of τότε introducing a concluding event or speech which may be interpreted as the delayed fulfillment of a goal.

6.1.2   Τότε in Mark, Luke, John, and Acts

As indicated in the table of section 6.1, τότε is not used in *Mark* as an intersentential conjunction. It occurs only following a 'when' clause and in the combination καί τότε.

Nor is τότε used as an intersentential conjunction in *John*. It occurs following time expressions and also when a conjunction such as οὖν is present.

In *Luke*, τότε is commonly found following 'when' clauses, highlighting the fact that the following event(s) occurred at the time just specified, sometimes with the additional implication 'and not at some previous time'. However, it occasionally links low-level narrative units, to indicate that the units share continuity of time and of other factors, and to introduce the next significant development in the storyline. In 24:45, for instance, τότε links two speeches by Jesus to the disciples on what the Scriptures had to say about what had happened to him (v. 44) and what was to happen as a result (vv. 46–48), perhaps with the implication, "at this time and not before" (Pope p.c.).[5]

In *Acts*, τότε is a fairly common intersentential conjunction. As in Luke, it occasionally provides a cohesive link between low-level narrative units (e.g., in 1:12 and 7:4). In the majority of instances, however, it introduces conclusions that achieve the goal of one of the participants in the previous events, as in 25:12, 27:32, and probably 15:22. In 4:8 and 26:1b, τότε introduces a key speech that may perhaps be viewed as a goal, in that it occurs in response to a question or invitation. (See Levinsohn 1987:151–53 for further discussion of τότε in Acts.)

Review Questions

(a) What are the two basic intersentential functions of τότε when used as an adverbial conjunction?

(b) Τότε and ἐν ἐκείνῳ τῷ καιρῷ 'at that time' both indicate that the units they link occur in the same general time frame. What additional information does τότε convey?

Suggested Answers

(a) When used as an intersentential conjunction, τότε most commonly signals divisions of an episode into subsections and provides cohesion between them by indicating continuity of time and of other factors. The event introduced by τότε is also presented as the next significant development of the episode. Τότε also introduces *conclusions* that fulfill the (at times delayed) goal or prediction of earlier events.

(b) Τότε indicates that the units it links belong together as part of the same episode.

Illustrative Passage 3: Luke 14:16b–24

(16b)   <u>Man certain</u> 3S.was.making supper great,

(16c)   καί 3S.invited many

(17)   καί 3S.sent the slave his at.the hour of.the supper to.say to.the invited.ones, "Come, for everything is now ready."

(18)   καί 3P.began from one all to.be.excused...

(21a)   καί having.arrived the slave 3S.reported to.the lord his these.things.

(21b)   τότε having.become.angry the house.owner 3S.said to.the slave his, "Go.out at once into the streets and lanes of.the town and bring in the poor, the crippled, the blind, and the lame."

(22)   καί 3S.said the slave, "Sir, what you ordered has been done, and there is still room."

(23)   καί 3S.said the lord to the slave, "Go.out into the roads and lanes, and compel people to come in, so that my house may be filled..."

Question

What is the function of τότε in v. 21b?

Suggested Answer

Τότε in v. 21b signals the division of the episode into subsections and indicates that the units it links enjoy continuity of time and of other factors (e.g., the goal, which remains the same even though the second unit involves a change of strategy from the first). It also introduces the next significant development in the episode. (The function of τότε is captured in English by the translation "thereupon.")

---

[5] Alternatively, τότε introduces and highlights a concluding "speech complex" (sec. 5.3.3) consisting of v. 45 καί vv. 46–49.

Passage 4: Acts 6:8–11

(8)   Stephen δέ full of.grace and of.power 3S.was.doing wonders and signs great among the people.

(9)   3P.rose.up δέ certain of.the from the synagogue of.the called of.freedmen... debating with.the Stephen,

(10)   καί not 3P.were.able to.contradict the wisdom and the spirit with.which 3S.was.speaking.

(11)   τότε 3P.secretly.instigated men saying that "We have heard him speak blasphemous words against Moses and God."

Question

What is the function of τότε in v. 11?

Suggested Answer: see Appendix under 6(4).

6.2   Non-Conjunctive Καί

All languages have some means of indicating that a sentence or proposition is to be related to its context by *addition*. English has several such devices, including "also," "too," "in addition," and "furthermore." However, additives are put to different uses in different languages. In this connection, Regina Blass has written several articles (e.g., Blass 1990) on additives in German and Sissala (a Niger-Congo language spoken in Burkina Faso and Ghana), describing how they differ from additives in English.

It is normal for additives to indicate *parallelism* between the proposition concerned and an earlier one. Thus, in the following pair of sentences, the additive (indicated by +) constrains sentence b to be interpreted in parallel with sentence a. In particular, "one" in sentence b is to be interpreted as 'a computer' because of the parallelism with sentence a.

(1)   a. Bill has a computer.
       b. + Susan has one.

However, in some languages the same additive also indicates *"(backwards) confirmation."*[6] In other words, the proposition concerned is added to confirm an earlier one. For instance (to cite Blass 1990:135), when speaker B uses an additive in the following context in Sissala, he does so to show that he is confirming what speaker A has asserted.

(2)   Speaker A: Zimpeale is a Dagaati.
       Speaker B: + he is; I know him.

The following are further instances in which some languages use the additive as a confirmation marker:

(3)   She told him to do it. + he did it.
(4)   He doesn't want to stop, + not for a little while.

English does not use the additive "also" to confirm an earlier proposition. Instead, it employs words like "indeed" and "even." Koiné Greek, in contrast, can use the same additive, non-conjunctive or "adverbial" καί (Porter 1992:211), to mark confirmation as well as parallelism. I now discuss this marker and, in sec. 6.3, contrast its function with that of τέ solitarium, another additive particle (Winer 1882:542).

Before illustrating the employment of non-conjunctive καί to indicate parallelism and confirmation, we need to be able to distinguish this use of καί from its conjunctive use, i.e., when its function is to

---

[6] Since *backwards* confirmation seems to me to be redundant, I will refer to this function of the additive simply as *confirmation*.

conjoin phrases, clauses, or sentences.[7] Titrud (op. cit. 8–9) distinguishes the two uses in clauses on the basis of their position:

> As a conjunction linking clauses, καί only occurs as the first word of a clause, never postpositionally... When καί does occur postpositionally, it is an adverb.

Titrud also points out (1991:9):

> The conjunctive καί is a coordinating conjunction; it coordinates grammatical units of equal rank... [For example, w]hen καί is found between an indicative verb and a participle..., the καί is an adverb and not a conjoiner.

In **2 Pet. 2:1** (below), καί occurs three times and each one is interpreted by Titrud's principles as an adverb. Since the first two do not begin a clause, they cannot be conjunctive. As for καί in v. 1d, Titrud (ibid.) considers it not to be a conjunction because, if it were, it would be coordinating an indicative and a participial clause.[8]

(1:21)   ... men spoke from God as they were carried along by the Holy Spirit.

(2:1a)   Ἐγένοντο   δὲ   καὶ   ψευδοπροφῆται   ἐν   τῷ   λαῷ,
         3P.became   DE   +   false.prophets   among   the   people

(1b)   ὡς   καὶ   ἐν   ὑμῖν   ἔσονται   ψευδοδιδάσκαλοι,
       as   +   among   you   3P.will.be   false.teachers

(1c)   οἵτινες   παρεισάξουσιν   αἱρέσεις   ἀπωλείας,
       who   3P.will.secretly.bring.in   opinions   of.destruction

(1d)   καὶ   τὸν   ἀγοράσαντα   αὐτοὺς   δεσπότην   ἀρνούμενοι,
       +   the   having.bought   them   master   denying

(1e)   bringing.on themselves swift destruction.

Heckert (1996:58) adds a second principle for distinguishing the conjunctive and non-conjunctive usages of καί:

> As a conjunction, καί almost invariably links contiguous constituents. If it occurs at the beginning of a clause, it is normally conjoining contiguous clauses.[9] Adverbial καί, in contrast, links noncontiguous constituents across clause or sentence boundaries... [I]t immediately precedes the constituent that it is adding to an earlier one.

This principle confirms that the first two instances of καί in 2 Pet. 2:1 are non-conjunctive. In both cases, the immediately following constituent is added to a noncontiguous constituent across a clause or sentence boundary. In v. 1a, καί immediately precedes ψευδοπροφῆται, and the constituent to which this is added is the reference in the previous sentence to the true prophets or ὑπὸ πνεύματος ἁγίου φερόμενοι ἄνθρωποι (by Spirit Holy being.borne men). Similarly, in v. 1b, καί immediately precedes ἐν ὑμῖν, and the constituent to which this is added is ἐν τῷ λαῷ, which is found in the previous clause, with ὡς intervening.

Review Question

How may non-conjunctive καί be distinguished from conjunctive καί?

---

[7] For a detailed discussion of καί as a conjunction in the Pastoral Epistles, see Heckert 1996:71-90.

[8] Most grammarians consider that, occasionally, καί is used to coordinate units of *unequal* rank. However, it is a good linguistic principle to start by assuming that the norms for interpreting καί have been followed, then see whether that assumption leads to an acceptable interpretation of the passage under consideration before proposing an interpretation based on failure to follow the norms.

[9] See Eph. 2:6a for an exception.

Suggested Answer

Non-conjunctive καί may be distinguished from conjunctive καί in the following ways:

- Conjunctive καί typically coordinates grammatical units of equal rank and, when linking clauses, only occurs as the first word of a clause, never postpositionally.
- Conjunctive καί typically links contiguous constituents, whereas non-conjunctive καί typically links noncontiguous constituents across clause or sentence boundaries.

The first two clauses of 2 Pet. 2:1 illustrate non-conjunctive καί used when the constituent that it modifies is *parallel* to the constituent to which it is added. In v. 1a, ψευδοπροφῆται is parallel to ὑπὸ πνεύματος ἁγίου φερόμενοι ἄνθρωποι. Similarly, in v. 1b, ἐν ὑμῖν is parallel to ἐν τῷ λαῷ.[10]

The following passages also illustrate non-conjunctive καί used when there is parallelism with a previous non-contiguous constituent.

In **2 Tim. 2:2b**, the constituent that immediately follows καί, ἑτέρους, is parallel to the non-contiguous constituent πιστοῖς ἀνθρώποις (reliable men) in v. 2a.

(2a)   and the things you have heard me say in the presence of many witnesses, these things entrust to reliable men

(2b)   οἵτινες   **ἱκανοὶ**   ἔσονται   **καὶ ἑτέρους**   διδάξαι.
         who   qualified   3S.will.be   +   others   to.teach

In **1 Tim. 2:5**, the constituent that immediately follows καί, μεσίτης θεοῦ καὶ ἀνθρώπων, is parallel to the non-contiguous constituent θεός.

(5)   εἷς   γὰρ   θεός,   εἷς   καὶ   μεσίτης   θεοῦ   καὶ   ἀνθρώπων,
         one   for   God   one   +   mediator of.God and   of.men

In **2 Tim. 2:12b**, the constituent that immediately follows καί, ἐκεῖνος, is parallel to the subject of the previous verb ('we').

(12b)   εἰ   ἀρνησόμεθα,   **κἀκεῖνος**   ἀρνήσεται   ἡμᾶς·
         if   we.shall.deny   +.that.one   3S.will.deny   us

As both Titrud and Heckert point out, non-conjunctive καί modifies the *immediately following* constituent (even when it is a verb—see below). As such, it differs from "also" in English, which does not have to be contiguous to the constituent it is modifying. Thus, the NIV translates 2 Tim. 2:12b, "If we disown him, he will *also* disown us."

Romans 5:7b provides an example of non-conjunctive καί used as a marker of *confirmation*. The presence of γάρ constrains v. 7b to be interpreted as strengthening v. 7a. In turn, the presence of καί confirms the possibility that one might *actually* have the courage to die for a good person, in the light of the fact that only rarely will one die for a righteous person.

(7a)   Indeed, rarely will anyone die for a righteous person;

(7b)   ὑπὲρ   γὰρ τοῦ   ἀγαθοῦ   τάχα   τις   καὶ τολμᾷ   ἀποθανεῖν·
         on.behalf.of for of.the good.(person) perhaps someone   +   3S.dares to.die

Most instances of non-conjunctive καί that are used for confirmation are traditionally called "ascensive" (Wallace 1995:670) and "arise in contexts that give rise to an interpretation of 'lowness of likelihood'" (Blass 1993:12). **1 Cor. 2:10b** illustrates this usage. The constituent that immediately follows καί, τὰ βάθη τοῦ θεοῦ, is added to the non-contiguous constituent πάντα in order to confirm that the Spirit truly examines *all* things. 'The depths of God' is judged to be the *least likely* member of the set of all things that the Spirit (or, more likely, Paul's opponents) might be able to examine.

(10b)   τὸ   γὰρ   πνεῦμα   **πάντα**   ἐραυνᾷ,   καὶ τὰ   βάθη   τοῦ   θεοῦ.
         the   for   Spirit   all.things   3S.examines   +   the   depths   of.the   God

---

[10] See below for discussion of καί in 2 Pet. 2:1d as a marker of confirmation.

In **James 2:19b**, the constituent that immediately follows καί, τὰ δαιμόνια, is added to the non-contiguous constituent σύ (you) in ironic confirmation that 'you' do well in believing that there is one God. 'The demons' are judged to be the beings that 'you' would least want to be compared with in connection with 'your' faith in God.

(19a)   You believe that there is one God. You do well!

(19b)   **καὶ τὰ δαιμόνια** πιστεύουσιν καὶ φρίσσουσιν.
         +   the demons   3P.believe   and 3P.shudder

2 Pet. 2:1d (cited above) provides a further example in which the constituent that immediately follows καί, τὸν ἀγοράσαντα αὐτοὺς δεσπότην (ἀρνούμενοι), is given as the most extreme instance of the 'destructive opinions' that the false teachers will bring in (v. 1c).

The constituent to which the constituent modified by καί is added is not always stated explicitly; it may be *contextually presupposed*. This is exemplified in **Gal. 5:12**, where the context speaks of circumcision (vv. 2–11). Paul adds to the contextually presupposed information that 'those who are troubling you' have been or had themselves circumcised the parallel act that they would be least likely to perform, viz. 'emasculate themselves'.[11]

(11)   But if I, brothers, am still preaching circumcision, why am I still being persecuted? In that case the offence of the cross has been removed.

(12)   ὄφελον καὶ ἀποκόψονται   οἱ   ἀναστατοῦντες ὑμᾶς.
        I.would +   3P.will.emasculate.selves the.ones troubling   you

In conclusion, Blass (ibid.) reminds her readers, "the implicature of 'low on the scale of likelihood' of 'even' is not part of the meaning of καί. Rather the scalar interpretation arises out of its use in context." In other words, it is when what is added in association with non-conjunctive καί is "low on the scale of likelihood" that its ascensive usage is recognized.

Review Questions

(a) To which constituent does non-conjunctive καί relate as an additive?
(b) What are the two relations with a corresponding noncontiguous constituent that may be discerned when non-conjunctive καί occurs?
(c) How does the ascensive sense of καί arise?

Suggested Answers

(a) Non-conjunctive καί relates as an additive to the constituent that immediately follows it.
(b) The relations with a corresponding noncontiguous constituent that may be discerned when non-conjunctive καί occurs are those of parallelism and confirmation.
(c) The ascensive sense of καί arises when the constituent it modifies is judged from the context to be the least likely or most extreme member of a set of possibilities.

I turn now to the *degree of prominence* that is to be associated with non-conjunctive καί, and claim that this is determined by the *position* in the clause or sentence of the constituent that it modifies (see chapters 2–3).[12]

- If the constituent modified by καί is preposed for *focus* (it *precedes* the verb), then it is indeed "intensified or emphasized" (Titrud 1992:242–43).
- If the constituent modified by καί is in its *default* position (it *follows* the verb), then it typically is given less prominence than when preposed for focus.
- If the constituent modified by καί is preposed as a *point of departure*, then it receives only such prominence as is associated with a switch from the corresponding constituent.[13]

---

[11] Lightfoot (1892:207) notes the juxtaposition of the concepts of circumcision and emasculation in Dion Cassius.

[12] In the case of *verbs* that are modified by καί, see sec. 3.5 on the placement of a verb at the end of its clause to bring it into focus (e.g. Rom. 5:7b—discussed above).

2 Pet. 2:1 (repeated below) illustrates all three of these positions. In v. 1d, καὶ τὸν ἀγοράσαντα αὐτοὺς δεσπότην precedes the verb and has been preposed for focus; this is the most common position when the ascensive sense of καί arises. In v. 1a, καί ψευδοπροφῆται follows the verb in its default position. This constituent does not warrant being preposed because the writer's interest in false prophets is only in passing, as he moves to the topic of his passage, the 'false teachers' who will be among 'you'. Finally, v. 1b has presentational articulation, with the subject ψευδοδιδάσκαλοι at the end of the sentence to bring it into focus (sec. 3.5). Καὶ ἐν ὑμῖν, in turn, is the preposed point of departure, which may well carry some thematic prominence as attention switches from the false prophets of v. 1a, but is not the primary focus of the sentence.[14]

(1a)   Ἐγένοντο   δὲ   καὶ   ψευδοπροφῆται   ἐν   τῷ   λαῷ,
       became   DE   +   false.prophets   among the people

(1b)   ὡς καὶ ἐν   ὑμῖν   ἔσονται   ψευδοδιδάσκαλοι,
       as + among you   3P.will.be false.teachers

(1c)   οἵτινες   παρεισάξουσιν   αἱρέσεις   ἀπωλείας
       who   will.secretly.bring.in opinions of.destruction

(1d)   **καὶ   τὸν   ἀγοράσαντα   αὐτοὺς   δεσπότην** ἀρνούμενοι,
       +   the   having.bought them   master   denying

James 2:19b (cited above) provides another example in which the constituent modified by καί is preposed to bring it into focus.[15] In the case of **1 Cor. 2:10b** (repeated below), although καὶ τὰ βάθη τοῦ θεοῦ follows the verb, it is in apposition to πάντα, which has been preposed for focus, so presumably receives the same degree of prominence.

(10b)   τὸ   γὰρ   πνεῦμα   **πάντα**   ἐραυνᾷ,   καὶ   τὰ   βάθη   τοῦ   θεοῦ.
        the   for   Spirit   all.things 3S.examines +   the   depths of.the God

In **Acts 21:16a**, the constituent modified by καί is in its default position after the verb. This is an entirely appropriate position for the focal constituent of the clause, as the concern of the verse is less with the disciples who 'came along with us' than with the person to whom 'we' were brought, viz., Mnason.[16]

(15)   ... We were going up to Jerusalem.

(16a)   συνῆλθον   δὲ   καὶ   τῶν   μαθητῶν   ἀπὸ   Καισαρείας   σὺν   ἡμῖν,
        3P.went.with DE   +   of.the disciples   from Caesarea   with us

(16b)   bringing us to the house of Mnason of Cyprus, an early disciple, with whom we were to lodge.

See also Eph. 6:21 (Ἵνα δὲ εἰδῆτε καὶ ὑμεῖς τὰ κατ' ἐμέ 'so that you also may know how I am').[17]

---

[13] Titrud (1992:242f) makes a stronger claim: "The adverbial καί seems to call special attention to what follows it, marking it with prominence... it appears that the primary function of the adverbial καί is to indicate that the following component(s) should be intensified or emphasized, just as a spotlight focuses our attention on something." However, he also concedes (p. 245), "In many cases, it is quite difficult to determine the degree of intensity the writer wishes to convey" by using non-conjunctive καί. This section argues that "the degree of intensity" is determined by the position of the constituent in the sentence.

[14] Among the constituents modified by καί in passages cited by Titrud (1991:4-7), the following appear to be preposed as points of departure: Matt. 18:33b, Mark 13:29, Luke 17:10 and 21:31.

[15] Titrud (1991:4-7) cites many passages in which the constituent modified by καί precedes the verb to bring it into focus. They include Matt. 5:46, Mark 4:41, John 7:47, 1 Pet. 2:21 and 3:19, 2 Pet. 1:14 and 3:16a.

[16] The order of constituents in Acts 21:16a has been determined by default principles 2 and 3, rather than 1 (secs. 3.1-3.3).

[17] I would interpret Matt. 6:10b (γενηθήτω τὸ θέλημά σου, ὡς ἐν οὐρανῷ καὶ ἐπὶ γῆς 'Thy will be done, as in heaven (so) also on earth') as having two "information units" (Halliday 1967:200), with the constituent modified by καί in its default position in the second. See also Acts 7:51.

In **Acts 9:24c**, Lenski (1934:372) treats non-conjunctive καί as ascensive, translating the clause, "were even guarding the gates." However, the constituent concerned is in its default position following the verb, and I think it more likely that the final anarthrous constituent, ἡμέρας τε καὶ νυκτος 'both day and night', is the focus of the comment. In any case, τὰς πύλας is scarcely the least likely or most extreme item that one might expect the Jews to watch in connection with their plot to kill Saul.[18] So, while τὰς πύλας does appear to be added to confirm the seriousness of the plot to kill Paul, the constituent is not given particular prominence.

(24a–b) the Jews plotted to kill him, but their plot became known to Saul.

(24c) παρετηροῦντο   δὲ καὶ τὰς πύλας ἡμέρας τε   καὶ νυκτὸς
      3P.were.watching DE +   the gates   by.day both and by.night

      ὅπως αὐτὸν ἀνέλωσιν·
      so.as him   to.destroy

Phil. 2:9 (διὸ καὶ ὁ θεὸς αὐτὸν ὑπερύψωσεν (therefore + the God him highly. exalted)) provides an instance in which the constituent modified by καί, ὁ θεός, is preposed as a point of departure, as attention switches from Jesus (the subject throughout vv. 6–8) to God. A number of commentators make observations like "The καί implies that God *on his side responds*" (Plummer 1919:47), which suggest that καί is to be interpreted as a marker of *confirmation*. In particular, God's act of highly exalting Jesus confirms what Jesus did in obedience. Alternatively, the hymn that Paul is citing draws a parallel between God highly exalting Jesus and Jesus being 'exalted' (ὑψωθῆναι—John 3:14) on the cross, which is mentioned at the end of v. 8.[19]

Finally, I look at **1 Pet. 3:5**, since this is an example about which Titrud expresses doubt as to "the degree of intensity the writer wishes to convey" (1992:245). The problem is that the constituent modified by καί may have been preposed either as a point of departure or for focus. If ἐκόσμουν ἑαυτὰς ὑποτασσόμεναι τοῖς ἰδίοις ἀνδράσιν is judged to be a comment about αἱ ἅγιαι γυναῖκες αἱ ἐλπίζουσαι εἰς θεόν, then it would function as a point of departure/propositional topic, which receives no special prominence. However, if ἐκόσμουν ἑαυτὰς ὑποτασσόμεναι τοῖς ἰδίοις ἀνδράσιν is judged to be presupposed information (the context concerns how women who are submissive to their husbands are to adorn themselves), then the constituent would be preposed for focus. This interpretation is reflected in English in a cleft sentence with two information foci (see NIV and NRSV): "It was **in this way** that <u>long ago</u> **the holy women who hoped in God** used to adorn themselves...". The focus of the first information unit is οὕτως, and the constituent modified by καί is the focus of the second, following the point of departure πότε.

(1) Likewise, wives, accept the authority of your husbands... (4)... let your adornment be the inner self with the lasting beauty of a gentle and quiet spirit, which is very precious in God's sight.

(5) οὕτως γάρ <u>ποτε</u> καὶ αἱ ἅγιαι γυναῖκες αἱ
     so   for then   +   the holy   women   the

     ἐλπίζουσαι εἰς θεὸν ἐκόσμουν ἑαυτὰς ὑποτασσόμεναι
     hoping   in   God   3P.adorned selves submitting.selves

     τοῖς ἰδίοις ἀνδράσιν,
     to.the own   husbands

In summary, then, the *presence* of non-conjunctive καί indicates that the constituent which immediately follows it is to be added to a corresponding constituent (whether explicit or contextually

---

[18] Non-conjunctive καί precedes τὰς πύλας, not παρετηροῦντο.

[19] See Greenlee 1992:118 for a summary of commentators' views as to the constituent with which this καί is connected. My discussion assumes that διὸ καί is a combination of διό and non-conjunctive καί, as seems clear in Luke 1:35 and 2 Cor. 5:9, rather than a complex conjunction. Some commentators connect καί with ὑπερύψωσεν 'exalted highly', even though it does not immediately follow καί. I consider such an analysis to be wrong!

presupposed) for parallelism or confirmation. The *position* in the clause or sentence of this constituent determines the degree of prominence to be allocated to it, whether as a point of departure, preposed to bring it into focus, or following the verb in its default position.

Review Question

How does the position in the sentence of a constituent modified by καί affect the prominence of that constituent?

Suggested Answer

The position in the sentence of a constituent modified by καί affects the prominence of that constituent as follows:
- If the constituent modified by καί is preposed for *focus* (it *precedes* the verb), then it is indeed "intensified or emphasized" (Titrud loc. cit.).
- If the constituent modified by καί is in its *default* position (it *follows* the verb), then it typically is given less prominence than when preposed for focus.
- If the constituent modified by καί is preposed as a *point of departure*, then it receives only such prominence as is associated with a switch from a corresponding constituent.

Illustrative Passage 5a: Philippians 2:23–24

(23)   <u>τοῦτον</u> μὲν οὖν ἐλπίζω πέμψαι ὡς ἂν ἀφίδω τὰ
       this.one   then   I.hope   to.send whenever I.see the

       περὶ   ἐμὲ   ἐξαυτῆς·
       concerning me   immediately

(24)   πέποιθα δὲ ἐν κυρίῳ ὅτι καὶ αὐτὸς ταχέως ἐλεύσομαι.
       I.trust   DE in Lord   that   +   self   shortly I.will.come

Question

In Phil. 2:24, in what sense is καί additive? How much prominence is given to αὐτός?

Suggested Answer

In Phil. 2:24, the presence of καί indicates parallelism with 'this one' (v. 23), i.e., Timothy (v. 19); "I also, as well as Timothy" will come (Greenlee 1992:156). Αὐτός is preposed to provide a new point of departure, with such prominence as is associated with a switch of attention from another participant. Ταχέως would then be interpreted as the focus of the comment about 'I myself'.

Illustrative Passage 5b: Philippians 2:4–5

(4)   μὴ   τὰ   ἑαυτῶν   ἕκαστος σκοποῦντες
      not   the.(things) of.selves each   looking.at

      ἀλλὰ [καὶ] τὰ   ἑτέρων   ἕκαστοι.
      but   +   the   of.others each

(5)   τοῦτο φρονεῖτε ἐν ὑμῖν   ὃ   καὶ ἐν Χριστῷ Ἰησοῦ,
      this   think   in you   which   +   in Christ   Jesus

Questions

(a) In Phil. 2:4, what difference does the presence versus the absence of καί make to the way in which the constituent it modifies relates to the context? How much prominence is given to this constituent? (See discussion above of 1 Cor. 2:10.)
(b) In Phil. 2:5, in what sense is καί additive? How much prominence is given to ἐν Χριστῷ Ἰησοῦ?

Suggested Answers

(a) In Phil. 2:4, the presence of καί marks the additive relationship between τὰ ἑτέρων and τὰ ἑαυτῶν. Without καί, it might be possible to understand the verse to be instructing its recipients to look to the interests of others *instead of* their own interests (but see sec. 7.1 on the use of ἀλλά following a negative). Since τὰ ἑαυτῶν is preposed to bring it temporarily into focus (sec. 4.3), τὰ ἑτέρων is also marked for prominence.

(b) In Phil. 2:5, καί is probably used to indicate that ἐν Χριστῷ ᾽Ιησοῦ is to be interpreted as being in *parallel* to ἐν ὑμῖν. ῝Ο καὶ ἐν Χριστῷ ᾽Ιησοῦ follows the verb in its default position, as befits the introduction of a secondary topic (the primary topic being exhortations to the Philippians—see vv. 1–5, 12ff). However, it is possible that καί is being used in a *confirmatory* sense, with the attitude of Christ Jesus being cited to strengthen the exhortation of vv. 1–4, in which case τοῦτο "refers to the generosity and humility exhorted in the preceding verses" (Greenlee 1992:103). This sense would certainly be preferred if the variant γάρ were read in v. 5.

Passage 6a: Matthew 10:29–30

(29)   Are not two sparrows sold for a penny? And not one of them will fall to the ground apart from the will of your Father.

(30)   ὑμῶν   δὲ   καὶ   αἱ   τρίχες   τῆς   κεφαλῆς   πᾶσαι   ἠριθμημέναι   εἰσίν.
         of.you DE   +   the   hairs   of.the head   all   numbered   3P.are

Passage 6b: 1 Corinthians 7:40

(40a)   She is happier if she stays as she is, in my judgment.

(40b)   δοκῶ   δὲ   κἀγὼ   πνεῦμα   θεοῦ   ἔχειν.
         I.think DE   +.I   Spirit   of.God   to.have

Questions

(a) In Matt. 10:30, why does ὑμῶν begin the sentence? (See sec. 4.5.)

(b) What is the function of καί in this verse? How much prominence is given to the constituent it modifies?

(c) In 1 Cor. 7:40b, what is the function of καί?

Suggested Answers: see Appendix under 6(6).

6.3   Τέ Solitarium

The form of τέ that I am discussing in this section occurs by itself without any subsequent corresponding καί or τέ, hence *solitarium*. It is to be distinguished from the correlative τέ, i.e., τέ used in the combinations τέ... καί and τέ... τέ and traditionally translated 'both... and,' 'not only... but also'.

Almost all of the intersentential occurrences of τέ solitarium in the New Testament are in Acts. The other instances in which it links contiguous clauses or sentences are in Matt. 28:12, Luke 24:20, John 4:42 and 6:18, Rom. 2:19 and 16:26, Eph. 3:19, Heb. 1:3 and 12:2, and Jude 6.[20] In many of these passages, δέ is a variant reading; in others, τέ is omitted. Where the apparatus in *Nestle-Aland* records a variant, the comment "(UBS text)" indicates that my comments are based on the preferred reading in the UBS 3rd. corrected edition.

We have seen that non-conjunctive καί adds *parallel* events or propositions (most often with different subjects), or propositions that *confirm* a previous proposition. Τέ solitarium, in contrast, adds distinct

---

[20] In Rom. 7:7, τέ solitarium links *non*contiguous constituents between clauses conjoined by γάρ; τὴν ἐπιθυμίαν 'the lust' is a specific instance of τὴν ἁμαρτίαν 'the sin'. As with other instances of τέ solitarium, the propositions concerned are characterized by *sameness*.

propositions that are characterized by *sameness*, in the sense that they refer to different aspects of the same event, the same occasion, or the same pragmatic unit.[21]

In **Acts 8:25**, τέ solitarium links propositions that refer to two aspects of the same *event*. The act of 'proclaiming the good news to many villages of the Samaritans' is a different aspect of the same event as 'they returned to Jerusalem', in the sense that the proclamation took place while the apostles were returning there (τέ solitarium is glossed as ADDitive).

(25a)   O̲ἱ̲   μὲν   οὖν   διαμαρτυράμενοι   καὶ   λαλήσαντες   τὸν   λόγον
        they   then   having.witnessed   and   having.spoken   the   word

        τοῦ   κυρίου   ὑπέστρεφον   εἰς   Ἱεροσόλυμα,
        of.the   Lord   3P.were.returning   to   Jerusalem

(25b)   **πολλάς**   τε   **κώμας**   **τῶν**   **Σαμαριτῶν**   εὐηγγελίζοντο.
        many   ADD   villages   of.the   Samaritans   3P.were.evangelizing

Other passages in which τέ solitarium links propositions that refer to different aspects of the same event include Acts 20:7 (Paul was lecturing to them... τέ he continued speaking [the same lecture] until midnight) and, between participial clauses, Matt. 28:12 (having met with the elders τέ having devised a plan [during that meeting]).

In **Acts 21:18** (UBS text), τέ solitarium links propositions that refer to two different aspects of the same *occasion*; the elders attended the meeting between Paul, ourselves, and James.

(18a)   τῇ̲   δὲ   ἐ̲π̲ι̲ο̲ύ̲σ̲ῃ̲   εἰσῄει   ὁ   Παῦλος   σὺν   ἡμῖν   πρὸς   Ἰάκωβον,
        on.the   DE   next.day   3S.went.in   the   Paul   with   us   to   James

(18b)   **πάντες**   τε   παρεγένοντο   οἱ   πρεσβύτεροι.
        all   ADD   3P.came   the   elders

Other passages in which τέ solitarium links propositions that refer to different aspects of the same occasion include:
Acts 1:15: Peter stood up among the believers τέ the group (among which he stood up) numbered about a hundred and twenty.
Acts 12:17 (UBS text): Peter described how the Lord had brought him out of prison τέ said (on the same occasion), "Tell this to James and the brothers."
John 4:41–42 (UBS text): Many more became believers because of Jesus' words τέ they said to the woman, "No longer do we believe just because of what you said; now we have heard for ourselves..."
Τέ links different aspects of their response to Jesus staying with them for two days.

If we apply the above conclusions to the presence of τέ solitarium in **Acts 17:14** (UBS text), the sentences concerned are to be interpreted as referring to different aspects of the same occasion. "The urgency of Paul's departure was such that Silas and Timothy had to be left behind" (Levinsohn 1987:129, see v. 15b). If the UBS text is followed, this means that the sentences are not in contrast, and 'but' is an inappropriate conjunction in English to express the relationship between them.

(14a)   **εὐθέως**   δὲ   τ̲ό̲τ̲ε̲   τὸν   **Παῦλον**   ἐξαπέστειλαν
        immediately   DE   then   the   Paul   3P.sent.away

        οἱ   ἀδελφοὶ   πορεύεσθαι   ἕως   ἐπὶ   τὴν   θάλασσαν,
        the   brothers   to.go   as.far.as   to   the   sea

(14b)   ὑπέμειναν   τε   ὅ   τε   Σιλᾶς   καὶ   ὁ   Τιμόθεος   ἐκεῖ.
        3P.remained   ADD   the   both   Silas   and   the   Timothy   there

Acts 5:41–42 illustrate the use of τέ solitarium to link sentences that belong to the same *pragmatic unit*, in the sense that it is the particular context that makes them belong together. These verses describe

---

[21] "It is additional, but in intimate relation with the preceding" (Robertson n.d.:1179)

the response of the apostles to the actions of the authorities, and may be viewed as different aspects of the same response, both being contrary to the intentions of the authorities.

(41) Οἱ   μὲν οὖν ἐπορεύοντο   χαίροντες ἀπὸ προσώπου τοῦ   συνεδρίου,
      they   then 3P.were.going   rejoicing   from presence   of.the   council

      ὅτι   κατηξιώθησαν   ὑπὲρ τοῦ ὀνόματος ἀτιμασθῆναι,
      that 3P.were.deemed.worthy for   the name   to.be.dishonored

(42) πᾶσάν τε   ἡμέραν ... οὐκ ἐπαύοντο   διδάσκοντες καὶ
      every   ADD   day   not 3P.were.ceasing teaching   and

      εὐαγγελιζόμενοι τὸν Χριστὸν Ἰησοῦν.
      preaching   the Christ   Jesus

A further example in which τέ solitarium links propositions that belong to the same pragmatic unit is found in Acts 10:33 (So I sent for you immediately τέ it was good of you to come). The context makes it clear that the reason Cornelius sent for Peter was to call him to come, so the two propositions together represent but complementary aspects of the fulfillment of the angel's command of v. 32.

Studies in a number of languages have revealed that, when an additive is used to indicate that distinct propositions belong to the same pragmatic unit, the effect is to identify the event with which the additive is associated as *being of particular significance* for the next development of the story. This is particularly evident when a coordinative conjunction has linked previous propositions.[22]

This effect may be illustrated for Greek by passages in which a proposition associated with τέ follows one or more introduced by καί. Typically, in such passages, the clause associated with τέ introduces the *specific lead-in* to the next development of the storyline. The presence of τέ, following a series of events introduced with καί, seems to increase tension (Pope p.c.) in anticipation of a significant development that will build specifically on the event associated with τέ.

This is illustrated in Acts 12:10–13 (below). Whereas the events of vv. 10–11 (Peter's escape from prison and his realization that the escape was miraculous) are linked with καί, the last part of his walk (v. 12) is introduced with τέ and presents the specific lead-in to the next development in the story (introduced, in v. 13, with δέ).

Passage 7: Acts 12:10–13

(10a) having.gone.through δέ first prison and second 3P.came on the gate the iron the leading to the city, which by.self 3S.was.opened to.them

(10b) καί having.gone.out 3P.went.along street one,

(10c) καί **immediately** 3S.departed the angel from him.

(11) καί the Peter **in self** having.become 3S.said, "Now I am sure that the Lord has sent his angel and rescued me from the hands of Herod..."

(12) having.realized τέ 3S.came on the house of.the Mary... where 3P.were many assembled and praying.

(13) having.knocked δέ he the door of.the gate, 3S.approached maidservant...

This pragmatic effect when τέ is used is found not only following a series of events introduced with καί; it may be discerned also when the event that is added, while applying to the same occasion, is otherwise *unrelated* to the one with which it is being associated. Acts 28:2a (below) illustrates this. The

---

[22] See, for example, Follingstad 1994:163-64 on the use of the additive *kìn* in the Tyap (Niger-Congo) language of Nigeria.

This pragmatic effect may be explained from the principles of Relevance Theory. When a speaker chooses to use a (marked) additive conjunction such as "also," even though an (unmarked) coordinative conjunction such as "and" would apparently have been appropriate, "he must have intended to convey special contextual effects" (Gutt 1991:103). Gutt's claim is based on the feature concerned being less common than another one. By choosing a less common or more marked form, "the communicator makes the utterance more costly to process... [and] this would entail that she intended to convey additional implicatures to compensate for the increase in processing effort" (Gutt 1991:41; see also Sperber and Wilson 1986:220).

sentence of v. 1 gives background information which is not of particular importance to the events that follow, whereas v. 2a, with its preposed constituent marking a switch of attention from 'us' to 'the natives', adds an unrelated event. It is this event that forms the specific lead-in to the development of v. 3.

Passage 8: Acts 28:1–3

(1)   καί having.been.saved τότε we.found.out that **Melita** the island 3S.is.called.

(2a)   the τέ natives 3P.were.showing not the ordinary kindness to.us,

(2b)   having.lit γάρ fire 3P.welcomed all us because.of the rain...

(3)   having.gathered δέ the Paul of.sticks certain quantity and having.placed.on on the fire, snake from the heat having.come.out 3S.fastened.on the hand his.

See also Acts 9:3 and 15:4 (discussed in Levinsohn 1987:132–33).

Because of such examples, the old Greek grammarians suggested that elements linked by τέ were not "homogeneous" (Winer 1882:542), in the sense that they were not of equal importance.[23] However, such a feature is probably not part of the *semantic* meaning of τέ (nor of "also"). Rather, the *pragmatic effect* of adding the last event of a series or of adding an event that is unrelated to the previous one, instead of merely conjoining it, is to indicate that it is of particular significance for a following significant development.[24]

Luke 24:20 (below) provides a *non-narrative* instance of τέ used to add a proposition that is of particular significance for what follows. The speech of vv. 19–24 refers in general to the things that their addressee must surely be aware of (v. 19b); τέ adds the specific event that is leading them to reexamine their expectations about Jesus (v. 21a).

Passage 9: Luke 24:18–21a (UBS text)

(18)   In answer δέ, one of them, whose name was Cleopas, said to him, "Are you the only stranger in Jerusalem who does not know the things that have taken place in these days?"

(19a)   καί 3S.said to.them, "What.things?"

(19b)   They δέ 3P.said to.him, "The.things about Jesus of.the Nazareth, who 3S.became man prophet powerful in deed and word before the God and all the people,

(20)   how τέ 3S.delivered.over him the chief.priests and the authorities our to condemnation of.death and 3P.crucified him.

(21a)   we δέ we.were.hoping that he 3S.is the about to.redeem the Israel..."

Review Questions

(a) What is the basic function of τέ solitarium? How does this differ from that of non-conjunctive καί?

(b) What pragmatic effect does τέ solitarium have, especially when it follows a series of propositions linked by καί?

Suggested Answers

(a) The basic function of τέ solitarium is to add distinct propositions that are characterized by *sameness*; they refer to the same event, the same occasion, or the same pragmatic unit. In contrast, non-conjunctive καί adds *parallel* events or propositions (most often with different subjects), or propositions that *confirm* a previous proposition.

(b) Especially when τέ solitarium follows a series of propositions linked by καί, it has the effect of increasing tension by marking the specific lead-in to a following significant development.

---

[23] In fact, Winer states that, usually, the second element is of *less* importance!

[24] In Luke 14:26 (UBS text), τέ adds the final and most significant object that a potential disciple is to 'hate'. Non-conjunctive καί is also used, since the referent (τὴν ψυχὴν ἑαυτοῦ 'his own life') is the least likely thing that one might be expected to hate.

Illustrative Passage 10: John 6:16–19a

(16)   When δέ evening 3S.became, 3P.went.down the disciples his to the sea

(17a)   καί having.embarked in boat 3P.were.going across the sea to Capernaum

(17b)   καί **darkness** already 3S.had.come

(17c)   καί not.yet 3S.had.come to them the Jesus,

(18)   the τέ sea, (with) **wind strong** blowing, 3S.was.becoming.roused.

(19a)   Having.rowed οὖν about furlongs 25 or 30, 3P.see the Jesus walking on the sea and **near the boat** becoming

Question

What does the function of τέ in v. 18 appear to be?

Suggested Answer

Τέ in v. 18 appears to add to the set of circumstances listed in v. 17 a circumstance applying to the same occasion that was of particular significance ('On top of that...'). This circumstance may be thought of as the specific lead-in to the significant development of v. 19 (introduced with οὖν); in Mark's account (6:48), it was this circumstance that led to Jesus' decision to approach them.

Illustrative Passage 11: Acts 21:27–32

In the following passage, τέ occurs in v. 30a and in v. 31 (UBS text).

(27a)   When δέ 3P.were.about the seven days to.be.completed, the from the Asia Jews having.seen him (Paul) in the temple, 3P.were.stirring.up all the crowd

(27b)   καί 3P.laid.on on him the hands, (28) shouting, "Men of Israel, help us! This is the man who teaches all men everywhere against our people and this place. And besides, he has brought Greeks into the temple area and defiled this holy place."

(29)   3P.were γάρ having.previously.seen Trophimus the Ephesian in the city with him, whom 3P.were.supposing that **into the temple** 3S.brought the Paul.

(30a)   3S.was.aroused τέ the city whole

(30b)   καί 3S.became running.together of.the people,

(30c)   καί having.seized the Paul, 3P.were.dragging him outside of.the temple

(30d)   καί **immediately** 3P.were.shut the gates.

(31)   3P.seeking τέ* him to.kill, 3S.came.up report to.the commander of.the troops that **all** 3S.is.in.confusion Jerusalem (*variant: δέ*)

(32a)   who **at.once** having.taken soldiers and officers, 3S.ran.down to them.

(32b)   They δέ having.seen the commander and the soldiers, 3P.stopped beating the Paul.

Questions

(a) What does the use of τέ in v. 30a indicate?

(b) What is the effect of using τέ in v. 31?

(c) What is the effect on the development of the story of reading δέ in v. 31?

Suggested Answers

(a) The use of τέ in v. 30a indicates that the arousing of the whole city was another aspect of the same event as the stirring up of the crowd by the Asian Jews (v. 27a). In other words, their being aroused is presented as the flip side of the stirring up, rather than as a new development.

(b) The effect of using τέ in v. 31, following the series of propositions linked with καί, is to identify the event as of particular significance. It, together with the 'continuative' relative clause of v. 32a (see sec. 11.2), is the specific lead-in to the next development in the story, viz., their ceasing to beat Paul (v. 32b). (Pope (p.c.) suggests that, "when you get two τέ's in a row... there is even more tension built up.")

(c) With τέ in both v. 30a and v. 31, the effect is to organize the story around Paul as patient. One step in the development of the episode involves him being seized, dragged out of the temple, and beaten. In the next step (v. 32b), the beating stops. If δέ is read in v. 31, the word of the riot reaching the Roman commander (v. 31) is presented as a separate development, and the story is not as clearly organized around Paul.

Passage 12: Acts 6:7–7:1

(7a)   καί the word of.the God/Lord 3S.was.increasing

(7b)   καί 3S.was.being.multiplied the number of.the disciples in Jerusalem greatly,

(7c)   **much** τέ **crowd of.the priests** 3P.were.obeying the faith.

(8)   Stephen δέ full of.grace and of.power 3S.was.doing wonders and signs great among the people.

(9)   3P.rose.up δέ certain of.the from the synagogue of.the called of.freedmen... debating with.the Stephen

(10)   καί not 3P.were.able to.contradict the wisdom and the spirit with.which 3S.was.speaking.

(11)   τότε 3P.secretly.instigated men saying that "We have heard him speak blasphemous words against Moses and God."

(12a)   3P.aroused τέ the people and the elders and the scribes

(12b)   καί coming.on 3P.seized him

(12c)   καί 3P.led to the council,

(13)   3P.set.up τέ witnesses false saying, "This man never ceases to speak words against this holy place..."

(15)   καί having.gazed at him all the sitting in the council 3P.saw the face his as face of.angel.

(7:1)   3S.said δέ the high.priest, "Is this so?"

Question

What is the function of τέ in vv. 7c, 12a, and 13?

Suggested Answer: see Appendix under 6(12).

7
THEMATIC DEVELOPMENT IN NON-NARRATIVE TEXT

This chapter concentrates on the four most common ways in which sentences in non-narrative text are formally related: by means of δέ (sec. 7.1); simple juxtaposition, i.e., asyndeton (sec. 7.2); conjunctive καί (sec. 7.3); and οὖν (sec. 7.4). Section 7.1 also contrasts the functions of δέ and ἀλλά in similar contexts.[1]

7.1   Δέ

The basic function of δέ is the same in narrative and non-narrative text. In both it is used to mark new developments, in the sense that the information it introduces builds on what has gone before and makes a distinct contribution to the argument (see Youngman 1987:152). In both, it also introduces background material (ibid.).

I begin this section by reviewing Heckert's argument (1996:47–56) that the "adversative" and "connective" senses that are traditionally attributed to δέ arise from the differing *contexts* in which this marker of distinctive information is used.[2]

Heckert (op. cit. p. 54) cites **1 Tim. 4:8b** (below) as a typical context in which δέ occurs and an adversative sense of *contrast* may be discerned; I produce his reasoning more or less verbatim. The use of γάρ at the beginning of v. 8 constrains the verse to be processed as strengthening some aspect of the assertion of v. 7b (γύμναζε σεαυτὸν πρὸς εὐσέβειαν). This strengthening material is in two parts, linked by δέ: ἡ σωματικὴ γυμνασία πρὸς ὀλίγον ἐστὶν ὠφέλιμος (v. 8a) and ἡ εὐσέβεια πρὸς πάντα ὠφέλιμός ἐστιν (v. 8b). The first part does not address the topic of 'godliness,' which was the focus of v. 7b. Rather, it provides the counterpoint (sec. 2.8) for the second part to contrast with. It is this second part that strengthens some aspect of v. 7b. Thus, within the strengthening material of v. 8, there is development from less relevant to more relevant material. The presence of δέ, in turn, constrains v. 8b to be processed as developing from the previous material.

(7b)	γύμναζε	δὲ	σεαυτὸν	πρὸς	εὐσέβειαν·		
	train	DE	yourself	for	godliness		

(8a)	ἡ	γὰρ	σωματικὴ	γυμνασία	πρὸς	ὀλίγον	ἐστὶν ὠφέλιμος,
	the	for	bodily	training	for	little	3S.is profitable

(8b)	ἡ	δὲ	εὐσέβεια	πρὸς	πάντα	ὠφέλιμός	ἐστιν
	the	DE	godliness	for	all	profitable	3S.is

Heckert (p. 48) cites **2 Tim. 1:5** (below) as an instance in which δέ is taken to have a *connective*, rather than an adversative sense. Πίστεως (v. 5a) is modified by a complex relative clause, the two parts of which are linked by δέ: ἐνῴκησεν πρῶτον ἐν τῇ μάμμῃ σου Λωΐδι καὶ τῇ μητρί σου Εὐνίκῃ (v. 5b) and πέπεισμαι ὅτι καὶ ἐν σοί (v. 5c).[3] Of these two clauses, it is v. 5c that relates directly to v. 5a. The presence of δέ constrains v. 5c to be processed as developing from the previous material, viz., v. 5b.

(5a)	**ὑπόμνησιν**	λαβὼν	τῆς	ἐν	σοὶ	ἀνυποκρίτου	πίστεως,
	remembrance	having.taken	of.the	in	you	genuine	faith

(5b)	ἥτις	ἐνῴκησεν	πρῶτον	ἐν	τῇ	μάμμῃ	σου
	which	3S.dwelt	first	in	the	grandmother	your

---

[1] On ἀλλά as a marker of contrast in the Pastoral Epistles, see Heckert 1996:13-28.

[2] The following paragraphs are based on sec. 2 of Levinsohn 1999a.

[3] As Heckert observes (loc. cit.), the presence of non-conjunctive καί tends to ensure that the material is interpreted in a connective, rather than an adversative sense.

Λωΐδι   καὶ   τῇ   μητρί   σου   Εὐνίκη,
Lois   and   the   mother   your   Eunice

(5c)   πέπεισμαι   δὲ   ὅτι   καὶ   ἐν   σοί.
I.have.been.persuaded   DE   that   +   in   you

If δέ is not an adversative marker, yet occurs most frequently in contexts in which contrast can be discerned,[4] what is it that conveys the adversative sense? For "true contrast" between propositions to be present, "there must be at least two opposed pairs of lexical items" (Longacre 1996:55). According to Mann & Thompson (1987:8), propositions are in prototypical contrast when they are:[5]

1. perceived as the same in certain respects
2. perceived as different in certain respects, and
3. compared with respect to one or more of these differences.

In the case of 1 Tim. 4:8, the common element between the two propositions is ἐστὶν ὠφέλιμος, while two opposed pairs of lexical items occur: ἡ σωματικὴ γυμνασία versus ἡ εὐσέβεια, and πρὸς ὀλίγον versus πρὸς πάντα. Thus, this verse is an instance of 'true' contrast, *whether or not δέ is present*. Furthermore, such instances of contrast in Greek have at least one member of one of the opposing pairs as a point of departure, which itself signals the switch from the other member of the pair. In 1 Tim. 4.8, ἡ εὐσέβεια is a point of departure, signaling a switch from the corresponding element ἡ σωματικὴ γυμνασία. I therefore conclude that, in the context of 'true' contrast, δέ is either redundant or *conveys something other than contrast*, viz., development.

Once one or more of the characteristics of 'true' contrast are absent, commentators often disagree as to whether δέ is used in an adversative or a connective sense. **2 Tim. 2:23a** (below) illustrates this. This exhortation to avoid negative behavior follows an exhortation to positive behavior (v. 22b), which leads Alford (1863.III:387) to translate δέ with 'but'. However, the difficulty (among other factors) of identifying two opposed pairs of lexical items between vv. 22b and 23 leads other commentators (e.g., Hendriksen 1957:274) to view δέ as connective, introducing a second admonition in parallel with that of v. 22a or vv. 20–22.[6] A developmental treatment of δέ readily fits the passage: within the general topic of behaviors to practice and to avoid (vv. 14–26), the point of departure τὰς μωρὰς καὶ ἀπαιδεύτους ζητήσεις indicates a switch to the next sub-topic, in the development of the overall topic.

(22a)   τὰς   δὲ   νεωτερικὰς   ἐπιθυμίας   φεῦγε,
the   DE   youthful   lusts   flee

(22b)   δίωκε   δὲ   δικαιοσύνην   πίστιν   ἀγάπην   εἰρήνην   μετὰ   τῶν
pursue   DE   righteousness   faith   love   peace   with   the

ἐπικαλουμένων   τὸν   κύριον   ἐκ   καθαρᾶς   καρδίας.
calling.on   the   Lord   out.of   heart   clean

(23a)   τὰς   δὲ   μωρὰς   καὶ   ἀπαιδεύτους   ζητήσεις   παραιτοῦ,
the   DE   foolish   and   ignorant   speculations   refuse

A majority of commentators take δέ in **2 Tim. 2:20a** (below) to be adversative. However, the points of contrast with the context are not explicit, and some writers therefore take it to be connective.[7] Once again, a developmental interpretation of δέ satisfactorily fits the context. Having stated (v. 19) that 'God's firm foundation stands, bearing this inscription: "The Lord knows those who are his" and "Let everyone who calls on the name of the Lord turn away from wickedness",' δέ constrains v. 20 to be processed as building on and developing from previous material. The nature of the development becomes

---

[4] According to Heckert (op. cit. 53), "out of 59 appearances of δέ in the P[astoral] E[pistles], 38 are contrastive."

[5] Linguists use the term *prototype* to denote "an ideal example of a category" (Whaley 1997:289).

[6] This admonition itself is viewed by some (e.g., Smith & Beekman 1981:62-63) as being a specific example of the exhortation of vv. 14-15, in parallel with vv. 16-19.

[7] In fact, 2 Tim. 2:20a has presentational articulation and is used to introduce new items to an ongoing argument; see sec. 5.4.1.

clear when the author moves from the illustration of v. 20 itself to the application in v. 21a. 'If anyone cleanses himself from these things' (compare Ἀποστήτω ἀπὸ ἀδικίας 'let (him) turn away from wickedness'—v. 19), 'he will be a special utensil, dedicated and useful to the master'.

(20a) Ἐν   μεγάλῃ δὲ οἰκίᾳ οὐκ ἔστιν μόνον σκεύη χρυσᾶ καὶ ἀργυρᾶ
       in   great   DE house not   3S.is only   vessels golden and silver

(20b) ἀλλὰ καὶ ξύλινα καὶ ὀστράκινα, κ.τ.λ.
       but   +   wooden and earthen

(21a) ἐὰν οὖν⁸ τις   ἐκκαθάρῃ   ἑαυτὸν ἀπὸ τούτων,
       if   then anyone 3S.cleanses self   from these

(21b) ἔσται   σκεῦος εἰς τιμήν, ἡγιασμένον, εὔχρηστον τῷ
       3S.will.be vessel to   honor sanctified   useful   to.the

       δεσπότῃ, εἰς πᾶν   ἔργον ἀγαθὸν ἡτοιμασμένον.
       master   to   every work   good   having.been.prepared

As Heckert notes (op. cit. p. 57), δέ in **1 Tim. 3:5** (below) occurs in connection with background material that interrupts the list of qualifications for an overseer. The material concerned builds on v. 4 and makes a new point. Although some versions (e.g., NRSV) translate δέ as "for," thus interpreting v. 5 as stating a reason for the injunction of v. 4, failure to use γάρ means that Fairbairn (1956 (1874]:142) is right in observing, "it introduces parenthetically a statement which forms an antithesis to the one immediately preceding, yet an antithesis which at the same time constitutes a reason..." In other words, the selection of δέ, rather than γάρ, constrains v. 5 to be processed as developing from the previous material, even though it happens also to strengthen that material.

(4)   τοῦ   ἰδίου οἴκου καλῶς προϊστάμενον κ.τ.λ.
      of.the own   house well   managing

(5)   εἰ δέ τις   τοῦ   ἰδίου οἴκου προστῆναι οὐκ οἶδεν,
      if DE anyone of.the own   house to.manage not 3S.knows

      πῶς ἐκκλησίας θεοῦ   ἐπιμελήσεται;
      how church   of.God 3S.will.care.for

Δέ versus Ἀλλά

We can see the developmental nature of δέ also by comparing its usage with that of ἀλλά in similar contexts. When ἀλλά links a negative characteristic or proposition with a following positive one, the negative proposition usually retains its relevance.[9] When δέ is used, the characteristic or proposition associated with δέ is more in focus; the negative proposition is usually discarded or replaced by the positive one.[10]

This is illustrated by comparing 1 Tim. 6:17 and 1:9. In **6:17**, the rich are *both* to avoid putting their confidence in riches and to set it on God.[11]

---

[8] See sec. 7.4 for a discussion of οὖν in v. 21a.

[9] The positive proposition or characteristic may be viewed as "the other side of the coin" from the negative one (Pope p.c.).

[10] According to Alford (1863.IV:355), δέ has the effect of "removing the thing previously negatived altogether out of our field of view, and substituting something totally different for it."

[11] See also 1 Tim. 3.3 and 2 Tim. 2.24. Combinations of constituents like οὐ μόνον A ἀλλὰ καί B also illustrate that 'A' remains to the fore when ἀλλὰ καί adds 'B'. See, for example, 2 Tim. 2:20a-b (above). See Heckert 1996:19-28 for discussion of further examples of ἀλλά in the Pastoral Epistles.

The negation of the constituent preceding ἀλλά may be *relative*, rather than absolute. In Acts 5:4, for example, Meyer (1883:106) notes that οὐκ ἐψεύσω ἀνθρώποις ἀλλὰ τῷ θεῷ means "*not so much... but rather.*"

(17) Τοῖς πλουσίοις ἐν τῷ νῦν αἰῶνι παράγγελλε
      to.the rich   in the present age   charge

      μὴ ὑψηλοφρονεῖν μηδὲ ἠλπικέναι ἐπὶ πλούτου
      not to.be.high.minded nor to.have.hope on of.riches

      ἀδηλότητι ἀλλ᾽ ἐπὶ θεῷ κ.τ.λ.
      uncertainty but on God

In **1 Tim. 1:9a**, in contrast, δικαίῳ is preposed within the point of departure (cf. sec. 4.5) in anticipation of a switch to the more focal list of types of people that is introduced with δέ.[12] Δέ constrains the list to be processed as developing from the preceding material.

(9a) εἰδὼς τοῦτο, ὅτι **δικαίῳ** νόμος οὐ κεῖται,
      knowing this that for.righteous law not 3S.exists

(9b) ἀνόμοις δὲ καὶ ἀνυποτάκτοις, κ.τ.λ.
      for.lawless DE and rebellious

Review Questions

(a) What conditions must be fulfilled for "true contrast" between propositions to be present, according to Longacre and Mann & Thompson?

(b) How do the "adversative" and "connective" senses associated with δέ arise?

(c) When linking a negative characteristic or proposition with a positive one, how do the functions of ἀλλά and δέ differ?

Suggested Answers

(a) For "true contrast" between propositions to be present, "there must be at least two opposed pairs of lexical items" (Longacre). According to Mann & Thompson, for propositions to be in prototypical contrast they must be:
1. perceived as the same in certain respects
2. perceived as different in certain respects, and
3. compared with respect to one or more of these differences.

(b) The "adversative" and "connective" senses associated with δέ arise from the context. An adversative sense may be perceived to the extent that the relation between two propositions or groups of propositions conforms to the conditions for 'true' contrast. If commentators are only able to identify one opposed pair of lexical items, then the relation will tend to be viewed as "connective."

(c) When ἀλλά links a negative characteristic or proposition with a positive one, the negative part usually retains its relevance. When δέ is used, there is development from the negative to the positive part, and the negative part is usually discarded or replaced by the positive one.

Illustrative Sentence: Titus 1:15

(15a) **πάντα** καθαρὰ τοῖς καθαροῖς·
       all.things pure to.the pure

(15b) τοῖς δὲ μεμιαμμένοις καὶ ἀπίστοις οὐδὲν καθαρόν,
       to.the DE defiled   and unbelieving nothing pure

(15c) ἀλλὰ μεμίανται   αὐτῶν καὶ ὁ νοῦς καὶ ἡ συνείδησις.
       but 3S.has.been.defiled their both the mind and the conscience

(a) Why do the propositions of vv. 15a–b provide an example of 'true' contrast?

---

[12] The order of constituents in 1 Tim. 1:9a indicates that the focus of the clause is not δικαίῳ but the negated verb (see sec. 4.1): 'a law for the righteous doesn't exist.'

(b) Why is ἀλλά, rather than δέ, the appropriate conjunction to link the negative and positive propositions of vv. 15b–c?

Suggested Answers

(a) The propositions of vv. 15a–b provide an example of 'true' contrast because they have a constituent in common ('be pure'), and two pairs of opposing lexical items: πάντα versus οὐδὲν and τοῖς καθαροῖς versus τοῖς μεμιαμμένοις καὶ ἀπίστοις. This last constituent is the point of departure in v. 15b, to mark the switch from τοῖς καθαροῖς.

(b) 'Αλλά, rather than δέ, is the appropriate conjunction to link the negative and positive propositions of vv. 15b–c because the negative proposition (οὐδὲν καθαρόν) retains its relevance, rather than being discarded or replaced by the positive proposition. In other words, it is still true as v. 15c is being asserted that nothing is pure to the defiled and unbelieving.

We now look at James 1:2–11 (below), to see how δέ marks steps in the development of the author's argument. Discussion of δέ in vv. 4, 5a, 6a, 9 and 10 follows the passage. (See sec. 2.8 for discussion of the presence and absence of points of departure in the passage.)

Passage 1: James 1:2–11

(2)	Ø **all joy** consider, brothers my, whenever **into.trials** you.fall into.various,
	(3) knowing that the testing of.your the faith 3S.works endurance.
(4)	the δέ endurance **work perfect** 3S.let.have, so.that you.may.be perfect and entire, **in nothing** lacking.
(5a)	if δέ any of.you 3S.lacks wisdom, 3S.let.ask from the giving God to.all unreservedly and not reproaching
(5b)	καί 3S.will.be.given to.him.
(6a)	3S.let.ask δέ in faith, nothing doubting;
(6b)	the γάρ doubting.one 3S.is.like wave of.sea being.blown.by.wind and being.tossed.
(7–8)	not γάρ 3S.let.think the man that that 3S.will.receive anything from the Lord, man double.minded unstable in all the ways his.
(9)	3S.let.boast δέ the brother the lowly in the exaltation his,
(10)	the δέ rich in the humiliation his, since **as flower of.grass** 3S.will.pass.away.
(11a)	3S.rose γάρ the sun with the burning.heat
(11b)	καί 3S.dried the grass
(11c)	καί the flower its 3S.fell
(11d)	καί the beauty of.the appearance its 3S.perished;
(11e)	Ø οὕτως + the rich in the goings his 3S.will.fade.away.

Δέ is used in James 1:2–11 to move from point to point; each point builds on the previous one.

Thus, the reference to endurance (ὑπομονήν) at the end of v. 3 is taken up in v. 4 as the point of departure/propositional topic, in connection with δέ. The assertions of v. 4 build on those of v. 3, but are distinct.

Verse 4 ends with the phrase 'lacking in nothing' (ἐν μηδενὶ λειπόμενοι), while v. 5 begins with a conditional clause that picks up the idea of lacking. Δέ in v. 5 indicates that this new assertion both builds on what has gone before and presents something distinct.

Verse 6 picks up the verb 'let him ask' (αἰτείτω) from v. 5 and adds the new concept of faith: 'let him ask in faith' (ἐν πίστει). Again, δέ reflects the fact that this verse both builds on what has preceded it and has something new to say.

The exact relationship of v. 9 to the context is unclear, but many commentators think that it builds on the assertion of v. 2 about 'trials' (πειρασμοῖς), in which case it operates at a higher level than in vv. 4–6 (see sec. 5.1). The presence of δέ simply indicates that v. 9 builds on and develops from what he has already said.

Finally, in v. 10, δέ is used in connection with a point of departure to indicate that the argument develops through a switch from 'the lowly brother' (ὁ ἀδελφὸς ὁ ταπεινὸς in v. 9) to 'the rich' (ὁ πλούσιος). This is clear from the content of v. 11, which concerns, not the lowly brother, but the rich man. (The relation between v. 10 and v. 9 meets the conditions for 'true' contrast—see above.)

As this discussion of James 1:9 has shown, the sense in which material introduced with δέ builds on and develops from the context is not always readily apparent. However, we do well to take the presence of δέ seriously.

Past editions of the SIL semantic structure analyses (SSAs) do not always capture the developmental nature of δέ, as for instance in **2 Peter 1:13**. I comment below on the presence of δέ in v. 13 and v. 15.

(12) Therefore I intend to keep on reminding you of these things, though you know them already and are established in the truth that has come to you.

(13) **δίκαιον** δὲ ἡγοῦμαι, ἐφ' ὅσον εἰμὶ ἐν τούτῳ τῷ σκηνώματι,
   right DE I.consider as.long.as I.am in this the tabernacle

   διεγείρειν ὑμᾶς ἐν ὑπομνήσει, κ.τ.λ.
   to.arouse you by reminder

(15) σπουδάσω δὲ καὶ ἑκάστοτε ἔχειν ὑμᾶς μετὰ τὴν
   I.will.be.eager DE + always to.have you after the

   ἐμὴν ἔξοδον τὴν τούτων μνήμην ποιεῖσθαι.
   my exodus the of.these.things memory to.cause.

Johnson (1988) considers that vv. 13–14 provide the reason for v. 12. However, the presence of δέ constrains v. 13 to be interpreted as either a new assertion that builds on v. 12 or background material (I prefer the former analysis). In v. 12, the author says, 'I intend to remind you'; in v. 13, 'I consider it right to do so'; and, in v. 15, he further develops the same line of reasoning ('I will be eager also always...'). Thus, although vv. 13–14 can be interpreted as relating semantically to v. 12 on the basis of reason, the *formal* relationship between the two verses is a developmental one.

Now, the purpose of SSAs, as the name suggests, is to reflect *semantic* relations between propositions or groups of propositions. Thus, when δέ relates two groups of propositions between which a specific semantic relation can be discerned, the SSA usually indicates the semantic relation. My problem with this is that it can mislead the Bible translator; the SSA indicates one type of relation (a semantic one), when the biblical author uses a different type (a developmental one).

Now read the following passage, in which Phil. 1:23a appears to be an amplification of v. 22b (Banker 1996:59) but the presence of δέ constrains the material with which it is associated to be interpreted as a further development of Paul's argument.

Illustrative Passage 2: Philippians 1:22–25

(22a) εἰ δὲ τὸ ζῆν ἐν σαρκί, τοῦτό μοι καρπὸς ἔργου,
    if DE the to.live in flesh this for.me fruit of.labor

(22b) καὶ τί αἱρήσομαι οὐ γνωρίζω.
    and what I.will.choose not I.know

(23a) συνέχομαι δὲ ἐκ τῶν δύο, τὴν ἐπιθυμίαν ἔχων
    I.am.hard.pressed DE from the two the desire having

    εἰς τὸ ἀναλῦσαι καὶ **σὺν** **Χριστῷ** εἶναι,
    to the to.depart and with Christ to.be

(23b) πολλῷ [γὰρ] μᾶλλον κρεῖσσον·
    much for more better

(24) τὸ   δὲ   ἐπιμένειν   [ἐν] τῇ   σαρκὶ   ἀναγκαιότερον δι᾽ ὑμᾶς.
      the DE   to.remain   in   the flesh   more.necessary   for you

(25) καὶ τοῦτο πεποιθὼς   οἶδα   ὅτι   μενῶ   κ.τ.λ.
      and this   having.been.persuaded.of I.know that I.will.remain

Question

How extensive is the unit that δέ in v. 23a constrains to be interpreted as a further development in Paul's argument?

Suggested Answer

The unit that δέ in v. 23a constrains to be interpreted as a further development in Paul's argument includes at least vv. 23–24 (and, probably, vv. 23–26). In v. 22, Paul presents his dilemma (to live versus to die—v. 21). In vv. 23–24 he further develops his argument by reaching the conclusion that to continue living is necessary for his addressees. Within this development unit, v. 23 provides the counterpoint for the main assertion of v. 24. (Καί then constrains vv. 25–26 to be added to and associated with v. 24—see sec. 7.3.)

7.2   Asyndeton

Strictly speaking, the absence of any conjunction between sentences of a Greek text should imply only that the author offered no processing constraint on how the following material was to be related to its context (see the introduction to part II). In practice, however, New Testament authors tend to use a conjunction whenever the relationship with the context concerned is strengthening (γάρ), developmental (δέ), associative or additive (καί), or inferential-cum-resumptive (οὖν), etc. Consequently, asyndeton tends to imply "*not* strengthening, *not* developmental, *not* associative, *not* inferential, etc." This is why asyndeton is often the norm when the relation of the following material to the context is not logical or chronological.[13]

Asyndeton is found in two very different contexts in non-narrative text:
- when there is a *close* connection between the information concerned (i.e., the information belongs together in the same unit)
- when there is *no* direct connection between the information concerned (i.e., the information belongs to different units).[14]

An example of asyndeton involving a *close* connection between propositions or groups of propositions is when the relation between them is *GENERIC-specific*. This is illustrated in Titus 2:1–3; v. 1 refers to healthy teaching in general, whereas vv. 2 and 3 introduce specific instances of such teaching.

Passage 3: Titus 2:1–3

(1) Σὺ   δὲ   λάλει   ἃ   πρέπει   τῇ   ὑγιαινούσῃ διδασκαλίᾳ.
     you DE   speak   what 3S.is suitable to.the healthy   teaching

---

[13] For those familiar with SIL's Semantic Structure Analyses (SSAs), the following are the relations that I have noted for which asyndeton is the norm:

orientation: orienter – CONTENT
restatement: GENERIC – specific_n and generic – SPECIFIC
associative: NUCLEUS – comment and NUCLEUS – parenthesis.

For background reading on such relations, see Beekman and Callow 1974:287-311.

[14] One way to recognize when no direct connection between juxtaposed information is intended is by the presence of *vocatives* like ἀδελφοί 'brothers' (Banker 1984:31), as in James 2:1, and of *orienters* (complement-taking predicates) like Ἠκούσατε 'You have heard' (Matt. 5:21); see further in sec. 17.2.1. (Phil. 3:13a is an exception; information from v. 12 is repeated to highlight the assertion of vv. 13b-14—see sec. 12.1.) Conversely, one would normally expect no vocatives or orienters to separate juxtaposed constituents when a close relationship between them is intended.

(2) Ø πρεσβύτας **νηφαλίους** εἶναι, σεμνούς, κ.τ.λ.
     older.men temperate to.be respectable

(3) Ø πρεσβύτιδας ὡσαύτως ἐν καταστήματι ἱεροπρεπεῖς, κ.τ.λ.
     older.women similarly in behavior as.befits.holiness

1 Tim. 3:1b provides another example of asyndeton involving a close connection between information. In this instance, the relation involved is *orienter-CONTENT*. The orienter is v. 1a and the CONTENT of ὁ λόγος, v. 1b.

(1a) Ø **Πιστὸς** ὁ λόγος.
      faithful the word

(1b) Ø Εἴ τις ἐπισκοπῆς ὀρέγεται, **καλοῦ ἔργου** ἐπιθυμεῖ.
      if anyone of.overseer 3S.aspires good work 3S.desires

The first clause of this same verse provides an example of asyndeton when *no* direct connection between units is intended. No direct connection is intended between "Directions with respect to Public Worship" (chapter 2) and "Directions with respect to the Institution of the Offices" (chapter 3) (Hendriksen 1957:90, 116).

Asyndeton is the norm between *paragraphs* with different topics[15] when the topic of the new paragraph is not considered to strengthen, develop from, be associated with, or be inferred from that of the previous one. Asyndeton is typically found at the following transitions:
- from the opening salutation to the body of each letter (e.g., James 1:2—passage 1)
- from the body of a letter to its closure (e.g. 1 Tim. 6:21b)[16]
- from one major or minor topic to another (e.g. 1 Tim. 3:1a above).[17]

Asyndeton is found also between *individual propositions* that are viewed as independent of each other. Thus, in **Tit. 3:15**, though both sentences involve greetings, they are not strictly parallel, and the second does not strengthen or develop from the first.

(15a) Ἀσπάζονταί σε οἱ μετ᾽ ἐμοῦ πάντες.
       3P.greet you the.ones with me all

(15b) Ἄσπασαι τοὺς φιλοῦντας ἡμᾶς ἐν πίστει.
       greet the loving us in faith

Other relations between propositions or groups of propositions that are characterized by asyndeton include:
- *Evaluations* of previous material,[18] commonly with the demonstrative pronoun οὗτος as the point of departure/propositional topic. See, for example, 1 Tim. 2:3 (τοῦτο[19] καλὸν καὶ ἀπόδεκτον ἐνώπιον τοῦ σωτῆρος ἡμῶν θεοῦ 'This is right and is acceptable in the sight of God our Savior'), which provides an evaluation of vv. 1–2.
- *Summaries* of previous material, again with οὗτος as the point of departure/propositional topic. See, for example, Titus 2:15 (Ταῦτα λάλει κ.τ.λ. 'Speak these things ...'), assuming that ταῦτα refers to "all the practical exhortations contained in chapter ii" (Guthrie 1957:202).[20]

---

[15] In SSA terms, the relationship between the paragraphs is NUCLEUS-NUCLEUS.

[16] Contrast Jude 24; δέ constrains vv. 24-25 to be interpreted as a new development.

[17] However, a change of topic may be signaled by a switch to a new point of departure in connection with δέ, as in 1 Cor. 8:1 (discussed in sec. 2.2). In such instances, the author views the new topic as further developing the overall purpose of the letter. Topic changes that involve a degree of parallelism may be characterized by the adverbial conjunction ὡσαύτως 'similarly,' as in Tit. 2:3 (passage 3 above) or 1 Tim. 2:9 (with non-conjunctive καί).

[18] The SSA term for an evaluation is an orienter.

[19] Γάρ is a variant to asyndeton, in which case 1 Tim. 2:3 would be constrained to be processed as strengthening all or part of vv. 1-2.

[20] For Banker (1987:45), the relation of Tit. 2:15 to vv. 1-14 is NUCLEUS-manner.

- Some *orienter-CONTENT* relations (see 1 Tim. 3:1 above), in which the first proposition introduces the second. See also Tit. 1:12 (passage 4 below).[21]
- *Generic-Specific* relations, in which the second proposition gives a specific instance of the more generic proposition that precedes it, as in Tit. 2.1–2 (above).

In the following passage from Titus 1 (see passage 6 of sec. 2.8 for the Greek text and consideration of the points of departure), asyndeton is found in vv. 12a (UBS text), 12b (see above), 13a, 15, and 16 (see discussion following the passage). The SSA analysis is based on Banker (1987); the labels NUCLEUS₁ and NUCLEUS₂ imply that the groups of propositions concerned are of equal importance and parallel to each other.

Passage 4: Titus 1:10–16

grounds for CONCLUSION of 13b–14 (10–13a)
    NUCLEUS₁ (10–11)
        (10a)   3P.are γάρ many [+] rebellious idle.talkers and deceivers,
                especially the.ones of the circumcision,
        (11a)   whom 3S.is necessary to.stop.mouth,
        (11b)   who **entire households** 3P.overturn
                teaching what not 3S.ought dishonest gain for.sake.of.
    NUCLEUS₂ (12–13a)
      orienter for 12b
        (12a)   Ø* 3S.said certain of them own their prophet, (*variants: γάρ, δέ)
      COMMENT
        (12b)   Ø Cretans always liars, wicked beasts, gluttons lazy.
      evaluation of 12b
        (13a)   Ø the witness this 3S.is true,
CONCLUSION (13b–14)
        (13b)   for which cause reprove them severely, (14) so.that 3P.may.be.healthy
                in the faith, not paying.attention to.Jewish myths and commandments
                of.men turning.away.from the truth.
comment about CONCLUSION of 13b–14 (15–16)
    NUCLEUS₁ (15a–c)
        (15a)   Ø all.things pure to.the pure;
        (15b)   to.the δέ defiled and unbelieving nothing pure,
        (15c)   ἀλλά 3S.has.been.defiled their both the mind and the conscience.
    NUCLEUS₂ (16)
        (16a)   Ø **God** 3P.profess to.know,
        (16b)   by.the δέ works 3P.deny, **detestable** being and disobedient
                and to every work good unfit.

In the above passage, the undisputed examples of asyndeton occur where the relation between the constituents is "not strengthening, not developmental, not associative, not inferential, etc."

In v.13a, the evaluation of the COMMENT of v. 12b begins with a point of departure/propositional topic that includes a form of the demonstrative οὗτος but no conjunction (see sec. 5.4.3).

In v. 15a, asyndeton introduces a comment about the NUCLEUS of vv. 13b–14 (Banker notes that the proposition of v. 15a probably is another saying, parallel to that of v. 12b). Alternatively, it may be a second NUCLEUS in parallel to vv. 13b–14.

In v. 16a, asyndeton introduces a NUCLEAR statement that is in parallel to the NUCLEAR statement of v. 15.

---

[21] Other orienter-CONTENT relationships require ὅτι to introduce the content. See chap. 16 on the use of ὅτι *recitativum* in Luke-Acts and John.

I turn now to consideration of v. 12a.

The asyndeton reading is consistent with vv. 12–13 being interpreted as a second NUCLEUS in parallel to vv. 10–11. Verses 10–13a are then taken as together providing the grounds for the CONCLUSION of vv. 13b–14.

There is a complication, however. As I noted in sec. 2.8, the order of the constituents in v. 12a indicates that attention remains on the 'rebellious people, idle talkers and deceivers', which might suggest that the quotation is made to confirm what v. 10 has said about the nature of Cretans. This would suggest a logical CONCLUSION-grounds relation between vv. 10–11 and vv. 12–13a, which is perhaps why one MS inserted γάρ. Further research is needed to determine whether asyndeton is acceptable when the relation is CONCLUSION-grounds, or whether the absence of γάρ excludes such a logical relation. (If the variant reading δέ is followed, v. 12a would further develop the argument of vv. 10–11, and the grounds for the CONCLUSION of vv. 13b–14 would then be only vv. 12–13a.)

We have seen that asyndeton is usually associated with the absence of the sort of relations signaled by γάρ, δέ, καί, οὖν, etc. On occasion, however, propositions on the same topic are juxtaposed and treated formally as independent of each other, when a conjunction might appear to be appropriate. This is particularly common towards the end of an epistle.

Such is the case in **1 Tim. 5:20a** (below), for which a variant with δέ exists. White (1970 (1909):136) observes that, whereas vv. 17–25 "form one section, marked by one prominent topic, the relation of Timothy to presbyters," "the sequence of thought in these concluding verses of the chapter is not formal and deliberate." The effect of adding δέ is to constrain v. 20 to be processed as developing from the previous material. Without δέ, τοὺς ἁμαρτάνοντας might refer to sinners in the congregation as a whole; with δέ, it more clearly refers just to presbyters.

(19)   Never accept any accusation against an elder except on the evidence of two or three witnesses.

(20a)   Ø*   τοὺς   ἁμαρτάνοντας   **ἐνώπιον πάντων** ἔλεγχε, (*variant*: δέ)
         the.ones sinning   before   all   expose

2 Tim. 4:17–18 (below) provides another instance in which the juxtaposition of propositions means that they are treated as formally independent of each other, yet their content suggests a relation between them that might have merited a conjunction. A number of commentators (e.g., Hendriksen 1957:327) consider v. 18 to be "a conclusion drawn from the preceding verse" (Minor 1992:148). The variant καί would then add this conclusion to the paragraph (see sec. 5.3.2). However, the relation between the propositions is left implicit in the UBS text.

(17d)   καὶ ἐρρύσθην   ἐκ   στόματος λέοντος.
         and I.was.rescued out.of mouth   of.lion

(18a)   Ø* ῥύσεταί   με ὁ   κύριος ἀπὸ παντὸς ἔργου πονηροῦ
         3S.will.rescue me the Lord   from every   work   evil
        (*variant:* καί)

Thus, although authors tend to juxtapose sentences to indicate "not strengthening, not developmental, not associative, not inferential," the possibility still exists, in individual passages, for asyndeton to indicate merely an absence of a constraint on processing. In this case the reader is left to deduce the relation between each new proposition and its context.

Kathleen Callow (1992:192) identifies a further motivation for asyndeton: "δέ characteristically occurs where there is linear development of thought, and … marks new developments in the progression of the message. It does not occur when the message is *emotional*, or when there is a *poetic or rhetorically motivated dwelling on one point*" (the emphasis is mine).

One passage "expressing strong emotion" (op. cit. p. 189) is 1 Cor. 6:1–11. In spite of the occurrence of μέν οὖν in v. 4 and μέν [οὖν] in v. 7, not a single δέ is used in this passage.

Review Questions

(a) What are the two very different contexts in which asyndeton is commonly found in non-narrative text?

(b) The absence of any conjunction between sentences of a Greek text should imply only that the author offered no processing constraint on how the following material was to be related to its context. In practice, what does asyndeton tend to imply?

(c) With which of the following relations between propositions or groups of propositions would you expect to find asyndeton: (i) orienter-CONTENT, (ii) GENERIC-specificₙ, (iii) NUCLEUS-NUCLEUS, (iv) CONCLUSION-grounds?

(d) What further motivation for asyndeton has Kathleen Callow identified?

Suggested Answers

(a) Asyndeton in non-narrative text is commonly found in two very different contexts:
- when there is a *close* connection between the information concerned (i.e., the information belongs together in the same unit)
- when there is *no* direct connection between the information concerned (i.e., the information belongs to different units).

(b) Asyndeton tends to imply *not* strengthening, *not* developmental, *not* associative, *not* inferential, etc.

(c) (i) Asyndeton is expected for some orienter-CONTENT relations (ὅτι is expected for others).

(ii) Asyndeton is expected for GENERIC-specificₙ relations.

(iii) Asyndeton is expected for some NUCLEUS-NUCLEUS relations. However, δέ may link them if a developmental relation between them is discerned.

(iv) Γάρ or ὅτι, rather than asyndeton, is expected for CONCLUSION-grounds relations.

(d) Kathleen Callow finds that asyndeton occurs where δέ might have been expected "when the message is emotional, or when there is a poetic or rhetorically motivated dwelling on one point."

Illustrative Passage 5: Galatians 3:1–14

The following passage should be studied with particular attention to how the sentences are linked. (Subordinating conjunctions, which are not discussed in this book, are indicated in parentheses. See passage 7 of sec. 2.8 for the Greek text. See passage 8 of sec. 7.4 on οὖν in v. 5.)

(1a)   Ø Oh senseless Galatians, **who** you 3S.bewitched,

(1b)   to.whom (οἷς) before eyes <u>Jesus</u> <u>Christ</u> 3S.was.portrayed crucified?

(2a)   Ø **this only** I.want to.learn from you;

(2b)   Ø **by works of.law** the Spirit you.received or by hearing of.faith?

(3a)   Ø **so senseless** you.are?

(3b)   Ø having.begun in.Spirit, <u>now</u> **in.flesh** are.you.perfected?

(4)   Ø **so.much** you.suffered in.vain—if really + in.vain?

(5)   the οὖν <u>supplying</u> to.you the <u>Spirit</u> and <u>working</u> <u>powerful.deeds</u> <u>among</u> <u>you</u>, by works of.law or by hearing of.faith?

(6a)   as (καθώς) <u>Abraham</u> 3S.believed in.the God,

(6b)   καί 3S.was.accounted to.him for righteousness.

(7a)   (you).know ἄρα (then)

(7b)   that (ὅτι) the.ones of <u>faith</u>, <u>these</u> **sons** 3P.are of.Abraham.

(8a)   having.foreseen δέ the Scripture

(8b)   that (ὅτι) **by faith** 3S.would.justify the nations the God,

(8c)   3S.before.preached to.the Abraham

(8d)   that (ὅτι) 3P.will.be.blessed in you all the nations;

(9)   so (ὥστε) **the.ones of faith** 3P.are.blessed with the faithful Abraham.

(10a)   <u>as.many.as</u> γάρ **of works of.law** 3P.are, **under curse** 3P.are;

(10b)   3S.has.been.written γάρ

(10c)   that (ὅτι) **Cursed** everyone who not 3S.abides by.all the having.been.written in the book of.the law of.the to.do them.

(11a)   that (ὅτι) δέ <u>by</u> <u>law</u> **none** 3S.is.justified <u>before</u> <u>the</u> <u>God</u> clear,

(11b)   since (ὅτι) <u>the</u> <u>just</u> **of faith** 3S.will.live;

(12a)   <u>the</u> δέ <u>law</u> not 3S.is of faith,

(12b)   ἀλλ' **The having.done them** 3S.will.live by them.

(13a)   Ø <u>Christ</u> **us** 3S.redeemed from the curse of.the law having.become on.behalf.of us curse,

(13b)   since (ὅτι) 3S.has.been.written,

(13c)   Ø **Cursed** everyone the having.hung on tree,

(14a)   so.that (ἵνα) to <u>the</u> <u>nations</u> the blessing of.the Abraham 3S.might.become in Christ Jesus,

(14b)   so.that (ἵνα) <u>the</u> <u>promise</u> <u>of.the</u> <u>Spirit</u> we.might.receive through the faith.

Questions

(a) First, look at the instances of asyndeton in vv. 1a, 2a, 2b, 3a, 3b, and 4. (Whether asyndeton is present in v. 6a depends on how καθώς is interpreted—see Rogers 1989:67.)
1. Which instances of asyndeton reflect a NUCLEUS-NUCLEUS relation between propositions or groups of propositions?
2. Which reflect an orienter-CONTENT relation between propositions?
3. What relation between vv. 1 and 2 would be consistent with asyndeton in v. 2a?
4. What relation between vv. 3 and 4 would be consistent with asyndeton in v. 4?

(b) Now look at the instances of δέ in vv. 8a, 11a, and 12a.
1. Why is δέ appropriate in v. 8a?
2. Why is δέ appropriate in vv. 11a and 12a?

(c) What does ἀλλά indicate in v. 12b?

(d) What does the presence of asyndeton in v. 13 suggest?

Suggested Answers

(a) Concerning asyndeton in vv. 1a, 2a, 2b, 3a, 3b, and 4.
1. Asyndeton in v. 1a links NUCLEUS-NUCLEUS statements at the beginning of a section (an analysis strengthened by the use of the vocative—see sec. 17.2.8). Rogers (1989) also suggests a NUCLEUS-NUCLEUS between vv. 1–2 and vv. 3–5.
2. Asyndeton in vv. 2b and 3b reflects an orienter-CONTENT relation between propositions (vv. 2a-Ø-2b and 3a-Ø-3b).
3. A generic-SPECIFIC relation between vv. 1 and 2 would be consistent with asyndeton in v. 2a (see Meyer's 1873 comment, "The foolishness of their error is now disclosed to them…").
4. A NUCLEUS-evaluation (or NUCLEUS-parenthesis) relation between vv. 3 and 4 would be consistent with asyndeton in v. 4.

(b) Concerning δέ in vv. 8a, 11a, and 12a.
1. A comparison of v. 7b and v. 9 indicates that the unit of vv. 8–9 relates closely to v. 7 (both concern οἱ ἐκ πίστεως 'the ones of faith'). At the same time, v. 9 has more to say than v. 7b (Rogers 1989:73 calls the relation contraction-NUCLEUS): in v. 7b, these people are 'sons of Abraham'; in v. 9, they are blessed with Abraham, which is the point of the quotation of v. 8d. Thus, vv. 8–9 both build on and develop from v. 7.
2. Verses 10–12 consist of a three-point line of reasoning, each point building on the last and being distinct from what has gone before. First, ἐν νόμῳ 'by law', a concept that was reintroduced in v. 10, is made the point of departure in v. 11a. This sentence makes a new assertion about the law, viz., that no one is justified before God by it. (See sec. 9.4 on the absence of the article in the initial expression ἐν νόμῳ.) Verse 12 then develops the argument further, this time with ὁ νόμος 'the law' as the point of departure/propositional topic. Once again, the material introduced with δέ builds on what preceded it and also makes a different assertion, viz., that the law has nothing to do with faith.

(c) The presence of ἀλλά in v. 12b indicates a non-developmental relationship between the negative and positive assertions of v. 12 and, in particular, that the assertion of v. 12a retains its relevance.

(d) The presence of asyndeton in v. 13 suggests that the line of reasoning in vv. 10–12 has come to an end, and a new point (NUCLEUS) is being presented.

7.3 Conjunctive Καί[22]

In sec. 6.2, we noted that conjunctive καί "is used to link items of equal status" (Porter 1992:211). In non-narrative text, it constrains the material it introduces to be processed as being added to and associated with previous material (i.e., it basically has the same function as that described in sec. 5.3.2 for John's Gospel). In contrast with δέ, the material it introduces does *not* represent a new development with respect to the context.

For most instances of conjunctive καί in non-narrative text, it is extremely obvious that it associates together the material it conjoins. Thus, in **1 Tim. 2:13-14**, it conjoins the two sentences that are introduced by γάρ. It is these sentences *together* that strengthen the previous verse. (Within the sentence introduced by καί, δέ in v. 14b functions developmentally.)

(12) I do not allow a woman to teach or to have authority over a man, but to keep silent.

(13)   Ἀδὰμ   γὰρ   **πρῶτος**   ἐπλάσθη,   εἶτα   Εὔα.
       Adam   for   first   3S.formed   then   Eve

(14a) καὶ   Ἀδὰμ   οὐκ   ἠπατήθη,
       and   Adam   not   3S.was.deceived

(14b) ἡ   δὲ   γυνὴ   ἐξαπατηθεῖσα   ἐν   παραβάσει   γέγονεν·
       the   DE   woman   having.been.deceived   in   transgression   3S.has.become

2 Tim. 4:17 describes two actions performed by the Lord (vv. 17a-b), together with their purpose (vv. 17c-d). The final καί of the verse (v. 17e) has the effect of associating the result of the actions described in vv. 17a-b with those actions.

(17a) ὁ   δὲ   **κύριός**   μοι   παρέστη
       the   DE   Lord   with.me   3S.stood

(17b) καὶ   ἐνεδυνάμωσέν   με,
       and   3S.empowered   me

(17c) ἵνα   δι'   ἐμοῦ   τὸ   κήρυγμα   πληροφορηθῇ
       so.that   through   me   the   proclamation   3S.might.be.fully.made

(17d) καὶ   ἀκούσωσιν   πάντα   τὰ   ἔθνη,
       and   3P.might.hear   all   the   Gentiles

(17e) **καὶ**   ἐρρύσθην   ἐκ   στόματος   λέοντος.
       and   I.was.rescued   out.of   mouth   of.lion

In **2 Tim. 3:11** (below), many commentators (e.g., Hendriksen 1957:292) interpret the καί of v. 11c as *adversative*. This cannot mean that καί itself conveys an adversative sense, but rather that καί conjoins propositions that are in an adversative relationship. Why, then, was καί used in this passage (associating the propositions together), rather than δέ (treating them as distinct discourse units)? The reason is found in the flow of the argument. This is from 'what persecutions I endured' (v. 11b) to 'and all who want to live a godly life in Christ Jesus will also be persecuted' (v. 12), which is constrained by δέ to be processed as developing from the previous material. Since v. 12 does not develop from v. 11c but from v. 11b, καί is the appropriate particle to associate v. 11c non-developmentally with the rest of v. 11.[23]

(10) Now you have observed my teaching, my conduct, my aim in life, my faith, my patience, my love, my steadfastness, (11a) my persecutions and suffering the things that happened to me in Antioch, in Iconium, in Lystra,

---

[22] This section is based on Heckert 1996:79-89 and sec. 3 of Levinsohn 1999a.

[23] "Καί links sentences W and X if the following events Y do not build upon the event described in X" but on W (Levinsohn 1987:112). In v. 12, non-conjunctive καί constrains πάντες to be processed as being in parallel with a corresponding constituent, viz., 'I' (Paul).

(11b) **οἵους** **διωγμοὺς** ὑπήνεγκα
what.kind.of persecutions I.endured

(11c) καὶ **ἐκ** **πάντων** με ἐρρύσατο ὁ κύριος.
and from all me 3S.rescued the Lord

(12) καὶ **πάντες** δὲ οἱ **θέλοντες** **εὐσεβῶς** **ζῆν**
+ all DE the.ones wanting godly to.live

ἐν Χριστῷ Ἰησοῦ διωχθήσονται.
in Christ Jesus 3P.will.be.persecuted

The καί of **1 Tim. 3:16a** is well motivated from a discourse perspective, without it being necessary to claim that it "heightens the force of the predication" (Ellicott 1883:194). Δέ in 4.1 constrains the material associated with it to be processed as developing from the discourse unit that preceded it. This unit first gives the motivation for writing (3:14–15a) and then, having emphasized the truth of the gospel, expands on the grandeur of the gospel (vv. 15b–16, see Knight 1992:182). Chapter 4 develops from the unit as a whole by informing the readers that some will depart from the faith and teach things that will be harmful to 'the household of God' (3:15a).

(14) These things I write to you hoping to come to you soon, (15a) but (δέ) if I delay, so that you may know how one ought to behave in the household of God,

(15b) which is the church of the living God, the pillar and bulwark of the truth.

(16a) καὶ **ὁμολογουμένως** **μέγα** ἐστὶν τὸ τῆς εὐσεβείας μυστήριον·
and confessedly great 3S.is the of.the godliness mystery

(16b) who was revealed in flesh, vindicated by (the) Spirit, seen by angels, proclaimed among Gentiles, believed in throughout the world, taken up in glory.

(4:1) Now (δέ) the Spirit expressly says that in later times some will renounce the faith...

Although sec. 6.2 offered some criteria for distinguishing conjunctive καί from non-conjunctive καί, it is not always easy to do so when καί begins a sentence and no (other) conjunction is present. As far as the development of the discourse is concerned, however, the implications of starting a sentence with καί are very similar, whether it is conjunctive or non-conjunctive. In either case, the material it introduces is to be associated with previous material, rather than representing a new development in the argument.

2 Tim. 1:18b illustrates this point. If this καί is viewed as conjunctive, then the sentence is to be conjoined to vv. 16–17, even though they are not contiguous to v. 18b. If it is viewed as non-conjunctive, then ὅσα ἐν Ἐφέσῳ διηκόνησεν is constrained to parallel processing with Onesiphorus' service in Rome. Either way, though, the material introduced by καί is to be associated at least with v. 17.

(16a) May the Lord grant mercy to the household of Onesiphorus,

(16b) ὅτι **πολλάκις** με ἀνέψυξεν
since often me 3S.refreshed

(16c) καὶ τὴν ἅλυσίν μου οὐκ ἐπαισχύνθη,
and the chain my not 3S.was.ashamed.of

(17) ἀλλὰ γενόμενος ἐν Ῥώμῃ **σπουδαίως** ἐζήτησέν με καὶ εὗρεν·
but becoming in Rome diligently 3S.sought me and 3S.found

(18a) δῴη αὐτῷ ὁ κύριος εὑρεῖν ἔλεος παρὰ κυρίου
3S.may.grant to.him the Lord to.find mercy from Lord

ἐν ἐκείνῃ τῇ ἡμέρᾳ.
in that the day

(18b) καὶ ὅσα **ἐν Ἐφέσῳ** διηκόνησεν, **βέλτιον** σὺ γινώσκεις.
+/and how.many.ways in Ephesus 3S.served very.well you you.know

Review Question

In non-narrative text, how does καί constrain the material it introduces to be processed?

Suggested Answer

In non-narrative text, καί constrains the material it introduces to be processed as being added to and associated with previous material.

Illustrative Passage 6: Titus 3:6–8

The NRSV inserts a paragraph break between vv. 8a and 8b, whereas the UBS third edition begins a new paragraph at v. 8a.[24] In the light of the presence of asyndeton in v. 8a and of καί in v. 8b, which is the most likely location for a paragraph break?

(6)   This Spirit he poured out on us richly through Jesus Christ our Savior, (7) so that, having been justified by his grace, we might become heirs according to the hope of eternal life.

(8a)   Ø Πιστὸς   ὁ   λόγος·
           trustworthy the   word

(8b)   καὶ περὶ   τούτων βούλομαί σε   διαβεβαιοῦσθαι,
           and concerning these   I.counsel you   to.strongly.affirm

(8c)   ἵνα   φροντίζωσιν   καλῶν ἔργων προΐστασθαι
           so.that 3P.may.take.thought of.good works to.be.involved

           οἱ   πεπιστευκότες   θεῷ·
           the.ones having.believed   in.God

Suggested Answer

Asyndeton is commonly found between paragraphs with different topics, so the presence of asyndeton in Titus 3:8a is consistent with a paragraph break at the beginning of v. 8. In turn, καί constrains the material it introduces to be processed as being added to and associated with previous material. A paragraph break at the beginning of v. 8a is therefore more likely than one between v. 8a and v. 8b.

7.4 Οὖν[25]

Section 5.3.3 described οὖν as a marked developmental conjunction, employed in John's Gospel in two ways: inferentially and as a resumptive (also called a "continuative"). Οὖν is used in the same two ways in non-narrative text (see Heckert 1996:96), viz.,[26]

- inferentially
- as a resumptive, usually following material of a digressional nature such as that introduced by γάρ to strengthen an assertion or assumption presented in or implied by the immediate context.

I consider these ways in turn.

1 Tim. 3:2a provides an example of οὖν used *inferentially*. Verse 1 states the topic (whoever aspires to the office of bishop desires a noble task). Οὖν then introduces the inferences that are to be drawn from this fact. Οὖν constrains the material with which it is associated to be processed as a new point on the topic of v. 1, and which develops from it in an inferential way.

---

[24] See Greenlee (1989:95-96) for a list of commentators who recognize the beginning of a discourse unit at v. 8a or at v. 8b.

[25] The following paragraphs are based on Heckert 1996:96-104 and sec. 4 of Levinsohn 1999a. See sec. 10.1 on μέν οὖν.

[26] One of the eight categories into which MGM (pp. 1104-09) classify οὖν is *summary* (e.g., Matt. 1:17), which I take to be an instance of inference. Further research is needed to determine whether these eight categories can be reduced to only two (inferential and resumptive) and whether, in practice, every example is interpretable as further development of the main topic or event line. See below on the suggestion that οὖν has an "adversative (but)" sense.

(1)   Ø **Πιστὸς**   ὁ   λόγος.   Εἴ   τις   ἐπισκοπῆς   ὀρέγεται,
       trustworthy   the   word   if   anyone   overseer   3S.aspires.to

     καλοῦ   **ἔργου**   ἐπιθυμεῖ.
     of.good   work   3S.desires

(2a)   δεῖ   οὖν   τὸν   ἐπίσκοπον   **ἀνεπίλημπτον**   εἶναι,
       3S.is.necessary   then   the   overseer   without.reproach   to.be

See also 2 Tim. 2:21 (discussed in sec. 7.1), concerning which Heckert notes (1996:97), "In 2 Tim. 2:20 Paul introduces the analogy of a royal household... From this analogy Paul draws an inference... introduced by οὖν (v. 21)."

We have already met the *resumptive* usage of οὖν in the narrative of John's Gospel (sec. 5.3.3). In fact, οὖν is used resumptively in nearly every New Testament epistle. Typically, it occurs after strengthening material associated with γάρ or ὅτι. In such situations, the *topic* that was under consideration before the strengthening material occurred is resumed and advanced, but οὖν conveys some "inferential force, since it also draws a conclusion from the supportive material introduced by γάρ" (Heckert 1996:118).

For example, **2 Tim. 1:8** resumes the topic of v. 6, following the material of v. 7 that strengthens the exhortation of v. 6, by giving a further exhortation that advances the argument.

(6)   for which reason I remind you to rekindle the gift of God that is within you through the laying on of my hands;

(7)   οὐ   γὰρ   ἔδωκεν   ἡμῖν   ὁ   θεὸς   πνεῦμα   δειλίας
       not   for   3S.gave   to.us   the   God   spirit   of.cowardice

       ἀλλὰ   δυνάμεως   καὶ   ἀγάπης   καὶ   σωφρονισμοῦ.
       but   of.power   and   of.love   and   of.self-discipline

(8)   μὴ   οὖν   ἐπαισχυνθῇς   τὸ   μαρτύριον   τοῦ   κυρίου   κ.τ.λ.
       not   then   be.ashamed.of   the   testimony   of.the   Lord

Heckert also classifies οὖν in **1 Tim. 2:1** as resumptive, returning to a main theme (topic) following a digression: "chapter 2, verses 1 and 2 not only resume the theme of what Timothy is directed to do, but also develop it by moving to a new point" (loc. cit.). However, he observes, "It is not apparent here that the function of οὖν in this text is inferential," i.e., that it relates inferentially to the comments of 1:19b–20 about those who have suffered shipwreck in the faith.

(18)   I am giving you this command, Timothy, my child, in accordance with the prophecies made earlier about you, so that by following them you may fight the good fight, (19a) having faith and a good conscience,

(19b)   which certain persons by rejecting conscience have suffered shipwreck in the faith; (20) among whom are Hymenaeus and Alexander, whom I have turned over to Satan, so that they may learn not to blaspheme.

(2:1)   Παρακαλῶ   οὖν   πρῶτον   πάντων   ποιεῖσθαι
       I.urge   then   first   of.all   to.be.made

       δεήσεις   προσευχὰς   ἐντεύξεις   εὐχαριστίας   κ.τ.λ.
       supplications   prayers   intercessions   thanksgivings

In such instances, then, the presence of οὖν constrains the material with which it is associated to be processed as a new point on the main topic under consideration, building on and developing from that earlier material, but without inferential overtones. (See also 2 Tim. 2:1. In the case of Heb. 4:14, where οὖν takes up the topic of Jesus as our high priest, which was last mentioned in 2:17, the intervening material has concerned a different topic.)

It appears, therefore, that οὖν is most likely to convey some inferential force when used as a resumptive if the amount of intervening material is short. Whether the amount of intervening material is short or long, the presence of οὖν only constrains what follows to be interpreted as further development of the topic that has been resumed.

The use of οὖν following strengthening material associated with γάρ may be contrasted with the use of δέ in the same situation. Each instance in the Pastoral Epistles in which δέ follows strengthening material associated with γάρ also involves a point of departure whose referent is a different subject from that of the previous material. In other words, following this strengthening material, the epistle develops in connection with a switch from the previous subject or topic to a different one.

This is illustrated in **2 Tim. 3:10**. This verse follows comments about the fate of those who 'oppose the truth' (vv. 8–9a). After v. 9b, which strengthens the assertion of v. 9a, however, it is not the topic of 'those who oppose the truth' that is resumed. Rather, δέ constrains v. 10 to be processed as developing from the previous material. The initial σύ and the content of the verse make it clear that that development is contrastive: 'you' is opposed to 'those who oppose the truth' and 'observed my teaching' is opposed to 'oppose the truth' (v. 8).

> (8)   As Jannes and Jambres opposed Moses, so also these oppose the truth, men of corrupt mind and counterfeit faith.

> (9a) ἀλλ' οὐ προκόψουσιν ἐπὶ πλεῖον,
>   but not 3P.will.advance yet further

> (9b) ἡ   γὰρ ἄνοια αὐτῶν ἔκδηλος ἔσται   πᾶσιν, κ.τ.λ.
>   the for folly their plain   3S.will.be to.all

> (10) Σὺ δὲ παρηκολούθησάς μου τῇ διδασκαλίᾳ κ.τ.λ.
>   you DE you.closely.followed my the teaching

See also 1 Tim. 6:9, 1 Tim. 6:11, and 2 Tim. 4:5.

I conclude that, whereas both δέ and οὖν constrain the material with which they are associated to be processed as developing from previous material, they differ in that, when οὖν is used, a previous main topic continues to be considered, whereas no such constraint applies to δέ.[27]

One of the categories into which MGM divide οὖν is "*Adversative* (but)." In each instance, οὖν introduces further development of the main topic or event line.

For example, in **1 Cor. 11:20**, Dana & Mantey (1955:257–58) translate συνερχομένων οὖν ὑμῶν ἐπὶ τὸ αὐτὸ "*However*, when ye assemble together." In fact, οὖν is used to *resume* and advance the topic of the problems that occur when 'you come together as a church' (vv. 17–18), following material in v. 19 that is introduced with γάρ to strengthen one of the assertions of v. 18.[28]

> (17) Now (δέ) in the following instructions I do not commend you, since it is not for the better but for the worse that you come together. (18) For (γάρ), to begin with, when you come together as a church, I hear that there are divisions among you; and to some extent I believe it.

> (19) Indeed (γάρ), there have to be factions among you, so that it will become clear who among you are genuine.

> (20) Συνερχομένων οὖν ὑμῶν ἐπὶ τὸ αὐτὸ
>   coming.together then you at the self

---

[27] In Jude 5, following strengthening material associated with γάρ, the topic under consideration in v. 3 appears to be resumed and advanced. This probably explains why οὖν is a variant reading to δέ in v. 5.

[28] Many translations into English begin v. 20 without a conjunction. An alternative would be to begin v. 20, 'When you come together, then,…'

οὐκ ἔστιν **κυριακὸν δεῖπνον** φαγεῖν·
not 3S.is Lord's supper to.eat

Romans 10:14 contains a further instance of οὖν that MGM classify as adversative; it is used to resume and advance the main topic of chapters 9–11 (the unbelieving Jews), following twelve verses (10:2–13) that strengthen previous assertions! Compare John 12:7 and Acts 26:22 (which MGM also classify as adversative), in which οὖν is used to resume and advance the event line or main topic following background material.

An adversative relation is readily perceived between the statement of **Acts 23:20** and the recommendation of v. 21. This is enhanced by the initial reference to 'you', marking a switch to the new point of departure/propositional topic. However, οὖν is not present to signal this adversative relation. Rather, it is there to constrain v. 21 to be processed as an *inference* that is to be drawn from v. 20.[29]

(20) He answered, "The Jews have agreed to ask you to bring Paul down to the council tomorrow, as though they were going to inquire more thoroughly into his case.

(21a) σὺ οὖν μὴ πεισθῇς αὐτοῖς·
you then not be.persuaded by.them

Review Questions

(a) In which two ways is οὖν used in non-narrative text?

(b) Δέ constrains the material with which it is associated to be processed as developing from previous material. What additional constraint does the presence of οὖν place on processing.

Suggested Answers

(a) In non-narrative text, οὖν is used:
   1. inferentially
   2. as a resumptive, usually following material of a digressional nature such as that introduced by γάρ or ὅτι to strengthen an assertion or assumption presented in or implied by the immediate context. Often, there are inferential overtones, too, especially if the intervening material is short.

(b) Whereas both δέ and οὖν constrain the material with which they are associated to be processed as developing from previous material, the presence of οὖν also indicates that the previous main topic continues to be considered.

Illustrative Passage 7: Matthew 5:43–48

(43) You have heard that it was said, "You shall love your neighbor and hate your enemy."

(44) ἐγὼ δὲ λέγω ὑμῖν, ἀγαπᾶτε τοὺς ἐχθροὺς κ.τ.λ.
I DE I.say to.you love the enemies

(45a) ὅπως γένησθε υἱοὶ τοῦ πατρὸς ὑμῶν τοῦ ἐν οὐρανοῖς,
so.that you.may.become sons of.the father your of.the in heaven

(45b) ὅτι τὸν ἥλιον αὐτοῦ ἀνατέλλει ἐπὶ πονηροὺς καὶ
since the sun his 3S.raises on evil.ones and

ἀγαθοὺς καὶ βρέχει ἐπὶ δικαίους καὶ ἀδίκους.
good.ones and 3S.rains on just.ones and unjust.ones

(46a) ἐὰν γὰρ ἀγαπήσητε τοὺς ἀγαπῶντας ὑμᾶς, τίνα μισθὸν ἔχετε;
if for you.love the.ones loving you what reward you.have

---

[29] Other instances of οὖν that MGM (ibid.) classify as adversative but may be interpreted as inferential include Matt. 26:54 (the adversative sense comes from the assumed premise from which the inference is drawn, 'But if I were to appeal to my Father'), John 8:38 (notice the presence of non-conjunctive καί modifying ὑμεῖς) and 9:18, and Rom. 11:19.

(46b)   οὐχὶ   καὶ   οἱ   τελῶναι   τὸ   αὐτὸ   ποιοῦσιν;
         not   +   the   tax.collectors   the   same   3P.do

(47a)   καὶ   ἐὰν ἀσπάσησθε   τοὺς   ἀδελφοὺς   ὑμῶν   μόνον,   τί   περισσὸν   ποιεῖτε;
         and   if   you.greet   the   brothers   your   only   what   extraordinary   you.do

(47b)   οὐχὶ   καὶ   οἱ   ἐθνικοὶ   τὸ   αὐτὸ   ποιοῦσιν;
         not   +   the   Gentiles   the   same   3P.do

(48)   Ἔσεσθε   οὖν   ὑμεῖς   τέλειοι   ὡς   ὁ   πατὴρ   ὑμῶν   ὁ
        you.will.be   then   you   perfect   as   the   father   your   the

         οὐράνιος   τέλειός   ἐστιν.
         heavenly   perfect   3S.is

Questions

(a) Why is asyndeton appropriate in v. 46b?
(b) Why is conjunctive καί appropriate in v. 47?
(c) Why is οὖν appropriate in v. 48?

Suggested Answers

(a) Asyndeton is appropriate in v. 46b because the clause is an evaluation of v. 46a.
(b) Καί is appropriate in v. 47 because the sentence provides a second example parallel to that of v. 46. As the presence of γάρ indicates, both of these examples are given to strengthen the exhortation of vv. 44–45 by elucidating "how the disciples as sons of the heavenly Father could not maintain their position if they should refuse to show love such as that of their Father" (Lenski 1943:250).
(c) Οὖν is appropriate in v. 48 because the topic of vv. 44–45a is resumed and advanced. 'You' are not only to 'love your enemies... so that you may be children of your Father in heaven'; you are to 'be perfect, as your heavenly Father is perfect'.

Illustrative Passage 8: Galatians 3:1–5 (see passage 7 of sec. 2.8 for the Greek text)

(1a)   Ø Oh senseless Galatians, **who** you 3S.bewitched
(1b)   to.whom before eyes Jesus Christ 3S.was.portrayed crucified?
(2a)   Ø **this only** I.want to.learn from you;
(2b)   Ø **by works of.law** the Spirit you.received or by hearing of.faith?
(3a)   Ø **so senseless** you.are?
(3b)   Ø having.begun in.Spirit, now **in.flesh** are.you.perfected?
(4)   Ø **so.much** you.suffered in.vain—if really + in.vain?
(5)   the οὖν supplying to.you the Spirit and working powerful.deeds among you, by works of.law or by hearing of.faith?

Question

Why is οὖν appropriate in v. 5?

Suggested Answer

Οὖν is appropriate in v. 5 because the topic of v. 2 is resumed (Lightfoot 1892:136), after the evaluative comment or parenthesis of v. 4. The argument of the topic has been advanced; whereas v. 2 concerned receiving the Spirit, v. 5 concerns the Galatians' current experience of the Spirit.

The questions following passage 9 concern both the conjunctions used and the order of constituents. (The variant readings in vv. 4–5a do not affect the points being considered here.)

Passage 9: Colossians 2:20–3:5a

(2:20) If you died with Christ to the elemental spirits of the world, why, as though you still belonged to the world, do you submit to regulations? (21) "Do not touch nor taste nor handle," (22) which refer to things that perish with use, according to the commandments and teachings of men, (23) which having indeed an appearance of wisdom in promoting self-imposed piety, humility, [and] severe treatment of the body, (are) not of any value in checking self-indulgence.

(3:1a) Εἰ   οὖν   συνηγέρθητε   τῷ   Χριστῷ,
        if   then you.were.raised.with the Christ

(1b) τὰ   ἄνω   ζητεῖτε,
      the above seek

(1c) οὗ   ὁ   Χριστός ἐστιν
      where the Christ   3S.is

(1d) ἐν   δεξιᾷ τοῦ   θεοῦ καθήμενος·
      in   right of.the God   sitting

(2) Ø τὰ   ἄνω   φρονεῖτε, μὴ   τὰ   ἐπὶ τῆς γῆς.
        the above think   not the on   the earth

(3a) ἀπεθάνετε γάρ
      you.died   for

(3b) καὶ ἡ   ζωὴ ὑμῶν κέκρυπται   σὺν τῷ   Χριστῷ ἐν τῷ   θεῷ.
      and the life your 3S.has.been.hidden with the Christ in the God

(4a) Ø ὅταν ὁ   Χριστὸς φανερωθῇ,   ἡ   ζωὴ ὑμῶν,
        when   the Christ   3S.may.be.manifested the life your

(4b) τότε καὶ ὑμεῖς σὺν αὐτῷ φανερωθήσεσθε   ἐν δόξῃ.
      then +   you   with him   3S.will.be.manifested in glory

(5a) Νεκρώσατε   οὖν   τὰ   μέλη   τὰ   ἐπὶ τῆς γῆς,
      put.to.death then the members the on   the earth

Questions[30]

(a) In 3:1a, why does the conditional clause begin the sentence? Why is οὖν used?

(b) In v. 2, why is asyndeton used?

(c) In v. 3b, why is conjunctive καί used? Why does ἡ ζωὴ ὑμῶν begin the clause? What is the implication of ending the clause with ἐν τῷ θεῷ?

(d) In v. 4a, why is asyndeton used, rather than γάρ, δέ, καί, or οὖν?

(e) In v. 4b, why is τότε used? Why is non-conjunctive καί used? How prominent is the constituent that it modifies? Why does σὺν αὐτῷ precede the verb?

(f) Why is οὖν used in v. 5a?

Suggested Answers: see Appendix 7(9).

---

[30] These questions only ask you to look at the constituent order of a few clauses. In fact, you should be able to explain the order of constituents in *every* clause, in terms of default and marked orderings.

III: PATTERNS OF REFERENCE

Part III of this book considers some factors that determine how an entity is referred to. It may be with a noun (e.g., ἄγγελος, Ἰησοῦς, νόμος), with an article[1] plus a noun (e.g., ὁ ἄγγελος, ὁ Ἰησοῦς, ὁ νόμος), with a pronoun (e.g., αὐτός, ἐκεῖνος), with an articular pronoun (e.g., ὁ), or with no overt reference other than the information conveyed by a verb about the person and number of the subject. Discussion of these forms of reference is divided between two chapters; chapter 8 considers the choice between a noun, a pronoun and no overt reference to a participant in a story, while chapter 9 concentrates on the presence versus the absence of the article with nouns.

Both chapters identify normal or *default* patterns of reference. Thus, section 8.2 indicates what is the default form of reference when the subject remains the same between clauses, when a non-subject in one clause becomes the subject of the next, etc. Similarly, section 9.2.1 describes the default rules for using or not using the article (introduce a participant without the article, make further reference to the participant with the article).

One reason for identifying these default patterns is in order to recognize when they are being broken, since it is the *marked* forms of reference that tell the reader that a new section is beginning or that a particular event or speech is being highlighted. They also reveal which parts of a book are being organized around a single participant and which parts take different participants in turn as focal (secs. 8.3 and 9.2.2).

These chapters also point out that the patterns of reference employed by each Gospel writer are not identical. This is particularly evident when the article is considered. Whereas Matthew and Luke-Acts employ basically the same principles, both Mark and John have their own characteristic reasons for using or omitting the article (secs. 9.2.2-3).

Perhaps the most significant claim in these chapters concerns what Wallace (1996:243) calls "anarthrous nouns" with "definite" force, i.e., nouns that are not preceded by the article yet have a uniquely identifiable referent. Such nouns lack the article for *prominence*, to focus on them or bring them to the attention of the reader for one reason or another (sec. 9.2.3). Section 9.3 argues that many nouns lack the article not because they describe a quality, but because they are focal.

---

[1] Porter (1992:103) points out, "the Greek article is best not called the 'definite article', since this implies a non-existent indefinite article."

8
PARTICIPANT REFERENCE

Greek, like all languages, has a variety of forms of reference to the participants in a story. They extend from an implicit reference conveyed only by the person of the verb, to sets of pronouns (articular and demonstrative, among others), to a full noun phrase (with or without the article—see chap. 9). In this chapter, factors that influence the use of these different forms are considered. An understanding of these factors sheds light on the author's intentions as to the status of the participants in the story, on whether or not certain events or speeches are highlighted, and on the degree to which successive episodes are associated together.

Section 8.1 briefly considers how major and minor participants are introduced to new and to existing scenes. Section 8.2 proposes rules for determining whether further reference to participants who have already been activated (introduced to the story) are "default" or "marked" encodings. Finally, section 8.3 considers how the system of reference is modified if one participant (the "VIP" or "very important participant"—*SIL-UND* sec. 17.2) is singled out for special treatment in part or all of a book. Such treatment has implications for identifying major divisions in the narrative and highlighted speeches or actions.

8.1   The Status and Introduction of Participants

The most common distinction that linguists make, as far as participant *status* is concerned, is between major and minor participants. "Notionally, MAJOR PARTICIPANTS are those which are active for a large part of the narrative and play leading roles; minor participants are activated briefly and lapse into deactivation" (*SIL-UND* sec. 17.2.1).

The distinction between major and minor participants is needed for one of the default encoding rules of sec. 8.2, but otherwise seems to be of little consequence.

New Testament authors *introduce* participants in a variety of ways.

The introductory reference to the first participant of a story or episode is often the *point of departure*/propositional topic of a sentence with topic-comment articulation. This is illustrated in Luke 15:11b (Ἄνθρωπός τις[1] εἶχεν δύο υἱούς 'A certain man had two sons') and Acts 10:1 (Ἀνὴρ δέ τις ἐν Καισαρείᾳ ὀνόματι Κορνήλιος... 'Now a certain man in Caesarea named Cornelius...'). See also the introduction to an existing scene of Simon's mother-in-law in Mark 1:30.

Introductions to a new section of an ongoing story most often involve a sentence with *presentational* articulation, as in Acts 9:10a (Ἦν δέ τις μαθητὴς ἐν Δαμασκῷ ὀνόματι Ἀνανίας 'Now there was a disciple in Damascus named Ananias'). Sentences with presentational articulation are sometimes used also in non-narrative to introduce new participants or objects to an ongoing argument, as in Titus 1:10 (discussed in sec. 2.8) and 2 Tim. 2:20a (discussed in sec. 7.1).

A participant may be introduced to an existing scene with a verb of *arrival*, as in John 4:7a (Ἔρχεται γυνὴ ἐκ τῆς Σαμαρείας ἀντλῆσαι ὕδωρ 'A Samaritan woman came to draw water').[2]

Participants are often introduced to an existing scene as the *object of a verb of perception*, as in Luke 5:27b (καὶ ἐθεάσατο τελώνην ὀνόματι Λευὶν κ.τ.λ. 'and he saw a tax collector named Levi...').

---

[1] Hopper and Thompson (1984:719) have shown that, in many languages, the presence versus absence of words like 'one' or 'a certain', in connection with the introduction of a participant, depends on whether or not "it figures in the discourse as a *salient* participant." In Koiné Greek, τις is often used as an adjective when major participants are introduced. Equally, however, it is often *not* used when others are introduced (see John 4:7a and Luke 5:27b below) and I do not discern a discourse explanation for its presence or absence. Τις is also used as an indefinite pronoun to introduce minor participants, as in Acts 5:25 (παραγενόμενος δέ τις ἀπήγγειλεν αὐτοῖς κ.τ.λ. 'then someone arrived and announced...').

[2] See sec. 12.2 on the use of the historical present in connection with the introduction of participants to existing scenes.

Participants may also be introduced by *association* with another participant. In Luke 15:11b (above), for instance, the two sons are introduced by association with their father.

The introduction of participants may be *highlighted* by placing ἰδού 'behold' immediately before the reference to them. Van Otterloo (1988:34) says that ἰδού is used in this way "to focus special attention on a major... participant as he/she/it is introduced onto the event line of an episode."[3] This usage, which is found mostly in Matthew's Gospel and Luke-Acts, is illustrated in **Matt. 2:1b**.

(1a) <u>Τοῦ</u> δὲ <u>Ἰησοῦ</u> γεννηθέντος   ἐν Βηθλέεμ τῆς Ἰουδαίας
     of.the DE Jesus   having.been.born   in Bethlehem of.the Judea

     ἐν ἡμέραις Ἡρῴδου τοῦ βασιλέως,
     in days   of.Herod the king

(1b) ἰδού   μάγοι ἀπὸ ἀνατολῶν παρεγένοντο εἰς Ἱεροσόλυμα
     behold magi from east   3P.arrived   in Jerusalem

Some participants are *never* introduced, presumably because their presence is assumed. Examples include Simon (Peter) in Luke 4:38, the angel of the Lord in Acts 5:19, and Felix the governor in Acts 23:24.

Although the presence of *supernatural* participants is generally assumed, their introduction to an existing scene may be highlighted. Such is the case for the angel of the Lord in **Matt. 1:20b**.

(20a) <u>ταῦτα</u> δὲ <u>αὐτοῦ</u> ἐνθυμηθέντος
      these DE his   thinking.on

(20b) ἰδού   ἄγγελος κυρίου κατ' ὄναρ ἐφάνη   αὐτῷ
      behold angel   of.Lord by   dream 3S.appeared to.him

8.2   Further Reference to Activated Participants

Once a participant has been introduced to the story, the way he or she is referred to depends on a number of factors, such as the number of participants on stage, their relative status, whether or not their role changes, and the position of the sentence in the text. Reflecting these factors, three tasks for a scheme of reference have been identified (*SIL-UND* sec. 16.2):

semantic: identify the referents unambiguously, distinguishing them from other possible ones
discourse-pragmatic: signal the activation status and prominence of the referents or the actions they perform
processing: overcome disruptions in the flow of information.

Note. The term "activation status" refers to whether the referent is being introduced (activated) or reintroduced (reactivated), or is already on stage (active).

Givón's "*Iconicity Principle*" (1983:18) partially accounts for the above tasks. It states:

The more disruptive, surprising, discontinuous or hard to process a topic is, the more *coding material* must be assigned to it.

---

[3] Van Otterloo fails to distinguish between instances of ἰδού in which the reference to the new participant occurs immediately after ἰδού and those in which ἰδού is followed by a verb. If this distinction is made, it turns out that, when a reference to a new participant immediately follows ἰδού, the participant typically has a major role to play in an existing scene. When ἰδού is followed by a verb, in contrast, it is a significant *act* that is introduced to the existing scene and any participant involved is cast in a non-active role. See, for example, Matt. 9:2 (καὶ ἰδού προσέφερον αὐτῷ παραλυτικὸν κ.τ.λ. 'and behold, they [unspecified] brought to him a paralytic...').

Groce (1991:128) points out that many participants introduced by ἰδού are "accorded only obscure reference, without a given name in most cases." Such participants might well not have been perceived to have a major role to play in the episode into which they were introduced, had ἰδού not been used.

See sec. 11.1.1 on the use of genitives absolute to highlight the introduction of participants to an existing scene.

For Koiné Greek, the coding material for *third person referents* would be on the following scale, with the least coding material at the top of the scale and the most at the bottom:

> implicit reference reflected in the person of the verb
> articular pronouns
> "independent" (demonstrative or intensive) pronouns
> full noun phrases (including proper names)

I find that Givón's Iconicity Principle works up to a point. For example, it correctly predicts that, when there is a discontinuity because a participant is being reactivated after an absence, it is normal to refer to him or her with a full noun phrase. Similarly, it is normal to use a full noun phrase when a sentence is highlighted because the event described is "disruptive, surprising" (ibid.). However, sentences may be highlighted and a full noun phrase employed when the information concerned is important but neither disruptive nor surprising (e.g., a key speech). Also, it is not clear whether the principle covers the use of full noun phrases at the beginning of new "narrative units" (Fox 1987:168) when the participants remain the same and occupy the same roles in successive paragraphs. (The term *narrative unit* covers episodes, sections, and subsections of a narrative—see fn. 4 of chap. 1.)

The following are three factors that Givón's principle does not seem to cover:
- the *status* of the participant, in particular whether two major participants are interacting or whether the interacting participants are one major and one minor (see below).
- the *salience* of the participant: a participant like Jesus who is central to a whole book (the "global VIP") is referred to in different ways than other major participants (sec. 8.3). In addition, references by name to a locally important participant ("local VIP") are often anarthrous (see chap. 9).
- whether or not the reference to a participant follows a *reported speech*: the articular pronoun is used almost exclusively to refer to the addressee of the last speech (see sec. 13.1).

An alternative to Givón's Iconicity Principle is to analyze the system of reference to activated participants in terms of *default and marked encoding*. First, default values are identified for various situations in which, in Givón's terms, there is no great discontinuity or surprise. Marked encodings are those that are other than the default encoding for a specific situation.

Default encoding for Koiné Greek narrative includes the following rules for *subjects*:[4]

1. If the subject is the *same* as in the previous clause, no overt reference is made to the subject (unless the construction used requires an overt subject—see rule 5 below).
2. If the subject was the *addressee* of an immediately preceding speech, an articular pronoun or no overt reference is used (depending on factors to be discussed in chaps. 13–14).
3. If a non-subject in one clause becomes the subject of the next and a major participant is interacting with a *minor* participant or is *alone*, no reference is made to the subject.
4. In all other occasions that involve a *change of subject*, a full noun phrase is used to refer to the subject. (These include occasions in which a participant is reactivated and those in which two major participants are interacting. See sec. 8.3 for a systematic exception to this rule.)
5. If the subject of a *genitive absolute* is the same as the subject of the previous clause, an independent pronoun is used (in genitives absolute, the subject generally is obligatory).[5] Similarly, if a *point of departure involving renewal* has the same subject as that of the previous sentence, an independent pronoun is used (see below). (In the case of *relative clauses* with the same subject as that of the previous clause, a *relative* pronoun is used—see sec. 11.2 for examples.)

---

[4] I do not discuss default or marked encodings of non-subjects, although this is a valid area of research. For a step-by-step methodology for analyzing reference to both subjects and non-subjects in a monologue discourse, see *SIL-UND* chap. 18.

[5] Genitives absolute occur without overt subjects in Luke 12:36 and Acts 21:31, plus as variants in other passages. If no overt reference were considered to be the default encoding for genitives absolute with the same subject as the previous clause, the presence of the independent pronoun could readily be explained in terms of new narrative units or of highlighting the event described in the following independent clause.

I now illustrate these rules from the parable of the Prodigal Son (Luke 15:11–32), before adding some provisos to rule 1.

Default rule 1 is illustrated in **Luke 15:13b**. The subject of v. 13b is the same as in v. 13a and there is no overt reference, other than the third person singular verb ending.

(13a)   καὶ   <u>μετ' οὐ πολλὰς ἡμέρας</u> συναγαγὼν
         and   after not many   days   having.gathered.together

         πάντα   ὁ   νεώτερος υἱὸς ἀπεδήμησεν εἰς χώραν μακράν
         everything the younger   son   3S.journeyed to   country far

(13b)   καὶ <u>ἐκεῖ</u>   διεσκόρπισεν τὴν οὐσίαν   αὐτοῦ ζῶν   ἀσώτως.
         and there   3S.squandered   the property his   living loosely

Default rule 2 is illustrated in **Luke 15:12b**. The subject of v. 12b was the addressee of the speech of v. 12a and is referred to by an articular pronoun or no overt reference, depending on the reading followed.[6]

(11b)   <u>Ἄνθρωπός τις</u>   εἶχεν δύο υἱούς.
         man   certain 3S.had two sons

(12a)   καὶ εἶπεν ὁ   νεώτερος αὐτῶν τῷ   πατρί,
         and 3S.said the younger   of.them to.the father

         Πάτερ, δός μοι τὸ ἐπιβάλλον μέρος τῆς   οὐσίας.
         father give to.me the belonging part   of.the property

(12b)   <u>ὁ</u> δὲ* διεῖλεν αὐτοῖς τὸν βίον.   (*variant for <u>ὁ</u> δὲ: καί)
         he DE 3S.gave to.them the property

Luke 15:22 illustrates an occasion in which the subject was the addressee of the previous speech but then speaks to someone other than the previous subject. The reference to the subject is therefore a full noun phrase, in conformity with default rule 4.

(21)   εἶπεν δὲ ὁ   υἱὸς αὐτῷ, Πάτερ, ἥμαρτον εἰς   τὸν οὐρανὸν
       3S.said DE the son to.him father I.sinned against the   heaven

       καὶ ἐνώπιόν σου, κ.τ.λ.
       and before   you

(22)   εἶπεν δὲ ὁ   πατὴρ πρὸς τοὺς δούλους αὐτοῦ, κ.τ.λ.
       3S.said DE the father to   the   slaves   his

Default rule 3 is illustrated in **Luke 15:15–16a**. These verses describe the interaction of a major participant (the younger son) and a minor participant (a citizen of the country). In both v. 15b and v. 16, the subject was a non-subject in the previous clause and no overt reference is made to him.

(15a)   καὶ πορευθεὶς ἐκολλήθη   ἑνὶ   τῶν   πολιτῶν
         and having.gone 3S.became.associated to.one of.the citizens

         τῆς   χώρας ἐκείνης,
         of.the country that

(15b)   καὶ ἔπεμψεν αὐτὸν εἰς τοὺς ἀγροὺς αὐτοῦ βόσκειν χοίρους,
         and 3S.sent   him   to   the   fields   his   to.feed   pigs

(16a)   καὶ ἐπεθύμει   χορτασθῆναι ἐκ   τῶν κερατίων ὧν
         and 3S.was.longing to.be.fed   from the   pods   which

---

[6] See passage 8 of sec. 5.1 on the significance of reading καί in v. 12b.

ἤσθιον   οἱ   χοῖροι,
3P.were.eating the pigs

Default rule 4 is illustrated in Luke 15:12a (above). There is a change of subject from v. 11b (a certain man) to the younger son and a full noun phrase is used. See also Luke 15:22 (above).

Default rule 5 is illustrated in **Luke 15:14a**. The subject of the genitive absolute of v. 14a is the same as the subject of v. 13b, so an independent pronoun (αὐτοῦ) is used.

(13b) καὶ ἐκεῖ διεσκόρπισεν τὴν οὐσίαν αὐτοῦ ζῶν ἀσώτως.
       and there 3S.squandered the property his living loosely

(14a) δαπανήσαντος δὲ αὐτοῦ πάντα κ.τ.λ.
       having.spent DE he everything

Luke 2:36–37a (repeated from sec. 2.3) illustrates default rule 5 when a point of departure involving renewal has the same subject as that of the previous sentence. In both v. 36b and v. 37, the point of departure is an independent pronoun.

(36a) Καὶ ἦν Ἄννα προφῆτις, θυγάτηρ Φανουήλ, κ.τ.λ.
       and 3S.was Anna prophetess daughter Phanuel

(36b) αὕτη προβεβηκυῖα ἐν ἡμέραις πολλαῖς,
       this having.become.advanced in days many

       ζήσασα μετὰ ἀνδρὸς ἔτη ἑπτὰ ἀπὸ τῆς παρθενίας αὐτῆς
       having.lived with husband years seven from the virginity her

(37a) καὶ αὐτὴ χήρα ἕως ἐτῶν ὀγδοήκοντα τεσσάρων,
       and she widow until years eighty four

In regard to rule 1 above, it should be noted that, if the subject is the same as in the last independent clause that describes a storyline event, no overt reference is made to it, even if intervening background material has a different subject. This is illustrated in **Acts 5:2c**; the subjects of vv. 2a and 2c are the same (Ananias), and no overt reference is made to him in v. 2c even though the intervening genitive absolute has a different subject.

(2a) καὶ ἐνοσφίσατο ἀπὸ τῆς τιμῆς,
      and 3S.misappropriated from the price

(2b) συνειδυίης καὶ τῆς γυναικός,
      having.known + the wife

(2c) καὶ ἐνέγκας μέρος τι **παρὰ τοὺς πόδας τῶν ἀποστόλων** ἔθηκεν.
      and having.brought part certain at the feet of.the apostles 3S.laid

A further proviso to rule 1 is that, when the subject and other participants in the action of the previous clause are included in a plural subject in the next clause, this is usually treated as the same subject for the purposes of participant reference encoding. An example is in **Luke 15:24b**; the subject of the speech of vv. 22–24a was the father and he, together with the addressees, is included in the plural subject of v. 24b. No overt reference is therefore made to the subject.

(22) εἶπεν δὲ ὁ πατὴρ πρὸς τοὺς δούλους αὐτοῦ, κ.τ.λ.
      3S.said DE the father to the slaves his

(23) καὶ φέρετε τὸν μόσχον τὸν σιτευτόν, θύσατε,
      and bring the calf the fattened sacrifice

      καὶ φαγόντες εὐφρανθῶμεν, (24a) ὅτι κ.τ.λ.
      and having.eaten let.us.be.merry since

(24b) καὶ ἤρξαντο εὐφραίνεσθαι.
       and 3P.began to.be.merry

However, the reverse is not true. When a member of a *group* of participants that featured in the previous clause becomes the subject of the next clause, a full noun phrase is used. This is illustrated in Luke 15:12a (above). The two sons as a group featured in the previous clause (v. 11b), whereas the subject of v. 12a is the younger son, so rule 4 applies.

Passage 1 (below) displays how the participants are referred to throughout the parable of the Prodigal Son and which default rule is operating. (I do not indicate how the participants are referred to within the reported speeches, as these are embedded in the overall narrative.)

The following abbreviations are used: art = articular pronoun; GA = genitive absolute; intro = introduction of a participant; NP = full noun phrase; pn = independent pronoun; Ø = no overt reference.

The numbers in parentheses refer to the referents: 1 is the father; 2, the younger son; 3, the older son; 4, the citizen of v. 15; 5, the slaves of v. 22; and 6, the lad of v. 26. The first three are major participants; the other three are minor ones.

The numbers in the default rule column indicate which of the five default rules for subject encoding is operating. The absence of a number in v. 14c indicates that the encoding is not a default value (see below).

Passage 1: Luke 15:11–32

verse	subject	non-subject	default rule	summary of contents
11	NP (1)	NP (2 + 3)	intro	(had)
12a	NP (2)	NP (1)	4	(said, 'Give me my share!')
12b	art (1)	pn (2 + 3)	2	(divided his property between)
13a	NP (2)		4	(departed to a far country)
13b	Ø (2)		1	(squandered the property)
14a	pn (2)		5	(when spent everything) (GA)
14b	famine		intro	(arose in that country)
14c	pn (2)		-	(began to be in want)
15a	Ø (2)	NP (4)	1	(joined himself to)
15b	Ø (4)	pn (2)	3	(sent into his fields)
16a	Ø (2)		3	(longed to feed on pods)
16b	no-one	pn (2)	4	(gave anything)
17	Ø (2)		3	(coming to himself, said)
20a	Ø (2)	NP (1)	1	(rising up, came to)
20b	pn (2)		5	(while yet at a distance) (GA)
20c	NP (1)	pn (2)	4	(saw)
20d	Ø (1)		1	(had compassion)
20e	Ø (1)	pn (2)	1	(running, embraced)
20f	Ø (1)	pn (2)	1	(kissed)
21	NP (2)	pn (1)	4	(said to)
22	NP (1)	NP (5)	-	(said to)
24b	Ø (1 +)		1	(began to make merry)
25a	NP (3)		4	(was in the field)
25b	Ø (3)		1	(as drew near, heard music)
26	Ø (3)	NP (6)	1	(calling, asked what music meant)
27	art (6)	pn (3)	2	(said, 'Your brother came')
28a	Ø (3)		3	(was angry)
28b	Ø (3)		1	(refused to go in)
28c	NP (1)	pn (3)	4	(coming out, besought)
29	art (3)	NP (1)	2	(answering, said to)
31	art (1)	pn (3)	2	(said to)

When *more* coding material occurs than the default rules predict, this typically marks the beginning of a narrative unit or highlights the action or speech concerned.

In passage 1 (above), the only subject that has more coding material than the default rules predict is in v. 14c. An independent pronoun is used, even though the referent is the only major participant on stage and the default encoding would have been no overt reference (rule 3). However, v. 14a appears to begin a new narrative unit, so more coding material is appropriate to mark that fact.

Passage 2 (below) illustrates the use of a full noun phrase in connection with the climactic event of an episode. In Acts 5:5, the default encoding of reference to Ananias would have been an articular pronoun, as he was the addressee of the previous speech (rule 2). This marked encoding contributes to the highlighting of v. 5. (The following abbreviations are used: A refers to Ananias, P to Peter, and Y to the youths of v. 6a.)

Passage 2: Acts 5:1–6

verse	subject	non-subject	default rule	summary of contents
1	NP (A)	NP (wife)	intro	(sold property with)
2a	Ø (A)		1	(appropriated part of the price)
2b	NP (wife)		4	(being aware of it) (GA)
2c	Ø (A)	NP (apostles)	1	(bringing, placed at the feet of)
3	NP (P)	Ø (A)	4	(said)
5a	NP (A)		-	(hearing, died)
5b	NP (fear)	NP (all)	intro	(fell on)
6a	NP (Y)	pn (A)	intro	(arising, wrapped)
6b	Ø (Y)	Ø (A)	1	(carrying out, buried)

In passage 3, which is a conversation between the Lord and Ananias (not the same Ananias as in Acts 5), several of the speeches are introduced with more coding material for the subject than the default rules predict. The instructions of the Lord (L) to Ananias (A) in Acts 9:11 and 15 may both be viewed as key speeches. Ananias' objection in v. 13 is also introduced with a full noun phrase; this is the norm when the previous addressee seeks to take control of the conversation (see sec. 14.1).

Passage 3: Acts 9:10–16

verse	subject	non-subject	default rule	summary of contents
10a	NP (A)		intro	(there was in Damascus)
10b	NP (L)	pn (A)	intro	(said to)
10c	art (A)	Ø (L)	2	(said)
11	NP (L)	pn (A)	-	([said] to)
13	NP (A)	Ø (L)	-	(answered)
15	NP (L)	pn (A)	-	(said to)

The above passages illustrate that, if more coding material is used than the default rules predict, either a new narrative unit has begun (as in Luke 15:14) or else an action or speech has been highlighted. In the case of speeches introduced with a full noun phrase rather than an articular pronoun, either the speech is a key one or else it represents a move to take control on the part of the speaker (sec. 14.1).

Once references to participants have been classified as default or marked encodings, this can be used to confirm or reject claims that a narrative unit begins at such and such a verse, or that such and such an action or speech has been highlighted. For example, if a certain sentence is considered to begin a new narrative unit but no overt reference to the subject occurs, then the validity of the proposed break in the narrative should be questioned.

Luke 20:20 (passage 4) is such a questionable sentence. In some versions (e.g., NIV, NRSV), it is considered to begin a new narrative unit. However, there is no overt reference in this verse to the subject. This is consistent with default rule 1 (the subject of v. 20 is the same as in v. 19a–c), but not with the expectation that new narrative units begin with more coding material. Furthermore, the reference to the scribes in v. 19a (the addressees of the previous speech) has more coding material than default rule 2 predicts. This is appropriate if the narrative unit begins at v. 19 rather than v. 20. (In this passage, which is discussed further in sec. 17.1, S refers to the scribes and J to Jesus.)

Passage 4: Luke 20:19–20

verse	subject	non-subject	default rule	summary of contents
19a	NP (S)	pn (J)	-	(sought to lay hands on)
19b	Ø (S)	NP (people)	1	(feared)
19c	Ø (S)		1	(for knew that)
19d	Ø (J)	pn (S)		(had told parable against)
20	Ø (S)	NP (spies)	1	(watching, sent, pretending to be honest, to catch his word)

(In v. 20, the subject is the same as in the last clause that describes a main event [v. 19b], so rule 1 applies, since v. 19d is an embedded clause introduced with ὅτι. See sec. 8.3 for why v. 19d contains no overt reference to Jesus.)

Review Questions

(a) If the subject is the same as in the last clause, what is the default encoding? In genitives absolute? If a point of departure is required?

(b) If the subject was the addressee of the previous speech (and vice versa, where appropriate), what is the default encoding?

(c) What is the default encoding if the subject was a non-subject in the previous clause and only one major participant is on stage? if two major participants are on stage?

(d) When more coding material is used than the default rules predict, what does this usually mark?

Suggested Answers

(a) If the subject is the same as in the last clause, the default encoding is no overt reference. In genitives absolute, however, it is an independent pronoun. An independent pronoun is also the default encoding if a point of departure is required.

(b) If the subject was the addressee of the last speech (and vice versa, where appropriate), the default encoding is an articular pronoun or no overt reference.

(c) If the subject was a non-subject in the previous clause, the default encoding is no overt reference if only one major participant is on stage; it is a full noun phrase, however, if two major participants are on stage.

(d) When more coding material is used than the default rules predict, this is usually to mark the beginning of a narrative unit or to highlight the action or speech concerned.

Illustrative Passage 5: Acts 8:26–40 (UBS text)

Note which references to the subjects in this passage are default encodings and which are marked ones. (P refers to Philip and E to the eunuch.)

verse	subject	non-subject	default rule	summary of contents
26a	NP (angel)	NP (P)		(spoke to, saying, "Go south!")
26b	pn (this)			(is deserted)
27a	Ø (P)			(rising, went)
27b	NP (E)			(had come to Jerusalem to worship)
28a	Ø (E)			(was returning)
28b	Ø (E)			(was sitting in his chariot)
28c	Ø (E)	NP (Isaiah)		(was reading)
29	NP (Spirit)	NP (P)		(said to, "Approach this chariot!")
30a	NP (P)	pn (E)		(heard reading Isaiah)

30b	Ø (P)	Ø (E)	(said, "Do you understand?")
31a	art (E)	Ø (P)	(said, "How can I?")
31b	Ø (E)	NP (P)	(invited to sit with him)
32–33	NP (passage)		(was this:…)
34	NP (E)	NP (P)	(said, "Who does he speak about?")
35	NP (P)	pn (E)	(preached Jesus to)
36a	Ø (P + E)		(came upon some water)
36b	NP (E)	Ø (P)	(says, "May I be baptized?")
38a	Ø (E)		(commanded the chariot to stop)
38b	NP (P + E)		(both went down into the water)
38c	Ø (P)	pn (E)	(baptized)
39a	Ø (P + E)		(when came up from the water)
39b	NP (Spirit)	NP (P)	(took away)
39c	NP (E)	pn (P)	(no longer saw)
39d	Ø (E)		(was going on his way rejoicing)
40a	NP (P)		(found himself in Azotus)
40b	Ø (P)		(was preaching to all the towns)

Questions

(a) In which clauses or sentences does default encoding rule 1 determine the form of reference to the subject?

(b) In which clauses or sentences does default rule 2 determine the form of reference to the subject?

(c) In which clauses or sentences is there *more* coding material than the default rules predict? Why has such marked encoding been used?

(d) In which clause is there *less* coding material than the default rules predict?

Suggested Answers

(a) In conformity with default encoding rule 1, no overt reference to the subject occurs in the following clauses or sentences: 28a, 28b, 28c, 30b, 31b, 38a, 39d, and 40b, plus 36a and 39a (the two participants involved in the previous clause make up the new plural subject).

(b) In conformity with default rule 2, a subject that was the addressee of the previous speech is referred to by either an articular pronoun or no overt reference in the following clauses or sentences: 27a (the background material of v. 26b intervenes) and 31a.

(c) More coding material than the default rules predict is found in the following clauses or sentences:
   - v. 30 (the subject was the previous addressee): a new narrative unit probably begins here; in vv. 26–29, the interactions were between Philip and an angel or the Spirit; in vv. 30ff., they are between Philip and the eunuch.
   - v. 34 (the same subject as in v. 31b, the intervening material is background information): a new narrative unit probably begins here, following the lengthy quotation of vv. 32–33.
   - v. 35 (the subject was the previous addressee): the first climax of the interaction between Philip and the eunuch is highlighted.
   - v. 38b (the two participants involved in the previous clause make up the new plural subject): the climactic event complex of vv. 38b–c is highlighted.

(d) Less coding material than the default rules predict is found in v. 38c (there is a change of subject to the singular from the plural of v. 38b—compare v. 36b). This may be because the respective roles of the two participants are unambiguous (see the passive βαπτισθῆναι in v. 36c) and the event is completely predictable. It is possible, however, that no overt reference to Philip is made because he is treated as the "VIP"—see sec. 8.3.

8.3   References to VIPs

The rules of sec. 8.2 for default encoding of references to participants are based on what Givón (1983:13) calls a "look-back" strategy. They depend on whether the new subject has remained the same as before or not and, if not, whether it was the previous addressee or was in some other non-subject role in the previous clause. In each case, the encoding was determined by looking back to the immediate context.

It appears that all languages in fact use at least *two* strategies of reference at different times: the look-back strategy and what chapter 17 of the *SIL-UND* volume calls a *"VIP"* strategy, where VIP stands for "very important participant."[7] In the VIP strategy, "one referent is distinguished from the rest" (Grimes loc. cit.). In the look-back strategy, in contrast, all the major participants are treated alike. The same document can use both strategies in different sections.

A VIP can be identified either on the *global* level (e.g., for a whole book of the New Testament), or on a *local* level (e.g., for a section of a book or even for a single episode). It appears that each Gospel treats Jesus as the global VIP. In the book of Acts, different Christian leaders in turn may be treated as the VIP, either at the local level (for one or two episodes) or, in the case of Paul, at a more global level (see sec. 9.2.2).

When the VIP strategy is being used, languages have a variety of ways of marking the VIP. Grimes noted that, in some Amerindian languages, "a special set of terms refer to it no matter how many other things have been mentioned more recently" (loc. cit.). For example, one pronoun set may be reserved exclusively for the VIP and another set for the other participants.

Another way in which a VIP strategy works is by *orientation* with respect to the VIP. For example, movement towards the location of the VIP may always be expressed with 'come' verbs, while movement in any other direction is expressed with 'go' verbs.[8] Similarly, kinship terms may be used so that other participants are related to the local VIP (e.g., 'the man', '*his* wife and child').

Of most significance for the topic of this chapter, however, is the tendency for references to the VIP to be *minimal*, once he or she has been activated (see Marchese 1984:234–35).

In the Gospels, Jesus is the global VIP. If we take the UBS paragraphing as an indication of the beginning of new narrative units, the norm there is for there to be no overt reference to Jesus (except in genitives absolute, where an independent pronoun is used), *even when Jesus was not the subject of the previous clause*. In other words, default encoding for the global VIP as subject, when he was in a non-subject role in the previous clause, is no overt reference (in violation of default rule 4). Examples in passage 6 (below) include, with various degrees of MS support, Matthew 4:12, 18, 23, and 5:1.[9] In such instances, I suggest, the author perceives sufficient continuity between the episodes concerned to omit any reference to Jesus, so the break in the story is minor.

Since the default encoding for the global VIP as subject is no overt reference, then any overt reference to Jesus as subject once he has been activated is marked encoding. Overt reference (typically, a full noun phrase) is indicative of one of two situations:

- a major break in the story (e.g., because of a significant change of theme or situation)
- a key speech or action.

Passage 6 illustrates default and marked encoding of reference to Jesus as global VIP. Lines across the page indicate new paragraphs in the UBS text. Note the clauses marked as not conforming to the default encoding rules of section 8.2. (A refers to Andrew, An to angels, D to the devil, J to Jesus, Ja to James, Jo to John, and P to Peter. "(VIP)" indicates an overt subject reference to Jesus as the VIP. Some manuscripts refer to Jesus by name in 4:12, 4:18a and 4:23.)

---

[7] Grimes (loc. cit.) calls the VIP strategy the "thematic strategy."

[8] Turnbull (1986:43) considers that the Greek verbs ἔρχομαι and πορεύομαι "do have directional-specificity," with ἔρχομαι generally coming to some "reference point assumed by the speaker for himself or for the hearer." Research is needed to determine whether the reference point may be the VIP.

[9] Alford (1863.I:30) comments concerning the presence of ὁ Ἰησοῦς as a variant reading in Matt. 4:12, "the commencement of an ecclesiastical portion, and the name was therefore supplied, as so frequently is the case." He makes a similar observation about vv. 18 and 23. However, Pope notes (p.c.) that "there are also a number of MSS that start a church reading at 5:1, but there is practically no evidence for referring to Jesus with a noun phrase at that point."

Passage 6: Matthew 4:1–5:1 (UBS text)

verse	subject	non-subject	default rule	summary of contents
1	NP (J)	NP (Spirit)	4 (VIP)	(was led into wilderness by)
		NP (D)		(to be tempted by)
2	Ø (J)		1	(after 40 days, hungered)
3	NP (D)	pn (J)	4	(approaching, said)
4	art (J)	Ø (D)	2	(answering, said)
5a	NP (D)	pn (J)	-	(takes into the holy city)
5b	Ø (D)	pn (J)	1	(stood on wing of temple)
6	Ø (D)	pn (J)	1	(says to)
7	NP (J)	pn (D)	- (VIP)	(said to)
8a	NP (D)	pn (J)	-	(takes to high mountain)
8b	Ø (D)	pn (J)	1	(shows all kingdoms, glory)
9	Ø (D)	pn (J)	1	(said to)
10	NP (J)	pn (D)	- (VIP)	(says to)
11a	NP (D)	pn (J)	-	(leaves)
11b	NP (An)		intro	(approached)
11c	Ø (An)	pn (J)	1	(ministered to)
12	Ø (J)		3	(hearing re Jo, departed to Gal)
13	Ø (J)		1	(leaving, dwelt in Caper.)
14–16				(quotation from Isaiah)
17	NP (J)		- (VIP)	(began to proclaim and say)
18a	Ø (J)	NP (P + A)	1	(walking, saw)
18b	Ø (P + A)		3	(for were fishermen)
19	Ø (J)	pn (P + A)	1	(says to)
20	art (P + A)	pn (J)	2	(leaving nets, followed)
21a	Ø (J)	NP (Ja + Jo)	3	(going on, saw)
21b	Ø (J)	pn (Ja + Jo)	1	(called)
22	art (Ja + Jo)	pn (J)	2	(leaving boat, followed)
23	Ø (J)		-	(went about teaching)
24a	NP (report)	pn (J)	intro	(of went into all Syria)
24b	unspecified	pn (J)		(brought all sick to)
24c	Ø (J)	pn (sick)	3	(healed)
25	NP (crowds)	pn (J)	intro	(followed from...)
5:1	Ø (J)	NP (crowds)	-	(seeing, went into mount)

(In 4:19 the subject is the same as in the last clause that describes a main event (v. 18a) and so rule 1 applies, even though there is intervening background material introduced with γάρ. As for v. 24b, it is the norm for plural subjects whose referent is unspecified to have no overt reference.)

In the above passage, reference to Jesus at the beginning of a new narrative unit is overt in the UBS text only in 4:1 and 4:17. The implication is that the author perceives a fair degree of continuity between the events of vv. 1–16, whereas v. 1 and v. 17 begin new narrative units following significant changes of theme or situation. (Concerning v. 17, Schooling 1985:21 observes that, in Matthew's Gospel, ἀπὸ τότε 'from that time' occurs at the beginning of major units.)

Similarly, there is a fair degree of continuity between the events of 4:17–25 (or 4:23–25 if ὁ Ἰησοῦς is read in v. 23) and the Sermon on the Mount (see the comment on passage 5 of sec. 5.1 for evidence that 4:23–25 set the scene for chapters 5–7).

In contrast, reference to the devil is overt at the beginning of each new narrative subunit (vv. 5a, 8a, 11a). In each instance, he was the addressee of the previous speech, so an articular pronoun or no overt reference would have been the default encoding (rule 2; compare vv. 20 and 22).

In 4:7 and 10, reference to Jesus is overt in connection with the introduction to a key speech that concludes the narrative unit.[10]

Review Question

The norm is for reference to Jesus as subject in the Synoptic Gospels not to be overt, even when he was in a non-subject role in the previous clause. However, there are two common reasons for referring overtly to Jesus in such circumstances. What are they?

Suggested Answer

Overt reference to Jesus as subject in the Synoptic Gospels is indicative of:
1. a major break in the story (e.g., because of a significant change of theme or situation)
2. a key speech or action.

Turning now to the book of Acts, references to Christian leaders are sometimes not overt when a full noun phrase would be expected according to the default rules of sec. 8.2. This suggests that they are being treated in such passages as the local VIP.

I have already noted Acts 8:38c as a possible instance in which failure to refer overtly to Philip may indicate that he is being treated as the local VIP (Suggested Answer (d) following passage 5). Passage 7 (below) provides instances in which failure to refer overtly to Saul may also suggest that he is being treated as the local VIP.

Illustrative Passage 7: Acts 9:17–30

In reading this passage, which follows on immediately from passage 3, note which references to the subject are default encodings and which are marked ones, according to the rules of sec. 8.2. (Lines across the page indicate new paragraphs in the UBS text. The abbreviations are as follows: A refers to Ananias; B to Barnabas; H to the Hellenists; Sa to Saul.)

verse	subject	non-subject	summary of contents
17a	NP (A)		(went away)
17b	Ø (A)		(entered the house)
17c	Ø (A)	pn(!) (Sa)	(putting hands on, said)
18a	NP (as scales)	pn (Sa)	(fell away from eyes of)
18b	Ø (Sa)		(saw again)
18c	Ø (Sa)		(rising up, was baptized)
19a	Ø (Sa)		(taking food, was strengthened)
19b	Ø (Sa)	NP (disciples)	(was with some days)
20	Ø (Sa)		(proclaimed Jesus in synagogues)
21a	NP (hearers)		(were amazed)
21b	Ø (hearers)		(were saying)
22a	NP (Sa)		(increased in power)
22b	Ø (Sa)	NP (Jews)	(was confounding)
23			(After some time had passed)
	NP (Jews)	pn (Sa)	(consulted together to kill)
24a	NP (plot)	NP (Sa)	(became known to)
24b	Ø (Jews)	pn (Sa)	(were watching gates to kill)
25	NP (disciples)	pn (Sa)	(taking, let down in basket)
26a	Ø (Sa)	NP (disciples)	(arriving in Jm., tried to join)
26b	all (disciples)	pn (Sa)	(feared)
27a	NP (B)	pn (Sa)	(taking)

---

[10] Although the UBS text of Matt. 9:12 reads ὁ δὲ, the textual variant ὁ δὲ Ἰησοῦς seems more probable, since vv. 12-13 present a key speech that concludes the narrative unit.

		NP (apostles)	(led to apostles)
27b	Ø (B)	pn (apostles)	(narrated to how he (Sa) saw Lord)
28	Ø (Sa)	pn (apostles)	(with, going in and out)
29a	Ø (Sa)	NP (H)	(spoke and discussed with)
29b	art (H)	pn (Sa)	(attempted to kill)
30	NP (brothers)	pn (Sa)	(knowing, brought to Caesarea)

Questions

(a) Which default rule accounts for the reference to the subject in v. 22a? In v. 26a? In v. 29b?

(b) Why is a full noun phrase used in v. 17a to refer to Ananias?

(c) Why is no overt reference to the subject used in v. 18b? In v. 24b? In v. 28?

Suggested Answers

(a) The default rules that account for the references to the subject in the following verses are as follows:
- in v. 22a: 4 (Saul was not involved in the events of v. 21)
- in v. 26a: 3 (Saul is the only participant on stage)
- in v. 29b: 2.

(b) A full noun phrase is used to refer to Ananias in v. 17a, even though he is the addressee of the last speech, because v. 17a begins a new narrative unit.

(c) No overt reference to the subject occurs in vv. 18b, 24b or 28, for the following reasons:
- by v. 18b, Ananias seems to have faded out of the scene, leaving Saul as the only (major) participant on stage
- in v. 24b, the same animate participants are acting as in vv. 23–24a (the plot is by the Jews), so there is no real change of subject
- in v. 28, it is possible that Barnabas and the apostles are viewed as minor participants, so rule 3 again applies. However, it is more likely that Saul is being treated as the local VIP. (See also the pronominal reference to Saul as object in v. 17c, when a full noun phrase would have been expected, and the failure to identify Saul by name in the reported speech of v. 27b.)

Passage 8 (below) is followed by questions on the forms of reference to the different participants. Some MSS have no overt reference to Jesus in Matt. 8:3a and 7; in others, ὁ Ἰησοῦς is present. (The abbreviations are as follows: C refers to the centurion, J to Jesus, L to the leper, and M to Peter's mother-in-law.)

Passage 8: Matthew 7:28–8:18

verse	subject	non-subject	summary of contents
28a	NP (J)		(when ended these sayings)
28b	NP (crowds)	pn (J)	(were astounded at teaching of)
29	Ø (J)	pn (crowds)	(for taught authoritatively)
8:1a	pn (J)		(as came down from mountain) (GA)
1b	crowds many	pn (J)	(followed)
2	NP (L)	pn (J)	(worshipped, saying)
3a	Ø/NP (J)	pn (L)	(stretching out hand, touched saying)
3b	leprosy	pn (L; 'his')	(was cleansed)
4	NP (J)	pn (L)	(says to)
5a	pn (J)		(as entered Capernaum) (GA)
5b	NP (C)	pn (J)	(approached, beseeching)
7	Ø/NP (J)	pn (C)	(says to)
8	NP (C)		(answering, said)
10a	NP (J)		(hearing, marveled)
10b	Ø (J)	followers	(said to)
13a	NP (J)	NP (C)	(said to)
13b	NP (boy)		(was healed that same hour)

14	NP (J)	NP (M)	(coming into house, saw sick)
15a	Ø (J)	pn (M)	(touched hand of)
15b	NP (fever)	pn (M)	(left)
15c	Ø (M)		(arose)
15d	Ø (M)	pn (J)	(ministered to)
16a	unspecified	pn (J)	(in eve, brought many possessed to)
16b	Ø (J)	NP (spirits)	(expelled with a word)
16c	Ø (J)	all ill	(healed)
17	Isaiah's prophecy		(was fulfilled)
18	NP (J)	NP (crowd[s])	(seeing…)

Questions

(a) Which default rule explains the use of the independent pronouns in 8:1a and 5a? If the paragraph breaks in the UBS text were classified as major or minor, which type would these be?

(b) Why is there no overt reference to the subject in 8:15c?

(c) Why is a full noun phrase used to refer to the centurion in 8:8, even though he is the addressee of the previous speech?

(d) Why is a full noun phrase used to refer to Jesus in 8:4? In 8:10a? In 8:13a? In 8:14? In 8:18? In 7:28a?

(e) If ὁ Ἰησοῦς is read in 8:3a, what would motivate this marked encoding? In 8:7?

Suggested Answers: see Appendix under 8(8).

9
THE ARTICLE WITH SUBSTANTIVES

Throughout the Greek New Testament, nouns whose referents are "known, particular" (BDF §252) are at times preceded by the article (they are said to be "articular or arthrous"—Porter 1992:104) and at times appear without it (they are said to be "anarthrous"). Wallace (1996:209) notes:

> The function of the article is *not* primarily to make something definite that would otherwise be indefinite... There are at least 10 ways in which a noun in Greek can be definite without the article. For example, proper names are definite even without the article (Παῦλος means "Paul," not "*a* Paul"). Yet, proper names sometimes take the article. Hence, when the article is used with them it must be for some other purpose.

This chapter is concerned with one such purpose. It claims that, if the referent of an *anarthrous* noun phrase is known and particular (or, to be more exact, if the author assumes that the reader will be able to assign it unique referential identity—see sec. 9.1), this gives it *prominence*. It is marked as prominent because it is of particular importance.

Thus, out of the cast of participants involved in events being described by an author, one (or, occasionally, two) may be marked as being most important because they are central to the story at that point. In other words, they are salient (sec. 8.2). Similarly, out of the constituents of a comment about a propositional topic, one or two may be marked as being most important because they are focal in the sentence. Anarthrous references to entities with unique referential identity have a part to play in identifying which participants or constituents are currently important.

To illustrate this claim, I consider the presence versus the absence of the article in three situations: with proper names for people in the Gospels and Acts (sec. 9.2), with other substantives[1] (sec. 9.3) and, in particular, with points of departure (sec. 9.4). First, though, I briefly review some general characteristics of the article.

9.1   Preliminaries

Porter (op. cit. 104) distinguishes two uses of the article with substantives: the "particular" use and the "categorical" use. "When the article is used, the substantive may refer to a particular item, or it may represent a category of items" (loc. cit.).

Thus, in **Luke 4:20a**, τὸ βιβλίον refers to the *particular* scroll from which Jesus had been reading; the phrase has a unique referent.

(20a)	καὶ	πτύξας		τὸ	βιβλίον ἀποδοὺς		τῷ	ὑπηρέτῃ	ἐκάθισεν·
	and	having.rolled.up		the	scroll	having.given.back	to.the	attendant	3S.sat.down

In **Luke 10:7b**, ὁ ἐργάτης represents the *category* of workers in general. The article "distinguishes one class from another" (Wallace op. cit. 227).

(7b)	**ἄξιος**	γὰρ	ὁ	ἐργάτης	τοῦ	μισθοῦ	αὐτοῦ.
	worthy	for	the	worker	of.the	wage	his

An observation is in order about substantives that are particular and have a unique referent because of their *association* with another substantive that has unique referential identity. When a semantic item is introduced, other items that the culture associates with that item are also "accessed." For example, if I refer in a Western culture to a *house*, I also presuppose the existence of its door, its roof, its windows, its kitchen, etc.

---

[1] Porter (op. cit. 313) defines a substantive as "any word which may be used like a noun. For example, in Greek, participles, infinitives, and especially adjectives, besides nouns, are often used as substantives."

This observation explains why it is appropriate in Luke 4:20a (above) to refer to the synagogue attendant with the article (τῷ ὑπηρέτῃ). As Wallace observes (op. cit. 217), "the attendant has not been mentioned." Nevertheless, once the synagogue is accessed (in v. 16),[2] the items that the culture associates with the synagogue are also accessed, including the attendant. Consequently, the article is used provided the substantive has unique referential identity.

Turning to the *absence* of the article with substantives, Wallace's chart of "The Semantics of Anarthrous Nouns" (op. cit. 243) presents three overlapping "forces" that an anarthrous substantive may have:

Concerning *indefinite* substantives, Givón states (1984:399), "Speakers code a referential nominal as indefinite if they think that they are *not* entitled to assume that the hearer can... assign it unique referential identity." For example, in John 4:7 (γυνὴ ἐκ τῆς Σαμαρείας 'a woman of Samaria'), the reader will not be able to identify which particular woman the author has in mind; the woman is simply one member of the class of "women of Samaria."

Concerning *qualitative* substantives, Wallace states (op. cit. 244), "A qualitative noun places the stress on quality, nature, or essence... most abstract nouns will be qualitative." An example of a qualitative substantive is ἀγάπη in 1 John 4:8 (ὁ θεὸς ἀγάπη ἐστίν 'God is love').

Definite substantives "have unique referential identity" (op. cit. 245) even when they are anarthrous and, since "by the nature of the case, a proper name is definite without the article" (loc. cit.), it is to proper names that we turn our attention in sec. 9.2.

One reason for the overlapping ovals in Wallace's chart of the semantics of anarthrous nouns (above) is the following. Whereas "indefinite" is opposed to "definite" (a noun cannot at the same time have an indefinite and a definite force), once a "qualitative" concept has been introduced, the reader can "assign it unique referential identity" and, where appropriate, refer to it with the article. This is seen in **James 1:3–4**, where the quality of endurance (ὑπομονή) is introduced in v. 3b, then becomes the propositional topic of v. 4a.

(3b) τὸ   δοκίμιον ὑμῶν   τῆς πίστεως κατεργάζεται ὑπομονήν.
      the testing   of.your the faith   3S.works   endurance

(4a) ἡ   δὲ ὑπομονὴ ἔργον τέλειον   ἐχέτω,
      the DE endurance work   complete 3S.let.have

As noted in the introduction to this chapter, my claim is that, if a reader can assign unique referential identity to an anarthrous noun, then it is prominent (the center of attention or focal). My interest is therefore in a *two*-way division of anarthrous substantives, between those that Wallace would classify as "definite" and those that Porter (loc. cit.) would call "non-particular," whether Wallace would view them as "indefinite" or "qualitative." The following diagram shows the division. (See further in sec. 9.3.)

(NON-PARTICULAR)	(PARTICULAR)
INDEFINITE	**DEFINITE**
(including QUALITATIVE without unique referential identity)	(including QUALITATIVE with unique referential identity)

---

[2] In the Jewish culture of the time, referring to a town like Nazareth would presuppose the existence of its synagogue.

Review Questions

(a) What does it mean if a participant is said to be *salient*?

(b) What does *anarthrous* mean? What is its opposite?

(c) Which two uses of the article with substantives does Porter distinguish?

(d) What are the three overlapping forces that an *anarthrous* substantive may have, according to Wallace?

Suggested Answers

(a) If a participant is said to be salient, it means that he or she is the center of attention (of particular importance).

(b) *Anarthrous* is used to refer to substantives that are not preceded by a modifying article. Its opposite is *arthrous* or *articular*, which is used to refer to substantives that are preceded by an article.

(c) Porter distinguishes the *particular* use of the article from its *categorical* use.

(d) The three overlapping forces that an anarthrous substantive may have, according to Wallace, are: indefinite, qualitative, and definite.

9.2   The Article with Proper Names for People[3]

Proper names for people in Koiné Greek occur sometimes with a preceding article and sometimes without. For example, both ὁ Γαλλίων (the Gallio) and Γαλλίωνος (of Gallio) occur (Acts 18:14, 12). Section 9.2.1 concerns default rules of usage of these two forms to introduce or *activate* and to refer to activated participants by name; sec. 9.2.2, the reactivation of participants after an absence or at the beginning of new episode; and sec. 9.2.3, anarthrous references to activated participants.

9.2.1   Default Rules

When a participant is activated (introduced for the first time), reference to him or her by name typically is anarthrous.[4] However, once he or she has been activated, subsequent references to him or her by name within the same episode are articular.

To activate a participant by name:	anarthrous reference
To refer by name to an activated participant:	articular reference

The references to Gallio in Acts 18:12, 14 and 17 (passage 1) illustrate this rule. The introductory reference to him in v. 12 is anarthrous (indicated by 'Ø'). Subsequent references, however, are articular (indicated by 'the'). (In the following charts, references to participants that do not involve a proper name are given in parentheses.)

Passage 1: Acts 18:12–18

	subject	non-subject	summary of contents
12	Ø Gallio		(being proconsul of Achaia)
	(the Jews)	the Paul	(rose up against)
		(him)	(brought before the tribunal)
14a	the Paul		(was about to speak)
	the Gallio	(the Jews)	(said to, "(14b–15)")
16		(them)	(dismissed from the tribunal)
17	(all)	Ø Sosthenes	(turned on)
	(none of these things)	the Gallio	(mattered to)
18	the Paul	(the brothers)	(said farewell to)
	Ø Priscilla and Aquila	(with him)	(sailed away)

---

[3] The material on Acts is adapted from Heimerdinger and Levinsohn 1992.

[4] "John's general rule is to *introduce* a personal name *without the article*" (Abbott 1906:57-58).

For the operation of the default rules of reference in the four Gospels, see the references to the following people (see sec. 9.2.2 on the *re*activation of participants):

- in Matthew 14, to Herod the tetrarch : activated with an anarthrous reference in v. 1, further references in vv. 3, 6a, and 6b are articular
- in Mark 15, to Pilate: activated with an anarthrous reference in v. 1 (UBS text), the nine further references in vv. 2–44 are all articular
- in Luke 9, to Peter: reactivated with an anarthrous reference in v. 28 (UBS text—see sec. 9.2.2), further references in vv. 32 and 33 are articular
- in John 18:15–18, to Peter: reactivated with an anarthrous reference in v. 15, further references in vv. 16, 17, and 18 are articular.

One restriction on the rule described above concerns *indeclinable* names (i.e., those of non-Greek origin). Typically, such names are articular if they are *not in the nominative*, even when the referent is being activated for the first time. As Wallace (op. cit. 240) notes, "The article is used with indeclinable nouns to show the case of the noun." For example, the first reference to Joseph in Matt. 1:18 is τῷ Ἰωσήφ, and the first reference to Isaac in Acts 7:8 is τὸν Ἰσαάκ.[5] In contrast, Sosthenes (a name of Greek origin) is introduced in the accusative case in Acts 18:17 without the article (Σωσθένην).

In *genitive phrases*, however, the genitive reference to a named possessor may be anarthrous even if the noun is indeclinable. For example, Acts 13:21 refers to υἱὸν Κίς 'son (of) Kish'.

Back in the second century, Apollonius Dyscolus "observed that both the head noun and genitive noun mimicked each other with regard to articularity" (Wallace op. cit. 239). However, Heimerdinger claims (p.c.), "When all the examples of a dependent genitive in an articular phrase are considered, it is found that the article is retained whenever the reference to the person is anaphoric. When the article is omitted, the reference is either a set phrase like 'the name of Jesus'... or a first mention."

This is illustrated by the two references to Simon in **Luke 4:38**, both of which are counterexamples to "Apollonius' Canon." Simon is mentioned for the first time in the Gospel in v. 38a and the reference is anarthrous, even though the head noun is articular. Once activated, however, the reference to him is articular even though the head noun is anarthrous.

(38a) Ἀναστὰς   δὲ   ἀπὸ τῆς συναγωγῆς
      having.arisen DE   from the synagogue

      εἰσῆλθεν   εἰς τὴν οἰκίαν Σίμωνος.
      3S.entered into the house of.Simon

(38b) πενθερὰ   δὲ τοῦ Σίμωνος ἦν   συνεχομένη πυρετῷ μεγάλῳ
      mother-in-law DE of.the Simon 3S.was suffering.with fever high

See also the anarthrous reference to Jason in Acts 17:5, following an articular head noun (τῇ οἰκίᾳ Ἰάσονος 'the house of Jason').

Review Questions

(a) Are participants typically activated by name with an articular or an anarthrous reference? What about the default way of referring to an activated participant?

(b) In John 1:45, the first reference to Nathanael is articular (εὑρίσκει Φίλιππος τὸν Ναθαναὴλ 'Philip finds Nathanael'). Why?

Suggested Answers

(a) Participants are typically activated by name with an *anarthrous* reference. The default way of referring by name to an activated participant is with an *articular* reference.

---

[5] However, see Teeple 1973:303. Heimerdinger (p.c.) also considers it possible "that it is not case which affects the article with O.T. names" and that my conclusions, as they involve such names, "will only work with certain MSS."

(b) In John 1:45, the first reference to Nathanael is articular to show the case of the noun, which is indeclinable.

9.2.2   The Reactivation of Participants

Section 8.3 introduced the concept of a *global VIP* around whom part or all of a book is organized. One of the characteristics of a global VIP is that he (together with his followers) tends to remain 'on stage' as one episode follows another. In contrast, other participants are often reintroduced or *reactivated* at the beginning of a new episode, even if they were active in the previous one. This is particularly evident in the first half of Acts, where different sections concern different Christian leaders, so I begin this section by describing the system of reactivation in Acts.

At the beginning of a new episode in Acts, the norm is for a major participant to be reactivated with an anarthrous reference, unless he is the global VIP around whom the section of the story is organized. The basic principle is as follows:

- reactivations of the *global VIP* after a temporary absence are articular (perhaps he is considered to be in the wings, rather than truly being reactivated)
- reactivations of participants other than the global VIP are anarthrous. (Typically, such a participant is also salient—see sec. 9.2.3.)

To reactivate the global VIP by name:	articular reference
To reactivate other participants by name:	anarthrous reference

The *first* half of the book of Acts concerns the activities of various Christian leaders (Peter, Stephen, Philip, and Saul) and none of them is treated as the global VIP. Instead, whenever one of them is reactivated after an absence, the reference is anarthrous. The same is true of other major participants who are reactivated.

This is illustrated in Acts 12 (passage 2 below), Peter is reactivated in v. 3 with an anarthrous reference (he last featured as an individual when he reported to the church in Jerusalem in 11:4–17). Similarly, Herod (who is introduced in 12:1) is reactivated in v. 19 with an anarthrous reference, as are Barnabas and Saul in v. 25 (they were last mentioned in 11:30). Once reactivated, however, further references are articular.

Passage 2: Acts 12:1–13:1

	subject	non-subject	summary of contents
1	Ø Herod	(some of the church)	(arrested)
2		Ø James	(killed)
3–4		Ø Peter	(arrested, put in prison)
5	the Peter		(was kept in prison)
6	the Herod	(him)	(when was about to bring out)
	the Peter		(was sleeping)
7	(Ø angel of.Lord)		(appeared)
		the Peter	(struck on side)
8	(the angel)	(to him)	(said, "Get dressed!")
	...		
11	the Peter		(came to himself)
12–13		of the[6] Mary the mother of Ø John the called Mark	(went to the house)
14	(maidservant)	of the Peter	(recognized the voice)
	...		
16	the Peter		(kept on knocking)

---

[6] Since Mary has not previously been activated, an anarthrous reference to her is to be expected, and this is the reading found in most MSS. Later in this section I discuss the implications of following the articular reading of the UBS text.

19	Ø Herod		(searching...)
20		Ø Tyrians and Sidonians	(was angry with)
		Ø Blastus	(having persuaded)
21	the Herod		(sat on throne)
	...		
25	Ø Barnabas and Saul		(returned from Jerusalem)
13:1	the Barnabas...		(list of prophets, etc.)

The *second* half of Acts generally revolves around a single major Christian leader, Paul, and this is reflected in the way he is referred to. Once he has been established as the global VIP, reactivating references to him after a brief absence typically are articular. See, for example, 18:18 (in passage 1 of sec. 9.2.1) and 25:23 (following a conversation between governor Festus and King Agrippa). (In the first half of the book, in contrast, reactivating references to Paul (Saul) are usually anarthrous, as in 12:25 of passage 2. See the discussion below of the articular reference to him in 9:1.)

Exceptions to this last pattern are limited to occasions when another major participant was on stage and Paul was definitely absent (not just in the wings).[7] Thus, his reintroduction in 19:1 (below) follows a section on the activities of Apollos (18:24–28) during which Paul was elsewhere (see v. 21).

Passage 3: Acts 18:21–19:1

	subject	non-subject	summary of contents
21	(he = Paul)		(set sail from Ephesus)
	...		
24	Ø Apollos		(came to Ephesus)
26	Ø Priscilla and Aquila	(him)	(heard)
	...		
19:1	the Apollos		(was at Corinth)
	Ø Paul		(arrived at Ephesus)

Throughout the second half of the book of Acts, participants *other* than Paul are reactivated anarthrously. For example, see the reactivation of Priscilla and Aquila in 18:18 (passage 1) and again in 18:26 (passage 3). To use a staging analogy, at the end of each episode or subsection of the second half of Acts, the stage is typically cleared of all the participants *except Paul*. As the next episode begins, Paul is already on stage, but the rest of the participants must be brought or brought back on stage.

Typically, then, participants other than the global VIP are reactivated by name with an anarthrous reference. I turn now to instances in Acts when a new episode or subsection has begun but the first reference to a previously activated participant is *articular*. The presence of the article constrains the reader to relate the referent to that previously activated participant.[8]

In Acts 10:17, for instance, there is an articular allusion to Cornelius (οἱ ἄνδρες οἱ ἀπεσταλμένοι ὑπὸ τοῦ Κορνηλίου 'the men sent by Cornelius'). This verse occurs in the scene that began in v. 9 when Peter was reactivated with an anarthrous reference. The presence of the article in v. 17 constrains the reader to relate the referent to the Cornelius who had been previously activated.

In **Acts 9:1**, the reference to Saul is articular. In addition, the following participial clause recalls the last scene in which Saul was present. The combination constrains the reader to relate the events of 9:1ff. to this last scene and to recognize the referent as the Saul who had been activated there. In other words, Luke is resuming the storyline he left after 8:3, rather than starting a completely new episode.[9]

---

[7] In 19:30, the reference to Paul in the UBS text is anarthrous (Παύλου), though most MSS have an articular reading. If the UBS text is followed, the anarthrous reference might underline the fact that Paul was not on stage for the events of vv. 23-29 (the allusion to him at the end of v. 29 is also anarthrous). See also the anarthrous reference to Jesus in Matt. 26:75.

[8] See below on *an*arthrous allusions to inactive participants in John's Gospel.

[9] It is possible that Saul is already being treated as a VIP. This is suggested also by the minimal references to him in Acts 9:17c and 9:28 (Suggested Answer (c) to passage 7 of sec. 8.3).

(8:3)   But Saul was ravaging the church by entering house after house; dragging off both men and women, he committed them to prison.

(9:1)
Ὁ   δὲ   Σαῦλος   ἔτι   ἐμπνέων   ἀπειλῆς   καὶ   φόνου
the   DE   Saul   still   breathing   threat   and   murder

εἰς   τοὺς   μαθητὰς   τοῦ   κυρίου,   κ.τ.λ.
to   the   disciples   of.the   Lord

See also the articular reference to Cornelius in Acts 10:24, when Peter arrives from Joppa with the messengers that Cornelius had sent to fetch him.

The Acts 10:17 example cited above related back to part of the same overall episode. In Acts 11:19, however, the allusion to Stephen (ἐπὶ Στεφάνῳ / ἐπὶ Στεφανοῦ/ ἀπὸ τοῦ Στεφανοῦ) relates to an event that occurred *after* Stephen's death (8:4), and most MSS omit the article when alluding to him. This suggests that Luke sees little benefit for the new episode in his readers recalling the details of the last scene in which Stephen was present.

In contrast, the contents of **Acts 15:38** make it clear that Luke wishes his readers to recall the previous episode in which John Mark was present, so the articular reading is warranted. (See passage 6 of sec. 9.2.3 for further discussion of these verses.)

(37)
Βαρναβᾶς   δὲ   ἐβούλετο   συμπαραλαβεῖν   καὶ   τὸν*   Ἰωάννην
Barnabas   DE   3S.was.wanting   to.take.along   +   the   John

τὸν   καλούμενον   Μᾶρκον·   (**variant*: omit τὸν)
the   called   Mark

(38)   But Paul was insisting not to take with them one who had deserted them in Pamphylia and had not accompanied them in the work.

I noted earlier that the reference to Mary in Acts 12:12 (passage 2 above) is anarthrous in most MSS, which is consistent with her not having previously been activated. Suppose the articular reading of the UBS text is followed (ἦλθεν ἐπὶ τὴν οἰκίαν τῆς Μαρίας τῆς μητρὸς Ἰωάννου τοῦ ἐπικαλουμένου Μάρκου 'he (Peter) went to the house of Mary, the mother of John whose other name was Mark'). This suggests that Mary was accessed by association with something in the context that was shared knowledge in Luke's time, such as a close relationship between Peter and John Mark or that the house church "to which Peter himself was attached—met in Mary's house" (Bruce 1988:238).

I now make a few observations about the reactivation of participants in the *Gospels*, excluding Mark.[10]

A cursory examination suggests that Matthew and Luke follow the same system of reactivation as for Acts. However, this is obscured by the fact that, if the apostles as a whole are present, the individual apostles such as Simon Peter do not need to be activated.

For example, in *Matthew*'s Gospel, Simon is introduced for the first time in 4:18 and reactivated in 8:14 with an anarthrous reference at the beginning of another episode. However, once the apostles have been called (10:2ff.), the first reference to Peter in each episode in which he has an individual part to play is normally articular (e.g. 14:28 (UBS text), 15:15, 16:22, 17:1, 17:24; see sec. 9.2.3 on the anarthrous reference in 16:16).

Luke's Gospel is similar. Simon is introduced for the first time in Luke 4:38a (see sec. 9.2.1) and reactivated with an anarthrous reference in 5:3 (if the UBS text is followed). Once the apostles have been called (6:13ff.), the first reference to Peter in each episode in which he has an individual part to play is usually articular (8:45, 12:41, 18:28 (UBS text), 22:54, 24:12). However, whenever Luke wishes to

---

[10] Although Mark occasionally has anarthrous references to participants who had previously been activated, he does not seem to follow the same principles as the other Gospel writers. See, for example, the anarthrous references to Simon in the UBS text of 1:30, 1:36, and 8:33, together with the articular reference to him in 3:16.

indicate that the apostles as a whole were not present during an episode, then the first reference to Peter in that episode is anarthrous (8:51, 9:28 (UBS text), 22:8).

In *John*'s Gospel, in contrast, individual apostles are always reactivated with anarthrous references, even when reference has already been made to the disciples as a whole. For example, following the reference to the disciples in 6:3, Philip (v. 5—UBS text) and Andrew (v. 8) are both reactivated with anarthrous references. Furthermore, allusions by name to inactive participants who have previously been activated are anarthrous (e.g., John the Baptist in 1:40, Andrew and Peter in 1:44, Simon Peter in 6:8, and Mary in 11:20b).

As for references to *Jesus* as the global VIP at the beginning of a new episode in the Gospels, on the relatively few occasions that they occur (see sec. 8.3), they are normally articular. See, for example, Matt. 3:13, Luke 4:14 (UBS text), and John 3:22. This makes the anarthrous references to Jesus of particular significance.

In the *Synoptic Gospels*, once Jesus has been activated for the first time (Matt. 1:16 and Mark 1:9, see below for Luke), he is treated as the global VIP and never reactivated until after his death and burial. Only when he reappears after the resurrection is he reactivated with a further anarthrous reference (Matt. 28:9, Luke 24:15b (UBS text)).

In the first three chapters of *Luke*'s Gospel, however, each reference to Jesus is anarthrous. This suggests that Luke does not treat him as the global VIP in these chapters but, rather, reactivates him (together with the other major participants) at the beginning of each new episode (see especially 2:52, 3:21, 3:23 (UBS text), and 4:1). See further in sec. 9.2.3.

There are so many variant readings in *John*'s Gospel that it is difficult to draw conclusions with any certainty. However, if the UBS text is right in choosing an anarthrous reference to Jesus in 5:1, 12:36b, 17:1 and 18:1, the implication would be that, at these points, John clears the stage for a new section of his book. (See also the less widely supported anarthrous variants in 7:1, 8:12, 10:23 and 21:1.) Thus, John 1–4 would constitute one section, as would chapter 17, etc.

Review Questions

(a) If a section of a book has a global VIP, what is the default way of referring to him by name after a brief absence?

(b) What is the normal way of reactivating by name participants other than the global VIP?

(c) In Acts, what is the significance of an articular allusion to a previously activated participant who is now inactive?

(d) How does the calling of the apostles in Luke 6:13ff. and Matt. 10:2ff. affect the way that individual apostles are referred to by name thereafter?

Suggested Answers

(a) If a section of a book has a global VIP, the default way of referring to him by name after a brief absence is with an *articular* reference.

(b) The normal way of reactivating by name participants other than the global VIP is with an *anarthrous* reference.

(c) In Acts, an articular allusion to a previously activated participant who is now inactive constrains the reader to relate the referent to that previously activated participant. In practice, this implies that Luke wishes his readers to recall the details of the last scene in which this participant was active.

(d) Once the apostles have been called, references by name to individual apostles are with an *articular* reference whenever the apostles as a group are with Jesus. Prior to their calling, they were reactivated by name with an *anarthrous* reference.

9.2.3   Anarthrous References to Activated Participants

According to the principle of sec. 9.2.1, further references to activated participants are normally articular. Anarthrous references to activated participants are therefore of particular significance. In particular, they make the participant and/or his or her initiative or speech *prominent*, because it is of particular importance. Once again, I illustrate this phenomenon first in Acts, then add examples from the Gospels (other than Mark).

Most anarthrous references to activated participants in Acts fall into two groups:

1. those that involve a switch of attention to a salient participant or local VIP
2. those that occur in connection with the introduction to a speech whose contents are particularly important.

The first of these groups, anarthrous references to a participant in connection with a switch of attention to that participant, may involve a switch from a less salient to a more salient participant or from one salient participant to another. Such references probably identify the participant as the *local VIP* (sec. 8.3). This participant usually takes initiatives that determine how the episode will work out. However, that is not always so (see below on Zechariah as the local VIP in Luke 1:8–20).

Switches from *a less salient to a more salient participant* or local VIP are illustrated in the interaction of Acts 3:1-6 (below) between the lame man and Peter. First, Peter and John are reactivated at the beginning of the episode (see sec. 9.2.2). Then, each time attention switches back to Peter, the reference to him is anarthrous (vv. 3, 4, and 6). From the perspective of the story as a whole, Peter is more salient than the lame man; he is the local VIP and his initiatives determine the outcome of the story. Note also the articular reference to John in v. 4, who now occupies a support role rather than an initiating one.

Passage 4: Acts 3:1–6

	subject	non-subject	summary of contents
1	Ø Peter & John		(were going to the temple)
2	(lame man)		(was being carried in)
3	(who)	Ø Peter & John	(seeing, was begging)
4	Ø Peter	(him)	(gazing at)
		the John	(with, said, "Look at us!")
5	(He)	(them)	(fixed his attention on)
6	Ø Peter		(said)

In Acts 7:58–8:3 (below), there are a couple of switches from Stephen to Saul. The references in 7:59 and 8:2 to Stephen are articular, since he is an activated participant. The introduction of Saul to the book is anarthrous (7:58), as expected. What is noteworthy is that, when attention switches to him again in 8:1 and 8:3, the references are again anarthrous. This is appropriate because, as Stephen dies and is buried, attention shifts from him to Saul and the persecution that he initiated. In other words, he is now more salient than Stephen.

Passage 5: Acts 7:58–8:3

	subject	non-subject	summary of contents
58	(the witnesses)	Ø Saul	(laid their clothes at the feet of)
59		the Stephen	(stoned)
8:1	Ø Saul		(was approving of his death)
2	(godly men)	the Stephen	(buried)
3	Ø Saul	(the church)	(began to destroy)

See also Acts 10:21 (most MSS—attention switches from what the Spirit said to Peter in vv. 19–20 to his active response). Acts 9:39 is similar (attention shifts from the men who summoned Peter to his active response). In both instances, Peter is the center of attention. In other words, he is salient.

Passage 6 illustrates switches of attention *from one salient participant to another* within the same scene. This involves a series of initiatives by Paul and Barnabas. Of particular note is the articular reference to Barnabas in Acts 15:39b, at the point that he ceases to be salient to the book because he leaves the scene. (See sec. 9.2.2 on the reactivation of John Mark in v. 37 and the textual variant at that point.)

Passage 6: Acts 15:36–40

	subject	non-subject	summary of contents
36	Ø Paul	Ø Barnabas	(said to, "Let's visit the churches")
37	Ø Barnabas	the John the called Mark	(wanted to take)
38	Ø Paul		(was insisting not to do so)
39a	(they)		(parted company)
39b	the Barnabas	the Mark	(taking, sailed for Cyprus)
40	Ø Paul	Ø Silas	(choosing, departed)

It is unusual for two participants to be salient at the same time, as is briefly the case in passage 6. It is more normal for different participants in turn to become salient (the local VIP). This is illustrated in passage 7. As attention switches to the significant contributions of Peter (Acts 15:7), then Barnabas and Paul (v. 12), and then James (v. 13), each reference is anarthrous, indicating that each in turn becomes salient. (See the discussion following passage 10 for the same phenomenon in Luke 1–3.)

Passage 7: Acts 15:6–13

	subject	non-subject	summary of contents
6	(the apostles and elders)	(met)	
7	Ø Peter		(said)
12	(the whole assembly)		(was silent)
		Ø Barnabas and Paul	(heard)
13	(they)		(when finished)
	Ø James		(spoke up)

I now consider anarthrous references in Acts to participants who make a *speech* that is particularly important. Such references appear to have the rhetorical effect of highlighting that speech. They differ from many of those considered above in that they involve, not a switch of attention to a different participant or local VIP, but a response by the addressee of the last speech. In such contexts, references to the speaker are typically anarthrous only if the speech is the climax of the episode or otherwise is of particular importance.

In passage 8 (below), for example, references to the speakers are articular until the speech of Acts 10:34ff., which is introduced by an anarthrous reference to Peter. It is this speech that the whole chapter has been leading up to from the time that the angel told Cornelius to send for Peter so that Cornelius could hear what he had to say (vv. 5 and 22).

Passage 8: Acts 10:25–34

	subject	non-subject	summary of contents
25	the Peter		(entered)
	the Cornelius	(him)	(meeting, worshipped)
26	the Peter	(him)	(raised, saying, "(26b-29)")
30	the Cornelius		(said)
34	Ø Peter		(said, "(climactic speech)")

In *reported speeches* in Acts, as in narrative, anarthrous references to activated participants indicate that the participant is salient to the argument or is the local VIP. This is illustrated in Stephen's speech in Acts 7 (passage 9). In the section that concerns Moses, references to him by name are anarthrous, each time attention returns to him (vv. 22, 29, 32). Only in v. 31 is the reference to him articular, reflecting the fact that he is only a spectator at this point, rather than an active participant in the story.

Passage 9: Acts 7:20–32

	subject	non-subject	summary of contents
20	Ø Moses		(was born)
21	(the daughter of.P)	(him)	(took, raised as her son)
22	Ø Moses		(was instructed in the wisdom of Egypt)
	...		
29	Ø Moses		(fled to Midian)
30	(Ø angel)	(him)	(appeared to)
31	the Moses		(seeing, was wondering at sight)
	(he [GA])		(approaching)
	(voice of.Lord)		(came)
32	Ø Moses		(trembled with fear)

One point to remember about reported speeches is that, even if a participant has already featured in the narrative in which a speech is embedded, the initial reference in the speech itself may be anarthrous because the reference is a first mention, as far as the addressee is concerned.

For example, in Acts 10:32, Cornelius tells Peter that the angel who had appeared to him had said, 'Send to Joppa for Simon [Σίμωνα]'. This is the first time that Cornelius had heard of Simon Peter, so the reference is anarthrous.

Contrast Acts 13:2, in which the Holy Spirit speaks to the group of prophets and teachers assembled in Antioch and says, 'Set apart for me Barnabas and Saul'. These names are articular (τὸν Βαρναβᾶν καὶ Σαῦλον), since the men are present when the speech is made and are not being introduced to the addressees for the first time.

Thus, the presence versus the absence of the article with proper names in Acts is systematic. Of particular significance is the absence of the article when activated participants are referred to by name. Such anarthrous references signal the importance of the participant and/or of his or her initiative or speech.[11]

I now turn to some observations about anarthrous references to activated participants in the *Gospels*.

In *Luke*'s Gospel, Jesus appears not to become the *global* VIP until chapter 4. Before this, anarthrous references to one of the activated participants in each episode indicate that he or she is the *local* VIP for that episode, i.e., the most salient participant. For example, in 1:39–56 (below), references to Mary are anarthrous whenever she takes the initiative (vv. 39, 46, 56a), while references to Elizabeth are articular. In contrast, v. 41a only reiterates the event of v. 40b from Elizabeth's point of view, so the reference to Mary is articular.

Passage 10: Luke 1:39–56

	subject	non-subject	summary of contents
39	Ø Mary		(traveled to the hill country)
40a		Ø Zechariah	(entered the house of)
40b		the Elizabeth	(greeted)
41a	the Elizabeth	the Mary	(when heard the greeting of)
	(the baby)		(leaped in her womb)
41b	the Elizabeth	Ø Spirit Holy	(was filled with)
42			(exclaimed, "(43–45)")
46	Ø Mary		(said, "(47–55)")
56a	Ø Mary	(with her)	(stayed about three months)
56b			(returned to her home)

---

[11] This phenomenon is not limited to Greek. Mfonyam (1994:202) writes concerning the Bafut (Grassfields) language of Cameroon, "When a previously introduced participant is referred to by name in Bafut, the norm is for the name to be followed by the demonstrative appropriate to the noun class... If the participant is highlighted, however, the demonstrative is omitted."

The rest of Luke 1–3 is structured in a similar way. The anarthrous references to activated participants that are listed in this paragraph indicate that the local VIP for each episode of chapter 1 is in turn Zechariah (1:12 and 18), Elizabeth (1:24), Mary (when interacting both with the angel [1:34 and 38a] and with Elizabeth [above]), and Zechariah (1:67). (In 1:57, the reference to Elizabeth is articular to indicate the case of the noun, since her name is indeclinable.) Similarly, the local VIPs in chapters 2–3 are Joseph and Mary (2:4 and 2:5), Simeon and Mary (2:34), and Jesus (2:43 and 2:52, 3:21 and 3:23 (UBS text)). (In 3:2, the reactivating reference to John the Baptist is also anarthrous, possibly indicating that he is the local VIP at that point.)

See also *Matthew* 2; the anarthrous references to Herod in vv. 7, 12, 15, and 16 may indicate that he is the local VIP. Then there is the genealogy of **Matt. 1:1ff.**; each new point of departure/propositional topic is anarthrous. This suggests that each ancestor in turn becomes salient and that the genealogy develops by switches from one salient ancestor to the next.[12]

(2a)   Ἀβραὰμ   ἐγέννησεν   τὸν   Ἰσαάκ,
        Abraham   3S.fathered   the   Isaac

(2b)   Ἰσαὰκ   δὲ   ἐγέννησεν   τὸν   Ἰακώβ,
        Isaac   DE   3S.fathered   the   Jacob

(2c)   Ἰακὼβ   δὲ   ἐγέννησεν   τὸν   Ἰούδαν κ.τ.λ.
        Jacob   DE   3S.fathered   the   Judah

Once Jesus is established as the global VIP, individual initiatives or speeches may be introduced with an anarthrous reference by name to an activated participant, to highlight that initiative or speech. In Matt. 16:16, for instance, Simon Peter's important pronouncement 'You are the Christ, the Son of the living God' is introduced with an anarthrous reference to Peter (ἀποκριθεὶς δὲ Σίμων Πέτρος εἶπεν, 'In answer, Simon Peter said'—see also the UBS text of Luke 9:20b). Matthew 14:29 (some MSS) also contains an anarthrous reference to Peter as an activated participant, when he walks on the water.

Anarthrous references to *Jesus* as an activated participant in Matthew's Gospel are rare. In the UBS text, they are found only in 17:8, where αὐτὸν Ἰησοῦν μόνον (Jesus alone) is the focus of the sentence (see sec. 9.3); in 21:1, as Jesus sends two of the disciples for the donkey on which he will enter Jerusalem; and in 21:12, when he enters the temple to drive out those who are selling and buying there; together with the variant reading in 20:17. In each of these instances, either Jesus or his initiative is particularly important.

In *Luke*'s Gospel, all the anarthrous references to Jesus as an activated participant that MGM list have articular variants. Some introduce a speech that could perhaps be judged to be the climax of an episode (5:10, 9:50, 23:28; see also 5:8 (many MSS), in which the reference to Simon Peter is also anarthrous when he confesses Jesus as Lord for the first time—see Plummer 1896:145). In 9:36 (as in Matt. 17:8), Ἰησοῦς μόνος is the focal constituent of the sentence. In 22:48, Jesus' rebuke could be judged to be important (see also some MSS of 4:4). In 8:41 and 18:40, however, I see no reason why the speech or action should be marked as especially important.

I turn now to *John*'s Gospel, where the number of anarthrous references to activated participants is much greater than in Matthew or Luke-Acts. For example, MGM list more than ninety anarthrous references to Jesus. It is very common for articular variants also to be found, but it does appear that the effect of choosing the anarthrous form of reference is to mark as important the referent or, more often, his initiative or speech.

Most anarthrous references to activated participants in John are found when the referent is the subject of an active verb and, therefore, in a position to take a significant initiative or make a significant speech.

---

[12] The articular references to Judah (v. 2c) and to other children whose names are declinable suggest that the purpose of the genealogy is not so much to make a comment and supply new information about each father (whom he fathered—see Bailey 1998:10). Rather, it is to enumerate the generations (see v. 17), which is best achieved by centering attention on the fathers.

See, for example, the anarthrous reference to Philip in **John 1:45**, following the background material of v. 44 in which the reference to him was articular.

(43)   The next day Jesus decided to go to Galilee and he finds Philip (Φίλιππον). And Jesus says to him, "Follow me."

(44)   ἦν   δὲ   ὁ   Φίλιππος   ἀπὸ   Βηθσαϊδά, κ.τ.λ.
         3S.was   DE   the   Philip   from Bethsaida

(45a)   εὑρίσκει   Φίλιππος   τὸν   Ναθαναὴλ
         3S.finds   Philip   the   Nathanael

(45b)   and says to him, "We have found him about whom Moses... wrote."

See also the anarthrous reactivating reference to Simon Peter in John 18:10, when he draws his sword and cuts off the right ear of the high priest's slave. In 20:18, the reference to Mary Magdalene is anarthrous when, following her conversation with the risen Jesus, she goes and tells the disciples that she has seen the Lord.

Points of departure that mark switches of attention from another participant to a salient participant (usually Jesus) typically have an anarthrous reference to the salient participant. See, for example, John 6:15, 8:59b, 11:33 and 11:38.

Focal constituents that involve a named reference to an activated participant are also anarthrous (see sec. 9.3), as in most MSS of John 4:2 (καίτοιγε Ἰησοῦς αὐτὸς οὐκ ἐβάπτιζεν ἀλλή οἱ μαθηταὶ αὐτοῦ 'although it was not Jesus himself who baptized but his disciples').

See sec. 15.1 for why speech margins of the form ἀπεκρίθη καὶ εἶπεν 'answered and said' usually have an anarthrous reference to the speaker when he is named.

Review Questions

(a) What is indicated by anarthrous references by name to activated participants?

(b) Most of the references to one of the participants in each episode of Luke 1–3 are anarthrous. What does this suggest?

Suggested Answers

(a) Anarthrous references by name to activated participants mark the participant as salient. They may indicate that he or she is the local VIP and/or that an initiative or speech by that participant is of particular importance.

(b) The anarthrous references by name to one of the participants in each episode of Luke 1–3 suggest that he or she is the local VIP, i.e., the most salient participant of that episode.

Illustrative Passage 11: Luke 23:1–13

Concentrate on the references by name to Pilate and to Herod.

	subject	non-subject	summary of contents
1	(the assembly)	the* Pilate (*variant: Ø)	(led him before)
2		(him)	(began to accuse)
3a	the Pilate	him	(questioned)
3b	(he)	him	(answered, "You say so")
4	the Pilate	(the chief priests)	(said to, "I find no guilt")
5	(they)		(were insisting)
6	Ø* Pilate (*var: ὁ)		(asked if Jesus is Galilean)
7a		Ø Herod's jurisdiction	(learning that he is of)
7b		Ø* Herod (*var: τὸν)	(sent him to)
8	the Herod	the Jesus	(seeing, rejoiced)
9a		(him)	(questioned at length)

9b	(he)	(him)	(answered nothing to)
10	(the chief priests)	(him)	(were vehemently accusing)
11a	the Herod	(him)	(treated with contempt)
11b		the* Pilate (*variant: Ø)	(sent him back to)
12	the Herod & the Pilate		(became friends)
13	Ø* Pilate (*var: ὁ)	(the chief priests)	(having called together)
		(to them)	(said, "I will release Jesus")

Questions

(a) If the UBS text is followed, why are the references to Pilate articular in vv. 3a, 4, 11b and 12, but anarthrous in vv. 6 and 13?

(b) Why would it be appropriate for *both* references to Herod in v. 7 to be anarthrous?

(c) Would you expect the reference to Pilate in v. 1 to be anarthrous or articular? (He was introduced in 3:1 and was mentioned in a reported speech in 13:1.) What would the alternative reading imply?

Suggested Answers

(a) The articular references to Pilate in Luke 23:3a, 4, 11b (UBS text), and 12 are the default way of referring to an activated participant (as are the articular variant readings in vv. 6 and 13). The anarthrous references to him in vv. 6 and 13 mark as important the initiatives concerned (to send Jesus to Herod and to call the Jews together to inform them that he was going to release Jesus). The anarthrous variant reading in v. 11b would have the same effect.

(b) The first reference to Herod in 23:7 occurs within a reported speech (Pilate heard, "He is of Herod's jurisdiction"). The anarthrous reference suggests that Herod is being activated *within* the speech. If the anarthrous variant is read in v. 7b, this would indicate that Herod is being reactivated in the narrative. (He last featured in the *narrative* in 9:9.)

(c) I would expect the reference to Pilate in 23:1 to be *anarthrous*, since he is being reactivated (and will be a salient participant). The articular variant reading implies that Luke intends his readers to relate this reference to the context, whether it be his introduction in 3:1 or some knowledge that his readers are assumed to share with him.

In the following passage, note whether references by name to the participants are articular or anarthrous.

Passage 12: Acts 8:4–26

	subject	non-subject	summary of contents
4	(the scattered ones)		(preached)
5	Ø Philip		(went to Samaria)
6	(the crowds)	the Philip	(heard)
	...		
9	Ø Simon		(used to practice sorcery)
10–11	(all)	(whom)	(used to heed)
12	(they)	the Philip	(believed, were baptized)
13	the Simon		(also believed)
		the Philip	(used to attach himself to)
14	(the in Jerusalem apostles)		(heard:)
	the* Samaria (*var: Ø)	(the word of the God)	(has received)
	(they)	Ø* Peter and John	(sent) (*variant: τὸν)
15	(who)	(them)	(going, prayed for)
	(they)	Ø Spirit Holy	(that might receive)
	...		
17	(they)	(them)	(laid hands on)
	(they)	Ø Spirit Holy	(received)
18	the Simon		(seeing that:)

	the Spirit	(the apostles)	(was given through)
	(he)	(them)	(offered money to, saying)
20	Ø Peter	(him)	(said to)
24	the* Simon (*variant: Ø)		(answering, said)
25	(they)		(returned)
26	(Ø angel of.Lord)	Ø Philip	(spoke to)

Questions

(a) Why are the references by name to Philip in vv. 5 and 26 anarthrous? Why is the reference in v. 12 articular? (Philip had previously been mentioned in Acts 6:5.)

(b) Why is the reference to Simon in v. 18 articular?

(c) Why is the reference to Peter in v. 20 anarthrous, but the reference to Simon in the UBS text of v. 24 is articular?

(d) In v. 14, why is it appropriate for the reference to Peter and John to be anarthrous? What would the articular textual variant imply?

Suggested Answers: see Appendix under 9(12).

9.3 Anarthrous References to Other Substantives

The principle of section 9.2.3 that anarthrous references to activated participants indicate prominence does not apply just to proper names for people. It can be applied to any noun with unique referential identity. If an anarthrous substantive has a unique referent and is activated, then its referent is prominent.

The references in Galatians to God (θεός) illustrate how this works. In the first three chapters of the letter, θεός is usually articular since the references to God are not the focal constituents of the clause or sentence concerned. Rather, they are supportive of the focal constituents. For example, in **Gal. 3:11a** ("Now it is evident that no man is justified before God by the law"—NRSV), the focal constituents are "no man" (οὐδείς) and "evident" (δῆλον) (see sec. 9.4 on ἐν νόμῳ "by the law"). If read orally, with the context taken into account, stress will fall on some or all of these constituents, but not on "before God" (παρὰ τῷ θεῷ).

(11a) ὅτι δὲ ἐν νόμῳ **οὐδείς** δικαιοῦται παρὰ τῷ θεῷ δῆλον,
that DE by law no.one 3S.is.justified before the God clear

(See also Gal. 2:21 and 3:18.)

In **Gal. 2:19b**, however, θεῷ is contrasted with νόμῳ, and is focal and central to the argument, so the reference to God is anarthrous.

(19a) ἐγὼ γὰρ διὰ νόμου νόμῳ ἀπέθανον,
I for through law to.law I.died

(19b) ἵνα **θεῷ** ζήσω.
that to.God I.might.live

Similarly, in Gal. 4:8–9, in which discussion centers on 'knowing God' and 'being known by God', the references to God are anarthrous. See also Gal. 4:14 and 6:7.[13]

References to 'the Spirit' in **Gal. 3:2b** (articular) and **Gal. 3:3b** (anarthrous) illustrate the operation of the same principle. In v. 2b, it is not necessary to argue that the reference is to the person rather than the power of the Holy Spirit (see Francis 1985:136–37, Swartz 1993). Rather, the reference to the Spirit is supportive, because the focus of the sentence is the contrast between 'by works of law' and 'by

---

[13] In Ephesians, references to God as an activated participant are anarthrous only when the constituent concerned is preposed for focus (2:8, 4:24) or otherwise is especially prominent (6:17). (The anarthrous references to God in 1:2 and 6:23 may be formulaic.) When a constituent is *postposed* for focus, the references to God are articular (3:9, 3:10, 5:20).

hearing with faith', with 'you received the Spirit by some means' as the presupposition (see sec. 4.3). In v. 3b, however, the contrast between 'in the Spirit' and 'in the flesh' is focal and central.

(2b)   **ἐξ ἔργων νόμου** τὸ πνεῦμα ἐλάβετε   ἢ   ἐξ ἀκοῆς πίστεως;
       by works of.law the Spirit you.received or by hearing of.faith

(3a)   **οὕτως ἀνόητοί** ἐστε;
       thus   foolish   are.you

(3b)   ἐναρξάμενοι πνεύματι <u>νῦν</u> **σαρκὶ** ἐπιτελεῖσθε;
       having.begun in.Spirit now in.flesh are.you.perfected

See also the references to the Holy Spirit in Acts 8:15–19 (below). In vv. 15b, 17b and 19, they are anarthrous, as befits focal constituents. In v. 18, however, τὸ πνεῦμα is the propositional topic about which a comment is made, so the reference is articular, while the focal constituent (διὰ τῆς ἐπιθέσεως τῶν χειρῶν τῶν ἀποστόλων) is preposed.[14]

Passage 13: Acts 8:14–19

(14)   Now when the apostles at Jerusalem heard that Samaria had accepted the word of God, they sent Peter and John to them (15a) who, having come down,

(15b)   προσηύξαντο περὶ αὐτῶν ὅπως λάβωσιν   πνεῦμα ἅγιον· κ.τ.λ.
        3P.prayed   for   them   that   3P.may.receive   Spirit   Holy

(17a)   τότε ἐπετίθεσαν   τὰς χεῖρας ἐπ' αὐτούς
        then   3P.were.laying   the   hands   on   them

(17b)   καὶ ἐλάμβανον   πνεῦμα ἅγιον.
        and   3P.were.receiving   Spirit   Holy

(18a)   ἰδὼν   δὲ   ὁ   Σίμων ὅτι **διὰ   τῆς ἐπιθέσεως**
        having.seen   DE   the   Simon   that   through   the   laying.on

        τῶν   χειρῶν τῶν   ἀποστόλων δίδοται   το πνεῦμα,
        of.the   hands   of.the   apostles   3S.is.given   the   Spirit

(18b)   he offered them money, (19) saying, "Give me also this power so that anyone on whom I lay my hands may receive the Holy Spirit (πνεῦμα ἅγιον)."

An observation is in order at this point about "Colwell's rule," part of which reads, "Definite predicate nouns which precede the verb usually lack the article" (1933:20). Since predicate nouns that precede the verb typically have been preposed for focus, it is appropriate that they should also lack the article. Thus, in Matt. 27:42 (βασιλεὺς Ἰσραήλ ἐστιν 'he is the king of Israel'—cited by Wallace (1996:263) as an instance of a clause containing a definite predicate nominative), the predicate noun phrase βασιλεὺς Ἰσραήλ has been preposed for focus, so it is appropriate that it be anarthrous.

The problem with any anarthrous substantive that is not a proper name is that, even if it has already been used in the passage (i.e., it has been activated), the new reference could still have an indefinite force. For example, various commentators have suggested that anarthrous instances of *law* (νόμος) in Romans and Galatians refer to law in general (i.e., it has indefinite force) or to "its quality *as law*" (Sanday & Headlam 1895:58), even after νόμος has been activated. However, Cranfield (1975:154 fn. 2) maintains, "The view... that it was Paul's custom to place the article before νόμος when he was using it with reference to the OT law and that, when he omits the article, he is using the word in a general sense, cannot be sustained."

Now, one cannot completely exclude interpretations such as that of Sanday & Headlam. Nevertheless, once a concept like law or faith has been activated, further anarthrous references to the concept may well have "definite force" if the reference occurs in a potentially focal position in the clause

---

[14] For further discussion of anarthrous references to the Holy Spirit, see Levinsohn 1993.

or sentence. This position is greatly strengthened if articular references to the concept are found in the same passage.

So, νόμος is activated in Gal. 2:16a (ἐξ ἔργων νόμου 'by works of law') and the articular form ὁ νόμος occurs in 3:12. Since most of the anarthrous references to law in chapters 2 and 3 occur in potentially focal positions in their clause or sentence (e.g., in 2:19a, 3:2b, 3:10a, 3:18), it is very likely that they have definite force and the article has been omitted because they are focal.

The same argument applies to the references to faith (πίστις) in Galatians 3. This concept is also activated in 2:16a (διὰ πίστεως Ἰησοῦ Χριστοῦ 'through faith in Jesus Christ') and the articular form διὰ τῆς πίστεως occurs in 3:14. Since most of the anarthrous references to faith in chapter 3 occur in potentially focal positions in their clause or sentence (e.g., in vv. 2b, 5b, 8a, 9), it is very likely that they have definite force and the article has been omitted because they are focal.

Review Questions

(a) If an anarthrous constituent is to be interpreted as marked for prominence, what conditions must it fulfill?

(b) Once an abstract concept like 'faith' has been activated (mentioned in a passage), what might suggest that later anarthrous references to the concept may well have definite force?

Suggested Answers

(a) If an anarthrous constituent is to be interpreted as marked for prominence, it must have unique referential identity; i.e., it must have been activated and have definite force.

(b) Once an abstract concept like 'faith' has been activated, later anarthrous references to the concept may well have definite force if they occur in a potentially focal position in their clause or sentence. This position is strengthened if articular references to the concept are found in the same passage.

Illustrative Passage 14: Romans 8:5–9b

The questions that follow this passage concern the references to God (θεός), spirit/Spirit (πνεῦμα), and flesh (σάρξ).

(5)　　For those who live according to the flesh set their minds on the things of the flesh, but those who live according to the Spirit set their minds on the things of the Spirit.

(6a)　τὸ　γὰρ　φρόνημα　τῆς　　σαρκὸς　θάνατος,
　　　　the　for　mind　　of.the　flesh　　death

(6b)　τὸ　δὲ　φρόνημα　τοῦ　　πνεύματος　ζωὴ　καὶ　εἰρήνη·
　　　　the　DE　mind　　of.the　spirit　　　life　and　peace

(7a)　διότι　τὸ　φρόνημα　τῆς　　σαρκὸς　ἔχθρα　εἰς　θεόν,
　　　　because　the　mind　of.the　flesh　　enmity　to　God

(7b)　τῷ　γὰρ　νόμῳ　τοῦ　θεοῦ　οὐχ　ὑποτάσσεται,
　　　　to.the　for　law　of.the　God　not　3S.is.subject

(7c)　οὐδὲ　γὰρ　δύναται·
　　　　neither　for　3S.is.able

(8)　　οἱ　　δὲ　ἐν　σαρκὶ　ὄντες　θεῷ　ἀρέσαι　οὐ　δύνανται.
　　　　the.ones　DE　in　flesh　being　God　to.please　not　3P.are.able

(9a)　ὑμεῖς　δὲ　οὐκ　ἐστὲ　ἐν　σαρκὶ　ἀλλὰ　ἐν　πνεύματι,
　　　　you　DE　not　you.are　in　flesh　but　in　spirit

(9b)　εἴπερ　πνεῦμα　θεοῦ　οἰκεῖ　ἐν　ὑμῖν.
　　　　since　spirit　of.God　3S.dwells　in　you

Questions

(a) Why is it a reasonable hypothesis to consider all the references in vv. 6–9 to God (θεός), Spirit/spirit (πνεῦμα), and flesh (σάρξ) to have "definite force"?

(b) Why are the references to flesh and Spirit/spirit anarthrous in v. 9a? Why are the references to them in v. 6 (and v. 7a) articular?

(c) Why is the reference to flesh anarthrous in v. 8?

(d) Why are the references to God anarthrous in vv. 7a and 8, but articular in v. 7b?

(e) Why is πνεῦμα θεοῦ anarthrous in v. 9b?

Suggested Answers

(a) It is a reasonable hypothesis to consider all the anarthrous references in vv. 6–9 to Θεός, πνεῦμα and σάρξ to have "definite force" because each has been activated (previously mentioned) and articular references to each occur in the passage.

(b) The references to flesh and Spirit/spirit are anarthrous in v. 9a because they are in contrast and the contrast is focal in the sentence (see Murray 1968:284). The references to them in v. 6 (and v. 7a) are articular because they are part of the propositional topic. For example, τὸ φρόνημα τῆς σαρκός is the propositional topic of v. 6a, with θάνατος the focus of the clause.

(c) The reference to flesh is anarthrous in v. 8 because, although it is part of the propositional topic (οἱ ἐν σαρκὶ ὄντες), it has been placed prior to its verb (ὄντες) to bring it into focus.

(d) In v. 7a, εἰς θεόν is anarthrous because it is the focus of the clause. In v. 7b, τῷ νόμῳ τοῦ θεοῦ is articular because the phrase is supportive, with the focus on the final verb (οὐχ ὑποτάσσεται)—see v. 7c, which strengthens the verb of v. 7b. In v. 8, θεῷ is anarthrous because it has been preposed for focus.

(e) Πνεῦμα θεοῦ is anarthrous in v. 9b because it has been preposed for focus.

9.4   Anarthrous Points of Departure

This section points out that, although points of departure are usually articular (sec. 3.8.2), they may be anarthrous. If an anarthrous point of departure has unique referential identity, then it (as well as some constituent of the comment) is especially prominent.

Delin (1989) has observed that, in some types of "it-cleft" sentence in English, *two* constituents are accented for prominence. One of the examples given is from the following exchange between teachers in a Scottish staff room, in which nuclear accent falls on the second part of the cleft and subsidiary accent on the first. In sentence b, "me" is the point of departure and propositional topic about which "can't type properly" is the comment, and this point of departure carries subsidiary accent for prominence.

a. Did the student really make this error?
b. No, it's just **me** that can't **type** properly.

Hebrews 11 provides a number of instances of anarthrous points of departure in Greek. Several paragraphs begin with πίστει, which provides a point of departure by renewal (sec. 2.3). The TEV uses it-cleft sentences to capture the prominent nature of the point of departure. For example, it translates **Heb. 11:3a**, "It is by faith that we understand that the universe was created by God's word." Appropriately, the focal constituent of the comment (ῥήματι θεοῦ) is also anarthrous.

(3a)   **Πίστει**   νοοῦμεν   κατηρτίσθαι   τοὺς   αἰῶνας   ῥήματι   θεοῦ,
       by.faith   we.understand   to.have.been.created   the   worlds   by.word   of.God

In **Gal. 3:11a** (discussed in sec. 9.3), ἐν νόμῳ appears to be the basis for relating the sentence to its context (νόμος was mentioned twice in v. 10), as well as providing the point of departure for the rest of the clause. In turn, οὐδεὶς and δῆλον are the focus respectively of the embedded and the main clauses. The absence of the article with ἐν νόμῳ is consistent with the point of departure being prominent. It may be prominent because it provides the counterpoint for the focal constituent of v. 11b (ἐκ πίστεως) to contrast with.

(10)   For all who rely on the works of the law (ἐξ ἔργων νόμου) are under a curse; for it is
         written, "Cursed is everyone who does not observe and obey all the things written in the
         book of the law (τοῦ νόμου)."

(11a)   ὅτι   δὲ   ἐν   νόμῳ   οὐδεὶς   δικαιοῦται   παρὰ   τῷ   θεῷ   δῆλον,
         that   DE   by   law   no.one   3S.is.justified before   the   God   clear

(11b)   ὅτι   Ὁ   δίκαιος   ἐκ   πίστεως   ζήσεται·
         since the   just   by   faith   3S.will.live

Review Questions

(a) Why is a point of departure usually articular? (If necessary, see sec. 3.8.2.).
(b) If a point of departure is anarthrous but the referent has already been activated, what does this
    indicate?

Suggested Answers

(a) A point of departure is usually articular because it either refers to or switches from information that
    is accessible in the context (sec. 3.8.2). Consequently, it usually has unique referential identity.
(b) If a point of departure is anarthrous but the referent has already been activated, this indicates that the
    point of departure is especially prominent.

Passage 15: Galatians 3:21–26

The questions that follow this passage concern references to παιδαγωγός 'trainer', νόμος 'law', and
πίστις 'faith'. (Except in genitive phrases, references to Χριστός are always anarthrous in Galatians, so
will not be discussed.)

(21a)   Ὁ   οὖν   νόμος   κατὰ   τῶν   ἐπαγγελιῶν   [τοῦ   θεοῦ];
         the   then   law   against the   promises   of.the   God

(21b)   μὴ   γένοιτο.
         not   3S.let.become

(21c)   εἰ   γὰρ   ἐδόθη   νόμος   ὁ   δυνάμενος   ζωοποιῆσαι,
         if   for   3S.was.given law   the   being.able   to.make.alive

(21d)   ὄντως   ἐκ   νόμου   ἂν ἦν   ἡ   δικαιοσύνη·
         really   by   law   3S.would.have.been   the   righteousness

(22a)   ἀλλὰ   συνέκλεισεν   ἡ   γραφὴ   τὰ   πάντα   ὑπὸ   ἁμαρτίαν,
         but   3S.shut.up   the   Scripture   the   all   under   sin

(22b)   ἵνα   ἡ   ἐπαγγελία   ἐκ   πίστεως   Ἰησοῦ   Χριστοῦ
         that   the   promise   by   faith   of.Jesus Christ

         δοθῇ   τοῖς   πιστεύουσιν.
         3S.may.be.given   to.the   believing.ones

(23a)   Πρὸ   τοῦ   δὲ   ἐλθεῖν   τὴν   πίστιν
         before the   DE   to.come   the   faith

(23b)   ὑπὸ   νόμον   ἐφρουρούμεθα
         under   law   we.were.guarded

(23c)   συγκλειόμενοι   εἰς   τὴν   μέλλουσαν   πίστιν   ἀποκαλυφθῆναι,
         being.shut.up   to   the   being.about   faith   to.be.revealed

(24a)   ὥστε   ὁ   νόμος   παιδαγωγὸς   ἡμῶν   γέγονεν   εἰς   Χριστόν,
         so.as   the   law   trainer   our   3S.has.become to   Christ

(24b) ἵνα ἐκ πίστεως δικαιωθῶμεν·
      that by faith   we.might.be.justified

(25a) ἐλθούσης   δὲ τῆς πίστεως
      having.come DE the faith

(25b) οὐκέτι   ὑπὸ   παιδαγωγόν ἐσμεν.
      no.longer   under trainer   we.are

(26) Πάντες γὰρ υἱοὶ θεοῦ   ἐστε   διὰ   τῆς πίστεως ἐν Χριστῷ Ἰησοῦ·
      all   for sons of.God you.are through the faith   in Christ   Jesus

Questions

(a) Why is the reference to 'trainer' in v. 25b anarthrous? And in v. 24a?

(b) Why are the references to 'law' articular in vv. 21a and 24a, but anarthrous in vv. 21c, 21d, and 23b?

(c) Why are the references to 'faith' articular in vv. 23a, 23c, 25a and 26, but anarthrous in vv. 22b and 24b?

Suggested Answers: see Appendix under 9(15).

PART IV: BACKGROUNDING AND HIGHLIGHTING DEVICES

Let me begin part IV of this book by telling you what chapters 10 and 11 are *not* going to be about! They are *not* going to be about distinguishing foreground information from background information. Rather, they are concerned with how certain material may be background*ed* with respect to other material and how certain material may be foreground*ed* or highlighted with respect to other material again. In other words, they are concerned with devices that make material *more* backgrounded or *more* foregrounded.

I will therefore devote this introductory section to a few words about foreground and background.

K. Callow (1974:52–53) relates foreground to *thematic prominence*: "this is what I'm talking about." Thematic material "carries the discourse forward, contributes to the progression of the narrative or argument... develops the theme of the discourse." In contrast, nonthematic or background material "serves as a commentary on the theme, but does not itself contribute directly to the progression of the theme... [it] fills out the theme but does not develop it."

Now, *narrative* is defined over against other discourse genres as "+ Agent oriented, + Contingent temporal succession" (Longacre 1996:9, see *SIL-UND* sec. 2.2). Consequently, the primary components of narrative are events that are performed in chronological sequence by participants. Non-event material such as "setting," "explanatory information," "evaluative information," "collateral information," and "performative information" (Grimes 1975:51–70) is classified as background material in narrative (see *SIL-UND* sec.12.3 for discussion of these terms).

Behavioral discourses such as parts of the Epistles differ from narrative in that the primary components are not generally organized in chronological sequence. In such discourses, assertions and imperatives with second person subjects may well make up the theme line.

The problem is that one discourse genre is frequently embedded in another. For example, the Epistle to the Galatians contains an embedded narrative (1:13–2:14), while each Gospel writer has probably arranged his narrative episodes with the goal of influencing his readers. Consequently, "material which might have a background function in narrative may be thematic in ... other types of discourse" (Callow op. cit. 56). So, in John's Gospel, a conclusion such as 20:31 ('But these are written so that you may come to believe that Jesus is the Messiah...') is background information as far as the immediately preceding narrative is concerned. However, it is to be interpreted as thematically prominent for the behavioral theme line that unites the narratives of the Gospel.

So, the same material can be viewed as background in one genre and as foreground in another. Consequently, I prefer to concentrate on the devices that authors use to indicate that certain material is backgrounded over against other material and that certain other material is highlighted over against other material.

Nevertheless, whatever the genre, certain types of material are *not* thematic. For example, γάρ constrains sentences it introduces to be interpreted as strengthening material in the immediate context, whatever the genre (though the sentence can itself be strengthened and, if the subsequent argument builds upon it, form part of some other theme line). Conversely, δέ or οὖν constrain sentences they introduce to be interpreted as developing a theme at some level (even if only within material introduced with γάρ).

Chapter 10 concentrates on devices that some NT authors use to indicate that a *sentence* is to be viewed as backgrounded, while chapter 11 discusses backgrounding *within* the sentence. Chapter 12 describes means of *highlighting*, then considers the role of the *historical present* in backgrounding and highlighting. See sec. 16.1 on the backgrounding of speeches by reporting them indirectly.

10

BACKGROUNDING OF SENTENCES

This chapter discusses three devices that some NT authors use to indicate that the sentence concerned has been backgrounded. Section 10.1 concerns prospective μέν (whether or not it is accompanied by οὖν), which frequently downgrades the importance of the sentence concerned with respect to a following sentence introduced with δέ. Section 10.2 begins by discussing the natural prominence that is reflected in the inherent properties of different verb forms, then considers the circumstances under which an imperfect might be indicating that the sentence concerned has been backgrounded. Finally, section 10.3 considers the use of ἐγένετο 'it happened' followed by a temporal expression and often an infinitival subject, to indicate that the preceding material forms the general background for the following foreground events.

10.1 Prospective Μέν

The term *prospective* is used in connection with μέν to mean that it anticipates, or at least implies, a corresponding sentence containing δέ. The old Greek grammarians considered μέν as always prospective, even when occurring in the combination μέν οὖν, and I have argued (Levinsohn 1987:137–50) that this is always true for Acts.

The presence of μέν not only anticipates a corresponding sentence containing δέ but frequently, in narrative, it also downgrades the importance of the sentence containing μέν. In particular, the information introduced with μέν is often of a secondary importance in comparison with that introduced with δέ.[1]

For instance, in **Luke 23:56b**, the presence of μέν anticipates the material introduced with δέ in 24:1 and implies that, in comparison, the information of v. 56b is of secondary importance. This seems evident from the fact that 24:1 refers back to the spices whose preparation had been noted in 23:56a.

(56a)   Then they returned, and prepared spices and ointments.

(56b)   Καὶ τὸ   μὲν σάββατον ἡσύχασαν κατὰ   τὴν ἐντολήν.
        and   the   sabbath   3P.rested according.to the commandment

(1)   τῇ   δὲ   μιᾷ   τῶν   σαββάτων ὄρθρου βαθέως ἐπὶ τὸ   μνῆμα
        the   DE   first of.the week   dawn   early   to   the tomb

        ἦλθον   φέρουσαι ἃ   ἡτοίμασαν ἀρώματα.
        3P.came   bringing   what 3P.prepared spices

When οὖν follows μέν, it is employed in one or other of the ways that were described in secs. 5.3.3 and 7.4, viz., inferentially or as a resumptive.

Acts 23:18 illustrates the *inferential* use of οὖν in connection with μέν. Paul asks a centurion to take his sister's son to the tribune, so (οὖν) he does so. At the same time, what is important is not the action of being taken to the tribune but the resulting opportunity to report something to him (see the end of v. 17). So the presence of μέν anticipates the material introduced with δέ in v. 19 and implies that, in comparison, the information of v. 18 is of secondary importance.

(17)   Paul called one of the centurions and said, "Take this young man to the tribune, for he has
        something to report to him."

(18)   ὁ   μὲν οὖν   παραλαβὼν   αὐτὸν ἤγαγεν   πρὸς τὸν
        the.one   then having.taken him   3S.brought to   the

---

[1] Phil. 1:15–17 may provide non-narrative instances in which μέν does *not* downgrade the information it introduces over against the material introduced with δέ. It could be argued that the assertions concerned are of equal importance, as is suggested by the English introducers "On the one hand... On the other hand."

170

χιλίαρχον καὶ φησίν,
tribune and 3S.affirms,

"The prisoner Paul called me and asked me to bring this young man to you; he has something to tell you."

(19) ἐπιλαβόμενος δὲ τῆς χειρὸς αὐτοῦ ὁ χιλίαρχος
having.grasped DE the hand his the tribune

καὶ ἀναχωρήσας κατ᾽ ἰδίαν ἐπυνθάνετο,
and having.withdrawn privately 3S.was.inquiring,

"What is it that you have to report to me?"

Acts 8:4 illustrates the *resumptive* use of οὖν in connection with μέν; the topic of the Christians who were scattered by the persecution described in v. 1b is resumed and advanced. The presence of μέν anticipates the material introduced with δέ in v. 5 and implies that, in comparison, the information of v. 4 is of secondary importance. Subsequent events show that the story indeed develops from the action of v. 5 rather than that of v. 4.

(1b) A severe persecution began that day against the church in Jerusalem, and all except the apostles were scattered throughout the countryside of Judea and Samaria.

(2) Devout men buried Stephen and made loud lamentation over him. (3) But Saul was ravaging the church by entering house after house; dragging off both men and women, he committed them to prison.

(4) Οἱ μὲν οὖν <u>διασπαρέντες</u> διῆλθον
the.ones then having.been.scattered 3P.went.about

εὐαγγελιζόμενοι τὸν λόγον.
preaching the word

(5) <u>Φίλιππος</u> δὲ κατελθὼν εἰς [τὴν] πόλιν τῆς Σαμαρείας
Philip DE going.down to the city of.the Samaria

ἐκήρυσσεν αὐτοῖς τὸν Χριστόν.
3S.was.proclaiming to.them the Christ

(6a) And the crowds with one accord listened eagerly to what was said by Philip,

Other examples in which the material introduced with μέν is of secondary importance in comparison with the following material introduced with δέ are found in Acts 8:25, 11:19, and 19:32 (οὖν is resumptive in each of these examples).

Illustrative Passage 1: Acts 15:1–4

(1) Then certain individuals came down from Judea and were teaching the brothers, "Unless you are circumcised according to the custom of Moses, you cannot be saved." (2) And after Paul and Barnabas had no small dissension and debate with them, the brothers appointed Paul and Barnabas and some of the others to go up to Jerusalem to discuss this question with the apostles and the elders.

(3) Οἱ μὲν οὖν <u>προπεμφθέντες</u> <u>ὑπὸ</u> <u>τῆς</u> <u>ἐκκλησίας</u>
the.ones then having.been.sent by the church

διήρχοντο τήν τε Φοινίκην καὶ Σαμάρειαν
3P.were.passing.through the both Phoenicia and Samaria

ἐκδιηγούμενοι τὴν ἐπιστροφὴν τῶν ἐθνῶν κ.τ.λ.
telling.in.detail the conversion of.the Gentiles

(4a)   παραγενόμενοι   δὲ   εἰς   Ἰερουσαλὴμ   παρεδέχθησαν   ἀπὸ
          having.come   DE   to   Jerusalem   3P.were.received   by

          τῆς   ἐκκλησίας   καὶ   τῶν   ἀποστόλων   καὶ   τῶν   πρεσβυτέρων,
          the   church   and   the   apostles   and   the   elders

Questions

(a) Why is μέν appropriate in v. 3?
(b) What is the function of οὖν in v. 3?

Suggested Answers

(a) Μέν is appropriate in v. 3 because the information it introduces is of secondary importance in comparison with that of v. 4. Paul and the others were sent to Jerusalem to meet with the apostles and elders (v. 2) and v. 4a describes them doing so.
(b) The function of οὖν in v. 3 is inferential; the group was appointed to go to Jerusalem, so it started passing through Phoenicia and Samaria in order to fulfill its commission.

In the following passage, the speech of Acts 25:4–5 is introduced with μέν οὖν.

Passage 2: Acts 25:2–6

(2b)   and they appealed to him (Festus), (3) requesting as a favor to have him (Paul) transferred to Jerusalem, planning an ambush to kill him along the way.

(4)   ὁ μέν οὖν   Φῆστος   ἀπεκρίθη   τηρεῖσθαι   τὸν   Παῦλον
        the   then   Festus   3S.answered   to.be.kept   the   Paul

        εἰς   Καισάρειαν,   ἑαυτὸν   δὲ   μέλλειν   ἐν τάχει   ἐκπορεύεσθαι·
        in   Caesarea   himself   DE   to.intend   shortly   to.go.forth

(5)   "So," he said, "let those of you who have the authority come down with me, and if there is anything wrong about the man, let them accuse him."

(6)   Διατρίψας   δὲ   ἐν   αὐτοῖς   ἡμέρας   οὐ   πλείους   ὀκτὼ   ἢ   δέκα,
        having.stayed   DE   among   them   days   not   more   eight   or   ten

        καταβὰς   εἰς   Καισάρειαν,   τῇ   ἐπαύριον   καθίσας
        going.down   to   Caesarea   on.the   morrow   having.sat

        ἐπὶ   τοῦ   βήματος   ἐκέλευσεν   τὸν   Παῦλον   ἀχθῆναι.
        on   the   judgment.seat   3S.ordered   the   Paul   to.be.brought

Questions

(a) How does the presence of μέν in v. 4 contribute to the relative prominence of the events of this passage?
(b) What is the function of οὖν in v. 4?

Suggested Answer: see Appendix under 10(2).

10.2   Natural Prominence and the Verb; The Imperfect

A number of linguists have shown that there is a significant correlation between the verb form used and foreground versus background information. For example, Foley and Van Valin (1984:371) show that there is a correlation between the "semantic verb type" (Longacre 1990:63) or "lexical meaning" (Fanning 1990:127) of the verb used in the clause and foreground versus background; this correlation is considered briefly in sec. 10.2.1. A correlation has also been observed between the verbal *aspect* and foreground versus background; this correlation is taken up in sec. 10.2.2, together with the extent to which the selection of the imperfect rather than the aorist in a narrative in NT Greek is indicative of background information.[2]

10.2.1 Verb Types and Natural Prominence

If we encounter a verb such as 'was' (ἦν) in a narrative, we expect the sentence concerned to be of a background nature. Foley and Van Valin (1984) go further; they discern a natural correlation between *four* basic verb classes and background versus foreground information. They use syntactic and semantic criteria proposed by Dowty (1979:60) to distinguish the following classes of verbs:

- achievement (e.g., recognize, find, die)[3]
- accomplishment (e.g., make something, paint a picture)
- activity (e.g., run, drive a car)
- state (e.g., know, have).

Foley and Van Valin point out (op. cit. 371) that clauses "with achievement and accomplishment verbs will strongly tend to occur in the temporal structure." In other words, such clauses will tend to present foreground information in narrative. In contrast, clauses "with activity and state verbs [will strongly tend to occur] in the durative/descriptive structure" (loc. cit.). In other words, such clauses will tend to present background information in narrative.

The selection of a particular semantic verb type therefore tends naturally to determine whether the clauses in which it appears will convey information of more or less importance for the genre concerned. What is significant for the Bible translator is that different languages tend to allocate individual verbs to the same semantic type, so that the verb that is most likely to be selected as the translation of an achievement verb in Greek is likely also to be an achievement verb, etc. In other words, the translator will probably preserve the natural prominence conveyed by a particular verb in Greek even if he or she has not classified the verbs of the receptor language into semantic types.

10.2.2 Verbal Aspect and Background versus Foreground

Before looking at the correlation between certain verbal aspects and background versus foreground, we need to understand what linguists mean by aspect. Verbal aspect is a way of *portraying* an event ("the speaker's subjective view of a process or event"—Reed & Reese 1996:183; it "reflects the subjective conception or portrayal by the speaker"—Fanning 1990:31).

For example, when the *imperfective* aspect is used to describe an event, the event is portrayed as *not completed*. The Greek imperfect is a past tense with imperfective aspect; thus, συνεπορεύετο αὐτοῖς 'he was journeying with them' (Luke 24:15b) indicates that the journeying is portrayed as an action that has not been completed at the point the story has reached. (For Fanning, this is the "internal" aspect, since it views the action "from a reference-point *within* the action, without reference to the beginning or end-point of the action"—op. cit. 84–85.)

When the *perfective* aspect is used to describe an event, the event is portrayed *as a whole* ("a complete and undifferentiated process"—Porter 1992:21). The Greek aorist has perfective aspect; thus, ἦλθον 'they came' indicates that the act of coming is viewed as a single journey, including its beginning and end. Though the use of the aorist presupposes that the journey was completed, it does not focus on the end of the journey; it simply views the journey as a whole. (For Fanning, this is the "external" aspect, which views the action "from a vantage-point *outside* the action... without reference to its internal structure"—loc. cit.)[4]

---

[2] In addition, Hopper & Thompson (1980:252) found that "high transitivity" correlates with foreground, while "low transitivity" correlates with background (using the term "transitivity" in a broader sense than that of having a direct object)—see *SIL-UND* sec. 12.1.

[3] Fanning (1990:129) divides achievements into "climaxes" (e.g., die, buy, sell) and "punctuals" (e.g., expire, hit).

[4] See Reed & Reese (1996:183–84) for comparison of the aspectual models of Porter, Fanning, and McKay.

Foley and Van Valin point out that there is an inherent correlation between perfective versus imperfective aspect and foreground versus background:[5]

> [T]he perfective aspect is the primary aspectual category found in the temporal structure of narrative discourse in a number of languages and imperfective aspect is primary in durational/descriptive structure. (op. cit. 373)
>
> This finding [the statement on p. 373] is not surprising, since perfective aspect codes completed actions and events and imperfective incomplete events and actions and the former fit more naturally into the temporal structure of narrative, the latter into durational/descriptive structure. (op. cit. 397)

Thus, it is natural in a narrative in Greek for a clause with the verb in the imperfect (which has imperfective aspect) to be conveying information of less importance than one with the verb in the aorist (perfective aspect); this is due to the nature of the respective aspects.

For example, the imperfect is used in Greek to encode *habitual* actions, since habits are not viewed as completed, and such actions are typically viewed as events of secondary importance in narrative. This is seen in **Luke 2:41–43**; the fact that Jesus' parents habitually went to Jerusalem for the festival of the Passover (v. 41) is of secondary importance to the events of vv. 43ff. that took place after they went there when he was twelve years old.

(41) Καὶ   ἐπορεύοντο   οἱ   γονεῖς   αὐτοῦ   κατ'   ἔτος
      and   3P.were.traveling the parents his   every year

      εἰς Ἰερουσαλὴμ τῇ   ἑορτῇ   τοῦ   πάσχα.
      to   Jerusalem   for.the feast   of.the passover

(42) καὶ ὅτε   ἐγένετο   ἐτῶν   δώδεκα, ἀναβαινόντων αὐτῶν
      and when 3S.became years twelve   going.up   they

      κατὰ   τὸ   ἔθος   τῆς   ἑορτῆς
      according.to the custom of.the feast

(43) καὶ τελειωσάντων   τὰς ἡμέρας, ἐν   τῷ   ὑποστρέφειν
      and having.fulfilled the days   in   the to.return

      αὐτοὺς ὑπέμεινεν   Ἰησοῦς ὁ   παῖς ἐν   Ἰερουσαλήμ, κ.τ.λ.
      them   3S.remained Jesus   the boy   in   Jerusalem

Thus, in narrative, the imperfect tends to correlate with background information and the aorist with foreground events, because of their inherent nature.

Nevertheless, the presence of the imperfect in a narrative in Greek is *not* a signal that the information concerned is necessarily of a background nature. This is seen in **Luke 2:38**. Verses 36–38 are all in the imperfect; v. 36 gives non-event information with ἦν, the relative clause of v. 37b describes a habitual action, and the foreground events of v. 38 are also portrayed as incomplete (see the NRSV translation, "began to praise God...").[6]

---

[5] See also Hopper 1979:215-16. Contrast Reed & Reese (1996:189), who argue for a correlation between the aorist (perfective aspect) and background information, and between the imperfective aspect and foreground information ("thematic prominence").

Incidentally, I disagree with Reed & Reese when they say that the use of the aorist *within* the quotation of Jude 14–15 shows "its relationship to the rest of the material in the book" (op. cit. 195). The quotation is the object of a speech verb and the tense-aspects of verbs used within embedded speeches need to be treated separately from the main verbs of the superstructure of a book.

[6] Robertson (n.d.:885) analyzes examples such as Luke 2:38 and John 8:31 (below) as "inchoative" imperfects, often translated "began."

Fanning (1997 lecture notes) contrasts passages like Luke 2:36-38 in which the imperfect is the only tense-aspect used with passages in which the imperfect contrasts with the aorist. In such passages, "the imperfect provides the background of the narrative." Mark 5:1-7 illustrates this; "the main narrative [is] carried by aorists and historical presents, with imperfects filling in background details."

My impression is that the correlation between the imperfect and background information is much stronger in Mark and John than in the other Gospels and Acts.

(36)   There was also a prophetess, Anna the daughter of Phanuel, of the tribe of Asher. She was of a great age, having lived with her husband seven years after her marriage, (37a) and as a widow to the age of eighty-four,

(37b)   ἢ   οὐκ   ἀφίστατο   τοῦ   ἱεροῦ   κ.τ.λ.
        who   not   3S.was.departing.from the   temple

(38)   καὶ   αὐτῇ   τῇ   ὥρᾳ   ἐπιστᾶσα   ἀνθωμολογεῖτο
        and   at.same the hour having.stood.nearby 3S.was.praising

        τῷ   θεῷ   καὶ   ἐλάλει   περὶ   αὐτοῦ   πᾶσιν   τοῖς
        the   God   and   3S.was.speaking about him   to.all   the.ones

        προσδεχομένοις   λύτρωσιν   Ἰερουσαλήμ.
        anticipating   redemption of.Jerusalem

This passage shows that the primary function of the imperfect in Greek is not to mark background but to portray events as incomplete. The tendency for habitual actions and other events of secondary importance in narrative to lend themselves to being portrayed as incomplete results in the correlation between the imperfect and background information.[7]

However, there appear to be occasions when the imperfect is used when *it is not obvious that the event described can be viewed as being incomplete*. The use of ἔλεγεν in **John 8:31** is a case in point. It does not seem likely that the imperfect is used here because Jesus habitually made this statement. Nor is there any suggestion that the speech is portrayed as incomplete because Jesus was interrupted.[8]

(30)   As he was saying these things, many believed in him.

(31)   ἔλεγεν   οὖν   ὁ   Ἰησοῦς   πρὸς τοῖς   πεπιστευκόσας   αὐτῳ   Ἰουδαίους,
        3S.was.saying then the   Jesus   to   the   having.believed   in.him Jews,

        "If you continue in my word, you are truly my disciples; (32) and you will know the truth, and the truth will make you free."

(33)   They answered him, "We are descendants of Abraham and have never been slaves to anyone. What do you mean by saying, 'You will be made free'?"

If an event cannot readily be viewed as incomplete yet the imperfect is used, we can consider such an imperfect to be used in a *marked* way. The message to the reader in this case is that, because the writer did not select the *natural* way of portraying a completed event (with, say, an aorist), there must be "added implicatures" (see fn. 22 of sec. 6.3). .

Ἔλεγεν in John 8:31 (above) could be such a marked usage of the imperfect. Possible confirmation for this interpretation is that the speech follows a paragraph break in some versions, so could readily be interpreted as the speech that incites or provokes the conversational exchange of the rest of the chapter.[9]

As I close this section, I must emphasize that the correlation between the imperfective aspect and background information, on the one hand, and between perfective aspect and foreground information, on the other, is specific to *narrative*.

Review Questions

(a) What are two correlations that Foley & Van Valin have observed in narrative between verb forms and foreground versus background?

(b) What is verbal aspect?

(c) What characterizes perfective aspect? And imperfective aspect?

---

[7] Reed & Reese (1996:190) make the same point: "the use of verbal aspect... to indicate prominence is a secondary role."

[8] Abbott (1906:342) renders ἔλεγεν "began to say."

[9] I am grateful to Mona Perrin (p. c.) for pointing this out.

(d) Under what circumstances might it be legitimate to view an imperfect in a Greek narrative as a signal of background information?

Suggested Answers

(a) The two correlations that Foley & Van Valin have observed in narrative between verb forms and foreground versus background are:
- the basic class (semantic type) of the verb: achievement and accomplishment verbs tend to correlate with foreground, whereas activity and state verbs tend to correlate with background
- verbal aspect: the perfective (external) aspect tends to correlate with foreground, whereas the imperfective (internal) aspect tends to correlate with background.

(b) Verbal aspect is the way that a speaker portrays an event.

(c) With perfective aspect an event is portrayed as a whole. With imperfective aspect an event is portrayed as incomplete.

(d) It may be legitimate to view an imperfect in a Greek narrative as a signal of background information if the event concerned cannot readily be viewed as incomplete.

Illustrative Sentence 3a: John 6:70–71a

(70)   Jesus answered them, "Did I not choose you, the twelve? Yet one of you is a devil."

(71a)   ἔλεγεν   δὲ   τὸν   Ἰούδαν   Σίμωνος   Ἰσκαριώτου·
        3S.was.saying   DE   the   Judas   of.Simon   Iscariot

Question

Why is it appropriate to use an imperfect in John 6:71a, even though an aorist is used to refer to the same speech in v. 70?

Suggested Answer

It is appropriate to use an imperfect in John 6:71a, even though an aorist is used to refer to the same speech in v. 70, because it is background material, not a foreground event of the narrative. Nevertheless, "[w]hen an utterance is not understood at first but only later, the event can be regarded as continuing beyond the initial time of voicing the utterance, and so the voicing itself can be referred to with imperfective aspect" (Pope p.c.—see also John 2:21).

Illustrative Passage 3b: Mark 15:11–15

(11)   But the chief priests stirred up (ἀνέσεισαν) the crowd to have him release Barrabas for them instead.

(12)   ὁ   δὲ   Πιλᾶτος   πάλιν   ἀποκριθεὶς   ἔλεγεν*   αὐτοῖς,
        the   DE   Pilate   again   answering   3S.was.saying   to.them,
        "Then what do you wish me to do with the man you call the King of the Jews?"
        (*variant: εἶπεν)

(13)   οἱ   δὲ   πάλιν   ἔκραξαν,
        they   DE   again   3P.cried.out,
        "Crucify him!"

(14a)   ὁ   δὲ   Πιλᾶτος   ἔλεγεν   αὐτοῖς,
        the   DE   Pilate   3S.was.saying   to.them,
        "Why, what evil has he done?"

(14b)   But they shouted (ἔκραξαν) all the more, "Crucify him!"

(15)   So Pilate, wishing to satisfy the crowd, released (ἀπέλυσεν) Barrabas for them; and after flogging Jesus, he handed him over (παρέδωκεν) to be crucified.

Question

If the UBS text is followed, why is an imperfect used in Mark 15:12 and 14a?

Suggested Answer

An imperfect may have been used in Mark 15:12 (UBS text) and 14 because Pilate was interrupted by the shouts of the crowd (vv. 13 and 15). Alternatively, they may have been used to background Pilate's questions because the crowd was controlling the exchange.

10.3   The Use of Ἐγένετο

This section concerns the combination of ἐγένετο ('it happened'—translating Hebrew *wayhi*) and a temporal expression, as in ἐγένετο δὲ ἐν ταῖς ἡμέραις ἐκείναις (now it happened in those days—Acts 9:37a). This combination is a device found in the LXX that Luke often uses to background information with respect to the following foreground events. Although BDF (§472) state that ἐγένετο is "meaningless," owing "its origin to an aversion to beginning a sentence with a temporal designation" (§442), it definitely is not! Rather, as Newman and Nida note (1972:93), it "is one of Luke's favorite devices for marking a transition in an episode." In particular, it picks out from the general background the *specific circumstance* for the foreground events that are to follow.

Particularly in Acts, ἐγένετο occurs with an infinitival clause that "is to be regarded as the (enlarged) subject of ἐγένετο" (Winer 1882:406). (An infinitival clause as subject of ἐγένετο is found occasionally also in Luke's Gospel. An infinitival clause is the subject of ἐγένετο also in Mark 2:15; this verse lacks a temporal expression in the UBS text, however.)

(In *Matthew*'s Gospel, the combination of ἐγένετο and a temporal expression almost invariably begins Καὶ ἐγένετο ὅτε ἐτέλεσεν ὁ Ἰησοῦς 'And it happened when Jesus had finished...' This occurs at major divisions in the book, rather than at a transition in an episode—see Matt. 11:1, 13:53, 19:1, and 26:1. See the suggested answer to question (d) on passage 8 of sec. 8.3 for discussion of 7:28, where the same expression occurs. In Matt. 9:10, however, ἐγένετο is followed by a genitive absolute at a transition in an episode; this verse is parallel to Mark 2:15—see above. *Mark* 1:9 and 4:4 are the only occasions in that Gospel when ἐγένετο is followed by a temporal expression. The combination is not used in *John*'s Gospel.)

One use of this construction that is *not* the main focus of this section is to indicate that an expected event materialized. For example, **Acts 27:22ff.** record Paul's prediction that everyone would be saved from the sea and, in v. 44b, the infinitival subject of ἐγένετο alludes to this.

(22)   "... not one of you will be lost..."

(44b)   καὶ   οὕτως   ἐγένετο   **πάντας**   διασωθῆναι   ἐπὶ   τὴν   γῆν.
        and   thus   3S.happened all   to.be.saved   on   the   land
        (i.e., and so everyone's escape to land materialized)

Other examples are found in Acts 10:25, 21:1, and 21:5, in each of which, the construction occurs *within* a temporal expression.

In the combination that is the concern of this section, however, the infinitival subject of ἐγένετο describes the specific circumstance for the following foreground events (see chap. 11 for other instances in which subordination is used as a means of backgrounding information). Typically, ἐγένετο is followed first by the temporal setting for these events and then by the infinitival subject itself. The temporal setting relates back to the general background described in the sentences immediately preceding ἐγένετο.

In **Acts 9:37a**, for example, the temporal expression ἐν ταῖς ἡμέραις ἐκείναις refers to a particular time within the period during which the general background situation of v. 36 held true. The infinitival clause ἀσθενήσασαν αὐτὴν ἀποθανεῖν, which is the subject of ἐγένετο, then presents the specific circumstance that leads to the following foreground events.

(36)   Now in Joppa there was a disciple whose name was Tabitha... who was devoted to good
        works and acts of charity.

(37a)   ἐγένετο   δὲ   ἐν ταῖς ἡμέραις ἐκείναις[10] ἀσθενήσασαν αὐτὴν ἀποθανεῖν·
        3S.happened DE   in   the   days   those   ailing   she   to.die

See also Acts 4:5, 19:23 and 28:17, plus 16:16 (with a genitive absolute).

This function of ἐγένετο is found also in Luke's Gospel. A particularly intriguing example occurs in
Luke 3:21-22. In this passage, the temporal setting of v. 21a relates back to the baptismal ministry of
John that was described in vv. 3-18. The coming of the Holy Spirit upon Jesus and the voice from
heaven are then expressed in infinitival clauses as the subjects of the ἐγένετο (vv. 21b-22b). The
implication is that the coming of the Spirit upon Jesus is but the specific circumstance for the following
foreground events, viz., his temptation by the devil and subsequent ministry.[11]

(21a)   Ἐγένετο   δὲ   ἐν τῷ   βαπτισθῆναι ἅπαντα τὸν λαὸν
        3S.happened DE   in   the   to.be.baptized all   the   people

(21b)   καὶ Ἰησοῦ βαπτισθέντος   καὶ προσευχομένου
        and   of.Jesus   having.been.baptized and   praying

        ἀνεῳχθῆναι   τὸν οὐρανὸν
        to.be.opened   the   heaven

(22a)   καὶ καταβῆναι   τὸ πνεῦμα τὸ ἅγιον ... ἐπ’ αὐτόν,
        and   to.come.down the   Spirit   the Holy   on   him

(22b)   καὶ **φωνὴν ἐξ οὐρανοῦ** γενέσθαι, κ.τ.λ.
        and   voice   from heaven   to.become

(23-38) (the genealogy of Joseph)
(4:1)   And Jesus, full of the Spirit, returned from the Jordan...

Notwithstanding examples like Luke 3:21-22, the specific circumstance is not usually expressed in
Luke's Gospel as the infinitival subject of ἐγένετο. Instead (as in Hebrew), it is presented in one or more
independent clauses. This is illustrated in **Luke 1:41,** in which the temporal setting immediately follows
ἐγένετο in v. 41a, while the specific circumstance is the independent clause of v. 41b.

(41a)   καὶ ἐγένετο   ὡς   ἤκουσεν τὸν ἀσπασμὸν
        and   3S.happened when 3S.heard the   greeting

        τῆς   Μαρίας ἡ   Ἐλισάβετ,
        of.the   Mary   the   Elizabeth

(41b)   ἐσκίρτησεν τὸ βρέφος ἐν τῇ κοιλίᾳ αὐτῆς,
        3S.leaped   the   babe   in   the   womb   her

(41c)   and Elizabeth was filled with the Holy Spirit, (42-43) and exclaimed with a loud cry,
        "Blessed are you among women... (44) For as soon as I heard the sound of your greeting,
        the child in my womb leaped for joy..."

See also Mark 1:9 and 4:4.

In some passages, the temporal setting that immediately follows ἐγένετο relates, not to earlier events
of the same episode, but to the previous episode. In such instances, the whole episode provides the
general background to the next one. For example, in **Acts 19:1,** the specific circumstance of Paul's
interaction with the disciples in Ephesus (vv. 2-6) is his encounter with them when he arrives there.
However, the temporal setting of v. 1 refers to the concluding events of the previous episode. It is clear

---

[10] Temporal expressions that immediately follow ἐγένετο are treated as points of departure.

[11] Note the parallel with the treatment of the coming of the Holy Spirit upon the early church (Acts 2:1-4) as part of the
setting for the events described in the rest of the book (see sec. 5.1).

from the answer of v. 3 that Apollos' earlier ministry in Ephesus (18:24ff.) provides the general background to the new episode (compare 'though he knew only the baptism of John' in 18:25 with 'into John's baptism' in 19:3b).

(24)   Apollos... (25) taught accurately the things about Jesus, though he knew only the baptism of John...

(1)
Ἐγένετο	δὲ	ἐν	τῷ	τὸν	Ἀπολλῶ	εἶναι	ἐν
3S.happened	DE	in	the	the	Apollos	to.be	in

Κορίνθῳ	Παῦλον	διελθόντα	τὰ	ἀνωτερικὰ	μέρη
Corinth	Paul	having.traveled.through	the	upper	regions

[κατ]ελθεῖν	εἰς	Ἔφεσον	καὶ	εὑρεῖν	τινας	μαθητὰς
to.come.down	to	Ephesus	and	to.find	some	disciples

(2)   and he said to them, "Did you receive the Holy Spirit when you became believers?" They replied, "No, we have not even heard that there is a Holy Spirit."

(3)   Then he said, "Into what then were you baptized?" They said, "Into John's baptism."

In Luke's Gospel, the temporal setting following ἐγένετο sometimes refers neither to earlier events of the same episode nor to the previous episode. Nevertheless, it appears that the presence of ἐγένετο indicates that the two episodes are to be related thematically, with the previous episode providing general background for the foreground events of the following one.

In Luke 9:18, for example, the time expression that immediately follows ἐγένετο (ἐν τῷ εἶναι αὐτὸν προσευχόμενον κατὰ μόνας 'as he was praying alone') appears to be unrelated to the previous episode (the feeding of the five thousand in vv. 12-17). Nevertheless, the question of v. 18 ('Who do the crowds say that I am?') suggests that the episodes are related thematically, with the feeding of the five thousand providing the general background for the following conversation.

Similarly, in Luke 7:11, ἐγένετο links the healing of the centurion's servant who was 'at the point of death' (v. 2) with the episode in which the son of the widow of Nain is raised from death (vv. 11-17). The use of ἐγένετο suggests that the episode involving someone at the point of death is to be taken as the general background to the one involving someone already dead.[12] (Matthew 9:10 provides a further instance in which the temporal setting following ἐγένετο refers neither to an earlier event of the same episode nor directly to the previous episode.)

Review Questions

(a) Is it true that Luke uses ἐγένετο as a device "for marking a transition in an episode" (Newman and Nida 1972)?

(b) What is the typical role of the infinitival subject of ἐγένετο in Acts?

Suggested Answers

(a) Yes. Luke uses ἐγένετο as a device "for marking a transition in an episode" in the sense that ἐγένετο marks the transition from events that contribute background details for the following foreground events to the foreground events themselves. In some instances, however, the presence of ἐγένετο indicates that the previous episode provides the general background for the following foreground events.

(b) In Acts, the infinitival subject of ἐγένετο typically presents an event that is the specific circumstance for the following foreground events. (In the case of Luke's Gospel, an independent clause following ἐγένετο is more often used to perform this function.)

---

[12] The main point, that ἐγένετο links the two episodes, is not affected if one reads ἐν τῇ ἑξῆς 'on the next day' instead of ἐν τῷ ἑξῆς 'soon afterwards'.

Illustrative Passage 4: Acts 16:13–17

(13)   On the sabbath day we went outside the gate by the river, where we supposed there was a place of prayer; and we sat down and spoke to the women who had gathered there. (14) A certain woman named Lydia, a worshiper of God, was listening to us... The Lord opened her heart to listen eagerly to what was said by Paul. (15) When she and her household were baptized, she urged us, saying, "If you have judged me to be faithful to the Lord, come and stay at my house." And she prevailed upon us.

(16)

Ἐγένετο	δὲ	πορευομένων	ἡμῶν	εἰς	τὴν	προσευχὴν
3S.happened	DE	going	our	to	the	prayer.place

παιδίσκην	τινὰ	ἔχουσαν	πνεῦμα	πύθωνα	ὑπαντῆσαι	ἡμῖν,
maid	certain	having	spirit	of.python	to.meet	with.us

ἥτις	ἐργασίαν	πολλὴν	παρεῖχεν	τοῖς	κυρίοις	αὐτῆς	μαντευομένη.
who	gain	much	3S.was.bringing	to.the	masters	her	prophesying

(17)   This one followed Paul and us, crying, "These men are slaves of the Most High God, who proclaim to you a way of salvation."

Question

What is the function of ἐγένετο in v. 16?

Suggested Answer

Since the genitive absolute that follows ἐγένετο in v. 16 relates to the previous episode (see v. 13), ἐγένετο indicates that that episode forms the general background to the one that follows. The infinitival subject of ἐγένετο (a slave girl who had a spirit of divination met us) presents the specific circumstance for the following foreground events (vv. 18ff.).

Passage 5: Luke 24:13–17

(13)   Now two of them were going on that same day to a village called Emmaus, about seven miles from Jerusalem,

(14)

καὶ	αὐτοὶ	ὡμίλουν	πρὸς	ἀλλήλους	περὶ	πάντων
and	they	3P.were.talking	to	each.other	about	all

τῶν	συμβεβηκότων	τούτων.
the	having.occurred	these

(15a)

καὶ	ἐγένετο	ἐν	τῷ	ὁμιλεῖν	αὐτοὺς	καὶ	συζητεῖν
and	3S.happened	in	the	to.talk	them	and	to.discuss

(15b)

καὶ	αὐτὸς*	Ἰησοῦς	ἐγγίσας	συνεπορεύετο	αὐτοῖς,
+	self	Jesus	having.drawn.near	3S.was.traveling.with	them

(*variant: insert ὁ)

(16)   but their eyes were kept from recognizing him. (17) And he said to them, "What are you discussing with each other while you walk along?"

Questions

(a) What is the function of ἐγένετο in v. 15a?
(b) If the UBS text is followed, why is the reference to Jesus in v. 15b anarthrous? (If necessary, see sec. 9.2.2.)

Suggested Answers: see Appendix under 10(5).

11
BACKGROUNDING WITHIN SENTENCES

This chapter discusses two ways in which information is backgrounded within sentences: through prenuclear anarthrous participial clauses (sec. 11.1) and in connection with a particular type of relative clause (sec. 11.2). Section 11.1 also considers the implications for continuity of situation and other factors of beginning a sentence with a participle rather than an adverbial clause of time.

11.1   Anarthrous Participial Clauses[1]

This section makes three points about anarthrous participial clauses, which are often called "circumstantial" participles. The first (in sec. 11.1.1) concerns the difference between nominative participial clauses (hereafter referred to as NPCs) and genitives absolute[2] (GAs). This difference can be described in terms of "switch reference" (Haiman & Munro 1983). In the vast majority of cases, this means that the subject of a NPC is the same as that of the clause to which it is subordinate (here called the *nuclear* clause), whereas the subject of a GA is different from that of the nuclear clause.

In section 11.1.2, I look at the significance of placing an anarthrous participial clause before its nuclear clause versus after its nuclear clause. I conclude that prenuclear participial clauses are always backgrounded with respect to their nuclear clause, whereas no such claim can be made about postnuclear participial clauses.

Finally, I return to the claim of sec. 2.4 that, when a sentence begins with a verb rather than a point of departure, no discontinuity has been indicated. I argue in sec. 11.1.3 that the same is true of sentences that begin with an anarthrous participle, and I present specific instances in Acts in which a continuity of situation and other factors is implied that might not be immediately evident were it not for the participle.

11.1.1   The Difference between NPCs and GAs

This section discusses two types of anarthrous or circumstantial participial clauses: those in the nominative case (NPCs) and those in the genitive (GAs) (see Healey & Healey 1990:179–80 and Wallace 1996:617 on distinguishing these types of participles from "attributive" or "adjectival" participles).

NPCs almost always have the *same subject* as their nuclear clause. Apparent exceptions (e.g., in Acts 19:34) typically involve the same *underlying* subject.

Thus in **Acts 5:17**, the subject of the NPC (v. 17a) is 'the high priest and all who were with him', and they are the subject also of the nuclear clause (v. 17b).

(17a)   Ἀναστὰς   δὲ   ὁ   ἀρχιερεὺς   καὶ   πάντες   οἱ   σὺν   αὐτῷ,   κ.τ.λ.
        having.arisen DE   the high.priest   and   all   the.ones   with   him

(17b)   ἐπλήσθησαν   ζήλου
        3P.were.filled   with.jealousy

Healey & Healey (1990:187) found that the subject of the GA typically "is not identical with the subject of the leading verb" (quoting Smyth 1956:457).

This is exemplified in **Acts 4:1**. The subject of the GA (v. 1a) is 'Peter and John' (3:11) and the subject of the nuclear clause (v. 1b) is 'the priests and the captain of the temple'.

---

[1] Greek grammarians traditionally call these participial *phrases*. Current linguistic practice is to call them *clauses*.

[2] I follow Healey & Healey (1990) in using the term absolute even when, as in Acts 4:1, the genitival subject of the participial clause is involved in the action of the nuclear clause.

(1a)   Λαλούντων   δὲ   αὐτῶν   πρὸς   τὸν   λαὸν
       speaking   DE   they   to   the   people

(1b)   ἐπέστησαν   αὐτοῖς   οἱ   ἱερεῖς   καὶ   ὁ   στρατηγὸς   κ.τ.λ.
       3P.approached   them   the   priests   and   the   captain

Healey and Healey (loc. cit.) found that, out of the 313 New Testament occurrences of the GA that they identified, only three or four did not strictly obey the rule that there be a change of subject between the GA and the nuclear clause. Even the apparent exceptions show changes consistent with the behavior of switch-reference markers in other languages.[3]

Thus, in **Acts 21:34b–c**, although the surface subject of the GA and the nuclear clause is the same, the *role* of the subject changes from experiencer to agent.[4]

(34b)   μὴ   δυναμένου   δὲ   αὐτοῦ   γνῶναι   τὸ   ἀσφαλὲς   διὰ   τὸν   θόρυβον
       not   being.able   DE   he   to.know   the   definite   because.of   the   noise

(34c)   ἐκέλευσεν   ἄγεσθαι   αὐτὸν   εἰς   τὴν   παρεμβολήν.
       3S.ordered   to.be.brought   him   into   the   barracks

Type of Anarthrous Participial Clause	Subject of Nuclear Clause is typically:
Nominative (NPC)	same
Genitive Absolute (GA)	different

Now, a construction that indicates switch reference provides a natural way of highlighting the introduction to an existing scene of participants who perform significant actions that change the direction of the story, etc. This is because, when the GA has the *same* subject as the *previous* clause, the scene is set for a *different* participant to be the subject of the nuclear clause. The employment of the GA with the same subject as the previous clause thus gives natural prominence to the event described in the following nuclear clause.

This is illustrated in Acts 4:1 (above). In the GA of v. 1a, αὐτῶν refers to the same speakers as those of the immediately preceding speech (3:12–26). Such a use of the GA anticipates the appearance of new participants who will perform a significant action that changes the direction of the story.

Review Question

How do NPCs and GAs differ in their relationship to their nuclear clause?

Suggested Answer

A NPC typically has the same subject as its nuclear clause; a GA typically has a different subject.

Illustrative Passage 1: Luke 15:13b–14

(13b)   καὶ   ἐκεῖ   διεσκόρπισεν   τὴν   οὐσίαν   αὐτοῦ   ζῶν   ἀσώτως.
       and   there   3S.squandered   the   property   his   living   loosely

(14a)   δαπανήσαντος   δὲ   αὐτοῦ   πάντα
       having.spent   DE   he   everything

(14b)   ἐγένετο   λιμὸς   ἰσχυρὰ   κατὰ   τὴν   χώραν   ἐκείνην,
       3S.happened   famine   severe   throughout   the   country   that

(14c)   καὶ   αὐτὸς   ἤρξατο   ὑστερεῖσθαι.
       and   he   3S.began   to.go.without

---

[3] In some languages, the system of switch-reference depends on whether the *topic* of the passage changes or remains the same.

[4] The Byzantine text "corrects" the text of v. 34b to μὴ δυναμένος δὲ γνῶναι κ.τ.λ. I have not investigated whether Luke always uses a GA when the subject remains the same but its role changes, or whether he normally uses a NPC.

Question

What is the effect of using a GA in v. 14a?

Suggested Answer

The subject of the GA in v. 14a is the same as that of v. 13b. So, the effect of using the GA is to set the scene for the introduction of a new participant (the famine) and to give prominence to this significant action that changes the direction of the story.

11.1.2 Anarthrous Participial Clauses and Backgrounding

This section argues that anarthrous participial clauses that *precede* their nuclear clause present information that is backgrounded. This means that the information they convey is of secondary importance vis-à-vis that of the nuclear clause. This claim does not hold for anarthrous participial clauses that follow their nuclear clauses.

It is generally recognized that the events described in anarthrous participial clauses relate semantically to their nuclear clauses in a variety of ways. Thus, Funk (1973:669) says, "The circumstantial participle as the equivalent of an adverbial clause may be taken (i.e., inferred from the context) to denote time, cause, means, manner, purpose, condition, concession, or attendant circumstances." However, Robertson (n.d.:1124) points out that "there is a constant tendency to read into this circumstantial participle more than is there. In itself, it must be distinctly noted, the participle does not express time... These ideas are not in the participle, but are merely suggested by the context."

Thus, the function of the anarthrous participle is not to specify any of the relationships that Funk lists. "Other more extended but more precise constructions are available for the same purpose: prepositional phrases, conditional, causal, temporal clauses, etc., and finally the grammatical coordination of two or more verbs" (BDF §417).

According to Greenlee (1963:66–67) and Healey and Healey (1990:247), an anarthrous participial clause that *precedes* the verb typically describes an event that is of secondary importance vis-à-vis the information conveyed by the nuclear clause.[5] I therefore consider that prenuclear participial clauses are so encoded specifically to *signal* that the information concerned is of secondary importance vis-à-vis the nuclear event.

This is illustrated in **Mark 5:25–27**. The effect of using the series of participial clauses is to signal that all the information prior to v. 27c is of secondary importance vis-à-vis the foreground event described in v. 27c.

(25) καὶ γυνὴ οὖσα ἐν ῥύσει αἵματος δώδεκα ἔτη
and woman being with flow of.blood twelve years

(26a) καὶ πολλὰ παθοῦσα ὑπὸ πολλῶν ἰατρῶν
and many.things having.suffered by many physicians

(26b) καὶ δαπανήσασα τὰ παρ' αὐτῆς πάντα
and having.spent the with her all

(26c) καὶ μηδὲν ὠφεληθεῖσα
and nothing having.benefited

---

[5] The term "*coordinate* circumstances" that Greenlee uses to describe such clauses is unfortunate, since the circumstances are always of secondary importance with respect to the action of the nuclear clause. As Wallace (1996:640) notes, "The participle... in effect, 'piggy-backs' on the mood of the main verb." Thus, in Matt. 28:19 (πορευθέντες οὖν μαθητεύσατε πάντα τὰ ἔθνη 'going, therefore, make disciples of all nations'), πορευθέντες is a necessary "attendant circumstance" (op. cit. p. 645) to the imperative μαθητεύσατε. The disciples have to go before they can make disciples. At the same time, the act of going is of secondary importance with respect to the act of making disciples.

(26d)   ἀλλὰ   μᾶλλον   **εἰς**   **τὸ**   **χεῖρον**   ἐλθοῦσα,
        but   rather   into   the   worse   having.come

(27a)   ἀκούσασα   περὶ   τοῦ   Ἰησοῦ,
        having.heard about the   Jesus

(27b)   ἐλθοῦσα   ἐν   τῷ   ὄχλῳ   ὄπισθεν
        having.come in   the   crowd   behind

(27c)   ἥψατο   τοῦ   ἱματίου   αὐτοῦ·
        3S.touched the   garment   his

It is true, then, that specific semantic relationships between a prenuclear anarthrous participial clause and the following nuclear clause may be deduced from the context. Nevertheless, the only relationship between them that has been signaled is a *pragmatic* one, that the event of the participial clause is of secondary importance vis-à-vis that of the nuclear clause. This is illustrated in John 9:25c, Matt. 6:27, and Heb. 1:1–2 (all of which are presented below).

In **John 9:25c**, a concessive relationship between the participial clause and the following nuclear clause is readily deduced. Nevertheless, the primary significance of using the participial clause is that the reference to having been blind provides the counterpoint for the assertion of the nuclear clause. Furthermore, τυφλός is preposed in the participial clause to bring it into temporary focus (sec. 4.3) in anticipation of the contrastive switch to the real focus of the sentence, βλέπω.

(25c)   **ἓν**   οἶδα   ὅτι   **τυφλὸς**   ὢν   <u>ἄρτι</u>   βλέπω.
        one   I.know   that   blind   being   now   I.see

In **Matt. 6:27**, the participial clause may be interpreted as describing the means of realizing the result that is described in the nuclear clause. Formally, however, μεριμνῶν (v. 27a) only reiterates the theme of the passage (see v. 25) and is of secondary importance in comparison with the desired result stated in v. 27b.

(25)   Therefore I tell you, do not be anxious about your life, what you will eat or what you will drink, or about your body, what you will wear...

(27a)   τίς   δὲ   ἐξ   ὑμῶν   μεριμνῶν
        who   DE   of   you   being.anxious

(27b)   δύναται   προσθεῖναι   ἐπὶ   τὴν   ἡλικίαν   αὐτοῦ   πῆχυν   ἕνα;
        3S.can   to.add   to   the   stature   his   cubit   one

Many versions translate **Heb. 1:2a** as being in a contrastive relationship with v. 1. However, it is not the participial clause that signals the contrast. Rather, as sec. 7.1 points out, the contrast is conveyed by there being at least two opposing pairs of lexical items (πάλαι plus τοῖς πατράσιν versus ἐπ’ ἐσχάτου τῶν ἡμερῶν τούτων plus ἡμῖν, and ἐν τοῖς προφήταις versus ἐν υἱῷ) and a common element (God speaking). The participial clause itself signals only that it is of secondary importance vis-à-vis the foreground assertion of v. 2a for which it provides the framework.

(1)   **Πολυμερῶς**   **καὶ**   **πολυτρόπως**   πάλαι   ὁ   θεὸς
        in.many.portions   and   in.many.ways   long.ago   the   God

        λαλήσας   τοῖς   πατράσιν   ἐν   τοῖς   προφήταις
        having.spoken to.the   fathers   by   the   prophets

(2a)   <u>ἐπ’</u>   <u>ἐσχάτου</u>   <u>τῶν</u>   <u>ἡμερῶν</u>   <u>τούτων</u>   ἐλάλησεν   ἡμῖν   ἐν   υἱῷ,
        in   last   of.the   days   these   3S.spoke   to.us   by   son

Participial clauses that *follow* the nuclear clause may be concerned with some aspect of the nuclear event itself. Alternatively, they may describe "a circumstance as merely accompanying the leading verb" (Greenlee 1986:57).

In **Matt. 28:18**, for instance, ἐλάλησεν and λέγων refer to the same event. The postnuclear participial clause of v. 18b details what it was that Jesus spoke to the disciples.

(18a) καὶ προσελθὼν ὁ Ἰησοῦς ἐλάλησεν αὐτοῖς
      and approaching the Jesus 3S.spoke with.them

(18b) λέγων, Ἐδόθη μοι πᾶσα ἐξουσία κ.τ.λ.
      saying 3S.was.given to.me all authority

In **Matt. 11:19a**, the postnuclear participles refer to the manner in which the action of the nuclear clause ('came') was carried out.

(19a) ἦλθεν ὁ υἱὸς τοῦ ἀνθρώπου ἐσθίων καὶ πίνων,
      3S.came the son of.the man eating and drinking

In **Acts 5:2b**, the postnuclear GA describes "a circumstance... accompanying the leading verb" (ibid.).

(2a) καὶ ἐνοσφίσατο ἀπὸ τῆς τιμῆς,
     and 3S.misappropriated from the price

(2b) συνειδυίης καὶ τῆς γυναικός,
     having.known + the wife

In some passages, however, the GA describes a modification in circumstances and appears to occur after the nuclear clause only to preserve the flow of the story. **Acts 24:10** provides an illustration. Here, Paul responds primarily, not to the governor's invitation to speak, but to the accusations of vv. 2–9. By placing the GA of v. 10b after the nuclear clause, it is perhaps clearer to whom the answer (ἀπεκρίθη) is made.

(2–8) (Tertullus' speech, outlining the accusations against Paul.)
(9) The Jews also joined in the charge by asserting that all this was true.

(10a) Ἀπεκρίθη τε ὁ Παῦλος
      3S.answered ADD the Paul

(10b) νεύσαντος αὐτῷ τοῦ ἡγεμόνος λέγειν,
      having.nodded to.him the governor to.speak

In **Acts 28:25**, the postnuclear GA describes rather more than a modification in circumstances! The effect of placing the GA after the verb is twofold. On the one hand, it allows attention to be kept on Paul's visitors at the beginning of the sentence (they were the subject in v. 24). More significantly, it allows Paul's speech of vv. 25–28 to occur last and therefore feature most prominently in the episode (if the UBS text is followed—this effect is lost if v. 29 is read), even though it was made before the Jews finally departed.

(24) Some were convinced by what he had said, while others refused to believe.

(25a) **ἀσύμφωνοι** δὲ ὄντες πρὸς ἀλλήλους ἀπελύοντο
      at.variance DE being toward one.another 3P.were.departing

(25b) εἰπόντος τοῦ Παύλου ῥῆμα ἕν, ὅτι
      having.said the Paul word one that

(25c) "The Holy Spirit was right in saying to your ancestors through the prophet Isaiah, (26) 'Go to this people and say,...'"

Whereas prenuclear anarthrous participial clauses describe information secondary in importance to that of the nuclear clause, the importance of postnuclear participial clauses is *not* determined by the fact that the information is encoded as a participial clause. Rather, the relative importance of the information conveyed in the two clauses has to be deduced from the context.[6]

This last claim is illustrated from the five examples of postnuclear clauses that appear above. In Matt. 28:18, the most important information is not that Jesus spoke (ἐλάλησεν), but the content of his speech, which is introduced with λέγων. In Matt. 11:19a, it is clear from the context (v. 18) that the significant information is not that the Son of Man came (ἦλθεν), but *how* he came. In Acts 28:25ff., Paul's speech which is the object of the GA appears to be the climax of at least the episode. In Acts 5:2, however, the information of the GA is only of importance later in the episode. Finally, in Acts 24:10, the information conveyed by the GA would appear to be of minor significance.

Review Questions

(a) What semantic or pragmatic relationship with a nuclear clause is signaled when an anarthrous (circumstantial) participial clause precedes it?

(b) For what purposes does an anarthrous participial clause typically follow its nuclear clause? What is the relative status of the information conveyed by the two clauses?

Suggested Answers

(a) When an anarthrous (circumstantial) participial clause precedes a nuclear clause, the information it conveys is of secondary importance vis-à-vis that conveyed in the nuclear clause. No specific semantic relationship with the nuclear clause is signaled; rather, it is to be deduced from the context.

(b) When an anarthrous participial clause follows a nuclear clause, it typically describes:
  • some aspect of the event presented in the nuclear clause, or
  • a circumstance accompanying the event presented in the nuclear clause.

The relative status of the information conveyed in the two clauses has to be deduced from the context.

Illustrative Passage 2: Acts 25:4–9

Note the anarthrous participial clauses that occur in this passage.

(4)   So Festus replied that Paul was being kept at Caesarea, and that he himself intended to go there shortly. (5) "So," he said, "let those of you who have the authority come down with me, and if there is anything wrong about the man, let them accuse him."

(6a)   Διατρίψας   δὲ   ἐν   αὐτοῖς ἡμέρας οὐ   πλείους ὀκτὼ ἢ   δέκα,
       having.stayed DE   with them   days   not more.than eight or ten

(6b)   καταβὰς   εἰς Καισάρειαν,
       having.come.down   to   Caesarea

(6c)   τῇ   ἐπαύριον καθίσας   ἐπὶ τοῦ βήματος
       on.the next.day having.sat on   the judgment.seat

(6d)   ἐκέλευσεν τὸν Παῦλον ἀχθῆναι.
       3S.ordered the Paul   to.be.brought

(7a)   παραγενομένου δὲ   αὐτοῦ
       having.arrived DE he

(7b)   περιέστησαν   αὐτὸν οἱ   ἀπὸ Ἱεροσολύμων καταβεβηκότες   Ἰουδαῖοι
       3P.stood.around him   the from Jerusalem   having.come.down Jews

(7c)   πολλὰ καὶ βαρέα αἰτιώματα καταφέροντες   ἃ   οὐκ
       many and serious charges   bringing.against which not

---

[6] Hwang likewise claims (1990:73) that, whereas prenuclear subordinate clauses in English present information of secondary importance, postnuclear subordinate clauses do not.

ἴσχυον   ἀποδεῖξαι,
3P.were.able to.prove

(8) <u>τοῦ   Παύλου</u>   ἀπολογουμένου   ὅτι
     the   Paul   defending.himself that
     "I have in no way committed an offense against the law of the Jews, or against the temple, or against the emperor."

(9a) ὁ <u>Φῆστος</u> δὲ θέλων   τοῖς 'Ιουδαίοις χάριν καταθέσθαι
      the Festus   DE wanting to.the Jews   favor to.grant

(9b) ἀποκριθεὶς   τῷ   Παύλῳ   εἶπεν,
      having.answered to.the Paul   3S.said
      "Do you wish to go up to Jerusalem and be tried there before me on these charges?"

Questions

(a) Five *prenuclear NPCs* occur in this passage; in which verses do they occur? What is the status of the information they convey vis-à-vis that of their nuclear clause?

(b) In which verse does a *postnuclear NPC* occur? What is the status of the information it conveys vis-à-vis that of its nuclear clause?

(c) In which verse does a *prenuclear GA* occur? What is the status of the information it conveys vis-à-vis that of the following clauses?

(d) In which verse does a *postnuclear GA* occur? What is the status of the information it conveys vis-à-vis that of its nuclear clause?

(e) In the light of your answers to questions (a) to (d), which are the foreground events and speeches of vv. 6–9?

Suggested Answers

(a) The five prenuclear NPCs of this passage occur in vv. 6a, 6b, 6c, 9a, and 9b. They supply information of secondary importance vis-à-vis that of their nuclear clauses (the event of v. 6d and the speech of v. 9b).

(b) A postnuclear NPC occurs in v. 7c. The information it conveys is more important than that conveyed in the nuclear clause of v. 7b.

(c) A prenuclear GA occurs in v. 7a. It supplies information of secondary importance vis-à-vis that of the following clauses (vv. 7b–c—see answer (b)).

(d) A postnuclear GA occurs in v. 8. Like the postnuclear NPC of v. 7c, the information it conveys is more important than that conveyed in the nuclear clause of v. 7b.

(e) The foreground events and speeches of vv. 6–9 are:
  - v. 6d: Festus ordered Paul to be brought
  - vv. 7b–c: the Jews from Jerusalem stood around Paul, bringing many serious charges against him which they could not prove
  - v.8: while Paul maintained that he had committed no offense against anyone
  - v 9b: Festus asked Paul if he was willing to go to Jerusalem to be tried.

11.1.3 Initial Participles and Continuity

Prenuclear anarthrous participial clauses often do more than just indicate that the information they convey is of secondary importance vis-à-vis that of the nuclear clause. If the sentence concerned begins with the participle (especially a NPC, see below on GAs), no discontinuity has been signaled (sec. 2.4). In practice, this means that continuity of situation and other relevant factors between the contiguous nuclear clauses is implied. Thus, while a prenuclear participial clause may present some modification in circumstances, if it begins with the participle the overall continuity of situation and other factors between the foreground events described in the nuclear clauses is preserved.

Acts 5:17 (repeated below) illustrates a prenuclear participial clause of this type. The religious authorities are reactivated in a clause with an initial participle (v. 17a) and it is thereby implied that they have been placed in the scene that was set by the previous sentence(s). In other words, there is an implied continuity of situation and other factors with the context, notwithstanding their reactivation. Consequently, when the following nuclear clause says that they were filled with jealousy, the reason for that jealousy is to be deduced from the immediate context.

(16)   A great number of people would also gather from the towns around Jerusalem, bringing the sick and those tormented by unclean spirits, and they were all cured.

(17a)   Ἀναστὰς   δὲ   ὁ   ἀρχιερεὺς   καὶ πάντες οἱ   σὺν   αὐτῷ, κ.τ.λ.
         having.arisen DE   the   high.priest   and   all   the.ones   with   him

(17b)   ἐπλήσθησαν   ζήλου
         3P.were.filled   with.jealousy

(When an anarthrous participial clause begins with a constituent other than the participle, the constituent is either a point of departure, as in Acts 25:8 and 9a of passage 2 above, or has been preposed for focus, as in Acts 25:7c.)

The relationship of sentence initial participles (especially GAs) to continuity of situation contrasts with the function of initial adverbial clauses of time, i.e., temporal points of departure. These signal *discontinuities* of time and express the temporal setting for the following event(s). When a participle begins the sentence, however, it implies continuity of situation and other relevant factors with the context, even if it also describes a modification of the temporal setting (see further in Levinsohn 1977a:21 and 1987:65ff.). The differences may be expressed as follows:[7]

sentence initial	signals:
adverbial clause of time	+ discontinuity of time
participle	– discontinuity

A comparison of Acts 18:6 and 9:23 illustrates the difference between beginning a sentence with a participle and with an adverbial clause of time.

In **Acts 18:6**, a participle begins the sentence. In this particular passage, continuity of *roles* between the foreground events of vv. 5–6 is particularly evident. "In 18:5–6, Paul is subject of both independent clauses, and the Jews are undergoers. Even though these roles are temporarily reversed in the GA itself, between the independent clauses they remain unchanged" (Levinsohn 1987:72).

(5)   When Silas and Timothy arrived from Macedonia, Paul was occupied with proclaiming the word, testifying to the Jews that the Messiah was Jesus.

(6a)   ἀντιτασσομένων   δὲ   αὐτῶν   καὶ   βλασφημούντων
         opposing   DE   they   and   blaspheming

(6b)   having shaken out his clothes, he said to them, "Your blood be on your own heads! I am innocent. From now on I will go to the Gentiles."

In **Acts 9:23**, an adverbial clause of time begins the sentence. "... in 9:22–23, Saul and the Jews change roles, between the independent clauses which are contiguous to the temporal clause" (loc. cit.)

(22)   Saul became increasingly more powerful and confounded the Jews who lived in Damascus by proving that Jesus was the Messiah.

(23a)   Ὡς   δὲ   ἐπληροῦντο   ἡμέραι   ἱκαναί,
         when   DE   3P.were.fulfilled   days   many

(23b)   the Jews plotted to kill him;

---

[7] Although the examples of this section are taken only from Acts, this contrast appears to hold also for the Gospels.

See Levinsohn 1987:71–79 for further pairs of examples from Acts that illustrate the difference between beginning a sentence with a participle and beginning one with an adverbial clause of time.[8]

In the majority of cases in which a participle begins the sentence in Acts, continuity with the context is obvious. However, in a few instances, the use of such a participle (especially if it is a GA) makes explicit a continuity that is not immediately apparent.

This is illustrated in **Acts 7:30**. Verse 23 begins with an adverbial clause of time, whereas v. 30 conveys very similar information with a GA. In the case of v. 23, the primary relationship with the context is temporal; the setting simply changes to forty years later. In contrast, notwithstanding a similar change of temporal setting between the material preceding and following the GA of v. 30, there is such continuity in Stephen's argument that it is undesirable for the temporal discontinuity to be to the fore. The nature of the continuity is made explicit in v. 35, when the speeches of v. 27 ('Who made you a ruler and judge over us?') and of v. 34 ('I will send you to Egypt') are brought together and contrasted.

(22)   And Moses was instructed in all the wisdom of the Egyptians and was powerful in his words and deeds.

(23)   Ὡς   δὲ   ἐπληροῦτο   αὐτῷ   τεσσερακονταετὴς   χρόνος,
       when   DE   3S.was.fulfilled   to.him   forty.years   time

it came into his heart to visit his relatives, the Israelites. (24) When he saw one of them being wronged, he defended the oppressed man and avenged him by striking down the Egyptian... (26) The next day he came to some of them as they were quarreling and tried to reconcile them... (27) But the man who was wronging his neighbor pushed him aside, saying, "Who made you a ruler and a judge over us? ..." (29) When he heard this, Moses fled and became a resident alien in the land of Midian, where he became the father of two sons.

(30)   Καὶ   πληρωθέντων   ἐτῶν   τεσσεράκοντα
       and   being.fulfilled   years   forty

an angel appeared to him in the wilderness of Mount Sinai, in the flame of a burning bush... (33) Then the Lord said to him, (34) "... I have come down to rescue them. Come now, I will send you to Egypt."

(35)   This Moses whom they rejected when they said, "Who made you a ruler and a judge?" God sent as both ruler and liberator through the angel who appeared to him in the bush.

Review Questions

If a sentence begins with a participle, what does this signal? And what implication follows?

Suggested Answers

If a sentence begins with a participle, no discontinuity has been signaled. It follows that continuity of situation and other factors with the context is implied.

Illustrative Passage 3: Acts 23:11–12

In this passage, note the initial GA in Acts 23:12.

---

[8] Three types of adverbial clause of time are common in narratives in Acts:

ἐν plus the dative typically describes a fairly stative situation *during* which the main events take place, as in 9:3;

ὅτε: if in the aorist, the following event is in chronological *sequence* with the event described in the temporal setting, as in 1:13; if in the imperfect, the events are *simultaneous*, as in 22:20;

ὡς: if in the imperfect, there is temporal *overlap* (while the event described in the adverbial clause was taking place, something else happened), as in 8:36; it is "used in temporal clauses but often with a slight *comparative or causal* sense" (op. cit. 242), as in 5:24.

(11)   The <u>following</u> <u>night</u> the Lord stood near Paul and said, 'Keep up your courage! For just as you have testified for me in Jerusalem, so you must bear witness also in Rome.'

(12)   Γενομένης   δὲ   ἡμέρας ποιήσαντες συστροφὴν οἱ   Ἰουδαῖοι
        having.become DE   day   having.made conspiracy the Jews

        ἀνεθεμάτισαν   ἑαυτοὺς   λέγοντες μήτε   φαγεῖν μήτε
        3P.bound.with.oath themselves saying   neither to.eat nor

        πιεῖν   ἕως οὗ ἀποκτείνωσιν τὸν Παῦλον.
        to.drink until   3P.may.kill   the Paul

Question

What is the effect of using a GA at the beginning of v. 12, rather than an adverbial clause of time?

Suggested Answer

The effect of beginning Acts 23:12 with a GA, rather than an adverbial clause of time, is to imply that there is a direct relationship between the Lord's promise of v. 11 that Paul is to be a witness in Rome and the plot of the Jews to kill him. Were it not for the GA, it might take several chapters for this relationship to be discerned.

Many versions treat v. 11 as a separate paragraph at the end of the episode "Before the Sanhedrin" and insert a title before v. 12 (e.g., "The Plot to Kill Paul"—NIV). Since v. 23 also begins with a participle, the title "Paul transferred to Caesarea" could appropriately introduce v. 11, rather than v. 23, in order to indicate the continuity in vv. 11ff.

11.2   Relative Clauses

Relative clauses in Greek begin with a relative pronoun which, as a general rule, "agrees in gender and number with its referent (the thing to which it refers) and in case with its function in its own clause" (Porter 1992:244). If the referent is overtly stated, then the relative clause follows it.

In **Acts 9:36**, for example, ἥ is feminine singular because it agrees with Ταβιθά, which is a feminine noun in the singular; ἥ is in the nominative because it is the subject of λέγεται. The relative clause follows Ταβιθά. (In the initial examples of this section, the relative clause is in curly brackets.)

(36)   Ταβιθά, {ἣ   διερμηνευομένη λέγεται   Δορκάς}
        Tabitha   which being.translated 3S.is.called Dorcas

Linguists commonly divide relative clauses into two types: restrictive and nonrestrictive.

A *restrictive* relative clause "serves to delimit the potential referents" (Comrie 1989:138), as in:

The man {who arrived yesterday} left this morning.

A *nonrestrictive* relative clause "serves merely to give the hearer an added piece of information about an already identified entity, but not to identify that entity" (loc. cit.), as in:

Mr. Smith, {who arrived yesterday}, left this morning.[9]

Both restrictive and nonrestrictive relative clauses are found in Koiné Greek.

Luke 1:26 contains a *restrictive* relative clause. The clause 'whose name is Nazareth' delimits the potential referents of 'a city of Galilee'.

(26)   εἰς πόλιν τῆς   Γαλιλαίας {ᾗ   ὄνομα Ναζαρὲθ}
        to   city   of.the Galilee   to.which name   Nazareth

---

[9] Many languages do not have nonrestrictive relative clauses, and only use restrictive relative clauses in very specific circumstances. See Pope 1993 and Levinsohn 1997 on this problem in some languages of West Africa.

Acts 9:36 (above) contains an example of a *nonrestrictive* relative clause. The clause 'which means Dorcas' adds a piece of information about an already identified entity.

Nonrestrictive relative clauses in Greek are traditionally subdivided into *appositional* (as in Acts 9:36) and *continuative* (Winer 1882:680).[10] Appositional relative clauses, as their name suggests, stand in apposition to the noun that they modify. Continuative relative clauses, in contrast, typically describe an event that involves the referent of the relative pronoun and occurs subsequent to the previous event or situation in which the referent featured.

An example of a continuative relative clause is found in **Acts 28:23c**. The referent of οἷς is the people who came to Paul in his lodging (v. 23b). Verse 23c describes an event that involves these referents and that occurs subsequent to the event of v. 23b.

(23b)   ἦλθον   πρὸς   αὐτὸν   εἰς   τὴν   ξενίαν   πλείονες
       3P.came   to   him   in   the   lodging   more

(23c)   οἷς   ἐξετίθετο   διαμαρτυρόμενος   τὴν   βασιλείαν   τοῦ   θεοῦ
       to.whom   3S.was.explaining   testifying.about   the   kingdom   of.the   God

Continuative relative clauses are most common in narrative, linking events in chronological sequence, though they are found in non-narrative. Characteristically, the information preceding the relative pronoun is *backgrounded* vis-à-vis what follows.

This is confirmed by the verbs that are used in the two parts of such sentences. The clause preceding the relative pronoun often contains a state or activity verb, which tends to correlate with background information in narrative, while the clause that follows the relative pronoun contains an achievement or accomplishment verb, which tends to correlate with foreground information (see sec. 10.2.1).

Luke 19:30 provides an example in which the clause preceding the relative pronoun (v. 30a) contains an activity verb,[11] but the continuative relative clause (v. 30b) contains an achievement verb. (The parallels in Matt. 21:2 and Mark 11:2 use καί to link the clauses, leaving the information they convey unranked for prominence.)

(30a)   Ὑπάγετε   εἰς   τὴν   κατέναντι   κώμην,
       go   into   the   opposite   village

(30b)   ἐν   ᾗ   εἰσπορευόμενοι   εὑρήσετε   πῶλον   δεδεμένον,
       in   which   entering   you.will.find   colt   tied

It is very common in the Gospels for a participant, prop or concept to be introduced in the clause that precedes the relative pronoun. This information may be viewed as backgrounded vis-à-vis the statement made about him, her or it in the continuative relative clause that follows.

In **Luke 6:48**, for instance, the 'man building a house' is introduced prior to the relative pronoun, while the events that he performs are described in the clauses that follow it. (The parallel passage in Matt. 7:24 also uses a continuative relative clause in this way.)

(48a)   **ὅμοιός**   ἐστιν   ἀνθρώπῳ   οἰκοδομοῦντι   οἰκίαν
       likened   3S.is   to.man   building   house

(48b)   ὃς   ἔσκαψεν   καὶ   ἐβάθυνεν   καὶ   ἔθηκεν
       who   3S.dug   and   3S.went.down.deep   and   3S.laid

         θεμέλιον   ἐπὶ   τὴν   πέτραν·
         foundation   on   the   rock

---

[10] Jespersen (1964:356) makes the same distinction for English. See also Depraetere 1996.

[11] Foley & van Valin (1984) consider "motional" verbs such as *go* to be activity verbs, even though the goal of the journey is stated.

In Acts, the clause prior to the relative pronoun commonly gives more extensive information than just the introduction of the participant, etc. Nevertheless, this information still forms the background to the event(s) that are described in the continuative relative clause that follows.

Acts 19:24–25 illustrates the presentation of extensive background information prior to the relative pronoun.

(24) Δημήτριος γάρ τις ὀνόματι, ἀργυροκόπος, ποιῶν ναοὺς ἀργυροῦς
    Demetrius for certain named silversmith making shrines silver

    Ἀρτέμιδος παρείχετο τοῖς τεχνίταις οὐκ ὀλίγην ἐργασίαν,
    of.Artemis 3S.was.providing to.the craftsmen not small profit

(25a) οὓς συναθροίσας ... εἶπεν,
    whom having.assembled 3S.said

Further examples of such continuative relative clauses include Acts 11:29–30 (the effect of using the relative pronoun is to background the intention with respect to the realization of that intention) and 17:10 (the effect of using the relative pronoun is to background the journey with respect to the event performed on arrival at the destination).

The rhetorical effect of using a continuative relative clause in narrative is apparently to move the story forward quickly by combining background and foreground information in a single sentence.[12] Since the clause prior to the relative pronoun commonly introduces participants, such sentences will tend to occur at the beginning of episodes, hence the appropriateness of moving as quickly as possible to the foreground events of the episode.

In **Acts 23:13–14a,** for example, the number of plotters is presented, not as a separate sentence, but in the same sentence as the next foreground event. This sentence is towards the beginning of the episode (see the discussion following passage 3 of sec. 11.1.3), so it is appropriate to move quickly to the next foreground event.

(12) In the morning, the Jews joined in a conspiracy and bound themselves by an oath neither to eat nor drink until they had killed Paul.

(13) ἦσαν δὲ πλείους τεσσεράκοντα οἱ ταύτην τὴν
    3P.were DE more forty the.ones this the

    συνωμοσίαν ποιησάμενοι,[13]
    plot having.made

(14a) οἵτινες προσελθόντες τοῖς ἀρχιερεῦσιν ... εἶπαν,
    who having.approached to.the chief.priests 3P.said

(Contrast Acts 19:14, in which background information is presented in a separate sentence, with the rhetorical effect of *slowing down* the story immediately prior to the climactic events of the episode—sec. 12.1.)

In continuative relative clauses in narrative, the material preceding the relative pronoun is often naturally background information. In non-narrative discourses such as reasoned argument, however, it may itself have been the foreground assertion, which then becomes the "ground" for another foreground

---

[12] In the UBS text, a colon sometimes separates the clause that precedes the relative pronoun from the relative clause itself, as though they were two separate sentences. I consistently use a comma to link continuative relative clauses with the clause in which the referent of the relative pronoun is found.

[13] English versions often use a relative pronoun to translate "substantive" or articular participial clauses such as οἱ ταύτην τὴν συνωμοσίαν ποιησάμενοι (see the NRSV translation "there were more than forty *who joined in this conspiracy*"). However, they are not classified as relative clauses, since they are not linked to their main clause by a relative pronoun.

assertion.[14] For example, **Acts 7:44–46** contains a chain of relative clauses. Each in turn becomes the ground for a following foreground assertion.

(44)   Ἡ   σκηνὴ   τοῦ   μαρτυρίου   ἦν   τοῖς   πατράσιν   ἡμῶν
the   tent   of.the   witness   3S.was   to.the   fathers   our

ἐν   τῇ   ἐρήμῳ   κ.τ.λ.
in   the   desert

(45a)   ἣν   καὶ   εἰσήγαγον   διαδεξάμενοι   οἱ   πατέρες   ἡμῶν
which   +   3P.brought.in   having.received   the   fathers   our

μετὰ   Ἰησοῦ   ἐν   τῇ   κατασχέσει   τῶν   ἐθνῶν,
with   Joshua   in   the   taking.possession   of.the   nations

(45b)   ὧν   ἐξῶσεν   ὁ   θεὸς   ἀπὸ   προσώπου   τῶν   πατέρων
whom   3S.drove.out   the   God   from   presence   of.the   fathers

ἡμῶν   ἕως   τῶν   ἡμερῶν   Δαυίδ,
our   until   the   days   of.David

(46a)   ὃς   εὗρεν   χάριν   ἐνώπιον   τοῦ   θεοῦ
who   3S.found   favor   before   the   God

Other chains of continuative relative clauses are found in Acts 5:36, Acts 7:38–39, and 1 Pet. 3:18–22.

Review Questions

(a) What is the difference between a restrictive and a nonrestrictive relative clause?

(b) What two types of nonrestrictive relative clauses are found in Koiné Greek?

Suggested Answers

(a) A restrictive relative clause delimits potential referents of the head noun. A nonrestrictive relative clause gives added information about an already identified entity.

(b) The two types of nonrestrictive relative clauses found in Koiné Greek are appositional and continuative. (The information prior to a continuative relative clause is backgrounded vis-à-vis the information in the continuative clause itself.)

Illustrative Sentence 4a: Acts 8:27

(27b)   καὶ   ἰδοὺ   ἀνὴρ   Αἰθίοψ   εὐνοῦχος   δυνάστης
and   behold   man   Ethiopian   eunuch   court.official

Κανδάκης   βασιλίσσης   Αἰθιόπων,
of.Candace   queen   of.Ethiopians

(27c)   ὃς   ἦν   ἐπὶ   πάσης   τῆς   γάζης   αὐτῆς,
who   3S.was   over   all   the   treasury   her

(27d)   ὃς   ἐληλύθει   προσκυνήσων   εἰς   Ἰερουσαλήμ,
who   3S.had.come   worshipping   to   Jerusalem

Question

What type of relative clause occurs in Acts 8:27c? And in v. 27d?

---

[14] Some languages employ a development marker or a "spacer" (Dooley 1990:477) within sentences to separate the ground and the foreground assertion. Such a marker has a very similar function to that of the relative pronoun which introduces continuative relative clauses.

Suggested Answer

The relative clause that occurs in Acts 8:27c could be viewed as restrictive, used to delimit the potential referents of δυνάστης Κανδάκης βασιλίσσης Αἰθιόπων (a court official of Candace queen of the Ethiopians). However, "Luke's readers can hardly be expected to have a detailed knowledge of the personages of the Candace's court, so the progression from courtier to treasurer hardly delimits him further" (Pope p.c.). If such is the case, then the relative clause is nonrestrictive and appositional (in apparent support of this interpretation, the UBS text inserts a comma at the end of v. 27b).[15] The relative clause that occurs in v. 27d is appositional, as it only supplies an added piece of information about an already identified entity.

Illustrative Sentence 4b: Acts 8:9–10

(9)   Now a certain man named Simon had previously practiced magic in the city and amazed the people of Samaria, saying that he was someone great,

(10)   ᾧ   προσεῖχον   πάντες ἀπὸ μικροῦ ἕως μεγάλου λέγοντες,
        to.whom 3P.were.paying attention all   from small   to   great   saying

        Οὗτός ἐστιν ἡ   δύναμις τοῦ   θεοῦ ἡ   καλουμένη Μεγάλη.
        this   3S.is the power   of.the God   the called   great

Question

What type of relative clause occurs in Acts 8:10?

Suggested Answer

The relative clause that occurs in Acts 8:10 is nonrestrictive and continuative. Verse 9 introduces Simon and supplies some information about his activities. This information provides the background for the response of the people to these activities, which is described in the continuative relative clause. (In vv. 10–12, the attention is on the people, not on Simon, as they first respond to his magic, but then believe Philip's teaching and are baptized. Only in v. 13 does attention switch back to Simon.)

Illustrative Passage 5: Acts 16:11–14 (UBS text)

Note the relative clauses in this passage.

(11)   So we set sail from Troas and took a straight course to Samothrace, and the following day to Neapolis,

(12a)   κἀκεῖθεν   εἰς Φιλίππους,
        and.from.there   to   Philippi

(12b)   ἥτις ἐστιν πρώτη[ς] μερίδος τῆς   Μακεδονίας πόλις, κολωνία.
        which 3S.is prominent of.district of.the Macedonia   city   colony

(12c)   ἦμεν   δὲ   ἐν ταύτῃ τῇ   πόλει διατρίβοντες ἡμέρας τινάς.
        we.were DE   in this   the city   staying   days   some

(13a)   τῇ   τε   ἡμέρᾳ τῶν   σαββάτων ἐξήλθομεν ἔξω
        on.the ADD day   of.the sabbaths we.went.out outside

        τῆς   πύλης παρὰ ποταμὸν
        of.the gate   beside river

(13b)   οὗ   ἐνομίζομεν   προσευχὴν   εἶναι,
        where we.were.supposing prayer.place to.be

---

[15] It is often unclear whether a relative clause in Greek is intended to be restrictive or nonrestrictive and appositional.

(13c) καὶ   καθίσαντες   ἐλαλοῦμεν   ταῖς   συνελθούσαις   γυναιξίν.
       and   having.sat.down   we.were.speaking to.the having.come.together women

(14a) καί   τις   γυνὴ   ὀνόματι   Λυδία,   πορφυρόπωλις   πόλεως
       and   certain   woman   named   Lydia   purple.cloth.dealer of.city

       Θυατείρων σεβομένη   τὸν   θεόν,   ἤκουεν,
       of.Thyatira worshipping the   God   3S.was.listening

(14b) ἧς   ὁ   κύριος   διήνοιξεν τὴν καρδίαν   προσέχειν
       of.whom the   Lord   3S.opened the heart   to.take.heed

       τοῖς   λαλουμένοις   ὑπὸ   τοῦ   Παύλου.
       to.the   being.spoken   by   the   Paul

Questions

(a) What type of relative clause occurs in Acts 16:12b?
(b) What type of relative clause occurs in v. 13b?
(c) What type of relative clause occurs in v. 14b?

Suggested Answers

(a) The relative clause of Acts 16:12b is nonrestrictive and appositional. It gives an added piece of information about Philippi.
(b) The relative clause of v. 13b is restrictive if it delimits the area outside the gate by the river to "where we supposed there was a place of prayer." Otherwise, it is nonrestrictive and appositional, supplying an added piece of information about an already identified place (outside the gate by the river).
(c) The relative clause of v. 14b is nonrestrictive and continuative. Verse 14a introduces Lydia and indicates that she was listening to what was being said. This information provides the background to the result of her listening.

Passage 6: Acts 21:3–11 (UBS text)

(3)   We came in sight of Cyprus; and leaving it on our left, we sailed to Syria and landed at Tyre, because the ship was to unload its cargo there.

(4a) ἀνευρόντες   δὲ   τοὺς   μαθητὰς
      having.searched.for DE   the   disciples

(4b) ἐπεμείναμεν αὐτοῦ ἡμέρας ἑπτά,
      we.stayed   there days   seven

(4c) οἵτινες   τῷ   Παύλῳ ἔλεγον   διὰ τοῦ πνεύματος
      who   to.the Paul   3P.were.saying by   the Spirit

      μὴ   ἐπιβαίνειν εἰς   Ἱεροσόλυμα.
      not   to.go.up   to   Jerusalem

(5a) ὅτε   δὲ   ἐγένετο   ἡμᾶς   ἐξαρτίσαι   τὰς   ἡμέρας,
      when   DE   3S.happened   us   to.be.finished the   days

(5b) ἐξελθόντες   ἐπορευόμεθα
      having.gone.out we.were.going

(5c) προπεμπόντων ἡμᾶς πάντων   σὺν   γυναιξὶ καὶ   τέκνοις
      accompanying us   everyone with wives   and   children

      ἕως   ἔξω   τῆς   πόλεως,
      as.far.as outside the   city

(5d)   καὶ θέντες   τὰ γόνατα ἐπὶ τὸν αἰγιαλὸν
        and having.bent the knees   on   the beach

(5e)   προσευξάμενοι[16]
        having.prayed

(6a)   ἀπησπασάμεθα ἀλλήλους
        we.said.farewell to.one.another

(6b)   and we went on board the ship, while they returned home. (7) We, having finished the
        voyage from Tyre, arrived at Ptolemais; and we greeted the brothers and stayed with them
        for one day.

(8)   On the next day we left and came to Caesarea; and we went into the house of Philip the
        evangelist, one of the seven, and stayed with him.

(9)   τούτῳ   δὲ ἦσαν   θυγατέρες τέσσαρες παρθένοι προφητεύουσαι.
        to.this.one DE 3P.were daughters   four   virgins   prophesying

(10a)   ἐπιμενόντων δὲ ἡμέρας πλείους
        remaining   DE days   many

(10b)   κατῆλθέν   τις   ἀπὸ τῆς Ἰουδαίας προφήτης ὀνόματι Ἄγαβος,
        3S.came.down certain from the Jews   prophet   named   Agabus

(11)   and, having come to us, he took Paul's belt, bound his own feet and hands with it, and
        said, "Thus says the Holy Spirit, 'This is the way the Jews in Jerusalem will bind the man
        who owns this belt and will hand him over to the Gentiles.'"

Questions

(a) Which of the verses for which the Greek is given contain prenuclear NPCs?

(b) What type of relative clause occurs in v. 4c?

(c) What is the relative status of the information contained in the three numbered clauses of v. 4?

(d) Which verse contains a postnuclear GA? What is the status of the information it conveys vis-à-vis
    that of its nuclear clause?

(e) Which verse contains a prenuclear GA? What is the effect of using a GA to begin v. 10, rather than
    an adverbial clause of time?

Suggested Answer: see Appendix under 11(6).

---

[16] Kilpatrick (1965:200) considers the textual variant (5e) προσηυξάμεθα (6a) καὶ ἀσπασάμενοι to be original.

12
HIGHLIGHTING AND THE HISTORICAL PRESENT

A variety of devices are employed to highlight a sentence and indicate that the information it conveys is of particular importance for the narrative episode or for the point that is being insisted upon. Those devices that have been encountered in previous chapters are listed in sec. 12.1, which also discusses the role of *tail-head linkage* in preparing the reader for the significant material that will be presented immediately afterwards. The presence of a *historical present* most often has the effect of highlighting what follows, as well; sec. 12.2 reports on progress in understanding the significance of this device in the Gospels of Matthew and John.

12.1   Devices for Highlighting in Koiné Greek

Sentences are typically highlighted when they relate to a *climax*[1] or when a particularly *significant development* or a *change of direction* occurs in the story. Typically, some of the same rhetorical devices are used for both, but climaxes are more extensively marked. These devices usually occur *prior* to the description of the highlighted event and often involve "redundancy" (Smith 1985), such as the use of a full noun phrase to refer to the same subject (sec. 8.2) or further reference to the same event (see below on tail-head linkage).

The devices already mentioned by which sentences are highlighted in Greek include the following:
- τότε, used to highlight concluding speeches (sec. 6.1.1), as in Matt. 15:28
- τέ solitarium, used in certain contexts to indicate the specific lead-in to the next development in the story (sec. 6.3), as in Acts 12:12
- ἰδού and ἴδε (sec. 8.1), used to highlight the introduction of a participant when followed immediately by reference to the participant, as in Matt. 2:1b, or to highlight an event when followed immediately by the verb, as in Matt. 9:2
- a *full noun phrase* or other marked encoding of participant reference, used to highlight events or speeches of particular significance (sec. 8.2), as in Luke 1:41a (below)
- *anarthrous* references to activated participants and other substantives, used to give them prominence (secs. 9.2.3, 9.3, and 9.4), as in Acts 10:34 (Πέτρος), Gal. 2:19b (θεῷ), and Heb. 11:3a (πίστει)
- a *genitive absolute* with the same subject as in the immediately preceding clause, to highlight the introduction to an existing scene of participants who will perform significant actions (sec. 11.1.1), as in Acts 4:1.

Highlighting devices that will be discussed in subsequent sections include:
- some instances of the *historical present* (sec. 12.2)
- ἀποκρίνομαι 'answer', used to introduce significant responses in a conversation (sec. 14.1).

In addition to the above devices, a form of repetition called *tail-head linkage* is sometimes employed immediately prior to a particularly significant event or speech, to highlight it (or to resume the event line—see below). Tail-head linkage in NT Greek involves the repetition, in an adverbial or participial clause at the beginning (the head) of the new sentence, of the main verb and other information that occurred in the previous sentence (the tail). This repetition may be thought of as a rhetorical device that slows the story down prior to the significant event or speech.

---

[1] I use the term *climax* to refer to "the event or point of greatest intensity or interest; a culmination or apex" (OED). Contrast Hwang (1997:301), for whom the notional climax is the "the highest tension point of the story." In the English story analyzed by Hwang, what I judge to be the climax or culminating event to which the story has been building up has been allocated to the "Postpeak Episode" (op. cit. 299–300), rather than to the "Peak Episode". The devices I describe in this chapter occur at what Longacre (1996:37) calls the "peak," which he uses "to refer to any episodelike unit set apart by special surface features and corresponding to the climax or denouement in the notional structure."

Luke 1:41a (below) provides an example of tail-head linkage as well as of marked encoding of participant reference. Verse 40b ends with the words, ἠσπάσατο τὴν Ἐλισάβετ. A nominalized reference to this action occurs in the adverbial clause of time that opens v. 41 (ὡς ἤκουσεν τὸν ἀσπασμὸν τῆς Μαρίας ἡ Ἐλισάβετ). This repetition has the rhetorical effect of slowing the story down prior to the reporting of a particularly significant event, viz., the babe leaping in Elizabeth's womb (v. 41b), which leads to Elizabeth's exclamation of vv. 42–45 (see sec. 10.3). A further highlighting device is the use of a full noun phrase to refer to Elizabeth in v. 41a, when default encoding of reference to a subject who was the addressee of the immediately preceding speech would be no more than an articular pronoun (sec. 8.2). (The use of a full noun phrase to refer to Mary in v. 41a is also a marked form of reference.)

(40a)   and she entered the house of Zechariah

(40b)   καὶ   ἠσπάσατο   τὴν   Ἐλισάβετ.
         and   3S.greeted   the   Elizabeth

(41a)   καὶ   ἐγένετο   ὡς   ἤκουσεν   τὸν   ἀσπασμὸν   τῆς   Μαρίας   ἡ   Ἐλισάβετ,
         and   3S.happened when   3S.heard the   greeting   of.the Mary   the Elizabeth

(41b)   ἐσκίρτησεν   τὸ   βρέφος   ἐν   τῇ   κοιλίᾳ   αὐτῆς,
         3S.leaped   the baby   in   the womb   her

(41c)   and Elizabeth was filled with the Holy Spirit, (42) and exclaimed with a loud cry, "Blessed are you among women, and blessed is the fruit of your womb…"

See also Acts 1:9, in which Jesus' speech of vv. 7–8, which is introduced with εἶπεν 'said', is followed by a further reference to that speech (καὶ ταῦτα εἰπὼν 'having said these things'), prior to the presentation of the next particularly significant event of the narrative, viz., Jesus' ascension to heaven.[2]

Following background material, it is quite common to use a form of tail-head linkage to refer back to the last event before this material and highlight the next development as the event line is *resumed*.

This is seen in **John 21:21**. Verse 20a presented the last event (Peter sees the disciple whom Jesus loved). A nonrestrictive and appositional relative clause gives an added piece of information about this disciple (v. 20b), following which the event line is resumed in v. 21 with a further reference to the event of v. 20a, thus highlighting the incident of vv. 21–23. (In this instance, a synonym of βλέπει—v. 20a—is used in v. 21a, viz., ἰδών.)

(20a)   Ἐπιστραφεὶς   ὁ   Πέτρος   βλέπει   τὸν   μαθητὴν   ὃν
         having.turned   the Peter   3S.sees   the   disciple   whom

         ἠγάπα   ὁ   Ἰησοῦς   ἀκολουθοῦντα,
         3S.was.loving the Jesus   following

(20b)   ὃς   καὶ   ἀνέπεσεν   ἐν   τῷ   δείπνῳ   ἐπὶ   τὸ   στῆθος   αὐτοῦ
         who   +   3S.reclined during the supper   upon the breast   his

         καὶ   εἶπεν,   Κύριε,   τίς   ἐστιν   ὁ   παραδιδούς   σε;
         and   3S.said   lord   who   3S.is   the.one betraying   you

(21a)   τοῦτον   οὖν   ἰδὼν   ὁ   Πέτρος
         this.one then   having.seen the   Peter

(21b)   λέγει   τῷ   Ἰησοῦ,   Κύριε,   οὗτος   δὲ   τί;
         3S.says   to.the Jesus   lord   this.one DE   what

---

[2]   However, when a completive verb such as τελέω is used in connection with tail-head linkage, as in Matt. 19:1 (ὅτε ἐτέλεσεν ὁ Ἰησοῦς τοὺς λόγους τούτους 'when Jesus had finished these words'), this is indicative of a discontinuity—see also sec. 10.3.

See also John 13:31 (the main verb of v. 30a is ἐξῆλθεν 'he went out'; following the background material of v. 30b, v. 31 begins with the adverbial clause of time Ὅτε ἐξῆλθεν). A further example is in Acts 4:23 (the main verb of v. 21 is ἀπέλυσαν 'they released'; following the background material of v. 22, v. 23 begins with the participle ἀπολυθέντες 'having been released').

Another device that languages use to slow down the recounting of an episode immediately before its climax, is to include background information at that point. This does not seem to be a common device in the Greek NT, but may well be the motivation for inserting the background material of **Acts 19:14** between the command of the Jewish exorcists (v. 13) and the response of the evil spirit (v. 15).

(13)　　Then some itinerant Jewish exorcists tried to use the name of the Lord Jesus over those who had evil spirits, saying, "I adjure you by the Jesus whom Paul proclaims."

(14)　　ἦσαν　　δὲ　　τινος　　Σκευᾶ　　Ἰουδαίου　　ἀρχιερέως　　ἑπτὰ
　　　　　　3P.were　DE　of.certain　Sceva　　Jewish　　　high.priest　seven

　　　　　　υἱοὶ　τοῦτο　τοιοῦντες.
　　　　　　sons　this　　doing

(15)　　But in reply, the evil spirit said to them, "Jesus I know, and Paul I know; but who are you?" (16) Then the man with the evil spirit leaped on them, mastered them all, and so overpowered them that they fled out of the house naked and wounded.

Further instances in which background information is inserted immediately before the climactic event include:

- John 2:9b: καὶ οὐκ ᾔδει πόθεν ἐστίν, οἱ δὲ διάκονοι ᾔδεισαν οἱ ἠντληκότες τὸ ὕδωρ 'and did not know where it came from—though the servants who had drawn the water knew' is inserted immediately before the climax of the episode
- Mark 5:28: ἔλεγεν γὰρ ὅτι Ἐὰν ἅψωμαι κἂν τῶν ἱματίων αὐτοῦ σωθήσομαι 'for she was saying, "If I but touch his clothes, I will be made well"' is inserted after the woman touches Jesus' cloak (v. 27), but before the result of her doing so is reported (v. 29).

Illustrative Passage 1: Matthew 28:8–10

Read through the following passage, noting the highlighting features.

(8)　　So they left the tomb quickly with fear and great joy, and ran to tell his disciples.

(9a)　　καὶ　ἰδοὺ　Ἰησοῦς　ὑπήντησεν　αὐταῖς　λέγων,　Χαίρετε.
　　　　　and　behold　Jesus　　3S.met　　　them　　saying　hello

(9b)　　αἱ　δὲ　προσελθοῦσαι　ἐκράτησαν　αὐτοῦ　τοὺς　πόδας
　　　　　they　DE　approaching　　3P.held　　his　　the　　feet

(9c)　　καὶ　προσεκύνησαν　αὐτῷ.
　　　　　and　3P.worshiped　　him

(10)　　τότε　λέγει　αὐταῖς　ὁ　Ἰησοῦς,
　　　　　then　3S.says　to.them　the　Jesus,
　　　　　"Do not be afraid; go and tell my brothers to go to Galilee; there they will see me."

Questions

(a) What three highlighting features mentioned in this section are found in Matt. 28:9–10? (The historical present in v. 10 is discussed in sec. 14.3.)

(b) In many MSS, the following clause is found at the beginning of v. 9a before καὶ ἰδού:

　　　　　ὡς　δὲ　ἐπορεύοντο　　ἀπαγγεῖλαι　τοῖς　μαθηταῖς　αὐτοῦ
　　　　　as　DE　3P.were.going　to.report　　to.the　disciples　　his

Why might this clause be appropriate in this context, according to the principles presented in this section?[3]

Suggested Answers

(a) The three highlighting features found in Matt. 28:9–10 that are mentioned in this section are:

- ἰδού (in v. 9a), highlighting the reactivation of Jesus (with an anarthrous reference to him—see sec. 9.2.2)
- τότε (in v. 10), highlighting the concluding speech of the episode
- the use of a full noun phrase to refer to Jesus (in v. 10), in connection with the same speech. Since Jesus is the global VIP, no overt reference to him would have been the default form of reference (sec. 8.3).

(b) According to the principles presented in this section, it would be appropriate to include the adverbial clause of time noted above at the beginning of v. 9 because this would constitute tail-head linkage. Such a slowing-down device is normal in languages immediately before a climactic event, and this appearance of Jesus after his resurrection is possibly the most climactic event of the Gospel.

The following passage is repeated from passage 5 of sec. 10.3, where a question was asked about the function of ἐγένετο.

Passage 2: Luke 24:13–17

(13)   Now two of them were going on that same day to a village called Emmaus, about seven miles from Jerusalem,

(14)   καὶ <u>αὐτοὶ</u> ὡμίλουν   πρὸς ἀλλήλους περὶ πάντων
         and they   3P.were.talking to   each.other about all

         τῶν συμβεβηκότων τούτων.
         the having.occurred these

(15a)   καὶ ἐγένετο   <u>ἐν</u> <u>τῷ</u> <u>ὁμιλεῖν</u> <u>αὐτοὺς</u> <u>καὶ</u> <u>συζητεῖν</u>
         and 3S.happened in   the   to.talk   them   and to.discuss

(15b)   καὶ <u>αὐτὸς</u> Ἰησοῦς ἐγγίσας   συνεπορεύετο   αὐτοῖς,
         +   self   Jesus   having.drawn.near 3S.was.traveling.with them

(16)   but their eyes were kept from recognizing him. (17)   And he said to them, "What are you discussing with each other while you walk along?"

Question

The temporal expression following ἐγένετο in v. 15a repeats part of v. 14. What is such repetition called? What is its rhetorical effect?

Suggested Answer: see Appendix under 12(2).

12.2 The Historical Present

I argue in this section that the primary motivation for using the historical present (hereafter, HP) is to *highlight* and that, particularly in Mark and John, what is highlighted by the HP is not so much the speech or act to which it refers but the event(s) that follow. In other words, like other devices employed for highlighting, the HP usually occurs *prior* to the event or group of events that are of particular significance.

---

[3] I am grateful to Tony Pope (p.c.) for pointing out the significance of this variant.

The historical or historic present is the name given to the use of the present tense in a narrative when the verb would be expected to have been in the past tense or perfective aspect. In Greek, this means that the verb would normally have been in the aorist.

Thus, in **Matt. 26:36a**, ἔρχεται 'comes' is used where the expected verb is ἦλθεν 'came'. Since the genre is narrative, ἔρχεται is said to be in the historical present.

(35b)   <u>ὁμοίως</u> καὶ **πάντες** οἱ **μαθηταὶ** εἶπαν.
        likewise +   all   the disciples 3P.said

(36a)   Τότε ἔρχεται μετ' αὐτῶν ὁ Ἰησοῦς εἰς χωρίον λεγόμενων Γεθσημανί
        then 3S.comes with them the Jesus to   place   called   Gethsemane

The HP is not peculiar to NT Greek, as it is found also in narrative texts in classical Greek and in the LXX translation of the Old Testament (see Fanning 1990:226–39). The frequency of the HP in the Gospels and Acts is as follows:[4]

Matthew	93	(including 68 speech verbs such as λέγει 'he says')
Mark	151	(including 72 speech verbs)
Luke-Acts	22	(including 17 speech verbs)
John	162	(including 127 speech verbs).

Note. It is normal to divide HPs in Koiné Greek into two types: those involving speech verbs (hereafter, "speech HPs") and those involving other verbs ("non-speech HPs").

Grammarians regularly associate the HP with two features:[5]
- boundaries in the discourse
- prominence.

I consider these features in turn.

Boundaries in the discourse

Thackeray (1909) claimed that the main function of the HP was to introduce "a fresh paragraph in the narrative," while Porter writes (1992:301), "Verb tense-forms are frequently shifted (e.g. aorist to present, and so forth) to indicate the boundaries of a discourse." Porter cites Mark 7:1 as an instance in which the "historical present (συνάγονται) introduces a new pericope, the previous one (which goes back at least as far as Mk 6.53) having ended with a series of aorist and imperfect tense-forms."

However, Porter also observes (op. cit. 31), "Some have argued that the historical present is used to mark significant changes in the narrative flow. Whereas... this category must be considered when formulating an explanation of this usage, the instances where it does not mark significant change are too manifest to endorse this scheme as a sufficient explanation." In **Mark 2:1–4**, for instance, the HPs of vv. 3 and 4b are used only *after* the episode has begun and are not contiguous, being separated by a verb in the aorist (v. 4a).

(1)   When he returned to Capernaum after some days, it was reported (ἠκούσθη) that he was at home. (2) So many gathered around (συνήχθησαν) that there was no longer room for them, not even in front of the door; and he was speaking (ἐλάλει) the word to them.

(3)   καὶ ἔρχονται φέροντες πρὸς αὐτὸν παραλυτικὸν αἰρόμενον ὑπὸ τεσσάρων.
        and 3P.come carrying to   him   paralytic   being.carried by four

(4a)   And, being unable to bring him to Jesus because of the crowd, they removed (ἀπεστέγασαν) the roof above him;

---

[4] The figures are from Hawkins (1909), as quoted by Fanning (op. cit. 234 fn. 75).

[5] Porter (1992:30–31) discusses *four* proposals concerning the use of the HP: dramatic use, tense reduction, change of setting or character, and verbal aspect.

(4b)   καὶ   ἐξορύξαντες   χαλῶσι   τὸν   κράβαττον   ὅπου
        and   having.opened   3P.lower   the   mattress   on.which

        ὁ   παραλυτικὸς   κατέκειτο.
        the   paralytic   3S.was.lying

In Matthew's Gospel, nearly every non-speech HP occurs at a generally recognized paragraph boundary. Nevertheless, there is still no need to claim that the HP is *marking* the boundary. This is because other features that tend to occur at boundaries are also present, such as τότε (e.g., in 26:36a above—see sec. 6.1.1) or a temporal point of departure (3:1, 17:1, 25:11, 25:19), including a genitive absolute (2:13, 2:19). Matthew 26:40 (καὶ ἔρχεται 'and he comes') is an exception.

I therefore conclude that it is not the presence of a HP per se that indicates the boundary (contra Levinsohn 1992:141–44). Rather, the nature of its function as a marker of prominence (see below) often leads to its occurrence early in a paragraph. (See sec. 17.2.10 for further discussion of shifts of tense forms, whether from the aorist to the HP or *vice versa*, as supporting evidence for a boundary.)

Prominence

Concerning the HP and prominence, Porter concludes (loc. cit.), "Whereas the aorist is merely used in its common narrative function, the present form draws added attention to the action to which it refers." He cites **Acts 10:11** as an instance in which the HP is used "to highlight Peter's vision" (see also sec. 12.2.2).

(9)   The next day, as they were on their journey and approaching the city, Peter went up (ἀνέβη) on the roof to pray about noon. (10) He became (ἐγένετο) hungry and was wanting (ἤθελεν) to eat something. While they were preparing it, a trance came (ἐγένετο) over him

(11)   and he sees (καὶ θεωρεῖ) heaven opened and something like a large sheet coming down, being lowered to the ground by its four corners, (12) in which were all kinds of four-footed creatures and reptiles and birds of the air.

(13)   And a voice came (ἐγένετο) to him, "Get up, Peter, kill and eat."

Particularly in Mark and John, however, the HP " does *not* draw attention to the event which the HP verb itself refers to, as those events, in themselves, are not particularly important—*to go, to say, to gather together, to see, etc.* ... [I]t has a *cataphoric* function; that is, it points on beyond itself into the narrative, it draws attention to what is following" (J. Callow 1996:2).

So, in **Mark 1:21**, it is not the action of entering Capernaum itself that is particularly important. Rather, the presence of the HP points on beyond itself and draws attention to the subsequent events that take place in Capernaum.

(20)   And immediately he (Jesus) called (ἐκάλεσεν) them; and, leaving their father Zebedee in the boat with the hired men, they followed (ἀπῆλθον) him.

(21a)   Καὶ   εἰσπορεύονται   εἰς   Καφαρναούμ·
        and   3P.enter   into   Capernaum

(21b)   And immediately, on the sabbath, having entered the synagogue, he was teaching (ἐδίδασκεν).

(22)   And they were amazed (ἐξεπλήσσοντο) at his teaching, for he was teaching them as one having authority, and not as the scribes.

Other instances in which the event presented in the HP appears to be particularly insignificant include Mark 8:6 (UBS text—and he gives orders (παραγγέλλει) to the crowd to recline on the ground) and Luke 7:40 (ὁ δέ, Διδάσκαλε, εἰπέ, φησίν 'and he, "Teacher, speak" says'). In both cases, it is what follows the event or speech associated with the HP that is highlighted. (See sec. 15.1 on how the distribution of articular and anarthrous references to speakers in John provides further evidence that HPs do not highlight the speech that they introduce but a later speech or event.)[6]

However, Callow also points out (loc. cit.), "While most speech HPs are cataphoric, Johnson [(1984)] maintains that when a speech HP closes off a verbal interchange... the content is important in itself, and is not pointing forward to something following it."[7]

In **Mark 2:17**, for example, the use of λέγει would appear to highlight Jesus' speech itself, not the episode of vv. 18ff. that follows it. (See also the reference to Jesus by name—sec. 8.3.)

(15)   And as he sat at dinner in Levi's house, many tax collectors and sinners were also sitting (συνανέκειντο) with Jesus and his disciples—for there were many who were following him. (16) When the scribes of the Pharisees saw that he was eating with sinners and tax collectors, they were saying (ἔλεγον) to his disciples, "Why does he eat with tax collectors and sinners?"

(17)   καὶ ἀκούσας   ὁ   Ἰησοῦς λέγει   αὐτοῖς,
         and having.heard the Jesus   3S.says   to.them
         "Those who are well have no need of a physician, but those who are sick; I have come to call not the righteous but sinners."

(18)   {This new episode concerns why the disciples of John and of the Pharisees fast, whereas Jesus' disciples do not.}

Nevertheless, I suggest that, even in such instances, the HP continues to have cataphoric overtones. The incident of Mark 2:15–17 is the first of four occasions in which Jesus interacts with the Pharisees (2:18–22, 2:23–28 and 3:1–5 are the others), culminating in 3:6: 'the Pharisees went out and immediately conspired with the Herodians against him how to destroy them.' If the HP of 2:17 has cataphoric overtones, it indicates that, even though the conclusion of one incident has been reached, more is to follow. (See secs. 14.3 and 15.1 for similar claims concerning HPs that introduce concluding speeches in Matthew and John.)

I now concentrate on the function of *non-speech* HPs in Matthew (sec. 12.2.1) and John (sec. 12.2.3; the five non-speech HPs found in Luke-Acts are discussed briefly in sec. 12.2.2). See secs. 14.2–3 for speech HPs in Matthew. See sec. 15.1 for speech HPs in John.

While there are similarities in the way Matthew and John use the HP, there are some important differences. For example, whereas HPs in Matthew mark as significant the participant they activate, the implications of using a HP to activate a participant in John are rather weaker. Instead, the cataphoric overtones of using the HP are more to the fore. (The use of the HP in Mark appears also to have primarily a cataphoric function—see Levinsohn 1977,[8] Johnson 1984 and J. Callow 1996—whereas non-speech HPs in Luke-Acts function more like those in Matthew.)

Section 12.2.1 identifies a number of *conditions* that must be met if a HP is to be used in Matthew. In addition, one condition that appears to be applicable to all the Gospels and Acts is the following:

It is used only in connection with *the interaction of two participants or groups of participants*. In other words, it is never used in situations in which the actions or speeches of only one participant are given... (Levinsohn 1977:14)

So, no HP is found when Jesus is praying to his Father, since no response is recorded. Nor is it used when Jesus is teaching but his listeners' response is not recorded. Thus, there is no HP in Matt. 11:20–30, for example.

---

[6] The cataphoric effect of using a HP may result naturally from portraying an event or speech as incomplete (the present tense prototypically has imperfective aspect—sec. 10.2.2).

[7] HPs that introduce concluding speeches are not taken to be cataphoric in the sense that they point forward to the speech that they introduce because, as Johnson (1984) notes, most speech HPs look beyond the speech they introduce to the following speeches or events.

[8] The HP in Mark "is always *cataphoric*, anticipatory, pointing to another action connected with it" (Levinsohn 1977:14).

The question of why a HP is *not* used when all the conditions have been met is left until sec. 14.3, after the function of speech HPs has been considered.

12.2.1 Non-Speech Historical Presents in Matthew

Non-speech HPs in Matthew may be divided into three categories, the first being by far the most common (the first two categories are found also in John—sec. 12.2.3):

- those that *activate* a participant who has a significant role to play by introducing him or her to the scene of a previous interaction between participants
- those that *move* activated participants to the location of the next significant events
- those that describe the *conclusion* of an interaction between participants when significant event(s) are still to follow.

What is noteworthy about these categories is that the HP is used only if it has been preceded by a subsection of a larger episode; see further below. Furthermore, while cataphoric overtones may well be present with the first two categories, the participant or location concerned is also significant, in the case of Matthew.

Historical Presents and the Activation of Participants

These next paragraphs show that, for a non-speech HP to be used in Matthew to activate a participant, two conditions must be met:

- the participant must have an active role to play (by taking an initiative)
- the participant must be introduced to the scene of a previous interaction between participants.

I first consider some examples that meet both conditions, so a HP is used. In **Matt. 3:13**, for instance, Jesus is introduced to the scene in which John has been baptizing people (see sec. 6.1 on the use of τότε to associate together subsections of an episode) and he has an active role to play in subsequent events at the scene. The HP marks the introduction of Jesus as significant.

(7–12)   {The previous subsection ends with John speaking (εἶπεν) to those who have come to him for baptism}

(13)   Τότε παραγίνεται ὁ ᾽Ιησοῦς ἀπὸ τῆς Γαλιλαίας ἐπὶ τὸν ᾽Ιορδάνην
       then 3S.arrives the Jesus from the Galilee at the Jordan

       πρὸς τὸν ᾽Ιωάννην τοῦ βαπτισθῆναι ὑπ᾽ αὐτοῦ.
       to the John of.the to.be.baptized by him

(14)   John was preventing (διεκώλυεν) him... (15) In answer, Jesus said (εἶπεν) to him...

See also Matt. 9:14, 15:1, and 25:11. (In each of these examples, the initiative taken by the participant who was introduced with the HP is the speech that is introduced in a postnuclear participial clause of the same sentence.)

The HPs in Matt. 26:40 and 26:45 may fit into the same category. In both instances, Jesus comes to the disciples (ἔρχεται πρὸς τοὺς μαθητὰς) with whom he had previously been interacting and says (καὶ λέγει) something to them. In the case of 26:45, the HPs point forward to the arrival of the armed band led by Judas (v. 47).[9]

When the participant to be introduced to the scene of a previous interaction does *not* subsequently have an active role to play in that he never takes an initiative, a HP is *not* used. This is seen in **Matt. 19:13**; the participants who are introduced (the children and those who brought them) have no active part to play in the ongoing events which, as in the previous subsection (vv. 10–12), involve an interaction between Jesus and his disciples.

---

[9] On the intervening occasion that Jesus returns to the disciples (26:43), no HP is used in most MSS, as there is no interaction between them; see the discussion below of Matt. 1:18–20.

(11-12) {The previous subsection ends with Jesus teaching (εἶπεν) his disciples about celibacy}

(13a) Τότε   προσηνέχθησαν   αὐτῷ   παιδία   ἵνα   **τὰς χεῖρας**
then   3P.were.brought   to.him children so.that the hand

ἐπιθῇ   αὐτοῖς καὶ προσεύξηται·
3S.may.put.on them and to.pray

(13b) But the disciples rebuked (ἐπετίμησαν) them. (14) But Jesus said (εἶπεν), "Let the little children come to me..." (15) And, having laid his hands on them, he departed (ἐπορεύθη) from there.

See also Matt. 12:22. Contrast 27:38, in which the two thieves are activated with a passive HP (σταυροῦνται 'are crucified'), but take the initiative later in the episode (v. 44).

A comparison of Matt. 2:19 and 1:20 suggests that, for a HP to be used to activate a participant, there must have been a previous interaction between participants. In both passages, following a genitive absolute, a supernatural participant is activated. In the case of **Matt. 2:19** (and 2:13), previous events have formed a separate subsection of a larger episode and a HP is used.

(17-18) {The previous subsection ends with a quotation from Jeremiah that was fulfilled (ἐπληρώθη) when Herod had the infants slaughtered—v. 16}

(19) <u>Τελευτήσαντος</u> δὲ <u>τοῦ</u> <u>Ἡρῴδου</u> ἰδοὺ ἄγγελος κυρίου
having.died   DE the Herod   behold angel   of.Lord

φαίνεται κατ᾽ ὄναρ τῷ   Ἰωσὴφ ἐν Αἰγύπτῳ (20) λέγων,
3S.appears in   dream to.the Joseph in Egypt   saying,
"Rising up, take the child and his mother, and go to the land of Israel..."

(21) Then he, rising up, took (παρέλαβεν) the child and his mother, and went to the land of Israel.

In contrast, **Matt. 1:18-19** do not describe a previous interaction between participants, but are simply part of the setting for the events that are to follow (the RSV translates vv. 18b-19 as a single sentence). This may be why no HP is used in v. 20.

(18) Now <u>the birth of Jesus Christ</u> took place in this way. <u>When his mother Mary had been engaged to Joseph</u>, before they lived together, she was found to be with child from the Holy Spirit; (19) and <u>Joseph her husband</u>, being a righteous man and unwilling to expose her to public disgrace, planned to dismiss her quietly.

(20) <u>ταῦτα</u> δὲ <u>αὐτοῦ</u> <u>ἐνθυμηθέντος</u> ἰδοὺ ἄγγελος κυρίου
these DE of.him thinking.on   behold angel   of.Lord

κατ᾽ ὄναρ ἐφάνη   αὐτῷ λέγων,
by   dream 3S.appeared to.him saying,...

To sum up, it appears that for a HP to be used to activate a participant in Matthew's Gospel, the participant must be introduced to the scene of a previous interaction between participants and must have an active role to play.

Historical Presents and the Movement of Activated Participants to a New Location

Sometimes, when Jesus has been interacting with other people, a HP is used to bring all the participants to the *location* of the next significant events in which they are involved. The HP gives prominence to the following events that take place at that location, or even to the location itself because of its significance for subsequent events.

In **Matt. 26:36**, for instance, two HPs are used: one to move all the activated participants to Gethsemane and a second to introduce Jesus' initial speech to his disciples. These HPs are readily interpreted as pointing forward to and highlighting "Our Lord's agony at Gethsemane" (Alford

1863.I:270). Furthermore, the location itself is significant for subsequent events, as it will be the place to which Judas will bring an armed group to arrest Jesus.

(35)   {The previous subsection ends with Peter saying (λέγει)[10] to Jesus, "Even though I must die with you, I will not deny you." And so said (εἶπαν) all the disciples.}

(36)   Τότε   ἔρχεται   μετ'   αὐτῶν   ὁ   Ἰησοῦς   εἰς   χωρίον
        then   3S.comes   with   them   the   Jesus   to   place

        λεγόμενον   Γεθσημανί   καὶ   λέγει   τοῖς   μαθηταῖς,
        called   Gethsemane   and   3S.says   to.the   disciples
        "Sit here while I go over there and pray."

(37)   And, having taken Peter and the two sons of Zebedee with him, he began (ἤρξατο) to be grieved and distressed.

See also Matt. 4:5, 4:8 (with πάλιν 'again').[11]

In contrast, when Jesus and the disciples move to a new location in Matt. 13:36, no HP is used (Τότε ἀφεὶς τοὺς ὄχλους ἦλθεν εἰς τὴν οἰκίαν 'then, having left the crowds, he went into the house'). This may be because the location itself is of no significance for subsequent events or because the interpretation of the parable of the weeds of the field (vv. 36–43) does not warrant being given special prominence.

Historical Presents and Conclusions

On two occasions, a HP is used in Matthew in connection with the *concluding event* of an interaction between participants. In both, the HP appears to be used not to highlight the concluding event itself but to point forward to and give prominence to the events that follow.[12]

In **Matt. 3:15**, for instance, the event presented with the HP concludes an interaction between John and Jesus. The HP points forward to and gives prominence to the coming of the Holy Spirit upon Jesus and the voice from heaven (vv. 16–17).

(13)   Then Jesus arrives (παραγίνεται) from Galilee to the Jordan to John, to be baptized by him.

(14)   John was preventing (διεκώλυεν) him... (15a) In answer, Jesus said (εἶπεν) to him, "Let it be so now; for it is proper for us in this way to fulfill all righteousness."

(15b)   τότε   ἀφίησιν   αὐτόν.
        then   3S.permits   him

(16)   And having been baptized, Jesus immediately came up (ἀνέβη) from the water (17) and behold, the heavens were opened (ἠνεῴχθησαν)...

See also Matt. 4:11a (Τότε ἀφίησιν αὐτὸν ὁ διάβολος 'then the devil leaves him'), which concludes the interaction between the devil and Jesus, and points forward to the arrival of the angels to serve him (see the use of ἰδού in v. 11b).

I argued above that a HP is only used to activate a participant in Matthew's Gospel when the participant is introduced to the scene of a previous interaction between participants and has an active role to play. If that conclusion is valid, then the use of a HP in **Matt. 3:1**, which activates John the Baptist, implies that the episode is to be understood as part of a larger whole, even though he is introduced to a different location than that of the events of the end of chapter 2 (Nazareth). In this connection, see

---

[10] See sec. 14.2 on the use of the HP in Matt. 26:35.

[11] Some MSS have a HP (λέγει) also in 4:9, which would result in every event and speech of vv. 8–11a being presented with a HP.

[12] Pope (p.c.) disagrees. He feels that, in both 3:15b and 4:11a, the concluding event is highlighted.

Alford's comment (1863.I:18), "the ἡμέραι ἐκεῖναι must be understood to mean that we take up the persons of the narrative where we left them."

(2:23)   And having come, he settled (κατῴκησεν) in a town called Nazareth, so that what had been spoken through the prophets might be fulfilled, "He will called a Nazorean."

(3:1)   Ἐν δὲ ταῖς ἡμέραις ἐκείναις παραγίνεται
in   DE the   days   those   3S.comes

Ἰωάννης ὁ βαπτιστὴς κηρύσσων ἐν τῇ ἐρήμῳ
John   the Baptist   preaching in the desert

τῆς Ἰουδαίας (2) [καὶ] λέγων,
of.the Judea   and   saying,
"Repent, for the kingdom of heaven has come near."

Review Questions

(a) If a HP is used to activate a participant in Matthew's Gospel, what does this imply?
(b) If a HP is used to move activated participants to a new location, to what does it give prominence?

Suggested Answers

(a) If a HP is used to activate a participant in Matthew's Gospel, this implies that the participant will have a significant role to play in the following events. Furthermore, a HP is used only if the participant is being introduced to the scene of a previous interaction between participants.
(b) If a HP is used to move activated participants to a new location, this gives prominence to the following events that take place at that location, or even to the location itself because of its significance for subsequent events.

Note the use of the HP in the following passages, then answer the questions.

Illustrative Passage 3: Matthew 25:14–20

(14-18)   {A man entrusted (παρέδωκεν) his property to three servants. Two gained (ἐκέρδησεν) more talents, whereas the third hid (ἔκρυψεν) the money in the ground.}

(19)   μετὰ δὲ πολὺν χρόνον ἔρχεται ὁ κύριος τῶν δούλων ἐκείνων
after DE much time   3S.comes the master of.the slaves   those

καὶ συναίρει λόγον μετ' αὐτῶν.
and 3S.settles accounts with them

(20)   And he who had received the five talents, approaching, brought (προσήνεγκεν) five more talents, saying, "Master, you handed over to me five talents; see, I have made five more talents."

Question

Why are HPs used in v. 19?

Suggested Answer

HPs are used in v. 19 to reactivate the master of the slaves (following a previous interaction between participants) and to indicate that he has an active role to play.

Passage 4: Matthew 16:28–17:2

(28)   "Truly, I say to you, some standing here will not taste death before they see the Son of Man coming in his kingdom."

(1a)   Καὶ μεθ’ ἡμέρας ἓξ παραλαμβάνει ὁ Ἰησοῦς τὸν Πέτρον
        and after days six 3S.takes the Jesus the Peter

        καὶ Ἰάκωβον καὶ Ἰωάννην τὸν ἀδελφὸν αὐτοῦ
        and James and John the brother his

(1b)   καὶ ἀναφέρει αὐτοὺς εἰς ὄρος ὑψηλὸν κατ’ ἰδίαν.
        and 3S.leads.up them to mount high privately

(2)   And he was transfigured (μετεμορφώθη) before them...

Question

What does the presence of the HPs in Matt. 17:1 imply?

Suggested Answer: see Appendix 12(4).

12.2.2 Non-Speech Historical Presents in Luke-Acts

Only five non-speech HPs are found in Luke-Acts. All involve introducing to an existing scene information that both is significant in its own right and leads to further significant events:
- the arrival of someone with the news that the daughter of the synagogue ruler has died (Luke 8:49)
- the sight of Abraham and Lazarus in his bosom (Luke 16:23)
- the sight of the linen cloths by themselves (Luke 24:12)
- the sight of heaven open and something like a sheet coming down (Acts 10:11)
- the discovery of many Gentiles assembled to hear Peter (Acts 10:27), which leads Peter to say what he did in vv. 28–29.

It appears, therefore, that, while HPs are seldom used in Luke-Acts, those that do occur function more or less like those found in Matthew's Gospel, viz., to mark as significant the information associated with the HP and to give prominence to what follows.

12.2.3 Non-Speech Historical Presents in John

HPs in John, whether or not they introduce a reported speech, are usually cataphoric, i.e., point forward to and highlight what follows.

A difference between John and Matthew is that it is the norm in John for non-speech HPs to be followed, often immediately, by speech HPs. (In Matthew, this only occurs in connection with the movement of activated participants to the location of the next significant events.) See sec. 15.1 for discussion of whether or not the speech HP is cataphoric.

A further difference between John and Matthew is that the conditions that must be met for a HP to be used appear to be less stringent in John than in Matthew. Thus, although the non-speech HPs of John may be divided into three categories, the first being by far the most common, the conditions attached to them are weaker:
- those that *activate* a participant by introducing him or her to the scene of a previous interaction between participants (whether or not he has a significant part to play)
- those that *move* activated participants to the location of the next significant events
- others that describe events that lead immediately to a highlighted event.

As in Matthew, the majority of non-speech HPs in John activate participants by *introducing them to an existing scene*. In **John 6:19a**, for instance, Jesus is introduced as the object of θεωροῦσιν to the scene in which the disciples are struggling against the elements.

(16)   When evening came, his disciples went down (κατέβησαν) to the sea (17) and, having embarked in a boat, were going (ἤρχοντο) across the sea to Capernaum. Darkness had

already come (ἐγεγόνει), and Jesus had not yet come (ἐληλύθει) to them. (18) Because a strong wind was blowing, the sea was becoming rough (διεγείρετο).

(19a) ἐληλακότες οὖν ὡς σταδίους εἴκοσι πέντε ἢ
having.rowed then about furlongs twenty five or

τριάκοντα θεωροῦσιν τὸν Ἰησοῦν περιπατοῦντα ἐπὶ τῆς
thirty 3P.see the Jesus walking on the

θαλάσσης καὶ ἐγγὺς τοῦ πλοίου γινόμενον,
sea and near the boat becoming

(19b) and they were afraid (ἐφοβήθησαν). (20) But he says (λέγει) to them, "It is I; do not be afraid." (21) Then they were willing (ἤθελον) to take him into the boat, and immediately the boat reached (ἐγένετο) the land to which they were going.

Similarly, following the Prologue to the Gospel (1:1–14), John the Baptist is activated in 1:15 with a HP that relates him to the existing scene (μαρτυρεῖ περὶ αὐτοῦ 'testifies about him', i.e., the Word), as is Jesus in 1:29, Simon in 1:41, Philip in 1:43, and Nathanael in 1:45. See also 2:9 (the bridegroom), 4:7 (a woman of Samaria), 5:14 (Jesus), 8:3! (a woman taken in adultery), 9:13 (the Pharisees), 12:22a (Andrew), 12:22b (Jesus), 13:6 (Simon Peter), 13:26 (Judas), 18:3 (Judas and those with him), 20:1 (Mary Magdalene), 20:2 (Simon Peter and the disciple whom Jesus loved), 20:6 (Simon Peter again), 20:12 (two angels), 20:14b (Jesus), 20:18 (the disciples), 20:26 (Jesus), and 21:20 (the disciple whom Jesus loved).

Significant objects are also introduced with a HP. See 20:1 (the stone taken away from the tomb) and 20:5 and 6 (the various cloths in the tomb).

At the beginning of an episode, in contrast, participants are activated without a HP. See, for example, **John 2:1–2**, where the mother of Jesus, Jesus, and his disciples are all activated without a HP. (The servants, in contrast, are activated as the addressees of λέγει in v. 5.)

(1) On the third day there was (ἐγένετο) a wedding in Cana of Galilee, and the mother of Jesus was (ἦν) there. (2) Both Jesus and his disciples were invited (ἐκλήθη) to the wedding.

Similarly, Nicodemus is activated without a HP at the beginning of chapter 3.

The participants who are activated with a HP are of varying importance. In 6:19a (above), Jesus is very significant, as is the action he is performing. In **John 2:9b**, in contrast, the bridegroom has no active role to play (in Matthew, the participant must have an active role to play before a HP may be used—sec. 12.2.1). Rather, what is significant is what is said to him (v. 10), which is also introduced with a HP.[13]

(9a) When the master of the feast tasted the water that had become wine, and did not know where it had come from (though the servants who had drawn the water knew),

(9b) φωνεῖ τὸν νυμφίον ὁ ἀρχιτρίκλινος
3S.calls the bridegroom the master.of.feast

(10) καὶ λέγει αὐτῷ,
and 3S.says to.him,
"Everyone serves the good wine first, and then the inferior wine after the guests have become drunk. But you have kept the good wine until now."

---

[13] The HP which introduces the speech of 2:10 may also be cataphoric, pointing forward to the conclusion of v. 11 ('This, the first of his signs, Jesus did in Cana of Galilee, and revealed his glory; and his disciples believed in him').

Similarly, in **John 12:22–23**, although HPs are used both to activate Andrew and Jesus, what is more significant is what Jesus says (vv. 23–28a) and in particular, since that speech is also introduced with a HP, the response of v. 28b.[14]

(20)   Now there were (ἦσαν) some Greeks among those who were going up to worship at the festival. (21) So they approached (προσῆλθον) Philip, who was from Bethsaida in Galilee, and were asking (ἠρώτων) him, saying, "Sir, we wish to see Jesus."

(22a)   ἔρχεται   ὁ   Φίλιππος   καὶ   λέγει   τῷ   Ἀνδρέᾳ,
        3S.comes   the   Philip   and   3S.says to.the   Andrew

(22b)   ἔρχεται   Ἀνδρέας καὶ Φίλιππος καὶ λέγουσιν τῷ   Ἰησοῦ.
        3S.comes   Andrew   and Philip   and 3P.say   to.the   Jesus

(23)   ὁ   δὲ   Ἰησοῦς   ἀποκρίνεται αὐτοῖς λέγων,
        the DE   Jesus   3S.replies   to.them saying,
        "The hour has come for the Son of Man to be glorified... (28a) Father, glorify your name."

(28b)   ἦλθεν   οὖν   φωνὴ   ἐκ   τοῦ   οὐρανοῦ,
        3S.came   then voice from   the   heaven,
        "I have glorified it, and I will glorify it again."

It appears, therefore, that the rhetorical effect of using a HP to activate a participant in John's Gospel is to highlight, but the reader must deduce from the context what is being highlighted. In particular, the participant activated with the HP may or may not be the one who performs the significant event(s) or speech.

In a few instances, when Jesus has already been activated, a HP is used to bring him to the *location* of the next significant events. In **John 4:5**, for instance, a HP is used to bring him to the city of Sychar. This is the location for the next significant interaction of his ministry.

(1)   When Jesus learned that the Pharisees had heard, "Jesus is making and baptizing more disciples than John" (2)—although it was not Jesus himself but his disciples who baptized—(3) he left (ἀφῆκεν) Judea and departed (ἀπῆλθεν) again for Galilee. (4) Now it was necessary (ἔδει) for him to pass through Samaria.

(5)   ἔρχεται   οὖν   εἰς   πόλιν   τῆς   Σαμαρείας λεγομένην Συχὰρ
        3S.comes then to   city   of.the Samaria   called   Sychar
        near the plot of ground that Jacob had given to his son Joseph.

(6a)   Jacob's well was (ἦν) there, and Jesus, tired out by his journey, was sitting (ἐκαθέζετο) by the well.

See also John 11:38 (Jesus comes to Lazarus' tomb) and 18:28 (they lead Jesus to the praetorium—with which Pilate is associated, as the articular reference to him in v. 29 suggests). In each of these examples, the location itself is important only insofar as significant events occur there, so the HP may be considered to have a cataphoric function.

Finally, HPs appear to be used cataphorically in **John 13:4a–b** (below) and again in v. 5a to highlight the immediately following event (vv. 4c and 5b respectively), which is presented in the aorist. (A similar effect is achieved in vv. 6b–7—see sec. 15.1. The HP in v. 6a is used to activate Simon Peter—see above.)[15]

---

[14] Pope (p.c.) suggests a possible parallel between a chain of HPs such as that found in John 12:22–23 and a series of τέ's such as that found in Acts 21:30–31 (see sec. 6.3). Both have the rhetorical effect of building up tension in anticipation of the next significant development.

[15] See also Rev. 12:4 (καὶ ἡ οὐρὰ αὐτοῦ σύρει τὸ τρίτον τῶν ἀστέρων τοῦ οὐρανοῦ καὶ ἔβαλεν αὐτοὺς εἰς τὴν γῆν 'and his tail drags the third part of the stars of heaven and threw them to the earth').

(1) Now before the festival of the Passover, since Jesus knew that his hour had come to depart from this world to go to the Father, having loved his own who were in the world, he loved (ἠγάπησεν) them to the end.

(2) While supper was taking place, since the devil had already put it into the heart of Judas the son of Simon Iscariot to betray him, (3) knowing that the Father had put all things into his hands, and that he had come from God and was going to God,

(4a) ἐγείρεται ἐκ τοῦ δείπνου
      3S.rises from the supper

(4b) καὶ τίθησιν τὰ ἱμάτια
      and 3S.puts.aside the garments

(4c) καὶ λαβὼν λέντιον διέζωσεν ἑαυτόν·
      and having.taken towel 3S.girded himself

(5a) εἶτα βάλλει ὕδωρ εἰς τὸν νιπτῆρα
      then 3S.puts water into the basin

(5b) καὶ ἤρξατο νίπτειν τοὺς πόδας τῶν μαθητῶν
      and 3S.began to.wash the feet of.the disciples

      καὶ ἐκμάσσειν τῷ λεντίῳ ᾧ ἦν διεζωσμένος.
      and to.wipe with.the towel with.which 3S.was girded

(6a) ἔρχεται οὖν πρὸς Σίμωνα Πέτρον·
      3S.comes then to Simon Peter

(6b) He says (λέγει) to him, "Lord, are you going to wash my feet?"

(7) Jesus answered (ἀπεκρίθη)...

Review Questions

(a) When a non-speech HP is used in John to activate a participant, does the participant necessarily have an active part to play in subsequent events?

(b) When a non-speech HP is used to move Jesus to a new location, what does this imply?

Suggested Answers

(a) When a non-speech HP is used in John to activate a participant, the participant concerned does not necessarily have an active part to play in subsequent events.

(b) When a non-speech HP is used to move Jesus to a new location, this implies that significant events involving Jesus will take place at that location.

Note the presence of non-speech HPs in the following illustrative passages.

Illustrative Passage 5: John 20:24–26

(24) But <u>Thomas</u>, one of the twelve, called the Twin, was not with them when Jesus came.

(25a) So the other disciples were saying (ἔλεγον) to him, "We have seen the Lord."

(25b) But he said (εἶπεν) to them, "Unless I see the mark of the nails in his hands, and put my finger in the mark of the nails and my hand in his side, I will not believe."

(26a) And <u>a</u> <u>week</u> <u>later</u> his disciples were (ἦσαν) again in the house, and Thomas with them.

(26b) ἔρχεται ὁ Ἰησοῦς <u>τῶν</u> <u>θυρῶν</u> κεκλεισμένων
      3S.comes the Jesus the doors having.been.shut

(26c) καὶ ἔστη εἰς τὸ μέσον καὶ εἶπεν, Εἰρήνη ὑμῖν.
      and 3S.stood in the midst and 3S.said peace to.you

Question

Why is a HP used in v. 26b?

Suggested Answer

A HP is used in v. 26b to introduce Jesus to the scene of a previous interaction between participants and to indicate that he has an active part to play.

Illustrative Passage 6: John 21:7b–14 (UBS text)

(7b)   <u>Simon Peter</u>, having heard, "It is the Lord," tied (διεζώσατο) his outer garment around himself, for he was naked, and threw (ἔβαλεν) himself into the sea. (8) But <u>the other disciples</u> came (ἦλθον) in the boat,... dragging the net full of the fish.

(9)

ὡς	οὖν	ἀπέβησαν	εἰς	τὴν	γῆν	βλέπουσιν	ἀνθρακιὰν
when	then	3P.disembarked	onto	the	land	3P.see	charcoal.fire

κειμένην	καὶ	ὀψάριον	ἐπικείμενον	καὶ	ἄρτον.
lying	and	fish	lying.upon	and	bread

(10)

λέγει	αὐτοῖς	ὁ	Ἰησοῦς,	
3S.says	to.them	the	Jesus,	"Bring some of the fish that you have just caught."

(11)   So Simon Peter went aboard (ἀνέβη) and dragged (εἵλκυσεν) the net ashore, full of large fish, 153 of them; and though there were so many, the net was not torn.

(12a)

λέγει	αὐτοῖς	ὁ	Ἰησοῦς,	
3S.says	to.them	the	Jesus,	"Come and have breakfast."

(12b)   Now none of the disciples was daring to ask him, "Who are you?" because they knew it was the Lord.

(13)

ἔρχεται	Ἰησοῦς	καὶ	λαμβάνει	τὸν	ἄρτον	καὶ	δίδωσιν
3S.comes	Jesus	and	3S.takes	the	bread	and	3S.gives

αὐτοῖς,	καὶ	τὸ	ὀψάριον	ὁμοίως.
to.them	and	the	fish	likewise

(14)   Thus Jesus now manifested (ἐφανερώθη) himself for the third time to the disciples after he was raised from the dead.

Questions

(a) Why is a HP used in v. 9?
(b) Why are HPs used in v. 13?
(c) What is the significance of the anarthrous reference to Jesus in the UBS text of v. 13? (Contrast the articular references to him in vv. 10 and 12.)

Suggested Answers

(a) A HP is used in v. 9 to introduce significant objects to the existing scene. These objects are the charcoal fire and especially the fish and the bread.
(b) The first HP in v. 13 brings Jesus to the location of the bread and fish, which implies that the events that occur there are of significance. Since the series of HPs continues, it appears that it is the act of giving the bread to the disciples that is particularly significant. Alternatively, the HPs point to the conclusion of v. 14.
(c) The anarthrous reference to Jesus in the UBS text of v. 13 has the effect of highlighting the events that he performs. In this connection, Beasley-Murray (1987:400) states, "The provision of a meal—

fish and bread—by Jesus, particularly in light of the language used in v 13, imparts to the occasion something of the quality of the Last Supper."[16]

---

[16] "Since the [MS] support for an anarthrous reference is so limited I am inclined to suspect that the highlighting it achieves is a deliberate heightening of prominence by liturgically-minded editors of the words which resemble the language of the Last Supper" (Pope p.c.).

PART V: THE REPORTING OF CONVERSATION

Reported conversations tend not to be structured like ordinary narrative events. In the case of NT Greek, we have already noted (sec. 8.2) that the default encoding of references to a speaker who was the previous addressee is often an articular pronoun, rather than a full noun phrase, even though the latter is the norm for many other changes of subject. Furthermore, the majority of examples of the historical present involve speech verbs (see the statistics cited in sec. 12.2). In other words, they most often introduce reported speeches. So, since reported conversation occupies so much of the Gospels and Acts, it is important that we understand the significance of the different ways in which it is handled.

Now for some terminology!

The term *closed conversation* refers to one in which each new speaker and addressee is drawn from the speakers and addressees of previous speeches of the conversation. Acts 10:3ff. provides an example of a closed conversation; the angel and Cornelius address each other in turn.

Passage 1: Acts 10:3–4

(3)   ... he clearly saw an angel of God coming in and saying to him, "Cornelius."

(4a)   ὁ   δὲ ... εἶπεν,
         he DE   3S.said,
         "What is it, Lord?"

(4b)   εἶπεν δὲ αὐτῷ,
         3S.said DE to.him,
         "Your prayers and your alms have ascended as a memorial before God..."

Luke 15:21–23 is an example of a conversation that is *not* closed, since the addressees of the speech of vv. 22–23 (the slaves) had not been involved in the conversation up to that point (unlike the son).

Passage 2: Luke 15:21–23

(21)   And the son said to him, "Father, I have sinned against heaven and before you; I am no longer worthy to be called your son..."

(22)   εἶπεν δὲ ὁ   πατὴρ πρὸς τοὺς δούλους αὐτοῦ,
         3S.said DE the father to   the   slaves   his,
         (23) "Quickly bring out a robe—the best one—and put it on him..."

For a reported conversation to be *tight-knit*, it must be a closed conversation, with the previous addressee becoming the new speaker and *vice versa*. In addition, each successive speaker "takes up the same topic as that of the previous speech and develops the conversation from the point at which the last speaker left off" (Levinsohn 1987:36).

Passage 1 above is a tight-knit conversation, since Cornelius responds to the angel in line with his greeting, while the angel in turn answers Cornelius' question.

Passage 3 (below) is not a tight-knit conversation. Although it starts off the same way as passage 1, with Ananias responding to the Lord in line with his greeting and the Lord then giving his instruction, Ananias then breaks the tight-knit nature of the exchange by voicing an objection (Acts 9:13–14). We shall see in sec. 14.1 that, when a speech in the Synoptic Gospels and Acts is introduced with some form of ἀποκρίνομαι 'answer', this signals that the tight-knit nature of the conversation has been broken because the new speaker attempts to take control of it.

Passage 3: Acts 9:10b–14

> (10b)   The Lord said to him in a vision, "Ananias."

> (10c)   ὁ   δὲ   εἶπεν,
>   he DE   3S.said,
>   "Here I am, Lord."

> (11-12) ὁ   δὲ   κύριος   πρὸς   αὐτόν,
>   the DE   Lord   to   him,
>   "Rising, go to the street called Straight, and at the house of Judas look for a man of Tarsus
>   named Saul."

> (13-14) ἀπεκρίθη   δὲ   Ἀνανίας,
>   3S.answered DE   Ananias,
>   "Lord, I have heard from many about this man, how much evil he has done to your saints
>   in Jerusalem..."

The term *speech orienter* refers to the clause that introduces the actual speech.[1] In Greek, speech orienters almost always occur before the speech, as in Acts 10:4b above (εἶπεν δὲ αὐτῷ). Occasionally, however, the orienter may occur within the speech, as in Matt. 14:8 (Δός μοι, φησίν, ὧδε ἐπὶ πίνακι τὴν κεφαλὴν Ἰωάννου τοῦ βαπτιστοῦ. '"Give me," she says, "here on a platter the head of John the Baptist"'—see sec. 14.3 for discussion of the historical present φησίν). Alternatively, the orienter may be split by the speech, as in Luke 7:40b (UBS text—ὁ δέ, Διδάσκαλε, εἰπέ, φησίν 'And he, "Teacher, say on," says'). In Rev. 1:8, the orienter follows the speech (Ἐγώ εἰμι τὸ Ἄλφα καὶ τὸ Ὦ, λέγει κύριος ὁ θεός '"I am the Alpha and the Omega," says the Lord God'). In John 1:21c (Ὁ προφήτης εἶ σύ; 'Are you the prophet?'), the orienter is omitted completely (see also Mark 8:20 and Luke 7:41). More often, though, it is the verb of the orienter that is omitted, as in Acts 9:11 above (ὁ δὲ κύριος πρὸς αὐτόν, 'and the Lord to him').

When an episode contains more than one conversation between the participants, each conversation may be thought of as a *round*. For example, the temptation of Jesus by the devil (Matt. 4:3–11) may be thought of as having three rounds. Peter's denial of Jesus (Matt. 26:69–75) is similar.

A speech may be reported *directly* or *indirectly*.

When a speech is reported directly, no significant changes are made to the speech. In particular, any use of the first or second person to refer to the speaker or addressee is preserved. In Luke 7:40b above, for instance, the second person form of the verb, εἰπέ, has been preserved.

When a speech is reported indirectly, it may be changed in a number of ways (see chap. 17 of Porter 1992 for a detailed discussion). A finite verb may be replaced by an infinitive or other non-finite form, as in Acts 12:15b (ἡ δὲ διϊσχυρίζετο οὕτως ἔχειν. 'She, however, 3S.was.insisting thus to.be'). Alternatively, the finite verb may be preserved but ὅτι or ἵνα follows the orienter, while any reference to the speaker or addressee is changed to third person. This is illustrated in **John 4:51** (UBS text). The orienter λέγοντες is followed by ὅτι and the reference to the addressee is in third person.

> (51b)   λέγοντες   ὅτι   ὁ   παῖς   αὐτοῦ   ζῇ.
>   saying   that the child his   3S.lives

A third way to report speech is directly but with ὅτι inserted between the orienter and the speech. When ὅτι occurs in this position, it is called *recitativum*. **John 4:42a** illustrates ὅτι *recitativum*.

> (42a)   τῇ   τε   γυναικὶ   ἔλεγον   ὅτι   Οὐκέτι
>   to.the and woman   3S.were.saying that no.longer
>
>   διὰ   τὴν   σὴν   λαλιὰν   πιστεύομεν,   αὐτοὶ   γὰρ   ἀκηκόαμεν   κ.τ.λ.
>   because.of the your word   we.believe   selves   for   we.have.heard

---

[1] Longacre (1996:89) uses the term "quotation formula."

I argue in chapter 16 that, whereas the norm is to report speech directly, reporting speech indirectly has the effect of backgrounding the speech, while using ὅτι *recitativum* signals that the speech culminates some unit.

I recognize two *strategies* for reporting conversations in the Synoptic Gospels and Acts, which are distinguished by whether the *non-initial* speeches are introduced with a conjunction or not.

- When a conjunction occurs in the orienter of non-initial speeches, as in passages 1 to 3 above, the *default* strategy has been employed; this strategy is discussed in chapter 13.
- If no conjunction occurs in the orienter of non-initial speeches, a *nondevelopmental* strategy has been employed—see sec. 14.2. What is notable about this strategy, which is used only in Matthew (and John—see chap. 15), is that the speech orienter is often in the historical present.

Passage 4 illustrates this nondevelopmental strategy, with no conjunction in the orienter of Matt. 17:25a. Since the question of v. 24b is negated by οὐ, the expected response is positive (Porter 1992:278). The actual response is also positive, so v. 25a does not represent a new development in the conversation.

Passage 4: Matthew 17:24–25a

(24a)   When they reached Capernaum, the collectors of the temple tax came to Peter

(24b)   καὶ   εἶπαν,   Ὁ   διδάσκαλος   ὑμῶν   οὐ   τελεῖ   [τὰ]   δίδραχμα;
      and   3P.said   the   teacher   your   not   3S.pays   the   two.drachma

(25a)   λέγει,   Ναί.
      3S.says   yes

The functions of the different speech orienters in John's Gospel differ in certain crucial respects from their functions in the Synoptic Gospels and Acts, so chapter 15 is devoted exclusively to the reporting of conversations in John.

13
THE DEFAULT STRATEGY FOR REPORTING CONVERSATIONS

I begin this chapter by considering the status of reported conversations in narrative. I look particularly at how the form of the orienter reflects whether the speech concerned is an end in itself or is but an intermediate step en route to the actions that result from the conversation (sec. 13.1). I then consider the status of the final speech of a conversation and note how the form of the speech orienter in Luke-Acts reflects whether or not the speech attains the goal of one of the participants (sec. 13.2).

The concept of intermediate steps en route to a goal may be related to bringing a referent into temporary focus (sec. 4.3), in anticipation of a switch of attention to another referent. Section 13.3 considers a few examples of such anticipatory points of departure that do not involve reported conversation.

13.1   The Status of Reported Speeches in the Overall Narrative

As I have already indicated, non-initial speeches of a reported conversation are generally not treated in the same way as sentences that describe actions other than speech. This is because, in many narratives, what is important is not so much the individual speeches themselves, but rather the result of the conversation, which may be expressed either in the final speech or in an action that occurs in response to the conversation.

In narratives in Luke-Acts and, to a lesser extent in the other Gospels, the orienters of non-initial speeches of a tight-knit, closed conversation begin with a reference to the speaker when they are simply *intermediate steps* en route to the goal of the conversation. Unless the speech is highlighted, this reference will be an articular pronoun (see sec. 8.2).[1] The articular pronoun is sometimes used also when the previous addressee responds to a speech with an action rather than a speech, provided that the action is viewed as but an intermediate step en route to the goal (see Luke 1:29 of passage 3 below).

Luke 10:25–28 (below) is typical of such conversations. The orienters that introduce the speeches of vv. 26 and 27 begin with an articular pronoun. This is because it is the speech of v. 28 that answers the question of v. 25, whereas the speeches of vv. 26 and 27 are only intermediate steps to the realization of that goal. (See sec. 13.2 on the significance of beginning the orienter of the final speech of v. 28 with a verb.)

Passage 1: Luke 10:25–28

(25)   INITIAL SPEECH
And behold, a lawyer stood up to test him, saying,
"Teacher, what must I do to inherit eternal life?"

(26)   INTERMEDIATE STEP

ὁ   δὲ   εἶπεν   πρὸς   αὐτόν,
he   DE   3S.said   to   him,
"What is written in the law? What do you read there?"

(27)   INTERMEDIATE STEP

ὁ   δὲ   ἀποκριθεὶς   εἶπεν,
he   DE   answering   3S.said,
"You shall love the Lord your God..."

---

[1] When an articular pronoun is used, δέ and μέν are the only conjunctions that occur with it. As I noted in sec. 5.1 (fn. 5), such instances of δέ mark development only within the conversation.

(28)   FINAL SPEECH (GOAL)

εἶπεν   δὲ   αὐτῷ,[2]
3S.said   DE   to.him,
"You have given the right answer; do this, and you will live."

In Acts 12:15 (below), every non-initial speech is introduced with an articular pronoun. This is because what is important to the ongoing story is not the individual speeches but the goal as it affects Peter; furthermore, this goal is not even attained by the conversation (see sec. 13.2) but only because Peter continues knocking (v. 16). (Note that the form of the speech orienter is not affected by whether the reported speech is direct or indirect.)

Passage 2: Acts 12:13–16

(13)   When he (Peter) knocked at the outer gate, a maid named Rhoda came to answer. (14) On recognizing Peter's voice, she was so overjoyed that she did not open the gate. Instead, running in, she announced that Peter was standing at the gate.

(15a)   οἱ   δὲ   πρὸς   αὐτὴν   εἶπαν,
        they   DE   to   her   3P.said,
        "You are out of your mind."

(15b)   ἡ   δὲ   διϊσχυρίζετο   οὕτως   ἔχειν.
        she   DE   3S.was.insisting   thus   to.be

(15c)   οἱ   δὲ   ἔλεγον,
        they   DE   3P.were.saying,
        "It is his angel."

(16)   Peter was continuing to knock; and when they opened the gate, they saw him and were amazed.

Although many non-initial speeches are introduced with a reference to the speaker, a number are not. One reason is that, for a speech to be treated as an intermediate step, the conversation must be *closed*. This is why none of the speeches of Paul's trial before Felix (Acts 24:2–23) are treated as intermediate steps; each speaker addresses Felix, rather than the previous speaker.

If a non-initial speech of a *closed* conversation begins with a verb, the speech has *greater status* than that of an intermediate step. This is illustrated in the conversation between the angel Gabriel and Mary (below). In Luke 1:29, Mary's non-verbal response to the angel's greeting is not an end in itself; rather, it is but an intermediate step en route to what the angel has to say next. In contrast, the orienters of the speeches of vv. 34, 35, and 38a all begin with a verb, implying that they are to be viewed as foreground events in their own right.

Passage 3: Luke 1:28–38a

(28)   And having come to her, he said, "Greetings, favored one! The Lord is with you."

(29)   ἡ   δὲ   ἐπὶ   τῷ   λόγῳ   διεταράχθη   καὶ
        she   DE   at   his   word   3S.was.perplexed   and

        διελογίζετο   **ποταπὸς**   εἴη   ὁ   ἀσπασμὸς   οὗτος.
        3S.was.pondering   of.what.sort   3S.may.be   the   greeting   this

(30)   καὶ   εἶπεν   ὁ   ἄγγελος   αὐτῇ,
        and   3S.said   the   angel   to.her,
        "Do not be afraid, Mary, for you have found favor with God (31) And now, you will conceive in your womb and bear a son..."

---

[2] See sec. 8.3 on the absence of any reference to the speaker (Jesus, the global VIP).

(34)   εἶπεν   δὲ   Μαριὰμ   πρὸς   τὸν   ἄγγελον,
       3S.said   DE   Mary   to   the   angel,
       "How can this be, since I am a virgin?"

(35)   καὶ   ἀποκριθεὶς   ὁ   ἄγγελος   εἶπεν   αὐτῇ,
       and   answering   the   angel   3S.said   to.her,
       "The Holy Spirit will come upon you..."

(38a) εἶπεν   δὲ   Μαριάμ,
       3S.said   DE   Mary,
       "Here am I, the servant of the Lord..."

The orienters of individual speeches of *debates*, such as those recorded in John 6:25–58 and 8:12–58, never begin with an articular pronoun, either; most of them are presented as foreground events in their own right. This may be why the articular pronoun is used so seldom in John's Gospel.

Incidentally, in *John*'s Gospel, the articular pronoun appears to be used *only* for single speeches or acts that are an intermediate step towards a goal. Its effect is to move attention on from the referent of the pronoun to the next speaker or actor.

John 6:20 is an interesting example, in that Jesus was not even the addressee of a previous speech but, rather, responds to their becoming afraid (v. 19b). The episode of vv. 16–21 is told from the point of view of the disciples (note θεωροῦσιν 'they see' in v. 19a—sec. 12.2.3), with Jesus' speech of v. 20 an intermediate step to their next response.

(19a) When they had rowed about twenty five or thirty furlongs, they see Jesus walking on the
       sea and coming near the boat, (19b) and they were afraid.

(20)   ὁ   δὲ   λέγει   αὐτοῖς,
       he   DE   3S.says   to.them,
       "It is I; do not be afraid."

(21a) Then they were willing to take him into the boat,

In the other passages in which an articular pronoun occurs in John's Gospel, the response (whether non-verbal or verbal) is to a speech. See, for example:
1:38b (the disciples' question is but an intermediate step between the two speeches of Jesus that bring the disciples into contact with him)
2:8b (UBS text—attention rests briefly on the servants before passing in v. 9 to the master of the feast)
5:11 (as the following verses indicate, John's concern is more with the Jews than with the man who has been healed—see also 5:17)
9:38a (the blind man's response is an intermediate step either to his worshipping Jesus or to the interaction of vv. 39–41 between Jesus and the authorities—on the use of καί in v. 39, see sec. 5.3.2).

On the articular pronoun of John 21:6a, see passage 7 of sec. 15.1.

Questions

(a) What is a closed conversation?
(b) What is a tight-knit conversation?
(c) What does it mean for a speech to be an intermediate step in a reported conversation?
(d) How is an intermediate step signaled?
(e) In what type of reported conversation may intermediate steps occur?

Suggested Answers

(a) A closed conversation is one in which each new speaker and addressee is drawn from the speakers and addressees of previous speeches.

(b) A tight-knit conversation is a closed conversation in which each successive speaker takes up the same topic as that of the previous speech and develops the conversation from the point at which the last speaker left off.

(c) A speech is an intermediate step in a reported conversation if it represents but a step en route to a resulting speech or action, rather than being an end in itself. (An intermediate step is never the first speech in the conversation.)

(d) An intermediate step is signaled by an initial reference to the speaker in the speech orienter. Most often, this reference is in the form of an articular pronoun.

Note. Although an intermediate step is signaled by an initial reference to the speaker, it does not follow that all sentences that begin with references to the speaker are intermediate steps—see Luke 15:31 in sec. 13.2.

(e) Intermediate steps occur only in reported conversations that are closed and tight-knit (except in John 6:20—see above).

13.2 The Status of the Final Speech in a Reported Conversation

In section 13.1 we looked at non-initial speeches of reported conversations. I now focus specifically on the final speech of such conversations, and distinguish two types:

- those in which the orienter for the final speech begins with a verb
- those in which the orienter for the final speech begins with a reference to the speaker, employing either an articular pronoun or a full noun phrase.

The significance of the two types varies from book to book. I begin this section by concentrating on their function in Luke-Acts, and then add brief comments on their use in Matthew.

In sec. 6.1.1 we noted that, when a final speech attains the goal sought or predicted in earlier events, it is introduced with τότε in Matthew and Acts, particularly if the realization of the goal has been delayed. This question of whether or not the goal of one of the participants has been attained (usually, through the willing compliance of the other) is crucial also in determining whether or not the speech orienter begins with a verb, particularly in Luke-Acts.

A final speech can be said to have attained the goal of one of the participants if the subsequent story develops from the exchange in line with the intention of the final speech. This is illustrated in **Acts 10:7–8**; Cornelius follows the angel's instruction of vv. 4b–5 to send men to Joppa, so the final speech of the exchange has attained its goal.

(3)   … he clearly saw an angel of God coming in and saying to him, "Cornelius."

(4a)   ὁ   δὲ … εἶπεν,
        he   DE   3S.said,
        "What is it, Lord?"

(4b)   εἶπεν   δὲ   αὐτῷ,
        3S.said   DE   to.him,
        "… (5) Now send men to Joppa for a certain Simon who is called Peter…"

(7)   When the angel who spoke to him had left, he called two of his slaves… (8) and after telling them everything, he sent them to Joppa.

Similarly, in **Acts 19:5**, the disciples follow Paul's advice of v. 4 and are baptized. This shows that the final speech of the exchange attained its goal.

(2a)   εἶπέν   τε   πρὸς   αὐτούς,
        3S.said   ADD   to   them,
        "Did you receive the Holy Spirit when you became believers?"

(2b) οἱ δὲ πρὸς αὐτόν,
they DE to him,
"No, we have not even heard that there is a Holy Spirit."

(3a) εἶπέν τε,[3]
3S.said ADD
"Into what then were you baptized?"

(3b) οἱ δὲ εἶπαν,
they DE 3P.said,
"Into John's baptism."

(4) εἶπεν δὲ Παῦλος,
3S.said DE Paul,
"John baptized with the baptism of repentance, telling the people to believe in the one who was to come after him, that is, in Jesus."

(5) On hearing this, they were baptized in the name of the Lord Jesus.

See also Luke 10:28 (passage 1), which is the final speech of the first part of a conversation and attains the goal of that part in the sense that it answers the question of v. 25.

However, final speeches do not always attain the goal of either of the participants in the exchange. There are two reasons for this:
- the participants fail to reach agreement
- the speech is still only an intermediate step en route to some goal (sec. 13.1).

When a final speech does not attain the goal of either of the participants, the speech orienter begins with a reference to the speaker, rather than with a verb.

An example in the final speech of which the participants *fail to reach agreement* is seen in passage 2 of sec. 13.1 (repeated below). Rhoda and the others are still in disagreement at the end of the conversation, so the orienter of **Acts 12:15c** begins with articular pronoun.

(13) When he (Peter) knocked at the outer gate, a maid named Rhoda came to answer. (14) On recognizing Peter's voice, she was so overjoyed that she did not open the gate. Instead, running in, she announced that Peter was standing at the gate.

(15a) οἱ δὲ πρὸς αὐτὴν εἶπαν,
they DE to her 3P.said,
"You are out of your mind."

(15b) ἡ δὲ διϊσχυρίζετο οὕτως ἔχειν.
she DE 3S.was.insisting thus to.be

(15c) οἱ δὲ ἔλεγον,
they DE 3P.were.saying,
"It is his angel."

(16) Peter was continuing to knock; and when they opened the gate, they saw him and were amazed.

Other exchanges in which the orienter for the final speech begins with a reference to the speaker because the participants fail to reach agreement include:

---

[3] If the UBS3 reading is followed in Acts 19:3a, the first part of the conversation is divided into two question-and-answer pairs or "couplets" (sec. 15.1), the second of which is added to the first (see the τέ). This may have been done to increase tension as the conversation moves towards its climax (sec. 6.3). If the UBS1 reading is followed (ὁ δὲ εἶπεν), then all the non-initial speeches are treated as intermediate steps en route to the speech of v. 4 which attains Paul's purpose.

- Acts 10:15: the voice from heaven fails to persuade Peter to change his mind about unclean animals, as is clear from the fact that the vision occurs three times (v. 16)
- Luke 15:31: the father's final speech to the elder son presumably fails to persuade him to enter the house.

In other passages, the orienter of the final speech begins with a reference to the speaker because the conversation is *interrupted* before the participants reach agreement. This is the case in **Acts 2:13**, for instance. Peter's speech of vv. 14ff. interrupts the conversation about the behavior of the apostles.

(12)   All were amazed and perplexed, saying to one another, "What does this mean?"

(13)   ἕτεροι   δὲ   διαχλευάζοντες   ἔλεγον   ὅτι
        others   DE   mocking   3P.were.saying   that
        "They are filled with new wine."

(14)   But Peter, standing with the eleven, raised his voice and addressed them,...

In some passages, the orienter of the final speech that has been reported begins with a reference to the speaker because, as in the examples of sec. 13.1, the speech is still only an *intermediate step* to a goal. On occasion, this is because the speech that has been reported is followed by another, usually by the same speaker. It is this speech which attains the goal of one of the participants, so the previous speech was but an intermediate step to that goal. In **Acts 16:31**, for instance, the orienter begins with a reference to the speaker not because the participants fail to reach agreement but because the speech is but an intermediate step en route to the result expressed in the further speech of v. 32 and the response of v. 33.

(30)   Having brought them outside, he said, "Sirs, what must I do to be saved?"

(31)   οἱ   δὲ   εἶπαν,
        they   DE   3P.said,
        "Believe on the Lord Jesus, and you will be saved, you and your household."

(32)   And they spoke the word of the Lord to him and to all who were in his house.

(33)   And, having taken them at the same hour of the night, he washed their wounds, and he and his entire family were baptized without delay.

See also Acts 28:21–22 (the initial clause of v. 23, ταξάμενοι αὐτῷ ἡμέραν 'having set a day (to meet) with him', indicates that further conversation ensued).[4]

Another example is Acts 25:4–5: when the Jews ask Festus to transfer Paul to Jerusalem to be tried (vv. 2–3), Festus' reply leaves the matter unresolved. As the use of prospective μὲν also suggests (see sec. 10.1), his reply is but an intermediate step to the later interaction of vv. 7–12, during which he returns to the request of the Jews (v. 9).

Passage 4: Acts 25:2–9

(2b)   and they appealed to him (Festus), (3) requesting as a favor to have him (Paul) transferred to Jerusalem, planning an ambush to kill him along the way.

(4)   ὁ   μὲν   οὖν   Φῆστος   ἀπεκρίθη   τηρεῖσθαι   τὸν   Παῦλον
        the   then   Festus   3S.answered   to.be.kept   the   Paul

        εἰς   Καισάρειαν,   ἑαυτὸν   δὲ   μέλλειν   ἐν τάχει   ἐκπορεύεσθαι·
        in   Caesarea   himself   DE   to.intend   shortly   to.go.forth

(5)   "So," he said (φησίν), "let those of you who have the authority come down with me, and if there is anything wrong about the man, let them accuse him."

---

[4] This observation corrects the comments made on p. 133 of Levinsohn 1992.

(6)   After he had stayed among them not more than eight or ten days, he went down to
         Caesarea; the next day he took his seat on the tribunal and ordered Paul to be brought...
         (9) But Festus, wishing to do the Jews a favor, asked Paul, "Do you wish to go up to
         Jerusalem and be tried there before me on these charges?"

In all three accounts of Saul's conversion, the final speech of his conversation with the voice from
heaven is introduced with a reference to the voice (Acts 9:5b, 22:10b, 26:15b). Although, in each
instance, this speech attains the immediate goal of the speaker (Saul does what he is told), a *higher level
purpose* determines that these speeches are to be viewed as but intermediate steps en route to a larger
goal. This goal is achieved by a later speech.

This is particularly clear in Acts 22 (below), in which Paul is justifying his call to the Gentiles. The
orienter of the final speech of the exchanges of both v. 10 and vv. 13–16 begins with a reference to the
speaker, as they simply provide another step en route to the speech of v. 21 that achieves Paul's overall
goal. (In contrast, the speech of v. 8b is not treated as an intermediate step, presumably because its
contents are of significance for Paul's audience.)

Passage 5: Acts 22:7–21

EXCHANGE 1

(7)   And I fell to the ground and heard a voice saying to me, "Saul, Saul, why are you
         persecuting me?"

(8a)   ἐγὼ   δὲ   ἀπεκρίθην,
         I   DE   I.answered,
         "Who are you, Lord?"

(8b)   εἶπέν   τε   πρός   με,
         3S.said ADD   to   me,
         "I am Jesus of Nazareth whom you are persecuting."

(9)   Now those who were with me saw the light but did not hear the voice of the one who was
         speaking to me.

EXCHANGE 2

(10a)   εἶπον   δέ,
         I.said DE
         "What am I to do, Lord?"

(10b)   ὁ   δὲ   κύριος   εἶπεν   πρός   με,
         the   DE   Lord   3S.said to   me,
         "Get up and go into Damascus; there you will be told everything that has been assigned to
         you to do."

(11)   And since I could not see... I was led by the hand by those who were with me and came
         into Damascus.

EXCHANGE 3

(12)   A certain Ananias... (13) came to me and, standing beside me, said, "Brother Saul, regain
         your sight!"

(13b)   κἀγὼ   αὐτῇ   τῇ   ὥρᾳ   ἀνέβλεψα   εἰς   αὐτόν.
         and.I   in.this the   hour I.looked.up at   him

(14)   ὁ   δὲ   εἶπεν,
         he   DE   3S.said,
         "The God of our ancestors has chosen you..."

FINAL EXCHANGE

(17) After I had returned to Jerusalem and while I was praying in the temple, I fell into a trance (18) and saw Jesus saying to me, "Hurry and get out of Jerusalem quickly, because they will not accept your testimony about me."

(19) κἀγὼ   εἶπον,
      and.I I.said,
      "Lord, they themselves know that in every synagogue I imprisoned and beat those who believed in you..."

(21) καὶ εἶπεν πρός με,
      and 3S.said to me,
      "Go, for I will send you far away to the Gentiles."

See also the exchange between Paul, Festus and Agrippa in Acts 26: the overall goal of the passage is achieved, not by Paul's final speech of v. 29, but by the conclusion of those present, "This man is doing nothing to deserve death or imprisonment" (v. 31).

Thus, in Luke-Acts, the orienter of the final speech of an exchange begins with a reference to the speaker only when the participants have not reached agreement or the speech is but an intermediate step en route to a goal. This is not the case for *Matthew*'s Gospel. Occasionally, when the final speech of an exchange begins with a reference to the speaker in Matthew, the speech appears to terminate the episode and there is no evidence that the participants are in disagreement.

This is illustrated in **Matt. 13:52** (UBS text). The speech concerned concludes a lengthy collection of parables (vv. 3–50) and what follows appears to be unrelated to it. This is confirmed by the overt reference to Jesus in v. 53, as befits the beginning of a new narrative unit (sec. 8.3).

(51a) "Have you understood all this?"

(51b) λέγουσιν αὐτῷ, Ναί.
       3P.say   to.him yes

(52)   ὁ   δὲ εἶπεν[5] αὐτοῖς,
       he DE 3S.said to.them,
       "So every scribe who has been trained for the kingdom of heaven is like the master of a household who brings out of his treasure what is new and what is old."

(53)   When Jesus had finished these parables, he went away from there.

See also Matt. 17:20 and 19:11–12.

Review Questions

(a) In reported conversations in Luke-Acts, what is the significance of beginning the orienter of the final speech with a verb?

(b) What are two reasons for beginning the orienter of the final speech of a reported conversation in Luke-Acts with a reference to the speaker?

Suggested Answers

(a) When the orienter of the final speech of a reported conversation in Luke-Acts begins with a verb, this implies that the goal of one of the participants in the exchange has been attained, usually because of the willing compliance of the other.

(b) The orienter of the final speech of a reported conversation in Luke-Acts begins with a reference to the speaker when:

---

[5] Λέγει is a variant; see sec. 14.2 on the use of asyndeton and the historical present in Matthew's Gospel.

- the participants fail to reach agreement (including when the conversation is interrupted before they reach agreement)
- the speech is but an intermediate step to a goal.

Illustrative Passage 6: Acts 5:7–10a

Look at the form of the non-initial speech orienters in this passage.

(7)   An interval of three hours passed and <u>his</u> (Ananias') <u>wife</u> came in, not knowing what had happened.

(8a)   Peter said to her, "Tell me whether you and your husband sold the land for such and such a price."

(8b)   ἡ   δὲ   εἶπεν,
        she   DE   3S.said,
        "Yes, that was the price."

(9)   ὁ   δὲ   Πέτρος πρὸς αὐτήν,
        the   DE   Peter   to   her,
        "How is it that you have agreed together to put the Spirit of the Lord to the test? Look, the feet of those who have buried your husband are at the door, and they will carry you out."

(10)   She fell immediately at his feet and died. When the young men came in they found her dead, so they carried her out and buried her beside her husband.

Questions

(a) Why does the speech orienter of v. 8b begin with an articular pronoun?
(b) Why does the speech orienter of v. 9 begin with a reference to the speaker? And why is the reference a full noun phrase?

Suggested Answers

(a) The orienter of v. 8b begins with an articular pronoun because the speech is an intermediate step en route to Peter's goal for the conversation.
(b) The orienter of v. 9 begins with a reference to the speaker because the participants remain in disagreement (Ananias' wife did not willingly comply with Peter's judgment on her). The reference is a full noun phrase to highlight the speech.

Illustrative Passage 7: Luke 10:25–37

We have already noted that the goal of the question of v. 25 is attained in v. 28. Now look at the form of the speech orienters in the remainder of the episode.

(25)   And behold, a lawyer stood up to test him, saying,
        "Teacher, what must I do to inherit eternal life?"

(26)   ὁ   δὲ   εἶπεν   πρὸς αὐτόν,
        he   DE   3S.said   to   him,
        "What is written in the law? What do you read there?"

(27)   ὁ   δὲ   ἀποκριθεὶς εἶπεν,
        he   DE   answering   3S.said,
        "You shall love the Lord your God... and your neighbor as yourself."

(28)   εἶπεν   δὲ   αὐτῷ,
        3S.said DE   to.him,
        "You have given the right answer; do this, and you will live."

(29)   ὁ δὲ θέλων δικαιῶσαι ἑαυτὸν εἶπεν πρὸς τὸν ᾽Ιησοῦν,
       he DE wishing to.justify himself 3S.said to the Jesus,
       "And who is my neighbor?"

(30)   ὑπολαβὼν ὁ ᾽Ιησοῦς εἶπεν,
       replying the Jesus 3S.said,
       "A man was going down from Jerusalem to Jericho..." (to v. 35)

(36)   "Which of these three, do you think, was a neighbor to the man who fell into the hands of the robbers?"

(37a)   ὁ δὲ εἶπεν,
       he DE 3S.said,
       "The one who showed him mercy."

(37b)   εἶπεν δὲ αὐτῷ ὁ ᾽Ιησοῦς,
       3S.said DE to.him the Jesus,
       "Go and do likewise."

Questions (in order of difficulty)

(a) Why does the speech orienter of v. 37a begin with an articular pronoun, but that of v. 37b with a verb?
(b) Why does the speech orienter of v. 30 begin with a verb? (If unsure, see sec. 13.1.)
(c) Why does the speech orienter of v. 29 begin with an articular pronoun?

Suggested Answers

(a) The speech orienter of v. 37a begins with an articular pronoun because the speech concerned is but an intermediate step to the speech of v. 37b, which attains Jesus' goal in telling the parable and so is introduced with a verb. The reference to Jesus by name highlights this final speech.
(b) The speech of v. 30 begins with a verb because the parable is a foreground event in its own right—see sec. 13.1. See also the reference to Jesus by name in the orienter of v. 30, which highlights what he has to say.
(c) The speech orienter of v. 29 probably begins with an articular pronoun because the speech does not open the exchange and is an intermediate step en route to the overall goal. However, comparison with the initial verb in the orienter of Acts 22:10a of passage 5 indicates that, when one round of an exchange has been completed, the next round may be treated as a separate conversation (in the case of passage 5, the background material of 22:9 intervenes).

Passage 8: Acts 22:24–30

See sec. 14.1 on the use a form of ἀποκρίνομαι in v. 28a to attempt to control the conversation. Note how each of the other speeches in this passage is introduced.

(24)   the tribune... ordered Paul to be examined by flogging, to find out the reason for this outcry against him. (25) But when they had tied him up with the thongs, Paul said to the centurion who was standing by, "Is it legal for you to flog a Roman citizen who is uncondemned?"

(26)   When the centurion heard that, he went to the tribune and said to him, "What are you about to do? This man is a Roman citizen."

(27a)   προσελθὼν δὲ ὁ χιλίαρχος εἶπεν αὐτῷ,
       having.approached DE the tribune 3S.said to.him,
       "Tell me, are you a Roman citizen?"

(27b)   ὁ δὲ ἔφη, Ναί.
       he DE 3S.affirmed yes

(28a)   ἀπεκρίθη   δὲ   ὁ   χιλίαρχος,
        3S.answered DE   the tribune,
        "It cost me a large sum of money to get my citizenship."

(28b)   ὁ   δὲ   Παῦλος   ἔφη,
        the DE   Paul   3S.affirmed,
        "But I was born a citizen."

(29)   Immediately those who were about to examine him drew back from him. The tribune also
        was afraid, having realized that Paul was a Roman citizen and that he had bound him.

(30)   On the next day, desiring to find out what he was being accused of by the Jews,...

Questions

(a) Which speeches of the above passage form a closed conversation?

(b) Why do the speech orienters of vv. 27b and 28b begin with a reference to the speaker? (See vv. 24
and 30.)

Suggested Answers: see Appendix under 13(8).

13.3   Intermediate Steps and Anticipatory Points of Departure

We have been considering speech orienters that begin with a reference to the speaker; i.e., in which
the reference to the speaker has been preposed. A theoretical question arises: why is it appropriate for
these references to be preposed? It could be because conversations are judged to develop by switches of
attention from one speaker to the other, which is best signaled when they are being reported by
preposing the reference to the speaker so that they are treated as points of departure. However, this does
not explain why the reference to the *final* speaker is not preposed when the goal of the exchange is
attained by this speech. So another possibility is that references are preposed to *anticipate* a switch of
attention from the subject of an intermediate step to the next speaker (compare the discussion of
temporary focus in sec. 4.3).[6]

I suggest this because anticipatory points of departure appear to occur in a number of circumstances
in NT Greek. One of these involves occasions when a member or *subgroup* of a group of participants
mentioned in the last sentence becomes the subject, but the story develops through the initiative of the
remaining member(s) of the group.

When a subgroup becomes subject and the story develops through the action(s) of that subgroup,
reference to the subject is *not* preposed. This is illustrated in **Acts 11:28**; the story builds on the initiative
of Agabus.

(27)   Now in those days prophets came down from Jerusalem to Antioch.

(28a)   ἀναστὰς   δὲ   εἷς   ἐξ   αὐτῶν   ὀνόματι   Ἄγαβος
        having.arisen DE   one   of   them   named   Agabus

        ἐσήμανεν   διὰ   τοῦ   πνεύματος   λιμὸν   μεγάλην
        3S.signified through the   Spirit   famine   great

        μέλλειν   ἔσεσθαι   ἐφ'   ὅλην   τὴν   οἰκουμένην,
        to.be.about to.be   on   all   the   inhabited.earth

(28b)   which took place during the reign of Claudius.

However, if the story develops, not through the action of the first subgroup, but through the initiative
of the remaining member(s) of the original group, then the reference to the first subgroup is preposed, in
anticipation of the switch to the second.

---

[6] See Levinsohn 1987:19ff. for a detailed discussion of anticipatory points of departure, there called "temporary focus."

This is illustrated in **Acts 18:19**; the story develops, not through Priscilla and Aquila (v. 18), but through Paul. This is reflected not only in treating αὐτός in v. 19c as a point of departure, as attention switches to Paul, but also in preposing ἐκείνους in v. 19b, in anticipation of this switch of attention.

(18)   As for Paul, after staying there for a considerable time, he said farewell to the brothers and sailed for Syria, accompanied by Priscilla and Aquila, having had his head shaved at Cenchrae, for he was under a vow.

(19a)   κατήντησαν   δὲ   εἰς   Ἔφεσον,
        3P.arrived   DE   at   Ephesus

(19b)   κἀκείνους   κατέλιπεν   αὐτοῦ,
        and.those   3S.left   there

(19c)   αὐτὸς δὲ   εἰσελθὼν   εἰς   τὴν   συναγωγὴν   διελέξατο   τοῖς   Ἰουδαίοις.
        he   DE   having.entered into   the   synagogue   3S.debated with.the Jews

(20)   And when they asked him to stay longer, he declined; (21) but on taking leave of them, he said, "I will return to you, if God wills." Then he set sail from Ephesus.

See also the preposed reference to John Mark in Acts 13:13b.

Anticipatory points of departure may be compared with the use of anticipatory contrastive stress in English when referring to a member of a group. For example, when two schoolchildren are asked, "What did you two do today?" and one of them responds, "I studied all day," the implication is, "But he didn't." Similarly, the preposing of reference to one subgroup, when the story develops through the initiative of the other, anticipates the switch of attention to the second subgroup.

Anticipatory points of departure are also found in NT Greek when the story does not develop through the intention of the preposed subject, because this intention is *frustrated* by the intervention of another participant.

This is illustrated in **Acts 27:42**. The reference to the soldiers is preposed (both in the sentence and within the genitive phrase—sec. 4.5) in anticipation of the switch of attention to the centurion who frustrates their plan (v. 43).

(41)   But striking a reef, they ran the ship aground; the bow stuck and remained immovable, but the stern was being broken up by the force of the waves.

(42)   τῶν   δὲ   στρατιωτῶν   βουλὴ   ἐγένετο   ἵνα   τοὺς   δεσμώτας
        of.the DE   soldiers   plan   3S.became that   the   prisoners

        ἀποκτείνωσιν,   μή   τις   ἐκκολυμβήσας   διαφύγῃ.
        3P.should.kill   lest anyone having.swum.away   3S.may.escape

(43a)   ὁ   δὲ   ἑκατοντάρχης βουλόμενος   διασῶσαι   τὸν   Παῦλον
        the   DE   centurion   desiring   to.save   the   Paul

        ἐκώλυσεν   αὐτοὺς   τοῦ   βουλήματος,
        3S.kept   them   from.the plan

Anticipatory points of departure may often be recognized from the following characteristics:[7]
- the referent of the point of departure was involved in the last event described
- there is no action discontinuity with the last event described (i.e., the events concerned are in natural sequence and there is no significant temporal gap between them).

---

[7] The following are additional passages in Acts in which the reference to a subgroup is preposed because the story develops through the activities of some other participant (see Levinsohn 1980:55): 4:36 (see 5:1), 14:2 (see v. 3), 15:32 (see v. 35), 15:39 (τόν Βαρναβᾶν), 16:14 (attention switches to 'a certain maid' in v. 16), 17:18b (see v. 18c), 19:9 (τινες), and 23:8, plus a number of other passages involving μέν.

In other words, the point of departure is apparently unmotivated, so the reader is constrained to interpret it as anticipating a further switch of attention.

Review Question

Under what circumstances is the reference to a subgroup of a group of participants preposed in a sentence?

Suggested Answer

The reference to a subgroup of a group of participants is preposed in a sentence when the story develops, not through the action of that subgroup, but through the initiative of the remaining member(s) of the group. This reference anticipates the switch of attention to the remaining member(s) of the group.

Illustrative Passage 9: Luke 24:28–29

(28a)   And they drew near to the village to which they were going.

(28b)   καὶ <u>αὐτὸς</u> προσεποιήσατο πορρώτερον πορεύεσθαι.
         and he   3S.pretended   farther   to.journey

(29)   And they urged him strongly, saying, "Stay with us, because it is almost evening and the day is now nearly over." So he went in to stay with them.

Question

Why is αὐτὸς preposed in v. 28b?

Suggested Answer

Αὐτὸς is preposed in v. 28b probably because the story develops, not through the action of Jesus (the first subgroup), but through that of the remaining participants, who "frustrate" his apparent intention of going on with his journey.

14
MORE ON REPORTED CONVERSATIONS IN THE SYNOPTIC GOSPELS AND ACTS

This chapter tackles three topics: the use of a form of ἀποκρίνομαι 'answer' to indicate that the new speaker is seeking to take control of the reported conversation or make an authoritative pronouncement (sec. 14.1), the significance of conjoining reported speeches in Matthew's Gospel with asyndeton (sec. 14.2), and the function of speech HPs in Matthew other than those discussed in sec. 14.2 (sec. 14.3).

14.1 Control in Reported Conversations in the Synoptic Gospels and Acts

As I indicated in the introduction to part V, in a tight-knit conversation, the previous addressee takes up the topic of the exchange at the point at which the last speaker left off. However, the previous addressee may seek instead to *take control* of the conversation with an objection or new initiative that typically breaks the tight-knit nature of the exchange.[1] This is reflected in the speech orienter, which often under such circumstances contains a form of ἀποκρίνομαι.

This is illustrated in **Acts 9:10–16**, a conversation that closely parallels that of Acts 10:3–4 (passage 1 of the introduction to part V), until Ananias breaks the tight-knit nature of the exchange by countering with an objection (9:13–14). This objection is introduced with ἀποκρίνομαι.

(10b)   The Lord said to him in a vision, "Ananias."

(10c)   ὁ   δὲ   εἶπεν,
        he   DE   3S.said,
        "Here I am, Lord."

(11–12) ὁ   δὲ   κύριος   πρὸς   αὐτόν,
        the   DE   Lord   to   him,
        "Get up and go to the street called Straight, and at the house of Judas look for a man of Tarsus named Saul..."

(13–14) ἀπεκρίθη   δὲ   Ἀνανίας,
        3S.answered   DE   Ananias,
        "Lord, I have heard from many about this man, how much evil he has done to your saints in Jerusalem..."

(15–16) εἶπεν   δὲ   πρὸς   αὐτὸν   ὁ   κύριος,
        3S.said   DE   to   him   the Lord,
        "Go, for he is an instrument whom I have chosen..."

(17a)   So Ananias went and entered the house.

Notice, incidentally, that, following Ananias' counter of vv. 13–14, the speech of vv. 15–16 achieves the goal of the exchange, so the orienter begins with a verb. In contrast, the speech that should have attained that goal (vv. 11–12) but was frustrated by Ananias' counter is treated as an intermediate step. Although the speech of vv. 11–12 does not attain the goal of the conversation, a full noun phrase is used, as befits a key speech—sec. 8.2.

Ἀποκρίνομαι may be used even when the participant who is seeking to take control was not the addressee of a previous speech. The stimulus may be non-verbal, as in **Acts 3:12**.

(11)   While he clung to Peter and John, all the people ran together to them in the portico called Solomon's Portico, utterly astonished.

---

[1] I would like to acknowledge my indebtedness to Tony Pope (p.c.) for his insightful observations about the function of ἀποκρίνομαι in speech orienters. A number of his suggestions have been incorporated into this section.

(12)   ἰδὼν   δὲ   ὁ   Πέτρος ἀπεκρίνατο πρὸς τὸν λαόν,
        having.seen DE the Peter   3S.answered to   the   people

In Acts, the form of ἀποκρίνομαι that is most commonly used to signal attempts to take control is a finite verb (see below for exceptions). In *Matthew*'s Gospel, however, it is much more common for a participial form of ἀποκρίνομαι plus εἶπεν to be used. This is illustrated in **Matt. 21:24** where, rather than replying to the question addressed to him, Jesus takes control of the conversation by countering with another question.

(23)   ... the chief priests and the elders of the people came to him as he was teaching and said, "By what authority are you doing these things and who gave you this authority?"

(24)   ἀποκριθεὶς δὲ   ὁ   Ἰησοῦς εἶπεν   αὐτοῖς,
        answering   DE the Jesus   3S.said   to.them,
        "I also will ask you a question; if you tell me the answer, then I will also tell you by what authority I do these things..."

In **Matt. 14:28**, it is a specific member of the group of previous addressees who takes control and gives a significant response to a speech that had been addressed to the group as a whole.

(27)   Immediately Jesus spoke to them, saying, "Take heart! It is I; do not be afraid."

(28)   ἀποκριθεὶς δὲ   αὐτῷ ὁ   Πέτρος εἶπεν,
        answering   DE to.him the Peter   3S.said,
        "Lord, if it is you, command me to come to you on the water."

I now address the question of when a finite form of ἀποκρίνομαι is used alone over against the aorist participle ἀποκριθεὶς plus εἶπεν. This varies from book to book.

In *Acts*, the combination of the participle plus εἶπεν is used sparingly. Typically, it is accompanied by a full noun phrase reference to the subject. With one exception (see below), it is used when the counter or new initiative concerned would not have been expected. Furthermore, this counter or new initiative is decisive in determining the outcome of the exchange (contrast Acts 9:13–14 above). It seems reasonable, therefore, to assume that the longer form of the speech orienter has been chosen to highlight the speech.[2]

In **Acts 19:15**, for instance, the evil spirit would have been expected to comply with the exorcists' adjuration. Instead, it takes control of the situation and determines the outcome of the exchange.

(13)   Then some itinerant Jewish exorcists tried to use the name of the Lord Jesus over those who had evil spirits, saying, "I adjure you by the Jesus whom Paul proclaims."

(14)   Seven sons of a Jewish high priest named Sceva were doing this.

(15)   ἀποκριθὲν δὲ   τὸ   πνεῦμα τὸ   πονηρὸν εἶπεν   αὐτοῖς,
        answering   DE the   spirit   the   evil   3S.said   to.them,
        "Jesus I know, and Paul I know; but who are you?"

(16)   Then the man with the evil spirit leaped on them, mastered them all, and so overpowered them that they fled out of the house naked and wounded.

After the high priest's assertion of **Acts 5:28**, the apostles would have been expected either to stay silent or to offer some excuse for their conduct. Instead, they counter with a decisive appeal to higher authority for what they are doing (vv. 29ff.). This largely determines the outcome of the trial (see Gamaliel's warning in v. 39 that the authorities might be found to be fighting against God if they put the apostles to death).

---

[2] Pope (p.c.) considers that the longer form of the speech orienter is used not to highlight the content of the speech, but to mark the fact that a reply is being made at all.

(27b)   The high priest questioned them, (28) saying, "We gave you strict orders not to teach in this name, yet here you have filled Jerusalem with your teaching and you are determined to bring this man's blood on us."

(29)   ἀποκριθεὶς   δὲ   Πέτρος καὶ οἱ ἀπόστολοι εἶπαν,
answering   DE Peter   and the apostles   3P.said,
"We must obey God rather than any human authority…"

See also Acts 4:19.

In Acts 25:9, Festus would have been expected to reach a verdict on the charges brought against Paul. Instead, "wishing to do the Jews a favor," he counters with the suggestion that the case be transferred to Jerusalem. This speech is decisive in determining the outcome of the trial, in that it forces Paul to appeal to Caesar (vv. 10–11).

I turn now to **Acts 8:34**—an exception to the above pattern, in that the eunuch would be expected to initiate the conversation once Philip joined him. Nevertheless, his speech is decisive in that it determines how Philip will respond (he starts with the same Scripture—v. 35). In addition, it is possible that the combination of ἀποκριθείς and εἶπεν is used because of the extensive quotation from Scripture (vv. 32–33) that interrupts the event line. A form of ἀποκρίνομαι would be appropriate because the eunuch takes the initiative when the event line is resumed.

(31b)   And he invited Philip to get in and sit beside him.
(32)   Now the passage of the scripture that he was reading was this…

(34)   Ἀποκριθεὶς   δὲ ὁ   εὐνοῦχος τῷ   Φιλίππῳ εἶπεν,
answering   DE the eunuch to.the Philip   3S.said,
"About whom, may I ask you, does the prophet say this, about himself or about someone else?"

The authoritative pronouncement to the Jerusalem Council by James (Acts 15:13–21) is introduced in v. 13 with ἀπεκρίθη Ἰάκωβος λέγων (James answered saying). A possible parallel between this pronouncement and "covenant statements in Genesis [that] receive special marking with the infinitive construct le'mor" (van den Berg p.c.) may be intended (see BDF §420).

When a form of ἀποκρίνομαι is used in a speech orienter in *Luke*, it is usually as a participle, as in 1:35 and 10:27 (passages 3 and 1 of sec. 13.1). Exceptions are found in 13:15 and 17:20 (ἀπεκρίθη καὶ εἶπεν 'answered and said'), 20:7 (ἀπεκρίθησαν with indirect speech—used to indicate that the authorities have ceased to deliberate among themselves and are now answering Jesus), and 3:16 (ἀπεκρίνατο λέγων 'answered about himself saying'—an authoritative pronouncement), plus 4:4 and 8:50 (ἀπεκρίθη—in both instances, some MSS add λέγων). In every passage except 20:7, the speaker responds to a verbal or non-verbal stimulus by attempting to take control of the conversation. There are insufficient examples to propose reasons for using most of the less common orienters that have been noted in this paragraph.

Mark is like Luke, in that, when a form of ἀποκρίνομαι is used in a speech orienter, it is usually a participle, as in 3:33 (UBS text) and 10:51 (with λέγει or εἶπεν), 9:19 and 6:37 (preceded by an articular pronoun and with λέγει or εἶπεν). It is used as a main verb in 8:4, 9:17 (UBS text) and 12:29, plus 7:28 (ἡ δὲ ἀπεκρίθη καὶ λέγει αὐτῷ 'but she answered and says to him') and 15:9 (ὁ δὲ Πιλᾶτος ἀπεκρίθη αὐτοῖς λέγων 'but Pilate answered them, saying'). It is possible that, when the orienter begins with a reference to the speaker, the speech is viewed as an intermediate step. Research is needed to determine the significance of each orienter.

In *Matthew*, the combination of a finite form of ἀποκρίνομαι plus λέγων is generally *not* used for formal pronouncements (see 12:38, 25:9, 25:37, 25:44 and 25:45—all but one of these instances follow τότε). Nevertheless, the speeches so introduced do represent attempts by the speaker to take control of the conversation. As I noted above, it is far more common in Matthew for the participial form ἀποκριθείς to be used in speech orienters, whether followed by a noun phrase reference to the speaker (as in 21:24 and 14:28 above) or preceded by an articular pronoun.

The combination of an articular pronoun and ἀποκριθείς in Matthew most commonly introduces the *second* speech of a conversation. It is used to reject a proposal, correction or suggestion (stated or implied), as in **Matt. 16:2**.

(1)   The Pharisees and Sadducees came and to test him they asked him to show them a sign from heaven.

(2-4) ὁ   δὲ   ἀποκριθεὶς εἶπεν   αὐτοῖς,
       he   DE   answering   3S.said   to.them,
       "When it is evening, you say, 'It will be fair weather...'... An evil and adulterous generation asks for a sign, but no sign will be given to it except the sign of Jonah."

Other examples are found in Matt. 12:39, 15:3, 15:13, 15:24, 15:26, 19:4, 20:13, 24:2 (UBS text), 25:12, and 26:23.

The combination of an articular pronoun and ἀποκριθείς is used also to introduce an authoritative answer to a request for information, as in **Matt. 13:37**.

(36b) And his disciples approached him, saying, "Explain to us the parable of the weeds of the field."

(37)   ὁ   δὲ   ἀποκριθεὶς εἶπεν,
       he   DE   answering   3S.said,
       "The one who sows the good seed is the Son of man..."

Other examples are found in Matt. 13:11, 17:11 (UBS text), and 26:66b.

Pope (p.c.) points out that most of the examples in Matthew in which the articular pronoun precedes ἀποκριθείς introduce speeches by a participant "with natural presupposed authority," such as Jesus. Nevertheless, the combination may be used even when the speaker does not naturally have such authority, provided he or she is attempting to take control of the conversation. In **Matt. 21:29a**, for example, the son does not have natural authority over his father, but is still attempting to be dominant in the conversation (see also v. 30b).

(28b) A man had two sons; he went to the first and said, "Son, go and work in the vineyard today."

(29a) ὁ   δὲ   ἀποκριθεὶς εἶπεν,   Οὐ   θέλω.
       he   DE   answering   3S.said,   not   I.want

(29b) Later, however, he changed his mind and went.

Review Questions

(a) What is indicated by the presence in a speech orienter of a form of ἀποκρίνομαι?
(b) In Acts, under what circumstances is a combination of ἀποκριθείς and εἶπεν typically used, rather than a finite form of ἀποκρίνομαι? Does it have the same function in Matthew?

Suggested Answers

(a) The presence in a speech orienter of a form of ἀποκρίνομαι indicates that the speaker, while responding to a verbal or non-verbal stimulus, is seeking to take control of the conversation.
(b) In Acts, a combination of ἀποκριθείς and εἶπεν, rather than a finite form of ἀποκρίνομαι, typically is used when the counter or new initiative concerned would not have been expected. In Matthew, however, this combination is the normal way of indicating that the new speaker is attempting to take control of the conversation.

Illustrative Passage 1: Acts 8:18–24

Note the form of the non-initial speech orienters in this passage.

(18)   Now when Simon saw that the Spirit was given through the laying on of the apostles' hands, he offered them money, (19) saying, "Give me also this authority so that anyone on whom I lay my hands may receive the Holy Spirit."

(20)   Πέτρος   δὲ   εἶπεν   πρὸς   αὐτόν,
          Peter   DE   3S.said   to   him,
          "May your silver perish with you, because you thought you could obtain God's gift with money! (21) You have no part or share in this, for your heart is not right before God. (22) Repent therefore of this wickedness of yours, and pray to the Lord that, if possible, the intent of your heart may be forgiven you. (23) For I see that you are in the gall of bitterness and the chains of wickedness."

(24)   ἀποκριθεὶς   δὲ   ὁ   Σίμων   εἶπεν,
          answering   DE   the   Simon   3S.said,
          "Pray for me to the Lord, that nothing of what you have said may happen to me."

Questions

(a) According to the principles of sec. 13.2, why does the orienter to the speech of vv. 20–23 begin with a reference to the speaker?
(b) Why is a form of ἀποκρίνομαι used in the orienter to the speech of v. 24?
(c) What is suggested by the use of the longer form of speech orienter in v. 24?

Answers

(a) According to the principles of sec. 13.2, the orienter to the speech of vv. 20–23 begins with a reference to the speaker because the speech is but an intermediate step in the exchange.
(b) A form of ἀποκρίνομαι is used in the orienter to the speech of v. 24 to indicate that Simon attempted to take control of the conversation.
(c) The longer form of the speech orienter suggests that Simon's reply has been highlighted because it was unexpected. (Simon's subsequent attitude to Christianity may have made it so unexpected. Alternatively, inaccurate stories about the outcome of the incident described here may have been circulating.)

14.2   Asyndeton in Reported Conversations in Matthew's Gospel

In sec. 5.3 we saw that asyndeton was a nondevelopmental way of conjoining sentences in John's Gospel. It is also used to conjoin reported speeches in Matthew's Gospel when the response to the speech concerned does not develop the conversation because it is *expected* or *predictable*. What is potentially confusing is that, when asyndeton conjoins reported speeches in Matthew, the speech orienter concerned is often in the historical present (HP).

The response of **Matt. 17:25a**, for example, does not represent a new development in the conversation because the question of v. 24b expected a positive answer (Porter 1992:278). The speech of v. 25a is conjoined to the previous speech with asyndeton and the orienter is in the HP.

(24a)   When they reached Capernaum, the collectors of the temple tax came to Peter

(24b)   καὶ   εἶπαν,   Ὁ   διδάσκαλος   ὑμῶν   οὐ   τελεῖ   [τὰ]   δίδραχμα;
          and   3P.said   the   teacher   your   not   3S.pays   the   two.drachma

(25a)   Ø   λέγει,   Ναί.
                3S.says   yes

See also Matt. 9:28b (following a speech introduced in v. 28a with καὶ λέγει—sec. 14.3), 13:51b (sec. 13.2), and 26:25b (Jesus agrees with what Judas has proposed).

Fanning (1990:233) has suggested that verbs like λέγει "occur in a stereotyped use." Since no orienter in Matthew's Gospel begins with asyndeton and εἶπεν, it is not unreasonable to consider that, when it is appropriate to begin a speech orienter with asyndeton, the HP is automatically used as well. In the following discussion, I shall therefore focus on the use of asyndeton to conjoin reported speeches, rather than on the HP.

Asyndeton is used to conjoin speeches when the response concerned is *predictable* and, therefore, does not represent a new development in the conversation. This is illustrated in **Matt. 20:33**; the blind men's reply to Jesus' question is predictable.

(31b)   but they shouted even more loudly, "Have mercy on us, Lord, Son of David!"

(32a)   And having stopped, Jesus called them

(32b)   καὶ   εἶπεν,   Τί   θέλετε   ποιήσω   ὑμῖν;
         and   3S.said what you.wish I.may.do for.you

(33)   Ø λέγουσιν αὐτῷ,   Κύριε, ἵνα   ἀνοιγῶσιν   οἱ   ὀφθαλμοὶ   ἡμῶν.
         3P.say   to.him   Lord   that 3P.be.opened the   eyes   our

(34)   Moved with compassion (δέ), Jesus touched their eyes and immediately they regained their sight and followed him.

See also Matt. 22:42b (below).

If a response to an initial speech is conjoined with asyndeton and this is followed by a final speech by the first speaker which represents the goal to which the initial interaction was leading, then this speech also is conjoined with asyndeton. This is illustrated in **Matt. 22:43**; the reason that Jesus asks the question of v. 42a is in order to lead up to the assertion of v. 43.

(41)   Now while the Pharisees were gathered together, Jesus asked them a question, (42a) saying, "What do you think of the Messiah? Whose son is he?"

(42b)   Ø λέγουσιν   αὐτῷ,
         3P.say   to.him,
         "The son of David."

(43)   Ø λέγει   αὐτοῖς,
         3S.says   to.them,
         "How is it then that David by the Spirit calls him Lord..."

See also Matt. 20:7a-b (following an initial speech introduced with καὶ λέγει), 21:31b-c, and 21:41-42. Matthew 22:21a-b is similar (following an initial speech introduced with καὶ λέγει), except that τότε is used to highlight the final speech (sec. 14.3).

We turn now to *multi-round* conversations in which non-initial rounds are conjoined with asyndeton. This happens when the intention of the speaker remains the same as the new round begins, so no development occurs between the rounds.

For example, **Matt. 16:15** follows an initial round that consists of a question and answer, the answer of which is introduced with an articular pronoun since the content of the answer is not predictable from the question. As the second round begins, Jesus' original intention remains unchanged, so his speech is introduced with asyndeton.[3]

(13)   Now when Jesus came into the district of Caesarea Philippi, he was asking (ἠρώτα) his disciples, "Who do people say that the Son of Man is?"

---

[3] Pope (p.c.) suggests that the HP is used to highlight the reply of v. 16 because of its significance.

(14)   οἱ   δὲ   εἶπαν,
       they DE   3P.said,
       "Some say John the Baptist, but others Elijah, and still others Jeremiah or one of the
       prophets."

(15)   Ø λέγει   αὐτοῖς,
          3S.says to.them,
       "But who do you say that I am?"

(16)   ἀποκριθεὶς   δὲ   Σίμων Πέτρος   εἶπεν,
       answering   DE   Simon Peter   3S.said,
       "You are the Messiah, the Son of the living God."

Matthew 27:22 provides two examples of asyndeton conjoining reported speeches. The first (v. 22a) introduces the second round of an exchange between Pilate and the crowd. Verse 20 has already stated what the intention of the Jewish authorities is (that Barabbas be released and Jesus be destroyed), and this intention remains unchanged as the second round begins, hence the use of asyndeton. The response of v. 22b is predictable from v. 20, so does not represent a new development. (Subsequent rounds of the exchange are presented with the default strategy, as they represent further developments in the conversation.)[4]

(20)   Now the chief priests and the elders persuaded the crowds to ask for Barabbas and to have
       Jesus killed.

(21a) In response, the governor said to them, "Which of the two do you want me to release for
       you?"

(21b) οἱ   δὲ   εἶπαν, Τὸν   Βαραββᾶν.
       they DE   3P.said the   Barabbas

(22a) Ø λέγει   αὐτοῖς   ὁ   Πιλᾶτος,
          3S.says to.them the Pilate,
       "Then what should I do with Jesus who is called the Messiah?"

(22b) Ø λέγουσιν   πάντες,
          3P.say   everyone,
       "Let him be crucified!"

(23a) ὁ   δὲ   ἔφη,
       he   DE   3S.said,
       "Why, what evil has he done?"

Asyndeton is sometimes used to link reported speeches when the response concerned is introduced with the aorist of φημί "say yes, affirm, assert, maintain, assure" (Liddell & Scott 1901:1665). This verb is often used when a speaker restates a position, so it is natural that it should be accompanied by asyndeton, since such a restatement will often not constitute a further development in the conversation.

For example, in **Matt. 26:34**, Jesus reaffirms the position he took earlier in the conversation (v. 31), so his speech is not viewed as a new development. Peter's speech is not viewed as a new development, either, since it likewise reaffirms the position he stated in v. 33.[5]

(31-32) Then Jesus says to them, "You will all become deserters because of me this night..."

(33)   ἀποκριθεὶς   δὲ   ὁ   Πέτρος   εἶπεν   αὐτῷ,
       answering   DE   the Peter   3S.said to.him,
       "Though they all become deserters because of you, I will never desert you."

---

[4] The default strategy may have been used in Matt. 27:21b because the response of the crowds was not entirely predictable (the reader could not be certain in advance that they would do as the authorities had counseled them).

[5] Pope (p.c.) suggests that the HP is used in v. 35a to highlight "the emotional tone of Peter's speech."

(34)   Ø ἔφη   αὐτῷ   ὁ   Ἰησοῦς,
        3S.affirmed to.him the Jesus,
        "Truly I tell you, this very night... you will deny me three times."

(35a)   Ø λέγει   αὐτῷ   ὁ   Πέτρος,
        3S.says   to.him the Peter,
        "Even though I must die with you, I will not deny you."

See also Matt. 21:27b, in which Jesus reaffirms the position he stated in v. 24.

In **Matt. 27:65** (UBS text), the new speaker, Pilate, does no more than agree to the request of the previous speakers. In other words, his speech is not viewed as a new development in the story, so the speech is conjoined by asyndeton, while ἔφη conveys the idea of confirmation. (If δέ is read, then Pilate's response is viewed as a further development within the conversation. The translation given in the NRSV margin, "Take a guard of soldiers..." would lend itself to being interpreted as a new development.)

(62)   The next day... the chief priests and the Pharisees gathered before Pilate (63) and said, "Sir, we remember what that impostor said while he was still alive, 'After three days I will rise again.' (64) Therefore command the tomb to be made secure..."

(65)   Ø* ἔφη   αὐτοῖς ὁ Πιλᾶτος,   (*variant: δέ)
        3S.affirmed to.them the Pilate,
        "You have a guard of soldiers; go, make it as secure as you can."

See also Matt. 25:23, in which the affirmation of v. 21 is repeated.[6]

Review Questions

(a) When reported speeches are conjoined by asyndeton, what does this indicate?
(b) When non-initial rounds of a multi-round conversation begin with asyndeton, what does this indicate?

Suggested Answers

(a) When reported speeches are conjoined by asyndeton, this indicates that the response concerned does not represent a new development in the conversation, because it is expected or predictable.
(b) When non-initial rounds of a multi-round conversation begin with asyndeton, this indicates that the new round does not represent a new development in the conversation, because the speaker's intention remains unchanged.

Illustrative Passage 2: Matthew 19:16–22

Note the use of asyndeton in vv. 18a, 20, and 21.

(16)   Then someone, approaching him, said (εἶπεν), "Teacher, what good deed must I do to have eternal life?"

(17)   ὁ   δὲ εἶπεν   αὐτῷ,
        he DE 3S.said   to.him,
        "Why do you ask me about what is good? There is only one who is good. If you wish to enter into life, keep the commandments."

(18a)   Ø λέγει*   αὐτῷ, Ποίας;   (*variant: φήσιν)
        3S.says   to.him which.ones

---

[6] In Matt. 25:21, many MSS read δέ, rather than asyndeton. The asyndeton readings in vv. 21 and 22 would indicate that the story develops only as the third servant approaches (v. 24).

(18b) ὁ   δὲ   Ἰησοῦς εἶπεν,
the   DE   Jesus 3S.said,
"You shall not murder; You shall not commit adultery..."

(20) Ø λέγει   αὐτῷ   ὁ   νεανίσκος,
3S.says   to.him the young.man,
"I have kept all these; what do I still lack?"

(21) Ø ἔφη*   αὐτῷ   ὁ   Ἰησοῦ, (*variant: λέγει)
3S.affirms to.him the Jesus,
"If you wish to be perfect, go, sell your possessions, and give the money to the poor, and you will have treasure in heaven; then come, follow me."

(22) Hearing δέ this word, the young man went away grieving, for he had many possessions.

Questions

(a) Why is asyndeton appropriate in vv. 18a and 20?

(b) What does the use of asyndeton in v. 21 suggest?

Suggested Answers

(a) Asyndeton is appropriate in vv. 18a and 20 because the speeches concerned begin non-initial rounds of a multi-round conversation and the intention of the young man remains the same in each round, viz., to find out how to have eternal life.

(b) The use of asyndeton in v. 21 suggests that Jesus' reply does not represent a further development in the story. The exchange has been concerned with the young man's persistence in finding out how to have eternal life. It is appropriate, therefore, that the next development in the story is his response (v. 22), especially as the next development concerns Jesus' comments of vv. 23–24 about how hard it will be for a rich person to enter the kingdom of heaven.

Passage 3: Matthew 4:3–7

Note the orienters employed in the non-initial speeches of the following passages.

(3)   And having approached, the tempter said to him,
"If you are the Son of God, command these stones to become loaves of bread."

(4)   ὁ   δὲ   ἀποκριθεὶς εἶπεν,
he   DE   answering 3S.said,
"It is written, 'One does not live by bread alone, but by every word that comes from the mouth of God.'"

(5)   Then the devil takes him to the holy city and placed him on the pinnacle of the temple,

(6)   and says to him, "If you are the Son of God, throw yourself down; for it is written..."

(7)   Ø ἔφη   αὐτῷ   ὁ   Ἰησοῦς,
3S.affirmed to.him the Jesus,
"Again, it is written, 'Do not put the Lord your God to the test.'"

Questions

(a) What is the significance of beginning the speech orienter of v. 4 with an articular pronoun plus ἀποκριθείς?

(b) Why is it appropriate for the speech of v. 7 to be conjoined with asyndeton?

Suggested Answers: see Appendix under 14(3).

Passage 4: Matthew 20:20–23

(20)   Then the mother of the sons of Zebedee came to him with her sons and, kneeling before him, asked a favor of him.

(21a)   ὁ   δὲ   εἶπεν   αὐτῇ,   Τί   θέλεις;
        he   DE   3S.said to.her, what you.wish

(21b)   Ø   λέγει   αὐτῷ,
             3S.says   to.him,
        "Declare that these two sons of mine will sit, one at your right hand and one at your left, in your kingdom."

(22a)   ἀποκριθεὶς   δὲ   ὁ   ᾿Ιησοῦς   εἶπεν,
        answering   DE   the Jesus   3S.said,
        "You do not know what you are asking. Are you able to drink the cup that I am about to drink?"

(22b)   Ø   λέγουσιν   αὐτῷ,   Δυνάμεθα.
             3P.say   to.him, we.are.able

(23)   Ø*   λέγει   αὐτοῖς,   (*variant: καί)
             3S.says   to.them,
        "You will indeed drink my cup, but to sit at my right hand and at my left, this is not mine to grant..."

Questions

(a) Why is it appropriate to conjoin the speech of v. 21b with asyndeton?
(b) Why does the speech orienter of v. 22a begin with ἀποκριθείς?
(c) Why are the speeches of vv. 22b and 23 (UBS text) conjoined with asyndeton?

Suggested Answers: see Appendix under 14(4).

14.3   Speech Verbs in the Historical Present in Matthew

We turn now to the remaining instances of speech HPs in Matthew's Gospel, viz., those that follow a conjunction such as καί, τότε or, occasionally, δέ. Such speech HPs are *cataphoric*, in that they point forward to one or more significant events that are the result of or follow from the speech.

In **Matt. 28:10**, for instance, τότε introduces and highlights Jesus' concluding speech, while the HP points forward to the events that follow from that speech, viz., the disciples going to Galilee (v. 16) and Jesus' final command to them (vv. 18–20).

(8)   So they left the tomb quickly with fear and great joy, and ran to tell his disciples.

(9a)   καὶ   ἰδοὺ   ᾿Ιησοῦς   ὑπήντησεν   αὐταῖς   λέγων,   Χαίρετε.
        and   behold Jesus   3S.met   them   saying   hello

(9b)   αἱ   δὲ   προσελθοῦσαι   ἐκράτησαν   αὐτοῦ   τοὺς   πόδας
        they   DE   approaching   3P.held   his   the   feet

(9c)   καὶ   προσεκύνησαν   αὐτῷ.
        and   3P.worshipped   him

(10)   τότε   λέγει   αὐταῖς   ὁ   ᾿Ιησοῦς,
        then   3S.says   to.them   the Jesus,
        "Do not be afraid; go and tell my brothers to go to Galilee; there they will see me."

{11–15 describe what happened when the guard at the tomb reported to the chief priests.}

(16)   Now (δέ) The eleven disciples went to Galilee, to the mountain to which Jesus had directed them.

Other passages in which τότε introduces and highlights a concluding speech, while the speech HP points forward to the result of that speech, include Matt. 4:10 (Jesus says, "Go away, Satan," and the devil leaves him—v. 11), 9:37-38 (Jesus tells the disciples to ask the Lord of the harvest to send out laborers into his harvest, and he sent the twelve out—10:5), and 26:52-54 (see v. 56). See also 9:6 and 12:13 and, following two speeches introduced with asyndeton and a HP (sec. 14.2), 22:21b.

Sometimes the first verb of a subsection that begins with τότε is λέγει. A speech that is introduced in this way is significant in its own right in that it represents a new initiative on the part of the speaker, usually in the light of the preceding events. At the same time, the resulting event(s) are even more significant than the speech (see sec. 13.1 on the tendency for nonverbal events to be more important than the reported speeches that lead to them). This is illustrated in **Matt. 22:8.**

(7)   So the king became angry and, having sent his troops, destroyed (ἀπώλεσεν) those murderers and burned (ἐνέπρησεν) their city.

(8)   τότε   λέγει   τοῖς   δούλοις   αὐτοῦ,
        then   3S.says   to.the   slaves   his,
        "The wedding is ready, but those invited were not worthy. (9) Go therefore..."

(10)   And, having gone out into the streets, those servants gathered together (συνήγαγον) all whom they found, both good and bad;...

Other examples in which a subsection begins with τότε and a speech HP are found in Matt. 15:12, 18:32, 26:31, 26:38, and 27:13.

Speech HPs are frequently conjoined by καί to a preceding clause whose verb may itself be in the HP (Matt. 26:36, 26:40, 26:45—see discussion in sec. 12.2.1), or else be in the imperfect or aorist. Once again, a speech that is introduced in this way may represent a significant initiative on the part of the speaker. However, the resulting event(s) are even more significant than the speech. See, for example, **Matt. 9:9.**

(9a)   And, going away from there, Jesus saw (εἶδεν) a man called Matthew sitting at the tax booth;

(9b)   καὶ   λέγει   αὐτῷ,   Ἀκολούθει   μοι.
        and   3S.says   to.him   follow   me

(9c)   And rising he followed (ἠκολούθησεν) him.

See also Matt. 4:19, 9:28b, 14:31b, 21:19, and 22:20.

In the case of **Matt. 20:6,** the use of a HP instead of the aorist, which was used on the previous occasions that the landowner went to hire laborers (vv. 4-5), is clearly cataphoric. This cataphoric effect is strengthened even more when another HP is used in v. 8 (see sec. 14.2 on the use of the HPs with asyndeton in v. 7).

(3)   When he went out about nine o'clock, he saw (εἶδεν) others standing idle in the market place; (4) and he said (εἶπεν) to them, "You also go into the vineyard, and I will pay you whatever is right." So they went (ἀπῆλθον). (5) When he went out again about noon and about three o'clock, he did (ἐποίησεν) likewise.

(6a)   And about five o'clock when he went out he found (εὗρεν) others standing around

(6b)   καὶ   λέγει   αὐτοῖς,
        and   3S.says   to.them,
        "Why are you standing here idle all day?"

(7a)   Ø λέγουσιν αὐτῷ,
        3P.say   to.him,
        "Because no one has hired us."

(7b)   Ø λέγει   αὐτοῖς,
        3S.says   to.them,
        "You also go into the vineyard."

(8)   ὀψίας δὲ γενομένης λέγει ὁ κύριος τοῦ ἀμπελῶνος
        evening DE having.come 3S.says the owner of.the vineyard

        τῷ   ἐπιτρόπῳ αὐτοῦ,
        to.the foreman   his,
        "Call the laborers and give them their pay, beginning with the last and then going to the
        first."

(9)   When those hired about five o'clock came, each received (ἔλαβον) a denarius.

See also Matt. 8:26a (the HP points forward to the concluding event of v. 26b, which is introduced
with τότε), as well as the pair of speeches in 15:33–34a (pointing forward, presumably, to the events of
vv. 35ff.). 14:17 (introduced with οἱ δὲ λέγουσιν) is similar. See 8:7 (UBS text—some MSS omit καί)
for a further example in which the HP is cataphoric, pointing forward to the response of the centurion in
vv. 8–9.

On other occasions, however, the speech that is introduced with the HP is highly significant. A
particularly clear example (though not involving καὶ λέγει) is in **Matt. 14:8**, where the position of
φησίν in the middle of the speech further highlights what it is that the daughter of Herodias wishes to be
given (notice, too, the marked order of constituents—sec. 3.5).

(6)   But when Herod's birthday came, the daughter of Herodias danced (ὠρχήσατο) before the
        company, and it pleased (ἤρεσεν) Herod, (7) wherefore with an oath he promised
        (ὡμολόγησεν) to grant her whatever she might ask.

(8)   ἡ   δὲ προβιβασθεῖσα ὑπὸ τῆς μητρὸς αὐτῆς,
        she DE prompted   by   the   mother   her

        Δός μοι, φησίν, ὧδε ἐπὶ πίνακι τὴν κεφαλὴν Ἰωάννου τοῦ βαπτιστοῦ.
        Give me 3S.affirms here on platter the head   of.John   the   Baptist

(9)   And, though the king was grieved, yet out of regard for his oaths and for the guests, he
        commanded (ἐκέλευσεν) that it be given.

There remain a few passages in which a HP introduces the *concluding* speech of an episode and it is
perhaps less obvious that it is used cataphorically. I examine these passages in turn.

The speech HPs of **Matt. 21:13** and **21:16** are probably cataphoric, pointing forward to a further
confrontation between Jesus and the religious authorities, viz., that of 21:23ff (on the barren fig tree as
relating to the same theme, see Hendriksen 1974:774).

(12)   And Jesus entered (εἰσῆλθεν Ἰησοῦς) into the temple and threw out (ἐξέβαλεν) all who
        were selling and buying in the temple, and he overturned (κατέστρεψεν) the tables of the
        money changers and the seats of those who sold doves.

(13)   καὶ λέγει   αὐτοῖς,
        and 3S.says to.them,
        "It is written, 'My house shall be called a house of prayer'; but you are making it a den of
        robbers."

(14)   And the blind and lame approached (προσῆλθον) him in the temple, and he cured
        (ἐθεράπευσεν) them. (15) But when the chief priests and the scribes saw the amazing
        things that he did and the children crying out in the temple, "Hosanna to the Son of

David," they became angry (ἠγανάκτησαν) (16) and said (εἶπαν) to him, "Do you hear what these are saying?"

(16b)   ὁ   δὲ   Ἰησοῦς   λέγει   αὐτοῖς,
the   DE   Jesus   3S.says   to.them,
"Yes, have you never read, 'Out of the mouths of infants and nursing babies you have prepared praise for yourself'?"

(17)   And, having left them, he went out (ἐξῆλθεν) of the city to Bethany and spent the night (ηὐλίσθη) there.

{18–22 relate the cursing of the fig tree}

(23)   And, when he entered the temple, the chief priests and the elders of the people approached (προσῆλθον) him while he was teaching, saying, "By what authority are you doing these things, and who gave you this authority?"

The speech HP of **Matt. 8:20** may also be interpreted as cataphoric, pointing forward to the exchange of vv. 21–22 (see sec. 5.1 on the use of καί in vv. 18–20). However, if the UBS text is followed in v. 22, it is not clear to what that HP is pointing (some MSS have εἶπεν instead of λέγει in v. 22).

(19)   And, having approached, a scribe said (εἶπεν) to him,
"Teacher, I will follow you wherever you go."

(20)   καὶ   λέγει   αὐτῷ   ὁ   Ἰησοῦς,
and   3S.says   to.him   the   Jesus,
"Foxes have holes, and birds of the air have nests; but the Son of Man has nowhere to lay his head."

(21)   And <u>another</u> of <u>the/his</u> disciples said (εἶπεν) to him,
"Lord, let me first go and bury my father."

(22)   ὁ   δὲ   Ἰησοῦς   λέγει   αὐτῷ,
the   DE   Jesus   3S.says   to.him,
"Follow me, and let the dead bury their own dead."

Matthew 17:20 presents a similar problem (the UBS text reads ὁ δὲ λέγει, while some MSS read εἶπεν, most of them with the addition of Ἰησοῦς).

Finally, **Matt. 8:4** also introduces a concluding speech with a HP. If the HP is cataphoric, then it presumably points forward to the prophecy of 8:17 (Allen (1907:73) groups together 8:1–17 as "three miracles of healing;" see sec. 5.1 on Matthew relating 8:14–16 to show that this prophecy was fulfilled by Jesus' actions).

(3b)   And immediately his leprosy was cleansed (ἐκαθαρίσθη).

(4)   καὶ   λέγει   αὐτῷ   ὁ   Ἰησοῦς,
and   3S.says   to.him   the   Jesus,
"See that you say nothing to anyone; but go, show yourself to the priest, and offer the gift that Moses commanded, as a testimony to them."

{5–13 concern the centurion who asks Jesus to heal his servant; they conclude:}

(13b)   And the servant was healed (ἰάθη) that very hour.

{14–15 concern the healing of Peter's mother-in-law.}

(16)   And when evening had come, they brought (προσήνεγκαν) to him many who were possessed with demons; and he cast out (ἐξέβαλεν) the spirits with a word, and cured (ἐθεράπευσεν) all who were sick.

(17)   Thus was fulfilled (ὅπως πληρωθῇ) what had been spoken through the prophet Isaiah, "He bore our infirmities and bore our diseases."

I conclude that, with the exception of two passages with variant readings, all occurrences of speech HPs in Matthew's Gospel have cataphoric overtones.

Review Questions

(a) When a concluding speech is introduced with τότε and a HP, what does this indicate?
(b) When an episode ends with a speech that is introduced with a HP, what does this indicate?

Suggested Answers

(a) When a concluding speech is introduced with τότε and a HP, τότε highlights the speech, while the HP points forward to subsequent event(s), such as the result of the speech.
(b) When an episode ends with a speech that is introduced with a HP, the HP is pointing forward to a later episode.

Note the use of the HP in the following passages and answer the questions.

Illustrative Passage 5: Matthew 13:27–30 (UBS text)

(27)   And the slaves of the householder, approaching, said (εἶπον) to him, "Master, did you not sow good seed in your field? Where, then, did these weeds come from?"

(28a) He affirmed (ἔφη), "An enemy has done this."

(28b) οἱ   δὲ   δοῦλοι   λέγουσιν   αὐτῷ,
       the   DE   slaves   3P.say   to.him,
       "Then do you want us to go and gather them?"

(29)   ὁ   δὲ   φησιν,
       he   DE   3S.affirms,
       "No; for in gathering the weeds you would uproot the wheat along with them. (30) Let both of them grow together until the harvest; and at harvest time I will tell the reapers, Collect the weeds first and bind them in bundles to be burned, but gather the wheat into my barn."

Question

Why are HPs used in Matt. 13:28b and 29?

Suggested Answer

According to the analysis presented in this section, the HPs in Matt. 13:28b and 29 are used cataphorically; they presumably point forward to the interpretation of the parable given in vv. 36–43.

Passage 6: Matthew 22:11–13

(11)   But when the king came in to see the guests, he noticed a man there who was not wearing a wedding robe,

(12a) καὶ   λέγει   αὐτῷ,
       and   3S.says   to.him,
       "Friend, how did you get in here without a wedding robe?"

(12b) And he was speechless (ἐφιμώθη). (13) Then (τότε) the king said (εἶπεν) to the attendants, "Bind him hand and foot, and throw him into the outer darkness..."

Question

What is the significance of using a HP in v. 12a?

Suggested Answer: see Appendix under 14(6).

I now consider why the HP is used in some episodes in Matthew, but not in others.

Three conditions on the use of the HP in Matthew have been noted (sec. 12.2.1):
- HPs are used only in connection with the interaction of more than one participant or group of participants, and never when the actions or speeches of only one participant are being described
- HPs are used at the beginning of episodes only when the episode concerned is a new subsection of a larger episode
- HPs are used to activate a participant only if that participant has an active part to play.

These conditions explain the absence of HPs in a number of episodes. Take the requirement that a HP be used at the beginning of an episode only when that episode is a new subsection of a larger episode, for instance. This explains the absence of a HP in the first round of two three-round episodes (the temptation of Jesus by the devil—Matt. 4:1–4 and Peter's denial of Jesus—26:69–70). However, the presence of a HP in 3:1 makes it difficult to predict when the author will view an episode as part of a larger episode.

Similarly, the requirement that a participant have an active part to play if he or she is to be activated with a HP explains the absence of a HP when the sick are introduced in 8:16 and when the 'tax collectors and sinners' are introduced in 9:10.

The above conditions are sufficient to explain the absence of non-speech HPs in other parts of chapters 1–4 of Matthew, too. As already noted, no HP is used to introduce the angel in 1:20, because no previous interaction between any participants has been recorded. Then, in 2:1, the magi are not introduced to an existing scene, but to Herod in Jerusalem. In 3:5 and 3:7, HPs are not used to introduce new participants to the existing scene because they do not take any initiative. Finally, in 4:1, a HP is not used to move Jesus to the wilderness because he goes alone, leaving John behind.

Matthew 8 contains four or five speech HPs, which have been analyzed as cataphoric, but no non-speech HPs. The conditions stated above possibly exclude the use of non-speech HPs when Jesus and his disciples move to new locations (vv. 1, 5, 14) or when new participants who have an active role to play are activated (vv. 2, 5, 19). However, another factor may be relevant, too. This is that there is a strong tendency throughout Matthew *either* to use HPs at the beginning of subsections *or* in connection with speeches (the main exception being those HPs that describe the movement of activated participants to the location of the next significant events, as in 4:5 and 26:36).

Wilson (1974:215) suggests that the presence of the HP in certain episodes of Mark's Gospel "serves to single out a main *theme* of the narrative, marking certain of the episodes, while being absent from intervening episodes ancillary to the theme so marked." However, Boos (1984:22) considers that some HPs relate to high-level themes, whereas others are only of local significance.[7]

If we apply these suggestions to Matthew, we may distinguish between those speech HPs that are of *local* significance only, in that they point forward and highlight an event later in the same episode, and those that have *wider* significance, in that they point to events in a later episode. These last may be recognized from the fact that the episode concludes with a speech that is introduced with a HP. Among instances of speech HPs identified above as pointing to a later episode were the following:
8:4 (pointing to the prophesy of 8:17 as the theme of Jesus healing is developed)
8:20 (pointing to further teaching on discipleship in 8:22)
9:37–38 (pointing to the sending out of the disciples in 10:5)
13:29 (UBS text—pointing to the interpretation of the parable in 13:36–43)
21:13 and 16 (pointing to a further confrontation with the religious authorities in 21:23–27)
28:10 (the HP points forward to Jesus' final instructions in 28:16–20).

As for the non-speech HPs that are found at the beginning of episodes and subsections (sec. 12.2.1), these indicate that the events concerned are part of a larger whole. They may also contribute, therefore,

---

[7] Boos made his observation about John's Gospel.

to the identification of higher-level themes (especially if the associative nature of τότε and of genitives absolute is also taken into account).

The tendency for Matthew either to use non-speech HPs or speech HPs may then imply that Matthew indicates the development of a theme over more than one episode either at the beginning of an episode or at the end of an episode, but not in both places.

So, a profitable area of research would be to consider the interplay of two factors:

1. the extent to which the conditions stated at the beginning of this subsection exclude the use of HPs in each episode of Matthew
2. the extent to which the use of the HP, τότε, genitives absolute and other cohesive devices such as the presence versus absence of overt references to Jesus indicate that episodes are to be grouped together because they share a common theme.

This would reveal whether we are close to accounting for the presence versus absence of HPs in the Gospel, and where further studies of the HP should be directed.

15
REPORTED CONVERSATIONS IN JOHN'S GOSPEL

An analysis of speech orienters in John's Gospel needs to account for at least four variables:

1. the means of conjoining units that is chosen (δέ, καί, οὖν or asyndeton—see sec. 5.3)
2. articular versus anarthrous references by name to the speaker (sec. 9.2)
3. the verb chosen (principally, λέγω/εἶπον or ἀποκρίνομαι)
4. the tense-aspect chosen (especially the aorist versus the historical present—HP).

See also the use of the articular pronoun to present intermediate steps (sec. 13.1).

As was noted in sec. 13.1, the status of reported conversations varies from episode to episode. In some of the episodes recorded in John's Gospel, the speeches are an end in themselves, as when Jesus debates with potential believers (e.g., Nicodemus in 3:2ff.). In others, the speeches lead to non-verbal signs, such as the healing of the official's son in 4:46–54. Then there are exchanges that contain an extensive debate but nevertheless lead to non-verbal results, such as the interaction between Jesus and the woman at the well in 4:7–26, which leads to many residents of Sychar believing that he is "the Savior of the world" (v. 42) . In yet others, the evidence of the non-verbal sign is expressed in a reported speech (2:10). In other words, there is no neat division between reported conversations in which the speeches are an end in themselves and those that are not.

There are significant correlations between the status of a reported conversation and some of the variables mentioned above. For example, the individual speeches of debates with opponents tend to be linked with οὖν and the speech verb usually is not in the HP. However, the correlation between these forms and "tension and conflict" (Reimer 1985:34) is only partial.

One reason that HPs tend not to occur in debates or with οὖν (a HP and οὖν are found together in a speech orienter only following background material) is that, as in Matthew, most speech HPs are *cataphoric* (Boos 1984:20–22). In other words, they point on from the current speech to a later speech or action (see sec. 15.1). In debates, in contrast, each speech is of importance, so the development of the debate would be marred if the reader were pointed on from the current speech to a later response.[1]

In sec. 14.1 we saw that forms of ἀποκρίνομαι are used in the Synoptic Gospels and Acts to break the tight-knit nature of a closed conversation. This effect is achieved in John by what I shall call the *long* orienter of ἀπεκρίθη καὶ εἶπεν; see sec. 15.2 for discussion of its functions.

However, when ἀπεκρίθη is used by itself in John (what I call the *short* orienter), the effect is not to break the tight-knit nature of a conversation. Rather, it is the default way of introducing a response to an initial speech. This is particularly evident when ἀπεκρίθη introduces the direct response to a question, as in **John 21:5b**; no attempt to control the conversation is suggested by answering a direct question with the expected answer.

(5a) λέγει   οὖν   αὐτοῖς   [ὁ]   Ἰησοῦς,   Παιδία,   μή   τι   προσφάγιον   ἔχετε;
     says   then   to.them   the   Jesus   children   not   any   fish   you.have

(5b) Ø   ἀπεκρίθησαν   αὐτῷ,   Οὔ.
     3P.answered   him   No

See also John 1:21e, 8:49, 13:26, and 18:5a. See sec. 15.1 for a long list of passages in which a form of ἀποκρίνομαι associates a response with a speech introduced with a HP.

---

[1] Boos (op. cit. 20) proposes a different explanation for the uneven distribution of HPs in John's Gospel, viz., "that the significant groupings of the historical present... signal that particular section as important in the plot development of the total discourse."

It appears to follow that, when ἀπεκρίθη does *not* introduce certain speeches of a conversation, the exchange falls into distinct parts, especially when a developmental conjunction is also used. This is illustrated in John 18:33–38 (below). The use and non-use of the short orienter ἀπεκρίθη has the effect of dividing the conversation into three parts: vv. 33b–36, v. 37a–b, and v. 38a. In v. 37a, οὖν marks the beginning of a new development unit and is accompanied by εἶπεν, as is normal (see also 4:48, 8:57, 9:26, 11:12 and 11:16, among others). The HP of v. 38a, in turn, points forward to the next series of events. This is confirmed by the use in v. 38b of καί (sec. 5.3.2) and tail-head linkage (τοῦτο εἰπὼν— sec. 12.1) to slow the story down prior to the next significant events.

Passage 1: John 18:33–38 (UBS text)

(33a)   Then Pilate entered the praetorium again and summoned Jesus,

(33b)   καὶ εἶπεν αὐτῷ,
and 3S.said to.him,
"Are you the king of the Jews?"

(34)   Ø ἀπεκρίθη Ἰησοῦς,
3S.answered Jesus,
"Do you ask this on your own, or did others tell you about me?"

(35)   Ø ἀπεκρίθη ὁ Πιλᾶτος,
3S.answered the Pilate,
"I am not a Jew, am I? Your own nation and the chief priests have handed you over to me. What have you done?"

(36)   Ø ἀπεκρίθη Ἰησοῦς,
3S.answered Jesus,
"My kingdom is not from this world..."

(37a)   εἶπεν οὖν αὐτῷ ὁ Πιλᾶτος,
3S.said then to.him the Pilate,
"So you are a king?"

(37b)   Ø ἀπεκρίθη ὁ Ἰησοῦς,
3S.answered the Jesus,
"You say that I am a king. For this I was born, and for this I came into the world, to testify to the truth. Everyone who belongs to the truth listens to my voice."

(38a)   Ø λέγει αὐτῷ ὁ Πιλᾶτος,
3S.says to.him the Pilate,
"What is truth?"

(38b)   Καὶ τοῦτο εἰπὼν πάλιν ἐξῆλθεν πρὸς τοὺς Ἰουδαίους κ.τ.λ.
and this having.said again 3S.went.out to the Jews

Incidentally, λέγει with asyndeton is not considered to be a stereotyped use of the HP in John, as εἶπεν is also possible with asyndeton; see John 6:10, 11:25 and 18:31b, though variant readings introduce a conjunction in each verse.

15.1   Historical Presents in Speech Orienters in John

As in Matthew, HPs in John's Gospel appear always to have a *prominence* function, while most HPs that occur in speech orienters are *cataphoric*. In other words, the use of a HP in a speech orienter most often points forward to and highlights a later speech or event.

Confirmation that many speech HPs are used for cataphoric effect is provided by the fact that so many occur in the orienter of the *first speech of a couplet.*[2]

The term *couplet* refers to a speech-speech or speech-action pair that belongs together because the initial speech calls for the specific response that is described in the second part. For example, a question calls for an answer, while a command calls for the execution of that command. If the second part of the couplet is a speech, it is often introduced in John's Gospel with ἀπεκρίθη.

John 5:6b-9a (below) consists of two couplets. Both begin with a speech HP (vv. 6b, 8), which points forward at least to the second part of each couplet, viz., the response of the sick man (v. 7) and his being healed (v. 9a). The speech that constitutes the second part of the first couplet is introduced with ἀπεκρίθη (v. 7).

Passage 2: John 5:6–9a

(6a)   When Jesus saw him lying there and knew that he had been lying there a long time,

(6b)   COUPLET 1:   QUESTION
Ø λέγει   αὐτῷ,
   3S.says   to.him,
"Do you want to be made well?"

(7)   ANSWER
Ø ἀπεκρίθη   αὐτῷ   ὁ   ἀσθενῶν,
   3S.answered   to.him   the.one   being.ill,
"Sir, I have no one to put me into the pool when the water is stirred up..."

(8)   COUPLET 2:   COMMAND
Ø λέγει   αὐτῷ   ὁ   Ἰησοῦς,
   3S.says   to.him   the   Jesus,
"Stand up, take your mat and walk."

(9a)   EXECUTION
And at once the man became (ἐγένετο) well, and he took up his mat and began to walk.

To illustrate how often a HP introduces the first speech of a couplet, here is a list of passages in which a speech HP in the first part of a couplet is followed by a form of ἀποκρίνομαι in the second: 1:48a, 3:4, 4:9, 4:11, 4:16, 5:6, 6:5, 7:50, 11:8, 13:6b, 13:8a, 13:25 and 13:37 (in this example and 13:25, the speech orienter of the reply is also in the HP), 13:36a, 14:22, 16:29, 18:4b (UBS text), 18:29b (UBS text), 19:6b, 19:9b, 19:10, 19:15b, 20:27, and 21:5a. In addition, on many occasions a HP in the first part of a couplet is followed by a nonverbal response such as that of 5:9a (above) which constitutes the second part of the couplet.

Among the many other examples of HPs that introduce the first speech or speeches of a conversation and have a cataphoric function are John 1:38a, 12:4 and 19:26–27a; see also the isolated speech in 19:28, which is followed by the nonverbal response of v. 29b. Still others introduce the first speech of a new round of a conversation, again with cataphoric effect, as in 6:8, 9:17, 11:11, and 21:12.

Now for the claim that the use of a speech HP usually *gives prominence to what follows*, rather than to the speech that it introduces. It is noteworthy that the norm in the UBS text is for references by name to a speaker to be articular when a HP is used, but to be anarthrous when a form of ἀποκρίνομαι is used (Abbott 1906:57), especially in the long orienter ἀπεκρίθη καὶ εἶπεν (see sec. 15.2).[3]

---

[2] Coulthard (1977:70) uses the term "adjacency pair" to refer to what is here called a couplet.

[3] Many references by name to Jesus in a speech orienter have articular and anarthrous variants. Unless indicated to the contrary, therefore, the examples cited follow the UBS text.

   Out of 39 references to Jesus in speech orienters that are accompanied by a form of ἀποκρίνομαι, only 6 are articular in the UBS text (plus 4 with some doubt). However, Pope (p.c.) considers that a further 7 or so references may also be articular.

form of speech verb	normal means of reference by name to speaker
λέγει	articular
ἀπεκρίθη (καὶ εἶπεν)	anarthrous

In other words, the way that speakers are referred to in speech orienters implies that the norm is for speeches introduced with a HP not to be accorded special prominence, but for speeches introduced with a form of ἀποκρίνομαι to be accorded such prominence (sec. 9.2). See, for instance, the articular reference to Jesus in John 5:8 (passage 2 above), but the anarthrous references to him in a number of MSS in 18:34, 18:36 and 18: 37b (passage 1).

If these norms are valid, then, taken together with the implications of using a speech HP in John's Gospel, they should help in the selection of variant readings. In John 3 (below), for instance, the HP of v. 4 has a cataphoric function, to point forward to and to highlight the response of v. 5. This in turn implies that an articular reference to Nicodemus is preferable in v. 4, whereas an anarthrous reference to Jesus is preferable in v. 5.

Passage 3: John 3:2–5

(2)   <u>οὗτος</u> ἦλθεν πρὸς αὐτὸν νυκτὸς καὶ εἶπεν αὐτῷ,
        this   3S.came to   him   by.night and 3S.said to.him,
       "Rabbi, we know that you are a teacher who has come from God; for no one can do these signs that you do apart from the presence of God."

(3)   Ø ἀπεκρίθη   * Ἰησοῦς καὶ εἶπεν   αὐτῷ,   (*variant: insert ὁ)
         3S.answered   Jesus   and 3S.said to.him,
       "Very truly, I tell you, no one can see the kingdom of God without being born from above."

(4)   Ø λέγει   πρὸς αὐτὸν [ὁ] Νικόδημος,
         3S.says to   him   the Nicodemus,
       "How can anyone be born after having grown old? Can one enter a second time into the mother's womb and be born?"

(5)   Ø ἀπεκρίθη   * Ἰησοῦς,   (*variant: insert ὁ)
         3S.answered   Jesus,
       "Very truly, I tell you, no one can enter the kingdom of God without being born of water and Spirit..."

Although the norm, when a speech orienter is in the HP, is for any reference by name to the speaker to be articular, occasionally the reference is *anarthrous*. When this happens, the speech itself is highlighted and it is less likely that the HP is being used cataphorically.[4]

For instance, all the speeches of John 20:15–17 are introduced with HPs (the HPs of vv. 14b and 18 are used to reactivate Jesus and the disciples—sec. 12.2.3). While it is possible to argue that they are all used cataphorically (pointing to the next time Jesus appears, presumably), the anarthrous references to Jesus (at least, in the UBS text) may suggest that it is the exchange between Mary Magdalene and the risen Jesus itself that is highlighted.

Passage 4: John 20:14–18

(14)   Having said these things, she turned (ἐστράφη) around and sees Jesus (θεωρεῖ τὸν Ἰησοῦν) standing, and did not know (ᾔδει) that it was Jesus.

---

[4] However, references in John's Gospel to Simon Peter are usually anarthrous when he is the speaker. This may imply in turn that the speech HPs of 13:8a and 9 have a cataphoric function, and that the speeches themselves are not highlighted. (A few MSS have an anarthrous reference to Jesus in v. 10.)

(15a)　Ø λέγει　αὐτῇ　*　Ἰησοῦς,　(*variant: insert ὁ)
　　　　3S.says　to.her　　Jesus,
　　　　"Woman, why are you weeping? Whom are you seeking?"

(15b)　Ø ἐκείνη　δοκοῦσα　ὅτι　ὁ　κηπουρός　ἐστιν λέγει　αὐτῷ,
　　　　that.one　supposing　that　the　gardener　3S.is　3S.says　to.him,
　　　　"Sir, if you have carried him away, tell me where you have laid him, and I will take him
　　　　away."

(16a)　Ø λέγει　αὐτῇ　*　Ἰησοῦς, Μαριάμ.　(*variant: insert ὁ)
　　　　3S.says　to.her　　Jesus,　Mary
　　　　3S.says　to.her

(16b)　Ø στραφεῖσα　ἐκείνη　λέγει　αὐτῷ　Ἑβραϊστί,
　　　　having.turned　that.one　3S.says　to.him　in.Hebrew,
　　　　"Rabbouni!" (which means Teacher).

(17)　Ø λέγει　αὐτῇ　*　Ἰησοῦς,　(*variant: insert ὁ)
　　　　3S.says　to.her　　Jesus,
　　　　"Do not hold on to me, because I have not yet ascended to the Father. But go to my
　　　　brothers and say to them, 'I am ascending to my Father and your Father, to my God and
　　　　your God.'"

(18)　Ø ἔρχεται　Μαριὰμ　ἡ　Μαγδαληνὴ　ἀγγέλλουσα τοῖς μαθηταῖς ὅτι
　　　　Ø 3S.comes　Mary　the　Magdalene　announcing　to.the disciples　that
　　　　"I have seen the Lord" and that he had said these things to her.

See also John 13:31–14:22 (the UBS text has articular references by name to Jesus in 14:6 and 14:9) and 21:15–17 (if the reference to Jesus in v. 17d is anarthrous).

In summary, the use of a speech HP typically has a *cataphoric* function, of pointing forward to a following speech or action. An *articular* reference to the speaker confirms that prominence is to be given to what follows, rather than to the speech itself. An *anarthrous* reference to the speaker, however, may imply that the speech itself is highlighted.

If the combination of a speech HP and an articular reference to the speaker indicates that the speech HP has a cataphoric function, the question arises as to which speech or action it points forward to. As noted above, the presence of the short orienter ἀπεκρίθη with a non-developmental form of conjoining tends to attach responses to an initial speech. It is possible, therefore, that the cataphoric effect of the combination of a speech HP and an answer introduced with ἀπεκρίθη is to point *beyond the couplet* so formed to a later speech or action, *unless* any reference by name to the respondent is anarthrous.

This would imply that, in John 5:6–9 (passage 2 above), the cataphoric effect of the speech HP of v. 6b would be to point beyond the answer of v. 7, perhaps to the healing of the man (v. 9a), which the speech HP of v. 8 would also point to. In contrast, in 3:4–5 (passage 3), the speech HP of v. 4 would point forward only to the response of v. 5, since the reference to Jesus is probably anarthrous.

In the examples considered to date, a speech HP has introduced the first part of a couplet, and the speech or action to which it points is sometimes the immediately following one (the second part of the couplet). When the speech introduced with a HP is *not* the first part of a couplet, the likelihood of the HP pointing forward to a *later* development is increased.

In John 1:21b, for instance, the speech introduced with the HP is in response to a question, so is not the first speech of a couplet. The speech is not of importance in its own right, as it reiterates the response of v. 20. Nor is it likely to be pointing forward to the immediately following couplet, as the response of v. 21d to the question of v. 21c is the same as in v. 21b. Rather, it points forward to the development of vv. 22–23, which is introduced with οὖν.

Passage 5: John 1:19–23

(19)   COUPLET 1:   QUESTION

And **this** is the testimony given by John when the Jews sent priests and Levites from Jerusalem to ask him, "Who are you?"

(20)   ANSWER

And he confessed and did not deny it, and confessed, "I am not the Messiah."

(21a)   COUPLET 2:   QUESTION

And they asked him, "What then? You are Elijah?"

(21b)   ANSWER

καὶ   λέγει,   Οὐκ εἰμί.
and 3S.says   not   I.am

(21c)   COUPLET 3:   QUESTION

"Are you the prophet?"

(21d)   ANSWER

καὶ   ἀπεκρίθη,   Οὔ.
and 3S.answered No

(22)   COUPLET 4:   QUESTION

εἶπαν   οὖν   αὐτῷ,
3P.said then to.him,

"Who are you? Let us have an answer for those who sent us. What do you say about yourself?"

(23)   ANSWER

Ø ἔφη,
   3S.affirmed,

"I am the voice of one crying out in the wilderness, 'Make straight the way of the Lord,' as the prophet Isaiah said."

Other examples in which the speech introduced with a HP is the second part of a couplet and the HP points forward to a later development include John 9:12b (pointing forward to the exchange of vv. 15ff.) and 11:34b. See also 7:6[5] and 18:5b.

As in Matthew (sec. 14.3), when a HP introduces the *final speech of an episode* and there is no evidence that the speech itself is being highlighted, then the HP is pointing forward to a subsequent episode. In John 1:51, for instance (καὶ λέγει αὐτῷ, "Truly, I tell you, you will see heaven opened and the angels of God ascending and descending upon the Son of Man"), Alford (1863.I:697) considers Jesus' words to refer to "the series of glories which was about to be unfolded in His Person and Work from that time forward" and which are described in subsequent chapters of John's Gospel. See also 20:29.

When more than one speech HP occurs in succession and any reference by name to the speaker is *articular* (contrast passage 4 above), each HP points forward to a later speech or action which, usually, is introduced without a HP. In John 11:21–25, for instance, the HPs of vv. 23 and 24 point forward to the speech of vv. 25f (assuming that the reference to Martha in v. 24 is articular).

---

[5] Note the preposed αὐτὸς in 7:9, marking this action as an intermediate step (sec. 13.3) en route to the event of v. 10.

Passage 6: John 11:21–25 (UBS text)

(21) εἶπεν   οὖν   ἡ   Μάρθα   πρὸς τὸν Ἰησοῦν,
3S.said   then   the   Martha   to   the   Jesus,
"Lord, if you had been here, my brother would not have died. (22) [But] even now I know that God will give you whatever you ask of him."

(23) Ø λέγει   αὐτῇ   ὁ   Ἰησοῦς,
3S.says   to.her   the   Jesus,
"Your brother will rise again."

(24) Ø λέγει   αὐτῷ   ἡ   Μάρθα,
3S.says   to.him   the   Martha,
"I know that he will rise again in the resurrection on the last day."

(25) Ø εἶπεν   αὐτῇ   ὁ   Ἰησοῦς,
3S.said   to.her   the   Jesus,
"I am the resurrection and the life..."

See also the series of speech HPs in John 4:49–50a, 11:38–40, 21:19b–22 and, possibly, 13:9–10 (see fn. 4). In the case of the speeches of 2:3–5, the last of which is "Do whatever he tells you," the HPs point forward to what Jesus tells the servants to do (vv. 7a, 8a). These instructions are also introduced with a speech HP.

In several passages, the series of speech HPs points beyond a rather inconsequential action that immediately follows to further exchanges involving the same or related participants. This is particularly evident when the action concerned has nothing to do with the topic of the preceding conversation.

In the case of John 4:19–26, for instance, the series of speech HPs does not point to the arrival of the disciples (the topic of the final speeches had been the coming Messiah). Rather, it points to the woman's response to the conversation ('He cannot be the Christ, can he?'—v. 29) and, ultimately, to the Samaritans coming to faith in Jesus (vv. 39–42—see the use of the HP in v. 28c to introduce the woman's speech of v. 29).

Similarly, the topic of the speeches of 18:17a–b concerns whether Peter is one of Jesus' disciples. The HPs point forward, not to Peter standing warming himself (v. 18), but to his later denials (vv. 25–26—an interaction between Jesus and his accusers also intervenes). As for the series of HPs in 20:12 (sees) –13, because the topic of the conversation is why Mary is weeping, they point, not to her turning around (v. 14a), but to the exchange between her and the risen Jesus, which has a further series of HPs (passage 4 above).

Review Questions

(a) When the reference to a participant in a speech orienter is *articular* and the speech verb is in the HP, what does this imply?
(b) When the reference to a participant in a speech orienter is *anarthrous* and the speech verb is in the HP, what may this imply?
(c) When a speech verb is in the HP and the orienter introduces the *final* speech of an episode, to what does the HP usually point forward?

Suggested Answers

(a) When the reference to a participant in a speech orienter is *articular* and the speech verb is in the HP, this implies that the HP has a cataphoric function; i.e., it points forward to a later speech or action.
(b) When the reference to a participant in a speech orienter is *anarthrous* and the speech verb is in the HP, this may imply that the speech or exchange itself is highlighted.
(c) When a speech verb is in the HP and the orienter introduces the *final* speech of an episode, the HP usually points forward to a following episode.

Illustrative Passage 7: John 21:1–6

The questions that follow the next two passages concern various aspects of the speech orienters.

(1)   After <u>these</u> <u>things</u> Jesus showed (ἐφανέρωσεν) himself again to the disciples by the Sea of Tiberias; and he showed (ἐφανέρωσεν) himself in this way. (2) There were (ἦσαν) together Simon Peter, Thomas called the Twin, Nathanael of Cana in Galilee, the sons of Zebedee, and two others of his disciples.

(3a)   Ø λέγει   αὐτοῖς Σίμων Πέτρος,[6]
         3S.says to.them Simon   Peter,
         "I am going fishing."

(3b)   Ø λέγουσιν αὐτῷ,
         3P.say   to.him,
         "We will also go with you."

(3c–d)   Ø ἐξῆλθον   καὶ ἐνέβησαν   εἰς   τὸ   πλοῖον,
         3P.went.forth and 3P.embarked into the boat

(3e)   καὶ ἐν ἐκείνῃ τῇ νυκτὶ ἐπίασαν οὐδέν.
         and in that   the night 3P.caught nothing

(4a)   **πρωΐας**   δὲ ἤδη γενομένης   ἔστη   Ἰησοῦς εἰς τὸν αἰγιαλόν,
         early.morning DE already having.become 3S.stood Jesus on the shore

(4b)   οὐ μέντοι   ᾔδεισαν   οἱ μαθηταὶ ὅτι **Ἰησοῦς** ἐστιν.
         not however 3P.had.realized the disciples that Jesus   3S.is

(5a)   λέγει   οὖν αὐτοῖς [ὁ] Ἰησοῦς,
         3S.says then to.them the Jesus,
         "Children, you have no fish, have you?"

(5b)   Ø ἀπεκρίθησαν αὐτῷ, Οὔ.
         3P.answered   him   No

(6a)   ὁ   δὲ εἶπεν αὐτοῖς,
         he DE 3S.said to.them,
         "Cast the net to the right side of the boat, and you will find some."

(6b)   ἔβαλον   οὖν,
         3P.threw   then

(6c)   καὶ οὐκέτι   **αὐτὸ** **ἑλκύσαι** ἴσχυον
         and no.longer it   to.draw   3P.were.strong

         ἀπὸ τοῦ πλήθους τῶν ἰχθύων.
         from the multitude of.the fish

Questions

(a) What is the effect of using HPs in 21:3a–b?
(b) What is the effect of using a HP in v. 5a?
(c) Why is οὖν also used in the speech orienter of v. 5a?
(d) What is the significance of introducing the speech of v. 6a with an articular pronoun? (If necessary, see sec. 13.1.)

---

[6] References in John's Gospel to Simon Peter are usually anarthrous when he is the speaker.

Suggested Answers

(a) The effect of using HPs in 21:3a–b is to point forward to the results of the conversation, viz., the events described in vv. 3c–e.

(b) The effect of using a HP in v. 5a is to point forward at least to the answer of v. 5b. Since a negative answer was expected, anyhow (Porter 1992:277), the cataphoric effect of the HP of v. 5a probably extends beyond this answer to the next couplet (see (d) below).

(c) Οὖν is used in the speech orienter of v. 5a because the storyline is resumed, following the background material of v. 4b, and the speech concerned represents a new development, as far as the author's purpose is concerned (sec. 5.3.3).

(d) The speech of v. 6a is introduced with an articular pronoun because it is an intermediate step en route to the events of vv. 6b–c, viz., the miraculous catch. This has the effect of keeping the attention on the execution of Jesus' command and the results, rather than on Jesus himself.

Passage 8: John 20:19–24

(19a–b) When it was evening on that day, the first day of the week, and <u>the doors</u> were locked where the disciples were for fear of the Jews, Jesus came (ἦλθεν) and stood (ἔστη) in the midst

(19c) καὶ λέγει αὐτοῖς,
and 3S.says to.them,
"Peace be with you."

(20a) καὶ τοῦτο εἰπὼν ἔδειξεν τὰς χεῖρας καὶ τὴν πλευρὰν αὐτοῖς.
and this having.said 3S.showed the hands and the side to.them

(20b) ἐχάρησαν οὖν οἱ μαθηταὶ ἰδόντες τὸν κύριον.
3P.rejoiced so the disciples having.seen the Lord

(21) εἶπεν οὖν αὐτοῖς [ὁ Ἰησοῦς] πάλιν,
3S.said then to.them the Jesus again,
"Peace with you. As the Father has sent me, so I send you."

(22a) καὶ τοῦτο εἰπὼν ἐνεφύσησεν
and this having.said 3S.breathed.on

(22b) καὶ λέγει αὐτοῖς,
and 3S.says to.them,
"Receive the Holy Spirit. (23) If you forgive the sins of any, they are forgiven; if you retain the sins of any, they are retained."

(24) But <u>Thomas, one of the twelve, the one called the Twin,</u> was not with them when Jesus came.

Questions

(a) What is the effect of beginning vv. 20 and 22 with τοῦτο εἰπών?
(b) What is the effect of using a HP in v. 19c?
(c) Why does the speech orienter of v. 21 begin with εἶπεν οὖν?
(d) What is the effect of using a HP in v. 22b?

Suggested Answers: see Appendix 15(8).

15.2   Ἀπεκρίθη καὶ εἶπεν in John

When a form of ἀποκρίνομαι occurs in a speech orienter in John's Gospel, it is always a finite verb. Whereas the short orienter ἀπεκρίθη is the default way of introducing a response to a previous speech or non-verbal stimulus (see the introduction to this chapter),[7] the long orienter ἀπεκρίθη καὶ εἶπεν *highlights* the response. The response is most often highlighted because it represents a significant counter (see sec. 14.1). Sometimes, it represents a significant new initiative, usually by other than the addressee of the previous speech. Occasionally, a direct answer to a question is highlighted because of its importance.[8]

John 4:9-17 illustrates the use of the long orienter to introduce significant countering speeches. Each of them is preceded by at least one speech introduced with a HP. The cataphoric implications of these HPs confirm the fact that the countering speeches are highlighted. Although Jesus' response of v. 10 deals with the topic of asking for a drink (see v. 9), he does not answer the Samaritan woman's question (whether real or rhetorical) about how it is that he is asking a Samaritan for one. Instead, he counters by directing her attention to himself and the gift of God which is 'living water'. Then, when she asks about the source of this living water (v. 11) and whether he is greater than Jacob (v. 12), he counters by speaking of the effect of drinking this water (vv. 13-14). Finally, when he tells her to call her husband (v. 16), she counters by saying that she has no husband (v. 17a), even though she is living with a man (v. 18)—a topic which Jesus takes up and thus reveals himself to be a prophet (v. 19). (See below on why the long orienter is not used in v. 16.)

(9)   λέγει   οὖν   αὐτῷ   ἡ   γυνὴ   ἡ   Σαμαρῖτις,
      3S.says then to.him the woman the Samaritan,
      "How is it that you, a Jew, ask a drink of me, a woman of Samaria?" (For Jews do not share things in common with Samaritans.)

(10) Ø ἀπεκρίθη   Ἰησοῦς   καὶ   εἶπεν   αὐτῇ,
         3S.answered Jesus   and   3S.said to.her,
      "If you knew the gift of God, and who it is that is saying to you, 'Give me a drink,' you would have asked him, and he would have given you living water."

(11) λέγει   αὐτῷ   [ἡ   γυνή],
      3S.says to.him the   woman,
      "Sir, you have no bucket, and the well is deep. Where do you get that living water? (12) Surely you are not greater than our ancestor Jacob...?"

(13) Ø ἀπεκρίθη   Ἰησοῦς   καὶ   εἶπεν   αὐτῇ,
         3S.answered Jesus   and   3S.said to.her,
      "Everyone who drinks of this water will be thirsty again, (14) but those who drink of the water that I will give them will never be thirsty..."

(15) λέγει   πρὸς   αὐτὸν   ἡ   γυνή,
      3S.says to   him   the woman,
      "Sir, give me this water, so that I may never be thirsty or have to keep coming here to draw water."

(16) λέγει   αὐτῇ,
      3S.says to.her,
      "Go, call your husband, and come back."

(17a) Ø ἀπεκρίθη   ἡ   γυνὴ   καὶ   εἶπεν   αὐτῷ,
          3S.answered the woman and   3S.said to.him,
       "I have no husband."

---

[7] John 5:17 and 10:32 follow non-verbal stimuli whose actor becomes the addressee, and whose undergoer becomes the speaker of the response.

[8] This section largely confirms Pope's (p.c.) conclusion that the long orienters are "used for revelations about or confessions of who Jesus is, final definitive replies, or mistaken opinions about Jesus' status. They come at significant points and relate to who Jesus is. This is, I suggest, in line with the purpose of John, which is a multi-stage debate... between the believing position of the disciples and the unbelieving position of the Jewish leaders."

Jesus' speech of v. 16 is *not* presented as a significant counter to the woman's request of v. 15. This is consistent with Alford's (1863.I:723) analysis of the verse: "I am persuaded that the right account is found, in viewing this command, as the *first step of granting her request*, δός μοι τοῦτο τὸ ὕδωρ."

Other countering speeches which are introduced with the long orienter include John 6:26, 7:21, 8:39a, 8:48, and 18:30. See also 2:18 (the Jews respond to Jesus' words and actions in the temple (vv. 15–16) by countering, 'What sign can you show us for doing this?'). In the case of 7:52, the counter is highlighted because it is the final word that brings the debate to an end.

The long orienter is used also when Jesus takes the initiative and responds in a significant way to a speech that was *not* addressed to him. In **John 12:30**, for example, Jesus responds to the speech of v. 29b but was not the addressee of that speech. His speech represents a significant new initiative, in that he introduces the topic of the Son of Man being lifted up from the earth (v. 32), which the crowd takes up in v. 34.

(29b)   Others were saying, "An angel has spoken to him."

(30)   Ø ἀπεκρίθη   Ἰησοῦς καὶ   εἶπεν,
         3S.answered Jesus   and   3S.said,
         "This voice has come not for my sake but for yours. (31) Now is the judgment of this world; now the ruler of this world will be driven out. (32) And I, when I am lifted up from the earth, will draw all people to myself."

See also John 5:19, 6:43, and 7:16.

The long orienter is used for highlighting even when the tight-knit nature of the conversation is not broken. This is evident in **John 6:29**, which answers the question of v. 28; the use of the 'redundant' introductory clause Τοῦτό ἐστιν τὸ ἔργον τοῦ θεοῦ also has the effect of highlighting the rest of the sentence.

(28)   Then they said to him, "What must we do to perform the works of God?"

(29)   Ø ἀπεκρίθη   [ὁ] Ἰησοῦς καὶ   εἶπεν   αὐτοῖς,
         3S.answered the Jesus   and   3S.said to.them,

         Τοῦτό ἐστιν τὸ   ἔργον τοῦ   θεοῦ, ἵνα   πιστεύητε
         this   3S.is the work   of.the God   that you.may.believe

         εἰς   ὃν   ἀπέστειλεν ἐκεῖνος.
         in   whom 3S.sent   that.one

See also John 2:19 (Jesus answers the question of v. 18), 8:14 (Jesus responds to the objection of v. 13), 9:20 (the blind man's parents respond to the question of v. 19), 13:7 (Jesus answers Peter's challenge of v. 6b), and 14:23 (Jesus answers Judas' question of v. 22—see Alford 1863.I:848). A further example is 1:26 (responding to the question of v. 25), but the combination ἀπεκρίθη ... λέγων is used.[9]

Similarly, Thomas' response in **John 20:28** to Jesus' invitation of v. 27 is introduced with the long orienter to highlight its significance.

(27)   εἶτα λέγει   τῷ   Θωμᾷ,
         then 3S.says to.the Thomas,
         "Put your finger here and see my hands. Reach out your hand and put it in my side. Do not doubt but believe."

(28)   Ø ἀπεκρίθη   Θωμᾶς καὶ   εἶπεν   αὐτῷ,
         3S.answered Thomas and   3S.said to.him,
         "My Lord and my God!"

_____

[9] The combination ἀποκρίνεται ... λέγων is found in John 12:23, introducing a significant new initiative on Jesus' part. See sec. 12.2.3 for the significance of using a HP to introduce this speech.

Review Questions

(a) What is the function of the short orienter? (See sec. 15.1, if necessary.)

(b) What is the effect of using the long orienter? Give three reasons for doing so!

Suggested Answers

(a) The short orienter is the default way of introducing a response to the previous speech or non-verbal stimulus.

(b) The effect of using the long orienter is to highlight the speech concerned. Most often, it is highlighted because it represents a significant counter. Sometimes, it represents a significant new initiative, usually by other than the addressee of the previous speech. Occasionally, a direct answer to a question is highlighted because of its importance.

Illustrative Passage 9: John 9:24–34

Look at the motivation for the short versus long orienters in vv. 27, 30, 34 and, finally, v. 25.

(24a)   So for the second time they called the man who had been blind,

(24b)   καὶ   εἶπαν   αὐτῷ,
         and   3P.said   to.him,
         "Give glory to God! We know that this man is a sinner."

(25)   ἀπεκρίθη   οὖν   ἐκεῖνος*   (*variant: add καὶ εἶπεν),
         3S.answered   then   that.one,
         "I do not know whether he is a sinner. One thing I do know, that though I was blind, now I see."

(26)   εἶπον   οὖν   αὐτῷ,
         3P.said   then   to.him,
         "What did he do to you? How did he open your eyes?"

(27)   Ø   ἀπεκρίθη   αὐτοῖς,
             3S.answered   to.them,
         "I have told you already, and you would not listen. Why do you want to hear it again? Do you also want to become his disciples?"

(28)   καὶ   ἐλοιδόρησαν   αὐτὸν   καὶ   εἶπον,
         and   3P.reviled   him   and   3P.said,
         "You are his disciple, but we are disciples of Moses. (29) We know that God has spoken to Moses, but as for this man, we do not know where he comes from."

(30)   Ø   ἀπεκρίθη   ὁ   ἄνθρωπος   καὶ   εἶπεν   αὐτοῖς,
             3S.answered   the   man   and   3S.said   to.them,
         "Here is an astonishing thing! You do not know where he comes from, and yet he opened my eyes. (31) We know that God does not listen to sinners... (33) If this man were not from God, he could do nothing."

(34)   Ø   ἀπεκρίθησαν   καὶ   εἶπαν   αὐτῷ,
             3P.answered   and   3P.said   to.him,
         "You were born entirely in sins, and are you trying to teach us?" And they drove him out.

Questions

(a) Why is the long orienter used in v. 30? In v. 34?

(b) Why is the short orienter used in v. 27, rather than the long orienter?

(c) If the variant (the long orienter) is followed in v. 25, what would this imply?

Suggested Answers

(a) The long orienter is used in v. 30 to highlight the countering speech of the blind man, presumably because of the conclusion that he reaches (v. 33). The speech of v. 34 is highlighted because it represents the authorities' final rejection of his insights.

(b) The short orienter is the default way of introducing a response. It is used in v. 27 because the author does not wish to highlight the response. Although the speech counters the authorities' questions of v. 26, it is treated as an ordinary reply, leading to their next attempt to discredit Jesus (v. 29).

(c) If the variant (the long orienter) is followed in v. 25, then the response is highlighted.

Illustrative Passage 10: John 3:2–12

Look at the motivation for the short versus long orienters in vv. 3, 5, 9 and 10.

(2) This one came to him by night and said to him, "Rabbi, we know that you are a teacher who has come from God; for no one can do these signs that you do apart from the presence of God."

(3) Ø ἀπεκρίθη Ἰησοῦς καὶ εἶπεν αὐτῷ,
    3S.answered Jesus and 3S.said to.him,
"Very truly, I tell you, no one can see the kingdom of God without being born from above."

(4) Ø λέγει πρὸς αὐτὸν [ὁ] Νικόδημος,
    3S.says to him the Nicodemus,
"How can anyone be born after having grown old? Can one enter a second time into the mother's womb and be born?"

(5) Ø ἀπεκρίθη Ἰησοῦς,
    3S.answered Jesus,
"Very truly, I tell you, no one can enter the kingdom of God without being born of water and Spirit. (6) What is born of the flesh is flesh, and what is born of the Spirit is spirit. (7) Do not be astonished that I said to you, 'You must be born from above.' (8) The wind blows where it chooses, and you hear the sound of it, but you do not know where it comes from or where it goes. So it is with everyone who is born of the Spirit."

(9) Ø ἀπεκρίθη Νικόδημος καὶ εἶπεν αὐτῷ,
    3S.answered Nicodemus and 3S.said to.him,
"How can these things be?"

(10) Ø ἀπεκρίθη Ἰησοῦς καὶ εἶπεν αὐτῷ,
    3S.answered Jesus and 3S.said to.him,
"Are you a teacher of Israel, and yet you do not understand these things? (11) Very truly, I tell you, we speak of what we know and testify to what we have seen; yet you do not receive our testimony. (12) If I have told you about earthly things and you do not believe, how can you believe if I tell you about heavenly things? ..."

Questions

(a) Why is the long orienter used in v. 3? And in v. 10?

(b) What does the use of the short orienter in v. 5 suggest?

(c) What does the use of the long orienter in v. 9 suggest?

Suggested Answers

(a) The long orienter is used in v. 3 because Jesus' response to Nicodemus' speech of v. 2 is a significant counter. The same is true of Jesus' response of vv. 10ff. (The speech is also the final one in the conversation, so one would expect it to be highlighted, anyhow.)

(b) The use of the short orienter in v. 5 indicates that Jesus' response is not specially highlighted, perhaps because it continues his argument of v.3.

(c) The use of the long orienter in v. 9 suggests that Nicodemus' question is a significant counter to Jesus' speech of vv. 5–8. Verse 11 suggests that it is in fact a rhetorical question of unbelief (Alford 1863.I:710).

Passage 11: John 1:48–50

(48a)   λέγει   αὐτῷ   Ναθαναήλ,
        3S.says   to.him   Nathanael,
        "How(ever) did you get to know me?"

(48b)   Ø ἀπεκρίθη   Ἰησοῦς καὶ εἶπεν   αὐτῷ,
        3S.answered Jesus   and 3S.said   to.him,
        "Before Philip called you, I saw you under the fig tree."

(49)   Ø ἀπεκρίθη   αὐτῷ   Ναθαναήλ* (*variants: add καὶ εἶπεν/λέγει αὐτῷ),
        3S.answered   to.him   Nathanael,
        "Rabbi, you are the Son of God! You are the King of Israel!"

(50)   Ø ἀπεκρίθη   Ἰησοῦς καὶ εἶπεν   αὐτῷ,
        3S.answered Jesus   and 3S.said   to.him,
        "Do you believe because I told you that I saw you under the fig tree? You will see greater things than these."

Questions:

(a) What is the significance of using the speech HP in v. 48a?

(b) Why is the long orienter used in v. 48b? In v. 50?

(c) In v. 49, what is the significance of following the UBS text? The variant reading with the addition of καὶ εἶπεν? The variant reading with the addition of καὶ λέγει?

Suggested Answers: see Appendix 15(11).

16
THREE WAYS OF REPORTING SPEECH[1]

As I noted in the introduction to part V, speeches may be reported in three ways in Greek: directly (with no significant changes to the content—the default way of reporting speech), indirectly (with significant changes to the content), and directly with ὅτι *recitativum* after the orienter.

I first suggest that, when a speech is reported indirectly, the speech is backgrounded with respect to what follows (sec. 16.1). I then address the significance of using ὅτι *recitativum* to introduce direct speech (sec. 16.2).

For grammarians, ὅτι *recitativum* "is practically equivalent to our quotation marks" (Moulton & Milligan 1974 (1930):463; see also Arndt & Gingrich 1957:593, BDF §470(1), Porter 1992:268 Robertson 1934:442, and Wallace 1996:454). However, they offer no explanation as to why ὅτι is sometimes present and sometimes absent with direct speech. One purpose of this chapter is to address that deficiency. My claim is that, in Luke-Acts and John, ὅτι *recitativum* is typically used to signal that the speech concerned culminates some unit or at least expands on some previous point.[2] This is true also of assertions that are introduced with the formula (ἀμὴν) λέγω σοι/ὑμῖν '(truly) I say to you' plus ὅτι (sec. 16.2.1).

This chapter does not discuss ὅτι following verbs that *require* a conjunction such as ὅτι when their complement is verbal. Such verbs denote sense perception (e.g. ἀκούω 'hear'), mental perception (e.g. γινώσκω 'know'), "thinking, judging, believing, hoping," and "verbs of swearing, affirming and corresponding formulae" (Arndt & Gingrich loc. cit.).

A second use of ὅτι that is not considered in this chapter is as a *causal* conjunction.[3] Following a verb of saying, though, it is not always clear whether ὅτι is causal or *recitativum*. In **John 20:13b**, for instance, the UBS text treats ὅτι as *recitativum*. However, the preceding question (v. 13a) asks the addressee *why* she is weeping, so it is reasonable to interpret v. 13b as giving the reason for her weeping (see the punctuation in Alford 1863.I:900).

(13a) καὶ λέγουσιν αὐτῇ ἐκεῖνοι, Γύναι, τί κλαίεις;
and 3S.say to.her those.ones woman why you.weep

(13b) λέγει αὐτοῖς ὅτι Ἦραν τὸν κύριόν μου,
3S.says to.them that/because 3P.took the lord my

καὶ οὐκ οἶδα ποῦ ἔθηκαν αὐτόν.
and not I.know where 3P.placed him

16.1 Indirect Reporting of Speech

The norm in Greek is for speeches to be reported in direct form, with indirect reporting used much less frequently. By using indirect speech, the reporter claims only that the contents are "truthful in relevant respects" (Follingstad forthcoming), and does not purport to reproduce the original words.

---

[1] I am grateful to Tony Pope for the many observations and suggestions that he made on a draft of an earlier article on this topic (Levinsohn 1999b).

[2] I have not studied the function of ὅτι *recitativum* in Matthew or Mark. Having read Levinsohn 1999b, Pope (p.c.) observed that most examples of ὅτι *recitativum* in Matthew "are culminating a unit or providing a strong reply or riposte which stops someone in their tracks. The latter don't fit well into this pattern; they seem to be simply exclamatory and/or shocking. This is related in the sense that they mark strong assertion, just as the climactic/culminating use, but they do not culminate the unit."

[3] Zerwick (1963:145 §422) suggests that ὅτι is often used to give "the reason not why the fact *is* so, but whereby it is *known* to be so."

Thus, the reported speech of **John 4:51b** (UBS text) conveys the sense of what the slaves said without communicating their actual words.[4]

(51b)	οἱ	δοῦλοι	αὐτοῦ	ὑπήντησαν	αὐτῷ	λέγοντες	ὅτι	ὁ	παῖς
	the	slaves	his	3P.met	him	saying	that	the	child

αὐτοῦ	ζῇ.
his	3S.lives

However, saying that indirect speech does not reproduce the original words does not explain *why* an author chooses to report certain speeches indirectly. One common motivation in languages for using an indirect form is to *background* the speech with respect to what follows. For example, Mfonyam (1994:195) observes concerning Bafut (Grassfields Bantu, Cameroon), "Another means by which background information is marked in Bafut is by indirect reported speech."

Indirect speech appears to be used in Luke-Acts and John for the same reason. This is illustrated in the following table, which gives an overview of the distribution of direct and indirect speech in **John 4:46b–54** (the UBS text is followed).

(46b)	Now there was a certain royal official whose son lay ill in Capernaum. (47) This man, having heard that Jesus had come from Judea to Galilee, went and was asking that (ἵνα) he come down and heal his son, for he was at the point of death.	(INDIRECT)
(48)	Then Jesus said to him, "Unless you see signs and wonders you will not believe."	(DIRECT)
(49)	The official says to him, "Sir, come down before my little boy dies."	(DIRECT)
(50a)	Jesus says to him, "Go, your son will live."	(DIRECT)
(50b)	The man believed the word that Jesus spoke to him and started on his way.	
(51)	As he was going down, his slaves met him and told him ὅτι his child was alive.	(INDIRECT)
(52a)	So he asked them the hour when he began to recover,	(INDIRECT)
(52b)	and they said to him ὅτι "Yesterday at one in the afternoon the fever left him."	(DIRECT + ὅτι)
(53a)	Then the father realized that this was the hour when Jesus had said to him, "Your son will live,"	(EMBEDDED DIRECT)
(53b)	and he himself believed, along with his whole household.	
(54)	This was the second sign that Jesus did after coming from Judea to Galilee.	

As John 4:54 indicates, the above passage recounts one of Jesus' 'signs'. The improvement in the child's health (v. 51) does not itself show that Jesus had healed him. What convinces the official that Jesus was responsible for the healing is that the child got better at the time that Jesus had stated that his son would live. The speeches of vv. 51–52a can, therefore, be viewed as *preliminary* to the rest of the episode of vv. 51–53. Similarly, the official's request of v. 47 can be viewed as preliminary to the rest of the episode of vv. 46b–50.

The following table gives an overview of the distribution of direct and indirect reported speech in **Acts 12:13–15** (passage 2 of sec. 13.1). In this exchange, Rhoda's speeches of vv. 14b and 15b, which are reported indirectly, may be viewed as backgrounded with respect to the responses of vv. 15a and 15c, which are reported directly.

(13)	When he knocked at the outer gate, a maid named Rhoda came to answer. (14a) On recognizing Peter's voice, she was so overjoyed that she did not open the gate.	
(14b)	Instead, running in, she announced that Peter was standing at the gate.	(INDIRECT)
(15a)	They said to her, "You are out of your mind."	(DIRECT)
(15b)	She was insisting that it was so.	(INDIRECT)
(15c)	They were saying, "It is his angel."	(DIRECT)

When a speech is introduced by ὅτι and there is no reference within it to the speakers or addressees, it is not possible to know for certain whether such a speech is in indirect or direct form. In the case of

---

[4] Although all MSS have ὅτι present in John 4:51, some read σου for αὐτου, in which case the speech would be reported directly.

John 7:12b, however, it is the first speech of an exchange and can readily be viewed as preliminary to the subsequent speech, so may be interpreted as indirect. Also, prospective μέν backgrounds the sentence (see sec. 10.1).

(12a)　And there was considerable complaining about him among the crowds.

(12b)　<u>οἱ</u>　μὲν　ἔλεγον　　　ὅτι　**Ἀγαθός**　ἐστιν,
　　　　some　　3P.were.saying　that　good　　　3S.is

(12c)　<u>ἄλλοι</u>　[δὲ]　ἔλεγον,　　　Οὔ,　ἀλλὰ　πλανᾷ　　τὸν　ὄχλον.
　　　　others　　DE　3P.were.saying　no　　rather　3S.deceives　the　crowd

For similar speeches introduced by ὅτι that are probably indirect, see John 9:9a (UBS text) and, in some MSS, 7:40, 7:41 and 9:9b. See also Luke 9:7b–8 (three speeches that may be viewed as preliminary to Herod's conclusion of v. 9) and 21:5a. In general, however, ὅτι appears not to be used in Luke-Acts to introduce indirect reported speech.

Ὅτι is often used when a speech is reported in a *subordinate clause*. This is not surprising, since subordinate clauses are often backgrounded with respect to their main clause. See, for example, **John 8:55c**, in which the conditional clause is the ground (protasis) for the assertion of the main clause (apodosis).

(55c)　<u>κἂν</u>　εἴπω　<u>ὅτι</u>　<u>οὐκ</u> <u>οἶδα</u>　<u>αὐτόν</u>,　ἔσομαι　ὅμοιος　ὑμῖν　ψεύστης·
　　　　+.if　I.say　that　not　I.know　him　　I.will.be　like　　you　　liar

(55d)　but I do know him and I keep his word.

See also John 8:54 and 9:19 (both within a relative clause).[5]

Ὅτι also tends to introduce speeches that are *hypothetical* and are introduced with negative orienters. Again, this is not surprising, since such speeches often provide the background ("collateral information"—Grimes 1975:64) to a following positive statement. Such is the case with the hypothetical speech of **John 21:23b**, which is the ground for the positive one of v. 23c.

(23b)　οὐκ　εἶπεν　δὲ　αὐτῷ　ὁ　Ἰησοῦς　ὅτι　οὐκ　ἀποθνήσκει
　　　　not　3S.said　DE　to.him　the　Jesus　　that　not　3S.would.die

(23c)　ἀλλ᾽,　Ἐὰν　αὐτὸν　θέλω　μένειν　　ἕως　ἔρχομαι　κ.τ.λ.
　　　　but　　if　　him　　I.want　to.remain　until　I.come

See also John 16:26.

When a reported speech begins indirectly but then becomes direct, the author's intention may well be to background the indirect part of the speech with respect to the direct part. This is illustrated in **Acts 25:4–5**; v. 4 is reported indirectly, whereas v. 5 is direct (v. 3 was also reported indirectly).

(4)　<u>ὁ</u>　μὲν　οὖν　**Φῆστος**　ἀπεκρίθη　τηρεῖσθαι　τὸν　Παῦλον
　　　the　　then　Festus　　3S.answered　to.be.kept　the　Paul

　　　εἰς　Καισάρειαν,　<u>ἑαυτὸν</u>　δὲ　μέλλειν　**ἐν τάχει**　ἐκπορεύεσθαι·
　　　in　Caesarea　　self　　　DE　to.intend　quickly　to.go.out

(5)　<u>Οἱ</u>　οὖν　<u>ἐν</u>　<u>ὑμῖν</u>,　φησίν,　<u>δυνατοὶ</u>　　συγκαταβάντες
　　　the　then　among　you　　3S.affirms　prominent.ones　having.come.down.with

　　　<u>εἴ</u> <u>τι</u>　<u>ἐστιν</u> ἐν　τῷ　ἀνδρὶ　ἄτοπον　κατηγορείτωσαν　　　αὐτοῦ.
　　　if　anything　3S.is　with　the　man　　wrong　3P.may.bring.charges.against　him

See also Luke 5:14 and Acts 1:4.

---

[5] All the speeches in *1 John* that are introduced with ὅτι occur in subordinate clauses; see 1 John 1:6, 1:8, 1:10, 2:4 (UBS text) and 4:20. See also Rev. 3:17 (UBS text) and 18:7 (most MSS).

Review Question

What appears to be the motivation for reporting speech indirectly?

Suggested Answer

The motivation for reporting speech indirectly appears to be to background the speech with respect to what follows.

Illustrative Passage 1: John 4:34–37

(34)   Jesus says to them, "My food is to do the will of him who sent me and to complete his work.

(35a)   οὐχ   ὑμεῖς   λέγετε   ὅτι   Ἔτι   τετράμηνός   ἐστιν   καὶ   ὁ   θερισμὸς   ἔρχεται;
        not   you   you.say   that   yet   four.months   3S.is   and   the   harvest   3S.comes

(35b)   ἰδοὺ   λέγω   ὑμῖν,   ἐπάρατε   τοὺς   ὀφθαλμοὺς   ὑμῶν   καὶ
        behold   I.say   to.you   lift.up   the   eyes   your   and

        θεάσασθε   τὰς   χώρας   ὅτι   λευκαί   εἰσιν   πρὸς   θερισμόν.
        see   the   fields   that   white   3S.are   to   harvest

Question

In v. 35a, why does ὅτι follow the speech orienter οὐχ ὑμεῖς λέγετε?

Suggested Answer

In v. 35a, ὅτι follows the speech orienter οὐχ ὑμεῖς λέγετε to background the speech of v. 35a with respect to the assertion of v. 35b.

16.2 Direct Reporting of Speech with Ὅτι Recitativum

In an earlier paper I argued that, in Luke-Acts, ὅτι *recitativum* "in some sense... is always used to introduce a [speech or] quotation which terminates or culminates some unit" (Levinsohn 1978:25). For example, in **Luke 4:43** it introduces the culminating word of the conversation with those who wanted to prevent Jesus from leaving them (v. 42).

(43)   ὁ   δὲ   εἶπεν   πρὸς   αὐτοὺς   ὅτι   Καὶ   ταῖς   ἑτέραις   πόλεσιν
        he   DE   3S.said   to   them   that   +   to.the   other   cities

        εὐαγγελίσασθαί   με   δεῖ   τὴν   βασιλείαν   τοῦ   θεοῦ,
        to.preach   me   3S.is.necessary   the   kingdom   of.the   God

        ὅτι   ἐπὶ   τοῦτο   ἀπεστάλην.
        since   to   this   I.was.sent

Similarly, in **Acts 25:16**, when the Jewish leaders ask Festus to pass sentence against Paul (v. 15—a request that is reported indirectly), his reply brings all discussion to an end.

(16)   πρὸς   οὓς   ἀπεκρίθην   ὅτι   οὐκ   ἔστιν   ἔθος   Ῥωμαίοις
        to   whom   I.answered   that   not   3S.is   custom   with.Romans

        χαρίζεσθαί   τινα   ἄνθρωπον   πρὶν ἢ   ὁ   κατηγορούμενος
        to.hand.over   any   man   before   the   one.being.accused

        κατὰ πρόσωπον   ἔχοι   τοὺς   κατηγόρους   τόπον   κ.τ.λ.
        face.to.face   may.have   the   accusers   place

See also Luke 1:25, 5:26, 5:36–39, 9:22, 19:9–10, 19:42–44, 22:61, and 24:46–49; Acts 20:38, 23:20, and 28:25.[6]

Ὅτι also precedes direct speech in John's Gospel to signal a culminating word. For example, the speech of **John 4:42** (UBS text) is the culmination of the interaction between Jesus and the woman at the well that has occupied most of the chapter.

(42)   τῇ   τε   <u>γυναικὶ</u>   ἔλεγον   ὅτι   Οὐκέτι   **διὰ**
        to.the and the.woman 3P.were.saying that no.longer because.of

        τὴν σὴν λαλιὰν πιστεύομεν, **αὐτοὶ** γὰρ ἀκηκόαμεν καὶ οἴδαμεν
        the your word we.believe selves for we.have.heard and we.know

        ὅτι <u>οὗτός</u> ἐστιν ἀληθῶς ὁ σωτὴρ τοῦ κόσμου.
        that this 3S.is truly the savior of.the world

Similarly, the speech of John 4:52b (sec. 16.1) is the culmination of the conversation reported in vv. 51–52. See also John 1:32–34, 6:14, 6:65, 9:9c (UBS text), 9:17b, 9:23, 10:41 (UBS text), 13:11 (UBS text—the conclusion of the explanation that was introduced with γάρ), and 16:15.[7]

In some instances in Luke-Acts, the speech introduced by ὅτι terminates only a sub-unit of the story. In **Acts 2:13**, for instance, ὅτι marks the last of the bystanders' reactions to the coming of the Holy Spirit upon the disciples (vv. 5–13), but the narrative continues with Peter's response to this final speech.[8]

(13)   <u>ἕτεροι</u> δὲ διαχλευάζοντες ἔλεγον   ὅτι **Γλεύκους**
        others DE mocking   3P.were.saying that of.sweet.wine

        μεμεστωμένοι εἰσίν.
        filled 3P.are

(14)   But Peter, standing with the eleven, raised his voice and addressed them, "... (15) Indeed, these are not drunk, as you suppose..."

See also Luke 1:61, 13:14, 15:27, and 19:34; and Acts 5:23. Nevertheless, ὅτι *recitativum* still signals that the speech terminates some unit.

In the next section I discuss the presence versus absence of ὅτι *recitativum* in Luke and John when a reported speaker uses (ἀμὴν) λέγω σοι/ὑμῖν '(truly) I say to you' to assert the truth of an assertion (sec. 16.2.1). This is followed by consideration of the use versus non-use of ὅτι in connection with a quotation from Scripture (sec. 16.2.2).

Many examples in these two sections involve the embedding of one speech or writing inside another, which means that the main speech contains an embedded orienter. If the orienter for the main speech is followed by ὅτι, the embedded orienter is not.

This is illustrated in **Luke 4:12**—the speech by which Jesus brings the devil's temptations to an end. Because ὅτι follows the orienter ἀποκριθεὶς εἶπεν αὐτῷ ὁ Ἰησοῦς, it is not used following εἴρηται, even though the quotation is the final point in the argument (sec. 16.2.2). Presumably, the scope of the first ὅτι includes the embedded quotation.

---

[6] All of these passages, and others, are discussed in Levinsohn 1978.

[7] Ὅτι is usually employed if the demonstrative οὗτος is used in the orienter to refer to the following speech. See, for example, John 21:23a (ἐξῆλθεν οὖν οὗτος ὁ λόγος εἰς τοὺς ἀδελφοὺς ὅτι...'So this word spread among the brothers that...'). Speeches that are introduced in this way 'culminate' the unit that begins with οὗτος by spelling out its content. See also Luke 24:44 and Acts 13:34 (following οὕτως).

[8] In some passages in Luke-Acts when the orienter is expressed as a postnuclear participial clause, the speech introduced with ὅτι seems to 'terminate' the sub-unit by giving the content of the nuclear verb. See, for example, Acts 11:2–3, in which the speech of v. 3 makes explicit what those of the circumcision were criticizing Peter for (διεκρίνοντο—v. 2). See also Luke 15:2 and 19:7; Acts 6:11, 15:5 and 18:13.

(12)   καὶ   ἀποκριθεὶς   εἶπεν   αὐτῷ   ὁ   Ἰησοῦς   ὅτι
        and   answering   3S.said to.him the Jesus   that

        Εἴρηται,   Οὐκ   ἐκπειράσεις   κύριον   τὸν   θεόν σου.
        3S.has.been.said not   you.shall.tempt lord   the   God your

Even when a causal ὅτι occurs in the immediate context of an embedded orienter, there appears to be
a preference for it not to be followed by ὅτι. This probably explains the existence of variants in **John
1:50** and John 3:28 (about which BDF (§470(1)) comment, "ὅτι is omitted before οὐκ because ὅτι
already comes before εἶπον").[9]

(50)   ἀπεκρίθη   Ἰησοῦς   καὶ   εἶπεν   αὐτῷ,   "Οτι   εἶπόν   σοι
        3S.answered Jesus   and   3S.said to.him   because I.said   to.you

        ὅτι   εἶδόν   σε   ὑποκάτω   τῆς   συκῆς,   πιστεύεις;
        that   I.saw   you underneath the   fig.tree you.believe

16.2.1 "Οτι Following Λέγω σοι/ὑμῖν

On 25 occasions in John's Gospel, Jesus is reported as introducing an assertion with the formula
ἀμὴν ἀμὴν λέγω σοι/ὑμῖν.[10] The norm is for ὅτι *not* to follow the formula; it is used only seven times.
When ὅτι does follow ἀμὴν ἀμὴν λέγω σοι/ὑμῖν, the following assertion "is a commentary" on what
has already been stated (Levinsohn 1978:28). In particular, it signals that the following assertion
explains, clarifies or otherwise explicates some previous point.[11] In contrast, assertions introduced with
ἀμὴν ἀμὴν λέγω σοι/ὑμῖν that lack ὅτι typically introduce new points.

This is seen by comparing **John 10:1** with **v. 7** (UBS text). The assertion of v. 1, which lacks ὅτι,
introduces the topic of "false and true shepherds" (Alford 1863.I:804), together with the image of the
gate of the sheepfold. This speech is followed by the observation (v. 6), 'Jesus used this figure with
them, but they did not understand what he was saying to them.' Consequently, the assertion of v. 7
interprets the figure for Jesus' audience. The presence of ὅτι signals that v. 7 does not introduce a new
point, but explicates some previous point.

(1)   Ἀμὴν   ἀμὴν   λέγω   ὑμῖν,   ὁ   μὴ   εἰσερχόμενος   διὰ
        truly   truly   I.say   to.you the not entering   through

        τῆς   θύρας   εἰς   τὴν   αὐλὴν   τῶν   προβάτων   ἀλλὰ
        the   door   into the   fold   of.the sheep   but

        ἀναβαίνων   ἀλλαχόθεν   ἐκεῖνος   κλέπτης   ἐστὶν   καὶ   λῃστής·
        going.up   another.way that.one   thief   3S.is   and   robber

(7)   Εἶπεν   οὖν   πάλιν   ὁ   Ἰησοῦς,   Ἀμὴν   ἀμὴν   λέγω   ὑμῖν
        3S.said then again   the Jesus   truly   truly   I.say   to.you

        ὅτι   ἐγώ   εἰμι   ἡ   θύρα   τῶν   προβάτων.   κ.τ.λ.
        that   I   I.am   the gate   of.the sheep

---

[9] See sec. 2 of Levinsohn 1999b for discussion of the extent to which the presence versus absence of ὅτι *recitativum* preceding
an embedded speech or quotation in John's Gospel is determined stylistically.

[10] In addition, Jesus' assertion of John 16:7 is introduced with ἐγὼ τὴν ἀλήθειαν λέγω ὑμῖν 'I tell you the truth.'

[11] I am grateful to Tony Pope (p.c.) for pointing this out to me.

A similar contrast is found in **John 13:18–21**. The absence of ὅτι in v. 20 is consistent with the assertion not relating closely to the context.[12] Its presence in v. 21 signals that the assertion explicates something that has already been said (vv. 18–19).

(18) "I am not speaking of all of you; I know whom I have chosen. But it is to fulfill the scripture, 'The one who ate my bread has lifted his heel against me.' (19) I tell you this now, before it occurs, so that when it does occur, you may believe that I am he.

(20) ἀμὴν ἀμὴν λέγω ὑμῖν, ὁ   λαμβάνων ἄν τινα
      truly truly I.say to.you the.one receiving whomever

      πέμψω   ἐμὲ λαμβάνει, κ.τ.λ.
      I.may.send me 3S.receives

(21) Ταῦτα εἰπὼν   [ὁ] Ἰησοῦς ἐταράχθη   τῷ πνεύματι
      this having.said the Jesus 3S.was.troubled in.the spirit

      καὶ ἐμαρτύρησεν καὶ εἶπεν, Ἀμὴν ἀμὴν λέγω ὑμῖν ὅτι
      and 3S.testified and 3S.said truly truly I.say to.you that

      εἷς ἐξ ὑμῶν παραδώσει με.
      one from you 3S.will.betray me

See also John 5:24 and 25 (explicating points made in vv. 22 and 21 in support of the assertion of v. 19), 8:34 (making explicit the implication of v. 32 that the hearers need to be freed from some sort of slavery), and 16:20–22 (explaining how v. 19 is to be understood). John 3:11 ('we speak of what we know and testify to what we have seen; yet you do not receive our testimony') gets "to the *heart* of the matter" (Pope p.c.) discussed in previous verses, especially the unbelief expressed in v. 9 by the question, 'How can these things be?'

The presence versus absence of ὅτι following (ἀμὴν) λέγω σοι/ὑμῖν in Luke's Gospel follows the same basic principle as that described for John. The main difference is that assertions introduced with ὅτι not only explicate what has already been said; they also terminate discussion of that topic or sub-topic.

This is seen in **Luke 4:24–25**. The presence of ὅτι in v. 24 indicates that v. 24 is a comment on vv. 22b–23 that also terminates the topic (the listeners' jealousy of Jesus—Alford 1863.I:476). Verse 25, in contrast, lacks ὅτι, as the verse begins the new topic of God's rejection of Israel (vv. 25–27).

(22b) They were saying, "Is not this Joseph's son?" (23) He said to them, "Doubtless you will quote to me this proverb, 'Doctor, cure yourself! Do here also in your hometown the things that we have heard you did at Capernaum.'"

(24) εἶπεν δέ, Ἀμὴν λέγω ὑμῖν ὅτι **οὐδεὶς προφήτης**
      3S.said DE truly I.say to.you that no   prophet

      δεκτός ἐστιν ἐν τῇ πατρίδι αὐτοῦ.
      welcome 3S.is in the country his

(25) ἐπ᾽ ἀληθείας δὲ λέγω ὑμῖν, **πολλαὶ χῆραι** ἦσαν
      in truth   DE I.say to.you many   widows 3P.were

      ἐν ταῖς ἡμέραις Ἠλίου ἐν τῷ Ἰσραήλ, κ.τ.λ.
      in the days   of.Elijah in the Israel

See also Luke 10:12, 10:24, 12:44, 14:24, 18:8, 21:3, 21:32, and 22:16 (all of which are discussed in Levinsohn 1978:28–29).

---

[12] "The connexion is very difficult, and variously set down" (op. cit. 838).

What is common, then, between Luke and John when ὅτι follows the formula (ἀμὴν) λέγω σοι/ὑμῖν, is that it signals that the assertion concerned is a commentary on some previous point. Whether the assertion is a terminating comment or whether it simply explicates some previous point seems to vary with the author.

16.2.2 Ὅτι with Quotations from Scripture

When a passage of Scripture is quoted as the final point to an argument in Luke-Acts and John, ὅτι follows γράφω 'write'. In **Luke 4:10–11**, for example, "the devil quotes two portions of Scripture, both introduced with ὅτι, to justify his call for Jesus to throw Himself off the pinnacle of the temple" (Levinsohn 1978:29).

(10)   γέγραπται   γὰρ   ὅτι   **Τοῖς ἀγγέλοις αὐτοῦ** ἐντελεῖται
         3S.is.written   for   that   to.the angels   his   3S.will.charge

         περὶ   σοῦ   τοῦ   διαφυλάξαι   σε,
         concerning   you   of.the   to.protect   you

(11)   καὶ   ὅτι   **Ἐπὶ** χειρῶν   ἀροῦσίν   σε,   μήποτε   προσκόψῃς
         and   that   upon   hands   3P.will.lift.up   you   lest   you.strike

         πρὸς   λίθον   τὸν   πόδα   σου.
         against   stone   the   foot   your

See also Luke 4:4, Acts 3:22 and 23:5. In the case of Luke 2:23, "Scripture is introduced using ὅτι to explain why Jesus had to be presented to the Lord in the temple (v. 22) (before Luke turns to another sacrifice, that which was made on behalf of Mary in v. 24)" (loc. cit.).[13]

Typically, when ὅτι *recitativum* is not used to introduce a quotation from Scripture, the quotation is *not* the final point to an argument. This is particularly clear when the quotation is followed by οὖν or διό, since these connectives introduce the next development in an argument. See, for instance, Luke 20:28 (the opening words of the Sadducees' speech), Luke 3:4–6 (in a narrative passage), Acts 1:20 and 15:15–18. See also Luke 4:17–19, 7:27 (the argument continues till v. 29), 19:46 and 20:17 (the argument continues till v. 18), and Acts 7:42–43.

When the quotation is the final point of the speech concerned, yet ὅτι is not used, this may still show that the quotation is not the final point of the argument. In the case of Luke 4:8, the exchange between Jesus and the devil is followed by another one (vv. 9–12). As for Acts 13:40–41, the final point of the main argument is the proclamation of Jesus in vv. 38–39, so the Scripture of vv. 40–41 that constitutes the warning is not introduced with ὅτι.

Several citations from a written source that are preceded by ὅτι in *John* are also quoted as the final point to an argument. Such is the case with **John 15:25**.

(23)   "Whoever hates me hates my Father also. (24) If I had not done among them the works that no one else did, they would not have sin. But now they have seen and hated both me and my Father.

(25)   ἀλλ᾽   ἵνα   πληρωθῇ   ὁ   λόγος   ὁ   ἐν   τῷ   νόμῳ   αὐτῶν
         but   that   3S.may.be.fulfilled   the   word   the   in   the   law   their

         γεγραμμένος   ὅτι   Ἐμίσησάν   με   δωρεάν.
         written   that   they.hated   me   without.cause

See also John 8:17 and 19:21b. The quotation in John 7:42 ('Has not the Scripture said...?') also concludes an argument, though it cites no Scripture directly.

---

[13] In other instances, a person, rather than Scripture, is quoted as the final point to an argument; see Luke 24:7, Acts 6:14 and 24:21.

Conversely, quotations from Scripture in John that do not culminate an argument are not introduced with ὅτι. For example, the following quotations are followed by a sentence introduced with οὖν or διὰ τοῦτο: John 2:17, 12:14-15, 12:38, and 19:24. See also John 6:31, 6:45, 12:39-40, 13:18, and 19:36-37 (although these quotations could be taken as the final point of the aside of vv. 35-37, the main narrative continues in v. 38).

I therefore conclude that ὅτι *recitativum* is used consistently in Luke-Acts and John to signal that the quotation it introduces culminates an argument.

Review Questions

(a) Is Turner (1963:326) right in claiming that ὅτι *recitativum* is to be taken as the "equivalent of inverted commas"?
(b) When ὅτι follows the formula (ἀμὴν) λέγω σοι/ὑμῖν in Luke or John, what does this signal?
(c) When ὅτι introduces a quotation in Luke-Acts or John, what does this signal?

Suggested Answers

(a) No! Rather, when introducing direct speech, the function of ὅτι *recitativum* is to signal that the speech terminates some unit or, at least, explicates some previous point.
(b) When ὅτι follows the formula (ἀμὴν) λέγω σοι/ὑμῖν in Luke or John, this signals that the assertion concerned is a commentary on some previous point. In Luke-Acts, this commentary typically terminates some unit or sub-unit. In John's Gospel, it simply explicates some previous point.
(c) When ὅτι introduces a quotation in Luke-Acts or John, this signals that the quotation culminates an argument.

Illustrative Passage 2: Luke 4:16–21

(16) He came to Nazareth, where he had been brought up, and went to the synagogue on the Sabbath day, as was his custom. He stood up to read, (17a) and the scroll of the prophet Isaiah was given to him.

(17b)
καὶ	ἀναπτύξας	τὸ	βιβλίον	εὗρεν	τὸν	τόπον
and	having.unrolled	the	scroll	3S.found	the	place

οὗ	ἦν	γεγραμμένον,	(18)	**Πνεῦμα**	**κυρίου**	ἐπ᾽	ἐμὲ	κ.τ.λ.
where	3S.was	written		spirit	of.lord	upon	me	

And, having rolled up the scroll and given it back to the attendant, he sat down. The eyes of all in the synagogue were fixed on him.

(21)
ἤρξατο	δὲ	λέγειν	πρὸς	αὐτοὺς	ὅτι	Σήμερον
3S.began	DE	to.say	to	them	that	today

πεπλήρωται	ἡ	γραφὴ	αὕτη	ἐν	τοῖς	ὠσὶν	ὑμῶν.
3S.has.been.fulfilled	the	scripture	this	in	the	ears	your

Questions

(a) Why does ὅτι *recitativum* not introduce the quotation from Scripture in Luke 4:18-19?
(b) Why does ὅτι *recitativum* introduce the reported speech of v. 21?

Suggested Answers

(a) Ὅτι *recitativum* does not introduce the quotation from Scripture in Luke 4:18-19 because the quotation is not the final point of the unit.
(b) Ὅτι *recitativum* introduces the reported speech of v. 21 because it is the culminating speech of the unit.

Illustrative Passage 3: John 11:38–41

(38)   Then Jesus, again greatly distressed, came to the tomb. It was a cave, and a stone was lying against it.

(39a)   Jesus says, "Take away the stone."

(39b)   Martha, the sister of the dead man, says to him, "Lord, already there is a stench because he has been dead four days."

(40)
λέγει	αὐτῇ	ὁ	Ἰησοῦς,	Οὐκ	εἶπόν	σοι	ὅτι	ἐὰν
3S.says	to.her	the	Jesus	not	I.said	to.you	that	if

πιστεύσῃς	ὄψῃ	τὴν	δόξαν	τοῦ	θεοῦ;
you.believed	you.will.see	the	glory	of.the	God

(41)   Then they took away the stone.

Question

Why does ὅτι *recitativum* introduce the embedded speech of v. 40?

Suggested Answer

῞Οτι *recitativum* introduces the embedded speech of v. 40 because it is the culminating speech of the conversation with Martha (which is a sub-unit of the larger discourse).

Illustrative Passage 4: Luke 6:3–6 (UBS text)

In some MSS, the speech of v. 5 is introduced with ὅτι *recitativum*.

(3)   Jesus answered, "Have you not read what David did when he and his companions were hungry, (4) how he entered the house of God and took and ate the bread of the Presence, which it is not lawful for any but the priests to eat, and gave some to his companions?"

(5)
καὶ	ἔλεγεν	αὐτοῖς,	**Κύριός**	ἐστιν	τοῦ	σαββάτου
and	3S.was.saying	to.them	lord	3S.is	of.the	Sabbath

ὁ	υἱὸς	τοῦ	ἀνθρώπου.
the	son	of.the	man

(6a)
Ἐγένετο	δὲ	ἐν	ἑτέρῳ	σαββάτῳ	εἰσελθεῖν	αὐτὸν
3S.happened	DE	on	another	Sabbath	to.enter	him

εἰς	τὴν	συναγωγὴν	καὶ	διδάσκειν.
into	the	synagogue	and	to.teach

Questions

(a) What does the absence of ὅτι *recitativum* in the UBS text of Luke 6:5 imply about the reported speech?

(b) What would the presence of ὅτι *recitativum* in the Luke 6:5 imply?

Suggested Answers: See Appendix 16(4).

PART VI: BOUNDARY FEATURES

This chapter concerns the criteria that enable the reader to recognize boundaries between paragraphs and larger semantic or pragmatic units such as 'sections' of a book. Because such units are characterized by having a single theme, the surface features considered in earlier chapters can only provide *supporting* evidence for boundaries established on other grounds. The problem is that supporting evidence can be cited for conflicting boundaries, so a need exists to discern *which* evidence is valid. I therefore suggest, in section 17.1, that the presence or absence of a *point of departure* has a major part to play in determining the validity of potential evidence. I then examine Beekman & Callow's (1974) list of potential supporting evidence from the point of view of its applicability in different situations (sec. 17.2).

17.1   Problems in Identifying Boundaries and a Partial Solution

This section begins by discussing three problems that arise when seeking to identify the boundaries of paragraphs or sections:

1. The paragraph or section is a semantic or pragmatic unit characterized by having a single theme, not by the presence of certain surface features
2. The presence of any specific surface feature is seldom a sufficient criterion on which to identify a paragraph or section boundary
3. Beekman and Callow's list of potential supporting evidence is sufficiently all-inclusive to justify alternative segmentations of the same passage.

However, the presence of a (sentence initial) point of departure partially alleviates these problems, since it indicates the primary basis for relating the information concerned to its context. The author's purpose and the text genre also influence low-level segmentation into paragraphs.

Problem 1: The paragraph or section is a semantic or pragmatic unit

Tomlin (1987:458) claims that "episodes are defined ultimately by the sustaining of attention on a particular paragraph level theme..." Beekman and Callow (1974:279) make a similar point:

> The basic criterion [for delineating a unit] is that a section or a paragraph deals with one theme. If the theme changes, then a new unit has started... what gives a section or paragraph its overall coherence as a semantic unit is the fact that one subject matter is being dealt with.

As a *semantic* unit,[1] then, the boundaries of a paragraph or section are defined on *semantic* grounds ("if the theme changes, then a new unit has started"), not with reference to the surface features discussed in earlier chapters (conjunctions, constituent order, etc.).

Although segmentation into paragraphs and sections is not *determined* by reference to surface features, there are many such features that occur at boundaries and can be taken as *supporting* evidence for the boundaries.

Problem 2: Surface features do not exclusively indicate boundaries

Although the presence of a surface feature can be taken as supporting evidence for a paragraph or section boundary, it must be emphasized that the presence of such a feature is seldom a sufficient criterion on which to base a boundary. Rather, if one of the reasons for the presence of a certain feature is because of a boundary between units, almost invariably there will be other reasons why that feature might be present.

---

[1] Randall Buth (p.c.) suggests that it would be better to call the paragraph a pragmatic unit, rather than a semantic one, since it reflects what the author views to be a single theme.

The use of 'redundant' noun phrase references to participants is a case in point. We have seen (sec. 8.2) that the default encoding of a subject in Greek, when it is the same as in the previous clause, is zero whereas, following a unit boundary, a noun phrase is used. However, a noun phrase is employed also when the sentence concerned is highlighted! Thus, though the presence of a 'redundant' noun phrase may provide supporting evidence for the existence of a boundary, it is not by itself sufficient evidence on which to posit the boundary (see further in sec. 17.2.7).

Now, suppose we discover a feature that does seem to occur systematically at boundaries in some particular text. It would be *wrong* to assume on that basis that the same feature will always mark boundaries since, in practice, different texts are arranged in different ways.

For example, Schooling (1985:21) observes that, in Matthew, ἀπὸ τότε 'from that time' "appears to occur very near those points where the book can be divided into four major units."[2] However, to argue from this observation that the presence of ἀπὸ τότε will always indicate a major boundary would be very foolish.

Another danger is to look for boundaries where they do not exist. For example, Luke has so designed the book of Acts that the major sections of the book are linked by *transitional* material. Commentators do not agree on where the sections begin and end, because the transitional material does not belong to one or the other; it bridges the gap.

A low-level case is **Acts 8:25–26**. Commentators consistently place a boundary before v. 26 (due, no doubt, to the use of the articular pronoun in v. 25 and the change of cast in v. 26), yet Luke introduces v. 25 with μὲν οὖν, anticipating a correlative δέ (found in v. 26) and the continuation of events involving Philip. The events of v. 25 are thus presented not so much as the conclusion of the first episode, but rather as transitional material uniting the two episodes that involve Philip, material that is *preliminary* to the second episode (see sec. 10.1).

| (25) | Οἱ | μὲν οὖν | διαμαρτυράμενοι | καὶ | λαλήσαντες | τὸν | λόγον |
| | the | then | having.witnessed | and | having.spoken | the | word |

| | τοῦ | κυρίου | ὑπέστρεφον | εἰς | Ἱεροσόλυμα, κ.τ.λ. |
| | of.the | Lord | 3P.were.returning | to | Jerusalem |

| (26) | Ἄγγελος | δὲ | κυρίου | ἐλάλησεν | πρὸς | Φίλιππον | λέγων, κ.τ.λ. |
| | angel | DE | of.Lord | 3S.spoke | to | Philip | saying |

Guthrie (1998:96) makes a similar point concerning the book of Hebrews. "The unit used to make an intermediary transition belongs neither exclusively to the discourse unit which precedes it nor the one which follows, but contains elements of both." He cites Heb. 8:1–2 as an example, which "functions as a direct intermediary transition between 5:1–7:28 and 8:3–10:18" (op. cit. p. 106).[3]

Problem 3: Beekman and Callow's list of potential supporting evidence is sufficiently all-inclusive to justify alternative segmentations of the same passage.

Beekman and Callow list the following as potential supporting evidence for boundaries (1974:279–80):[4]

- the conjunctions δέ, διό, καί, οὖν, τότε, etc.
- indications of change of time or location in narrative
- summary statements, such as 'when Jesus had finished these sayings' (Matt. 7:28, 11:1, 13:53, 19:1, 26:1)

---

[2] A more accurate claim is that asyndeton and ἀπὸ τότε signals a major boundary in Matthew (4:17, 16:21). The combination καὶ ἀπὸ τότε, which is found in 26:16, does not signal a major boundary in the Gospel.

[3] Note, however, the use of δέ and a point of departure in Heb. 8:1, following the strengthening material at the end of chapter 7. This indicates a switch from the previous topic to a different one (see sec. 7.4).

[4] Callow & Callow (1992:23) also mention "change of writer's mood (evidenced by strongly positive or negative vocabulary), change from casual to formal style, and so on" as a signal of "boundaries where import changes."

- rhetorical questions that introduce a new theme or topic
- the use of the vocative form of address
- changes in the cast of participants
- changes in the tense-aspect or mood of a verb.

This list is so inclusive that the presence of one or another of the features can often be cited as supporting evidence for alternative analyses of the same passage. Consider, for example, the grounds for recognizing a boundary at Luke 20:19 versus v. 20 (below; vv. 9–18 relate the parable of the vineyard and the tenants).

Passage 1: Luke 20:18–20

(18) [Jesus said, "..."] Everyone who falls on that stone will be broken to pieces; and it will crush anyone on whom it falls."

(19a) Καὶ ἐζήτησαν οἱ γραμματεῖς καὶ οἱ ἀρχιερεῖς
and 3P.sought the scribes and the chief.priests

ἐπιβαλεῖν ἐπ᾽ αὐτὸν τὰς χεῖρας ἐν αὐτῇ τῇ ὥρᾳ,
to.lay.on on him the hands in same the hour

(19b) καὶ ἐφοβήθησαν τὸν λαόν,
and 3P.feared the people

(19c) ἔγνωσαν γὰρ ὅτι **πρὸς αὐτοὺς** εἶπεν τὴν παραβολὴν ταύτην.
3P.knew for that against them 3S.said the parable this

(20) Καὶ παρατηρήσαντες ἀπέστειλαν ἐγκαθέτους κ.τ.λ.
and having.watched.carefully 3P.sent spies

ἵνα ἐπιλάβωνται αὐτοῦ λόγου, ὥστε παραδοῦναι αὐτὸν κ.τ.λ.
so.that 3P.might.seize his word so.as to.deliver him

There are several grounds for recognizing a boundary *after* v. 19. Semantically, v. 19 refers to the parable recounted in the previous verses, whereas v. 20 introduces a new theme. Supporting evidence for the boundary includes the following:
- the same participants are involved in the event described in v. 19 as in the previous events, whereas there is a partial change of cast in v. 20
- there is an implied time lapse ('having watched carefully') between the events of v. 19 and v. 20
- there is an implied movement off- and on-stage ('they sent').

At the same time, there are several grounds for a boundary to be recognized *before* v. 19. Semantically, there is a change of theme from challenging Jesus' authority (vv. 1–18) to finding a means of arresting him (vv. 19ff.). Supporting evidence for a boundary includes:
- a 'redundant' noun phrase reference to the scribes and chief priests in v. 19, but no overt reference to them in v. 20
- the events of v. 19 and v. 20 have the same initiators
- an initial participle at the beginning of v. 20, which tends to imply continuity with the context (sec. 11.1.3).

Since the potential supporting evidence for a boundary before versus after v. 19 is in conflict, we need to be able to discern *which* evidence is valid at each potential boundary.

A partial solution: The presence of a point of departure

Of the "linguistic clues as to the nature of the changes on which the segmentation is based" (Levinsohn 1980:517), foremost is the presence or absence of a point of departure, as it signals some sort of discontinuity.[5] What is of particular significance for determining boundaries in the presence of a point of departure is that it indicates the *primary basis* for relating what follows to the context. It thus gives some indication as to which of the potential supporting evidence is or is not valid.

In the case of passage 1 above, for instance, it is inappropriate to cite a lapse of time between Luke 20:19 and v. 20 as supporting evidence for a boundary after v. 19. This is because Luke chooses to begin v. 20 with a participle (implying continuity) rather than a temporal point of departure (indicating a temporal discontinuity).

A complicating factor: Low-level paragraph breaks

Although a major clue in determining the validity of some supporting evidence for boundaries is the presence of a point of departure, potential boundaries in many instances do not involve points of departure. In Acts, for instance, the different versions introduce paragraph breaks whenever there is a change in a relevant feature within strings of more than three sentences or colons (which, in the case of Acts, are Development Units [DUs] introduced by δέ). The following principle is helpful (Levinsohn 1980:523):

> If Event-type DUs E_1, E_2... E_m have feature X_1 in common and E_n... E_z have corresponding but different feature X_2 in common, then a paragraph break is discerned between E_m and E_n, provided that neither of the paragraphs produced by the posited break would contain only one event-type DU.[6]

As to which features are relevant to segmentation, I found that, whereas the division of a book into larger units is largely determined by the *purpose* of the book, the primary *genre* of the book produces many low-level divisions.

For example, different sections of the book of Acts are concerned with different Christian leaders. As a result, the book can be divided to some extent on the ground of which leader is to the fore (e.g., in chapters 6–9, Stephen, Philip, Saul, or Peter). Similarly, it can be divided to some extent on the ground of changes in the cast of participants who interact with an ongoing Christian leader (e.g., in chapter 16, Paul and Lydia, Paul and the girl with a spirit of divination, Paul and the Philippian jailer). Such divisions reflect the *purpose* of the book. However, because the primary genre of the book is narrative, many sections naturally *subdivide* on the ground of changes of temporal setting.

Review Questions

(a) On what grounds are the boundaries of paragraphs or sections defined?
(b) Is the presence of a particular surface feature usually a sufficient criterion on which to base a paragraph or section boundary?
(c) Why is the presence of a point of departure of particular value for recognizing the presence of a paragraph or section boundary?
(d) If the primary genre of a book is narrative, on what ground do many sections of the book subdivide?

Suggested Answers

(a) The boundaries of paragraphs or sections are defined on semantic or pragmatic grounds ("if the theme changes, then a new unit has started"—Beekman & Callow 1974:279), not with reference to surface features such as constituent order or the presence of a particular conjunction.
(b) No, the presence of a particular surface feature is seldom a sufficient criterion on which to base a paragraph or section boundary. Typically, there will be other reasons why that feature might be present.

---

[5] In the case of Acts, I even claimed (op. cit. 508) that "the principal divisions in the narrative must co-occur with sentences which begin with a... basis," i.e., a point of departure. Acts is a special case, in that the whole book develops a single theme, but this claim does have some validity also for other books.

[6] In English, paragraphs consisting of a single sentence tend to be avoided.

(c) The presence of a point of departure is of particular value for recognizing the presence of a paragraph or section boundary because it signals some sort of discontinuity and indicates the primary basis for relating what follows to the context. It thus gives some indication as to which of the potential supporting evidence is or is not valid.

(d) If the primary genre of a book is narrative, many sections of the book subdivide on the ground of changes of temporal setting.

17.2   Knowing When Supporting Evidence Is Valid

My aim in this section is to show when potentially supportive evidence should be taken as valid confirmation of the existence of a boundary. In the following subsections, the surface features mentioned in sec. 17.1 that Beekman and Callow (1974) cite as providing supporting evidence for a boundary are discussed. The list is supplemented by features mentioned in Neeley (1987).

17.2.1 Conjunctions and Asyndeton

The conjunctions δέ and τότε and asyndeton often occur at paragraph and section boundaries, whereas καί and τέ are less frequently found at such boundaries.

First, concerning δέ and καί (chaps. 5 and 7), I argued for Acts that "paragraph breaks must not violate the boundaries of D[evelopment] U[nit]s (with certain well-defined exceptions)" (1980:507).[7] In particular, if καί is used to associate information at the beginning or end of an episode in which each new development in the story is marked by the presence of δέ, then new paragraphs will tend not to begin with such a καί. Titrud (1991:18) makes a similar claim for the Epistles, "a new paragraph should not be made where a conjunctive καί begins a sentence in the Greek text."[8]

Nevertheless, if introductory material united by καί extends over several sentences and the events described by them occur at different times, then they will naturally fall into distinct paragraphs (see the principle stated at the end of sec. 17.1). Such is the case even when the absence of δέ may imply that they only form the setting for what is to follow (see sec. 5.1 for a discussion of the use of καί rather than δέ in Acts 1:9–2:4 and other passages).

Furthermore, it is common in the Synoptic Gospels and Acts for καί to introduce episodes that do not build directly on the last episode, so the presence of καί in no way excludes a paragraph break.

Té solitarium (sec. 6.3), because of its additive nature, tends not to occur at the beginning of a paragraph.[9] In particular, as with καί, paragraphs introduced with τέ should not violate the boundaries of development units introduced with δέ.

For this reason, the generally recognized paragraph break at **Acts 21:37** is inappropriate if it is proposed *instead of* a break at v. 35:

> The generally recognised paragraph break at xxi.37 reflects Paul's change of role to that of initiator and the interruption of the tribune's order of v. 34b. However, it does not do justice to the presence of τέ, which indicates that v. 37 occurs against the general background of the crowd's violence of v. 35... If the incident is begun at v. 35 rather than at v. 37, it becomes clearer that this part of the story is orientated primarily, not around Paul and the tribune, but around Paul and the crowd. (v. 39a shows that Paul's initiative in v. 37 is occasioned by his desire to speak to the crowd.) (Levinsohn 1980:503)

(33a)   τότε having drawn near, the tribune arrested him,
(33b)   καί ordered him to be bound with two chains;
(33c)   καί he was inquiring who he was and what he had done.

---

[7] "I therefore maintain that any analysis of the structure of Acts should take the DU as the basic element or building block of paragraphs. Exceptions to this norm are found only (a) when an additional break does not violate the boundaries of DUs; (b) immediately following a lengthy reported speech" (op. cit. 506).

[8] These remarks about δέ and καί do not apply to Mark's Gospel.

[9] Acts 24:10 and 27:21 are acceptable exceptions, since lengthy reported speeches typically occupy a paragraph by themselves—see fn. 6 and Neeley 1987:18–19.

(34a) <u>Some</u> δέ in the crowd were shouting one thing, some another;

(34b) not being able δέ to learn the facts because of the uproar, he ordered him to be brought into the barracks.

(35) <u>When</u> δέ <u>he came to the steps</u>, the violence of the mob was so great that he had to be carried by the soldiers.

(36) The crowd that was following γάρ kept shouting, "Away with him!"

(37a) Just as Paul was about τέ to be brought into the barracks, he said to the tribune, "May I say something to you?"

(37b) he δέ said, "Do you know Greek?..."

(39) Paul said δέ, "... I beg you, let me speak to the people."

(Supporting evidence for a boundary at v. 35 is the use of a temporal point of departure, whereas v. 37 begins with a participle. However, the fact that the background material of v. 36 relates back to v. 35 and Paul is referred to by name in v. 37 means that an *additional* paragraph break in v. 37 can be justified.)

As I noted at the beginning of part II, material introduced with γάρ strengthens an assertion or assumption that has been presented in or implied by the immediate context. Consequently, such material naturally belongs with the assertion to which it relates. However, if the strengthening material extends over several sentences, it may well be presented in its own paragraph.

See, for example, the citations from Scripture in Heb. 1:5–14. Because they strengthen the assertion of v. 4 that God's Son has 'become as much superior to angels as the name he has inferred is more excellent than theirs,' they are introduced with γάρ. Nevertheless, because they share a common theme (they are all quotations from the Old Testament), v. 5 often begins a new paragraph.

Tότε (sec. 6.1) occurs at "low level divisions within an episode" (Schooling 1985:18). It is thus a good piece of supporting evidence for a low-level boundary. However, since it is also used to introduce key concluding speeches, its presence does not guarantee a paragraph break.

Asyndeton (sec. 7.2) is commonly found at the beginning of a new paragraph or section if that unit has its own nucleus. This is true especially in the Epistles, since parallel statements in them commonly are juxtaposed without a conjunction. However, asyndeton is typically found also in connection with restatements and other relations that would suggest an association of the proposition concerned with its nucleus. Therefore, the absence of a conjunction is significant only in connection with other potential boundary features such as *vocatives* (see sec. 17.2.8) and some classes of *orienters* ("complement-taking predicates" —Noonan 1985:110) such as Ἠκούσατε ὅτι 'you heard that' (Matt. 5:21) or Ἐλπίζω ... ἵνα 'I hope... that' (Phil. 2:19).

In addition to the conjunctions mentioned above, Neeley (1987:18) has observed that the use of particles such as "οὖν, διὰ τοῦτο, ὅθεν, ἄρα... to indicate return to backbone from supportive material often also indicates a paragraph break." The longer the amount of intervening material, the more major is the boundary likely to be. See, for example, the use of οὖν at Heb. 4:14 to mark the resumption of the topic of Jesus as our high priest, which was last mentioned in 3:1. (For further examples of οὖν used as a resumptive, see sec. 7.4.)

17.2.2 Spatiotemporal Changes

References to new *temporal* settings are normally sentence initial, indicating that the basis for relating the new information to the context is temporal (see sec. 2.2 and sec. 17.1 above). When a temporal expression is not initial, this consistently indicates that the basis for relating to the context is not temporal (sec. 2.4). For a temporal change to be supporting evidence for a boundary, reference to it must therefore be initial; i.e., it must be a point of departure.

Spatial changes are less clear-cut, as most commonly they are indicated in connection with travel. In the case of Acts, there is no evidence "that changes of location per se constitute grounds for a paragraph break. Rather, events at location L₁ usually are separated from those which occur at L₂, because the two sets of events involve different casts" (Levinsohn 1980:538). Note that "travel from the scene of one incident to the scene of the next is usually appended to the description of events at the one location or the other" (loc. cit.). In other words, whereas changes of location may coincide with the presence of a boundary, such changes should not normally be cited as supporting evidence independent of changes of cast or time.

17.2.3 Summary Statements

By their nature, summary statements unite together the information they summarize and thereby indicate that the preceding material should be treated as a block, over against what is to follow. Summary statements thus provide good supporting evidence for boundaries (Larsen 1991c:51). See, for example, Heb. 11:39–40; the point of departure οὗτοι πάντες (these all) brings together all the heroes of the faith who were cited in earlier verses of the chapter.

Summary statements may terminate or begin units. In Matt. 7:28–29, the summary statement 'when Jesus had finished these sayings' introduces what is usually treated as a short *concluding* paragraph describing how the people responded to the Sermon on the Mount, before the next episode is presented (but see sec. 8.3). In Luke 7:1, in contrast, the summary statement *begins* the introductory sentence of the next episode ('After he had ended all his sayings in the hearing of the people, he entered Capernaum').

17.2.4 Chiastic Structures

Chiastic structures indicate that the material concerned forms a self-contained unit (see Neeley 1987:13–18), which should be treated as a block over against that which precedes and follows.

Neeley cites **Heb. 5:1–10** as an example of a chiastic structure. She uses A, A' (etc.) to refer to the corresponding parts of the structure, and superscript numbers to mark the corresponding elements in each part; the italics are also Neeley's.

A	For every *high priest*[1] taken from among men *is appointed*[2] on behalf of men in relation to things of God, that he may offer gifts and sacrifices for sins,
B	being able to deal gently with the ignorant and deceived, since he himself also is surrounded with weakness, and for this reason he ought, just as for the people, so also for himself, to offer for sins.
C	And no one takes this honor to himself,[3] but he who is called by God,[4] just as Aaron was.
C'	So also Christ did not glorify himself to become a high priest,[3] but the one who said to him,[4] You are my son, today I have begotten you. Just as also in another place he says, You are a priest forever after the order of Melchizedek.[4]
B'	who in the days of his flesh having offered up prayers and petitions with strong cries and tears to him who was able to save him from death and having been heard because of his fear of God, although he was a Son, learned obedience through what he suffered and having been perfected, he became the source of eternal salvation to those who obey him,
A'	*being designated by God*[2] a *high priest*[1] after the order of Melchizedek.

17.2.5 *Inclusio* Structures

Guthrie (1998:14) defines *inclusio* structures as "The bracketing of a pericope by making a statement at the beginning of the section, an approximation of which is repeated at the conclusion of the section." Callow and Callow (1992:27) call such structures "semantic sandwich" structures. Like chiasm, *inclusio* may indicate that the material concerned forms a self-contained unit. Romans 8:35–39 is such a structure, since it begins, τίς ἡμᾶς χωρίσει ἀπὸ τῆς ἀγάπης τοῦ Χριστοῦ; 'who will separate us from the love of Christ?' (v. 35) and ends, δυνήσεται ἡμᾶς χωρίσαι ἀπὸ τῆς ἀγάπης τοῦ θεοῦ κ.τ.λ. 'will be able to separate us from the love of God...' See also Heb. 5:1–10 (sec. 17.2.4 above).

See Guthrie (op. cit. 76–89) for instances of *inclusio* in Hebrews. See sec. 17.2.11 on the need to distinguish back-reference from *inclusio*.

17.2.6 Rhetorical Questions

Sometimes, as Beekman and Callow (1974:243) claim, "rhetorical questions are... used to signal the start of a new subject [theme] or some new aspect of the same subject." However, Neeley (1987:10–11) finds that "rhetorical questions... can mark introduction, point 1, peak or conclusion." See, for example, Heb. 1:5–2:2, in which rhetorical questions mark point 1 (1:5), two conclusions (1:13, 14), and an introduction (2:2–3).

A cursory inspection of the examples cited by Beekman and Callow and by Neeley suggests that those rhetorical questions that occur at generally recognized boundaries are usually accompanied by a developmental conjunction (δέ or οὖν). The question and conjunction *together* provide the supporting evidence for a boundary.

17.2.7 Participant Reference by Means of a Noun Phrase

If a 'redundant' noun phrase reference to a participant occurs, the context should be examined to see why it is present. It is generally not too difficult to decide whether its occurrence is due to highlighting or not, since highlighted sentences tend not to begin units. If the context suggests that it is used to highlight, it probably does not mark the beginning of a unit.

In the Gospels, references to Jesus by name at the beginning of a paragraph usually indicate a major break. See, for example, Mark 1:14 and 3:7.

The *absence* of a 'redundant' noun phrase at what may otherwise seem to be a boundary is useful counterevidence, at least against a high-level boundary (see sec. 8.3 and the discussion of Luke 20:20 in sec. 17.1).

17.2.8 Vocatives

I see a parallel between the presence of a vocative and the use of a 'redundant' noun phrase reference to a participant. Both are found at the beginning of units and in connection with key statements such as nuclear propositions. As such, they may be cited as supporting evidence for a boundary, but their presence does not automatically indicate a boundary.

As Banker's good treatment of the vocative ἀδελφοί 'brothers' concludes (1984:36), the vocative acts with other forms and constructions to signal the beginning of new units in discourse on various levels. It also seems to reinforce conjunctions such as ὥστε and ἄρα οὖν when they introduce commands that are nuclear propositions in paragraphs and sections. See also Longacre (1992:272–76) on vocatives in 1 John.

17.2.9 Changes of Cast and Role

I argued for Acts that a change of *cast* in narrative must directly affect the global VIP of the section if it is to constitute sufficient grounds to support a paragraph or section break. For example, "the introduction of participant A as initiator... must directly affect the central character [global VIP] of the narrative (a Christian leader, in the case of Acts) if a paragraph break is warranted" (Levinsohn 1980:533).

In **Acts 16:27**, for instance, the reintroduction of the jailer does not provide supporting evidence for a paragraph break, because his initiative does not directly affect Paul and Silas (the Christian leaders).

> (25)   About midnight Paul and Silas were praying and singing hymns to God, and the prisoners were listening to them. (26) Suddenly there was an earthquake, so violent that the foundations of the prison were shaken; and immediately all the doors were opened and everyone's chains were unfastened.

> (27)   ἔξυπνος   δὲ   γενόμενος   ὁ   δεσμοφύλαξ   καὶ   ἰδὼν
>   awake   DE   having.become the jailer   and having.seen

ἀνεῳγμένας   τὰς θύρας τῆς   φυλακῆς,
having.been.opened the doors of.the jail

having drawn his sword, was about to kill himself...

A significant change in the *role* of the global VIP also constitutes grounds for supporting a paragraph or section break. This is particularly the case if it involves a change from overall initiator to undergoer because of the emergence of a new initiator or if it involves a change from inactive bystander to overall initiator.

In **Acts 16:19**, for example, the introduction of the owners of the slave girl result in a change in Paul's role from overall initiator to undergoer, so provides supporting evidence for a paragraph break.

(17) This one, following Paul and us, would cry out, "These men are slaves of the Most High God, who proclaim to you a way of salvation." (18) She kept doing this for many days. But Paul, very much annoyed, turned and said to the spirit, "I order you in the name of Jesus Christ to come out of her." And it came out that very hour.

(19) ἰδόντες   δὲ οἱ κύριοι αὐτῆς ὅτι ἐξῆλθεν
having.seen DE the masters her   that 3S.left

ἡ ἐλπὶς τῆς ἐργασίας αὐτῶν,
the hope of.the profit   their

having seized Paul and Silas, dragged them into the market-place before the authorities (20) and, having brought them before the magistrates, said, "These men are disturbing our city..."

In summary, a change in participant cast or roles provides supporting evidence for a boundary if it affects the global VIP.

17.2.10 Changes of Verb Tense-Aspect, Mood and/or Person

Changes of tense-aspect and mood may provide supporting evidence for a boundary (Porter 1992:301). As an example of this, Neeley (1987:19) cites **Heb. 3:12–18**, "where, at the break [between v. 15 and v. 16], the verbs change in person, tense and mood" (from second person to third and from present imperative to past declarative). The change of person presumably parallels a change of cast in narrative.

(12) Βλέπετε, ἀδελφοί, μήποτε ἔσται   ἔν τινι ὑμῶν καρδία
look   brothers   lest   3S.shall.be in any of.you heart

πονηρὰ ἀπιστίας ἐν τῷ ἀποστῆναι ἀπὸ θεοῦ ζῶντος,
evil   of.unbelief in the to.depart from God living

(13) ἀλλὰ παρακαλεῖτε ἑαυτοὺς καθ' ἑκάστην ἡμέραν, κ.τ.λ.
but   exhort   selves each   day

(14) **μέτοχοι** γὰρ **τοῦ** **Χριστοῦ** γεγόναμεν,   ἐάνπερ
sharers for of.the Christ   we.have.become if.indeed

τὴν ἀρχὴν τῆς ὑποστάσεως μέχρι τέλους βεβαίαν
the beginning of.the assurance until end   firm

κατάσχωμεν, (15) ἐν τῷ λέγεσθαι, Σήμερον κ.τ.λ.
we.hold.fast   in the to.be.said today

μὴ σκληρύνητε τὰς καρδίας ὑμῶν κ.τ.λ.
not harden   the hearts your

(16a) τίνες γὰρ ἀκούσαντες παρεπίκραναν;
some   for hearing   3P.provoked

(16b) ἀλλ᾽ οὐ πάντες οἱ   ἐξελθόντες ἐξ Αἰγύπτου διὰ   Μωϋσέως;
       but not all the.ones coming.out out of.Egypt through Moses

(17a) τίσιν   δὲ προσώχθισεν τεσσεράκοντα ἔτη;
       with.whom DE 3S.was.angry forty   years

(17b) οὐχὶ τοῖς   ἁμαρτήσασιν,
       not with.the.ones sinning

(17c) ὧν   τὰ κῶλα ἔπεσεν ἐν τῇ ἐρήμῳ;
       of.whom the corpses 3S.fell in the desert

(18)   τίσιν   δὲ ὤμοσεν μὴ εἰσελεύσεσθαι εἰς τὴν κατάπαυσιν αὐτοῦ
       to.whom DE 3S.swore not to.enter   into the rest   his

       εἰ μὴ τοῖς   ἀπειθήσασιν;
       if not to.the.ones having.disobeyed

The use of the *historical present* (HP) may be included under this same heading. Since non-speech HPs commonly occur at the beginning of a subsection, switches from an aorist or imperfect to a non-speech HP may provide supporting evidence of a boundary. It must be remembered, though, that non-speech HPs do not always occur at the beginning of a subsection (see discussion in sec. 12.2).

17.2.11 Back-Reference

"Back-reference involves reference to the preceding paragraph or paragraphs or to a point or points within preceding paragraphs. Back-reference often occurs at the beginning of a new paragraph" (Neeley 1987:19). In **Acts 4:23**, there is a back-reference to an earlier verb (v. 21) in the preceding paragraph, in connection with the resumption of the main event line after the occurrence of the supportive material of v. 22.

(21)   οἱ   δὲ προσαπειλησάμενοι   ἀπέλυσαν αὐτούς,
       they DE having.threatened.more 3P.released them

       μηδὲν   εὑρίσκοντες τὸ πῶς κολάσωνται   αὐτούς,
       nothing finding   the how 3P.might.punish them

       διὰ   τὸν λαόν, κ.τ.λ.
       on.account.of the people

(22)   ἐτῶν   γὰρ ἦν   πλειόνων τεσσεράκοντα ὁ   ἄνθρωπος
       of.years for 3S.was more   forty   the man

       ἐφ᾽ ὃν   γεγόνει   τὸ σημεῖον τοῦτο τῆς ἰάσεως.
       upon whom 3S.has.become the sign   this of.the healing

(23)[10] Ἀπολυθέντες   δὲ ἦλθον   πρὸς τοὺς ἰδίους κ.τ.λ.
        having.been.released DE 3P.went to   the own

Although Guthrie (1998:78) considers **Heb. 4:14** to be an instance of *inclusio* with **Heb. 3:1** (see sec. 17.2.5), most of the terms common to the two verses are repeated in the NPC that introduces 4:14, rather than in the nuclear clause. This suggests that 4:14 is an instance of back-reference at the beginning of a new topic, as the topic of Jesus as our high priest is resumed (see sec. 17.2.1 on οὖν in 4:14).

(3:1) Ὅθεν,   ἀδελφοὶ ἅγιοι, κλήσεως ἐπουρανίου
       for.which.reason brothers holy   calling heavenly

       μέτοχοι, κατανοήσατε   τὸν ἀπόστολον καὶ ἀρχιερέα
       partners consider.carefully the apostle   and high.priest

---

10

τῆς   ὁμολογίας ἡμῶν   Ἰησοῦν,
of.the confession our   Jesus

(4:14) Ἔχοντες οὖν   ἀρχιερέα μέγαν διεληλυθότα   τοὺς οὐρανούς,
       having   then high.priest great having.gone.through the   heavens

Ἰησοῦν τὸν υἱὸν τοῦ θεοῦ, κρατῶμεν   τῆς ὁμολογίας.
Jesus   the son   of.the God   let.us.hold.firmly the   confession

(Hebrews 10:19-23 may be similar. Guthrie (op. cit. pp. 79-82) recognizes *inclusio* with 4:14-16, but the combination of the prenuclear NPC and the presence of οὖν suggests that the topic of 4:14-16 is being resumed, notwithstanding the repetition of the imperatives of those verses in 10:22-23.)

Guthrie also discusses "*hook words*" in Hebrews: "a rhetorical device used in the ancient world to tie two sections of material together. A word was positioned at the end of one section and at the beginning of the next to effect a transition between the two" (op. cit. p. 12). For instance, **Heb. 7:1** begins with the point of departure Οὗτος ὁ Μελχισέδεκ (this the Melchizedek), and Melchizedek was mentioned at the end of the previous section (6:20).

(6:20) ὅπου **πρόδρομος** ὑπὲρ ἡμῶν εἰσῆλθεν Ἰησοῦς, **κατὰ**   **τὴν τάξιν**
       where forerunner   for   us   3S.entered Jesus   according.to the order

Μελχισέδεκ **ἀρχιερεὺς** γενόμενος   εἰς τὸν αἰῶνα.
Melchizedek   high.priest   having.become to   the   age

(7:1) <u>Οὗτος</u> γὰρ <u>ὁ</u> <u>Μελχισέδεκ</u> κ.τ.λ.
      this   for the Melchizedek

Note, however, that the unusually heavy encoding of reference to Melchizedek in Heb. 7:1 is what particularly contributes to the identification of a paragraph break (see sec. 17.2.7). This is because a concept may be introduced at the end of one sentence and become the point of departure/propositional topic of the next, yet no paragraph break is recognized. See, for instance, James 1:3-4 (discussed in sec. 2.8).

One type of back-reference is *tail-head linkage* (sec. 12.1). Since it is not unusual for such repetition to be sentence initial, as in **Heb. 2:8b**, it may often be viewed as a specific instance of a point of departure (at a point of discontinuity).

(8a) **πάντα** ὑπέταξας   ὑποκάτω τῶν ποδῶν αὐτοῦ.
     all   you.subjected under   the   feet   his

(8b) <u>ἐν</u> <u>τῷ</u> γὰρ <u>ὑποτάξαι</u> [αὐτῷ]   <u>τὰ</u>   <u>πάντα</u>
     in   the   for   to.subject   to.him   the   all

οὐδὲν   ἀφῆκεν αὐτῷ   ἀνυπότακτον.
nothing 3S.left to.him unsubjected

As with οὖν used as a resumptive (sec. 17.2.1), the greater the distance between the back-reference and the material to which it refers, the more major is the boundary likely to be. Compare, for example, the degree of discontinuity implied by the references back to Acts 8:1 in 8:4 and 11:19.

Before going on to examine two passages that illustrate features of supporting evidence for boundaries, we do well to recognize that:

> The discussion does not imply the criteria are always so clear and unambiguous that the boundaries of these larger semantic units may be established without any problem cases at all... But it does imply that, as these criteria are consciously applied and more skill is gained, it will rarely be impossible to decide with certainty on a boundary. (Beekman & Callow 1974:280)

Review Questions

(a) Which of the following *conjunctions* are most likely to occur at paragraph and section boundaries: δέ, καί, τέ, τότε?

(b) What condition must be met for a *temporal* change to provide supporting evidence for a boundary?

(c) Under what circumstances does a *spatial* change in connection with travel provide supporting evidence for a boundary?

(d) Why do *summary statements* provide good supporting evidence for a boundary?

(e) Under what circumstances does a *rhetorical question* provide supporting evidence for a boundary?

(f) What other factor must be considered before it is judged that the presence of a *'redundant' noun phrase* reference provides supporting evidence for a boundary?

(g) Under what circumstances does a *change in participant cast or role* provide supporting evidence for a boundary?

Suggested Answers

(a) The conjunctions most likely to occur at paragraph and section boundaries are δέ and τότε. Because καί and τέ are used to associate information together, they typically occur either within paragraphs or at supplementary boundaries.

(b) For a temporal change to provide supporting evidence for a boundary, it must be expressed sentence initial, i.e., in a point of departure.

(c) A spatial change in connection with travel provides supporting evidence for a boundary only when accompanied by other supporting evidence such as a change of cast or time.

(d) Summary statements provide good supporting evidence for a boundary because they indicate that the preceding material is to be treated as a block.

(e) A rhetorical question provides supporting evidence for a boundary when accompanied by other supporting evidence such as a developmental conjunction.

(f) Before it is judged that the presence of a 'redundant' noun phrase reference provides supporting evidence for a boundary, the possibility that it is present to highlight the sentence concerned must be discounted.

(g) A change in participant cast or role provides supporting evidence for a boundary when it affects the global VIP.

Illustrative Passage 2: Acts 18:18–24

This passage describes the completion of Paul's second missionary journey and the beginning of his third. Because of this, a number of commentators introduce a major division in the book of Acts between 18:22 and 23. However, we must consider whether there is supporting evidence for such a boundary.

(18)   Paul δέ having stayed there for a considerable time and said farewell to the brothers, sailed away for Syria, accompanied by Priscilla and Aquila....

(19a)   They came down δέ to Ephesus,

(19b)   καί them he left there,

(19c)   he δέ going into the synagogue, had a discussion with the Jews.

(20)   On them asking δέ him to stay longer, he declined;

(21)   ἀλλά on taking leave of them, saying, "I will return to you if God wills," he set sail from Ephesus.

(22)   καί having landed at Caesarea, gone up and greeted the church, he went down to Antioch.

(23)   καί ποιήσας   χρόνον τινὰ ἐξῆλθεν   διερχόμενος
        and having.spent time   some 3S.went.out passing.through

        καθεξῆς τὴν Γαλατικὴν χώραν   καὶ Φρυγίαν, ἐπιστηρίζων
        in.order the Galatian   country and Phrygia   strengthening

        πάντας τοὺς μαθητάς.
        all   the disciples

(24) Ἰουδαῖος   δέ   τις   Ἀπολλῶς   ὀνόματι...   κατήντησεν   εἰς   Ἔφεσον,   κ.τ.λ.
      Jew   DE   certain Apollos   named   3S.arrived   in   Ephesus

Question

What evidence is there that a boundary is *not* to be perceived after Acts 18:22?

Suggested Answer

The evidence against a boundary after Acts 18:22 is:
- the use of καί introducing v. 23, but δέ in vv. 20 and 24 (δέ introduces what Luke perceives to be the new developments in the storyline)
- the use of an initial participle to introduce v. 23
- the failure to use a noun phrase to refer to Paul in v. 23.

Passage 3: Galatians 5:22–6:6

Commentators do not agree as to where the boundaries of this passage are. Read the passage carefully, applying the criteria discussed in the preceding sections. Remember that potential supporting evidence for a boundary generally has more than one interpretation. Asyndeton, for instance, may be used between parallel statements (e.g., between the nuclei of different units), but may also be used to introduce a restatement of a nucleus.

(22) Ὁ   δὲ   καρπὸς   τοῦ   πνεύματός   ἐστιν   ἀγάπη   χαρὰ   κ.τ.λ.
      the DE fruit   of.the Spirit   3S.is   love   joy

(23b) Ø   κατὰ   τῶν   τοιούτων   οὐκ   ἔστιν   νόμος.
       against the   such.things not   3S.is   law

(24) οἱ   δὲ   τοῦ   Χριστοῦ   [Ἰησοῦ]   τὴν   σάρκα
      the.ones DE of.the Christ   Jesus   the   flesh

      ἐσταύρωσαν   σὺν   τοῖς   παθήμασιν   καὶ   ταῖς   ἐπιθυμίαις.
      3P.crucified with the   passions   and   the   lusts

(25) Ø   εἰ   ζῶμεν   πνεύματι,   πνεύματι   καὶ   στοιχῶμεν.
       if   we.live by.spirit   with.spirit +   we.should.be.in.line

(26) Ø   μὴ   γινώμεθα   κενόδοξοι,   ἀλλήλους   προκαλούμενοι,
       not let.us.become conceited   one.another provoking

      ἀλλήλοις   φθονοῦντες.
      one.another envying

(6:1) Ø   Ἀδελφοί,   ἐὰν   καὶ   προλημφθῇ   ἄνθρωπος   ἔν   τινι   παραπτώματι,
       brothers, if   +   3S.is.overtaken man   in   some   transgression

      ὑμεῖς   οἱ   πνευματικοὶ   καταρτίζετε
      you   the   spiritual.ones restore

      τὸν   τοιοῦτον   ἐν   πνεύματι   πραΰτητος,
      the   such.a.one   in   spirit   of.meekness

      σκοπῶν   σεαυτὸν   μὴ   καὶ   σὺ   πειρασθῇς.
      watching.out for.self not +   you   you.be.tempted

(2a) Ø   Ἀλλήλων   τὰ   βάρη   βαστάζετε
       of.one.another the loads bear

(2b) καὶ   οὕτως   ἀναπληρώσετε   τὸν   νόμον   τοῦ   Χριστοῦ.
      and   thus   you.will.fulfill the   law   of.the Christ

(3)   εἰ γὰρ δοκεῖ   τις   εἶναί τι   **μηδὲν** ὤν,   φρεναπατᾷ ἑαυτόν.
         if for 3S.thinks anyone to.be something nothing being 3S.deceives self

(4a)   τὸ δὲ ἔργον ἑαυτοῦ δοκιμαζέτω ἕκαστος,
         the DE work of.self 3S.let.prove each.person

(4b)   καὶ τότε **εἰς ἑαυτὸν μόνον** τὸ καύχημα ἕξει
         and then in self   alone   the boast 3S.will.have

         καὶ οὐκ εἰς τὸν ἕτερον·
         and not in the other

(5)   ἕκαστος γὰρ **τὸ ἴδιον φορτίν** βαστάσει.
         each   for the own   load   3S.will.bear

(6)   Κοινωνείτω δὲ ὁ   κατηχούμενος   τὸν λόγον τῷ
         3S.let.share DE the.one being.instructed the word with.the.one

         κατηχοῦντι ἐν πᾶσιν ἀγαθοῖς.
         instructing in all   good.things

(7)   Ø Μὴ πλανᾶσθε, **θεὸς** οὐ μυκτηρίζεται. κ.τ.λ.
           not be.led.astray God   not 3S.is.mocked

Questions

Different commentators have suggested boundaries before Gal. 5:25, 5:26, 6:1, 6:6 and 6:7. Assuming that each of these boundaries can be justified on the ground of a change of theme:

(a) what supporting evidence is there for a boundary before 5:25?
(b) what supporting evidence, if any, is there for a boundary before 5:26?
(c) what supporting evidence is there for a boundary before 6:1?
(d) what supporting evidence is there *against* a boundary before 6:6?

Suggested Answers: see Appendix under 17(3).

APPENDIX
Suggested Answers to Illustrative Passages

2(4) Answers to Questions re Luke 2:22–28

(a) Verse 23b begins with the subject to establish the point of departure for the complement of γέγραπται (see the comment on 14:16b, passage 3).

(b) Verse 25b begins with the subject because the sentence is non-event material about Simeon, rather than the next event in sequence.

(c) Verse 28a begins with αὐτός to relate this sentence to the context on the basis of a switch back to Simeon, even though the event concerned may have been in natural sequence with the arrival in the temple of Jesus and his parents. This enables attention on Simeon to be maintained, notwithstanding the introduction to the scene of the other participants.

2(6) Answers to Questions re Galatians 3:1–14

(a) In v. 5, ὁ ἐπιχορηγῶν ὑμῖν τὸ πνεῦμα καὶ ἐνεργῶν δυνάμεις ἐν ὑμῖν begins the sentence because it is the point of departure for the following material; there is a switch to 'the one supplying to you the Spirit and working powerful deeds among you' from 'you' in vv. 2b–4.

(b) In v. 6a, 'Αβραάμ begins the sentence because it is the point of departure for the following material; there is a switch to 'Abraham' from 'you' in vv. 2b–4 and 'the one supplying to you the Spirit...' in v. 5.

(c) In v. 8a, ἡ γραφή does not begin the sentence because the topic of the passage does not switch from οἱ ἐκ πίστεως (v. 7) to 'the Scripture'; see v. 9.

(d) In v. 14a, εἰς τὰ ἔθνη begins the adverbial clause of purpose to indicate a switch from 'us' (ἡμᾶς) in v. 13a (see Meyer 1873:152).

3(1) Answers to Questions re Galatians 4:1–7

(a) The propositional topic ὁ κληρονόμος is initial in v. 1b to establish it as the point of departure for the sentence. Νήπιός probably precedes the verb because that is the normal position for a focal complement with a copula.

(b) The primary basis for relating v. 3a to the context is ἡμεῖς, which indicates a switch from comments about 'the heir' (v. 1b) to comparable comments about 'us' (ὅτε ἦμεν νήπιοι provides a second point of departure, involving a return to the time of v. 1b).

(c) Νήπιοι follows the copula in v. 3a because 'infants' is not a theme (topic) that will be developed in the following material.

(d) Ὑπὸ τὰ στοιχεῖα τοῦ κόσμου precedes the verb in v. 3b because it is focal. (Periphrastic imperfects such as ἤμεθα δεδουλωμένοι probably function like copulas, in which case ὑπὸ τὰ στοιχεῖα τοῦ κόσμου occurs in the normal place for a focal complement with a copula.)

(e) The adverbial clause of time ὅτε ἦλθεν τὸ πλήρωμα τοῦ χρόνου is initial in v. 4. The passage develops by a switch to that time from the time when we were infants (v. 3a).

(f) In v. 4a, τὸ πλήρωμα τοῦ χρόνου is final because it is the subject of a clause with presentational articulation and so is the focus of the clause.

(g) In v. 4b, ὁ θεὸς is not initial because the topic of 'we' (in v. 3a) is still being developed (see v. 5b), so a switch to 'God' is not warranted.

(h) Τοὺς ὑπὸ νόμον (v. 5a) precedes the verb because the verb ἐξαγοράσῃ has been placed at the end of the sentence to bring it into focus.

(i) In my opinion, τὴν υἱοθεσίαν (v. 5b) precedes the verb to bring it into focus, since it is the ultimate purpose of redemption (Erdman 1930:90). This assumes that the ἵνα clauses of vv. 5a and 5b are not parallel (see discussion in Rogers 1989:117).

4(1) Answers to Questions re Sentences from James

(a) The position of the negative in 1:20 indicates that part or all of the comment ('works God's righteousness') about the propositional topic ὀργὴ ἀνδρὸς 'man's anger' has been negated.

(b) The position of the negative in 2:1 indicates that the constituent that immediately follows the negative particle (ἐν προσωπολημψίαις) has been brought into focus.

4(2) Answers to Questions re Gal. 5:7

(a) In v. 7b, the presupposition is that someone 'hindered you from obeying the truth'; the focus is on τίς 'who'.

(b) In v. 7c, ἀληθείᾳ precedes the verb either to bring it into focus, for example, because it is particularly surprising that it is the truth which they fail to obey, or to bring the verb into focus (sec. 3.8.1). This latter is the preferred interpretation if the articular reading is followed (see sec. 9.3).

4(3) Answers to Questions re John 18:7–9

(a) In v. 8a, ἐγώ precedes εἰμι to bring it into focus. The answer to the question of v. 7 was 'Jesus the Nazarene' and v. 8a focuses on which person he is. (This analysis neither confirms nor excludes the possibility that an allusion to Exodus 3:14 is also intended.)

(b) In v. 8b, ἐμὲ precedes ζητεῖτε because it is brought into temporary focus, in anticipation of a switch of attention to τούτους.

4(4) Answers to the Questions re Passages from James

(a) In James 1:2b, πειρασμοῖς ποικίλοις is discontinuous because only the preposed part (πειρασμοῖς) is focal ('trials' will be the theme of the section); ποικίλοις is supportive.

(b) In 2:15b, γυμνοὶ καὶ λειπόμενοι τῆς ἐφημέρου τροφῆς is discontinuous because it is a complex focal constituent (the coordinative complement of the copula ὑπάρχωσιν).

(c) In 4:6a, μείζονα χάριν is discontinuous because the quotation that follows relates only to the second part (χάριν).

4(5) Answers to Questions re Matthew 5:20b and John 18:10

(a) In Matt. 5:20b, ὑμῶν may precede ἡ δικαιοσύνη and immediately follow the verb (by analogy with default ordering principle 1) because its referent is thematically salient; the sentence is organized around 'you' and is a comment about 'you'.

(b) In John 18:10b, τοῦ ἀρχιερέως precedes δοῦλον to bring it into focus, probably because Peter's denials occur in the high priest's courtyard (see especially v. 26). In v. 10c, αὐτοῦ may precede τὸ ὠτάριον τὸ δεξιόν and immediately follow the verb (by analogy with default ordering principle 1) to give extra prominence to τὸ ὠτάριον τὸ δεξιόν.

5(10) Answers to Questions re Luke 24:13–31

(a) Δέ is used in v. 17a but not in connection with the earlier events of the episode, because it is only at this point that the participants begin to interact. The events described prior to this may be viewed as setting the scene for the interaction.

(b) Although vv. 17b and 19a both involve a change of subject, the event (in v. 17b) or speech (in v. 19a) concerned does not constitute a development of any significance. Rather, they are little more than steps to a following speech of substance.

(c) The absence of δέ in vv. 25–30 suggests that Luke's purpose in relating the episode is advanced only as the two disciples recognize the fact of Jesus' resurrection for themselves and the evidences of his bodily resurrection are set forth. It is only when the physical evidence has been accumulated that Jesus' relating what had happened to the Scriptures is treated as a new development (v. 44).

5(18) Answers to Questions re John 6:12–21

(a) Καί is used in v. 21b to introduce the concluding event of the episode of vv. 16–21.

(b) Καί is used in v. 17a to associate the events it links into an event cluster. It is used in vv. 17b and 17c to associate together the events and circumstances that set the scene for the foreground events of vv. 19ff.

(c) Οὖν is used in v. 13a to introduce the logical response to Jesus' command of v. 12 (v. 21a is similar). It is used in vv. 14 and 15 in connection with preposed subjects marking switches of attention to different participants, to indicate that the events so introduced are also in logical sequence. In v. 19a it is probably functioning as a resumptive, following the background material of vv. 17b–18; v. 19 describes the next development involving the disciples (the episode of vv. 16–21 is told from their point of view—see sec. 13.1).

(d) Δέ is used in vv. 12 and 16, in connection with a temporal point of departure because, notwithstanding the change of setting, the same storyline is being further developed. Use of asyndeton would have implied a new scene and theme. Use of οὖν would have implied a logical relationship between the events so linked. With δέ, Jesus' order to gather the fragments is to be viewed as a new development, reinforcing the miracle, but not as a logical consequence of so many people having eaten. Similarly, the disciples' departure for Capernaum is presented as a new development, but not as a logical consequence of Jesus' departure to the mountain to be alone.

5(19) Answer to the Question re John 6:1–6

The background material of v. 4 does not strengthen anything in the context or refer to any item of the context, but presents distinctive information, so is introduced with δέ. Some commentators consider it to be not a mere episodeal time reference, but a theological comment that is relevant for the subsequent development of the story (see Carson 1991:268–69).

Although the comment of v. 6a refers back to the question of v. 5 (see the initial τοῦτο), it presents distinctive information, perhaps to prepare the reader for another of Jesus' "signs," so is introduced with δέ. If its intention had been solely to explain why Jesus asked the question, then γάρ would have been used.

The comment of v. 6b strengthens v. 6a by explaining why the question was a test, so is introduced with γάρ.

6(4) Answer to Question re Acts 6:8–11

Τότε is used in v. 11 to signal the division of the episode into subsections, indicate that the low-level narrative units it links enjoy continuity of time and of other factors (including the cast and the goal), and introduce the next significant development in the episode. Stephen's critics have tried one strategy and failed (vv. 9–10), *thereupon* they try another way of silencing him.

6(6) Answers to Questions re Matthew 10:29–30 and 1 Corinthians 7:40

(a) In Matt. 10:30, ὑμῶν begins the sentence because it is the new point of departure, signaling a switch of attention from the sparrows of v. 29.

(b) Καί is used in Matt. 10:30 for confirmation. It occurs in the context of God caring for individuals. Αἱ τρίχες τῆς κεφαλῆς is the least likely member of the set of individual items directly connected with 'you' that God might be expected to have numbered. This constituent has been preposed to bring it into focus (πᾶσαι ἠριθμημέναι is supportive information, being implied from v. 29).

(c) In 1 Cor. 7:40b, καί is used for parallelism, according to the majority of the commentators cited by Trail (1995:340): "'I, as well as others'… He may be referring to those who claimed to possess the Spirit of God." While Fee (1987:356-7) concedes that this interpretation is possible, he thinks it more likely that καί is confirmatory: the sentence "may simply be a strengthening of this 'opinion,' as in v. 25, that he is not simply on this own in this matter." The problem with treating καί as confirmatory is that it modifies ἐγώ, rather than the part of the sentence that confirms the validity of 'my judgment'.

6(12) Answer to Question re Acts 6:7–7:1

Τέ is used in v. 7c to add to v. 7b another aspect of the same event; the 'crowd of priests' is part of the group of 'disciples' whose number was increasing greatly.

Τέ may have been used in v. 12a for the same reason: Stephen's critics had two parts to the same strategy of discrediting him; τέ adds the second (v. 12) to the first (v. 11). In v. 13, however, τέ may have been used to introduce the specific lead-in to the next development (7:1); it is the last of a series of events designed to ensure that Stephen is found guilty. (The information of 6:15 is by way of an aside, before the high priest responds to the charge brought against Stephen.) Alternatively, τέ is used in v. 12a as well as v. 13 to increase tension, in anticipation of the speeches of 7:1ff.

7(9) Answers to Questions re Colossians 3:1–5a

(a) In 3:1a, the conditional clause begins the sentence because it is a point of departure, marking a switch from the corresponding conditional clause of 2:20 (Εἰ ἀπεθάνετε σὺν Χριστῷ κ.τ.λ.).
Οὖν is used in v. 1a to "resume the thought already expressed in 2:12, 13" and provide the "counterpart of 2:20" (Hendriksen 1974:139). The rhetorical question of 2:20 has an underlying exhortation to not continue submitting to regulations as though you still belonged to the world. 2:21–23 then expand on these regulations. 3:1 returns to the exhortations: not only are you to cease submitting to these regulations, but you are to seek the things that are above.

(b) Asyndeton is used in v. 2 because the clause restates and amplifies v. 1b (in SSA terms, the relation is contraction-amplification).

(c) In v. 3b, conjunctive καί is used because the material that strengthens the exhortation of v. 2 is v. 3a plus v. 3b.
Ἡ ζωὴ ὑμῶν begins v. 3b because it is the new point of departure/propositional topic, marking a switch from 'you died' (v. 3a) to 'your life'.
Ending v. 3b with ἐν τῷ θεῷ suggests that it, rather than the other peripheral constituent (σὺν τῷ Χριστῷ) is focal.

(d) Callow (1983:167) considers 3:4 to provide a second ground for v. 2. Asyndeton is the appropriate linkage between parallel propositions.

(e) In 3:4b, τότε is probably used, following the adverbial clause of time, to highlight the remainder of v. 4b (see sec. 6.1).
Non-conjunctive καί is used in 3:4b to constrain ὑμεῖς to be processed in parallel to ὁ Χριστός. It has been preposed for focus, following the temporal point of departure (v. 4a), so is very prominent. As noted in sec. 3.8.1, when a point of departure and a focal constituent both precede the verb, it is common for a supportive pronominal constituent (in this instance, σὺν αὐτῷ) also to precede it.

(f) Οὖν is used in 3:5 to resume and advance the topic of v. 2 with inferential overtones, following the strengthening material of v. 3.

8(8) Answers to Questions re Matthew 7:28–8:18

(a) Default rule 5 of sec. 8.2 explains the use in 8:1a and 5a of the independent pronoun to refer to the same subject as in the previous clause (subjects are generally obligatory in genitives absolute). Default encoding of reference to Jesus indicates that the author perceived sufficient continuity between the episodes to omit any reference to him, so the paragraph breaks are minor.

(b) There is no overt reference to the subject in v. 15c because one major and one minor participant are interacting (default rule 3).

(c) A full noun phrase is used in v. 8 to refer to the centurion, even though he is the addressee of the previous speech, because he takes control of the conversation (see further in sec. 14.1).

(d) A full noun phrase is used to refer to Jesus in 8:4, 10a and 13a because his speeches are viewed as key ones and, in 8:14 and 18, because there is sufficient discontinuity between the episodes to begin a new narrative unit (i.e., the paragraph breaks are major).
In 7:28a, it is possible that a full noun phrase is used to refer to Jesus to highlight the response to Jesus' words. However, I think it more likely that it is used because vv. 28–29 begin the next major

section; in 8:1a, only a pronoun is used in the genitive absolute. See sec. 10.3 on the use of ἐγένετο plus a temporal expression in Matthew's Gospel.

(e) If ὁ Ἰησοῦς is read in 8:3a, this marked encoding would highlight the action; as Pope (p.c.) observes, "Touching and healing a leper was certainly a very significant act."

In 8:7, the speech was intended to conclude the conversation (unless it is taken as a question), but it is unclear to me why it should be highlighted.

9(12) Answers to Questions re Acts 8:4–26

(a) The references to Philip by name in 8:5 and 8:26 are anarthrous because he is being reactivated after an absence (and is salient to the story). Verse 12 refers back to an earlier activity involving Philip (v. 6), so the articular reference to him would be consistent with him having already been activated.

(b) The reference to Simon in v. 18 is probably articular because he was an observer of the events of vv. 15–17, so was judged to have been "in the wings" during that time.

(c) The reference to Peter in v. 20 is anarthrous because of the significance of the speech that he makes. In contrast, Simon's reply is not viewed as particularly significant, so the reference to him in v. 24 is articular, as is normal for a reference to an activated participant.

(d) In v. 14, it is appropriate for the reference to Peter and John to be anarthrous, because they are being reactivated after an absence and are salient to the story. The articular textual variant would imply that they were reactivated by the expression οἱ ἐν Ἱεροσολύμοις ἀπόστολοι (the apostles in Jerusalem).

9(15) Answers to Questions re Galatians 3:21–26

(a) The reference to 'trainer' in v. 25b is anarthrous because the referent is not particular (hence the translation into English as "a trainer"). This may be the case also in v. 24a. However, παιδαγωγὸς ἡμῶν has been preposed for focus, so would be anarthrous, anyhow.

(b) The references to 'law' in vv. 21a and 24a are articular because the referent is the propositional topic and is not focal. The reference to 'law' in v. 21c is anarthrous because it is "indefinite." The references to 'law' in vv. 21d and 23b are anarthrous because, in both cases, they have been preposed for focus.

(c) The references to 'faith' in vv. 23a and 25a are articular because their referent is the propositional topic and is not focal.

The references to 'faith' in vv. 23c and 26 are articular because they are not focal. In the case of v. 23c, there is no suggestion of a change of focus from the preverbal constituent of v. 23b (ὑπὸ νόμου). In v. 26, the focal constituent is also preverbal (υἱοὶ θεοῦ).

The references to 'faith' in vv. 22b and 24b are anarthrous because they are preposed for focus.

10(2) Answers to Questions re Acts 25:1–6

(a) The prospective nature of μέν suggests that the speech of vv. 4–5 is of secondary importance in comparison with the events associated with the corresponding δέ (viz., those of vv. 6ff.). The effect is to shift attention back to Caesarea, where Paul is.

(b) The function of οὖν in v. 4 is inferential (not adversative, *contra* MGM); "the fact that Festus later asks Paul whether he is willing to go to Jerusalem to be tried (v 9) suggests that v 4 is not an outright refusal of the request. Rather, he may have thought that he was expediting it. Being unaware of the plot, he indicates to the Jews that the easiest way for the matter to be handled would be for them to accompany him to Caesarea, since he was going there anyway *en tachei*" (Levinsohn 1987:143). See also Lenski's translation of μέν οὖν as "accordingly" (1961:990).

10(5) Answers to Questions re Luke 24:13–17

(a) Ἐγένετο in v. 15a indicates that the events of vv. 13–14 form the general background to the following foreground events. The next clause (v. 15b) presents the specific circumstance for the foreground events of vv. 17ff.

(b) The reference to Jesus is anarthrous (UBS text) because he is being reactivated following his absence from the story during the events of vv. 1–14.

11(6) Answers to Questions re Acts 21:3–11

(a) The verses that contain prenuclear NPCs are vv. 4a, 5b, 5d, and (UBS text) 5e.

(b) The relative clause that occurs in v. 4c is nonrestrictive and continuative.

(c) The information in the NPC of v. 4a is backgrounded with respect to what follows. In turn, the clause that precedes the relative pronoun (v. 4b) provides the background for the speech of v. 4c. So, the information of v. 4a is less important than the information of v. 4b, which in turn is less important than the information of v. 4c.

(d) Verse 5c contains a postnuclear GA. Since the events described in vv. 5dff. "build as much on the action of the GA as on that of the preceding independent clause" (Levinsohn 1980:195), they are probably of equal importance.

(e) Verse 10a contains a prenuclear GA. The use of a GA rather than an adverbial clause of time implies continuity of situation and other relevant factors between the arrival of the prophet Agabus and the presence in the house of Philip the evangelist of his seven daughters who had the gift of prophecy. In line with this, Alexander states (1963 (1857):264), "That the prophesying of Philip's daughters had respect to Paul's captivity, is rendered still more probable by this verse, which immediately connects with it another intimation of the same sort from a very different quarter."

12(2) Answer to Question re Luke 24:13–17

The repetition of information from an earlier sentence, such as is found in the temporal expression of v. 15a, is called tail-head linkage. Its rhetorical effect is to slow down the story and thus highlight a significant event that follows, viz., Jesus' joining the disciples and his subsequent interaction with them.

12(4) Answer to the Question re Matthew 16:28–17:2

The HPs in Matt. 17:1 imply that this verse begins a new subsection of a larger episode, and gives prominence to the events that will take place at the location to which Jesus and the three disciples have moved.

13(8) Answers to Questions re Acts 22:24–30

(a) The four speeches of vv. 27a–28b form a closed conversation, in that each successive speaker and addressee were respectively the addressee and subject of the last speech.

(b) The speech orienters of vv. 27b and 28b begin with a reference to the speaker because the larger issue of the reason for the outcry against Paul (v. 24) remains unresolved—see v. 30. (The speech of v. 27b answered the immediate question as to whether or not Paul was a Roman citizen, so the orienter of v. 27b would have begun with a verb, had that been the goal that the tribune was seeking to attain.)

14(3) Answers to Questions re Matthew 4:3–7

(a) Verse 4 begins with an articular pronoun plus ἀποκριθείς because Jesus takes control of the conversation by rejecting the proposal of v. 3.

(b) It is appropriate for the speech of v. 7 to be conjoined with asyndeton because Jesus is reaffirming his rejection of the devil's proposal on the same ground (the Scriptures) as in his speech of v. 4.

14(4) Answers to Questions re Matthew 20:20–23

(a) It is appropriate to conjoin the speech of v. 21b with asyndeton because this speech begins the second round of the conversation (the first round being vv. 20–21a) and the mother's intention remains the same.

(b) The speech orienter of v. 22a begins with ἀποκριθείς because Jesus takes control of the conversation by countering the request of v. 21b with a question that is addressed, not to the mother (the previous speaker), but to the sons.

(c) The speech of v. 22b is probably conjoined with asyndeton because the response was expected (even though the question of v. 22a does not contain οὐ). Certainly, the final speech of v. 23 represents the goal to which the question of v. 22a was leading, so does not represent a new development with respect to that speech.

14(6) Answer to Question re Matthew 22:11–13

The HP of v. 12a points forward to the concluding speech of v. 13 which is introduced with τότε (the response of v. 12b is readily interpreted as an intermediate step—see sec. 13.1).

15(8) Answers to Questions re John 20:19–24

(a) The effect of beginning 20:20 and v. 22 with τοῦτο εἰπών, which is a form of tail-head linkage (sec. 12.1), is to slow the story down prior to the significant events described in the immediately following clauses.

(b) The effect of using a HP in v. 19c is to point forward to a following speech or event. Since v. 20 begins with τοῦτο εἰπών, this event is the one described in v. 20a.

(c) The speech orienter of v. 21 begins with εἶπεν οὖν because vv. 21ff. represent a new development in the storyline, and it is normal to use a speech verb in the aorist, rather than the HP, at the beginning of a development unit.

(d) The effect of using a HP in v. 22b to introduce the final speech of the scene is probably to point forward to the next scene (vv. 24ff.). However, since the speech itself concerns receiving the Holy Spirit and the forgiveness of sins, it is possible that John was pointing forward to other events.

15(11) Answer to Questions re John 1:48–50

(a) The speech HP in v. 48a is cataphoric, pointing forward to Jesus' response of v. 48b.

(b) The long orienter is used in 1:48b to highlight Jesus's response, probably because it is a countering speech (see Alford's (1863.I:696) comment, "there is probably no reference at all to the question which Nathanael had just asked") which leads to Nathanael's exclamation of v. 49. The long orienter is used to highlight Jesus' response of v. 50 because it is a significant counter, introducing the topic of the greater things that Nathanael will see (see also v. 51).

(c) If the UBS text is followed in v. 49, then Nathanael's response ("Rabbi, you are the Son of God! You are the King of Israel") is not specially highlighted (perhaps because Jesus' assertion of v. 50 is judged to be more important). The variant reading with the addition of καὶ εἶπεν would highlight Nathanael's response. The variant reading with the addition of καὶ λέγει would both highlight Nathanael's response and point forward to Jesus' assertion of v. 50.

16(4) Answers to Questions re Luke 6:3–6

(a) The absence of ὅτι *recitativum* in the UBS text of Luke 6:5 implies that the reported speech is not to be viewed as the culmination of the episode. Rather, as the presence of ἐγένετο implies, the episode that terminates with v. 5 provides the general background for and is related thematically to the following episode.

(b) The presence of ὅτι *recitativum* in the Luke 6:5 would imply that the speech was the culmination of the episode.

17(3) Answers to Questions re Galatians 5:22–6:7

(a) Supporting evidence for a boundary before 5:25 includes the sentence initial conditional clause (a point of departure) and the change of mood and person from third person declaratives in vv. 22–24 to first person plural exhortations in vv. 25–26.

(b) There appears to be no supporting evidence for a boundary before 5:26.

(c) Supporting evidence for a boundary before 6:1 includes the combination of the vocative and asyndeton, and the sentence initial conditional clause. There is also a change from first to second person.

(d) Supporting evidence against a boundary before 6:6 includes the absence of a point of departure, which might suggest continuity of topic. (Eadie 1869, commenting on this verse, says, "It is somewhat difficult to trace the connection; but it seems to be suggested by the last verse. The δέ may continue the thought under another aspect; thus, he had said, 'Bear one another's burdens'—now—δέ, this is one form in which the precept may be obeyed...").

GLOSSARY

This section presents definitions of some technical terms used in this volume. However, some introductory sections have been devoted to the definition and illustration of terms, in which case only a cross-reference to the relevant section has been provided.[1] Words in italics are defined elsewhere in the glossary.

anarthrous—without the article (introduction to chap. 9)

articular—with the article (introduction to chap. 9)

asyndeton—"the omission of a conjunction" (OED)

articulations of the sentence—see sec. 2.1

background material—"supportive material that does not itself narrate the main events" (Hopper 1979:213—introduction to part IV)

backgrounded—material that is *marked* as being of less importance than other material in the immediate context (introduction to part IV)

cast—group of characters present during an *episode*

cataphora—term used "for the process or result of a LINGUISTIC UNIT referring forward to another unit" (Crystal 1991:49)

circumstantial participial clauses—cover term for *anarthrous* participial clauses in the nominative case (NPCs) and genitives absolute (GAs—sec. 11.1)

closed conversation—reported conversation such that each successive speaker and addressee was a speaker or addressee of a previous speech (introduction to part V)

coherent—descriptive of a text if a reader "is able to fit its different elements into a single overall mental representation" (*SIL-UND* p. 10) or conceptual framework—chap. 1)

cohesion—use of linguistic means such as articles, pronouns and conjunctions to signal *coherence* (*SIL-UND* p. 12—chap. 1)

constituent—"basic term in GRAMMATICAL analysis for a LINGUISTIC UNIT which is a component of a larger CONSTRUCTION" (Crystal 1991:75)

continuity of action—see chap. 1

continuity of situation—relationship between two independent clauses such that, apart from modifications described in any anarthrous participial clause which precedes the second independent clause, the setting of the events described in the independent clauses remains unchanged, as do the participants involved (chap. 1, sec. 11.1.3)

core constituents—verb, subject, object and other nominal *constituents* of a clause which are not preceded by a preposition (sec. 3.2)

counterpoint—"contrasting ... idea, used to set off the main element" (*OED*—sec. 2.8)

couplet—speech-speech or speech-action pair that belongs together because the initial speech calls for the specific response that is described in the second part (sec. 15.1)

development marker (DE)—conjunction such as δέ or οὖν that constrains the material with which it is associated to be interpreted as a new step or development in the author's story or argument (secs. 5.1, 5.3, 7.1)

development unit (DU)—one or more *sentences* introduced by a *development marker* and associated by καί, τέ, or asyndeton which presents a new development in the story (sec. 17.1)

discrete—descriptive of linguistic elements that have "definable boundaries, with no gradation or continuity between them" (Crystal 1991:107—chap. 1)

episode—group of events that belong together and are described in one or more *paragraphs* (chap. 1)

---

[1] Some of the definitions provided here have been taken verbatim from Levinsohn 1987:178–81.

event cluster—group of events that are linked by καί and which are introduced by a *development marker* (sec. 5.1)

focus—that part of an utterance "which is intended to make the most important... change in the hearer's mental representation" (*SIL-UND* sec. 11.1—sec. 3.4)

focus-presupposition articulation—see sec. 2.1

foreground—material that "carries the discourse forward, contributes to the progression of the narrative or argument... develops the theme of the discourse" (K. Callow 1974:52–53—introduction to part IV); foreground events form the actual story line of the *narrative*, as distinct from *background material*

highlighted—material that is *marked* as being of more importance than other material in the immediate context (introduction to part IV)

initial events—events that set the scene for the *foreground* events of an *episode* or story

intermediate step—speech or act which potentially leads to the goal of a reported conversation, but is not itself the goal (sec. 13.1)

lead-in—in contrast with a previous *initial event*, the specific event on which the next development of the storyline builds (sec. 6.3)

major participant—see *participant, major*

marked, unmarked—presence or absence of a particular linguistic feature (Introduction on "Markedness")

minor participant—see *participant, minor*

narrative—material whose overall framework is chronological and which is concerned with actions performed by specific people or groups

narrative unit—term used by Fox (1987:168) for an *episode, section,* or *subsection* of a narrative (sec. 8.2).

paragraph—grouping of *sentences* that deal with the same theme (sec. 17.1)

participant, major—person or group that is active for a large part of an *episode* and plays a leading role (sec. 8.1)

participant, minor—person or group that is activated briefly and lapses into deactivation (sec. 8.1)

peripheral constituents—prepositional and adverbial *constituents* of a clause (sec. 3.2)

point of departure—element that is placed at the beginning of a clause or *sentence* with a dual function:
1. to provide a starting point for the communication; and
2. to cohesively anchor the subsequent clause(s) to something which is already in the context (sec. 2.2)

preposed—descriptive of a *constituent* placed earlier in a clause or *sentence* than its default position, usually to provide a *point of departure* or to bring it into *focus* (sec. 3.6)

presentational articulation—see sec. 2.1

prominence—"any device whatever which gives certain events, participants, or objects more significance than others in the same context" (K. Callow 1974:50) (chap. 2)

propositional topic—see *topic, propositional*

round—"recurring succession or series of activities" (OED) which, in this volume, are reported conversations, usually involving the same speakers (introduction to part V)

salient—descriptive of participants such as *VIPs* that are of particular importance or the center of attention (introduction to chap. 9)

section—grouping of *paragraphs* that deal with the same theme (chap. 1), part of a book or epistle

sequential, in sequence—descriptive of a chronological relationship between two events such that the second event occurs after the first (chap. 1)

sentence—single independent clause, together with those clauses that are subordinated to it setting—"where, when and under what circumstances actions take place" (Grimes 1975:51)

speech orienter—clause that introduces the content of a reported speech (introduction to part V)

subsection—subdivision of a *section* or *episode*, which may or may not be larger than a *paragraph* (chap. 1)

supportive—descriptive of those *constituents* of the comment about a *propositional topic* that are not *focal* (sec. 3.8.1)

temporary focus, in—descriptive of a *constituent* that is brought into *focus* by *preposing* it, in anticipation of a switch of attention to a corresponding *constituent* that is presented later (sec. 4.3)

tight-knit—descriptive of a relationship between reported speeches such that each successive speaker continues to develop the theme of the previous speech (introduction to part V)

topic-comment articulation—see sec. 2.1

topic, propositional—topic (usually the subject) about which a comment is made in a *sentence* with *topic-comment articulation* (sec. 2.1), so designated to distinguish it from the theme of a *paragraph* or *section*

unmarked—see *marked*

VIP (very important participant)—*major participant* who is distinguished from the rest (sec. 8.3)

REFERENCES

Abbott, Edwin A. 1906. *Johannine Grammar*. London: Adam & Charles Black.

Akin, D. L. 1987. A discourse analysis of the temptation of Jesus Christ as recorded in Matthew 4:1–11. *OPTAT* 1:78–86.

Aland, K., M. Black, C. M. Martini, B. M. Metzger, and A. Wikgren. 1968. *The Greek New Testament*. 2nd. ed. London, New York: United Bible Societies.

Alexander, J. A. 1857 (1963). *A Commentary on the Acts of the Apostles*. Edinburgh and Carlisle, Penn: The Banner of Truth Trust.

Alford, Henry. 1863. *The Greek Testament* (4 vols.). 5th. ed. London: Rivingtons.

Allen, Willoughby C. 1907. *A Critical and Exegetical Commentary on the Gospel according to S. Matthew*. 3rd. edition. Edinburgh: T. and T. Clark.

Andrews, A. 1985. The major functions of the noun phrase. *Language Typology and Syntactic Description*, edited by T. Shopen, I.62–154. Cambridge: Cambridge University Press.

Arichea, D. C. Jr., and E. A. Nida. 1976. *A Translator's Handbook on Paul's Letter to the Galatians*. New York: United Bible Societies.

Arndt, William F., and F. Wilbur Gingrich. 1957. *A Greek-English Lexicon of the New Testament and Other Early Christian Literature*. Chicago: University of Chicago Press and Cambridge: Cambridge University Press.

Bailey, Nicholas A. 1998. "What's wrong with my word order?" *JOTT* 10:1–29.

Banker, J. 1984. The position of the vocative ἀδελφοί in the clause. *START* 11:29–36.

———. 1987. *Semantic Structure Analysis of Titus*. Dallas: Summer Institute of Linguistics.

——— 1996. *A Semantic Structure Analysis of Philippians*. Dallas: Summer Institute of Linguistics.

Barnett, Paul. 1997. *The Second Epistle to the Corinthians*. The New International Commentary on the New Testament. Grand Rapids, MI: Eerdmans.

Beasley-Murray, George R. 1987. *John*. Word Biblical Commentary 36. Dallas: Word Inc.

Beekman, John, and John C. Callow. 1974. *Translating the Word of God*. Grand Rapids, MI: Zondervan.

Beneš, E. 1962. Die Verbstellung im Deutschen, von der Mitteilungsperspektive her betrachtet. *Philologica Pragensia* 5:6–19.

Black, David Alan, Katharine Barnwell, and Stephen Levinsohn (eds.). 1992. *Linguistics and New Testament Interpretation: Essays on Discourse Analysis*. Nashville: Broadman.

Blakemore, Diane. 1987. *Semantic Constraints on Relevance*. Oxford: Basil Blackwell.

Blass, F., A. Debrunner, and R. W. Funk. 1961. *A Greek Grammar of the New Testament*. Chicago: Chicago University Press.

Blass, Regina. 1990. *Relevance Relations in Discourse: A Study with Special Reference to Sissala*. Cambridge: Cambridge University Press.

———. 1993. *Constraints on Relevance in Koiné Greek in the Pauline Letters* (Nairobi, Summer Institute of Linguistics, Exegetical Seminar, May 29 – June 19, 1993).

Boos, D. 1984. The historic present in John's Gospel. *START* 11:17–24.

Boutin, M. E. 1988. *Transitivity and Discourse Grounding in Banggi*. Paper presented at International Symposium on Language and Linguistics, Bangkok, Thailand, August 1988.

Bratcher, R. G. 1984. *A Translator's Guide to the Letters from James, Peter and Jude*. London, New York, Stuttgart: United Bible Societies.

Brown, Robert K., Philip W. Comfort (translators), and J.D. Douglas (editor). 1990. *The New Greek-English Interlinear New Testament*. Wheaton, IL: Tyndale House Publishers Inc.

Bruce, F. F. 1982. The epistle to the Galatians. *The New International Greek Testament Commentary*. Grand Rapids, MI: Eerdmans.

———. 1988. *The Book of the Acts* (revised edition). Grand Rapids, MI: Eerdmans.

Burton, Ernest de Witt. 1921. *A Critical and Exegetical Commentary on the Epistle to the Galatians*. Edinburgh: T. and T. Clark.

Buth, R. 1982. Perspective in Gospel discourse studies, with notes on εὐθύς, τότε and the temptation pericopes. *START* 6:3–14.

———. 1990. *'Edayin*/τότε—anatomy of a Semitism in Jewish Greek. *Maarav* 5–6:33–48.

————. 1992. Οὖν, δέ, καί, and asyndeton in John's Gospel. In *Linguistics and New Testament Interpretation: Essays on Discourse Analysis*, edited by David Alan Black, Katharine Barnwell, and Stephen Levinsohn, 144–61. Nashville: Broadman.

Callow, John C. 1983. *A Semantic Structure Analysis of Colossians*, edited by Michael F. Kopesec. Dallas: Summer Institute of Linguistics.

————. 1992. Constituent order in copula clauses: a partial study. In *Linguistics and New Testament Interpretation: Essays on Discourse Analysis*, edited by David Alan Black, Katharine Barnwell, and Stephen Levinsohn, 68–89. Nashville: Broadman.

————. 1996. *The Historic Present in Mark*. (seminar handout).

Callow, Kathleen. 1974. *Discourse Considerations in Translating the Word of God*. Grand Rapids, MI: Zondervan.

————. 1992. The disappearing δέ in 1 Corinthians. In *Linguistics and New Testament Interpretation: Essays on Discourse Analysis*, edited by David Alan Black, Katharine Barnwell, and Stephen Levinsohn, 183–93. Nashville: Broadman.

————. 1992. Patterns of thematic development in 1 Corinthians 5:1–13. In *Linguistics and New Testament Interpretation: Essays on Discourse Analysis*, edited by David Alan Black, Katharine Barnwell, and Stephen Levinsohn, 194–206. Nashville: Broadman.

Callow, Kathleen, and John C. Callow. 1992. Text as purposive communication: a meaning-based analysis. In *Discourse Description: Diverse Linguistic Analyses of a Fund-Raising Text*, edited by William C. Mann and Sandra A. Thompson, 5–34. Amsterdam, Philadelphia: Benjamins.

Carson, D. A. 1991. *The Gospel according to John*. Grand Rapids, MI: Eerdmans.

Cervin, Richard S. 1993. A critique of Timothy Friberg's dissertation: New Testament Greek word order in light of discourse considerations. *JOTT* 6.1:56–85.

Chafe, Wallace L. 1976. Givenness, contrastiveness, definiteness, subjects, topics and point of view. In *Subject and Topic*, edited by C. N. Li, 25–55. New York, San Francisco, London: Academic Press.

Colwell, E. C. 1933. A definite rule for the use of the article in the Greek New Testament. *JBL* 52:12–21.

Comrie, Bernard. 1989. *Language Universals and Linguistic Typology*. Chicago: University of Chicago Press.

Coulthard, Malcolm. 1977. *An Introduction to Discourse Analysis*. London: Longmans.

Cranfield, C. E. B. 1975. *A Critical and Exegetical Commentary on the Epistle to the Romans*. Edinburgh: T. and T. Clark.

Crystal, David. 1991. *A Dictionary of Linguistics and Phonetics*. 3rd edition. Oxford: Basil Blackwell.

Dana, H. E., and J. R. Mantey. 1955. *A Manual Grammar of the Greek NT*. Macmillan.

Davison, M. E. 1989. NT Greek word order. *Literacy and Linguistic Computing* 4:19–28.

Delin, J. 1989. *The Focus Structure of It-Clefts*. Centre for Cognitive Science, Edinburgh.

Denniston, J. D. 1952. *Greek Prose Style*. Oxford: Clarendon Press.

————, 1959. *The Greek Particles*. Oxford: Clarendon Press.

Depraetere, Ilse. 1996. Foregrounding in English relative clauses. *Linguistics* 34:699–731.

Dik, Simon C. 1978. *Functional Grammar*. Amsterdam: N-Holland.

————. 1989. *The Theory of Functional Grammar. Part I: The Structure of the Clause*. Dordrecht, Providence, RI: Foris.

————, Maria E. Hoffman, Jan R. de Jong, Sie Ing Djiang, Harry Stroomer, and Lourens de Vries. 1981. On the typology of focus phenomena. In *Perspectives on Functional Grammar*, edited by Teun Hoekstra, Harry van der Hulst, and Michael Moortgat, 41–74. Dordrecht: Foris.

Dooley, Robert A. 1989. *Functional Approaches to Grammar: Implications for SIL Training*. MS.

————. 1990. The positioning of non-pronominal clitics and particles in lowland South American languages. In *Amazonian Linguistics: Studies in Lowland South American Languages*, edited by D. L. Payne, 457–83. Austin: University of Texas Press.

Dowty, D. 1979. *Word Meaning and Montague Grammar*. Dordrecht: Reidel.

Dryer, Matthew S. 1997. On the six-way word order typology. *Studies in Language* 21.1:69–103.

Eadie, J. [1869] 1979. A commentary on the Greek text of the epistle of Paul to the Galatians. *The John Eadie Greek Text Commentaries, Vol. 1*. Grand Rapids, MI: Baker Book House.

Ellicott, C. J. 1883. *The Pastoral Epistles of St. Paul*. London: Longmans.

Ellingworth, Paul. 1995. The dog in the night: a note on Mark's non-use of καί. *The Bible Translator* 46(1):125–28.

Erdman, C. R. 1930. *The Epistle of Paul to the Galatians*. Philadelphia: Westminster Press.

Everett, D. L. 1989. Clitic doubling, reflexives and word order alternations in Yagua. *Language* 65:339–72.

Fairbairn, B. 1956 (1874). *Commentary on the Pastoral Epistles*. Grand Rapids, MI: Zondervan.

Fanning, Buist M. 1990. *Verbal Aspect in New Testament Greek*. Oxford: Clarendon Press.

Fee, Gordon D. 1987. *The First Epistle to the Corinthians*. Grand Rapids, MI: Eerdmans.

Firbas, Jan. 1959. Thoughts on the communicative function of the verb in English, German and Czech. *BRNO Studies in English* 1:39–63.

——— 1964. From comparative word-order studies. *BRNO Studies in English* 4:111–26.

———, and K. Pala. 1971. Review of Ö. Dahl, 1969. Topic and comment: a study in Russian and general transformational grammar. Göteburg: Slavica Gothburgensia. *Journal of Linguistics* 7:91–101.

Fitzmyer, J. A. 1981. The Gospel according to Luke (I–IX). *The Anchor Bible*. Garden City, NY: Doubleday.

Foley, W. A., and R. D. Van Valin. 1984. *Functional Syntax and Universal Grammar*. Cambridge: Cambridge University Press.

Follingstad, Carl M. 1994. Thematic development and prominence in Tyap discourse. In *Discourse Features of Ten Languages of West-Central Africa*, edited by Stephen H. Levinsohn, 151–90. Dallas: Summer Institute of Linguistics and the University of Texas at Arlington.

——— forthcoming. *Modality and Perspective. A Distributionally-Based Function and Cognitive Analysis of the Biblical Hebrew Particle Kî*. Ph.D. thesis, Free University of Amsterdam.

Fox, B. 1987. Anaphora in popular written English narratives. In *Coherence and Grounding in Discourse*, edited by R. S. Tomlin, 157–74. Amsterdam, Philadelphia: Benjamins.

France, R. T. 1985. *The Gospel According to Matthew: An Introduction and Commentary*. Grand Rapids, MI: Eerdmans.

Francis, D. P. 1985. The Holy Spirit: a statistical inquiry. *The Expository Times* 96(5):136–37.

Fung, R. Y. K. 1992. "Justification" in the epistle of James. In *Right With God: Justification in the Bible and the World*, edited by D.A. Carson, 146–52. Grand Rapids MI: Baker Book House/The Paternoster Press.

Funk, R. W. 1973. *A Beginning-Intermediate Grammar of Hellenistic Greek. Part II: Syntax*. Atlanta: Scholars Press.

Garvin, P. L. 1963. Czechoslovakia. In *Current Trends in Linguistics*, edited by T. E. Sebeok, 1:499–522. The Hague: Mouton.

Gault, J. A. 1990. The discourse function of *kai egeneto* in Luke and Acts. *OPTAT* 4(4): 388–99.

Givón, Talmy. 1983. *Topic Continuity in Discourse*. Philadelphia: Benjamins.

——— 1984 and 1990. *Syntax: A Functional-Typological Introduction* (2 vols.). Amsterdam, Philadelphia: Benjamins.

Godet, Frederic Louis. 1977 (1883). *Commentary on Romans*. Grand Rapids, MI: Kregel Publications.

Greenlee, J. Harold. 1963 (3rd ed.) and 1986 (5th ed.). *A Concise Exegetical Grammar of New Testament Greek*. Grand Rapids, MI: Eerdmans.

——— 1989. *An Exegetical Summary of Titus and Philemon*. Dallas: Summer Institute of Linguistics.

——— 1992. *An Exegetical Summary of Philippians*. Dallas: Summer Institute of Linguistics.

Grimes, J. E. 1975. *The Thread of Discourse*. The Hague: Mouton.

Groce, W. W. Jr. 1991. *A Salience Scheme Approach to the Narrative of Matthew in the Greek New Testament*. M.A. thesis, University of Texas at Arlington.

Guthrie, D. 1957. *The Pastoral Epistles*. The Tyndale New Testament Commentaries. Grand Rapids, MI: Eerdmans.

Guthrie, George H. 1998. *The Structure of Hebrews: A Text-Linguistic Analysis*. Grand Rapids, MI: Baker Books.

Gutt, E.-A. 1991. *Translation and Relevance: Cognition and Context*. Oxford: Basil Blackwell.

Haiman, J., and P. Munro, eds. 1983. *Switch Reference and Universal Grammar*. Philadelphia: Benjamins.

Halliday, M. A. K. 1967. Notes on transitivity and theme in English. *Journal of Linguistics* 3:199–244.

Harbeck, W. 1970. Mark's use of γάρ in narration. *Notes on Translation* 38:10–15.

Hawkins, John C. 1909. *Horae Synopticae: Contributions to the Study of the Synoptic Problem*. 2nd edition. Oxford: Clarendon Press.

Healey, A. 1984. Split phrases and clauses in Greek. *START* 11:3–9.

Healey, P., and A. Healey. 1990. Greek circumstantial participles: tracking participants with participles in the Greek New Testament. *OPTAT* 4.3.

Heckert, Jakob A. 1996. *Discourse Function of Conjoiners in the Pastoral Epistles*. Dallas: Summer Institute of Linguistics.

Heimerdinger, J., and Levinsohn, Stephen H. 1992. The use of the definite article before names of people in the Greek text of Acts, with particular reference to Codex Bezae. *Filología Neotestamentaria* V:15–44.

Hendriksen, William. 1957. *A Commentary on I–II Timothy and Titus*. Ann Arbor: Cushing-Malloy Inc.

———. 1971. *A Commentary on Colossians and Philemon*. London: The Banner of Truth Trust.

———. 1974. *The Gospel of Matthew*. Edinburgh: The Banner of Truth Trust.

Hopper, Paul J. 1979. Aspect and foregrounding in discourse. In *Syntax and Semantics 12: Discourse and Syntax*, edited by Talmy Givón, 213–41. New York: Academic Press.

———, and Sandra A. Thompson. 1980. Transitivity in grammar and discourse. *Language* 56:251–99.

———, and ———. 1984. The discourse basis for lexical categories in universal grammar. *Language* 60:703–52.

Hwang, Shin Ja J. 1990. Foreground information in narrative. *Southwest Journal of Linguistics* 9(2):63–90.

———. 1997. A profile and discourse analysis of an English short story. *Language Research* 33(2):293–320.

Jespersen, Otto. 1964. *Essentials of English Grammar*. Alabama: University of Alabama Press.

Johnson, David. 1984. *A Study of the Use of the Historic Present in the Gospel of Mark*. Dissertation submitted to London Bible College in partial fulfillment of the requirements for an MA degree of the CNAA.

Johnson, Edna. 1988. *Semantic Structure Analysis of 2 Peter*. Dallas: Summer Institute of Linguistics.

Johnson-Laird, P. N. 1983. *Mental Models*. Cambridge MA: Harvard University Press.

Johnstone, B. 1987. "He says ... so I said": verb tense alternation and narrative depictions of authority in American English. *Linguistics* 25:33–52.

Kilpatrick, G. D. 1965. The Greek New Testament text of today and the *Textus Receptus*. In *The New Testament in Historical and Contemporary Perspective*, edited by H. Anderson and W. Barclay, 189–208. Oxford: Basil Blackwell.

Kistemaker, Simon J. 1993. *New Testament Commentary: Exposition of the First Epistle to the Corinthians*. Grand Rapids, MI: Baker Books.

Knight, G. W. 1992. *Commentary on the Pastoral Epistles*. Grand Rapids, MI: Eerdmans.

Lambrecht, Knud. 1994. *Information Structure and Sentence Form: Topic, Focus, and the Mental Representations of Discourse Referents*. Cambridge: Cambridge University Press.

Larsen, I. 1991a. Word order and relative prominence in New Testament Greek. *Notes on Translation* 5(1):29–34.

———. 1991b. Notes on the function of γάρ, οὖν, μέν, δέ, καί and τέ in the Greek New Testament. *Notes on Translation* 5(1):35–47.

———. 1991c. Boundary features. *Notes on Translation* 5(1):48–54.

———. 1991d. Quotations and speech introducers in narrative texts. *Notes on Translation* 5(1):55–60.

Lenski, R. C. H. 1937. *The Interpretation of St. Paul's Epistles to the Galatians, to the Ephesians, and to the Philippians*. Minneapolis: Augsburg Publishing House.

———. 1943. *The Interpretation of St. Matthew's Gospel*. Minneapolis: Augsburg Publishing House.

———. 1943. *The Interpretation of St. John's Gospel*. Minneapolis: Augsburg Publishing House.

———. 1961 (1934). *The Interpretation of the Acts of the Apostles*. Minneapolis: Augsburg Publishing House.

Levinsohn, Stephen H. 1975. Functional sentence perspective in Inga (Quechuan). *Journal of Linguistics* 11:13–37.

———. 1976. Progression and digression in Inga (Quechuan) discourse. *Forum Linguisticum* 1:122–47.

———. 1977a. The grouping and classification of events in Mark 14. *Notes on Translation* 66:19–28.

———. 1977b. The function of δέ in the narrative of Mark 14:1–16:8. *Notes on Translation* 67:2–9.

———. 1978. Luke's recitative usage of *hoti*. *Notes on Translation* 70:25–36.

———. 1980. *Relationships Between Constituents Beyond the Clause in the Acts of the Apostles*. Ph.D. Thesis, University of Reading.

———. 1987. *Textual Connections in Acts*. Atlanta: Scholars Press.

———. 1989. Phrase order and the article in Galatians. *OPTAT* 3(2):44–64.

———. 1990. Review of M. Hammond, E. A. Moravsik, and J. R. Wirth. 1988, eds. Studies in syntactic typology. Amsterdam: Benjamins. *Journal of Linguistics* 26:286–88.

———. 1992. The historic present and speech margins in Matthew. In *Language in Context: Essays for Robert E. Longacre*, edited by Shin Ja J. Hwang and William R. Merrifield, 451–73. Dallas: Summer Institute of Linguistics and the University of Texas at Arlington.

———. 1993. Anarthrous references to the Holy Spirit: another factor. *The Bible Translator* 44(1):138–44.

———. 1995. A discourse study of constituent order and the article in Philippians. In *Discourse Analysis and Other Topics in Biblical Greek*, edited by Stanley E. Porter and D. A. Carson, 60–74. Sheffield: JSOT Press.

———. 1997. A report on research into the functions of relative clauses in languages of Cameroon. *Notes on Translation* 11(3):38–40.

———. 1999a. Some constraints on discourse development in the Pastoral Epistles. In *Discourse Analysis of the New Testament: Approaches and Results*, edited by Jeffrey T. Reed and Stanley E. Porter, 316–33. JSNT Supplement Series 170. Sheffield: Sheffield Academic Press.

———. 1999b. Ὅτι *recitativum* in John's Gospel: a stylistic or a pragmatic device? *Work Papers of the Summer Institute of Linguistics, University of North Dakota Session* 43.

Li, Charles N. 1986. Direct and indirect speech: a functional study. In Florian Coulmas (ed.), *Direct and Indirect Speech. Trends in Linguistics: Studies and Monographs 31*. Berlin, New York, Amsterdam: Mouton de Gruyter.

Liddell, Henry George, and Robert Scott. 1901. *A Greek-English Lexicon.* 8th edition. Oxford: Clarendon Press.

Lightfoot, J.B. 1892. *Saint Paul's Epistle to the Galatians.* 10th edition. London: Macmillan.

Longacre, Robert E. 1976. *An Anatomy of Speech Notions.* Lisse: The Peter de Ridder Press.

———. 1990. Storyline concerns and word order typologies in East and West Africa. *Studies in African Linguistics*, Supplement 10.

———. 1992. Towards an exegesis of 1 John based on the discourse analysis of the Greek text. In *Linguistics and New Testament Interpretation: Essays on Discourse Analysis*, edited by David Alan Black, Katharine Barnwell, and Stephen Levinsohn, 271–86 Nashville: Broadman.

———. 1995. Left shifts in strongly VSO languages. In *Word Order in Discourse*, edited by Pamela Downing and Michael Noonan, 331–54. Amsterdam, Philadelphia: Benjamins.

———. 1996. *The Grammar of Discourse.* 2nd edition. New York: Plenum.

Mann, W. C., and Sandra A. Thompson. 1987. *Antithesis: A Study in Clause Ordering and Discourse Structure.* Marina del Rey: Information Sciences Institute.

Marchese, L. 1984. Pronouns and full nouns: a case of misrepresentation. *The Bible Translator* 35(2).

Marshall, I. Howard, 1978. *The Gospel of Luke: A Commentary on the Greek Text.* Exeter: The Paternoster Press.

McKay, K. L. 1994. *A New Syntax of the Verb: An Aspectual Approach.* Studies in Biblical Greek no. 5. New York: Peter Lang.

Meyer, Heinrich August Wilheim. 1873. *Critical and Exegetical Handbook to the Epistle to the Galatians,* translated by G. H. Venables. Edinburgh: T. and T. Clark.

———. 1883. *Critical and Exegetical Handbook to the Epistle to the Philippians,* translated by G. H. Venables. Edinburgh: T. and T. Clark.

Mfonyam, Joseph Ngwa. 1994. Prominence in Bafut: syntactic and pragmatic devices. In *Discourse Features of Ten Languages of West-Central Africa*, edited by Stephen H. Levinsohn, 191–210. Dallas: Summer Institute of Linguistics and the University of Texas at Arlington.

Minor, Eugene E. 1992. *An Exegetical Summary of 2 Timothy.* Dallas: Summer Institute of Linguistics.

Moffat, James. 1924. *A Critical and Exegetical Commentary on the Epistle to the Hebrews.* Edinburgh: T. and T. Clark.

Moulton, James Hope, and George Milligan. 1974 (1930). *The Vocabulary of the Greek Testament.* Grand Rapids, MI: Eerdmans.

Moulton, W. F., A. S. Geden, and H. K. Moulton. 1978. *Concordance to the Greek Testament.* Edinburgh: T. and T. Clark.

Murray, John. 1968. *The Epistle to the Romans.* Grand Rapids, MI: Eerdmans.

Neeley, L. L. 1987. A discourse analysis of Hebrews. *OPTAT* 3-4:1–146.

Nestle-Aland: 1994. *Novum Testamentum Graece* (27th. edition revised), edited by Barbara and Kurt Aland, Johannes Karavidopoulos, Carlo M. Martini, and Bruce M. Metzger. Stuttgart: Deutsche Bibelgesellschaft.

Newman, B. M., and E. A. Nida. 1972. *A Translator's Handbook on the Acts of the Apostles.* London: United Bible Societies.

Noonan, Michael. 1985. Complementation. In *Language Typology and Syntactic Description*, edited by Timothy Shopen, II.42-140. Cambridge: Cambridge University Press.

Payne, Doris L. 1995. Verb initial languages and information order. In *Word Order in Discourse*, edited by Pamela Downing and Michael Noonan, 449–85. Amsterdam/Philadelphia: Benjamins.

Perrin, Mona J. 1994. Rheme and focus in Mambila. In *Discourse Features of Ten Languages of West-Central Africa*, edited by Stephen H. Levinsohn, 231–41. Dallas: Summer Institute of Linguistics and the University of Texas at Arlington.

Pierpont, W. G. 1986. Studies in word order: personal pronoun possessives in nominal phrases in the New Testament. *START* 15:8–25.

Plummer, Alfred. 1896. *A Critical and Exegetical Commentary on the Gospel according to St. Luke*. Edinburgh: T. and T. Clark.

———. 1919. *A Commentary on St. Paul's Epistle to the Philippians*. London: Robert Scott.

Pope, Kathrin. 1993. The use of subordinate clauses in Waama and how this affects translation. *Notes on Translation* 7(2):1–11.

Porter, Stanley E. 1992. *Idioms of the Greek New Testament*. Sheffield: JSOT Press.

———. 1995. How can Biblical discourse be analyzed?: a response to several attempts. In *Discourse Analysis and Other Topics in Biblical Greek*, edited by Stanley E. Porter and D. A. Carson, 107–16. Sheffield: JSOT Press.

Poythress, V. S. 1984. The use of the intersentence conjunctions δέ, οὖν, καί and asyndeton in the Gospel of John. *Novum Testamentum* 26:312–40.

Radney, J. R. 1988. Some factors that influence fronting in Koine clauses. *OPTAT* 2(3):1–79.

Ramsey, V. 1987. The functional distribution of preposed and postposed "if" and "when" clauses in written discourse. In *Coherence and Grounding in Discourse*, edited by R. S. Tomlin, 383–408. Philadelphia: Benjamins.

Reed, Jeffrey T. 1997. *A Discourse Analysis of Philippians: Method and Rhetoric in the Debate over Literary Integrity*. JSNT Supplement Series 136. Sheffield: Sheffield Academic Press.

———, and Ruth A. Reese. 1996. Verbal aspect, discourse prominence, and the letter of Jude. *Filología Neotestamentaria* IX.181–99.

Reiling, J. 1965. The use and translation of καί ἐγένετο "and it happened," in the New Testament. *The Bible Translator* 16:153–63.

Reimer, M. 1985. The functions of οὖν in the Gospel of John. *START* 13:28–36.

Robertson, A. T. n.d. (copyrighted 1934). *A Grammar of the Greek New Testament in the Light of Historical Research*. New York, London: Harper.

Robinson, John. 1985. *The Priority of John*. London: SCM Press.

Rogers, E. 1984. Vocatives and boundaries. *START* 11:24–29.

———. 1989. *Semantic Structure Analysis of Galatians*. Dallas: Summer Institute of Linguistics.

Sanday, William, and Arthur C. Headlam. 1895. *A Critical and Exegetical Commentary on the Epistle to the Romans*. Edinburgh: T. and T. Clark.

Schooling, S. 1985. More on Matthew's brackets: a study of the function of time references in Matthew's Gospel. *START* 13:14–27.

SIL-UND: Dooley, Robert A., and Stephen H. Levinsohn. 1997. *Analyzing Discourse: Basic Concepts*. Summer Institute of Linguistics and University of North Dakota.

Smith, R. E. 1985. Recognizing prominence features in the Greek New Testament. *START* 14:16–25.

———, and John Beekman. 1981. *A Literary-Semantic Analysis of Second Timothy*. Dallas: Summer Institute of Linguistics.

Smyth, H. W. 1956. *Greek Grammar*. Preface and revision of the 1920 edition by G. M. Messing. Harvard: Harvard University Press.

Sperber, D., and D. Wilson. 1986. *Relevance: Communication and Cognition*. Oxford: Basil Blackwell.

Swartz, 1993. Person and power, the Greek article and *pneuma*. *The Bible Translator* 44(1):124–38.

Teeple, H. M. 1973. The Greek article with personal names in the Synoptic Gospels. *New Testament Studies* 19(3):302–17.

Terry, Ralph Bruce. 1995. *A Discourse Analysis of First Corinthians*. Dallas: Summer Institute of Linguistics and the University of Texas at Arlington.

Thackery, H. St. J. 1909. *A Grammar of the Old Testament in Greek According to the Septuagint*. Cambridge.

Thompson, Sandra A. 1985. Grammar and written discourse: initial vs. final purpose clauses in English. *Text* 5:55–84.

Thrall, M. E. 1962. *Greek Particles in the New Testament: Linguistic and Exegetical Studies*. Leiden: E. J. Brill.

Titrud, Kermit 1991. The overlooked καί in the Greek New Testament. *Notes on Translation* 5(1):1–28.

———. 1992. The function of καί in the Greek New Testament and an application to 2 Peter. In *Linguistics and New Testament Interpretation: Essays on Discourse Analysis*, edited by David Alan Black, Katharine Barnwell, and Stephen Levinsohn, 240–70. Nashville: Broadman.

Tomlin, R. S. 1986. *Basic Word Order: Functional Principles*. London, New York, Sydney: Croom Helm.

———, ed. 1987. *Coherence and Grounding in Discourse*. Philadelphia: Benjamins.

Trail, Ronald. 1995. *An Exegetical Summary of 1 Corinthians 1–9*. Dallas: Summer Institute of Linguistics.

Turnbull, Bruce F. 1986. A comment on Ross McKerras's article "Some ins and outs of 'come' and 'go'". *START* 16:42–43.

———. 1997. *Some Features of Genitives, English and Greek*. Paper read at seminar on Features of Greek Discourse, Dallas.

Turner, N. 1963. *Syntax. Vol. 3, A Grammar of New Testament Greek*, edited by J. H. Moulton. Edinburgh: T. and T. Clark.

Unger, Christoph. 1996. The scope of discourse connectives: implications for discourse organization. *Journal of Linguistics* 32:403–38.

Van Otterloo, Roger. 1988. Towards an understanding of "lo" and "behold": functions of ἰδού and ἴδε in the Greek New Testament. *OPTAT* 2(1):34–64.

Wallace, Daniel B. 1995. *Greek Grammar Beyond the Basics: An Exegetical Syntax of the New Testament*. Grand Rapids, MI: Zondervan.

Waltz, Nathan. 1976. Discourse patterns in John 11. *Notes on Translation* 59:2–8.

Waugh, L. R., and M. Monville-Burston. 1986. Aspect and discourse function: the French simple past in newspaper usage. *Language* 62:846–77.

Werth, Paul. 1984. *Focus, Coherence and Emphasis*. London, New York, Sydney: Croom Helm.

Whaley, Lindsay J. 1997. *Introduction to Typology: The Unity and Diversity of Language*. London: SAGE Publications.

White, N. J. D. 1970 (1909). The first and second epistles to Timothy and the epistle to Titus. *The Expositor's Greek Testament*, vol. 4, edited by W. R. Nicoll. Grand Rapids, MI: Eerdmans.

Wilson, W. A. A. 1974. Notes on the function of the historic present in Mark's Gospel. In *Understanding and Translating the Bible: Papers in Honor of Eugene A. Nida*, edited by Robert G. Bratcher, John J. Kijne, and William A. Smalley, 205–17. New York: American Bible Society.

Winer, G. B. 1882. *A Treatise on the Grammar of New Testament Greek*. Edinburgh: T. and T. Clark.

Youngman, S. 1987. *Stratificational Analysis of a Hortatory Text: 1 Corinthians 8.1–11.1*. M.A. thesis, University of Texas at Arlington.

Zegarac, Vladimir. 1989. Relevance theory and the meaning of the English progressive. *University College London Working Papers in Linguistics 1:19–31*.

Zerwick S. J., Maximilian. 1963. *Biblical Greek*. English edition adapted from 4th. Latin edition by Joseph Smith S. J. Rome: Scripta Pontificii Instituti Biblici.

INDEX OF SCRIPTURE REFERENCES

(fn = footnote; + = suggested answer found on the following page number in the Appendix)

10:32	80
10:51	233
11:1-9	81
11:2	191
12:29	233
12:35	13 fn
12:38	13-14
13:22	70
13:29	103 fn
14:1-16:8	80
14:60	50 fn
14:61	50, 50 fn
15:1-44	151
15:9	233
15:11-15	177-78
15:16	80
15:25	92
15:33	81 fn

Luke

1:5-2:7	76
1:8	76
1:8-20	156
1:11	7
1:12, 18	159
1:24	76, 159
1:25	265
1:26	76, 190
1:28-38	219-20
1:29	218, 219
1:34	159
1:35	104 fn, 233
1:38	159
1:39	76
1:39-56	158
1:41	178, 197, 198
1:56	76
1:57	11-12, 76, 159
1:59-65	15
1:61	265
1:65-67	76-77
1:67	76, 159
1:80	76
2:1	76
2:1-20	75-76
2:2	92
2:4, 5	159
2:6	76
2:21-40	74
2:22-28	21-22 + 285
2:23	268
2:25	60
2:34	159
2:36-37	12-13, 92, 138

2:36-38	174-75, 174 fn
2:41-43	174
2:43	159
2:52	155, 159
3:1	76, 161
3:2	159
3:4-6	268
3:15	76
3:16	233
3:21	76 155, 159
3:21-22	76, 178
3:23	155, 159
3:23-38	76, 178
4:1	76, 155
4:4	159, 233, 268
4:8	268
4:10-11	268
4:12	265-66
4:14	76, 155
4:16	76, 149
4:16-21	269
4:17-19	268
4:20	148, 149
4:24-25	267
4:31	76
4:31-37	18-19, 79
4:33	15 fn, 90, 90 fn
4:38	135, 151, 154
4:43	264
5:3	154
5:8, 10	159
5:14	264
5:26	265
5:27	36, 134, 134 fn
5:27-32	18, 71, 72, 74
5:29	19-20, 90
5:33-39	74
5:36-39	265
5:37	32
6:3-6	270 + 291
6:13	154, 155
6:47	64
6:48	191
7:1	277
7:11-17	179
7:27-29	268
7:40	202, 216
7:41	216
8:41	159
8:45	154
8:49	84, 208
8:50	233
8:51	155
9:7-8	263

9:12-17	179
9:18	179
9:20	159
9:22	265
9:28	155
9:28-33	151
9:36	159
9:42	84 fn
9:50	159
10:7	148
10:12, 24	267
10:25-28	218-19, 222
10:25-37	226-27
10:27	233
10:28	222
10:37	82 fn
12:30	66
12:36	136 fn
12:41	154
12:44	267
13:14	265
13:15	233
14:16-24	20-21, 98
14:24	267
14:26	109 fn
15:2	265 fn
15:11	134, 135
15:11-13	3-4
15:11-14	77
15:11-32	137, 139-40
15:12	30, 77 fn, 137-39
15:13	9, 137
15:13-14	182
15:14	138, 140
15:15-16	137-38
15:20	84 fn
15:21-23	215
15:22	137, 138
15:24	138
15:25	7
15:27	265
15:31	221, 223
16:20	14
16:23	208
17:10	103 fn
17:20	233
18:8	267
18:28	154
18:40	159
19:7	265 fn
19:9	30
19:9-10	265
19:28-37	81
19:30	191

INDEX OF TOPICS

(References are to Sections)

Discourse Features of New Testament Greek
Second Edition, 2000 by Stephen H. Levinsohn
ERRATA and ADDENDA

p. 7, fn. 1. Add 'The topic of a proposition is of *current interest*; the referent must either be already established in the discourse or easily related to one that is already established (op. cit. 164). See p. 42 for a similar comment about points of departure.'

p. 59. Ed Condra (p.c.) suggests that, in both Gal. 2:20d and Gal. 2:9, the constituent is discontinuous because only the first part is in focus, with the remainder supportive. This may imply that constituents are never discontinuous 'because only the second part relates to what follows' (p. 58). If so, the suggested answers on discontinuous constituents in Heb. 2:3b (p. 61) and James 4:6a (p. 286) would need to be modified. Further investigation is needed.

p. 62, sec. 4.5 on adjectival modifiers. Rev. 4:7 provides a good example of adjectival preposing within a point of departure. Verse 7a has default Art N Art Adj order (τὸ ζῷον τὸ πρῶτον). Verses 7b-d have marked Art Adj N order (e.g. τὸ δεύτερον ζῷον) to indicate the switch from the first to the second, third and fourth living beings.

p. 63, sec. 4.5 on Turner's 'emphatic' and 'unemphatic' pronominal genitives. By 'unemphatic' genitives, Turner means personal pronouns such as μου and αὐτοῦ. 'Emphatic' genitives refer to reflexive pronouns such as ἑαυτοῦ.

pp. 63–64. Replace the last three paragraphs with the following:

I now look at sentences in which an *unemphatic pronominal* genitive precedes a noun. As Turner (loc. cit.) notes, such genitives are *not* necessarily in focus.[fn.17] I am particularly concerned with Turner's set (b); viz., those that occur before the article, as in αὐτοῦ τὸν ἀστέρα 'his the star' (Matt. 2:2).

In 51 of the sample of 55 "unemphatic" examples which Turner cites, the phrase as a whole is a core constituent which immediately follows the verb, so that the order is:

verb – pronominal genitive – rest of the noun phrase.

The reader may notice a similarity with ordering principle 1 of sec. 3.1 (pronominal constituents of the comment precede nominal constituents). However, pronominal genitives sometimes *follow* the rest of a core noun phrase (as in Matt. 9:29a below), so it is not sufficient to say that they have been preposed by analogy with principle 1.[fn.18]

It appears that two of the other principles discussed in chapter 3 contribute, at least by analogy, to the pronominal genitive being preposed to immediately after the verb without being brought into focus:

the principle of sec. 3.5 that a focal constituent whose default position is not the end of a clause or sentence is placed at the end to give it extra prominence

default ordering principle 3, that propositional topics precede comments about their topics (sec. 3.3).

Then, on p. 64, change 'Secondly' to Firstly' and 'Thirdly' to 'Secondly'.

p. 114. Note that ἀλλά is a countering conjunction which 'corrects an expectation' (Heckert op. cit. 22) even when it follows a positive proposition. See Gal. 2:3, Phil. 1:18, 2 Tim. 3:9.

p. 116, next to last paragraph. If v. 9 had been developing from the exhortation of v. 6, resumptive οὖν would have been used, following the propositions introduced by γάρ— see sec. 7.4.

p. 123, Suggested Answer (a) concerning asyndeton in vv. 1a, 2a, 2b, 3a, 3b, and 4. The absence of conjunctions may be because 'the message is emotional' (K. Callow).

p. 125, (18a). Insert Ø at the beginning of the sentence.

p. 127, 2 Tim. 2:21. Οὖν probably marks the *resumption* of the topic of vv. 14-19 (see the discussion of v. 20a on pp. 113f.), following the introduction of new objects to an ongoing argument—see paragraph 5 of sec. 8.1, p. 134.

p. 127, end of second paragraph. Add the following footnote: When used with the inferential particle ἄρα 'so, as a result, consequently, οὖν is always resumptive ("here ἄ expresses the inference and οὖν the transition"—BAG p. 103); see Rom. 7:3, 9:16,18; Gal. 6:10, 1 Th. 5:6.

p. 130, (46b). Insert Ø at the beginning of the sentence.

p. 137, Luke 15:22. Delete this example, which illustrates marked encoding to highlight the father's unexpected initiative and is a key speech, so should be referred to in the second paragraph of p. 140.

p. 143, end of next to last paragraph. Add 'in the Synoptic Gospels.[fn.]' The footnote reads, 'Overt references to Jesus are much more frequent in John's Gospel. See chapter 15 on participant reference in John.'

p. 151, paragraph 1. Delete points 3 & 4 ('in Luke 9...' & 'in John 18:15-18...'). These comments illustrate the operation of the principle of sec. 9.2.2, not 9.2.1 (see the use of the word 'reactivated').

p. 155, lines 1-2. The three references to Peter may be anarthrous because they are focal constituents—see sec. 9.3.

pp. 150-51, 155-62. For 'activated', it is often clearer to read 'active'.

p. 170. Begin fn. 1 with '"[T]he inclusion of μέν throws the emphasis on the second member (indicated by δέ)" (BDF §447(5)).'

p. 173, fn. 1. Add 'There is also a correlation between *tense* and background information. In particular, events encoded in the pluperfect will always be backgrounded in narrative, because they occur prior to the time of the foreground events.'

pp. 197, 204-08. For 'activated', it is often clearer to read 'active'.

p. 244, Suggested Answer on the HP of Matt. 13:29. Add, 'Alternatively, since much of the interpretation concerns the time of "the harvest" (v. 39), the HP points forward to the unstated fulfilment of the command of v. 30b, "Collect the weeds first and bind them in bundles to be burned, but gather the wheat into my barn."'

p. 289, 9(15) (a). Following the first sentence, add, 'However, Philips translates παιδαγωγόν in v. 25b as "the trainer," in which case the reference is anarthrous because it is preposed for focus.'

p. 291, 17(3) (a). Further potential supporting evidence for a boundary before 5:25 is the back-reference in v. 25 to the Spirit (v. 22).

January 2005

Made in the USA